Springer Series in Statistics

Advisors:
D. Brillinger, S. Fienberg, J. Gani,
J. Hartigan, K. Krickeberg

Springer Series in Statistics

Andrews/Herzberg: Data: A Collection of Problems from Many Fields for the Student and Research Worker.
Anscombe: Computing in Statistical Science through APL.
Berger: Statistical Decision Theory and Bayesian Analysis, 2nd edition.
Brémaud: Point Processes and Queues: Martingale Dynamics.
Brockwell/Davis: Time Series: Theory and Methods.
Daley/Vere-Jones: An Introduction to the Theory of Point Processes.
Dzhaparidze: Parameter Estimation and Hypothesis Testing in Spectral Analysis of Stationary Time Series.
Farrell: Multivariate Calculation.
Goodman/Kruskal: Measures of Association for Cross Classifications.
Hartigan: Bayes Theory.
Heyer: Theory of Statistical Experiments.
Jolliffe: Principal Component Analysis.
Kres: Statistical Tables for Multivariate Analysis.
Leadbetter/Lindgren/Rootzén: Extremes and Related Properties of Random Sequences and Processes.
Le Cam: Asymptotic Methods in Statistical Decision Theory.
Manoukian: Modern Concepts and Theorems of Mathematical Statistics.
Miller, Jr.: Simulaneous Statistical Inference, 2nd edition.
Mosteller/Wallace: Applied Bayesian and Classical Inference: The Case of *The Federalist Papers.*
Pollard: Convergence of Stochastic Processes.
Pratt/Gibbons: Concepts of Nonparametric Theory.
Read/Cressie: Goodness-of-Fit Statistics for Discrete Multivariate Data.
Reiss: Approximate Distributions of Order Statistics: With Applications to Nonparametric Statistics.
Sachs: Applied Statistics: A Handbook of Techniques, 2nd edition.
Seneta: Non-Negative Matrices and Markov Chains.
Siegmund: Sequential Analysis: Tests and Confidence Intervals.
Tong: The Multivariate Normal Distribution
Vapnik: Estimation of Dependences Based on Empirical Data.
West/Harrison: Bayesian Forecasting and Dynamic Models
Wolter: Introduction to Variance Estimation.
Yaglom: Correlation Theory of Stationary and Related Random Functions I: Basic Results.
Yaglom: Correlation Theory of Stationary and Related Random Functions II: Supplementary Notes and References.

Y.L. Tong

The Multivariate Normal Distribution

Springer-Verlag
New York Berlin Heidelberg
London Paris Tokyo Hong Kong

Y.L. Tong
School of Mathematics
Georgia Institute of Technology
Atlanta, GA 30332-0160
U.S.A.

AMS Mathematics Subject Classifications (1980): 60E05, 62H99

Library of Congress Cataloging in Publication Data
Tong, Y.L. (Yung Liang), 1935-
The multivariate normal distribution / Y.L. Tong.
P. cm. — (Springer series in statistics)
Includes bibliographical references.
ISBN 0-387-97062-2 (alk. paper)
1. Distribution (Probability theory) 2. Multivariate analysis.
I. Title. II. Series.
QA273.6.T67 1990
519.2'4—dc20 89-21929
CIP

Printed on acid-free paper

Typeset by Asco Trade Typesetting Ltd., Hong Kong.
Printed and bound by R.R. Donnelley & Sons, Harrisonburg, Virginia.
Printed in the United States of America.

9 8 7 6 5 4 3 2 1

ISBN 0-387-97062-2 Springer-Verlag New York Berlin Heidelberg
ISBN 3-540-97062-2 Springer-Verlag Berlin Heldelberg New York

To My Family

Contents

Preface

The multivariate normal distribution has played a predominant role in the historical development of statistical theory, and has made its appearance in various areas of applications. Although many of the results concerning the multivariate normal distribution are classical, there are important new results which have been reported recently in the literature but cannot be found in most books on multivariate analysis. These results are often obtained by showing that the multivariate normal density function belongs to certain large families of density functions. Thus, useful properties of such families immediately hold for the multivariate normal distribution.

This book attempts to provide a comprehensive and coherent treatment of the classical and new results related to the multivariate normal distribution. The material is organized in a unified modern approach, and the main themes are dependence, probability inequalities, and their roles in theory and applications. Some general properties of a multivariate normal density function are discussed, and results that follow from these properties are reviewed extensively. The coverage is, to some extent, a matter of taste and is not intended to be exhaustive, thus more attention is focused on a systematic presentation of results rather than on a complete listing of them.

Most of the classical results on distribution theory, sampling distributions, and correlation analysis are presented in Chapters 2 and 3. Chapter 4 deals with the log-concavity, unimodality, total positivity, Schur-concavity, and arrangement increasing properties of a multivariate normal density function and related results. Notions of dependence and their application to the multivariate normal distribution are discussed in Chapter 5; not surprisingly, the results involve the covariance matrix of the distribution. Chapter 6 includes distribution theory and dependence results for the order statistics of normal variables. Chapter 7 contains inequalities and bounds for the multivariate normal distribution, including dependence-related inequalities, dimension-related inequalities, and inequalities for the probability contents of geometric regions in a certain class. Problems on statistical computing, mainly the generation of multivariate normal variates and the evaluation of multivariate normal probability integrals, are treated in Chapter 8; tables of equicoordinate one-sided and two-sided percentage points and probability integrals for exchangeable normal variables are given in the Appendix. A short chapter (Chapter 9) on the multivariate t distribution presents results concerning related distribution theory and convergence to the multivariate normal distribution. Chapters 2–9 contain sets of complementary problems. Finally, a combined list of references can be found at the end of the volume.

This book assumes a basic knowledge of matrix algebra and mathematical statistics at the undergraduate level, and is accessible to graduate students and advanced uhndergraduate students in statistics, mathematics, and related applied areas. Although it is not intended as a textbook, it can be used as a main reference in a course on multivariate analysis. And, of course, it can be used as a reference book on the multivariate normal distribution by researchers.

This work was partially supported by National Science Foundation grants DMS-8502346 and DMS-8801327 at Georgia Institute of Technology. Needless to say, I am indebted to the extensive literature in related areas. Professors Theodore W. Anderson, Herbert A. David, Kai-Tai Fang, Kumar Joag-Dev, Mark E. Johnson, Samuel Kotz, and Moshe Shaked read all or parts of the manuscript, and their comments and suggestions resulted in numerous significant improvements. However, I am solely responsible for errors and omissions. I am grateful to Professors Ingram Olkin and Frank Proschan for their inspiration, continuing encouragement, and constructively critical comments, and to Professor Milton Sobel for his strong influence on my work concerning the multivariate t distribution. I wish to thank Ms. Annette Rohrs for her skillful typing and wonderful cooperation, and also, the staff at Springer-Verlag for the neat appearance of the volume. Finally, I thank my wife Ai-Chuan and our children Frank, Betty, and Lily for their understanding and support. Frank read Chapter 1 and made some helpful comments, and Betty spent many long hours with me at the office.

Atlanta, Georgia Y.L. Tong
November 1988

Basic Notation and Numbering System

All vectors and matrices are in boldface type and, unless specified otherwise, all vectors are column vectors.

The following notation is used throughout this book:

(1) $\mathfrak{R} = (-\infty, \infty)$.
(2) $\mathfrak{R}^n = \{\mathbf{x}: \mathbf{x} = (x_1, \ldots, x_n)', -\infty < x_i < \infty \text{ for } i = 1, \ldots, n\}$.
(3) $\phi(z) = \dfrac{1}{\sqrt{2\pi}} e^{-z^2/2}, \ -\infty < z < \infty$.
(4) $\Phi(z) = \displaystyle\int_{-\infty}^{z} \frac{1}{\sqrt{2\pi}} e^{-u^2/2}\, du, \ -\infty < z < \infty$.
(5) The symbol "□" denotes the end of a proof or the end of an example.
(6) For an $n \times n$ symmetric matrix $\mathbf{\Sigma}$, $\mathbf{\Sigma} > 0$ denotes that $\mathbf{\Sigma}$ is positive definite.
(7) $\mathcal{N}(\mu, \sigma^2)$ denotes a univariate normal distribution with mean μ and variance σ^2.
(8) $\mathcal{N}_n(\boldsymbol{\mu}, \mathbf{\Sigma})$ denotes a multivariate normal distribution with mean vector $\boldsymbol{\mu}$ and covariance matrix $\mathbf{\Sigma}$.

Definitions, propositions, theorems, lemmas, facts, examples, remarks, and equations are numbered sequentially within each section. Results which are of general interest are stated as propositions, and results which concern only the multivariate normal distribution are given as theorems.

CHAPTER 1

Introduction

The multivariate normal distribution is undoubtedly one of the most well-known and useful distributions in statistics, playing a predominant role in many areas of applications. In multivariate analysis, for example, most of the existing inference procedures for analyzing vector-valued data have been developed under the assumption of normality. In linear model problems, such as the analysis of variance and regression analysis, the error vector is often assumed to be normally distributed so that statistical analysis can be performed using distributions derived from the normal distribution. In addition to appearing in these areas, the multivariate normal distribution also appears in multiple comparisons, in the studies of dependence of random variables, and in many other related areas.

1.1. Some Fundamental Properties

There are, of course, many reasons for the predominance of the multivariate normal distribution in statistics. These result from some of its most desirable properties as listed below:

(a) It represents a natural extension of the univariate normal distribution and provides a suitable model for many real-life problems concerning vector-valued data.
(b) Even if, in an experiment, the original data cannot be fitted satisfactorily with a multivariate normal distribution (as is the case when the measurements are discrete random vectors), by the central limit theorem the distribution of the sample mean vector is asymptotically normal. Thus the

multivariate normal distribution can be used for approximating the distribution of the same mean vector in the large sample case.

(c) The density function of a multivariate normal distribution is uniquely determined by the mean vector and the covariance matrix of the random variable (see Definitions 3.2.1, 3.2.2, and 3.2.3).

(d) Zero correlations imply independence; that is, if all the correlation coefficients between two sets of components of a multivariate normal variable are zero, then the two sets of components are independent (Theorem 3.3.2).

(e) The family of multivariate normal distributions is closed under linear transformations and linear combinations. In other words, the distributions of linear transformations or linear combinations of multivariate normal variables are again multivariate normal (Theorem 3.3.3 and Corollaries 3.3.3 and 3.3.4).

(f) The marginal distribution of any subset of components of a multivariate normal variable is also multivariate normal (Theorem 3.3.1).

(g) The conditional distribution in a multivariate normal distribution is multivariate normal. Furthermore, the conditional mean vector is a linear function and the conditional covariance matrix depends only on the covariance matrix of the joint distribution (Theorem 3.3.4). This property yields simple and useful results in regression analysis and correlation analysis (see Section 3.4).

(h) For the bivariate normal distribution, positive and negative dependence properties of the components of a random vector are completely determined by the sign and the size of the correlation coefficient (Section 2.3). Similar results also exist for the multivariate normal distribution (Section 5.1). Thus it is often chosen as an ideal model for studying the dependence of random variables.

1.2. Historical Remarks

Studies of the bivariate normal distribution seem to begin in the middle of the nineteenth century, and moved forward dramatically when Galton (1888) published his work on the applications of correlation analysis in genetics (see Pearson, 1920). As Pearson noted, "In 1885 Galton had completed the theory of bi-variate normal correlation" but, because he "was very modest and throughout his life underrated his own mathematical powers, he did not at once write down the equation" of the bivariate normal density function (Pearson, 1920). Consequently, it was Pearson (1896) himself who "gave a definitive mathematical formulation" of the bivariate normal distribution (Seal, 1967). The development of the multivariate normal distribution theory originated mainly from the studies of regression analysis and multiple and partial correlation analysis, and was treated comprehensively for the first time by Edgeworth (1892) (see Seal, 1967; Pearson and Kendall, 1970; Stigler, 1986,

Chaps. 8–10). The developments of the sampling distribution theory under the assumption of normality (as in Fisher's work on the distributions of sample correlation coefficients, Hotelling's T^2 distribution, and the Wishart distribution) then followed. Today, multivariate normal theory has become a fully grown area in statistics and plays a central role in statistical applications.

1.3. Characterization

Characterization of distributions is an important problem in mathematical statistics (see Kagan, Linnik, and Rao, 1973). For the multivariate normal distribution, there exist a number of interesting results and many of them involve specific transformations of random variables. For example, one result states that an n-dimensional random variable $\mathbf{Z}$ has a multivariate normal distribution with means 0, variances 1, and correlation coefficients 0, if and only if it is the observation obtained by selecting a point at random on the n-dimensional sphere with radius R, where R^2 has a chi-square distribution with n degrees of freedom. Furthermore, $\mathbf{X}$ has a multivariate normal distribution with an arbitrary mean vector and an arbitrary covariance matrix if and only if $\mathbf{X}$ and a linear function of $\mathbf{Z}$ are identically distributed (Theorems 4.1.1 and 3.2.2). Another characterization result concerns the transformations of variables from the polar system to the n-dimensional rectangular system, and a necessary and sufficient condition involves the independence of the radius variable and the angle vector (Theorem 4.1.2). Other characterization results can be given in terms of marginal and conditional distributions (see Theorem 4.1.3, Kagan, Linnik, and Rao (1973, pp. 475–477) and related references in Johnson and Kotz (1972, Chaps. 35 and 36)).

Exchangeable normal variables make their appearance in many areas of statistical applications. A characterization of exchangeable normal variables is just normality with a common mean, a common variance, and a common nonnegative correlation coefficient. Another characterization result states that the joint distribution of exchangeable normal variables is a mixture, and the common mean is a random variable with a univariate normal distribution (Theorem 5.3.1).

1.4. Scope and Organization

In view of the fact that there already exist many good books in the area of multivariate analysis (a standard reference is Anderson (1984)), and that statistical inference problems and procedures for analyzing vector-valued data have been extensively treated, we shall not make an attempt to include inference problems and data analysis methods in this book. Instead, we shall confine our attention to the *distribution* aspects of the multivariate normal theory. Toward this end we treat the following topics:

(a) *Basic distribution properties of the bivariate* (Chapter 2) *and multivariate* (Chapter 3) *normal distributions.* This includes the marginal and conditional distributions, the distributions of linear transformations and linear combinations of normal variables, dependence, regression analysis and correlation analysis, and distributions concerning the sample mean vector, the sample covariance matrix, and the sample correlation coefficients.

(b) *Some general properties of the multivariate normal density function and related results* (Chapter 4). The multivariate normal density function is known to be log-concave and unimodal. Furthermore, it is multivariate totally positive of order 2, Schur-concave, and arrangement increasing under certain additional conditions on the mean vector and the covariance matrix. Thus useful properties of such families of density functions immediately hold for the multivariate normal family.

(c) *Positively dependent and exchangeable normal variables* (Chapter 5). Several partial orderings of positive dependence of random variables exist in the literature. Here we present a comprehensive review and discuss their special applications to the multivariate normal distribution. For the special case when the distribution is permutation symmetric, positively dependent normal variables are just exchangeable normal variables with a common nonnegative correlation coefficient. This type of normal variable can be found in variance-component models, Bayes theory, and other related areas, and will be studied in Section 5.3.

(d) *Order statistics of normal variables.* Order statistics have important applications in statistical inference, multiple comparisons, reliability theory, and several other areas. In Chapter 6 we discuss the distribution properties and related results of order statistics of correlated normal variables. Special attention will be focused on the case of exchangeable normal variables, and the effects of their positive dependence on the order statistics will be treated.

(e) *Inequalities for the multivariate normal distribution.* Inequalities have become an integral part in many areas of statistics, particularly in multivariate analysis and reliability theory. In Chapter 7 we present a comprehensive and up-to-date treatment of the probability and moment inequalities for the multivariate normal distribution, and discuss some of their applications. This includes inequalities and bounds for the distribution function, for the probability contents of a class of geometric regions, and for the distributions of linear combinations of normal variables.

(f) *Statistical computing related to the multivariate normal distribution* (Chapter 8). This includes methods for generating n-dimensional normal variates with a given mean vector and a given positive definite covariance matrix, and methods for evaluating and approximating multivariate normal probability integrals. Special results are given for exchangeable normal variables. Tables of the equicoordinate one-sided and two-sided percentage points and probability integrals for exchangeable normal variables have been computed, and can be found in the Appendix of this book.

(g) *The multivariate t distribution.* The multivariate t distribution is a multivariate version of Student's t distribution, and it converges to the multivariate normal distribution when the number of degrees of freedom tends to infinity. In Chapter 9 we study its distribution properties and its relationship with the multivariate normal distribution.

The collection of results is not intended to be exhaustive. Instead of a complete gathering of the results, our attention will be focused on a comprehensive and coherent treatment of them related to the topics listed above.

CHAPTER 2

The Bivariate Normal Distribution

In the univariate case, a random variable X is said to have a normal distribution with mean μ and variance $\sigma^2 > 0$ (in symbols, $\mathcal{N}(\mu, \sigma^2)$) if its density function is of the form

$$f(x; \mu, \sigma^2) = \frac{1}{\sqrt{2\pi}\sigma} e^{-Q_1(x; \mu, \sigma^2)/2}, \qquad x \in \mathfrak{R},$$

where

$$Q_1(x; \mu, \sigma^2) = \frac{1}{\sigma^2}(x - \mu)^2 = (x - \mu)(\sigma^2)^{-1}(x - \mu),$$

$\mu \in \mathfrak{R}$, and $\sigma^2 \in (0, \infty)$. The bivariate normal density function given below is a natural extension of this univeriate normal density.

Definition 2.0.1.

(a) A two-dimensional random variable $\mathbf{X} = (X_1, X_2)'$ is said to have a nonsingular bivariate normal distribution if its density function is of the form

$$f(\mathbf{x}; \boldsymbol{\mu}, \boldsymbol{\Sigma}) = \frac{1}{2\pi|\boldsymbol{\Sigma}|^{1/2}} e^{-Q_2(\mathbf{x}; \boldsymbol{\mu}, \boldsymbol{\Sigma})/2}, \qquad \mathbf{x} \in \mathfrak{R}^2, \tag{2.0.1}$$

where

$$Q_2(\mathbf{x}; \boldsymbol{\mu}, \boldsymbol{\Sigma}) = (\mathbf{x} - \boldsymbol{\mu})'\boldsymbol{\Sigma}^{-1}(\mathbf{x} - \boldsymbol{\mu}), \tag{2.0.2}$$

$$\boldsymbol{\mu} = (\mu_1, \mu_2)', \qquad \boldsymbol{\Sigma} = \begin{pmatrix} \sigma_1^2 & \sigma_{12} \\ \sigma_{12} & \sigma_2^2 \end{pmatrix}, \tag{2.0.3}$$

$\sigma_i^2 > 0$ $(i = 1, 2)$, and $|\sigma_{12}| < \sigma_1\sigma_2$.

(b) $\mathbf{X}$ is said to have a singular bivariate normal distribution if there exist real numbers $\sigma_1, \sigma_2, \mu_1, \mu_2$ such that $\mathbf{X}$ and $(\sigma_1 Z + \mu_1, \sigma_2 Z + \mu_2)'$ are identically distributed, where Z has an $\mathcal{N}(0, 1)$ distribution.

2.1. Some Distribution Properties

2.1.1. Marginal and Conditional Distributions

Let $\rho = \sigma_{12}/\sigma_1\sigma_2$. Since $|\boldsymbol{\Sigma}| = \sigma_1^2\sigma_2^2(1-\rho^2)$, the inverse of $\boldsymbol{\Sigma}$ exists if and only if $|\rho| < 1$. Straightforward calculation shows that

$$\boldsymbol{\Sigma}^{-1} = \frac{1}{\sigma_1^2\sigma_2^2(1-\rho^2)}\begin{pmatrix} \sigma_2^2 & -\rho\sigma_1\sigma_2 \\ -\rho\sigma_1\sigma_2 & \sigma_1^2 \end{pmatrix}. \tag{2.1.1}$$

Thus for $|\rho| < 1$ we can write

$$f(\mathbf{x}; \boldsymbol{\mu}, \boldsymbol{\Sigma}) = \frac{1}{2\pi\sigma_1\sigma_2\sqrt{1-\rho^2}} \exp\left\{-\frac{1}{2(1-\rho^2)}\left[\left(\frac{x_1-\mu_1}{\sigma_1}\right)^2 - 2\rho\left(\frac{x_1-\mu_1}{\sigma_1}\right)\left(\frac{x_2-\mu_2}{\sigma_2}\right) + \left(\frac{x_2-\mu_2}{\sigma_2}\right)^2\right]\right\}. \tag{2.1.2}$$

From the identity

$$\left(\frac{x_1-\mu_1}{\sigma_1}\right)^2 - 2\rho\left(\frac{x_1-\mu_1}{\sigma_1}\right)\left(\frac{x_2-\mu_2}{\sigma_2}\right) + \left(\frac{x_2-\mu_2}{\sigma_2}\right)^2 = (1-\rho^2)\left(\frac{x_2-\mu_2}{\sigma_2}\right)^2 + \left[\left(\frac{x_1-\mu_1}{\sigma_1}\right) - \rho\left(\frac{x_2-\mu_2}{\sigma_2}\right)\right]^2,$$

the density function in (2.1.2) can be rewritten as

$$f(\mathbf{x}; \boldsymbol{\mu}, \boldsymbol{\Sigma}) = f_2(x_2; \mu_2, \sigma_2^2) f_{1|2}(x_1; \mu, \Sigma | x_2), \tag{2.1.3}$$

where

$$f_2(x_2; \mu_2, \sigma_2^2) = \frac{1}{\sqrt{2\pi}\sigma_2} \exp\left[-\frac{1}{2\sigma_2^2}(x_2-\mu_2)^2\right] = \frac{1}{\sigma_2}\phi\left(\frac{x_2-\mu_2}{\sigma_2}\right), \tag{2.1.4}$$

$$f_{1|2}(x_1; \mu, \Sigma | x_2) = \frac{1}{\sqrt{2\pi}\sigma_1\sqrt{1-\rho^2}} \exp\left[-\frac{1}{2\sigma_1^2(1-\rho^2)}\left(x_1 - \left(\mu_1 + \rho\frac{\sigma_1}{\sigma_2}(x_2-\mu_2)\right)\right)^2\right] = \frac{1}{\sigma_1\sqrt{1-\rho^2}}\phi\left(\frac{x_1 - (\mu_1 + \rho(\sigma_1/\sigma_2)(x_2-\mu_2))}{\sigma_1\sqrt{1-\rho^2}}\right), \tag{2.1.5}$$

and

$$\phi(z) = \frac{1}{\sqrt{2\pi}} e^{-z^2/2} \tag{2.1.6}$$

denotes the univariate standard normal density function.

This expression yields the following result.

Theorem 2.1.1. *Let* $\mathbf{X} = (X_1, X_2)'$ *be distributed according to a bivariate normal distribution with parameters* $\boldsymbol{\mu}$ *and* $\boldsymbol{\Sigma}$ *given in* (2.0.3). *Then*:

(a) *the marginal distribution of* X_i *is* $\mathcal{N}(\mu_i, \sigma_i^2)$ *for* $i = 1, 2$;
(b) *the correlation coefficient between* X_1 *and* X_2 *is* $\rho = \sigma_{12}/\sigma_1\sigma_2$;
(c) *for* $|\rho| < 1$, *the conditional distribution of* X_1 *given* $X_2 = x_2$ *is normal with mean* $\mu_1 + \rho(\sigma_1/\sigma_2)(x_2 - \mu_2)$ *and variance* $\sigma_1^2(1 - \rho^2)$;
(d) X_1 *and* X_2 *are independent if and only if* $\rho = 0$.

PROOF. (a) The statement is immediate when $|\sigma_{12}| = \sigma_1\sigma_2$. For $|\sigma_{12}| < \sigma_1\sigma_2$, the marginal density function of X_2 is

$$\begin{aligned}\int_{-\infty}^{\infty} & f_2(x_2; \mu_2, \sigma_2^2) f_{1|2}(x_1; \boldsymbol{\mu}, \boldsymbol{\Sigma}|x_2)\, dx_1 \\ &= f_2(x_2; \mu_2, \sigma_2^2) \int_{-\infty}^{\infty} f_{1|2}(x_1; \boldsymbol{\mu}, \boldsymbol{\Sigma}|x_2)\, dx_1 \\ &= f_2(x_2; \mu_2, \sigma_2^2),\end{aligned}$$

which is normal with mean μ_2 and variance σ_2^2. By symmetry, the marginal density function of X_1 is also normal with mean μ_1 and variance σ_1^2.

(b) If $\sigma_{12} = \sigma_1\sigma_2$ $(= -\sigma_1\sigma_2)$, then $P[X_1 = cX_2 + b] = 1$ holds for some $c > 0$ $(c < 0)$; thus $\rho = 1$ $(\rho = -1)$. If $|\sigma_{12}| < \sigma_1\sigma_2$ then, by (2.1.3)–(2.1.5) and the identities

$$\int_{-\infty}^{\infty} \frac{1}{\tau}\phi\left(\frac{z-\mu}{\tau}\right) dz = 1, \qquad \int_{-\infty}^{\infty} (z-\mu)\frac{1}{\tau}\phi\left(\frac{z-\mu}{\tau}\right) dz = 0$$

for all μ and $\tau > 0$, we have

$$\begin{aligned}&\operatorname{Cov}(X_1, X_2) \\ &= \int_{-\infty}^{\infty}\int_{-\infty}^{\infty} (x_1 - \mu_1)(x_2 - \mu_2) f(\mathbf{x}; \boldsymbol{\mu}, \boldsymbol{\Sigma})\, dx_1\, dx_2 \\ &= \sigma_1\sigma_2 \int_{-\infty}^{\infty} z_2\phi(z_2)\left[\int_{-\infty}^{\infty} ((z_1 - \rho z_2) + \rho z_2)\frac{1}{\sqrt{1-\rho^2}}\phi\left(\frac{z_1 - \rho z_2}{\sqrt{1-\rho^2}}\right) dz_1\right] dz_2 \\ &= \sigma_1\sigma_2 \int_{-\infty}^{\infty} z_2(0 + \rho z_2)\phi(z_2)\, dz_2 \\ &= \sigma_1\sigma_2\rho \; (= \sigma_{12}),\end{aligned}$$

where $z_i = (x_i - \mu_i)/\sigma_i$ $(i = 1, 2)$. Thus $\operatorname{Corr}(X_1, X_2) = \sigma_{12}/\sigma_1\sigma_2$.

(c) For $|\rho| < 1$, the conditional density of X_1 given $X_2 = x_2$ is

$$\frac{f(\mathbf{x}; \boldsymbol{\mu}, \boldsymbol{\Sigma})}{f_2(x_2; \mu_2 \sigma_2^2)} = f_{1|2}(x_1; \boldsymbol{\mu}, \boldsymbol{\Sigma}|x_2),$$

where $f_{1|2}$ is defined in (2.1.5). Thus the conditional distribution is normal with mean and variance

$$\mu_{1|2} = \mu_1 + \rho\frac{\sigma_1}{\sigma_2}(x_2 - \mu_2), \qquad \sigma_{1|2}^2 = \sigma_1^2(1 - \rho^2), \tag{2.1.7}$$

respectively.

(d) $\rho = 0$ if and only if the conditional density function $f_{1|2}(x_2; \boldsymbol{\mu}, \boldsymbol{\Sigma}|x_2)$ of X_1 given in (2.1.5) becomes the marginal density of X_1 or, equivalently, the joint density function $f(\mathbf{x}; \boldsymbol{\mu}, \boldsymbol{\Sigma})$ equals the product of the marginal densities of X_1 and X_2. □

Remark 2.1.1. From Theorem 2.1.1 it now becomes clear that $\boldsymbol{\mu}$ and $\boldsymbol{\Sigma}$, defined in (2.0.3), satisfy

$$E\mathbf{X} = \begin{pmatrix} EX_1 \\ EX_2 \end{pmatrix} = \boldsymbol{\mu},$$

$$E(\mathbf{X} - \boldsymbol{\mu})(\mathbf{X} - \boldsymbol{\mu})' = \begin{pmatrix} \mathrm{Var}(X_1) & \mathrm{Cov}(X_1, X_2) \\ \mathrm{Cov}(X_1, X_2) & \mathrm{Var}(X_2) \end{pmatrix} = \boldsymbol{\Sigma}.$$

Thus $\boldsymbol{\mu}$ and $\boldsymbol{\Sigma}$ are said to be, respectively, the mean vector and the covariance matrix of the bivariate normal distribution. For notational convenience, we shall use $\mathcal{N}_2(\boldsymbol{\mu}, \boldsymbol{\Sigma})$ to denote a bivariate normal distribution with mean vector $\boldsymbol{\mu}$ and covariance matrix $\boldsymbol{\Sigma}$.

Remark 2.1.2. Since the absolute value of the correlation coefficient of any pair of random variables must be bounded above by 1, we always have $|\sigma_{12}| \leq \sigma_1\sigma_2$. (This is why, in Definition 2.0.1, the case of $|\sigma_{12}| > \sigma_1\sigma_2$ need not be considered.) Furthermore, $\boldsymbol{\Sigma}$ is positive definite (so that $\boldsymbol{\Sigma}^{-1}$ exists) if and only if $|\sigma_{12}| < \sigma_1\sigma_2$ or, equivalently, $|\rho| < 1$.

For any given $\boldsymbol{\mu}$ and $\boldsymbol{\Sigma}$ such that $|\boldsymbol{\Sigma}| > 0$ (i.e., $|\rho| < 1$), the quadratic form $Q_2(\mathbf{x}; \boldsymbol{\mu}, \boldsymbol{\Sigma})$ defines an ellipse; i.e. the set of points

$$\{\mathbf{x}: \mathbf{x} \in \Re^2, Q_2(\mathbf{x}; \boldsymbol{\mu}, \boldsymbol{\Sigma}) = \lambda\}$$

is an ellipse in $\Re^2$, centered at $\boldsymbol{\mu}$, for every fixed $\lambda > 0$. Thus the value of the density function is a constant for all $\mathbf{x}$ on this ellipse and decreases as λ increases. If $\rho = 0$, then the major axis is parallel to either the x-axis or the y-axis.

2.1.2. Rotation of Axes and Orthogonal Transformations

A special case of interest is for $\boldsymbol{\mu} = \mathbf{0}$ and $\sigma_1^2 = \sigma_2^2$ ($= \sigma^2$, say). In this case we have

$$Q_2(\mathbf{x}; \mathbf{0}, \boldsymbol{\Sigma}) = \frac{1}{\sigma^2}(x_1^2 - 2\rho x_1 x_2 + x_2^2), \tag{2.1.8}$$

which is permutation symmetric in x_1 and x_2. Thus for all $\rho \in (-1, 1)$ the density function is symmetric about the 45-degree line defined by $x_1 = x_2$. For every fixed $\lambda > 0$, the set of points

$$\left\{(x_1, x_2)': \frac{1}{\sigma^2}(x_1^2 - 2\rho x_1 x_2 + x_2^2) = \lambda\right\}$$

must satisfy $x_2^2 - 2\rho x_1 x_2 + (x_1^2 - \lambda\sigma^2) = 0$, or

$$x_2 = \rho x_1 \pm (\lambda\sigma^2 - (1 - \rho^2)x_1^2)^{1/2},$$

for $|x_1| \leq \sigma(\lambda/(1 - \rho^2))^{1/2}$. The ellipse can be computed and plotted for selected values of ρ. It follows that after rotating the axes by 45 degrees in the counterclockwise direction, the major axis of the ellipse is parallel to either the new x-axis or the new y-axis. This involves linear transformations of bivariate normal variables and the following theorem is useful for this purpose. Since it is a special case of Theorem 3.3.3, its proof is omitted.

Theorem 2.1.2. *Let* $\mathbf{C} = (c_{ij})$ *be a given* 2×2 *real matrix and let* $\mathbf{b} = (b_1, b_2)'$ *be a real vector. If* $\mathbf{X} = (X_1, X_2)'$ *is distributed according to an* $\mathcal{N}_2(\boldsymbol{\mu}, \boldsymbol{\Sigma})$ *distribution, then*

$$\mathbf{Y} = \begin{pmatrix} Y_1 \\ Y_2 \end{pmatrix} = \begin{pmatrix} \sum_{j=1}^{2} c_{1j}X_j + b_1 \\ \sum_{j=1}^{2} c_{2j}X_j + b_2 \end{pmatrix} = \mathbf{CX} + \mathbf{b}$$

is distributed according to $\mathcal{N}_2(\mathbf{C}\boldsymbol{\mu} + \mathbf{b}, \mathbf{C}\boldsymbol{\Sigma}\mathbf{C}')$.

If in Theorem 2.1.2 we choose $\mathbf{b} = -\boldsymbol{\mu}$ and

$$\mathbf{C} = \begin{pmatrix} \sigma_1^{-1} & 0 \\ 0 & \sigma_2^{-1} \end{pmatrix},$$

where $\sigma_i = \sqrt{\sigma_i^2}$ is the standard deviation of X_i $(i = 1, 2)$, then $\mathbf{Y}$ is a bivariate normal variable with means 0, variances 1, and correlation coefficient ρ. Now consider a linear transformation of $\mathbf{Y}$ by rotating the xy axes by 45 degrees counterclockwise. Since a rotation of axes in $\Re^2$ can be accomplished by multiplying a vector by an orthogonal matrix, we may consider the linear transformation

$$\mathbf{Y}^* = \begin{pmatrix} Y_1^* \\ Y_2^* \end{pmatrix} = \frac{1}{\sqrt{2}}\begin{pmatrix} 1 & -1 \\ 1 & 1 \end{pmatrix}\begin{pmatrix} Y_1 \\ Y_2 \end{pmatrix}.$$

It is easy to verify that $\mathbf{Y}^*$ is a bivariate normal variable with means 0, variances $1 - \rho$ and $1 + \rho$, respectively, and correlation coefficient 0. Then the random variables

$$Z_1 = \frac{1}{\sqrt{1 - \rho}} Y_1^*, \qquad Z_2 = \frac{1}{\sqrt{1 + \rho}} Y_2^*,$$

are independent $\mathcal{N}(0, 1)$ variables.

Summarizing the steps given above, we conclude that if $\mathbf{X}$ is an $\mathcal{N}_2(\boldsymbol{\mu}, \boldsymbol{\Sigma})$ variable such that $|\rho| < 1$, then

$$\mathbf{Z} = \begin{pmatrix} Z_1 \\ Z_2 \end{pmatrix}$$

$$= \begin{pmatrix} (1-\rho)^{-1/2} & 0 \\ 0 & (1+\rho)^{-1/2} \end{pmatrix} \begin{pmatrix} 1/\sqrt{2} & -1/\sqrt{2} \\ 1/\sqrt{2} & 1/\sqrt{2} \end{pmatrix} \begin{pmatrix} \sigma_1^{-1} & 0 \\ 0 & \sigma_2^{-1} \end{pmatrix} \begin{pmatrix} X_1 - \mu_1 \\ X_2 - \mu_2 \end{pmatrix}$$

is an $\mathcal{N}_2(0, \mathbf{I}_2)$ variable (where $\mathbf{I}_2$ is the 2×2 identity matrix). Here the first step (from right) is to reduce the mean vector to $\mathbf{0}$, the second step is to achieve variables having variances 1. The third step, as described above, consists of the rotation of axes so that the new random variables Y_1^*, Y_2^* are uncorrelated (hence independent); and finally, the last step is to achieve variaces = 1.

On the other hand, by reversing this process we can always obtain a bivariate normal variable $(X_1, X_2)'$ with any mean vector $\boldsymbol{\mu}$, variances σ_1^2, σ_2^2, and correlation coefficient $\rho \in (-1, 1)$ through a transformation of two independent $\mathcal{N}(0, 1)$ variables. Since

$$\begin{pmatrix} d_1 & 0 \\ 0 & d_2 \end{pmatrix}^{-1} = \begin{pmatrix} d_1^{-1} & 0 \\ 0 & d_2^{-1} \end{pmatrix} \quad \text{and} \quad \frac{1}{\sqrt{2}}\begin{pmatrix} 1 & -1 \\ 1 & 1 \end{pmatrix}^{-1} = \frac{1}{\sqrt{2}}\begin{pmatrix} 1 & 1 \\ -1 & 1 \end{pmatrix},$$

the required transformation is given by

$$\begin{pmatrix} X_1 \\ X_2 \end{pmatrix} = \mathbf{C}\begin{pmatrix} Z_1 \\ Z_2 \end{pmatrix} + \begin{pmatrix} \mu_1 \\ \mu_2 \end{pmatrix}, \tag{2.1.9}$$

where

$$\mathbf{C} = \begin{pmatrix} \sigma_1\sqrt{(1-\rho)/2} & \sigma_1\sqrt{(1+\rho)/2} \\ -\sigma_2\sqrt{(1-\rho)/2} & \sigma_2\sqrt{(1+\rho)/2} \end{pmatrix}$$

$$= \begin{pmatrix} \sigma_1 & 0 \\ 0 & \sigma_2 \end{pmatrix} \begin{pmatrix} 1/\sqrt{2} & 1/\sqrt{2} \\ -1/\sqrt{2} & 1/\sqrt{2} \end{pmatrix} \begin{pmatrix} \sqrt{1-\rho} & 0 \\ 0 & \sqrt{1+\rho} \end{pmatrix}$$

is nonsingular if and only if $|\rho| < 1$. Furthermore, $\mathbf{C}$ satisfies $\mathbf{CC}' = \boldsymbol{\Sigma}$ and the steps in the transformation in (2.1.9) can be interpreted similarly.

We note in passing that there are other transformations which yield the same result. In particular, a suitably chosen triangular matrix serves exactly the same purpose (see, e.g., Proposition 8.1.1).

2.1.3. A Characterization and Related Transformation

In many applications, such as in certain Monte Carlo studies, we are concerned with the generation of a sequence of two-dimensional (pseudo) random variates $\{\mathbf{X}_t\}_{t=1}^N$ such that $\mathbf{X}_t$ is distributed according to an $\mathcal{N}_2(\boldsymbol{\mu}, \boldsymbol{\Sigma})$ distribution for given $\boldsymbol{\mu}$ and $\boldsymbol{\Sigma}$. In such applications it is usually easier to generate the independent univariate $\mathcal{N}(0, 1)$ variates Z_1 and Z_2 first, and then apply a transformation such as the one given in (2.1.9). The question that remains to be answered, of course, is how to generate independent $\mathcal{N}(0, 1)$ variates. A result of Box and Muller (1958), stated below, gives an answer to this question and provides a characterization of the bivariate normal distribution.

Theorem 2.1.3. *Let U_1, U_2 be independent uniform* $[0, 1]$ *variables, and define*

$$Z_1 = \sqrt{-2 \ln U_1} \sin(2\pi U_2), \qquad Z_2 = \sqrt{-2 \ln U_1} \cos(2\pi U_2). \quad (2.1.10)$$

Then Z_1, Z_2 are independent $\mathcal{N}(0, 1)$ variables.

Proof. By (2.1.10) we can write

$$U_1 = e^{-(Z_1^2+Z_2^2)/2}, \qquad U_2 = \frac{1}{2\pi} \tan^{-1}\left(\frac{Z_2}{Z_1}\right). \quad (2.1.11)$$

Since the Jacobian of the transformation

$$u_1(z_1, z_2) = e^{-(z_1^2+z_2^2)/2}, \qquad u_2(z_1, z_2) = \frac{1}{2\pi} \tan^{-1}\left(\frac{z_2}{z_1}\right)$$

is

$$|J| = \left|\frac{\partial u_i}{\partial z_j}\right| = \frac{1}{2\pi} e^{-(z_1^2+z_2^2)/2},$$

the joint density function of $(Z_1, Z_2)'$ is

$$f(z_1, z_2) = 1 \cdot |J| = \phi(z_1)\phi(z_2)$$

by calculus. □

Note that $Z_1^2 + Z_2^2$ has a chi-square distribution with 2 degrees of freedom, that is, its density function is negative exponential with mean 2. Thus Theorem 2.1.3 essentially says that for generating two independent $\mathcal{N}(0, 1)$ variates, we first choose the square of a radius at random according to this exponential distribution. After this radius is observed, we then choose, independently, an angle at random from the uniform $[0, 2\pi]$ distribution. The observed values of Z_1, Z_2 are determined by the projections on the x-axis and the y-axis of this random point with the given radius. But the selection of an angle from the uniform distribution is equivalent to selecting a point at random on the circle with given radius. Therefore Theorem 2.1.3 together with the transformation given in (2.1.9) yield the following characterization result for the bivariate normal distribution.

Theorem 2.1.4. *A two-dimensional random variable $(X_1, X_2)'$ is distributed according to an $\mathcal{N}_2(\boldsymbol{\mu}, \boldsymbol{\Sigma})$ distribution for some positive definite matrix $\boldsymbol{\Sigma}$ if and only if it is a random variable corresponding to the following experiment:*

(a) *observe the value of a random variable V from an exponential distribution with mean 2;*

(b) *for given* $V = v$, *observe a point at random on the circle with radius* $\sqrt{v}$, *and identify this point in* $\mathfrak{R}^2$ *as* $(Z_1, Z_2)'$;
(c) *apply the transformation* $(X_1, X_2)' = \mathbf{C}(Z_1, Z_2)' + \boldsymbol{\mu}$ *where* $\mathbf{C}$ *satisfies* $\mathbf{CC}' = \boldsymbol{\Sigma}$.

This characterization result has an n-dimensional generalization. In Theorem 4.1.1 we shall see that a multivariate normal variable corresponds to a similar experiment by:

(a) selecting a distance at random such that the square of the distance has a chi-square distribution with n degrees of freedom;
(b) selecting a point at random on the n-dimensional sphere with the observed radius; and
(c) applying a similar transformation.

Also note that a result of Tamhankar (1967) states that if Z_1, Z_2 are independent, then a characterization of normality is the independence of the random variable V and the angle variable arc $\tan(Z_2/Z_1)$. A general statement of that result for the multivariate normal distribution can be found in Theorem 4.1.2.

The transformation from independent $\mathcal{N}(0, 1)$ variables to a bivariate normal variable described above is from $\mathfrak{R}^2$ to $\mathfrak{R}^2$, that is, *two* independent $\mathcal{N}(0, 1)$ variables are transformed into a bivariate normal variable. There exist certain other useful transformations, one of them involves the transformation of three independent $\mathcal{N}(0, 1)$ variables. We state such a result below.

Fact 2.1.1. *Let* Z_0, Z_1, Z_2 *be independent* $\mathcal{N}(0, 1)$ *variables. For arbitrary but fixed* $\boldsymbol{\mu}$ *and* $\boldsymbol{\Sigma}$ *such that* $|\rho| < 1$, *let*

$$\begin{aligned} X_1 &= \sigma_1(\sqrt{1-|\rho|}\,Z_1 + \sqrt{|\rho|}\,Z_0) + \mu_1, \\ X_2 &= \sigma_2(\sqrt{1-|\rho|}\,Z_2 + \delta_\rho\sqrt{|\rho|}\,Z_0) + \mu_2, \end{aligned} \tag{2.1.12}$$

where

$$\delta_\rho = \begin{cases} 1 & \text{if} \quad \rho \geq 0, \\ -1 & \text{if} \quad \rho < 0. \end{cases} \tag{2.1.13}$$

Then $(X_1, X_2)'$ *is distributed according to an* $\mathcal{N}_2(\boldsymbol{\mu}, \boldsymbol{\Sigma})$ *distribution.*

This simple representation yields a number of useful applications. One of them is for expressing the joint distribution function of $(X_1, X_2)'$ in the form of a single integral. This will be discussed in the next section.

The proof of Fact 2.1.1 follows from Theorem 3.3.3 as a special case, and most of the other distribution properties of a bivariate normal variable follow immediately from more general results for the multivariate normal distribution given in Chapter 3.

2.2. The Distribution Function and Sampling Distributions

2.2.1. A Representation for the Distribution Function

If $\mathbf{X} = (X_1, X_2)'$ is distributed according to an $\mathcal{N}_2(\boldsymbol{\mu}, \boldsymbol{\Sigma})$ distribution such that $|\rho| < 1$ then, by definition, the distribution function of $\mathbf{X}$ is simply

$$F(x_1, x_2) = \int_{-\infty}^{x_1} \int_{-\infty}^{x_2} \frac{1}{2\pi\sigma_1\sigma_2\sqrt{1-\rho^2}} e^{-Q_2(\mathbf{u};\boldsymbol{\mu},\boldsymbol{\Sigma})/2}\, d\mathbf{u}. \tag{2.2.1}$$

The numerical values of the distribution function have been tabulated for selected parameters using various methods of evaluation and approximations (see Section 8.2). Also, in certain special cases, this double integral has a simple expression. For example, it is known that if $\mu_1 = \mu_2 = 0$, then $F(0, 0) = \frac{1}{4} + (1/2\pi) \arcsin \rho$ for all $\rho \in (-1, 1)$ and all σ_1^2, σ_2^2. The reader is referred to Johnson and Kotz (1972, Chap. 36, Sec. 4) for other related results.

The distribution function in (2.2.1) depends on a double integral and is difficult to evaluate numerically. In the following we provide an expression which depends only on a single integral. Let

$$\Phi(z) = \int_{-\infty}^{z} \frac{1}{\sqrt{2\pi}} e^{-u^2/2}\, du \tag{2.2.2}$$

denote the $\mathcal{N}(0, 1)$ distribution function. If $\rho \geq 0$, then by the expression in (2.1.12), we can write

$$\begin{aligned} F(x_1, x_2) &= P\left[\sqrt{1-\rho} Z_i \leq -\sqrt{\rho} Z_0 + \frac{x_i - \mu_i}{\sigma_i}, i = 1, 2\right] \\ &= P\left[Z_i \leq \frac{-\sqrt{\rho} Z_0 + a_i}{\sqrt{1-\rho}}, i = 1, 2\right], \end{aligned}$$

where $a_i = (x - \mu_i)/\sigma_i$ $(i = 1, 2)$. Since Z_1, Z_2, and Z_0 are independent $\mathcal{N}(0, 1)$ variables, Z_1 and Z_2 are independent $\mathcal{N}(0, 1)$ variables under the condition $Z_0 = z$ for all z. Thus, by first conditioning on $Z_0 = z$ then unconditioning and by $\phi(z) = \phi(-z)$, we have

$$F(x_1, x_2) = \int_{-\infty}^{\infty} \prod_{i=1}^{2} \Phi\left(\frac{\sqrt{\rho} z + a_i}{\sqrt{1-\rho}}\right) \phi(z)\, dz.$$

Similarly, for $\rho < 0$ we have

$$\begin{aligned} F(x, x_2) &= P\left[Z_1 \leq \frac{-\sqrt{|\rho|} Z_0 + a_1}{\sqrt{1-|\rho|}}, Z_2 \leq \frac{\sqrt{|\rho|} Z_0 + a_2}{\sqrt{1-|\rho|}}\right] \\ &= \int_{-\infty}^{\infty} \Phi\left(\frac{\sqrt{|\rho|} z + a_1}{\sqrt{1-|\rho|}}\right) \Phi\left(\frac{-\sqrt{|\rho|} z + a_2}{\sqrt{1-|\rho|}}\right) \phi(z)\, dz. \end{aligned}$$

Combining, we then have

$$F(x_1, x_2) = \int_{-\infty}^{\infty} \Phi\left(\frac{\sqrt{|\rho|}\,z + a_1}{\sqrt{1 - |\rho|}}\right) \Phi\left(\frac{\delta_\rho\sqrt{|\rho|}\,z + a_2}{\sqrt{1 - |\rho|}}\right) \phi(z)\,dz \qquad (2.2.3)$$

for $\rho \in (-1, 1)$, where δ_ρ is defined in (2.1.13). This expression provides a useful method for computing $F(x_1, x_2)$ numerically on a computer; a multivariate version of this result will be discussed in Section 8.3.

To study sampling distributions derived from the bivariate normal distribution, we consider $\mathbf{X}_1, \mathbf{X}_2, \ldots, \mathbf{X}_N$ which are independent $\mathcal{N}_2(\boldsymbol{\mu}, \boldsymbol{\Sigma})$ variables were $\mathbf{X}_t = (X_{1t}, X_{2t})'$ $(t = 1, \ldots, N)$. It is known that for

$$\bar{X}_i = \frac{1}{N} \sum_{t=1}^{N} X_{it}, \qquad i = 1, 2, \qquad (2.2.4)$$

$$S_{ij} = \frac{1}{N-1} \sum_{t=1}^{N} (X_{it} - \bar{X}_i)(X_{jt} - \bar{X}_j), \qquad i, j = 1, 2, \qquad (2.2.5)$$

the sample mean vector $\bar{\mathbf{X}}$ and sample covariance matrix $\mathbf{S}$ given by

$$\bar{\mathbf{X}} = \begin{pmatrix} \bar{X}_1 \\ \bar{X}_2 \end{pmatrix}, \qquad \mathbf{S} = \begin{pmatrix} S_{11} & S_{12} \\ S_{21} & S_{22} \end{pmatrix} \qquad (2.2.6)$$

are jointly sufficient for $(\boldsymbol{\mu}, \boldsymbol{\Sigma})$. Furthermore, $\bar{\mathbf{X}}$, $(N-1)S_{ii}/N$ $(i = 1, 2)$ and

$$r = \frac{S_{12}}{\sqrt{S_{11}S_{22}}} = \frac{\sum_{t=1}^{N} (X_{1t} - \bar{X}_1)(X_{2t} - \bar{X}_2)}{\left\{\left[\sum_{t=1}^{N} (X_{1t} - \bar{X}_1)^2\right]\left[\sum_{t=1}^{N} (X_{2t} - \bar{X}_2)^2\right]\right\}^{1/2}} \qquad (2.2.7)$$

are maximum likelihood estimators of $\boldsymbol{\mu}$, σ_i^2, and ρ, respectively (see Anderson (1984, Sec. 3.2)).

Since the distributions of $\bar{\mathbf{X}}$ and $\mathbf{S}$ immediately follow from the n-dimensional results given in Section 3.5, we shall restrict our attention here to the distribution of the sample correlation coefficient r.

2.2.2. Distribution of the Sample Correlation Coefficient

It is clear that $S_{12} = S_{21}$ holds, and that the joint distribution of S_{11}, S_{12}, and S_{22} does not depend on $\boldsymbol{\mu}$. Furthermore, for given positive variances σ_1^2 and σ_2^2, we have

$$r = \left(\frac{S_{12}}{\sigma_1\sigma_2}\right) \Big/ \left(\frac{\sqrt{S_{11}S_{22}}}{\sigma_1\sigma_2}\right) = \frac{S_{12}}{\sqrt{S_{11}S_{22}}}.$$

Thus in deriving the distribution of r we may assume that $\boldsymbol{\mu} = \mathbf{0}$ and $\sigma_1^2 = \sigma_2^2 = 1$.

The following theorem concerns the distribution of r when the components of $\mathbf{X}$ are independent.

Theorem 2.2.1. *Let* $\mathbf{X}_1, \ldots, \mathbf{X}_N$ $(N \geq 4)$ *be independent* $\mathcal{N}_2(\boldsymbol{\mu}, \boldsymbol{\Sigma})$ *random variables. If* $\rho = 0$, *then the density function of r is*

$$h(r) = \frac{\Gamma(\frac{1}{2}(N-1))}{\sqrt{\pi}\,\Gamma(\frac{1}{2}(N-2))}(1-r^2)^{(N-4)/2}, \qquad r \in (-1, 1). \tag{2.2.8}$$

Equivalently, $\sqrt{N-2}\,r/\sqrt{1-r^2}$ *has a Student's t distribution with* $N-2$ *degrees of freedom.*

Proof. Without loss of generality assume $\boldsymbol{\mu} = \mathbf{0}$ and $\sigma_1^2 = \sigma_2^2 = 1$. If $\rho = 0$, then $X_{11}, \ldots, X_{1N}, X_{21}, \ldots, X_{2N}$ are independent $\mathcal{N}(0, 1)$ variables. Thus, by conditioning on

$$(X_{21}, \ldots, X_{2N})' = (x_{21}, \ldots, x_{2N})',$$

$X_{11}, \ldots, X_{1N}$ are independent $\mathcal{N}(0, 1)$ variables for every given $(x_{21}, \ldots, x_{2N})'$. Now define two $N \times N$ matrices $\mathbf{B} = (b_{rs})$ and $\mathbf{C} = (c_{rs})$, where

$$b_{rs} = \frac{(x_{2r} - \bar{x}_2)(x_{2s} - \bar{x}_2)}{\left[\sum_{t=1}^{N} (x_{2t} - \bar{x}_2)^2\right]^{1/2}},$$

$$c_{rs} = \frac{1}{\sqrt{N}} \qquad \text{for all } r, s,$$

where $\bar{x}_2 = (1/N)\sum_{t=1}^{N} x_{2t}$; then for $\mathbf{Z} = (X_{11}, \ldots, X_{1N})'$ consider the quadratic forms

$$V_1 = \mathbf{Z}'\mathbf{B}\mathbf{Z} = \frac{\left(\sum_{t=1}^{N} (x_{2t} - \bar{x}_2)X_{1t}\right)^2}{\sum_{t=1}^{N} (x_{2t} - \bar{x}_2)^2},$$

$$V_2 = \mathbf{Z}'\mathbf{C}\mathbf{Z} = N\bar{X}_1^2,$$

and

$$V_3 = \mathbf{Z}'(\mathbf{I}_N - \mathbf{B} - \mathbf{C})\mathbf{Z} = \mathbf{Z}'(\mathbf{I}_N - \mathbf{C})\mathbf{Z} - V_1 = \sum_{t=1}^{N} (X_{1t} - \bar{X}_1)^2 - V_1.$$

Since $V_1 + V_2 + V_3 = \mathbf{Z}'\mathbf{Z}$ has a $\chi^2(N)$ distribution, by the Fisher–Cochran Theorem (Rao, 1973, p. 185) V_1, V_2, V_3 are *independent* chi-squared variables with degrees of freedom 1, 1, and $N-2$, respectively. But

$$\sum_{t=1}^{N} (x_{2t} - \bar{x}_2)(X_{1t} - \bar{X}_1) = \sum_{t=1}^{N} (x_{2t} - \bar{x}_2)X_{1t},$$

so that

$$r^2 = \frac{V_1}{V_1 + V_3}.$$

holds for every given $(x_{21}, \ldots, x_{2N})'$. Simple algebra shows that

$$\frac{r^2}{(1 - r^2)/(N - 2)} = \frac{V_1}{V_3/(N - 2)}$$

has an $F(1, N - 2)$ distribution. Since it does not depend on the vector $(x_{21}, \ldots, x_{2N})'$, the same distribution holds after unconditioning. Consequently, the random variable $\sqrt{N - 2}r/\sqrt{1 - r^2}$ has a Student's t distribution with $N - 2$ degrees of freedom. The density function of r in (2.2.8) then follows from the density function of the t distribution and by a change of variable given by $r = t/[(N - 2) + t^2]^{1/2}$. The details are left to the reader. □

Note that when $\rho = 0$, the density function $h(r)$ of r is symmetric about the origin. Furthermore, the percentage points of the distribution of r can be obtained from the t distribution in the following way: For $\alpha < 0.5$ choose t_α from the Student's t table with degrees of freedom $N - 2$ to satisfy

$$P[|t| > t_\alpha] = 2\alpha.$$

Then clearly we have

$$2\alpha = P\left[\frac{(N - 2)r^2}{1 - r^2} > t_\alpha^2\right] = P\left[r^2 > \frac{t_\alpha^2}{(N - 2) + t_\alpha^2}\right].$$

Thus

$$P\left[r \le \frac{t_\alpha}{\sqrt{(N - 2) + t_\alpha^2}}\right] = 1 - \alpha$$

holds for all $\alpha < 0.5$.

For the general case in which ρ is not necessarily 0, the problem becomes more complicated due to the lack of independence. The density function of r for $\rho \neq 0$ was first derived by Fisher (1915) using a geometric argument. In the following theorem we state the result with a sketch of the proof given in Anderson (1984, pp. 110–112).

Theorem 2.2.2. *Let* $\mathbf{X}_1, \ldots, \mathbf{X}_N$ $(N \ge 4)$ *be independent* $\mathcal{N}_2(\boldsymbol{\mu}, \boldsymbol{\Sigma})$ *random variables. Then for* $\rho \in (-1, 1)$ *the density function of* r *is*

$$h_\rho(r) = \frac{1}{\pi(N - 3)!} 2^{N-3}(1 - \rho^2)^{(N-1)/2}(1 - r^2)^{(N-4)/2} \times \sum_{j=0}^{\infty} \frac{(2\rho r)^j}{j!} \Gamma^2\left(\frac{N + j - 1}{2}\right). \tag{2.2.9}$$

Sketch of the Proof. Without loss of generality again assume that $\boldsymbol{\mu} = \mathbf{0}$ and $\sigma_1^2 = \sigma_2^2 = 1$.

(a) By Theorem 2.1.1, the conditional distribution of X_{1t} given $X_{2t} = x_{2t}$ is $\mathcal{N}(\rho x_{2t}, 1 - \rho^2)$ for $t = 1, \ldots, N$. Thus, by conditioning on $(X_{21}, \ldots, X_{2N})' =$

$(x_{21}, \ldots, x_{2N})'$:

(i)
$$\frac{S_{12}}{\sqrt{S_{22}}} = \frac{\sum_{t=1}^{N} (x_{2t} - \bar{x}_2)(X_{1t} - \bar{X}_1)}{\left[\sum_{t=1}^{N} (x_{2t} - \bar{x}_2)^2\right]^{1/2}}$$

is a normal variable with mean $\rho(\sum_{t=1}^{N} (x_{2t} - \bar{x}_2)^2)^{1/2}$ and variance $(1 - \rho^2)$;

(ii) $(N - 1)(S_{11} - S_{12}^2/S_{22})$ is a chi-squared variable with $N - 2$ degrees of freedom; and

(iii) $S_{12}/\sqrt{S_{22}}$ and $(N - 1)(S_{11} - S_{12}^2/S_{22})$ are conditionally independent.

(b) From (a) and the fact that $X_{21}, \ldots, X_{2N}$ are independent $\mathcal{N}(0, 1)$ variables, we can write out the joint density of

$$\left(\frac{S_{11}}{\sqrt{S_{22}}}, (N - 1)\left(S_{11} - \frac{S_{12}^2}{S_{22}}\right), (X_{21}, \ldots, X_{2N})'\right)'.$$

Then, after integrating out over the N-dimensional sphere we obtain the joint density function of

$$\left(\frac{S_{11}}{\sqrt{S_{22}}}, (N - 1)\left(S_{11} - \frac{S_{12}^2}{S_{22}}, S_{22}\right)\right)'.$$

(c) From (b), the density function of $(S_{11}, S_{12}, S_{22})'$ can be derived through a transformation of variables. From this density function we can obtain the joint density of $(r = S_{12}/\sqrt{S_{11}S_{22}}, S_{11}, S_{22})$ through another transformation of variables. Finally, the marginal density of r can be found by integrating out the other two variables. □

The density function of r given by Fisher (1915) is of the form

$$h_\rho(r) = \frac{1}{\pi(N - 3)!}(1 - \rho^2)^{(N-1)/2}(1 - r^2)^{(N-4)/2}\left[\frac{d^{N-2}}{dx^{N-2}}\left\{\frac{\cos^{-1}(-x)}{\sqrt{1 - x^2}}\right\}\Bigg|_{x=\rho r}\right], \tag{2.2.10}$$

which is different from, but is equivalent to (2.2.9). In addition to (2.2.9) and (2.2.10) Hotelling (1953) also obtained another expression for $h_\rho(r)$. But it also involves infinite series and is quite complicated. For selected values of ρ and N, the percentage points and probability integrals for r were tabulated by David (1938).

In addition to the existing tables, an approximation can be made using Fisher's z-transformation when N is large. Fisher (1915) studied the moments of the transformation

$$z = \tfrac{1}{2} \ln\left(\frac{1 + r}{1 - r}\right), \tag{2.2.11}$$

and found that the mean and the variance of z are approximately

$$\xi = \frac{1}{2}\ln\left(\frac{1+\rho}{1-\rho}\right) \tag{2.2.12}$$

and $1/(N-3)$, respectively, for large N. Furthermore, it was found that the distribution of the standardized z is closer to $\mathcal{N}(0, 1)$ than is the distribution of the standardized r. We summarize this result in the following theorem.

Theorem 2.2.3. *Let* $\mathbf{X}_1, \ldots, \mathbf{X}_N$ *be independent* $\mathcal{N}_2(\boldsymbol{\mu}, \boldsymbol{\Sigma})$ *variables. Let* r *denote the sample correlation coefficient given in* (2.2.7), *and let* z, ξ *be defined as in* (2.2.11) *and* (2.2.12), *respectively. Then, as* $N \to \infty$, *the limiting distribution of* $\sqrt{N-3}\,(z-\xi)$ *is* $\mathcal{N}(0, 1)$.

2.3. Dependence and the Correlation Coefficient

In the studies of dependence of random variables, various notions have been discussed in the literature. The bivariate normal distribution is an ideal model for illustrating those notions. Generally speaking, if $(X_1, X_2)'$ is distributed according to an $\mathcal{N}_2(\boldsymbol{\mu}, \boldsymbol{\Sigma})$ distribution, then:

(i) X_1 and X_2 are positively dependent if their correlation coefficient ρ is positive;
(ii) they are negatively dependent if ρ is negative; and
(iii) of course, they are independent if $\rho = 0$.

The strongest condition for studying the positive dependence of a pair of random variables X_1, X_2 appears to be:

(a) the TP_2 property: The joint density $f(x_1, x_2)$ satisfies

$$f(x_1^*, x_2)f(x_1, x_2^*) \leq f(x_1, x_2)f(x_1^*, x_2^*) \tag{2.3.1}$$

for all $x_1^* < x_1$ and $x_2^* < x_2$. This condition simply means that the likelihood becomes larger when both coordinates take larger values together and smaller values together at the same time. It is known that this condition is equivalent to saying that the family of conditional densities of X_1 given $X_2 = x_2$ has the monotone likelihood ratio property, that is,

$$\frac{f_{1|2}(x_1|x_2)}{f_{1|2}(x_1|x_2^*)} \text{ is a nondecreasing function of } x_1 \tag{2.3.2}$$

for all $x_2^* < x_2$.

Furthermore, it is known that this condition implies

(b) The Positive Regression Dependence (PRD) condition: $P[X_1 \leq x_1 | X_2 = x_2]$ is nonincreasing (thus $P[X_1 > x_1 | X_2 = x_2]$ is nondecreasing) in x_2 for all fixed x_1.

The notion of PRD depends on the conditional distribution of X_1 given $X_2 = x_2$, and implies

(c) Association (A) Property:

$$\mathrm{Cov}(g_1(X_1, X_2), g_2(X_1, X_2)) \geq 0 \tag{2.3.3}$$

holds for all nondecreasing functions g_1, g_2 such that the covariance exists. By choosing

$$g_i(X_1, X_2) = \begin{cases} -1 & \text{if } X_i \leq x_i, \\ 0 & \text{otherwise,} \end{cases}$$

for $i = 1, 2$, the association property implies

(d) The Positive Quadrant Dependence (PQD) condition:

$$P[X_1 \leq x_1, X_2 \leq x_2] \geq P[X_1 \leq x_1]P[X_2 \leq x_2] \qquad \text{for all } x_1, x_2. \tag{2.3.4}$$

The left-hand side in (2.3.4) is the probability that both X_1 and X_2 simultaneously take smaller values, and the right-hand side is the corresponding probability when X_1 and X_2 are independent. It is known that this probability inequality yields the following condition:

(e) The correlation coefficient ρ is nonnegative.

All of these conditions in (a)–(e) indicate the trend that a smaller X_1 value tends to be associated with a smaller X_2 value stochastically. They were introduced by Lehmann (1966), Esary, Proschan, and Walkup (1967), and others; a convenient reference is Tong (1980, Sec. 5.1). For bivariate random variables, the notions in (a), (b), (d), (e) can be modified for negative dependence by reversing the direction of the inequalities. It is also known that the implications from (a)–(e) are strict. Thus in general the sign of the correlation coefficient of X_1, X_2 determines the weakest condition on their positive or negative dependence.

For the bivariate normal distribution, however, all of these conditions are equivalent. This statement follows from the fact that the conditional distribution of X_1, given $X_2 = x_2$, is $\mathcal{N}(\mu_1 + \rho(\sigma_1/\sigma_2)(x_2 - \mu_2), \sigma_1^2(1 - \rho^2))$ (see Theorem 2.1.1(c)). Simple algebra then shows

$$\frac{f_{1|2}(x_1|x_2)}{f_{1|2}(x_1|x_2^*)} = \exp\left\{\frac{1}{\sigma_1^2(1-\rho^2)}[u_1(x_1, x_2, x_2^*) + u_2(x_2, x_2^*)]\right\}, \tag{2.3.5}$$

where u_2 does not depend on x_1 and $u_1(x_1, x_2, x_2^*) = (\rho\sigma_1/\sigma_2)(x_2 - x_2^*)x_1$ is increasing in x_1 (decreasing in x_1) for $\rho > 0$ (for $\rho < 0$). Since (2.3.1) is equivalent to (2.3.2), the statement follows. Thus, simply by the sign of ρ, we immediately have the results in (b)–(d). (For $\rho < 0$ the direction of the inequalities are reversed.)

For some of the notions of dependence discussed above, certain stronger results for the bivariate normal distribution are also known. For example, it is well known (Slepian's inequality, see Theorem 5.1.7) that the value of the bivariate normal distribution function $P_\rho[X_1 \le x_1, X_2 \le x_2]$ is increasing in ρ for all $\rho \in [-1, 1]$ and all fixed $(x_1, x_2)'$. This result yields the result in (2.3.4) as a special case. Consequently, we may obtain a partial ordering of the "strength" of (positive or negative) dependence for the bivariate normal distribution simply by the sign and the magnitude of the correlation coefficient. Similar results for the multivariate normal distribution will be given in Section 5.1.

PROBLEMS

In the following problems $(X_1, X_2)'$ is assumed to have an $\mathcal{N}_2(\boldsymbol{\mu}, \boldsymbol{\Sigma})$ distribution with density function $f(\mathbf{x}; \boldsymbol{\mu}, \boldsymbol{\Sigma})$ where $|\rho| < 1$.

2.1. Show directly by definition that $\{\mathbf{x}: \mathbf{x} \in \Re^2, Q_2(\mathbf{x}; \boldsymbol{\mu}, \boldsymbol{\Sigma}) \le \lambda\}$ is a convex set, where $Q_2(\mathbf{x}; \boldsymbol{\mu}, \boldsymbol{\Sigma})$ is defined in (2.0.2).

2.2. Assuming $\boldsymbol{\mu} = \mathbf{0}$, show that $f(\mathbf{x}; \boldsymbol{\mu}, \boldsymbol{\Sigma})$ is symmetric about the origin; i.e., $f(\mathbf{x}; \boldsymbol{\mu}, \boldsymbol{\Sigma}) = f(-\mathbf{x}; \boldsymbol{\mu}, \boldsymbol{\Sigma})$.

2.3. Assuming $\boldsymbol{\mu} = \mathbf{0}$, show that $f((x_1, x_2)'; \mathbf{0}, \boldsymbol{\Sigma}) = f((x_1, -x_2)'; \mathbf{0}, \boldsymbol{\Sigma})$ holds if and only if $\rho = 0$.

2.4. Assuming $\mu_1 = \mu_2$ and $\sigma_1^2 = \sigma_2^2$, show that $f(\mathbf{x}; \boldsymbol{\mu}, \boldsymbol{\Sigma})$ is a decreasing function of $|x_1 - x_2|$ for every fixed $x_1 + x_2 = \lambda$.

2.5. Let $\boldsymbol{\Sigma}$ be the covariance matrix given in (2.0.3) such that $|\sigma_{12}| < \sigma_1\sigma_2$. Find a 2×2 orthogonal matrix $\mathbf{C}$ such that $\mathbf{D} = \mathbf{C}\boldsymbol{\Sigma}\mathbf{C}'$ is a diagonal matrix with positive diagonal elements. (For the existence of $\mathbf{C}$, see Anderson (1984, p. 587)).

2.6. Find the matrix $\mathbf{D}$ in Problem 2.5. Then find $\mathbf{H}$ such that $\mathbf{H}\boldsymbol{\Sigma}\mathbf{H}' = \mathbf{I}_2$.

2.7. Verify the Jacobian of the transformation given in the proof of Theorem 2.1.3.

2.8. Assuming $\boldsymbol{\mu} = \mathbf{0}$, show that $P_\rho[X_1 \le 0, X_2 \le 0] = \frac{1}{4} + (1/2\pi) \arcsin \rho$. Then show that this probability is strictly increasing in $\rho \in [-1, 1]$.

2.9. Show that $F(x_1, x_2)$ defined in (2.2.3) can be written as

$$F(x_1, x_2) = \frac{1}{\sqrt{\pi}} \int_{-\infty}^{\infty} \Phi\left(\frac{\sqrt{2|\rho|}\,u + a_1}{\sqrt{1 - |\rho|}}\right) \Phi\left(\frac{\delta_\rho\sqrt{2|\rho|}\,u + a_2}{\sqrt{1 - |\rho|}}\right) e^{-u^2}\, du,$$

where $a_i = (x_i - \mu_i)/\sigma_i$ $(i = 1, 2)$.

2.10. (Continuation.) Let V denote an exponential random variable with mean 1. Show that $F(x_1, x_2) = E\psi(V; x_1, x_2)$ where

$$\psi(v; x_1, x_2) = \frac{1}{2\sqrt{\pi v}} \left\{ \Phi\left(\frac{\sqrt{2|\rho| v} + a_1}{\sqrt{1 - |\rho|}}\right) \Phi\left(\frac{\delta_\rho\sqrt{2|\rho| v} + a_2}{\sqrt{1 - |\rho|}}\right) + \Phi\left(\frac{-\sqrt{2|\rho| v} + a_1}{\sqrt{1 - |\rho|}}\right) \Phi\left(\frac{-\delta_\rho\sqrt{2|\rho| v} + a_2}{\sqrt{1 - |\rho|}}\right) \right\}.$$

2.11. Use the transformation in (2.1.12) in a similar fashion to express the probability $P[|X_1| \leq x_1, |X_2| \leq x_2]$ as a single integral.

2.12. Complete the proof of Theorem 2.2.1 by showing that if t has Student's t distribution with $N - 2$ degrees of freedom and $r = t/[(N - 2) + t^2]^{1/2}$, then the density function of r is that given in (2.2.8).

2.13. Show that both (2.2.9) and (2.2.10) reduce to (2.2.8) when $\rho = 0$.

2.14. Assuming $\rho = 0$, let r denote the sample correlation coefficient with $N = 28$ and let r_α denote the αth percentage point such that $P[r > r_\alpha] = \alpha$. Find r_α for $\alpha = 0.05$ and 0.01 using Student's t table.

2.15. Use Theorem 2.2.3 and the normal table to approximate r_α for $N = 28$ and $\alpha = 0.05, 0.01$.

2.16. Find a density function $g(y_1, y_2)$ of $(Y_1, Y_2)'$ such that $\text{Corr}(Y_1, Y_2) \geq 0$ but that $P[Y_1 \leq y_1, Y_2 \leq y_2] \geq P[Y_1 \leq y_1]P[Y_2 \leq y_2]$ does not hold for all $(y_1, y_2)'$.

CHAPTER 3

Fundamental Properties and Sampling Distributions of the Multivariate Normal Distribution

In this chapter we study some fundamental properties of the multivariate normal distribution, including distribution properties and related sampling distributions.

We first observe several different definitions of the multivariate normal distribution and show their equivalence. In Section 3.3 we consider a partition of the components of a multivariate normal variable, then derive the marginal and conditional distributions and the distributions of linear transformations and linear combinations of its components. The multiple and partial correlations, the canonical correlations, and the principal components are defined and studied in Section 3.4. Finally, in Section 3.5, we derive sampling distributions of the sample mean vector, the sample covariance matrix, and the sample correlation coefficients.

3.1. Preliminaries

In order to properly define the multivariate normal distribution and to study its distribution properties more efficiently, we begin with a review of some basic facts concerning the covariance matrix and the characteristic function of an n-dimensional random variable.

For $n \geq 2$ let $\mathbf{X} = (X_1, \ldots, X_n)'$ be an n-dimensional random variable. Let μ_i and σ_{ii} denote, respectively, the mean and the variance of X_i $(i = 1, \ldots, n)$, and let σ_{ij} denote the covariance between X_i and X_j $(1 \leq i < j \leq n)$. Then

$$\boldsymbol{\mu} = \begin{pmatrix} \mu_1 \\ \mu_2 \\ \vdots \\ \mu_n \end{pmatrix}, \qquad \boldsymbol{\Sigma} = \begin{pmatrix} \sigma_{11} & \sigma_{12} & \cdots & \sigma_{1n} \\ \sigma_{21} & \sigma_{22} & \cdots & \sigma_{2n} \\ & & \cdots & \\ \sigma_{n1} & \sigma_{n2} & \cdots & \sigma_{nn} \end{pmatrix}, \tag{3.1.1}$$

are, respectively, the mean vector and the covariance matrix of $\mathbf{X}$. For notational convenience we shall occasionally write σ_{ii} as σ_i^2 $(i = 1, \dots, n)$.

Fact 3.1.1. *For $k \geq 1$, let $\mathbf{C}$ be a $k \times n$ real matrix and let $\mathbf{b}$ be a $k \times 1$ real vector. Let $\mathbf{Y} = \mathbf{CX} + \mathbf{b}$. Then the mean vector and the covariance matrix of $\mathbf{Y}$ are, respectively,*

$$\boldsymbol{\mu}_{\mathbf{Y}} = \mathbf{C}\boldsymbol{\mu} + \mathbf{b}, \qquad \boldsymbol{\Sigma}_{\mathbf{Y}} = \mathbf{C}\boldsymbol{\Sigma}\mathbf{C}'.$$

Proof. For each fixed $i = 1, \dots, k$, we have

$$Y_i = \sum_{s=1}^{n} c_{is} X_s + b_i, \qquad i = 1, \dots, k.$$

Thus

$$EY_i = \sum_{s=1}^{n} c_{is} \mu_s + b_i, \qquad i = 1, \dots, k,$$

which is the ith row of $\mathbf{C}\boldsymbol{\mu} + \mathbf{b}$. Furthermore,

$$\begin{aligned} E(Y_i - EY_i)(Y_j - EY_j) &= E\left[\left\{\sum_{s=1}^{n} c_{is}(X_s - \mu_s)\right\}\left\{\sum_{t=1}^{n} c_{jt}(X_t - \mu_t)\right\}\right] \\ &= \sum_{s=1}^{n} \sum_{t=1}^{n} c_{is} c_{jt} \sigma_{ij}, \end{aligned}$$

which is just the (i, j)th element of $\mathbf{C}\boldsymbol{\Sigma}\mathbf{C}'$. □

Choosing $k = 1$ and $\mathbf{C} = \mathbf{c}' = (c_1, \dots, c_n)$ in Fact 3.1.1 we have

Fact 3.1.2. *For $\mathbf{c}' = (c_1, \dots, c_n)$ the variance of $Y = \mathbf{c}'\mathbf{X} = \sum_{i=1}^{n} c_i X_i$ is*

$$\sigma_Y^2 = \sum_{i=1}^{n} \sum_{j=1}^{n} c_i c_j \sigma_{ij} = \mathbf{c}'\boldsymbol{\Sigma}\mathbf{c}.$$

An $n \times n$ symmetric matrix $\boldsymbol{\Sigma}$ is said to be positive definite (p.d.) if $\mathbf{c}'\boldsymbol{\Sigma}\mathbf{c} \geq 0$ holds for all real vectors $\mathbf{c}$, and equality holds only for $\mathbf{c} = \mathbf{0}$. It is said to be positive semidefinite (p.s.d.) if $\mathbf{c}'\boldsymbol{\Sigma}\mathbf{c} \geq 0$ holds for all real vectors $\mathbf{c}$, and equality holds for some $\mathbf{c} = \mathbf{c}_0 \neq \mathbf{0}$. It is known that if $\boldsymbol{\Sigma}$ is p.d. (p.s.d.), then $|\boldsymbol{\Sigma}| > 0$ $(|\boldsymbol{\Sigma}| = 0)$ or, equivalently, the rank of $\boldsymbol{\Sigma}$ is n (is less than n).

The distribution of $\mathbf{X}$ is said to be singular if there exists a vector $\mathbf{c}_0 \neq \mathbf{0}$ such that $Y = \mathbf{c}_0'\mathbf{X}$ is singular (that is, $P[Y = \mu_Y] = 1$). But the variance of Y is $\mathbf{c}'\boldsymbol{\Sigma}\mathbf{c}$ and Y is singular if and only if $\sigma_Y^2 = 0$. Thus we have

Fact 3.1.3. *A covariance matrix $\boldsymbol{\Sigma}$ is either p.d. or p.s.d. Furthermore,*

$$\begin{aligned} \boldsymbol{\Sigma} \text{ is p.s.d.} \quad &\Leftrightarrow \quad |\boldsymbol{\Sigma}| = 0, \\ &\Leftrightarrow \quad \text{the rank of } \boldsymbol{\Sigma} \text{ is less than } n, \\ &\Leftrightarrow \quad \text{the corresponding distribution is singular.} \end{aligned}$$

We shall say that the distribution of $\mathbf{X}$ is nonsingular if it is not singular. Furthermore, for notational convenience we write $\boldsymbol{\Sigma} > 0$ instead of $|\boldsymbol{\Sigma}| > 0$ when $\boldsymbol{\Sigma}$ is p.d.

The characteristic function (c.f.) of an n-dimensional random variable $\mathbf{X}$ is given by

$$\psi_{\mathbf{X}}(\mathbf{t}) = Ee^{i\mathbf{t}'\mathbf{X}}, \qquad \mathbf{t} \in \Re^n,$$

where $i^2 = -1$. Through an application of the following known result:

Fact 3.1.4 (Uniqueness Theorem). *The c.f. of a random variable* $\mathbf{X}$ *determines its distribution uniquely*;

c.f.'s can be used for finding the distribution of a random variable.

For linear transformations of random variables, the following fact can easily be established:

Fact 3.1.5. *Let* $\mathbf{X}$ *be an n-dimensional random variable with c.f.* $\psi_{\mathbf{X}}(\mathbf{t})$. *Let* $\mathbf{C}$ *be an* $n \times n$ *real matrix and let* $\mathbf{b}$ *be an* $n \times 1$ *vector. Then the c.f. of* $\mathbf{Y} = \mathbf{CX} + \mathbf{b}$ *is* $\psi_{\mathbf{Y}}(\mathbf{t}) = e^{i\mathbf{t}'\mathbf{b}}\psi_{\mathbf{X}}(\mathbf{C}'\mathbf{t})$.

PROOF.

$$\begin{aligned}\psi_{\mathbf{Y}}(\mathbf{t}) &= Ee^{i\mathbf{t}'\mathbf{Y}}\\ &= Ee^{i\mathbf{t}'(\mathbf{CX}+\mathbf{b})}\\ &= e^{i\mathbf{t}'\mathbf{b}}Ee^{i(\mathbf{C}'\mathbf{t})'\mathbf{X}}.\end{aligned}$$ □

Now consider the partition of the components of an n-dimensional random variable $\mathbf{Y}$ given by $\mathbf{Y} = (\mathbf{Y}_1, \mathbf{Y}_2)'$, where $\mathbf{Y}_1$ is $k \times 1$ and $\mathbf{Y}_2$ is $(n-k) \times 1$.

Fact 3.1.6. *If the c.f. of* $\mathbf{Y}$ *is* $\psi_{\mathbf{Y}}(\mathbf{t})$, $\mathbf{t} \in \Re^n$, *then the c.f. of* $\mathbf{Y}_1$ *is* $\psi_{\mathbf{Y}}(\mathbf{t}_1, \mathbf{0})$, $\mathbf{t}_1 \in \Re^k$.

PROOF.

$$\psi_{\mathbf{Y}_1}(t_1, \ldots, t_k) = E\exp\left(i\sum_1^k t_jY_j\right) = E\exp\left[i\left(\sum_1^k t_jY_j + \sum_{k+1}^n 0Y_j\right)\right] = \psi_{\mathbf{Y}}(\mathbf{t}_1, \mathbf{0}).$$

□

If $\mathbf{H}$ is a $k \times n$ real matrix $(k < n)$ and if we are interested in finding the distribution of $\mathbf{Y}_1 = \mathbf{HX}$, a standard procedure is:

(i) Find $\psi_{\mathbf{Y}}(\mathbf{t})$, the c.f. of

$$\begin{pmatrix}\mathbf{Y}_1\\ \mathbf{Y}_2\end{pmatrix} = \begin{pmatrix}\mathbf{H} & \mathbf{0}\\ \mathbf{0}' & \mathbf{I}_{n-k}\end{pmatrix}\mathbf{X}$$

by applying Fact 3.1.5, where $\mathbf{0}$ is the $k \times (n-k)$ matrix with elements 0, and $\mathbf{I}_{n-k}$ is the $(n-k) \times (n-k)$ identity matrix;

(ii) find $\psi_{\mathbf{Y}_1}(\mathbf{t}_1)$ from $\psi_{\mathbf{Y}}(\mathbf{t})$, where $\mathbf{t}_1 = (t_1, \ldots, t_k)' \in \Re^k$;

(iii) identify the density $f_1(\mathbf{y}_1)$ associated with the c.f. $\psi_{\mathbf{Y}_1}(\mathbf{t}_1)$, then apply the uniqueness theorem (Fact 3.1.4) to claim that the density function of $\mathbf{Y}_1$ is $f_1(\mathbf{y}_1)$.

This method will be used in the proof of Theorem 3.3.1 for deriving the marginal distributions of a multivariate normal distribution.

3.2. Definitions of the Multivariate Normal Distribution

We first give a definition of the nonsingular multivariate normal distribution.

Definition 3.2.1. An n-dimensional random variable $\mathbf{X}$ with mean vector $\boldsymbol{\mu}$ and covariance matrix $\boldsymbol{\Sigma}$ is said to have a nonsingular multivariate normal distribution, in symbols $\mathbf{X} \sim \mathcal{N}_n(\boldsymbol{\mu}, \boldsymbol{\Sigma})$, $\boldsymbol{\Sigma} > 0$, if (i) $\boldsymbol{\Sigma}$ is positive definite, and (ii) the density function of $\mathbf{X}$ is of the form

$$f(\mathbf{x}; \boldsymbol{\mu}, \boldsymbol{\Sigma}) = \frac{1}{(2\pi)^{n/2} |\boldsymbol{\Sigma}|^{1/2}} e^{-Q_n(\mathbf{x}; \boldsymbol{\mu}, \boldsymbol{\Sigma})/2}, \qquad \mathbf{x} \in \Re^n, \tag{3.2.1}$$

where

$$Q_n(\mathbf{x}; \boldsymbol{\mu}, \boldsymbol{\Sigma}) = (\mathbf{x} - \boldsymbol{\mu})' \boldsymbol{\Sigma}^{-1} (\mathbf{x} - \boldsymbol{\mu}). \tag{3.2.2}$$

Remark 3.2.1. For this definition to be consistent, we must verify that if $\mathbf{X}$ has the density function $f(\mathbf{x}; \boldsymbol{\mu}, \boldsymbol{\Sigma})$, then the mean vector and the covariance matrix of $\mathbf{X}$ are indeed $\boldsymbol{\mu}$ and $\boldsymbol{\Sigma}$, respectively. This is postponed and will be given in Remark 3.3.1.

Now let $\mathbf{X} \sim \mathcal{N}_n(\boldsymbol{\mu}, \boldsymbol{\Sigma})$, $\boldsymbol{\Sigma} > 0$, and consider the transformation

$$\mathbf{Y} = \mathbf{C}\mathbf{X} + \mathbf{b}, \tag{3.2.3}$$

where $\mathbf{C} = (c_{ij})$ is an $n \times n$ real matrix and $\mathbf{b}$ is a real vector.

Theorem 3.2.1. *Let* $\mathbf{Y}$ *be defined as in* (3.2.3). *If* $\mathbf{X} \sim \mathcal{N}_n(\boldsymbol{\mu}, \boldsymbol{\Sigma})$, $\boldsymbol{\Sigma} > 0$, *and* $\mathbf{C}$ *is an* $n \times n$ *real matrix such that* $|\mathbf{C}| \neq 0$, *then* $\mathbf{Y} \sim \mathcal{N}_n(\boldsymbol{\mu}_{\mathbf{Y}}, \boldsymbol{\Sigma}_{\mathbf{Y}})$, $\boldsymbol{\Sigma}_{\mathbf{Y}} > 0$, *where*

$$\boldsymbol{\mu}_{\mathbf{Y}} = \mathbf{C}\boldsymbol{\mu} + \mathbf{b}, \qquad \boldsymbol{\Sigma}_{\mathbf{Y}} = \mathbf{C}\boldsymbol{\Sigma}\mathbf{C}'. \tag{3.2.4}$$

Proof. The mean vector and the covariance matrix of $\mathbf{Y}$ given in (3.2.4) follow immediately from Fact 3.1.1. To show normality we note that if $|\mathbf{C}| \neq 0$, then $\mathbf{C}^{-1}$ and $(\mathbf{C}\boldsymbol{\Sigma}\mathbf{C}')^{-1} = \mathbf{C}'^{-1}\boldsymbol{\Sigma}^{-1}\mathbf{C}^{-1}$ both exist. Thus we can write (by $\mathbf{y} = \mathbf{C}\mathbf{x} + \mathbf{b}$) $\mathbf{x} = \mathbf{C}^{-1}(\mathbf{y} - \mathbf{b})$. The density function of $\mathbf{Y}$ is then given by

$$\begin{aligned} g(\mathbf{y}; \boldsymbol{\mu}_{\mathbf{Y}}, \boldsymbol{\Sigma}_{\mathbf{Y}}) &= f(\mathbf{C}^{-1}(\mathbf{y} - \mathbf{b}), \boldsymbol{\mu}, \boldsymbol{\Sigma})|J| \\ &= \frac{1}{(2\pi)^{n/2}|\boldsymbol{\Sigma}|^{1/2}} e^{-((\mathbf{C}^{-1}(\mathbf{y}-\mathbf{b})-\boldsymbol{\mu})'\boldsymbol{\Sigma}^{-1}(\mathbf{C}^{-1}(\mathbf{y}-\mathbf{b})-\boldsymbol{\mu}))/2}|J|, \end{aligned}$$

where $|J|$ is the absolute value of $|\mathbf{C}^{-1}|$ and f is defined in (3.2.1). But $|\mathbf{C}^{-1}| = 1/|\mathbf{C}|$, so that $|\boldsymbol{\Sigma}|^{-1/2}|J| = |\mathbf{C}\boldsymbol{\Sigma}\mathbf{C}'|^{-1/2}$. Furthermore, it is straightforward to verify that

$$\begin{aligned}(\mathbf{C}^{-1}(\mathbf{y}-\mathbf{b})-\boldsymbol{\mu})'\boldsymbol{\Sigma}^{-1}(\mathbf{C}^{-1}(\mathbf{y}-\mathbf{b})-\boldsymbol{\mu})& \\ &= (\mathbf{y}-(\mathbf{C}\boldsymbol{\mu}+\mathbf{b}))'(\mathbf{C}\boldsymbol{\Sigma}\mathbf{C}')^{-1}(\mathbf{y}-(\mathbf{C}\boldsymbol{\mu}+\mathbf{b}))\\ &= Q_n(\mathbf{y};\boldsymbol{\mu}_{\mathbf{Y}},\boldsymbol{\Sigma}_{\mathbf{Y}}).\end{aligned}$$

Thus we have

$$g(\mathbf{y};\boldsymbol{\mu}_{\mathbf{Y}},\boldsymbol{\Sigma}_{\mathbf{Y}}) = \frac{1}{(2\pi)^{n/2}|\boldsymbol{\Sigma}_{\mathbf{Y}}|^{1/2}}e^{-Q_n(\mathbf{y};\boldsymbol{\mu}_{\mathbf{Y}},\boldsymbol{\Sigma}_{\mathbf{Y}})/2}, \qquad \mathbf{y}\in\Re^n. \qquad \square$$

A special case of interest is the standard multivariate normal variable, denoted by $\mathbf{Z} = (Z_1, \ldots, Z_n)'$, with means 0, variances 1, and correlation coefficients 0. In this case we can write $\mathbf{Z} \sim \mathcal{N}_n(\mathbf{0}, \mathbf{I}_n)$ with the density function given by

$$f(\mathbf{z};\mathbf{0},\mathbf{I}_n) = \frac{1}{(2\pi)^{n/2}}\exp\left(-\frac{1}{2}\sum_{j=1}^{n} z_j^2\right), \qquad \mathbf{z}\in\Re^n.$$

Thus $Z_1, \ldots, Z_n$ are independent random variables. After integrating out, we see that the marginal distribution of Z_i is univariate normal with mean 0 and variance 1.

Consider any given random variable $\mathbf{X}$ which has an $\mathcal{N}_n(\boldsymbol{\mu}, \boldsymbol{\Sigma})$ distribution, $\boldsymbol{\Sigma} > 0$. We now show how $\mathbf{X}$ and $\mathbf{Z}$ are related. For this purpose we recall a result in linear algebra.

Proposition 3.2.1. *Let $\boldsymbol{\Sigma}$ be an $n \times n$ symmetric matrix with rank r such that $\boldsymbol{\Sigma}$ is either positive definite ($r = n$) or positive semidefinite ($r < n$).*

(i) *If $r = n$, then there exists a nonsingular $n \times n$ matrix $\mathbf{H}$ such that $\mathbf{H}\boldsymbol{\Sigma}\mathbf{H}' = \mathbf{I}_n$.*

(ii) *If $r < n$, then there exists a nonsingular $n \times n$ matrix $\mathbf{H}$ such that*

$$\mathbf{H}\boldsymbol{\Sigma}\mathbf{H}' = \begin{pmatrix}\mathbf{I}_r & \mathbf{0}_{12}\\ \mathbf{0}_{21} & \mathbf{0}_{22}\end{pmatrix} \equiv \mathbf{D}, \tag{3.2.5}$$

where $\mathbf{0}_{12}, \mathbf{0}_{21}, \mathbf{0}_{22}$ are $r \times (n-r)$, $(n-r) \times r$, and $(n-r) \times (n-r)$ matrices with elements 0.

Letting $\mathbf{B} = \mathbf{H}^{-1}$ we have:

(i)$'$ *if $r = n$, then there exists a nonsingular $n \times n$ matrix $\mathbf{B}$ such that $\mathbf{B}\mathbf{B}' = \boldsymbol{\Sigma}$;*

(ii)$'$ *if $r < n$, then there exists a nonsingular $n \times n$ matrix $\mathbf{B}$ such that $\mathbf{B}\mathbf{D}\mathbf{B}' = \boldsymbol{\Sigma}$.*

PROOF. See Anderson (1984, Theorem A.2.2). $\square$

By choosing $\mathbf{C} = \mathbf{B}$ in Proposition 3.2.1(i) we immediately have

Theorem 3.2.2. $\mathbf{X} \sim \mathcal{N}_n(\boldsymbol{\mu}, \boldsymbol{\Sigma})$, $\boldsymbol{\Sigma} > 0$, *holds if and only if there exists a nonsingular $n \times n$ matrix $\mathbf{C}$ such that*

(i) $\mathbf{CC}' = \boldsymbol{\Sigma}$; *and*
(ii) $\mathbf{X}$ *and* $\mathbf{CZ} + \boldsymbol{\mu}$ *are identically distributed, where* $\mathbf{Z} \sim \mathcal{N}_n(\mathbf{0}, \mathbf{I}_n)$.

Next we direct our attention to the more general case in which the covariance matrix is not necessarily positive definite. To this end, we state a natural generalization of Definition 2.0.1(b).

Definition 3.2.2. An n-dimensional random variable $\mathbf{X}$ with mean vector $\boldsymbol{\mu}$ and covariance matrix $\boldsymbol{\Sigma}$ is said to have a singular multivariate normal distribution (in symbols, $\mathbf{X} \sim \mathcal{N}_n(\boldsymbol{\mu}, \boldsymbol{\Sigma})$, $|\boldsymbol{\Sigma}| = 0$) if:

(i) $\boldsymbol{\Sigma}$ is positive semidefinite; and
(ii) for some $r < n$ there exists an $n \times r$ real matrix $\mathbf{C}$ such that $\mathbf{X}$ and $\mathbf{CZ}_r + \boldsymbol{\mu}$ are identically distributed, where $\mathbf{Z}_r \sim \mathcal{N}_r(\mathbf{0}, \mathbf{I}_r)$.

Combining the nonsingular (Definition 3.2.1) and singular (Definition 3.2.2) cases, we have

Definition 3.2.3. An n-dimensional random variable with mean vector $\boldsymbol{\mu}$ and covariance matrix $\boldsymbol{\Sigma}$ is said to have a multivariate normal distribution (in symbols $\mathcal{N}_n(\boldsymbol{\mu}, \boldsymbol{\Sigma})$) if either $\mathbf{X} \sim \mathcal{N}_n(\boldsymbol{\mu}, \boldsymbol{\Sigma})$, $\boldsymbol{\Sigma} > 0$, or $\mathbf{X} \sim \mathcal{N}_n(\boldsymbol{\mu}, \boldsymbol{\Sigma})$, $|\boldsymbol{\Sigma}| = 0$.

By Theorem 3.2.2 and Definition 3.2.2, Definition 3.2.3 is equivalent to:

Definition 3.2.4. An n-dimensional random variable $\mathbf{X}$ with mean vector $\boldsymbol{\mu}$ and covariance matrix $\boldsymbol{\Sigma}$ is said to have a multivariate normal distribution (in symbols $\mathbf{X} \sim \mathcal{N}_n(\boldsymbol{\mu}, \boldsymbol{\Sigma})$) if there exists an $n \times r$ matrix $\mathbf{C}$ with rank $r \leq n$ such that:

(i) $\mathbf{CC}' = \boldsymbol{\Sigma}$; and
(ii) $\mathbf{X}$ and $\mathbf{CZ}_r + \boldsymbol{\mu}$ are identically distributed, where $\mathbf{Z}_r \sim \mathcal{N}_r(\mathbf{0}, \mathbf{I}_r)$.

Definition 3.2.4 was proposed by P.L. Hsu (Fang, 1988). It applies to both the nonsingular and singular cases, and is convenient for obtaining the marginal distributions and distributions of linear transformations of normal variables. Another useful application of Definition 3.2.4 is for obtaining the characteristic function (c.f.) of a multivariate normal variable. Since the c.f. of a univariate $\mathcal{N}(0, 1)$ variable is $e^{-t^2/2}$, the c.f. of $\mathbf{Z}_r$ is

$$\psi_{\mathbf{Z}_r}(\mathbf{t}) = e^{-\mathbf{t}'\mathbf{t}/2}, \qquad \mathbf{t} \in \Re^r.$$

By Definition 3.2.4 and Facts 3.1.4 and 3.1.5 we have, for all $r \leq n$:

Theorem 3.2.3. $\mathbf{X} \sim \mathcal{N}_n(\boldsymbol{\mu}, \boldsymbol{\Sigma})$ *holds if and only if its characteristic function is of the form*

$$\psi_{\mathbf{X}}(\mathbf{t}) = e^{i\mathbf{t}'\boldsymbol{\mu} - \mathbf{t}'\boldsymbol{\Sigma}\mathbf{t}/2}, \qquad \mathbf{t} \in \Re^n. \tag{3.2.6}$$

The next definition involves a closure property of linear combinations of the components of $\mathbf{X}$.

Definition 3.2.5. An n-dimensional random variable $\mathbf{X}$ with mean vector $\boldsymbol{\mu}$ and covariance matrix $\boldsymbol{\Sigma}$ is said to have a multivariate normal distribution if the distribution of $\mathbf{c}'\mathbf{X}$ is (univariate) $\mathcal{N}(\mathbf{c}'\boldsymbol{\mu}, \mathbf{c}'\boldsymbol{\Sigma}\mathbf{c})$ for all real vectors $\mathbf{c}$.

It should be noted that for a given n-dimensional random variable $\mathbf{X}$, $\mathbf{c}'\mathbf{X}$ may have a univariate normal distribution for some $\mathbf{c} \neq \mathbf{0}$ but not for all $\mathbf{c}$. In this case, of course, $\mathbf{X}$ is not normally distributed. To see this fact, consider the following example given in Anderson (1984, pp. 47–48).

EXAMPLE 3.2.1. Let $n = 2$, and define

$$A_1 = \{(x_1, x_2)': 0 \le x_i \le 1, i = 1, 2\},$$
$$A_2 = \{(x_1, x_2)': -1 \le x_1 \le 0, 0 \le x_2 \le 1\},$$
$$A_3 = \{(x_1, x_2)': -1 \le x_i \le 0, i = 1, 2\},$$
$$A_4 = \{(x_1, x_2)': 0 \le x_1 \le 1, -1 \le x_2 \le 0\}.$$

Let the density function of $\mathbf{X} = (X_1, X_2)'$ be

$$f(\mathbf{x}) = \begin{cases} \dfrac{1}{\pi} e^{-(x_1^2+x_2^2)/2} & \text{for} \quad \mathbf{x} \in A_1 \cup A_3, \\ 0 & \text{for} \quad \mathbf{x} \in A_2 \cup A_4, \\ \dfrac{1}{2\pi} e^{-(x_1^2+x_2^2)/2} & \text{otherwise.} \end{cases}$$

Then the marginal distributions of X_1 and X_2 are both $\mathcal{N}(0, 1)$, hence $\mathbf{c}'\mathbf{X}$ is $\mathcal{N}(0, 1)$ for $\mathbf{c} = (1, 0)'$ or $\mathbf{c} = (0, 1)'$. But clearly $\mathbf{X}$ does not have a bivariate normal distribution. □

We now prove the equivalence of all the definitions of the multivariate normal distribution stated above.

Theorem 3.2.4. *Definitions* 3.2.3, 3.2.4, *and* 3.2.5 *are equivalent.*

PROOF. The equivalence of Definitions 3.2.3 and 3.2.4 is clear. Thus it suffices to show the equivalence of Definitions 3.2.4 and 3.2.5.

It is immediate that if $\mathbf{X} \sim \mathcal{N}_n(\boldsymbol{\mu}, \boldsymbol{\Sigma})$, then $\mathbf{c}'\mathbf{X}$ is a univariate $\mathcal{N}(\mathbf{c}'\boldsymbol{\mu}, \mathbf{c}'\boldsymbol{\Sigma}\mathbf{c})$ variable for all $\mathbf{c}$. Conversely, suppose that $\mathbf{c}'\mathbf{X}$ has an $\mathcal{N}(\mathbf{c}'\boldsymbol{\mu}, \mathbf{c}'\boldsymbol{\Sigma}\mathbf{c})$ distribution for all $\mathbf{c} \in \Re^n$, then

$$\psi_{\mathbf{c}'\mathbf{X}}(t) = E \exp\left(it \sum_{j=1}^{n} c_j X_j \right) = e^{it\mathbf{c}'\boldsymbol{\mu} - (\mathbf{c}'\boldsymbol{\Sigma}\mathbf{c})t^2/2} \tag{3.2.7}$$

holds for all $t \in \mathfrak{R}$ and $\mathbf{c} \in \mathfrak{R}^n$. Thus

$$\psi_{\mathbf{c}'\mathbf{X}}(1) = Ee^{i\mathbf{c}'\mathbf{X}} = e^{i\mathbf{c}'\boldsymbol{\mu} - \mathbf{c}'\boldsymbol{\Sigma}\mathbf{c}/2} \equiv \psi^*_{\mathbf{X}}(\mathbf{c}), \qquad \mathbf{c} \in \mathfrak{R}^n.$$

But $\psi^*_{\mathbf{X}}(\mathbf{c})$ is just the characteristic function of a multivariate normal variable with mean vector $\boldsymbol{\mu}$ and covariance matrix $\boldsymbol{\Sigma}$. Thus by Theorem 3.2.3 and Fact 3.1.4 we have $\mathbf{X} \sim \mathcal{N}_n(\boldsymbol{\mu}, \boldsymbol{\Sigma})$. □

3.3. Basic Distribution Properties

In this section we describe certain distribution properties of the multivariate normal distribution.

3.3.1. Marginal Distributions and Independence

First we show that the marginal distributions of a multivariate normal variable are normal. For fixed $k < n$, consider the partitions of $\mathbf{X}$, $\boldsymbol{\mu}$, and $\boldsymbol{\Sigma}$ given below:

$$\mathbf{X} = \begin{pmatrix} \mathbf{X}_1 \\ \mathbf{X}_2 \end{pmatrix}, \qquad \boldsymbol{\mu} = \begin{pmatrix} \boldsymbol{\mu}_1 \\ \boldsymbol{\mu}_2 \end{pmatrix}, \qquad \boldsymbol{\Sigma} = \begin{pmatrix} \boldsymbol{\Sigma}_{11} & \boldsymbol{\Sigma}_{12} \\ \boldsymbol{\Sigma}_{21} & \boldsymbol{\Sigma}_{22} \end{pmatrix}, \tag{3.3.1}$$

where

$$\mathbf{X}_1 = (X_1, \ldots, X_k)', \qquad \mathbf{X}_2 = (X_{k+1}, \ldots, X_n)', \tag{3.3.2}$$

$$\boldsymbol{\mu}_1 = (\mu_1, \ldots, \mu_k)', \qquad \boldsymbol{\mu}_2 = (\mu_{k+1}, \ldots, \mu_n)', \tag{3.3.3}$$

$\boldsymbol{\Sigma}_{ii}$ is the covariance matrix of $\mathbf{X}_i$ ($i = 1, 2$), and $\boldsymbol{\Sigma}_{12} = (\sigma_{ij})$ is such that $\sigma_{ij} = \operatorname{cov}(X_i, X_j)$ for $1 \le i < j \le n$. Let $\mathbf{R} = (\rho_{ij})$ be such that

$$\rho_{ij} = \frac{\sigma_{ij}}{\sqrt{\sigma_{ii}\sigma_{jj}}}, \qquad i, j = 1, \ldots, n. \tag{3.3.4}$$

Then $\mathbf{R}$ is called the correlation matrix of $\mathbf{X}$. The diagonal elements of $\mathbf{R}$ are 1 and the off-diagonal elements are the correlation coefficients. For the partition of $\boldsymbol{\Sigma}$ defined in (3.3.1), a corresponding partition of $\mathbf{R}$ is

$$\mathbf{R} = \begin{pmatrix} \mathbf{R}_{11} & \mathbf{R}_{12} \\ \mathbf{R}_{21} & \mathbf{R}_{22} \end{pmatrix}. \tag{3.3.5}$$

In the following theorem we first derive the marginal distributions of $\mathbf{X}_1$ and $\mathbf{X}_2$.

Theorem 3.3.1. *If $\mathbf{X} \sim \mathcal{N}_n(\boldsymbol{\mu}, \boldsymbol{\Sigma})$, then for every fixed $k < n$ the marginal distributions of $\mathbf{X}_1$ and $\mathbf{X}_2$ are $\mathcal{N}_k(\boldsymbol{\mu}_1, \boldsymbol{\Sigma}_{11})$ and $\mathcal{N}_{n-k}(\boldsymbol{\mu}_2, \boldsymbol{\Sigma}_{22})$, respectively.*

PROOF. By Theorem 3.2.3 and Fact 3.1.6, the characteristic function of $\mathbf{X}_1$ is

$$\psi_{\mathbf{X}_1}(t_1, \ldots, t_k) = \psi_{\mathbf{X}}(t_1, \ldots, t_k, 0, \ldots, 0)$$
$$= e^{i\mathbf{t}'\boldsymbol{\mu}_1 - \mathbf{t}'\boldsymbol{\Sigma}_{11}\mathbf{t}/2}, \qquad \mathbf{t} \in \Re^k.$$

Thus, again by Theorem 3.2.3, $\mathbf{X}_1$ has an $\mathcal{N}_k(\boldsymbol{\mu}_1, \boldsymbol{\Sigma}_{11})$ distribution. The distribution of $\mathbf{X}_2$ follows similarly. □

If $\mathbf{X}$ has a nonsingular normal distribution, then $\boldsymbol{\Sigma} > 0$. This in turn implies $\boldsymbol{\Sigma}_{11} > 0$ and $\boldsymbol{\Sigma}_{22} > 0$. Consequently, we have

Corollary 3.3.1. *If* $\mathbf{X} \sim \mathcal{N}_n(\boldsymbol{\mu}, \boldsymbol{\Sigma})$, $\boldsymbol{\Sigma} > 0$, *then* $\mathbf{X}_1 \sim \mathcal{N}_k(\boldsymbol{\mu}_1, \boldsymbol{\Sigma}_{11})$, $\boldsymbol{\Sigma}_{11} > 0$, *and* $\mathbf{X}_2 \sim \mathcal{N}_{n-k}(\boldsymbol{\mu}_2, \boldsymbol{\Sigma}_{22})$, $\boldsymbol{\Sigma}_{22} > 0$.

Remark 3.3.1. Choosing $k = 2$ in Corollary 3.3.1 we observe, from Theorem 2.1.1, that if $\mathbf{X}$ has the density function given in (3.2.1), then the marginal distribution of $(X_1, X_2)'$ is bivariate normal with means μ_1, μ_2 and variances σ_{11}, σ_{22}, respectively, and covariance σ_{12}. By symmetry we conclude that if $\mathbf{X}$ has the density function given in (3.2.1), then the mean vector and the covariance matrix of $\mathbf{X}$ are, respectively, $\boldsymbol{\mu}$ and $\boldsymbol{\Sigma}$. This observation shows that Definition 3.2.1 is indeed consistent as noted in Remark 3.2.1.

It is well known that, in general, uncorrelated random variables are not necessarily independent. But for the multivariate normal variables those two conditions are equivalent. This is shown below.

Theorem 3.3.2. *Let* $\mathbf{X}_1$, $\mathbf{X}_2$ *be the random variables defined in* (3.3.1) *where* $\mathbf{X} \sim \mathcal{N}_n(\boldsymbol{\mu}, \boldsymbol{\Sigma})$. *Then they are independent if and only if* $\boldsymbol{\Sigma}_{12} = \mathbf{0}$.

PROOF. Let $\psi_{\mathbf{X}}(t_1, \ldots, t_n)$ denote the characteristic function of $\mathbf{X}$ then, by (3.2.6),

$$\boldsymbol{\Sigma}_{12} = 0 \quad \Leftrightarrow \quad (t_1, \ldots, t_n)\boldsymbol{\Sigma}(t_1, \ldots, t_n)' = \mathbf{t}_1'\boldsymbol{\Sigma}_{11}\mathbf{t}_1 + \mathbf{t}_2'\boldsymbol{\Sigma}_{22}\mathbf{t}_2$$
$$\Leftrightarrow \quad \psi_{\mathbf{X}}(\mathbf{t}) = \psi_{\mathbf{X}_1}(\mathbf{t}_1)\psi_{\mathbf{X}_2}(\mathbf{t}_2)$$

for all $\mathbf{t}_1 = (t_1, \ldots, t_k)' \in \Re^k$ and $\mathbf{t}_2 = (t_{k+1}, \ldots, t_n)' \in \Re^{n-k}$. Since $\mathbf{X}_1$, $\mathbf{X}_2$ are independent if and only if their joint characteristic function is the product of the marginal characteristic functions, the proof is complete. □

Remark 3.3.2. If the distribution of $\mathbf{X}$ in Theorem 3.3.2 is nonsingular, then an alternative proof exists: Let $f_1(\mathbf{x}_1)$, $f_2(\mathbf{x}_2)$ be the marginal density functions of $\mathbf{X}_1$, $\mathbf{X}_2$ given by

$$f_1(\mathbf{x}_1) = \frac{1}{(2\pi)^{k/2}|\boldsymbol{\Sigma}_{11}|^{1/2}} e^{-Q^{(1)}(\mathbf{x}_1; \boldsymbol{\mu}_1, \boldsymbol{\Sigma}_{11})/2},$$

$$f_2(\mathbf{x}_2) = \frac{1}{(2\pi)^{(n-k)/2}|\boldsymbol{\Sigma}_{22}|^{1/2}} e^{-Q^{(2)}(\mathbf{x}_2; \boldsymbol{\mu}_2, \boldsymbol{\Sigma}_{22})/2},$$

where

$$Q^{(i)}(\mathbf{x}_i; \boldsymbol{\mu}_i, \boldsymbol{\Sigma}_{ii}) = (\mathbf{x}_i - \boldsymbol{\mu}_i)'\boldsymbol{\Sigma}_{ii}^{-1}(\mathbf{x}_i - \boldsymbol{\mu}_i), \qquad i = 1, 2.$$

If $\boldsymbol{\Sigma} > 0$ and $\boldsymbol{\Sigma}_{12} = \mathbf{0}$, then

$$\boldsymbol{\Sigma}^{-1} = \begin{pmatrix} \boldsymbol{\Sigma}_{11} & \mathbf{0} \\ \mathbf{0} & \boldsymbol{\Sigma}_{22} \end{pmatrix}^{-1} = \begin{pmatrix} \boldsymbol{\Sigma}_{11}^{-1} & \mathbf{0} \\ \mathbf{0} & \boldsymbol{\Sigma}_{22}^{-1} \end{pmatrix}. \tag{3.3.6}$$

Simple calculation yields the identity

$$Q_n(\mathbf{x}; \boldsymbol{\mu}, \boldsymbol{\Sigma}) = Q^{(1)}(\mathbf{x}_1; \boldsymbol{\mu}_1, \boldsymbol{\Sigma}_{11}) + Q^{(2)}(\mathbf{x}_2; \boldsymbol{\mu}_2, \boldsymbol{\Sigma}_{22}). \tag{3.3.7}$$

This implies that

$$f(\mathbf{x}; \boldsymbol{\mu}, \boldsymbol{\Sigma}) = f_1(\mathbf{x}_1; \boldsymbol{\mu}_1, \boldsymbol{\Sigma}_{11}) f_2(\mathbf{x}_2; \boldsymbol{\mu}_2, \boldsymbol{\Sigma}_{22}),$$

as desired.

3.3.2. Linear Transformations and Linear Combinations

For the univariate case, the normal family of distributions is closed under linear transformations and linear combinations of random variables. In the following we show that the family of multivariate normal distributions also possesses such closure properties.

Theorem 3.3.3. *If* $\mathbf{X} \sim \mathcal{N}_n(\boldsymbol{\mu}, \boldsymbol{\Sigma})$ *and* $\mathbf{Y} = \mathbf{C}\mathbf{X} + \mathbf{b}$, *where* $\mathbf{C}$ *is any given* $m \times n$ *real matrix and* $\mathbf{b}$ *is any* $m \times 1$ *real vector, then* $\mathbf{Y} \sim \mathcal{N}_m(\mathbf{C}\boldsymbol{\mu} + \mathbf{b}, \mathbf{C}\boldsymbol{\Sigma}\mathbf{C}')$.

Proof. (i) For $m = n$, the proof follows immediately from Fact 3.1.5 and Theorem 3.2.3.

(ii) For $m < n$, consider the transformation

$$\mathbf{Y}^* = \begin{pmatrix} \mathbf{Y}_1 \\ \mathbf{Y}_2 \end{pmatrix} = \begin{pmatrix} \mathbf{C} \\ \mathbf{B} \end{pmatrix} \mathbf{X} + \begin{pmatrix} \mathbf{b} \\ \mathbf{0}_{n-m} \end{pmatrix}, \tag{3.3.8}$$

where $\mathbf{B}$ is any given $(n - m) \times n$ matrix. Since

$$\begin{pmatrix} \mathbf{Y}_1 \\ \mathbf{Y}_2 \end{pmatrix} \sim \mathcal{N}_n\left(\begin{pmatrix} \mathbf{C}\boldsymbol{\mu} + \mathbf{b} \\ \mathbf{B}\boldsymbol{\mu} \end{pmatrix}, \begin{pmatrix} \mathbf{C}\boldsymbol{\Sigma}\mathbf{C}' & \mathbf{C}\boldsymbol{\Sigma}\mathbf{B}' \\ \mathbf{B}\boldsymbol{\Sigma}\mathbf{C}' & \mathbf{B}\boldsymbol{\Sigma}\mathbf{B}' \end{pmatrix}\right),$$

$\mathbf{Y} = \mathbf{Y}_1 = \mathbf{C}\mathbf{X} + \mathbf{b} \sim \mathcal{N}_m(\mathbf{C}\boldsymbol{\mu}, \mathbf{C}\boldsymbol{\Sigma}\mathbf{C}')$.

(iii) For $m > n$, by Definition 3.2.4, there exists an $n \times r$ matrix $\mathbf{C}^*$ such that $\mathbf{X}$ and $\mathbf{C}^*\mathbf{Z}_r + \boldsymbol{\mu}$ are identically distributed, where $r \leq n$ is the rank of $\boldsymbol{\Sigma}$. Thus $\mathbf{C}\mathbf{X} + \mathbf{b}$ and $\mathbf{C}\mathbf{C}^*\mathbf{Z}_r + (\mathbf{C}\boldsymbol{\mu} + \mathbf{b})$ are both distributed according to a singular $\mathcal{N}(\mathbf{C}\boldsymbol{\mu} + \mathbf{b}, \mathbf{C}\boldsymbol{\Sigma}\mathbf{C}')$ distribution (again by Definition 3.2.4). □

If $\mathbf{X}$ is a nonsingular normal variable and, for $m < n$, if the $m \times n$ matrix $\mathbf{C}$ has rank m, then there exists an $(n - m) \times n$ matrix $\mathbf{B}$ such that the matrix

$\binom{\mathbf{C}}{\mathbf{B}}$ in (3.3.8) is nonsingular. This implies that the distribution of $\mathbf{Y}^*$, and hence the distribution of $\mathbf{Y}$, is nonsingular. Combining the result for $r = n$ already stated in Theorem 3.2.1 we have

Corollary 3.3.2. *If* $\mathbf{X} \sim \mathcal{N}_n(\boldsymbol{\mu}, \boldsymbol{\Sigma})$, $\boldsymbol{\Sigma} > 0$, $\mathbf{C}$ *is an* $m \times n$ *real matrix with rank* $m \leq n$, *and* $\mathbf{b}$ *is an* $m \times 1$ *real vector, then* $\mathbf{CX} + \mathbf{b}$ *has a nonsingular* $\mathcal{N}_m(\mathbf{C}\boldsymbol{\mu} + \mathbf{b}, \mathbf{C}\boldsymbol{\Sigma}\mathbf{C}')$ *distribution.*

Next we consider linear combinations of the components of a multivariate normal variable. Let $\mathbf{C}_1$, $\mathbf{C}_2$ be $m \times k$ and $m \times (n-k)$ matrices. For the partition defined in (3.3.1) consider the linear combination $\mathbf{Y} = \mathbf{C}_1\mathbf{X}_1 + \mathbf{C}_2\mathbf{X}_2$. Rewriting this as $\mathbf{Y} = \mathbf{CX}$, where $\mathbf{C} = (\mathbf{C}_1 \;\; \mathbf{C}_2)$ is an $m \times n$ matrix, and applying Theorem 3.3.3 yield

Corollary 3.3.3. *Let* $\mathbf{X}$ *be partitioned as in* (3.3.1), *and let* $\mathbf{C}_1$, $\mathbf{C}_2$ *be two* $m \times k$ *and* $m \times (n-k)$ *real matrices, respectively. If* $\mathbf{X} \sim \mathcal{N}_n(\boldsymbol{\mu}, \boldsymbol{\Sigma})$, *then*

$$\mathbf{Y} = \mathbf{C}_1\mathbf{X}_1 + \mathbf{C}_2\mathbf{X}_2 \sim \mathcal{N}_m(\boldsymbol{\mu}_{\mathbf{Y}}, \boldsymbol{\Sigma}_{\mathbf{Y}}),$$

where

$$\boldsymbol{\mu}_{\mathbf{Y}} = \mathbf{C}_1\boldsymbol{\mu}_1 + \mathbf{C}_2\boldsymbol{\mu}_2, \tag{3.3.9}$$

$$\boldsymbol{\Sigma}_{\mathbf{Y}} = \mathbf{C}_1\boldsymbol{\Sigma}_{11}\mathbf{C}_1' + \mathbf{C}_2\boldsymbol{\Sigma}_{22}\mathbf{C}_2' + \mathbf{C}_1\boldsymbol{\Sigma}_{12}\mathbf{C}_2' + \mathbf{C}_2\boldsymbol{\Sigma}_{21}\mathbf{C}_1'. \tag{3.3.10}$$

A special case of interest is $\mathbf{Y} = c_1\mathbf{X}_1 + c_2\mathbf{X}_2$ where c_1, c_2 are real numbers and $n = 2k$. This can be treated in Corollary 3.3.3 by taking $\mathbf{C}_i = c_i\mathbf{I}_k$ $(i = 1, 2)$. If in addition $\boldsymbol{\Sigma}_{12} = \mathbf{0}$, then clearly $\mathbf{Y}$ is distributed according to an $\mathcal{N}_k(c_1\boldsymbol{\mu}_1 + c_2\boldsymbol{\mu}_2, c_1^2\boldsymbol{\Sigma}_{11} + c_2^2\boldsymbol{\Sigma}_{22})$ distribution. Generalizing this result to several variables by induction we have

Corollary 3.3.4. *If* $\mathbf{X}_1, \mathbf{X}_2, \ldots, \mathbf{X}_N$ *are independent* $\mathcal{N}_n(\boldsymbol{\mu}_j, \boldsymbol{\Sigma}_j)$ *variables* $(j = 1, \ldots, N)$, *then* $\mathbf{Y} = \sum_{j=1}^N c_j\mathbf{X}_j$ *is distributed according to an* $\mathcal{N}_n(\sum_{j=1}^N c_j\boldsymbol{\mu}_j, \sum_{j=1}^N c_j^2\boldsymbol{\Sigma}_j)$ *distribution.*

3.3.3. Conditional Distributions

For $1 \leq k < n$ consider the partition of $\mathbf{X}$ defined in (3.3.1) and the linear transformation

$$\mathbf{Y} = \begin{pmatrix} \mathbf{Y}_1 \\ \mathbf{Y}_2 \end{pmatrix} = \begin{pmatrix} \mathbf{I}_k & -\mathbf{B} \\ \mathbf{0} & \mathbf{I}_{n-k} \end{pmatrix} \begin{pmatrix} \mathbf{X}_1 \\ \mathbf{X}_2 \end{pmatrix} \equiv \mathbf{CX}, \tag{3.3.11}$$

where $\mathbf{Y}_1$ and $\mathbf{Y}_2$ are $k \times 1$ and $(n-k) \times 1$ random variables, respectively, and $\mathbf{B}$ is a $k \times (n-k)$ real matrix. If $\mathbf{X} \sim \mathcal{N}_n(\boldsymbol{\mu}, \boldsymbol{\Sigma})$, then by Theorem 3.3.3 the joint distribution of $\mathbf{Y}_1, \mathbf{Y}_2$ is $\mathcal{N}_n(\boldsymbol{\mu}_{\mathbf{Y}}, \boldsymbol{\Sigma}_{\mathbf{Y}})$, where

$$\boldsymbol{\mu}_{\mathbf{Y}} = \begin{pmatrix} \boldsymbol{\mu}_1 - \mathbf{B}\boldsymbol{\mu}_2 \\ \boldsymbol{\mu}_2 \end{pmatrix},$$

$$\boldsymbol{\Sigma}_{\mathbf{Y}} = \begin{pmatrix} \boldsymbol{\Sigma}_{11} + \mathbf{B}\boldsymbol{\Sigma}_{22}\mathbf{B}' - \mathbf{B}\boldsymbol{\Sigma}_{21} - \boldsymbol{\Sigma}_{12}\mathbf{B}' & \boldsymbol{\Sigma}_{12} - \mathbf{B}\boldsymbol{\Sigma}_{22} \\ (\boldsymbol{\Sigma}_{12} - \mathbf{B}\boldsymbol{\Sigma}_{22})' & \boldsymbol{\Sigma}_{22} \end{pmatrix}.$$

If $\boldsymbol{\Sigma}$ is nonsingular, then $\boldsymbol{\Sigma}_{11}^{-1}$ and $\boldsymbol{\Sigma}_{22}^{-1}$ both exist. Thus if we choose $\mathbf{B}$ to satisfy $\boldsymbol{\Sigma}_{12} - \mathbf{B}\boldsymbol{\Sigma}_{22} = \mathbf{0}$, that is, if $\mathbf{B}$ is chosen to be

$$\mathbf{B} = \boldsymbol{\Sigma}_{12}\boldsymbol{\Sigma}_{22}^{-1}, \tag{3.3.12}$$

then $\mathbf{Y}_1$ and $\mathbf{Y}_2$ are uncorrelated (and thus independent). Consequently, we have

$$\begin{pmatrix} \mathbf{Y}_1 \\ \mathbf{Y}_2 \end{pmatrix} = \begin{pmatrix} \mathbf{X}_1 - \boldsymbol{\Sigma}_{12}\boldsymbol{\Sigma}_{22}^{-1}\mathbf{X}_2 \\ \mathbf{X}_2 \end{pmatrix} \sim \mathcal{N}_n\left(\begin{pmatrix} \mathbf{v}_{1\cdot 2} \\ \boldsymbol{\mu}_2 \end{pmatrix}, \begin{pmatrix} \boldsymbol{\Sigma}_{11\cdot 2} & \mathbf{0} \\ \mathbf{0} & \boldsymbol{\Sigma}_{22} \end{pmatrix}\right), \tag{3.3.13}$$

where

$$\mathbf{v}_{1\cdot 2} = \boldsymbol{\mu}_1 - \boldsymbol{\Sigma}_{12}\boldsymbol{\Sigma}_{22}^{-1}\boldsymbol{\mu}_2, \tag{3.3.14}$$

$$\boldsymbol{\Sigma}_{11\cdot 2} = \boldsymbol{\Sigma}_{11} - \boldsymbol{\Sigma}_{12}\boldsymbol{\Sigma}_{22}^{-1}\boldsymbol{\Sigma}_{21}. \tag{3.3.15}$$

Since $\mathbf{X}_1 - \boldsymbol{\Sigma}_{12}\boldsymbol{\Sigma}_{22}^{-1}\mathbf{X}_2$ and $\mathbf{X}_2$ are independent normal variables with marginal densities

$$g(\mathbf{x}_1; \boldsymbol{\mu}, \boldsymbol{\Sigma}|\mathbf{x}_2) = \frac{1}{(2\pi)^{k/2}|\boldsymbol{\Sigma}_{11\cdot 2}|^{1/2}} e^{-Q_k(\mathbf{x}_1 - \boldsymbol{\Sigma}_{12}\boldsymbol{\Sigma}_{22}^{-1}\mathbf{x}_2; \mathbf{v}_{1\cdot 2}, \boldsymbol{\Sigma}_{11\cdot 2})/2},$$

$$f_2(\mathbf{x}_2; \boldsymbol{\mu}, \boldsymbol{\Sigma}) = \frac{1}{(2\pi)^{(n-k)/2}|\boldsymbol{\Sigma}_{22}|^{1/2}} e^{-Q_{n-k}(\mathbf{x}_2; \boldsymbol{\mu}_2, \boldsymbol{\Sigma}_{22})/2},$$

respectively, their joint density is given by $g(\mathbf{x}_1; \boldsymbol{\mu}, \boldsymbol{\Sigma}|\mathbf{x}_2)f_2(\mathbf{x}_2; \boldsymbol{\mu}, \boldsymbol{\Sigma})$. From this joint density function we can rewrite the joint density of $(\mathbf{X}_1, \mathbf{X}_2)'$ by a linear transformation, which yields

$$f(\mathbf{x}_1, \mathbf{x}_2; \boldsymbol{\mu}, \boldsymbol{\Sigma}) = g(\mathbf{x}_1; \boldsymbol{\mu}, \boldsymbol{\Sigma}|\mathbf{x}_2)f_2(\mathbf{x}_2; \boldsymbol{\mu}, \boldsymbol{\Sigma}). \tag{3.3.16}$$

But

$$f(\mathbf{x}_1, \mathbf{x}_2; \boldsymbol{\mu}, \boldsymbol{\Sigma}) = f_{1|2}(\mathbf{x}_1; \boldsymbol{\mu}, \boldsymbol{\Sigma}|\mathbf{x}_2)f_2(\mathbf{x}_2; \boldsymbol{\mu}, \boldsymbol{\Sigma}) \tag{3.3.17}$$

also holds where $f_{1|2}$ is the conditional density function of $\mathbf{X}_1$, given $\mathbf{X}_2 = \mathbf{x}_2$. Thus the conditional density function of $\mathbf{X}_1$, given $\mathbf{X}_2 = \mathbf{x}_2$, must be $g(\mathbf{x}_1; \boldsymbol{\mu}, \boldsymbol{\Sigma}|\mathbf{x}_2)$. Since

$$Q_k(\mathbf{x}_1 - \boldsymbol{\Sigma}_{12}\boldsymbol{\Sigma}_{22}^{-1}\mathbf{x}_2; \nu_{1\cdot 2}, \boldsymbol{\Sigma}_{11\cdot 2}) = (\mathbf{x}_1 - \boldsymbol{\mu}_{1\cdot 2})'\boldsymbol{\Sigma}_{11\cdot 2}^{-1}(\mathbf{x}_1 - \boldsymbol{\mu}_{1\cdot 2}), \tag{3.3.18}$$

where

$$\boldsymbol{\mu}_{1\cdot 2} = \boldsymbol{\mu}_1 + \boldsymbol{\Sigma}_{12}\boldsymbol{\Sigma}_{22}^{-1}(\mathbf{x}_2 - \boldsymbol{\mu}_2), \tag{3.3.19}$$

we then obtain

Theorem 3.3.4. *Let* $\mathbf{X}$ *be partitioned as in* (3.3.1). *If* $\mathbf{X} \sim \mathcal{N}_n(\boldsymbol{\mu}, \boldsymbol{\Sigma})$, $\boldsymbol{\Sigma} > 0$, *then for any fixed* $k < n$ *the conditional distribution of* $\mathbf{X}_1$, *given* $\mathbf{X}_2 = \mathbf{x}_2$, *is* $\mathcal{N}_k(\boldsymbol{\mu}_{1\cdot 2}, \boldsymbol{\Sigma}_{11\cdot 2})$ *where* $\boldsymbol{\mu}_{1\cdot 2}$ *and* $\boldsymbol{\Sigma}_{11\cdot 2}$ *are defined in* (3.3.19) *and* (3.3.15), *respectively.*

We note in passing that $\boldsymbol{\mu}_{1\cdot 2}$ *is the conditional mean vector and* $\boldsymbol{\Sigma}_{11\cdot 2}$ is the conditional covariance matrix of $\mathbf{X}_1$, given $\mathbf{X}_2 = \mathbf{x}_2$. Furthermore, $\boldsymbol{\mu}_{1\cdot 2}$ is a linear function of $\mathbf{x}_2$ and $\boldsymbol{\Sigma}_{11\cdot 2}$ does not depend on $\mathbf{x}_2$. The matrix $\mathbf{B} = \boldsymbol{\Sigma}_{12}\boldsymbol{\Sigma}_{22}^{-1}$ is called the regression matrix of $\mathbf{X}_2$ on $\mathbf{X}_1$, and will be discussed more extensively in the next section.

3.4. Regression and Correlation

Consider the partition of the components of $\mathbf{X}$ into $\mathbf{X}_1$ and $\mathbf{X}_2$ defined in (3.3.1). In this section we study:

(a) the best predictor of a component of $\mathbf{X}_1$ based on $\mathbf{X}_2 = \mathbf{x}_2$;
(b) the multiple correlation coefficient between a component of $\mathbf{X}_1$ and the components of $\mathbf{X}_2$;
(c) the partial correlation coefficient between two components of $\mathbf{X}_1$, given $\mathbf{X}_2 = \mathbf{x}_2$;
(d) the canonical correlation coefficients between $\mathbf{X}_1$ and $\mathbf{X}_2$; and
(e) the principal components of $\mathbf{X}$.

3.4.1. Best (Linear) Predictors

For fixed $1 \le i \le k$ suppose that we are interested in predicting the value of X_i, given $\mathbf{X}_2 = \mathbf{x}_2$. Let $\hat{x}_i = \lambda(\mathbf{x}_2)$ denote a predictor which is a function of $\mathbf{x}_2$. The problem of interest is to find the optimal choice of such a function. For this purpose we define

Definition 3.4.1. $\hat{x}_i^* = \lambda^*(\mathbf{x}_2)$ is said to be the best predictor of X_i based on $\mathbf{X}_2 = \mathbf{x}_2$, using the loss function

$$L(X_i, \lambda(\mathbf{x}_2)) = (X_i - \lambda(\mathbf{x}_2))^2,$$

if

$$\inf_{\lambda} E[(X_i - \lambda(\mathbf{x}_2))^2 | \mathbf{X}_2 = \mathbf{x}_2] = E[(X_i - \lambda^*(\mathbf{x}_2))^2 | \mathbf{X}_2 = \mathbf{x}_2]$$

holds for all $\mathbf{x}_2$.

For certain multivariate distributions, the best predictor is difficult to find. Since linear functions of $\mathbf{x}_2$ are simpler, we often restrict attention to the subset of all linear functions of $\mathbf{x}_2$ and then obtain the best linear predictor. In the following we show that, for the multivariate normal distribution, the "overall" best predictor is in fact a linear predictor.

To see this, first note that

$$\begin{aligned} E[(X_i - \lambda(\mathbf{x}_2))^2 | \mathbf{X}_2 = \mathbf{x}_2] &= E[\{(X_i - \mu_{i\cdot 2}(\mathbf{x}_2)) + (\mu_{i\cdot 2}(\mathbf{x}_2) - \lambda(\mathbf{x}_2))\}^2 | \mathbf{X}_2 = \mathbf{x}_2] \\ &= \mathrm{Var}(X_i | \mathbf{X}_2 = \mathbf{x}_2) + (\mu_{i\cdot 2}(\mathbf{x}_2) - \lambda(\mathbf{x}_2))^2, \end{aligned}$$

where

$$\mu_{i\cdot 2}(\mathbf{x}_2) = E(X_i | \mathbf{X}_2 = \mathbf{x}_2)$$

is the conditional mean. If $\mathrm{Var}(X_i|\mathbf{X}_2 = \mathbf{x}_2)$ does not depend on $\mathbf{x}_2$, then clearly $E[(X_i - \lambda(\mathbf{x}_2))^2|\mathbf{X}_2 = \mathbf{x}_2]$ is minimized when the second term is zero.

If $X \sim \mathcal{N}_n(\boldsymbol{\mu}, \boldsymbol{\Sigma})$, $\boldsymbol{\Sigma} > 0$, then by Theorems 3.3.4 and 3.3.1 the conditional distribution of X_i, given $\mathbf{X}_2 = \mathbf{x}_2$, is normal with mean

$$\mu_{i\cdot 2}(\mathbf{x}_2) = \mu_i + \boldsymbol{\sigma}_i \boldsymbol{\Sigma}_{22}^{-1}(\mathbf{x}_2 - \boldsymbol{\mu}_2) \tag{3.4.1}$$

(a linear function of $\mathbf{x}_2$) and variance

$$\sigma_{ii\cdot k+1,\ldots,n} = \sigma_{ii} - \boldsymbol{\sigma}_i \boldsymbol{\Sigma}_{22}^{-1} \boldsymbol{\sigma}_i', \tag{3.4.2}$$

where

$$\boldsymbol{\sigma}_i = (\sigma_{i,k+1}, \ldots, \sigma_{i,n}) \tag{3.4.3}$$

is the ith row of the submatrix $\boldsymbol{\Sigma}_{12}$. Since $\sigma_{ii\cdot k+1,\ldots,n}$ does not depend on $\mathbf{x}_2$, we have

Theorem 3.4.1. *If* $\mathbf{X} \sim \mathcal{N}_n(\boldsymbol{\mu}, \boldsymbol{\Sigma})$, $\boldsymbol{\Sigma} > 0$, *then for all* $i \leq k$ *the best predictor of* X_i, *based on* $\mathbf{X}_2 = \mathbf{x}_2$, *is* $\mu_{i\cdot 2}(\mathbf{x}_2)$ *given in* (3.4.1).

We note that for given $\mathbf{X}_2 = \mathbf{x}_2$ the smallest value of $E(X_i - \lambda(\mathbf{x}_2))^2$ is $\sigma_{ii\cdot k+1,\ldots,n}$. The infimum occurs, of course, at $\lambda^*(\mathbf{x}_2) = \mu_{i\cdot 2}(\mathbf{x}_2)$. Also note that $\mu_{i\cdot 2}(\mathbf{x}_2)$ is just the ith row of the vector $\boldsymbol{\mu}_1 + \mathbf{B}(\mathbf{x}_2 - \boldsymbol{\mu}_2)$ where $\mathbf{B}$ is the regression matrix defined in (3.3.12).

3.4.2. Multiple Correlation Coefficient

The theory of partial and multiple correlation coefficients treated in this section was originally developed by Pearson (1896) and Yule (1897a, b). The reader is referred to Pearson (1920) for the historical developments.

Assume that $\mathbf{X} \sim \mathcal{N}_n(\boldsymbol{\mu}, \boldsymbol{\Sigma})$, $\boldsymbol{\Sigma} > 0$. Then, for fixed $1 \leq i \leq k$ and given real vector $\mathbf{c}$, the joint distribution of $(X_i, \mathbf{c}'\mathbf{X}_2)'$ can be obtained by the transformation

$$\begin{pmatrix} X_i \\ \mathbf{c}'\mathbf{X}_2 \end{pmatrix} = \begin{pmatrix} \delta_{i1} \ldots \delta_{ik} & 0 \ldots 0 \\ 0 \ldots 0 & c_1 \ldots c_{n-k} \end{pmatrix} \mathbf{X},$$

where

$$\delta_{ij} = \begin{cases} 1 & \text{for} \quad i = j, \\ 0 & \text{otherwise.} \end{cases}$$

By Theorem 3.3.3, this distribution is bivariate normal with means μ_i and $\mathbf{c}'\boldsymbol{\mu}_2$, and variances σ_{ii} and $\mathbf{c}'\boldsymbol{\Sigma}_{22}\mathbf{c}$, respectively, and covariance $\mathbf{c}'\boldsymbol{\sigma}_i$ where $\boldsymbol{\sigma}_i$ is given in (3.4.3). Thus for $\mathbf{c} \neq \mathbf{0}$ the correlation coefficient between X_i and $\mathbf{c}'\mathbf{X}_2$ is simply $\mathbf{c}'\boldsymbol{\sigma}_i'/(\sigma_{ii}\mathbf{c}'\boldsymbol{\Sigma}_{22}\mathbf{c})^{1/2}$.

In certain applications, we are interested in the best linear combination of the components of $\mathbf{X}_2$ such that the correlation coefficient between X_i and $\mathbf{c}'\mathbf{X}_2$ is maximized.

Definition 3.4.2. Let $\mathbf{X}$ be partitioned as in (3.3.1). For $1 \leq i \leq k$ the multiple correlation coefficient between X_i and $\mathbf{X}_2$ is defined by

$$R_{i\cdot k+1,\ldots,n} = \sup_{\mathbf{c}} \operatorname{Corr}(X_i, \mathbf{c}'\mathbf{X}_2). \tag{3.4.4}$$

In the following theorem we show that the $\mathbf{c}'$ vector which maximizes the right-hand side of (3.4.4) is $\boldsymbol{\sigma}_i\boldsymbol{\Sigma}_{22}^{-1}$, the *same* vector that yields the best predictor for X_i, when $\mathbf{X}_2 = \mathbf{x}_2$ is given.

Theorem 3.4.2. *If* $\mathbf{X} \sim \mathcal{N}_n(\boldsymbol{\mu}, \boldsymbol{\Sigma})$, $\boldsymbol{\Sigma} > 0$, *and the components of* $\mathbf{X}$ *are partitioned as in* (3.3.1), *then for every fixed* $i = 1, \ldots, k$ *the supremum of the right-hand side of* (3.4.4) *is attained at* $\mathbf{c}' = \boldsymbol{\sigma}_i\boldsymbol{\Sigma}_{22}^{-1}$, *and*

$$R_{i\cdot k+1,\ldots,n} = \left(\frac{\boldsymbol{\sigma}_i\boldsymbol{\Sigma}_{22}^{-1}\boldsymbol{\sigma}_i'}{\sigma_{ii}}\right)^{1/2}. \tag{3.4.5}$$

PROOF. We shall follow the core of the argument given in Anderson (1984, p. 40). Since the correlation coefficient does not depend on the means, without loss of generality it may be assumed that $\boldsymbol{\mu} = \mathbf{0}$. By Theorem 3.4.1, the inequality

$$E[(X_i - \boldsymbol{\sigma}_i\boldsymbol{\Sigma}_{22}^{-1}\mathbf{x}_2)^2 | \mathbf{X}_2 = \mathbf{x}_2] \leq E[(X_i - \alpha\mathbf{c}'\mathbf{x}_2)^2 | \mathbf{X}_2 = \mathbf{x}_2]$$

holds for all real numbers α, real vectors $\mathbf{c}$, and all $\mathbf{x}_2 \in \mathfrak{R}^{n-k}$. After unconditioning we have

$$E(X_i - \boldsymbol{\sigma}_i\boldsymbol{\Sigma}_{22}^{-1}\mathbf{X}_2)^2 \leq E(X_i - \alpha\mathbf{c}'\mathbf{X}_2)^2 \tag{3.4.6}$$

for all α and $\mathbf{c}$. Expanding both sides of (3.4.6) we have

$$\operatorname{Var}(\boldsymbol{\sigma}_i\boldsymbol{\Sigma}_{22}^{-1}\mathbf{X}_2) - 2\operatorname{Cov}(X_i, \boldsymbol{\sigma}_i\boldsymbol{\Sigma}_{22}^{-1}\mathbf{X}_2) \leq \alpha^2\operatorname{Var}(\mathbf{c}'\mathbf{X}_2) - 2\alpha\operatorname{Cov}(X_i, \mathbf{c}'\mathbf{X}_2).$$

After rearranging the terms and dividing $(\sigma_{ii}\operatorname{Var}(\boldsymbol{\sigma}_i\boldsymbol{\Sigma}_{22}^{-1}\mathbf{X}_2))^{1/2}$ throughout, we then obtain

$$\frac{\operatorname{Cov}(X_i, \boldsymbol{\sigma}_i\boldsymbol{\Sigma}_{22}^{-1}\mathbf{X}_2) - \alpha\operatorname{Cov}(X_i, \mathbf{c}'\mathbf{X}_2)}{(\sigma_{ii}\operatorname{Var}(\boldsymbol{\sigma}_i\boldsymbol{\Sigma}_{22}^{-1}\mathbf{X}_2))^{1/2}}$$

$$\geq \frac{1}{2}\left[\left(\frac{\operatorname{Var}(\boldsymbol{\sigma}_i\boldsymbol{\Sigma}_{22}^{-1}\mathbf{X}_2)}{\sigma_{ii}}\right)^{1/2} - \frac{\alpha^2\operatorname{Var}(\mathbf{c}'\mathbf{X}_2)}{(\sigma_{ii}\operatorname{Var}(\boldsymbol{\sigma}_i\boldsymbol{\Sigma}_{22}^{-1}\mathbf{X}_2))^{1/2}}\right].$$

The inequality

$$\operatorname{Corr}(X_i, \boldsymbol{\sigma}_i\boldsymbol{\Sigma}_{22}^{-1}\mathbf{X}_2) - \operatorname{Corr}(X_i, \mathbf{c}'\mathbf{X}_2) \geq 0$$

now follows by choosing

$$\alpha = \left(\frac{\operatorname{Var}(\boldsymbol{\sigma}_i\boldsymbol{\Sigma}_{22}^{-1}\mathbf{X}_2)}{\operatorname{Var}(\mathbf{c}'\mathbf{X}_2)}\right)^{1/2}.$$

Consequently, we have

$$\begin{aligned} R_{i\cdot k+1,\ldots,n} &= \frac{\operatorname{Cov}(X_i, \boldsymbol{\sigma}_i\boldsymbol{\Sigma}_{22}^{-1}\mathbf{X}_2)}{(\sigma_{ii}\operatorname{Var}(\boldsymbol{\sigma}_i\boldsymbol{\Sigma}_{22}^{-1}\mathbf{X}_2))^{1/2}} \\ &= \frac{\boldsymbol{\sigma}_i\boldsymbol{\Sigma}_{22}^{-1}\boldsymbol{\sigma}_i'}{(\sigma_{ii}(\boldsymbol{\sigma}_i\boldsymbol{\Sigma}_{22}^{-1}\boldsymbol{\sigma}_i'))^{1/2}} \\ &= \left(\frac{\boldsymbol{\sigma}_i\boldsymbol{\Sigma}_{22}^{-1}\boldsymbol{\sigma}_i'}{\sigma_{ii}}\right)^{1/2}. \end{aligned}$$ □

For the nonsingular multivariate normal distribution, the multiple correlation coefficient given in (3.4.5) is always larger than or equal to zero and less than or equal to one. Furthermore, since $\boldsymbol{\Sigma}_{22}^{-1}$ is positive definite (because $\boldsymbol{\Sigma}_{22}$ is positive definite), it is equal to zero if and only if $\boldsymbol{\sigma}_i = \mathbf{0}$; that is, if and only if X_i and $\mathbf{X}_2$ are independent.

Since $(X_i, \boldsymbol{\sigma}_i\boldsymbol{\Sigma}_{22}^{-1}\mathbf{X}_2)'$ has a bivariate normal distribution with means μ_i, $\boldsymbol{\sigma}_i\boldsymbol{\Sigma}_{22}^{-1}\boldsymbol{\mu}_2$, variances σ_{ii}, $\boldsymbol{\sigma}_i\boldsymbol{\Sigma}_{22}^{-1}\boldsymbol{\sigma}_i'$, and correlation coefficient $R_{i\cdot k+1,\ldots,n}$, the conditional distribution of X_i, given $\boldsymbol{\sigma}_i\boldsymbol{\Sigma}_{22}^{-1}\mathbf{x}_2$, is normal with variance

$$\sigma_{ii}(1 - R^2_{i\cdot k+1,\ldots,n}) = \sigma_{ii} - \boldsymbol{\sigma}_i\boldsymbol{\Sigma}_{22}^{-1}\boldsymbol{\sigma}_i'. \tag{3.4.7}$$

This is the smallest possible variance of the conditional distribution of X_i, given $\mathbf{c}'\mathbf{X}_2 = \mathbf{c}'\mathbf{x}_2$, where $\mathbf{c}$ is a nonzero real vector, and is obtained when $\mathbf{c}'$ is chosen to be $\boldsymbol{\sigma}_i\boldsymbol{\Sigma}_{22}^{-1}$.

3.4.3. Partial Correlation Coefficients

The partial correlation coefficient between two random variables is their correlation coefficient after allowing for the effects of a set of other variables. For $i, j = 1, \ldots, k$, $i \neq j$, if we consider the correlation between X_i and X_j, when $\mathbf{X}_2 = (X_{k+1}, \ldots, X_n)'$ is fixed, then this correlation coefficient can be obtained from the conditional distribution of $(X_i, X_j)'$, given $\mathbf{X}_2 = \mathbf{x}_2$.

Definition 3.4.3. Let $\mathbf{X}$ be partitioned as in (3.3.1). Then for given $\mathbf{X}_2 = \mathbf{x}_2$ the partial correlation coefficient between X_i and X_j is

$$\rho_{ij\cdot k+1,\ldots,n} = \frac{\operatorname{Cov}((X_i, X_j)|\mathbf{X}_2 = \mathbf{x}_2)}{(\operatorname{Var}(X_i|\mathbf{X}_2 = \mathbf{x}_2)\operatorname{Var}(X_j|\mathbf{X}_2 = \mathbf{x}_2))^{1/2}}$$

for $i, j = 1, \ldots, k$, $i \neq j$.

For the general case, the partial correlation coefficient might depend on $\mathbf{x}_2$. But for the multivariate normal distribution the result is quite simple, depending only on the elements of the covariance matrix.

Theorem 3.4.3. *If* $\mathbf{X} \sim \mathcal{N}_n(\boldsymbol{\mu}, \boldsymbol{\Sigma})$, $\boldsymbol{\Sigma} > 0$, *and the components of* $\mathbf{X}$ *are partitioned as in* (3.3.1), *then*

$$\rho_{ij\cdot k+1,\ldots,n} = \frac{\sigma_{ij} - \boldsymbol{\sigma}_i \boldsymbol{\Sigma}_{22}^{-1} \boldsymbol{\sigma}_j'}{((\sigma_{ii} - \boldsymbol{\sigma}_i \boldsymbol{\Sigma}_{22}^{-1} \boldsymbol{\sigma}_i')(\sigma_{jj} - \boldsymbol{\sigma}_j \boldsymbol{\Sigma}_{22}^{-1} \boldsymbol{\sigma}_j'))^{1/2}} \tag{3.4.8}$$

for $i, j = 1, \ldots, k$, $i \neq j$.

PROOF. By Theorem 3.3.4, the conditional distribution of $\mathbf{X}_1$, given $\mathbf{X}_2 = \mathbf{x}_2$, is normal with the conditional covariance matrix $\boldsymbol{\Sigma}_{11\cdot 2} = \boldsymbol{\Sigma}_{12} - \boldsymbol{\Sigma}_{12}\boldsymbol{\Sigma}_{22}^{-1}\boldsymbol{\Sigma}_{21}$. Thus by Theorem 3.3.1 the conditional distribution of $(X_i, X_j)'$, given $\mathbf{X}_2 = \mathbf{x}_2$, is bivariate normal with the conditional covariance matrix

$$\begin{pmatrix} \sigma_{ii} & \sigma_{ij} \\ \sigma_{ij} & \sigma_{jj} \end{pmatrix} - \begin{pmatrix} \boldsymbol{\sigma}_i \\ \boldsymbol{\sigma}_j \end{pmatrix} \boldsymbol{\Sigma}_{22}^{-1} (\boldsymbol{\sigma}_i' \ \ \boldsymbol{\sigma}_j'). \qquad \square$$

Note that the partial correlation coefficient in (3.4.8) is nonnegative if and only if $\sigma_{ij} \geq \boldsymbol{\sigma}_i \boldsymbol{\Sigma}_{22}^{-1} \boldsymbol{\sigma}_j'$. Thus it is possible to have a covariance matrix $\boldsymbol{\Sigma}$ such that the correlation coefficient between X_i and X_j (which is $\rho_{ij} = \sigma_{ij}/\sqrt{\sigma_{ii}\sigma_{jj}}$) is positive while the partial correlation coefficient is negative. As an illustration consider the following example:

EXAMPLE 3.4.1. Let $\mathbf{X} = (X_1, X_2, X_3)'$ be distributed according to an $\mathcal{N}_3(\mathbf{0}, \boldsymbol{\Sigma})$ distribution, where $\sigma_{ii} = 1$ $(i = 1, 2, 3)$ and $\sigma_{12} = 1 - 2\varepsilon$, $\sigma_{13} = \sigma_{23} = 1 - \varepsilon$, $0 < \varepsilon < \frac{1}{2}$. For every fixed $\mathbf{c} = (c_1, c_2, c_3)' \in \mathfrak{R}^3$ we have

(a) $$\begin{aligned} \mathbf{c}'\boldsymbol{\Sigma}\mathbf{c} &= (c_1^2 + c_2^2 + c_3^2) + 2(1 - \varepsilon)(c_1c_2 + c_1c_3 + c_2c_3) - 2\varepsilon c_1 c_2 \\ &= (1 - \varepsilon)(c_1 + c_2 + c_3)^2 + \varepsilon(c_1 - c_2)^2 + \varepsilon c_3^2. \end{aligned}$$

Since $\mathbf{c}'\boldsymbol{\Sigma}\mathbf{c} \geq 0$ holds, and the equality holds if and only if $c_1 = c_2 = c_3 = 0$, $\boldsymbol{\Sigma}$ is a positive definite matrix.

(b) The conditional distribution of $(X_1, X_2)'$, given $X_3 = x_3$, is bivariate normal with the covariance matrix

$$\boldsymbol{\Sigma}_{11\cdot 2} = \begin{pmatrix} 1 & 1 - 2\varepsilon \\ 1 - 2\varepsilon & 1 \end{pmatrix} - (1 - \varepsilon)^2 \begin{pmatrix} 1 & 1 \\ 1 & 1 \end{pmatrix} = \varepsilon \begin{pmatrix} 2 - \varepsilon & -\varepsilon \\ -\varepsilon & 2 - \varepsilon \end{pmatrix}.$$

Thus $\rho_{12} = 1 - 2\varepsilon > 0$ and $\rho_{12\cdot 3} = -\varepsilon/(2 - \varepsilon) < 0$. $\square$

3.4.4. Canonical Correlation Coefficients

The theory of canonical correlation was developed by Hotelling (1936), and may be regarded as a generalization of the notion of the multiple correlation.

Let us again consider the partition of $\mathbf{X}$ into $\mathbf{X}_1$ and $\mathbf{X}_2$, defined in (3.3.1), where $\mathbf{X}_1 = (X_1, \ldots, X_k)'$ and $\mathbf{X}_2 = (X_{k+1}, \ldots, X_n)'$. Recall that the multiple correlation coefficient between X_i and $\mathbf{X}_2$ is the largest possible correlation coefficient between X_i and $\mathbf{c}'\mathbf{X}_2$ over all possible choices of real vectors $\mathbf{c}$, where $1 \le i \le k$ is fixed. In canonical correlation analysis we are interested in finding two real vectors $\mathbf{c}_1, \mathbf{c}_2$ such that the correlation coefficient between $\mathbf{c}_1'\mathbf{X}_1$ and $\mathbf{c}_2'\mathbf{X}_2$ is maximized.

This maximization process can be carried out in the following fashion: First, we choose $\mathbf{c}_2$ to maximize the correlation coefficient between $\mathbf{c}_1'\mathbf{X}_1$ and $\mathbf{c}_2'\mathbf{X}_2$ for fixed $\mathbf{c}_1$, then we find its maximum over all possible choices of $\mathbf{c}_1$. Second, we choose $\mathbf{c}_1$ to maximize the correlation coefficient between $\mathbf{c}_2'\mathbf{X}_2$ and $\mathbf{c}_1'\mathbf{X}_1$ for fixed $\mathbf{c}_2$, then we find the optimal solution for $\mathbf{c}_2$. After completing these two steps we then choose the larger of the two resulting correlation coefficients.

Now, for every fixed $\mathbf{c}_1$ and $X_0 = \mathbf{c}_1'\mathbf{X}_1$ (say), the best choice of $\mathbf{c}_2'$ is simply the regression vector of $\mathbf{X}_2$ on X_0. Thus the largest possible correlation coefficient is just $(\mathbf{c}_1'\boldsymbol{\Sigma}_{12}\boldsymbol{\Sigma}_{22}^{-1}\boldsymbol{\Sigma}_{21}\mathbf{c}_1/\mathbf{c}_1'\boldsymbol{\Sigma}_{11}\mathbf{c}_1)^{1/2}$, the multiple correlation coefficient between X_0 and $\mathbf{X}_2$. Furthermore, since correlation coefficients are scale invariant, without loss of generality it may be assumed that

$$\mathbf{c}_1'\boldsymbol{\Sigma}_{11}\mathbf{c}_1 = 1. \tag{3.4.9}$$

Using Lagrange's method of multipliers, this amounts to the maximization of

$$g(\mathbf{c}_1, \lambda) = \mathbf{c}_1'\boldsymbol{\Sigma}_{12}\boldsymbol{\Sigma}_{22}^{-1}\boldsymbol{\Sigma}_{21}\mathbf{c}_1 - \lambda(\mathbf{c}_1'\boldsymbol{\Sigma}_{11}\mathbf{c}_1 - 1), \tag{3.4.10}$$

subject to the constraint in (3.4.9). After taking partial derivatives with respect to the components of $\mathbf{c}_1$ and letting them equal zero, we have

$$(-\lambda\boldsymbol{\Sigma}_{11} + \boldsymbol{\Sigma}_{12}\boldsymbol{\Sigma}_{22}^{-1}\boldsymbol{\Sigma}_{21})\mathbf{c}_1 = \mathbf{0}. \tag{3.4.11}$$

Multiplying the left-hand side of (3.4.11) by $\mathbf{c}_1'$ and using the identity in (3.4.9), we then obtain

$$\lambda = \mathbf{c}_1'\boldsymbol{\Sigma}_{12}\boldsymbol{\Sigma}_{22}^{-1}\boldsymbol{\Sigma}_{21}\mathbf{c}_1. \tag{3.4.12}$$

For $\mathbf{c}_1$ to have a nontrivial solution in (3.4.11) we must have

$$h_1(\lambda) = |-\lambda\boldsymbol{\Sigma}_{11} + \boldsymbol{\Sigma}_{12}\boldsymbol{\Sigma}_{22}^{-1}\boldsymbol{\Sigma}_{21}| = 0. \tag{3.4.13}$$

But $h_1(\lambda)$ is a polynomial of degree k. It can be verified that (see Anderson (1984, p. 483)) if $\boldsymbol{\Sigma}$ is positive definite, then $h_1(\lambda)$ has k nonnegative real roots.

Similarly, the maximization of the multiple correlation coefficient $(\mathbf{c}_2'\boldsymbol{\Sigma}_{21}\boldsymbol{\Sigma}_{11}^{-1}\boldsymbol{\Sigma}_{12}\mathbf{c}_2/\mathbf{c}_2'\boldsymbol{\Sigma}_{22}\mathbf{c}_2)^{1/2}$, subject to the constraint

$$\mathbf{c}_2'\boldsymbol{\Sigma}_{22}\mathbf{c}_2 = 1, \tag{3.4.14}$$

leads to the equation

$$(-\lambda\boldsymbol{\Sigma}_{22} + \boldsymbol{\Sigma}_{21}\boldsymbol{\Sigma}_{11}^{-1}\boldsymbol{\Sigma}_{12})\mathbf{c}_2 = \mathbf{0}. \tag{3.4.15}$$

In order to have a nonsingular solution we must have

$$h_2(\lambda) = |-\lambda\mathbf{\Sigma}_{22} + \mathbf{\Sigma}_{21}\mathbf{\Sigma}_{11}^{-1}\mathbf{\Sigma}_{12}| = 0, \tag{3.4.16}$$

which has $n - k$ nonnegative real roots.

Let $\lambda_1, \lambda_2, \ldots, \lambda_n$ be the collection of roots of the two equations $h_1(\lambda) = 0$ and $h_2(\lambda) = 0$ and, without loss of generality, assume that

$$\lambda_1 \geq \lambda_2 \geq \cdots \geq \lambda_n \geq 0. \tag{3.4.17}$$

Then by (3.4.12) the largest canonical correlation coefficient is simply $\sqrt{\lambda_1}$. The vectors $\mathbf{c}_1$, $\mathbf{c}_2$, which yield this largest canonical correlation coefficient, can be obtained from either (3.4.11) or (3.4.15) with $\lambda = \lambda_1$, depending on which equation has the root λ_1. Let $(\mathbf{c}_{1,1}, \mathbf{c}_{2,1})$ denote such a solution. Then the random variables $\mathbf{c}'_{1,1}\mathbf{X}_1$, $\mathbf{c}'_{2,1}\mathbf{X}_2$ are called the first pair of canonical variables.

This process can be continued to find all the λ_j values and the corresponding canonical variables. Without loss of generality, let

$$\lambda_1 > \lambda_2 > \cdots > \lambda_r \geq 0$$

denote the r $(r \leq n)$ distinct roots of $h_1(\lambda) = 0$ and $h_2(\lambda) = 0$. Then $\sqrt{\lambda_j}$ is called the jth canonical correlation coefficient, and the corresponding vector $(\mathbf{c}'_{1,j}\mathbf{X}_1, \mathbf{c}'_{2,j}\mathbf{X}_2)'$ is called the jth pair of canonical variables. Using Lagrange's method of multipliers it can be shown that (see Anderson (1984, p. 484)) the vectors $\{\mathbf{c}_{1,j}\}_{j=1}^r$, $\{\mathbf{c}_{2,j}\}_{j=1}^r$ also satisfy the conditions, for all $s \neq t$,

(i) $\quad \mathbf{c}'_{1,s}\mathbf{X}_1$ and $\mathbf{c}'_{1,t}\mathbf{X}_1$ are independent, (3.4.18)

(ii) $\quad \mathbf{c}'_{2,s}\mathbf{X}_2$ and $\mathbf{c}'_{2,t}\mathbf{X}_2$ are independent, (3.4.19)

(iii) $\quad \mathbf{c}'_{1,s}\mathbf{X}_1$ and $\mathbf{c}'_{2,t}\mathbf{X}_2$ are independent. (3.4.20)

Summarizing the above result, we say

Definition 3.4.4. Let $\mathbf{X}$ be partitioned as in (3.3.1), and let

$$\tau_j = \sup_{\mathbf{c}_{1,j},\mathbf{c}_{2,j}} \mathrm{Corr}(\mathbf{c}'_{1,j}\mathbf{X}_1, \mathbf{c}'_{2,j}\mathbf{X}_2)$$

subject to (3.4.18)–(3.4.20) and the condition

$$\mathbf{c}'_{1,j}\mathbf{\Sigma}_{11}\mathbf{c}_{1,j} = \mathbf{c}'_{2,j}\mathbf{\Sigma}_{22}\mathbf{c}_{2,j} = 1.$$

The distinct values $\tau_1 > \tau_2 > \cdots > \tau_r$ $(r \leq n)$ are called the canonical correlation coefficients between $\mathbf{X}_1$ and $\mathbf{X}_2$.

If $\mathbf{X}$ is a nonsingular $\mathcal{N}_n(\boldsymbol{\mu}, \mathbf{\Sigma})$ variable, then $\mathbf{\Sigma}_{11}$ and $\mathbf{\Sigma}_{22}$ are both nonsingular. Thus we obtain

Theorem 3.4.4. *If* $\mathbf{X} \sim \mathcal{N}_n(\boldsymbol{\mu}, \mathbf{\Sigma})$, $\mathbf{\Sigma} > 0$, *and* $\mathbf{X}$ *is partitioned as in* (3.3.1), *then the* j*th canonical correlation coefficient between* $\mathbf{X}_1$ *and* $\mathbf{X}_2$ *is* $\sqrt{\lambda_j}$, $j = 1, \ldots, r$, *where* $\lambda_1 > \lambda_2 > \cdots > \lambda_r \geq 0$ *are the* r *distinct roots of* $h_1(\lambda) = 0$ *and* $h_2(\lambda) = 0$, *defined in* (3.4.13) *and* (3.4.16), *respectively.*

3.4.5. Principal Components

Principal component analysis, originally proposed and studied by Hotelling (1933), concerns a method for obtaining a set of linear combinations of components of an n-dimensional random variable with certain desirable properties. Suppose that $\mathbf{X} \sim \mathcal{N}_n(\boldsymbol{\mu}, \boldsymbol{\Sigma}), \boldsymbol{\Sigma} > 0$. When the X_i's are independent, then a measure of dispersion of the distribution of $\mathbf{X}$ is the sum of the variances (which are the diagonal elements of $\boldsymbol{\Sigma}$). Furthermore, the larger the variance of X_i, the more it contributes to this dispersion. Thus the problem of interest is to define and obtain the principal (or the most influential) components with large variances when the X_i's are correlated. In this case it is not adequate just to consider each of the components separately because they tend to hang together.

In principal component analysis, we look for linear combinations of the X_i's such that the variances are maximized under certain constraints. Let $\mathbf{c}_1' = (c_{11}, \ldots, c_{1n})$ be a real vector such that $\mathbf{c}_1'\mathbf{c}_1 = 1$ and

$$\sup_{\{\boldsymbol{\alpha}:\boldsymbol{\alpha}'\boldsymbol{\alpha}=1\}} \operatorname{Var}(\boldsymbol{\alpha}'\mathbf{X}) = \operatorname{Var}(\mathbf{c}_1'\mathbf{X}).$$

Then $\mathbf{c}_1$ is the vector with norm 1 such that the variance of $\mathbf{c}_1'\mathbf{X}$ is maximized over all linear combinations of the components under this constraint. To find $\mathbf{c}_1$ note that $\operatorname{Var}(\boldsymbol{\alpha}'\mathbf{X}) = \boldsymbol{\alpha}'\boldsymbol{\Sigma}\boldsymbol{\alpha}$ for all $\boldsymbol{\alpha}$. Thus, by Lagrange's method of multipliers, this amounts to maximizing the function

$$g_1(\boldsymbol{\alpha}, \lambda) = \boldsymbol{\alpha}'\boldsymbol{\Sigma}\boldsymbol{\alpha} - \lambda(\boldsymbol{\alpha}'\boldsymbol{\alpha} - 1),$$

subject to $\boldsymbol{\alpha}'\boldsymbol{\alpha} = 1$. By calculus it follows that

$$\frac{\partial}{\partial \boldsymbol{\alpha}} g_1(\boldsymbol{\alpha}, \lambda) = 2(\boldsymbol{\Sigma}\boldsymbol{\alpha} - \lambda\boldsymbol{\alpha}) = 2(\boldsymbol{\Sigma} - \lambda\mathbf{I}_n)\boldsymbol{\alpha},$$

where $\mathbf{I}_n$ is the $n \times n$ identity matrix. The system of linear equations $(\partial/\partial\boldsymbol{\alpha})g_1(\boldsymbol{\alpha}, \lambda) = 0$ has a nontrivial solution if and only if

$$h(\lambda) \equiv |\boldsymbol{\Sigma} - \lambda\mathbf{I}_n| = 0 \tag{3.4.21}$$

holds. Thus λ must be an eigenvalue of $\boldsymbol{\Sigma}$. Furthermore, if $\mathbf{c}_1$ satisfies $2(\boldsymbol{\Sigma} - \lambda\mathbf{I}_n)\mathbf{c}_1 = 0$ then, by $\boldsymbol{\alpha}'\boldsymbol{\alpha} = 1$, we must have

$$\boldsymbol{\Sigma}\mathbf{c}_1 = \lambda\mathbf{c}_1 \tag{3.4.22}$$

and

$$\mathbf{c}_1'\boldsymbol{\Sigma}\mathbf{c}_1 = \lambda\mathbf{c}_1'\mathbf{I}_n\mathbf{c}_1 = \lambda. \tag{3.4.23}$$

Thus λ is actually the variance of $\mathbf{c}_1'\mathbf{X} \equiv Y_1$. Let λ_1 denote the value of this λ.

After Y_1 and λ_1 are obtained, we then look for another randm variable $Y_2 = \mathbf{c}_2'\mathbf{X}$ such that:

(i) $\mathbf{c}_2'\mathbf{c}_2 = 1$;
(ii) Y_2 is independent of Y_1; and

(iii) Y_2 has the largest variance among all linear combinations of components of $\mathbf{X}$ that satisfy (i) and (ii).

If $\boldsymbol{\alpha}$ is any vector that satisfies (i) and (ii), then $\boldsymbol{\alpha}'\boldsymbol{\alpha} = 1$ and, by (3.4.22),

$$\operatorname{Cov}(Y_1, Y_2) = \mathbf{c}_1'\boldsymbol{\Sigma}\boldsymbol{\alpha} = \boldsymbol{\alpha}'\boldsymbol{\Sigma}\mathbf{c}_1 = \lambda_1\boldsymbol{\alpha}'\mathbf{c}_1 = 0; \tag{3.4.24}$$

that is, $\boldsymbol{\alpha}$ and $\mathbf{c}_1$ must be orthogonal. Applying Lagrange's method of multipliers one more time leads to the maximization of the function

$$g_2(\boldsymbol{\alpha}, \lambda, \eta) = \boldsymbol{\alpha}'\boldsymbol{\Sigma}\boldsymbol{\alpha} - \lambda(\boldsymbol{\alpha}'\boldsymbol{\alpha} - 1) - \eta\boldsymbol{\alpha}'\boldsymbol{\Sigma}\mathbf{c}_1,$$

subject to $\boldsymbol{\alpha}'\boldsymbol{\alpha} = 1$ and (3.4.24). By

$$\frac{\partial}{\partial \boldsymbol{\alpha}} g_2(\boldsymbol{\alpha}, \lambda, \eta) = 2(\boldsymbol{\Sigma}\boldsymbol{\alpha} - \lambda\boldsymbol{\alpha} - \eta\boldsymbol{\Sigma}\mathbf{c}_1)$$

and (3.4.24) it follows that if $\mathbf{c}_2$ is a solution of $(\partial/\partial\boldsymbol{\alpha})g_2(\boldsymbol{\alpha}, \lambda, \eta) = 0$, then

$$\mathbf{c}_1'\boldsymbol{\Sigma}\mathbf{c}_2 - \lambda\mathbf{c}_1'\mathbf{c}_2 - \eta\mathbf{c}_1'\boldsymbol{\Sigma}\mathbf{c}_1 = -\eta\mathbf{c}_1'\boldsymbol{\Sigma}\mathbf{c}_1 = 0,$$

$$\mathbf{c}_2'\boldsymbol{\Sigma}\mathbf{c}_2 - \lambda\mathbf{c}_2'\mathbf{c}_2 - \eta\mathbf{c}_2'\boldsymbol{\Sigma}\mathbf{c}_1 = 0.$$

Thus we have $\eta = 0$. This implies that $\mathbf{c}_2$ and λ also satisfy the equations

$$\lambda = \mathbf{c}_2'\boldsymbol{\Sigma}\mathbf{c}_2, \qquad (\boldsymbol{\Sigma} - \lambda\mathbf{I}_n)\mathbf{c}_2 = 0.$$

Consequently, if $\mathbf{c}_2$ has a nontrivial solution, then λ also satisfies (3.4.21). Let the value of this λ be denoted by λ_2.

It is known that if $\boldsymbol{\Sigma}$ is an $n \times n$ positive definite matrix, then it has n positive real eigenvalues. Let $\lambda_1, \ldots, \lambda_n$ be the eigenvalues and, without loss of generality, assume that

$$\lambda_1 \geq \lambda_2 \geq \cdots \geq \lambda_n > 0. \tag{3.4.25}$$

Then using a similar argument we can continue this process to find n real vectors $\mathbf{c}_1, \mathbf{c}_2, \ldots, \mathbf{c}_n$ such that:

(i) $\mathbf{c}_i'\mathbf{c}_i = 1$ $(i = 1, \ldots, n)$;
(ii) $\mathbf{c}_i'\mathbf{c}_j = 0$ for all $i \neq j$; and
(iii) the variance of $Y_i = \mathbf{c}_i'\mathbf{X}$ is λ_i $(i = 1, \ldots, n)$.

Expressing the linear transformation in a matrix form we have

Theorem 3.4.5. *Let* $\mathbf{X} \sim \mathcal{N}_n(\boldsymbol{\mu}, \boldsymbol{\Sigma})$, $\boldsymbol{\Sigma} > 0$, *and let* $\lambda_1, \ldots, \lambda_n$ *be the eigenvalues of* $\boldsymbol{\Sigma}$ *satisfying* (3.4.25). *Then there exists an orthogonal matrix* $\mathbf{C} = (\mathbf{c}_1, \mathbf{c}_2, \ldots, \mathbf{c}_n)$ *satisfying* $\mathbf{Y} = \mathbf{C}'\mathbf{X} \sim \mathcal{N}_n(\mathbf{C}'\boldsymbol{\mu}, \mathbf{D})$, *where* $\mathbf{D} = (d_{ij})$ *is a diagonal matrix such that* $d_{ii} = \lambda_i$ $(i = 1, \ldots, n)$.

We now provide a formal definition of the principal components of $\mathbf{X}$ when it has a multivariate normal distribution.

Definition 3.4.5. Let $\mathbf{X} \sim \mathcal{N}_n(\boldsymbol{\mu}, \boldsymbol{\Sigma})$, $\boldsymbol{\Sigma} > 0$, and let $\mathbf{Y} = (Y_1, \ldots, Y_n)'$ be the random variable defined in Theorem 3.4.5. Then Y_i is said to be the ith principal component of $\mathbf{X}$ $(i = 1, \ldots, n)$.

Remark 3.4.1. If the components are independent, then $\mathbf{\Sigma}$ is already a diagonal matrix. In this case, Y_1 is the component of $\mathbf{X}$ with the largest variance, Y_2 is the component of $\mathbf{X}$ with the second largest variance, and so on; and $\mathbf{c}_i' = (0, \ldots, 0, 1, 0, \ldots, 0)$ which has a "1" in one of the n positions.

Remark 3.4.2. As a measure of the contributions to the sum of the variances of the Y_i's, the ratios $\lambda_i / \sum_{i=1}^n \lambda_j$ $(i = 1, \ldots, n)$ are of interest. In particular, $\lambda_1 / \sum_{i=1}^n \lambda_j$ represents the contribution of the first principal component of $\mathbf{X}$.

We note in passing that applications of the results of principal component analysis are not limited to the multivariate normal distribution because Theorem 3.4.5 does not require the assumption of normality.

3.4.6. An Example

We complete this section with an example.

EXAMPLE 3.4.2. Let $n = 5$, $k = 2$, and $\mathbf{X} \sim \mathcal{N}_5(\boldsymbol{\mu}, \mathbf{\Sigma})$. Consider the partition $\mathbf{X}_1 = (X_1, X_2)'$, $\mathbf{X}_2 = (X_3, X_4, X_5)'$,

$$\boldsymbol{\mu} = \begin{pmatrix} \boldsymbol{\mu}_1 \\ \boldsymbol{\mu}_2 \end{pmatrix}, \qquad \mathbf{\Sigma} = \begin{pmatrix} \mathbf{\Sigma}_{11} & \mathbf{\Sigma}_{12} \\ \mathbf{\Sigma}_{21} & \mathbf{\Sigma}_{22} \end{pmatrix},$$

where

$$\mathbf{\Sigma}_{11} = \begin{pmatrix} 1 & \rho_2 \\ \rho_2 & 1 \end{pmatrix}, \qquad \mathbf{\Sigma}_{22} = \begin{pmatrix} 1 & \rho_2 & \rho_2 \\ \rho_2 & 1 & \rho_2 \\ \rho_2 & \rho_2 & 1 \end{pmatrix},$$

$$\mathbf{\Sigma}_{12} = \mathbf{\Sigma}_{21}' = \begin{pmatrix} \rho_1 & \rho_1 & \rho_1 \\ \rho_1 & \rho_1 & \rho_1 \end{pmatrix},$$

and $0 \le \rho_1 \le \rho_2 < 1$. That is, the random variables are partitioned into two groups; the correlation coefficients within each group are ρ_2, and the correlation coefficients between groups are ρ_1.

(a) $\mathbf{X}$ is a nonsingular normal variable, i.e., $\mathbf{\Sigma} > 0$. To see this, for all nonzero vectors $\mathbf{c}' = (c_1, c_2, c_3, c_4, c_5) \neq \mathbf{0}$ we have

$$\begin{aligned}
&\mathbf{c}'\mathbf{\Sigma}\mathbf{c} \\
&= \sum_{i=1}^{5} c_i^2 + 2\rho_2(c_1c_2 + c_3(c_4 + c_5) + c_4c_5) + 2\rho_1(c_1 + c_2)(c_3 + c_4 + c_5) \\
&= \left(\sqrt{\rho_1} \sum_{i=1}^{5} c_i\right)^2 + (\rho_2 - \rho_1)((c_1 + c_2)^2 + (c_3 + c_4 + c_5)^2) + (1 - \rho_2) \sum_{i=1}^{5} c_i^2 \\
&> 0.
\end{aligned}$$

(b) Simple calculation shows

$$\mathbf{\Sigma}_{22}^{-1} = \frac{1}{(1+2\rho_2)(1-\rho_2)}\begin{pmatrix} 1+\rho_2 & -\rho_2 & -\rho_2 \\ -\rho_2 & 1+\rho_2 & -\rho_2 \\ -\rho_2 & -\rho_2 & 1+\rho_2 \end{pmatrix}.$$

Thus

$$\mathbf{\Sigma}_{12}\mathbf{\Sigma}_{22}^{-1} = \frac{\rho_1}{1+2\rho_2}\begin{pmatrix} 1 & 1 & 1 \\ 1 & 1 & 1 \end{pmatrix},$$

$$\begin{aligned}\mathbf{\Sigma}_{11\cdot 2} &= \mathbf{\Sigma}_{11} - \mathbf{\Sigma}_{12}\mathbf{\Sigma}_{22}^{-1}\mathbf{\Sigma}_{21} \\ &= \frac{1}{1+2\rho_2}\begin{pmatrix} 1+2\rho_2-3\rho_1^2 & \rho_2+2\rho_2^2-3\rho_1^2 \\ \rho_2+2\rho_2^2-3\rho_1^2 & 1+2\rho_2-3\rho_1^2 \end{pmatrix};\end{aligned} \tag{3.4.26}$$

and the conditional distribution of $\mathbf{X}_1$, given $\mathbf{X}_2 = \mathbf{x}_2$, is normal with mean vector

$$\begin{pmatrix} \mu_1 + \dfrac{\rho_1}{1+2\rho_2}\displaystyle\sum_{i=3}^{5}(x_j - \mu_j) \\ \mu_2 + \dfrac{\rho_1}{1+2\rho_2}\displaystyle\sum_{j=3}^{5}(x_j - \mu_j) \end{pmatrix}$$

and covariance matrix $\mathbf{\Sigma}_{11\cdot 2}$ given in (3.4.26).

(c) The best predictor for X_i $(i = 1, 2)$, given $(X_3, X_4, X_5)' = (x_3, x_4, x_5)'$, is

$$\hat{x}_i = \mu_i + \frac{\rho_1}{1+2\rho_2}\sum_{j=3}^{5}(x_j - \mu_j).$$

(d) The multiple correlation coefficient between X_i and $\mathbf{X}_2$ is

$$R_{i\cdot 345} = \frac{\sqrt{3}\rho_1}{\sqrt{1+2\rho_2}}, \qquad i = 1, 2,$$

and $R_{i\cdot 345} = 0$ if and only if $\rho_1 = 0$. When $\rho_1 = \rho_2 = \rho$, it becomes $\sqrt{3}\rho/\sqrt{1+2\rho}$.

(e) The partial correlation coefficient between X_1 and X_2 is

$$\rho_{12\cdot 345} = \frac{\rho_2 + 2\rho_2^2 - 3\rho_1^2}{1 + 2\rho_2 - 3\rho_1^2},$$

and is equal to ρ_2 when $(X_1, X_2)'$ and $(X_3, X_4, X_5)'$ are independent. When $\rho_1 = \rho_2 = \rho$, it reduces to $\rho/(1+3\rho)$.

(f) The determinants of the matrices $-\lambda\mathbf{\Sigma}_{11} + \mathbf{\Sigma}_{12}\mathbf{\Sigma}_{22}^{-1}\mathbf{\Sigma}_{21}$ and $-\lambda\mathbf{\Sigma}_{22} + \mathbf{\Sigma}_{21}\mathbf{\Sigma}_{11}^{-1}\mathbf{\Sigma}_{12}$ are, respectively,

$$h_1(\lambda) = (1-\rho_2)\lambda\left[(1+\rho_2)\lambda - \frac{6\rho_1^2}{1+2\rho_2}\right], \tag{3.4.27}$$

$$h_2(\lambda) = -(1-\rho_2)^2\lambda^2\left[(1+2\rho_2)\lambda - \frac{6\rho_1^2}{1+\rho_2}\right]. \tag{3.4.28}$$

Thus $h_1(\lambda) = 0$ and $h_2(\lambda) = 0$ have a common unique positive root $\lambda_1 = 6\rho_1^2/((1 + \rho_2)(1 + 2\rho_2))$ and all the other roots are zero. Consequently, it follows that:

(i) the largest canonical correlation coefficient between $\mathbf{X}_1$ and $\mathbf{X}_2$ is $\sqrt{6}\rho_1/\sqrt{(1 + \rho_2)(1 + 2\rho_2)}$, which is $\sqrt{6}\rho/\sqrt{(1 + \rho)(1 + 2\rho)}$ when $\rho_1 = \rho_2 = \rho$;

(ii) the canonical variables that yield this canonical correlation coefficient can be obtained by either finding a solution for $\mathbf{c}_1$ in (3.4.11) or finding a solution for $\mathbf{c}_2$ in (3.4.15), with $\lambda = \lambda_1$;

(iii) all other pairs of canonical variables that are uncorrelated with (hence independent of) the first pair must also be independent.

This is so because all other canonical correlation coefficients are zero.

(g) It is straightforward to verify that

$$|\mathbf{\Sigma} - \lambda\mathbf{I}_5| = (1 - \lambda - \rho_2)^3[(1 - \lambda + \rho_2)(1 - \lambda + 2\rho_2) - 6\rho_1^2]. \quad (3.4.29)$$

Thus the eigenvalues of $\mathbf{\Sigma}$ are

$$\lambda_1 = 1 + \tfrac{3}{2}\rho_2 + \tfrac{1}{2}(\rho_2^2 + 24\rho_1^2)^{1/2},$$
$$\lambda_2 = 1 + \tfrac{3}{2}\rho_2 - \tfrac{1}{2}(\rho_2^2 + 24\rho_1^2)^{1/2},$$
$$\lambda_3 = \lambda_4 = \lambda_5 = 1 - \rho_2.$$

In the special case when $\rho_1 = \rho_2 = \rho$, we have

$$\lambda_1 = 1 + 4\rho, \qquad \lambda_2 = \lambda_3 = \lambda_4 = \lambda_5 = 1 - \rho;$$

and a set of solutions for $\mathbf{c}_i$ in $(\mathbf{\Sigma} - \lambda_i\mathbf{I}_5)\mathbf{c}_i = \mathbf{0}$ is

$$\mathbf{c}_1' = \frac{1}{\sqrt{5}}(1 \;\; 1 \;\; 1 \;\; 1 \;\; 1), \qquad \mathbf{c}_2' = \frac{1}{\sqrt{20}}(-4 \;\; 1 \;\; 1 \;\; 1 \;\; 1),$$

$$\mathbf{c}_3' = \frac{1}{\sqrt{12}}(0 \;\; -3 \;\; 1 \;\; 1 \;\; 1), \qquad \mathbf{c}_4' = \frac{1}{\sqrt{6}}(0 \;\; 0 \;\; -2 \;\; 1 \;\; 1),$$

and

$$\mathbf{c}_5' = \frac{1}{\sqrt{2}}(0 \;\; 0 \;\; 0 \;\; -1 \;\; 1).$$

Thus the orthogonal matrix $\mathbf{C} = (\mathbf{c}_1 \;\; \mathbf{c}_2 \;\; \mathbf{c}_3 \;\; \mathbf{c}_4 \;\; \mathbf{c}_5)'$ satisfies the condition that $\mathbf{Y} = \mathbf{C}'\mathbf{X} \sim N_5(\mathbf{C}'\boldsymbol{\mu}, \mathbf{D})$, where $\mathbf{D}$ is the diagonal matrix with diagonal elements $\lambda_1, \ldots, \lambda_5$. The components of $\mathbf{Y}$, $Y_i = \mathbf{c}_i'\mathbf{X}$ $(i = 1, \ldots, 5)$, are the principal components of $\mathbf{X}$. When $\rho_1 = \rho_2 = \rho$, the variance of the first principal component $Y_1 = \mathbf{c}_1'\mathbf{X}$ is $\lambda_1 = \mathbf{c}_1'\mathbf{\Sigma}\mathbf{c}_1 = 1 + 4\rho$, and its contribution to the sum of the variances of the principal components is $20(1 + 4\rho)\%$. □

3.5. Sampling Distributions

For fixed positive integer N let $\mathbf{X}_1, \ldots, \mathbf{X}_N$ be a random sample of size N from an $\mathcal{N}_n(\boldsymbol{\mu}, \boldsymbol{\Sigma})$ distribution, that is, $\mathbf{X}_1, \ldots, \mathbf{X}_N$ are i.i.d. random variables with a common $\mathcal{N}_n(\boldsymbol{\mu}, \boldsymbol{\Sigma})$ distribution. Let

$$\bar{\mathbf{X}}_N = \frac{1}{N}\sum_{t=1}^{N} \mathbf{X}_t = (\bar{X}_1, \ldots, \bar{X}_n)', \tag{3.5.1}$$

$$\mathbf{S} = \begin{pmatrix} S_{11} & S_{12} & \cdots & S_{1n} \\ S_{21} & S_{22} & \cdots & S_{2n} \\ & & \cdots & \\ S_{n1} & S_{n2} & \cdots & S_{nn} \end{pmatrix} \tag{3.5.2}$$

denote the sample mean vector and the sample covariance matrix, respectively, where

$$\bar{X}_i = \frac{1}{N}\sum_{t=1}^{N} X_{it}, \tag{3.5.3}$$

$$S_{ij} = \frac{1}{N-1}\sum_{t=1}^{N} (X_{it} - \bar{X}_i)(X_{jt} - \bar{X}_j), \tag{3.5.4}$$

for $i, j = 1, \ldots, n$ (X_{it} is the ith component of $\mathbf{X}_t$). After arranging $\mathbf{X}_1, \ldots, \mathbf{X}_N$ in a matrix form by defining the $n \times N$ data matrix

$$\mathbf{X} = (\mathbf{X}_1, \ldots, \mathbf{X}_N), \tag{3.5.5}$$

the sample covariance matrix can be expressed as

$$\begin{aligned} \mathbf{S} &= \frac{1}{N-1}\left(\sum_{t=1}^{N} \mathbf{X}_t\mathbf{X}_t' - N\bar{\mathbf{X}}_N\bar{\mathbf{X}}_N'\right) \\ &= \frac{1}{N-1}(\mathbf{X}\mathbf{X}' - N\bar{\mathbf{X}}_N\bar{\mathbf{X}}_N'). \end{aligned} \tag{3.5.6}$$

By the identity

$$N\bar{\mathbf{X}}_N\bar{\mathbf{X}}_N' = \mathbf{X}\left(\frac{1}{N}\mathbf{1}_N\right)\mathbf{X}', \tag{3.5.7}$$

where $\mathbf{I}_N$ is the $N \times N$ identity matrix and $\mathbf{1}_N$ is the $N \times N$ matrix with elements one, we can write

$$\mathbf{S} = \frac{1}{N-1}\mathbf{X}\left(\mathbf{I}_N - \frac{1}{N}\mathbf{1}_N\right)\mathbf{X}'. \tag{3.5.8}$$

Note that $\mathbf{S}$ is symmetric, thus it involves only $n(n+1)/2$ random variables.

It is known that for $N > n$ $(\bar{\mathbf{X}}_N, (N-1)\mathbf{S}/N)$ is the maximum likelihood estimator of $(\boldsymbol{\mu}, \boldsymbol{\Sigma})$ (see Anderson (1984, Sec. 3.2)). Furthermore, almost all of the useful inference procedures in multivariate analysis depend on the data matrix $\mathbf{X}$ only through $(\bar{\mathbf{X}}_N, \mathbf{S})$. Thus the (marginal and joint) distributions of $\bar{\mathbf{X}}_N$ and $\mathbf{S}$ are of great interest.

3.5.1. Independence of $\bar{\mathbf{X}}_N$ and $\mathbf{S}$

Before deriving their distributions we first observe a basic fact. For the univariate normal distribution, it is well known that the sample mean and the sample variance are independent. We show below that a similar statement holds for the multivariate normal distribution.

Theorem 3.5.1. *For $N > n$, let $\mathbf{X}_1, \ldots, \mathbf{X}_N$ be i.i.d. $\mathcal{N}_n(\boldsymbol{\mu}, \boldsymbol{\Sigma})$ variables, $\boldsymbol{\Sigma} > 0$. Let $\bar{\mathbf{X}}_N$ and $\mathbf{S}$ be defined as in* (3.5.1) *and* (3.5.2), *respectively. Then $\bar{\mathbf{X}}_N$ and $\mathbf{S}$ are independent.*

There exist two independent proofs for this result.

First Proof. The proof depends on the following known result: Let $\mathbf{X}$ be defined as in (3.5.5), and let $\mathbf{C}_1$, $\mathbf{C}_2$ be two given $N \times N$ symmetric real matrices. If $\mathbf{C}_1\mathbf{C}_2 = \mathbf{0}$, then the quadratic forms $\mathbf{X}\mathbf{C}_1\mathbf{X}'$ and $\mathbf{X}\mathbf{C}_2\mathbf{X}'$ are independent. (See, e.g., Anderson and Styan (1982); a less general result was given earlier by Craig (1943).) Thus, by (3.5.7), (3.5.8) and

$$\left(\frac{1}{N}\mathbf{1}_N\right)\left(\mathbf{I}_N - \frac{1}{N}\mathbf{1}_N\right) = \mathbf{0},$$

$\bar{\mathbf{X}}_N\bar{\mathbf{X}}_N'$ and $\mathbf{S}$ are independent. Consequently, $\bar{\mathbf{X}}_N$ and $\mathbf{S}$ are independent. □

Second Proof. The second proof depends on an orthogonal transformation of the elements of $\mathbf{X}$. For every fixed $N \geq 2$ there exists an $N \times N$ orthogonal matrix $\mathbf{C} = (c_{rt})$ satisfying

$$c_{N1} = \cdots = c_{NN} = \frac{1}{\sqrt{N}}. \tag{3.5.9}$$

Since $\mathbf{C}\mathbf{C}' = \mathbf{C}'\mathbf{C} = \mathbf{I}_N$, we must have

$$\sum_{t=1}^{N} c_{rt}^2 = 1 \qquad \text{for all } r, \tag{3.5.10}$$

and

$$\sum_{t=1}^{N} c_{rt}c_{st} = 0 \qquad \text{for all} \quad r \neq s. \tag{3.5.11}$$

This implies

$$\sum_{t=1}^{N} c_{rt} = \sqrt{N} \sum_{t=1}^{N} c_{rt}c_{Nt} = 0 \qquad \text{for all} \quad r < N. \tag{3.5.12}$$

Let us define an $n \times N$ random matrix $\mathbf{Y}$ by

$$\mathbf{Y} = (\mathbf{Y}_1 \ldots \mathbf{Y}_N) = \mathbf{X}\mathbf{C}', \qquad \text{or equivalently,} \qquad \mathbf{Y}' = \mathbf{C}\mathbf{X}'.$$

Obviously, the joint distribution of the nN elements of $\mathbf{Y}$ is multivariate normal. Their means, variances, and covariances can be obtained from (3.5.9)–(3.5.12):

(i) For $1 \le i \le n$ and $1 \le r \le N - 1$,

$$EY_{ir} = \sum_{t=1}^{N} c_{rt} EX_{it} = \mu_i \sum_{t=1}^{N} c_{rt} = 0.$$

(ii) For $1 \le i, j \le n$ and $1 \le r \le N$,

$$\begin{aligned}\operatorname{Cov}(Y_{ir}, Y_{jr}) &= \operatorname{Cov}\left(\sum_{t=1}^{N} c_{rt} X_{it}, \sum_{t=1}^{N} c_{rt} X_{jt}\right) \\ &= \sum_{t=1}^{N} c_{rt}^2 \operatorname{Cov}(X_{it}, X_{jt}) \\ &= \sigma_{ij},\end{aligned}$$

which is the (i, j)th element of $\boldsymbol{\Sigma}$.

(iii) For $1 \le r < s \le N$,

$$\begin{aligned}\operatorname{Cov}(Y_{ir}, Y_{js}) &= \operatorname{Cov}\left(\sum_{t=1}^{N} c_{rt} X_{it}, \sum_{t=1}^{N} c_{st} X_{jt}\right) \\ &= \sum_{t=1}^{N} c_{rt} c_{st} \operatorname{Cov}(X_{it}, X_{jt}) \\ &= 0.\end{aligned}$$

It is easy to verify that the last row of $\mathbf{Y}'$, and hence the transpose of the last column of $\mathbf{Y}$, is

$$\sqrt{N}\bar{\mathbf{X}}_N' = (\sqrt{N}\bar{X}_1, \ldots, \sqrt{N}\bar{X}_n).$$

Combining (i)–(iii) with this fact we conclude that: The column vectors $\mathbf{Y}_1, \ldots, \mathbf{Y}_{N-1}$ of $\mathbf{Y}$ are i.i.d. $\mathcal{N}_n(\mathbf{0}, \boldsymbol{\Sigma})$ variables and are independent of its last column (which is $\sqrt{N}\bar{\mathbf{X}}$ and thus has an $\mathcal{N}_n(\sqrt{N}\boldsymbol{\mu}, \boldsymbol{\Sigma})$ distribution). Now by $\mathbf{C}'\mathbf{C} = \mathbf{I}_N$ we have $\mathbf{X}\mathbf{X}' = \mathbf{Y}\mathbf{Y}'$. But we also have

$$\mathbf{Y}\mathbf{Y}' = \sum_{t=1}^{N-1} \mathbf{Y}_t \mathbf{Y}_t' + N\bar{\mathbf{X}}_N \bar{\mathbf{X}}_N',$$

and (by (3.5.6))

$$(N - 1)\mathbf{S} = \mathbf{X}\mathbf{X}' - N\bar{\mathbf{X}}_N \bar{\mathbf{X}}_N'.$$

Thus $(N - 1)\mathbf{S}$ and $\sum_{t=1}^{N-1} \mathbf{Y}_t \mathbf{Y}_t'$ are identically distributed. Consequently, $\mathbf{S}$ and $\bar{\mathbf{X}}_N$ are independent. □

Remark 3.5.1. It should be pointed out that, although the statement of Craig's (1943) result is correct, his proof contains an error that cannot be patched up easily. Correct proofs seem to be first obtained independently by Ogawa (1949) and P.L. Hsu (Fang, 1988). For details, see Anderson ad Styan (1982) and Fang and Zhang (1988, Sec. 2.8).

This useful by-product, obtained in the second proof of Theorem 3.5.1 and stated below, will be applied to derive the Wishart distribution and the Hotelling T^2 distribution.

Proposition 3.5.1. *Let* $\mathbf{X}_1, \ldots, \mathbf{X}_N$ *be i.i.d.* $\mathcal{N}_n(\boldsymbol{\mu}, \boldsymbol{\Sigma})$ *variables,* $\boldsymbol{\Sigma} > 0$, *and let*

$$\mathbf{S} = \frac{1}{N-1}\left(\sum_{t=1}^{N} \mathbf{X}_t\mathbf{X}_t' - N\overline{\mathbf{X}}\overline{\mathbf{X}}'\right)$$

be the sample covariance matrix. Then $\mathbf{S}$ *and* $(N-1)^{-1}\sum_{t=1}^{N-1} \mathbf{Y}_t\mathbf{Y}_t'$ *are identically distributed where* $\mathbf{Y}_1, \ldots, \mathbf{Y}_{N-1}$ *are i.i.d.* $\mathcal{N}_n(\mathbf{0}, \boldsymbol{\Sigma})$ *variables.*

3.5.2. Sampling Distributions Concerning $\overline{\mathbf{X}}_N$

In view of the fact that $\overline{\mathbf{X}}_N$ and $\mathbf{S}$ are independent, their joint distribution is uniquely determined from the marginal distributions.

For the univariate normal case, it is well known that $\overline{X}_N$ and $N(\overline{X}_N - \mu)^2/\sigma^2$ are, respectively, $\mathcal{N}(\mu, \sigma^2/N)$ and $\chi^2(1)$ variables. We show that similar results hold for the sample mean vector $\overline{\mathbf{X}}_N$ of a multivariate normal distribution.

Theorem 3.5.2. *Let* $\mathbf{X}_1, \ldots, \mathbf{X}_N$ *be i.i.d.* $\mathcal{N}_n(\boldsymbol{\mu}, \boldsymbol{\Sigma})$ *variables,* $\boldsymbol{\Sigma} > 0$, *and* $\overline{\mathbf{X}}_N$ *be the sample mean vector defined in* (3.5.1). *Then* $\overline{\mathbf{X}}_N$ *has an* $\mathcal{N}_n(\boldsymbol{\mu}, (1/N)\boldsymbol{\Sigma})$ *distribution.*

PROOF. Immediate by Corollary 3.3.4. □

Theorem 3.5.3. *Under the conditions stated in Theorem* 3.5.2, $N(\overline{\mathbf{X}}_N - \boldsymbol{\mu})'\boldsymbol{\Sigma}^{-1}(\overline{\mathbf{X}}_N - \boldsymbol{\mu})$ *has a* $\chi^2(n)$ *distribution.*

PROOF. Let $\mathbf{C}$ be a nonsingular $n \times n$ matrix such that $\mathbf{C}\boldsymbol{\Sigma}\mathbf{C}' = \mathbf{I}_n$ (the existence of $\mathbf{C}$ follows from Proposition 3.2.1). Let $\mathbf{Z} = \sqrt{N}\mathbf{C}(\overline{\mathbf{X}}_N - \boldsymbol{\mu})$. Then, by Theorems 3.5.2 and 3.3.3, $\mathbf{Z}$ has an $\mathcal{N}_n(\mathbf{0}, \mathbf{I}_n)$ distribution; thus $\mathbf{Z}'\mathbf{Z}$ has a $\chi^2(n)$ distribution. But by $\sqrt{N}(\overline{\mathbf{X}}_N - \boldsymbol{\mu}) = \mathbf{C}^{-1}\mathbf{Z}$ we have

$$\begin{aligned} N(\overline{\mathbf{X}}_N - \boldsymbol{\mu})'\boldsymbol{\Sigma}^{-1}(\overline{\mathbf{X}}_N - \boldsymbol{\mu}) &= \mathbf{Z}'\mathbf{C}^{-1\prime}\boldsymbol{\Sigma}^{-1}\mathbf{C}^{-1}\mathbf{Z} \\ &= \mathbf{Z}'(\mathbf{C}\boldsymbol{\Sigma}\mathbf{C}')^{-1}\mathbf{Z} \\ &= \mathbf{Z}'\mathbf{Z}. \end{aligned}$$

Consequently, $N(\overline{\mathbf{X}}_N - \boldsymbol{\mu})'\boldsymbol{\Sigma}^{-1}(\overline{\mathbf{X}}_N - \boldsymbol{\mu})$ also has a $\chi^2(n)$ distribution. □

3.5.3. The Wishart and Related Distributions

The Wishart distribution is the joint distribution of the $n(n+1)/2$ variables $(N-1)S_{ij}$, $1 \le i \le j \le n$, which are elements of the random matrix $(N-1)\mathbf{S}$. The density function of this distribution is given in the following theorem.

Theorem 3.5.4. *Let $\mathbf{X}_1, \ldots, \mathbf{X}_N$ be i.i.d. $\mathcal{N}_n(\boldsymbol{\mu}, \boldsymbol{\Sigma})$ variables, $\boldsymbol{\Sigma} > 0$. Let $\mathbf{S}$ be the sample covariance matrix defined in (3.5.2). Then for $N > n$, the density function of $\mathbf{W} = (N-1)\mathbf{S}$ is*

$$f_{\boldsymbol{\Sigma}, N-1}(\mathbf{w}) = \frac{c_{N-1} |\mathbf{w}|^{(N-n-2)/2}}{|\boldsymbol{\Sigma}|^{(N-1)/2}} e^{-tr\boldsymbol{\Sigma}^{-1}\mathbf{w}/2} \tag{3.5.13}$$

for $\mathbf{w}$ in the set of all $n \times n$ positive definite matrices and 0 otherwise, where

$$c_{N-1} = \left[2^{n(N-1)/2} \pi^{n(n-1)/4} \prod_{j=1}^{n} \Gamma\left(\frac{N-j}{2}\right)\right]^{-1}. \tag{3.5.14}$$

There exist many different methods and approaches for deriving this density function. Wishart's (1928) original proof has a strong geometric flavor. Other proofs were given by Mahalanobis, Bose, and Roy (1937), Hsu (1939), Olkin and Roy (1954), and others. In view of Proposition 3.5.1 we may consider the distribution of the random matrix $\mathbf{W} = \mathbf{Y}\mathbf{Y}'$, where $\mathbf{Y}_1, \ldots, \mathbf{Y}_{N-1}$ are i.i.d. $\mathcal{N}_n(\mathbf{0}, \boldsymbol{\Sigma})$ variables and $\mathbf{Y} = (\mathbf{Y}_1, \ldots, \mathbf{Y}_{N-1})$. The proof adopted here depends on the following lemma give in Anderson (1984, p. 533):

Lemma 3.5.1. *If the density function of the $n \times (N-1)$ random matrix $\mathbf{Y}$ is $g(\mathbf{y}\mathbf{y}')$, then the density function of $\mathbf{W} = \mathbf{Y}\mathbf{Y}'$ is*

$$f(\mathbf{w}) = \frac{\pi^{(1/2)n[(N-1)-(n-1)/2]} |\mathbf{w}|^{(N-n-2)/2} g(\mathbf{w})}{\prod_{j=1}^{n} \Gamma((N-j)/2)}.$$

The proof of this lemma involves the joint distribution of the characteristic roots of $\mathbf{W}$, as shown in Anderson (1984, p. 533).

Proof of Theorem 3.5.4. The joint density function of $\mathbf{Y} = (\mathbf{Y}_1, \ldots, \mathbf{Y}_{N-1})'$ is

$$\begin{aligned} g(\mathbf{y}) &= \prod_{t=1}^{N-1} \frac{1}{(2\pi)^{n/2} |\boldsymbol{\Sigma}|^{1/2}} e^{-\mathbf{y}_t'\boldsymbol{\Sigma}^{-1}\mathbf{y}_t/2} \\ &= [(2\pi)^{n(N-1)/2} |\boldsymbol{\Sigma}|^{(N-1)/2}]^{-1} \exp\left(-\frac{1}{2}\sum_{t=1}^{N-1} \mathbf{y}_t'\boldsymbol{\Sigma}^{-1}\mathbf{y}_t\right) \\ &= [(2\pi)^{n(N-1)/2} |\boldsymbol{\Sigma}|^{(N-1)/2}]^{-1} e^{-tr\boldsymbol{\Sigma}^{-1}\mathbf{y}\mathbf{y}'/2}. \end{aligned}$$

The statement now follows immediately from Lemma 3.5.1. □

A special case of interest for $\boldsymbol{\Sigma} = \mathbf{I}_n$ in Theorem 3.5.4 is:

Corollary 3.5.1. *Let* $\mathbf{X}_1, \ldots, \mathbf{X}_N$ *be i.i.d.* $\mathcal{N}_n(\boldsymbol{\mu}, \mathbf{I}_n)$ *variables and let* $\mathbf{S} = (S_{ij})$ *be the sample covariance matrix. Then for* $N > n$, *the density function of* $(N-1)\mathbf{S}$ *is*

$$f_{\mathbf{I}_n, N-1}(\mathbf{w}) = c_{N-1}|\mathbf{w}|^{(N-n-2)/2}e^{-\operatorname{tr}\mathbf{w}/2} \tag{3.5.15}$$

for $\mathbf{w}$ *in the set of all* $n \times n$ *positive definite matrices, and* 0 *otherwise, where* c_{N-1} *is the constant defined in* (3.5.14).

A problem of great importance concerns the distribution of a transformation of the submatrices of a Wishart matrix. Let $\mathbf{Y}_1, \ldots, \mathbf{Y}_{N-1}$ be i.i.d. $\mathcal{N}_n(\mathbf{0}, \boldsymbol{\Sigma})$ variables such that, for $t = 1, \ldots, N-1$, $\mathbf{Y}_t$ is partitioned as

$$\mathbf{Y}_t = \begin{pmatrix} \mathbf{Y}_{1,t} \\ \mathbf{Y}_{2,t} \end{pmatrix} \sim \mathcal{N}_n\left(\mathbf{0}, \boldsymbol{\Sigma} = \begin{pmatrix} \boldsymbol{\Sigma}_{11} & \boldsymbol{\Sigma}_{12} \\ \boldsymbol{\Sigma}_{21} & \boldsymbol{\Sigma}_{22} \end{pmatrix}\right), \tag{3.5.16}$$

where $\mathbf{Y}_{1,t}$ is $k \times 1$ and $\mathbf{Y}_{2,t}$ is $(n-k) \times 1$. Consider the corresponding partition of $\mathbf{W} = \mathbf{YY}'$ given by

$$\mathbf{W} = \begin{pmatrix} \mathbf{W}_{11} & \mathbf{W}_{12} \\ \mathbf{W}_{21} & \mathbf{W}_{22} \end{pmatrix}, \tag{3.5.17}$$

where $\mathbf{W}_{11}$, $\mathbf{W}_{12} = \mathbf{W}'_{21}$, and $\mathbf{W}_{22}$ are, respectively, $k \times k$, $k \times (n-k)$, and $(n-k) \times (n-k)$. Clearly, we have

$$\mathbf{W}_{ii} = (\mathbf{Y}_{i,1} \cdots \mathbf{Y}_{i,N-1})(\mathbf{Y}_{i,1} \cdots \mathbf{Y}_{i,N-1})', \qquad i = 1, 2$$

and

$$\mathbf{W}_{12} = (\mathbf{Y}_{1,1} \cdots \mathbf{Y}_{1,N-1})(\mathbf{Y}_{2,1} \cdots \mathbf{Y}_{2,N-1})'.$$

The following lemma concerns the distribution of the matrix $\mathbf{W}_{11} - \mathbf{W}_{12}\mathbf{W}_{22}^{-1}\mathbf{W}_{21}$.

Lemma 3.5.2. *Let* $\mathbf{Y}_1, \ldots, \mathbf{Y}_{N-1}$ *be defined as in* (3.5.16) *and let* $\mathbf{W}$ *be partitioned as in* (3.5.17). *If* $\boldsymbol{\Sigma} > 0$, *then* $\mathbf{V} = \mathbf{W}_{11} - \mathbf{W}_{12}\mathbf{W}_{22}^{-1}\mathbf{W}_{21}$ *and* $\sum_{t=1}^{(N-1)-(n-k)} \mathbf{U}_t\mathbf{U}'_t$ *are identically distributed where* $\mathbf{U}_1, \ldots, \mathbf{U}_{(N-1)-(n-k)}$ *are i.i.d.* $\mathcal{N}_k(\mathbf{0}, \boldsymbol{\Sigma}_{11\cdot 2})$ *variables and* $\boldsymbol{\Sigma}_{11\cdot 2} = \boldsymbol{\Sigma}_{11} - \boldsymbol{\Sigma}_{12}\boldsymbol{\Sigma}_{22}^{-1}\boldsymbol{\Sigma}_{21}$.

Proof. For given $\mathbf{Y}_{2t} = \mathbf{y}_{2t}$ the conditional distribution of $\mathbf{Y}_{1t}$ is $\mathcal{N}_k(\mathbf{B}\mathbf{x}_{2t}, \boldsymbol{\Sigma}_{11\cdot 2})$ for $t = 1, \ldots, N-1$, where $\mathbf{B} = \boldsymbol{\Sigma}_{12}\boldsymbol{\Sigma}_{22}^{-1}$ is the regression matrix (Theorem 3.3.4). We show that for given $\mathbf{y}_{21}, \ldots, \mathbf{y}_{2,N-1}$ the conditional distribution of

$$\sum_{t=1}^{N-1} \mathbf{Y}_{1t}\mathbf{Y}'_{1t} - \mathbf{T}\mathbf{w}_{22}\mathbf{T}' = \sum_{t=1}^{N-1} \mathbf{Y}_{1t}\mathbf{Y}'_{1t} - \left(\sum_{t=1}^{N-1} \mathbf{Y}_{1t}\mathbf{y}'_{2t}\right)\mathbf{w}_{22}^{-1}\left(\sum_{t=1}^{N-1} \mathbf{Y}_{1t}\mathbf{y}'_{2t}\right)'$$

and the distribution of $\sum_{t=1}^{(N-1)-(n-k)} \mathbf{U}_t\mathbf{U}'_t$ are identical, where

$$\mathbf{w}_{22} = \sum_{t=1}^{N-1} \mathbf{y}_{2t}\mathbf{y}'_{2t}$$

and $\mathbf{T}$ is a $k \times (n-k)$ random matrix given by

$$\mathbf{T} = \left(\sum_{t=1}^{N-1} \mathbf{Y}_{1t}\mathbf{y}'_{2t}\right)\mathbf{w}_{22}^{-1}.$$

The lemma then follows from the fact that the underlying conditional distribution does not depend on the $\mathbf{y}_{2t}$'s. The proof given below, which follows the steps of Anderson's (1984, pp. 130–131) proof, depends on an orthogonal transformation of the matrix

$$\mathbf{Y} = \begin{pmatrix} \mathbf{Y}_{11}\mathbf{Y}_{12}\cdots\mathbf{Y}_{1,N-1} \\ \mathbf{y}_{21}\mathbf{y}_{22}\cdots\mathbf{y}_{2,N-1} \end{pmatrix} \equiv \begin{pmatrix} \mathbf{Y}^{(1)} \\ \mathbf{y}^{(2)} \end{pmatrix}$$

when the $\mathbf{y}_{2t}$'s are given. The basic idea is similar to that in the second proof of Theorem 3.5.1, except that it is more general.

Let $\mathbf{C}$ be a nonsingular matrix such that $\mathbf{C}\mathbf{w}_{22}\mathbf{C}' = \mathbf{I}_{n-k}$ and, for given $\mathbf{y}^{(2)} = (\mathbf{y}_{21}, \ldots, \mathbf{y}_{2,N-1})$, let $\mathbf{G}_2 = \mathbf{C}\mathbf{y}^{(2)}$ or, equivalently, $\mathbf{y}^{(2)} = \mathbf{C}^{-1}\mathbf{G}_2$. Then

$$\begin{aligned}\mathbf{G}_2\mathbf{G}'_2 &= \mathbf{C}\mathbf{y}^{(2)}(\mathbf{y}^{(2)})'\mathbf{C}' \\ &= \mathbf{C}\mathbf{w}_{22}\mathbf{C}' = \mathbf{I}_{n-k}.\end{aligned}$$

By Anderson (1984, p. 598), there exists an $((N-1)-(n-k)) \times (N-1)$ matrix $\mathbf{G}_1$ such that

$$\mathbf{G} = \begin{pmatrix} \mathbf{G}_1 \\ \mathbf{G}_2 \end{pmatrix}$$

is an orthogonal matrix. Now consider the orthogonal transformation of the matrix $\mathbf{Y}$ given by

$$\mathbf{U} = (\mathbf{U}_1, \ldots, \mathbf{U}_{N-1}) = \mathbf{Y}^{(1)}\mathbf{G}', \tag{3.5.18}$$

or, equivalently, $\mathbf{Y}^{(1)} = \mathbf{G}\mathbf{U}$. Clearly, we have

$$\begin{aligned}\sum_{t=1}^{N-1} \mathbf{U}_t\mathbf{U}'_t &= \mathbf{U}\mathbf{U}' \\ &= \mathbf{Y}^{(1)}\mathbf{G}'\mathbf{G}(\mathbf{Y}^{(1)})' = \mathbf{Y}^{(1)}(\mathbf{Y}^{(1)})'.\end{aligned}$$

On the other hand, by $\mathbf{T} = \mathbf{Y}^{(1)}(\mathbf{y}^{(2)})'\mathbf{w}_{22}^{-1}$ and $\mathbf{T}\mathbf{w}_{22}\mathbf{T}' = (\mathbf{T}\mathbf{w}_{22}\mathbf{T}')'$, we have

$$\begin{aligned}\mathbf{T}\mathbf{w}_{22}\mathbf{T}' &= (\mathbf{G}\mathbf{U}(\mathbf{C}^{-1}\mathbf{G}_2)'\mathbf{w}_{22}^{-1}(\mathbf{C}^{-1}\mathbf{G}_2)(\mathbf{G}\mathbf{U})')' \\ &= \mathbf{U}(\mathbf{G}\mathbf{G}'_2)(\mathbf{C}\mathbf{w}_{22}\mathbf{C}')^{-1}(\mathbf{G}_2\mathbf{G}')\mathbf{U}' \\ &= \mathbf{U}\begin{pmatrix} \mathbf{0} \\ \mathbf{I}_{n-k} \end{pmatrix}(\mathbf{0}\ \ \mathbf{I}_{n-k})\mathbf{U}' \\ &= \sum_{t=N-(n-k)}^{N-1} \mathbf{U}_t\mathbf{U}'_t.\end{aligned}$$

This implies that $\sum_{t=1}^{N-1} \mathbf{Y}_{1t}\mathbf{Y}'_{1t} - \mathbf{T}\mathbf{w}_{22}\mathbf{T}'$ and $\sum_{t=1}^{(N-1)-(n-k)} \mathbf{U}_t\mathbf{U}'_t$ are identically distributed. By (3.5.18) and the fact that $\mathbf{G}$ is an orthogonal matrix, it is easy to verify that $\mathbf{U}_1, \ldots, \mathbf{U}_{(N-1)-(n-k)}$ are independent $\mathcal{N}_k(\mathbf{0}, \boldsymbol{\Sigma}_{11\cdot 2})$ variables. Hence Lemma 3.5.2 follows. □

Combining Proposition 3.5.1 and Lemma 3.5.2 we immediately have

Theorem 3.5.5. *Let $\mathbf{X}_1, \ldots, \mathbf{X}_N$ be i.i.d. $\mathcal{N}_n(\boldsymbol{\mu}, \boldsymbol{\Sigma})$ variables and let $\mathbf{S}$ be the sample covariance matrix defined in* (3.5.2). *For fixed $1 \le k < n$, let $\mathbf{S}$ be partitioned as*

$$\mathbf{S} = \begin{pmatrix} \mathbf{S}_{11} & \mathbf{S}_{12} \\ \mathbf{S}_{21} & \mathbf{S}_{22} \end{pmatrix},$$

where $\mathbf{S}_{11}, \mathbf{S}_{12} = \mathbf{S}'_{21}$, and $\mathbf{S}_{22}$ are, respectively, $k \times k, k \times (n-k)$, and $(n-k) \times (n-k)$. If $N > n$, then

$$\mathbf{V} = (N-1)(\mathbf{S}_{11} - \mathbf{S}_{12}\mathbf{S}_{22}^{-1}\mathbf{S}_{21}) \tag{3.5.19}$$

and $\sum_{t=1}^{(N-1)-(n-k)} \mathbf{U}_t\mathbf{U}'_t$ are identically distributed where $\mathbf{U}_1, \ldots, \mathbf{U}_{(N-1)-(n-k)}$ are i.i.d. $\mathcal{N}_k(\mathbf{0}, \boldsymbol{\Sigma}_{11\cdot 2})$ variables ad $\boldsymbol{\Sigma}_{11\cdot 2} = \boldsymbol{\Sigma}_{11} - \boldsymbol{\Sigma}_{12}\boldsymbol{\Sigma}_{22}^{-1}\boldsymbol{\Sigma}_{21}$. Consequently, the density function of $\mathbf{V}$ can be obtained by substituting (i) *$\boldsymbol{\Sigma}_{11\cdot 2}$ for $\boldsymbol{\Sigma}$,* (ii) *$N - (n-k)$ for N, and* (iii) *k for n in the density function given in* (3.5.13).

Of special interest is the case $\boldsymbol{\Sigma}_{12} = \mathbf{0}$. This result is stated below and will be used to derive the distribution of the sample multiple correlation coefficient.

Corollary 3.5.2. *Let $\mathbf{X}_1, \ldots, \mathbf{X}_N$ be i.i.d. $\mathcal{N}_n(\boldsymbol{\mu}, \boldsymbol{\Sigma})$ variables, $\boldsymbol{\Sigma} > 0$, and $\boldsymbol{\Sigma}_{12} = \mathbf{0}$. Then*:

(a) *$\mathbf{V}$ in* (3.5.19) *is distributed as $\sum_{t=1}^{(N-1)-(n-k)} \mathbf{U}_t\mathbf{U}'_t$, and $(N-1)\mathbf{S}_{12}\mathbf{S}_{22}^{-1}\mathbf{S}_{21}$ is distributed as $\sum_{t=N-(n-k)}^{N-1} \mathbf{U}_t\mathbf{U}'_t$, where $\mathbf{U}_1, \ldots, \mathbf{U}_{N-1}$ are i.i.d. $\mathcal{N}_n(\mathbf{0}, \boldsymbol{\Sigma}_{11})$ variables; and*
(b) *$\mathbf{V}$ and $\mathbf{S}_{12}\mathbf{S}_{22}^{-1}\mathbf{S}_{21}$ are independent.*

Note that in (3.5.19) the random matrix $\mathbf{V}$ is properly defined only if $\mathbf{S}_{22}$ is invertible with probability one. This is possible when $\mathbf{S}$ itself is invertible with probability one. A more important question is whether $\mathbf{S}$ is positive definite (in symbols $\mathbf{S} > 0$) which, of course, implies that $\mathbf{S}$ is invertible. The answer to this question is given below.

Theorem 3.5.6. *Let $\mathbf{X}_1, \ldots, \mathbf{X}_N$ be i.i.d. $\mathcal{N}_n(\boldsymbol{\mu}, \boldsymbol{\Sigma})$ variables, $\boldsymbol{\Sigma} > 0$, and let $\mathbf{S}$ be the sample covariance matrix defined in* (3.5.2). *Then $P[\mathbf{S} > 0] = 1$ holds if and only if $N > n$.*

Proof. The proof given here is due to Dykstra (1970). Note that the assumption of normality is not needed, so that the statement also holds for other multivariate distributions.

By Proposition 3.5.1, $(N-1)\mathbf{S}$ and $\sum_{t=1}^{N-1} \mathbf{U}_t\mathbf{U}'_t = \mathbf{U}\mathbf{U}'$ are identically distributed where $\mathbf{U}_1, \ldots, \mathbf{U}_{N-1}$ are i.i.d. $\mathcal{N}_n(\mathbf{0}, \boldsymbol{\Sigma})$ variables and $\mathbf{U} =$

$(\mathbf{U}_1, \ldots, \mathbf{U}_{N-1})$. Thus, it is equivalent to showing that $P[\mathbf{U}\mathbf{U}' > 0] = 1$ holds if and only if $N > n$. Scheffé (1959, p. 399) states that:

(i) $\mathbf{U}$ and $\mathbf{U}\mathbf{U}'$ have the same rank; and
(ii) $\mathbf{U}\mathbf{U}' > 0$ ($\mathbf{U}\mathbf{U}'$ is positive semidefinite) if and only if the rank of $\mathbf{U}$ is n (is $< n$).

If $N < n$, then clearly the rank of $\mathbf{U}$ is $< n$. On the other hand, since

$$\text{rank}(\mathbf{U}_1, \ldots, \mathbf{U}_m) \leq \text{rank}(\mathbf{U}_1, \ldots, \mathbf{U}_{m+1})$$

for all $m \geq n$, it suffices to show that

$$P[\text{rank}(\mathbf{U}_1, \ldots, \mathbf{U}_n) < n] = 0.$$

For every fixed $i = 1, \ldots, n$, and for given

$$\mathbf{U}^{(i)} \equiv (U_1, \ldots, U_{i-1}, U_{i+1}, \ldots, U_n) = (u_1, \ldots, u_{i-1}, u_{i+1}, \ldots, u_n) \equiv \mathbf{u}^{(i)},$$

let $B_i(\mathbf{u}^{(i)})$ be the subspace spanned by $\mathbf{u}^{(i)}$. Then by $\mathbf{\Sigma} > 0$,

$$P[\mathbf{U}_i \in B_i(\mathbf{u}^{(i)})] = 0$$

holds for all $\mathbf{u}^{(i)}$ except perhaps on a set of probability zero. Consequently,

$$\begin{aligned} P[\text{rank}(\mathbf{U}_1, \ldots, \mathbf{U}_n) < n] &= P[\mathbf{U}_1, \ldots, \mathbf{U}_n \text{ are linearly dependent}] \\ &\leq \sum_{i=1}^{n} EP[\mathbf{U}_i \in B_i(\mathbf{u}^{(i)}) | \mathbf{U}^{(i)} = \mathbf{u}^{(i)}] \\ &= 0. \end{aligned}$$

□

3.5.4. Hotelling's T^2 Distribution

When applying Theorem 3.5.2 or 3.5.3 to make statistical inference on $\boldsymbol{\mu}$ based on $\bar{\mathbf{X}}_N$, the covariance matrix $\mathbf{\Sigma}$ must be known. If $\mathbf{\Sigma}$ is unknown, then a new statistic (a generalization of Student's t statistic) is needed. This was proposed and studied by Hotelling (1931): The statistic

$$T^2 = N(\bar{\mathbf{X}}_N - \boldsymbol{\mu})'\mathbf{S}^{-1}(\bar{\mathbf{X}}_N - \boldsymbol{\mu}) \tag{3.5.20}$$

is called Hotelling's T^2 statistic. Note that, by Theorem 3.5.6, $\mathbf{S}$ is positive definite with probability one, so that $\mathbf{S}^{-1}$ is positive definite and T^2 is a properly defined quadratic form with probability one.

Theorem 3.5.7. *Let $\mathbf{X}_1, \ldots, \mathbf{X}_N$ be i.i.d. $\mathcal{N}_n(\boldsymbol{\mu}, \mathbf{\Sigma})$ variables, $\mathbf{\Sigma} > 0$. Let $\bar{\mathbf{X}}$ and $\mathbf{S}$ be the sample mean vector and sample covariance matrix, respectively, and let T^2 be given in* (3.5.20). *Then for $N > n$, $((N - n)/((N - 1)n))T^2$ has an $F(n, N - n)$ distribution.*

Remark 3.5.2. We first note that the distribution of T^2 is invariant under the transformation $\mathbf{Z}_t = \mathbf{H}\mathbf{X}_t + \mathbf{b}$ ($t = 1, \ldots, N$) where $\mathbf{H}$ is any nonsingular $n \times n$

matrix and $\mathbf{b}$ is any real vector. The fact that it does not depend on $\mathbf{b}$ is easy to verify. To show that it also does not depend on $\mathbf{H}$, suppose that $\boldsymbol{\mu} = \mathbf{b} = \mathbf{0}$ and $\mathbf{Z}_t = \mathbf{H}\mathbf{X}_t$. Then $\bar{\mathbf{Z}}_N = \mathbf{H}\bar{\mathbf{X}}_N$ and $\mathbf{Z} = (\mathbf{Z}_1, \ldots, \mathbf{Z}_N) = \mathbf{H}(\mathbf{X}_1, \ldots, \mathbf{X}_N) = \mathbf{H}\mathbf{X}$. Consequently,

$$\begin{aligned}(N-1)\mathbf{S}_{\mathbf{Z}} &= \mathbf{Z}\mathbf{Z}' - N\bar{\mathbf{Z}}_N\bar{\mathbf{Z}}_N' \\ &= \mathbf{H}(\mathbf{X}\mathbf{X}' - N\bar{\mathbf{X}}_N\bar{\mathbf{X}}_N')\mathbf{H}',\end{aligned}$$

and this implies

$$\begin{aligned}\bar{\mathbf{Z}}_N'\mathbf{S}_{\mathbf{Z}}^{-1}\bar{\mathbf{Z}}_N &= (N-1)\bar{\mathbf{X}}_N'\mathbf{H}'\mathbf{H}'^{-1}(\mathbf{X}\mathbf{X}' - N\bar{\mathbf{X}}_N\bar{\mathbf{X}}_N')^{-1}\mathbf{H}^{-1}\mathbf{H}\bar{\mathbf{X}}_N \\ &= \bar{\mathbf{X}}_N'\mathbf{S}_{\mathbf{X}}^{-1}\bar{\mathbf{X}}_N.\end{aligned}$$

PROOF OF THEOREM 3.5.7. There are different methods for deriving the distribution of T^2. The proof given here, adopted from Anderson (1984, p. 161–162), depends on an orthogonal transformation for given $\bar{\mathbf{X}}_N = \bar{\mathbf{x}}_N$. After it is shown that the conditional distribution of T^2 does not depend on $\bar{\mathbf{x}}_N$, the statement follows by unconditioning.

Without loss of generality we may assume that $\mathbf{X}_1, \ldots, \mathbf{X}_N$ are i.i.d. $\mathcal{N}_n(\mathbf{0}, \mathbf{I}_n)$ variables. For given $\bar{\mathbf{X}}_N = \bar{\mathbf{x}}_N$ let $\mathbf{C}$ be an $n \times n$ orthogonal matrix such that the first row of $\mathbf{C}$ is $\bar{\mathbf{x}}_N/\sqrt{\bar{\mathbf{x}}_N'\bar{\mathbf{x}}_N}$, and let the c_{ij}'s ($i = 2, \ldots, n; j = 1, \ldots, n$) depend on $\bar{\mathbf{x}}_N$ through the c_{1j}'s. Now consider the linear transformation $\mathbf{U} = (U_1, \ldots, U_n)' = \mathbf{C}\bar{\mathbf{x}}_N$, and define $\mathbf{B} = \mathbf{C}\mathbf{S}\mathbf{C}'$. Since

$$\sum_{j=1}^{n} c_{ij}c_{1j} = \frac{(c_{i1} \ldots c_{in})\bar{\mathbf{x}}_N}{\sqrt{\bar{\mathbf{x}}_N'\bar{\mathbf{x}}_N}} = 0,$$

clearly we have

$$U_1 = \sqrt{\bar{\mathbf{x}}_N'\bar{\mathbf{x}}_N} \qquad \text{and} \qquad U_i = 0 \qquad \text{for} \quad i = 2, \ldots, n.$$

Thus we have, for given $\bar{\mathbf{X}}_N = \bar{\mathbf{x}}_N$,

$$\frac{T^2}{(N-1)} = \bar{\mathbf{x}}_N'\mathbf{S}^{-1}\bar{\mathbf{x}}_N = \mathbf{U}'\mathbf{B}^{-1}\mathbf{U} = U_1^2 b^{11},$$

where $\mathbf{B}^{-1} = (b^{ij})$. But $1/b^{11} = b_{11} - \mathbf{b}_1'\mathbf{B}_{22}^{-1}\mathbf{b}_1$. Since $\bar{\mathbf{X}}_N$ and $\mathbf{S}$ are independent (Theorem 3.5.1) and $\mathbf{C}$ depends only on $\bar{\mathbf{x}}_N$, the conditional distribution of $\mathbf{B}$ is identical to that of $\sum_{t=1}^{N-1} \mathbf{Z}_t\mathbf{Z}_t'$ where the $\mathbf{Z}_t$'s are i.i.d. $\mathcal{N}_n(\mathbf{0}, \mathbf{I}_n)$ variables. Thus by Theorem 3.5.5 (with $k = 1$), $(N-1)/b^{11}$ has a chi-square distribution with $(N-n)$ degrees of freedom for every fixed $U_1^2 = \bar{\mathbf{x}}_N'\bar{\mathbf{x}}_N$. But $NU_1^2 = N\bar{\mathbf{X}}_N'\bar{\mathbf{X}}_N$ itself has a chi-square distribution with n degrees of freedom (Theorem 3.5.3) and is independent of b^{11}. Consequently,

$$\frac{(N-n)}{(N-1)n}T^2 = \frac{NU_1^2/n}{((N-1)/b^{11})/(N-n)}$$

has an $F(n, N-n)$ distribution. □

Other results for the distribution of T^2 can be obtained by studying the random variable

$$T_0^2 = N(\bar{\mathbf{X}}_N - \boldsymbol{\mu}_0)'\mathbf{S}^{-1}(\bar{\mathbf{X}}_N - \boldsymbol{\mu}_0),$$

where μ_0 is not necessarily the mean vector of $\bar{\mathbf{X}}_N$. The distribution of T_0^2 involves a noncentral F distribution, and was given by Bose and Roy (1938), Hsu (1938), Bowker (1960), and others. The distribution of T^2 can be obtained from the distribution of T_0^2 by letting $\boldsymbol{\mu}_0 = \boldsymbol{\mu}$ (the mean vector of $\bar{\mathbf{X}}_N$) as a special case.

3.5.5. Sample Correlation Coefficients

To investigate the distributions of the sample multiple correlation coefficient and the sample partial correlation coefficient, we once again consider the partition of the components of an n-dimensional normal variable defined in (3.3.1). For fixed $N > n$, let $\{\mathbf{X}_t\}_{t=1}^N$ be a sequence of i.i.d. $\mathcal{N}_n(\boldsymbol{\mu}, \boldsymbol{\Sigma})$ variables, $\boldsymbol{\Sigma} > 0$, and let $\mathbf{S}$ be the sample covariance matrix defined in (3.5.2). We consider a corresponding partition of this sample covariance matrix given by

$$\mathbf{S} = \begin{pmatrix} \mathbf{S}_{11} & \mathbf{S}_{12} \\ \mathbf{S}_{21} & \mathbf{S}_{22} \end{pmatrix} = \frac{1}{N-1}\begin{pmatrix} \mathbf{W}_{11} & \mathbf{W}_{12} \\ \mathbf{W}_{21} & \mathbf{W}_{22} \end{pmatrix} = \frac{1}{N-1}\mathbf{W}, \tag{3.5.21}$$

where $\mathbf{S}_{11}$ is $k \times k$, $\mathbf{S}_{12} = \mathbf{S}'_{21}$ is $k \times (n-k)$, and $\mathbf{S}_{22}$ is $(n-k) \times (n-k)$.

The population multiple correlation coefficient between X_i and $(X_{k+1}, \ldots, X_n)'$, defined in Definition 3.4.2, can be estimated by substituting S_{ij}'s for σ_{ij}'s in (3.4.5). Without loss of generality it may be assumed that $i = k = 1$. (Because otherwise we need to consider only the marginal distribution of $(X_i, X_{k+1}, \ldots, X_n)'$ instead of the joint distribution of $\mathbf{X}$.) Then the sample multiple correlation coefficient is given by

$$\hat{R}_{1\cdot 2\ldots n} = \left(\frac{\mathbf{S}_1\mathbf{S}_{22}^{-1}\mathbf{S}'_1}{S_{11}}\right)^{1/2}, \tag{3.5.22}$$

where $\mathbf{S}_1 = (S_{12}, \ldots, S_{1n})$. It is known that $\hat{R}_{1\cdot 2\ldots n}$ is the maximum likelihood estimator of the population correlation coefficient $R_{1\cdot 2\ldots n}$ and has certain desirable properties.

In the following theorem we state a result for the distribution of $\hat{R}_{1\cdot 2\ldots n}$. When $R_{1\cdot 2\ldots n} > 0$, its density function has several different expressions, and the one given here is due to Fisher (1928). Since the proof is quite involved algebraically, it is outlined without details.

Theorem 3.5.8. *Let* $\mathbf{X}_1, \ldots, \mathbf{X}_N$ *be i.i.d.* $\mathcal{N}_n(\boldsymbol{\mu}, \boldsymbol{\Sigma})$ *variables,* $\boldsymbol{\Sigma} > 0$. *Let* $\hat{R} = \hat{R}_{1\cdot 2\ldots n}$ *be the sample multiple correlation coefficient defined in* (3.5.22).

(a) *If the population multiple correlation coefficient* $R_{1\cdot 2\ldots n}$ *is zero, then* $(N-n)\hat{R}^2/((n-1)(1-\hat{R}^2))$ *has an* $F(n-1, N-n)$ *distribution.*

(b) *If $R_{1\cdot 2\dots n}$ is not zero, the density function of $\hat{R}^2$ is*

$$g_{\hat{R}^2}(r^2) = \frac{(1-r^2)^{(N-n-2)/2}(1-R^2)^{(N-1)/2}}{\Gamma(\frac{1}{2}(N-n))\Gamma(\frac{1}{2}(N-1))} \sum_{j=1}^{\infty} \frac{(R^2)^j (r^2)^{(n-1)/2+j-1}\Gamma^2(\frac{1}{2}(N-1)+j)}{j!\Gamma(\frac{1}{2}(n-1)+j)}, \tag{3.5.23}$$

where $R^2 = R^2_{1\cdot 2\dots n}$. Thus the density function of $\hat{R}$ is $2rg_{\hat{R}^2}(r^2)$ for $r \geq 0$.

PROOF. (a) First note the identity

$$\frac{\hat{R}^2}{1-\hat{R}^2} = \frac{\mathbf{S}_1\mathbf{S}_{22}^{-1}\mathbf{S}_1'}{S_{11} - \mathbf{S}_1\mathbf{S}_{22}^{-1}\mathbf{S}_1'}.$$

Since $R_{1\cdot 2\dots n} = 0$ if and only if $\mathbf{\Sigma}_{12} = \mathbf{0}$, by Corollary 3.5.2 we immediately have:

(i) $(N-1)\mathbf{S}_1\mathbf{S}_{22}^{-1}\mathbf{S}_1'/\sigma_{11}$ has a $\chi^2(n-1)$ distribution;
(ii) $(N-1)(S_{11} - \mathbf{S}_1\mathbf{S}_{22}^{-1}\mathbf{S}_1')/\sigma_{11}$ has a $\chi^2(N-n)$ distribution; and
(iii) the two random variables in (i) and (ii) are independent.

Thus $(N-n)\hat{R}^2/((n-1)(1-\hat{R}^2))$ has an $F(n-1, N-n)$ distribution.

(b) Without loss of generality assume that $\boldsymbol{\mu} = \mathbf{0}$.

(i) First, let us consider the conditional distribution of the random variable $(N-n)\hat{R}^2/((n-1)(1-\hat{R}^2))$ for given

$$\mathbf{X}_{2t} \equiv (X_{2t}, \dots, X_{nt})' = (x_{2t}, \dots, x_{nt})' \equiv \mathbf{x}_{2t}, \qquad t = 1, \dots, N.$$

Since the conditional distribution of X_{1t} is

$$\mathcal{N}(\boldsymbol{\sigma}_1\mathbf{\Sigma}_{22}^{-1}\mathbf{x}_{2t}, \sigma_{11} - \boldsymbol{\sigma}_1\mathbf{\Sigma}_{22}^{-1}\boldsymbol{\sigma}_1' \equiv \sigma_{11\cdot 2}),$$

by applying the transformation in the proof of Lemma 3.5.2 we can show that $(N-1)\mathbf{S}_1\mathbf{S}_{22}^{-1}\mathbf{S}_1')/\sigma_{11\cdot 2}$ has a noncentral chi-square distribution with $n-1$ degrees of freedom and noncentrality parameter $(N-1)\boldsymbol{\beta}\mathbf{s}_{22}\boldsymbol{\beta}'/\sigma_{11\cdot 2}$, where $\boldsymbol{\beta} = \boldsymbol{\sigma}_1\mathbf{\Sigma}_{22}^{-1}$. Thus, for given $\mathbf{X}_{2t} = \mathbf{x}_{2t}$ $(t = 1, \dots, N)$, the conditional distribution of $(N-n)\hat{R}^2/((n-1)(1-\hat{R}^2))$ is a noncentral F distribution with degrees of freedom $(n-1, N-n)$ and noncentrality parameter $(N-1)\boldsymbol{\beta}\mathbf{s}_{22}\boldsymbol{\beta}'/\sigma_{11\cdot 2}$.

(ii) By the result in (i) we can write out the joint density function of $(\hat{R}^2, \mathbf{X}_{21}, \dots, \mathbf{X}_{2N})'$ and then integrate out $\mathbf{x}_{21}, \dots, \mathbf{x}_{2N}$ over the $(n-1)N$-dimensional space to obtain $g_{\hat{R}^2}(r^2)$. □

The population partial correlation coefficient $\rho_{ij\cdot k+1,\dots,n}$ defined in Definition 3.4.3 is the correlation between X_i and X_j $(1 \leq i < j \leq k)$ in the conditional distribution of $(X_1, \dots, X_k)'$, given $(X_{k+1}, \dots, X_n)' = (x_{k+1}, \dots, x_n)'$. Now let the sample covariance matrix $\mathbf{S}$ be partitioned as in (3.5.21). Then for fixed $(X_{2t}, \dots, X_{nt})' = (x_{2t}, \dots, x_{nt})'$ $(t = 1, \dots, N)$ the sample partial correlation coefficient is

$$r_{ij\cdot k+1,\ldots,n} = \frac{s_{ij\cdot k+1,\ldots,n}}{(s_{ii\cdot k+1\ldots n}\cdot s_{jj\cdot k+1\ldots n})^{1/2}},$$

where $s_{ij\cdot k+1,\ldots,n}$ is the (i, j)th element of the matrix $\mathbf{S}_{11} - \mathbf{S}_{12}\mathbf{S}_{22}^{-1}\mathbf{S}_{21}$. The following theorem concerns the distribution of $r_{ij\cdot k+1,\ldots,n}$.

Theorem 3.5.9. *Let* $\mathbf{X}_1, \ldots, \mathbf{X}_N$ *be i.i.d.* $\mathcal{N}_n(\boldsymbol{\mu}, \boldsymbol{\Sigma})$ *variables,* $\boldsymbol{\Sigma} > 0$. *Let*

$$\boldsymbol{\Sigma}_{11\cdot 2} = \boldsymbol{\Sigma}_{11} - \boldsymbol{\Sigma}_{12}\boldsymbol{\Sigma}_{22}^{-1}\boldsymbol{\Sigma}_{21} = (\sigma_{ij\cdot k+1,\ldots,n}).$$

Let r_{12} *be the sample correlation coefficient between* Y_1 *and* Y_2 *based on a random sample of size* $N - (n - k)$ *from a bivariate normal distribution with means* 0, *variances* 1, *and correlation coefficient*

$$\rho = \frac{\sigma_{ij\cdot k+1,\ldots,n}}{(\sigma_{ii\cdot k+1,\ldots,n}\sigma_{jj\cdot k+1,\ldots,n})^{1/2}}.$$

Then $r_{ij\cdot k+1,\ldots,n}$ *and* r_{12} *are identically distributed.*

This result, due to Fisher (1924), can be obtained by applying Theorem 3.5.5. The details are left to the reader.

Problems

3.1. Let $\mathbf{X}$ be any $r \times m$ real matrix for $r \leq m$. Show that $\mathbf{XX}'$ is either positive definite (p.d.) or positive semidefinite (p.s.d.). Furthermore, show that if the rank of $\mathbf{X}$ is r, then $\mathbf{XX}'$ is p.d.

3.2. Show that $\boldsymbol{\Sigma}$ is a p.d. matrix if and only if $\boldsymbol{\Sigma}^{-1}$ is a p.d. matrix.

3.3. Show that if $\boldsymbol{\Sigma}$ is a p.d. matrix, then its determinant is positive.

3.4. Show that if $\boldsymbol{\Sigma}$ is a p.d. matrix, then $c\boldsymbol{\Sigma}$ is a p.d. matrix for all $c > 0$.

3.5. Show that if $\boldsymbol{\Sigma}_1, \boldsymbol{\Sigma}_2$ are two $n \times n$ p.d. matrices, then $\boldsymbol{\Sigma}_1 + \boldsymbol{\Sigma}_2$ is a p.d. matrix.

3.6. Show that if $\boldsymbol{\Sigma}_1, \ldots, \boldsymbol{\Sigma}_m$ are $n \times n$ p.d. matrices, then $\sum_{j=1}^{m} c_j\boldsymbol{\Sigma}_j$ is a p.d. matrix for all $c_j > 0$ $(j = 1, \ldots, m)$.

3.7. Let $\boldsymbol{\Sigma} = (\sigma_{ij})$ be a 3×3 symmetric matrix such that

$$\sigma_{11} = \sigma_{22} = \sigma_{33} = 1, \qquad \sigma_{12} = 0.$$

Show that, at least for $(\sigma_{13} + \sigma_{23}) > \frac{3}{2}$, $\boldsymbol{\Sigma}$ is *not* a p.d. matrix.

In Problems 3.8–3.10, $\boldsymbol{\Sigma}$ denotes an $n \times n$ symmetric matrix; $\boldsymbol{\Sigma}_{11}$ and $\boldsymbol{\Sigma}_{22}$ are the corresponding submatrices defined in (3.3.1).

3.8. Show that if $\boldsymbol{\Sigma}$ is p.d., then both $\boldsymbol{\Sigma}_{11}$ and $\boldsymbol{\Sigma}_{22}$ are p.d.

3.9. Show that if $\boldsymbol{\Sigma}_{11}$ is not p.d., then $\boldsymbol{\Sigma}$ is not p.d.

3.10. Verify the statement in (3.3.6) cooncerning the inverse of $\boldsymbol{\Sigma}$.

3.11. Show that if $\mathbf{\Sigma}$ is p.s.d., then there exists a sequence of p.d. matrices $\{\mathbf{\Sigma}_t\}_{t=1}^{\infty}$ such that $\lim_{t\to\infty} \mathbf{\Sigma}_t = \mathbf{\Sigma}$.

3.12. Verify the equivalence statements in the proof of Theorem 3.3.2.

3.13. Verify the identity in (3.3.18).

3.14. Let $\mathbf{Z} \sim \mathcal{N}_n(\mathbf{0}, \mathbf{I}_n)$. Let $\mathbf{Y}_1 = \mathbf{C}_1\mathbf{Z}$ and $\mathbf{Y}_2 = \mathbf{C}_2\mathbf{Z}$ where $\mathbf{C}_i$ is $k_i \times n$, $k_i \le n$ $(i = 1, 2)$. Find a necessary and sufficient condition for the independence of $\mathbf{Y}_1, \mathbf{Y}_2$.

3.15. Let $\mathbf{X}$ be partitioned as in (3.3.1), for fixed $k + 1 \le m \le n$ let $\mathbf{X}_2^{(m)} = (X_{k+1}, \ldots, X_m)'$. Let $\lambda^*(\mathbf{x}_2^{(m)})$ be the best predictor of X_i $(1 \le i \le k)$, given $\mathbf{X}_2^{(m)} = \mathbf{x}_2^{(m)}$. Show that $E((X_i - \lambda^*(\mathbf{x}_2^{(m)}))^2 | \mathbf{X}_2^{(m)} = \mathbf{x}_2^{(m)})$ is a nonincreasing function of m.

3.16. Let $\mathbf{X}$ and $\mathbf{X}_2^{(m)}$ be defined as in Problem 3.15, and let $R_{i\cdot k+1,\ldots,n}$ be the multiple correlation coefficient between X_i and $\mathbf{X}_2^{(m)}$. Show that $R_{i\cdot k+1,\ldots,m}$ is a nondecreasing function of m.

3.17. Show that the multiple correlation coefficient $R_{i\cdot k+1,\ldots,n}$ is nonnegative and is bounded above by one.

3.18. Show that the canonical correlation coefficients are nonnegative and are bounded above by one.

3.19. Verify the statement in (3.4.10).

3.20. Verify (3.4.27) and (3.4.28).

3.21. Verify (3.4.29).

In Problems 3.22–3.28, $\mathbf{X} = (\mathbf{X}_1, \mathbf{X}_2)' = ((X_1, X_2), (X_3, X_4))'$ is assumed to have a multivariate normal distribution with means μ, variances σ^2, and correlation coefficients

$$\rho_{12} = \rho_{34} = \rho_2, \qquad \rho_{ij} = \rho_1 \qquad \text{for} \quad i \le 2 \text{ and } j \ge 3,$$

where $0 \le \rho_1 \le \rho_2$.

3.22. Find the marginal distributions of $\mathbf{X}_1$ and $\mathbf{X}_2$.

3.23. Find the conditional distribution of $\mathbf{X}_1$ given $\mathbf{X}_2 = \mathbf{x}_2$.

3.24. Find the best predictor $\lambda^*(\mathbf{x}_2)$ of X_1 and find $E((X_1 - \lambda^*(\mathbf{x}_2))^2 | \mathbf{X}_2 = \mathbf{x}_2)$.

3.25. Find the multiple correlation coefficient $R_{1\cdot 34}$.

3.26. Find the partial correlation coefficient $\rho_{12\cdot 34}$.

3.27. Find the canonical correlation coefficients between $\mathbf{X}_1$ and $\mathbf{X}_2$.

3.28. Find the principal components of $\mathbf{X}$ and their variances.

3.29. Verify the identities in (3.5.6), (3.5.7), and (3.5.8).

It is known that a sequence of m-dimensional random vectors $\{(U_{1N}, \ldots, U_{mN})'\}_{N=1}^{\infty}$ converges to a constant vector $\mathbf{c} = (c_1, \ldots, c_m)'$ in probability if and only if $\{U_{iN}\}_{N=1}^{\infty}$ converges to c_i in probability for each $i = 1, \ldots, m$. Use this result to establish the facts in Problems 3.30 and 3.31.

3.30. Let $\bar{\mathbf{X}}_N$ denote the sample mean vector from an $\mathcal{N}_n(\boldsymbol{\mu}, \boldsymbol{\Sigma})$ population. Show that $\bar{\mathbf{X}}_N$ converges to $\boldsymbol{\mu}$ in probability as $N \to \infty$.

3.31. Let $\mathbf{S}_N$ be the sample covariance matrix of a random sample of size N from an $\mathcal{N}_n(\boldsymbol{\mu}, \boldsymbol{\Sigma})$ population, $\boldsymbol{\Sigma} > 0$. Show that $\mathbf{S}_N$ converges to $\boldsymbol{\Sigma}$ in probability as $N \to \infty$.

3.32. Let $\mathbf{W}$ denote a Wishart matrix and $\mathbf{W}_{11}$ the submatrix defined in (3.5.17). Show that $\mathbf{W}_{11}$ has a Wishart distribution.

3.33. Verify that in the proof of Lemma 3.5.2, $\mathbf{U}_1, \ldots, \mathbf{U}_{(N-1)-(n-k)}$ are i.i.d. $\mathcal{N}_k(\mathbf{0}, \boldsymbol{\Sigma}_{11\cdot 2})$ variables.

3.34. Let T^2 be Hotelling's T^2 statistic defined in (3.5.20). Show that as $N \to \infty$, the limiting distribution of T^2 is $\chi^2(n)$.

3.35. Let $\hat{R} = \hat{R}_{1\cdot 2\ldots n}$ be the sample multiple correlation coefficient of a random sample of size N from an $\mathcal{N}_n(\boldsymbol{\mu}, \boldsymbol{\Sigma})$ population, $\boldsymbol{\Sigma} > 0$. Show that if $R_{1\cdot 2\ldots n} = 0$, then the limiting distribution of $N\hat{R}^2/(1 - \hat{R}^2)$ is $\chi^2(n-1)$.

3.36. Show that when $n = 2$, the distribution of the sample multiple correlation coefficient given in Theorem 3.5.8 reduces to that given in Theorems 2.2.1 and 2.2.2.

3.37. Complete the proof of Theorem 3.5.9.

CHAPTER 4

Other Related Properties

In Chapter 3 we have studied the fundamental properties and related distribution theory of the multivariate normal distribution using the specific functional form of its density function. Most of the results given there have been obtained by direct algebraic calculations. In this chapter we study some related properties with a more general approach. We show that the multivariate normal density function belongs to certain large classes of density functions. Consequently, it has all the common properties possessed by density functions in those classes. This approach allows us to apply more general and powerful mathematical tools for deriving useful results.

In Section 4.1 we show that the multivariate normal distribution belongs to the class of elliptically contoured distributions. Since a characterization for the elliptically contoured distributions is already available, a characterization for the multivariate normal distribution can be obtained by a simple modification. Section 4.2 concerns log-concavity and unimodality properties. Two important theorems, Prékopa's theorem (for families with log-concave density functions) and Anderson's theorem (for symmetric and unimodal density functions), are shown to be applicable to the multivariate normal distribution. Section 4.3 deals with the monotone likelihood ratio property and the multivariate total positivity property of a subclass of the multivariate normal density functions. In Sections 4.4 and 4.5 we discuss the Schur-concavity and arrangement-increasing properties for permutation-symmetric normal variables, and we present some useful results.

4.1. The Elliptically Contoured Family of Distributions and the Multivariate Normal

Let $\mathbf{X} = (X_1, \ldots, X_n)'$ denote an n-dimensional random variable. Let $\boldsymbol{\Sigma}$ be an $n \times n$ positive definite matrix and let $\boldsymbol{\mu}$ be an n-dimensional real vector.

Definition 4.1.1. $\mathbf{X}$ is said to have an elliptically contoured distribution if its density function is of the form

$$f_{\boldsymbol{\mu},\boldsymbol{\Sigma}}(\mathbf{x}) = |\boldsymbol{\Sigma}|^{-1/2} g((\mathbf{x}-\boldsymbol{\mu})'\boldsymbol{\Sigma}^{-1}(\mathbf{x}-\boldsymbol{\mu})), \qquad \mathbf{x} \in \mathfrak{R}^n, \tag{4.1.1}$$

where $g\colon \mathfrak{R} \to [0, \infty)$ is nonincreasing.

Several important distributions are known to belong to this family of distributions. The multivariate normal distribution can be shown to be a member of this family by choosing

$$g(u) = (2\pi)^{-n/2} e^{-(1/2)u}, \qquad u \in \mathfrak{R}. \tag{4.1.2}$$

Another member of this family is the multivariate t distribution which will be treated in Chapter 9 of this volume.

There are many known results concerning elliptically contoured distributions, including closure properties of the marginal and conditional distributions, results on the moments and sampling distributions, on the distributions of quadratic forms (Anderson and Fang, 1984), and on related statistical inference problems (Anderson, Fang, and Hsu, 1986). A comprehensive treatment can be found in the book by Fang and Zhang (1988), and all the results for this family apply to the multivariate normal distribution.

4.1.1. Marginal and Conditional Distributions

The distribution theory for elliptically contoured distributions appears to be comprehensively studied for the first time by Kelker (1970). Later Das Gupta, Eaton, Olkin, Perlman, Savage, and Sobel (1972) obtained probability inequalities for this class of distributions. To state results on the marginal and conditional distributions of an n-dimensional elliptically contoured random variable $\mathbf{X} = (X_1, \ldots, X_n)'$, consider the partitions of $\mathbf{X}$, $\boldsymbol{\mu}$, and $\boldsymbol{\Sigma}$ defined in (3.3.1). For $k < n$, let $\mathbf{X}_1 = (X_1, \ldots, X_k)'$, $\mathbf{X}_2 = (X_{k+1}, \ldots, X_n)'$, and denote $\boldsymbol{\Sigma}_{11\cdot 2} = \boldsymbol{\Sigma}_{11} - \boldsymbol{\Sigma}_{12}\boldsymbol{\Sigma}_{22}^{-1}\boldsymbol{\Sigma}_{21}$. By the known facts

$$|\boldsymbol{\Sigma}| = |\boldsymbol{\Sigma}_{11\cdot 2}| \cdot |\boldsymbol{\Sigma}_{22}| \tag{4.1.3}$$

(see Anderson (1984, p. 54)) and

$$\begin{aligned} \mathbf{y}'\boldsymbol{\Sigma}^{-1}\mathbf{y} &= \mathbf{y}_2'\boldsymbol{\Sigma}_{22}^{-1}\mathbf{y}_2 + (\mathbf{y}_1 - \boldsymbol{\Sigma}_{12}\boldsymbol{\Sigma}_{22}^{-1}\mathbf{y}_2)'\boldsymbol{\Sigma}_{11\cdot 2}^{-1}(\mathbf{y}_1 - \boldsymbol{\Sigma}_{12}\boldsymbol{\Sigma}_{22}^{-1}\mathbf{y}_2) \\ &\equiv v_2(\mathbf{y}_2; \boldsymbol{\Sigma}_{22}) + v_{1\cdot 2}(\mathbf{y}_1, \mathbf{y}_2; \boldsymbol{\Sigma}), \end{aligned} \tag{4.1.4}$$

we immediately obtain the identity

$$\begin{aligned} &|\boldsymbol{\Sigma}|^{-1/2} g((\mathbf{x}-\boldsymbol{\mu})'\boldsymbol{\Sigma}^{-1}(\mathbf{x}-\boldsymbol{\mu})) \\ &\quad = |\boldsymbol{\Sigma}_{22}|^{-1/2} |\boldsymbol{\Sigma}_{11\cdot 2}|^{-1/2} g(v_2((\mathbf{x}_2-\boldsymbol{\mu}_2); \boldsymbol{\Sigma}_{22}) + v_{1\cdot 2}((\mathbf{x}_1-\boldsymbol{\mu}_1), (\mathbf{x}_2-\boldsymbol{\mu}_2); \boldsymbol{\Sigma})). \end{aligned} \tag{4.1.5}$$

By applying this identity we then obtain

Proposition 4.1.1. *Let* $\mathbf{X}$ *be an n-dimensional random variable which has an elliptically contoured distribution with density function given in* (4.1.1). *Then for every fixed* $1 \le k < n$:

(a) *the marginal distribution of* $\mathbf{X}_1$ *(of* $\mathbf{X}_2$*) is elliptically contoured, and depends on* $\boldsymbol{\mu}$ *and* $\boldsymbol{\Sigma}$ *only through* $\boldsymbol{\mu}_1$ *and* $\boldsymbol{\Sigma}_{11}$ *(only through* $\boldsymbol{\mu}_2$ *and* $\boldsymbol{\Sigma}_{22}$*);*
(b) *the conditional distribution of* $\mathbf{X}_1$, *given* $\mathbf{X}_2 = \mathbf{x}_2$, *is also elliptically contoured.*

Proof. (a) The marginal density function of $\mathbf{X}_2$ is

$$|\boldsymbol{\Sigma}|^{-1/2}\int_{\Re^k} |\boldsymbol{\Sigma}_{11\cdot 2}|^{-1/2} g(v_2((\mathbf{x}_2-\boldsymbol{\mu}_2); \boldsymbol{\Sigma}_{22}) + v_{1\cdot 2}((\mathbf{x}_1-\boldsymbol{\mu}_1), (\mathbf{x}_2-\boldsymbol{\mu}_2); \boldsymbol{\Sigma}))\, d\mathbf{x}_1$$

$$= |\boldsymbol{\Sigma}_{22}|^{-1/2}\int_{\Re^k} g\left(v_2((\mathbf{x}_2-\boldsymbol{\mu}_2); \boldsymbol{\Sigma}_{22}) + \sum_{i=1}^k y_i^2\right)\prod_{i=1}^k dy_i$$

$$\equiv |\boldsymbol{\Sigma}_{22}|^{-1/2} g_2(v_2((\mathbf{x}_2-\boldsymbol{\mu}_2); \boldsymbol{\Sigma}_{22}))$$

$$= |\boldsymbol{\Sigma}_{22}|^{-1/2} g_2((\mathbf{x}_2-\boldsymbol{\mu}_2)'\boldsymbol{\Sigma}_{22}^{-1}(\mathbf{x}_2-\boldsymbol{\mu}_2)), \qquad \mathbf{x}_2 \in \Re^{n-k}.$$

It is easy to verify that g_2 is nonincreasing. The marginal density function of $\mathbf{X}_1$ follows by symmetry.

(b) The conditional density of $\mathbf{X}_1$, given $\mathbf{X}_2 = \mathbf{x}_2$, is

$$f_{1|2}(\mathbf{x}_1|\mathbf{x}_2) = \frac{|\boldsymbol{\Sigma}_{11\cdot 2}|^{-1/2} g(v_2((\mathbf{x}_2-\boldsymbol{\mu}_2), \boldsymbol{\Sigma}_{22}) + v_{1\cdot 2}((\mathbf{x}_1-\boldsymbol{\mu}_1), (\mathbf{x}_2-\boldsymbol{\mu}_2); \boldsymbol{\Sigma}))}{g_2(v_2((\mathbf{x}_2-\boldsymbol{\mu}_2); \boldsymbol{\Sigma}_{22}))}$$

$$\equiv |\boldsymbol{\Sigma}_{11\cdot 2}|^{-1/2} g_{1|2}((\mathbf{x}_1-\boldsymbol{\mu}_{1\cdot 2})'\boldsymbol{\Sigma}_{11\cdot 2}^{-1}(\mathbf{x}_1-\boldsymbol{\mu}_{1\cdot 2})|\mathbf{x}_2),$$

where

$$\boldsymbol{\mu}_{1\cdot 2} = \boldsymbol{\mu}_1 + \boldsymbol{\Sigma}_{12}\boldsymbol{\Sigma}_{22}^{-1}(\mathbf{x}_2-\boldsymbol{\mu}_2)$$

and $g_{1|2}$ is also nonincreasing. □

For the multivariate normal distribution, g_2 can be obtained by applying the identity

$$\int_{\Re^k} (2\pi)^{-k/2}\exp\left(-\frac{1}{2}\sum_{i=1}^k y_i^2\right)\prod_{i=1}^k dy_i = 1$$

to integrate out $(y_1, \ldots, y_k)'$. Since in this case

$$g\left((\mathbf{x}_2-\boldsymbol{\mu}_2)'\boldsymbol{\Sigma}_{22}^{-1}(\mathbf{x}_2-\boldsymbol{\mu}_2) + \sum_{i=1}^k y_i^2\right)$$

$$= (2\pi)^{-(n-k)/2} e^{(-1/2)(\mathbf{x}_2-\boldsymbol{\mu}_2)'\boldsymbol{\Sigma}_{22}^{-1}(\mathbf{x}_2-\boldsymbol{\mu}_2)}\cdot(2\pi)^{-k/2}\exp\left(-\frac{1}{2}\sum_{i=1}^k y_i^2\right)$$

the marginal density function of $\mathbf{X}_2$ is just

$$f_2(\mathbf{x}_2) = (2\pi)^{-k/2}|\boldsymbol{\Sigma}_{22}|^{-1/2} e^{(-1/2)(\mathbf{x}_2-\boldsymbol{\mu}_2)'\boldsymbol{\Sigma}_{22}^{-1}(\mathbf{x}_2-\boldsymbol{\mu}_2)}, \qquad \mathbf{x}_2 \in \Re^{n-k},$$

as shown in Theorem 3.3.1. Similarly, we have

$$f_{1|2}(\mathbf{x}_1; \boldsymbol{\mu}, \boldsymbol{\Sigma}|\mathbf{x}_2) = \frac{1}{(2\pi)^{k/2}|\boldsymbol{\Sigma}_{11\cdot 2}|^{1/2}} e^{(-1/2)(\mathbf{x}_1-\boldsymbol{\mu}_{1\cdot 2})'\boldsymbol{\Sigma}_{11\cdot 2}^{-1}(\mathbf{x}_1-\boldsymbol{\mu}_{1\cdot 2})}, \qquad x \in \Re^k,$$

which is the result given previously in Theorem 3.3.4.

4.1.2. A Characterization of the Multivariate Normal Distribution

A useful characterization theorem given by Cambanis, Huang, and Simons (1981) for the elliptically contoured distributions can be applied to obtain a characterization result for the multivariate normal distribution. Their theorem states

Proposition 4.1.2. *An n-dimensional random variable* $\mathbf{X}$ *has an elliptically contoured distribution, with density function given in* (4.1.1), *if and only if there exist a real vector* $\boldsymbol{\mu}$, *an* $n \times n$ *positive definite matrix* $\mathbf{C}$ *such that* $\mathbf{CC}' = \boldsymbol{\Sigma}$, *and a nonnegative random variable* R^2 *such that*:

(i) *for given* $R^2 = r^2$, $\mathbf{Z}$ *is uniformly distributed on the sphere* $\{\mathbf{z}: \mathbf{z} \in \Re^n, \sum_{i=1}^n z_i^2 = r^2\}$; *and*
(ii) $\mathbf{X}$ *and* $\mathbf{CZ} + \boldsymbol{\mu}$ *are identically distributed.*

If the distribution of R^2 in Proposition 4.1.2 is specified, then the distribution of $\mathbf{X}$ is uniquely determined. Thus an application of this proposition yields the following characterization result for the multivariate normal distribution.

Theorem 4.1.1. *An n-dimensional random variable* $\mathbf{X}$ *has an* $\mathcal{N}_n(\boldsymbol{\mu}, \boldsymbol{\Sigma})$ *distribution,* $\boldsymbol{\Sigma} > 0$, *if and only if* $\mathbf{X}$ *is the random variable corresponding to the following experiment*:

(i) *observe the value of* $V = R^2$ *which has a chi-square distribution with n degrees of freedom;*
(ii) *for given* $V = v$, *choose a point at random on the n-dimensional sphere with radius* $r = \sqrt{v}$ *and identify this point as* $\mathbf{Z} = (Z_1, \ldots, Z_n)'$;
(iii) *for a given mean vector* $\boldsymbol{\mu}$ *and a covariance matrix* $\boldsymbol{\Sigma}$ *choose* $\mathbf{C}$ *to satisfy* $\mathbf{CC}' = \boldsymbol{\Sigma}$, *and then obtain* $\mathbf{X} = \mathbf{CZ} + \boldsymbol{\mu}$. (*Note that the existence of* $\mathbf{C}$ *follows from Proposition* 3.2.1.)

PROOF. (a) If $\mathbf{X} \sim \mathcal{N}_n(\boldsymbol{\mu}, \boldsymbol{\Sigma})$, $\boldsymbol{\Sigma} > 0$, then by Corollary 3.3.2, $\mathbf{Z} = \mathbf{C}^{-1}(\mathbf{X} - \boldsymbol{\mu})$ has an $\mathcal{N}_n(\mathbf{0}, \mathbf{I}_n)$ distribution. Thus $V = \sum_{i=1}^n Z_i^2$ has a chi-square distribution with n degrees of freedom.

(b) By Corollary 3.3.2 it suffices to show that if $V = \sum_{i=1}^n Z_i^2$ has a chi-square distribution with n degrees of freedom, then $(Z_1, \ldots, Z_n)'$ has an

$\mathcal{N}_n(\mathbf{0}, \mathbf{I}_n)$ distribution. By Proposition 4.1.2 the joint density function of $\mathbf{Z}$ is of the form $g_0((\sum_{i=1}^n z_i^2)^{1/2})$ for some nonincreasing function g_0: $\mathfrak{R} \to [0, \infty)$. Let $R = \sqrt{V} = (\sum_{i=1}^n Z_i^2)^{1/2}$, then clearly we have

$$P[R \le \lambda] = \int_{\{\mathbf{z}: (\sum_{i=1}^n z_i^2)^{1/2} \le \lambda\}} g_0\left(\left(\sum_{i=1}^n z_i^2\right)^{1/2}\right) \prod_{i=1}^n dz_i.$$

After a change of variable from the n-dimensional rectangular system to the polar system and integrating out we have, for $r^2 = v$,

$$\begin{aligned} P[R \le \lambda] &= c_n \int_0^\lambda r^{n-1} g_0(r)\, dr \\ &= c_n \int_0^{\lambda^2} \tfrac{1}{2} v^{n/2-1} g_0(\sqrt{v})\, dv \qquad \text{for all} \quad \lambda > 0, \end{aligned} \tag{4.1.6}$$

where (by calculus) $c_n = 2\pi^{n/2}/\Gamma(n/2)$ (see, e.g., Iyanaga and Kawada (1980, p. 1427)). But $V = R^2$ has a chi-square distribution with n degrees of freedom. Thus we also have

$$\begin{aligned} P[R \le \lambda] &= P[V \le \lambda^2] \\ &= \int_0^{\lambda^2} \left[\Gamma\left(\frac{n}{2}\right) 2^{n/2}\right]^{-1} v^{n/2-1} e^{-v/2}\, dv \qquad \text{for all} \quad \lambda > 0. \end{aligned} \tag{4.1.7}$$

Since the integrands in (4.1.6) and (4.1.7) must be equal almost everywhere, we have

$$g_0(\sqrt{v}) = (2\pi)^{-n/2} e^{-v/2}, \qquad v > 0.$$

Consequently, the joint density function of $\mathbf{Z}$ is

$$g_0(\mathbf{z}) = (2\pi)^{-n/2} \exp\left(-\frac{1}{2} \sum_{i=1}^n z_i^2\right), \qquad \mathbf{z} \in \mathfrak{R}^n. \qquad \square$$

Remark 4.1.1. In the proof of Theorem 4.1.1, Proposition 4.1.2 is used only to establish the fact that the joint density of $\mathbf{Z}$ depends on $\mathbf{z} = (z_1, \ldots, z_n)'$ through $\sum_{i=1}^n z_i^2$. This fact can easily be justified even without applying Proposition 4.1.2. Thus the proof given here provides a direct verification for this characterization theorem for the multivariate normal distribution. Also note that a similar result was given by Khatri and Mukerjee (1987). Their result depends on the Taylor's series expansion of the density function of V and its Laplace transform.

Remark 4.1.2. As a special application of Theorem 4.1.1, the standard multivariate normal variate $\mathbf{Z} \sim \mathcal{N}_n(\mathbf{0}, \mathbf{I}_n)$ can be generated by first observing a random variate V from the $\chi^2(n)$ distribution then, for given $V = v$, choosing a point at random on the n-dimensional sphere with radius $\sqrt{v}$. For $n = 2$

this was discussed in Theorem 2.1.4 in connection with the Box–Muller method (Theorem 2.1.3) for generating bivariate normal variates.

Another characterization result, given by Tamhankar (1967), is closely related to Theorem 4.1.1. Let $f_1(x_1, \ldots, x_n)$ be the joint density function of the rectangular coordinates (random variables) $X_1, \ldots, X_n$, and assume that it is related to the joint density $f_2(r, \theta_1, \ldots, \theta_{n-1})$ of the polar coordinates (random variables) $R, \Theta_1, \ldots, \Theta_{n-1}$ by

$$f_1(x_1, \ldots, x_n)r^{n-1}\left(\prod_{j=1}^{n-2} (\sin \theta_j)^{n-j-1}\right) = f_2(r, \theta_1, \ldots, \theta_{n-1}),$$

where the coordinates are related by

$$\begin{aligned} x_1 &= r \cos \theta_1, \\ x_2 &= r \sin \theta_1 \cos \theta_2, \\ &\cdots \\ x_{n-1} &= r\left(\prod_{j=1}^{n-2} \sin \theta_j\right) \cos \theta_{n-1}, \\ x_n &= r\left(\prod_{j=1}^{n-1} \sin \theta_j\right), \end{aligned}$$

for $(x_1, \ldots, x_n)' \in \Re^n$, $r \geq 0$, and $\theta_j \in [0, 2\pi)$ $(j = 1, \ldots, n-1)$. Tamhankar's (1967) result states:

Theorem 4.1.2. *Assume that f_1, f_2 are absolutely continuous with respect to the Lebesgue measure, and that*

$$\frac{f_2(r, \theta_1, \ldots, \theta_{n-1})}{r^{n-1}\left(\prod_{j=1}^{n-2} (\sin \theta_j)^{n-j-1}\right)}$$

is well defined and nonzero everywhere, continuous in r for $r \geq 0$, and equal to $f_1(x_1, \ldots, x_n)$ which is continuous in x_i for each $i = 1, \ldots, n$. Then the following statements are equivalent:

(a) *$X_1, \ldots, X_n$ are independent random variables and R is independent of $(\Theta_1, \ldots, \Theta_{n-1})'$.*
(b) *$X_1, \ldots, X_n$ are i.i.d. $\mathcal{N}(0, \sigma^2)$ variables, where $\sigma^2 = (1/n)ER^2$.*

The key point in this theorem is that if $X_1, \ldots, X_n$ are independent, then the independence of the radius R and the angle vector $(\Theta_1, \ldots, \Theta_{n-1})'$ characterizes normality with i.i.d. $\mathcal{N}(0, \sigma^2)$ components. Note that the assertion is no longer true if the condition of independence of $X_1, \ldots, X_n$ is removed.

4.1.3. Other Related Characterization Results for the Multivariate Normal Distribution

Theorem 4.1.1 states that if the distribution of an n-dimensional random variable is elliptically contoured, then it is a multivariate normal distribution if and only if $V = R^2$ has a $\chi^2(n)$ distribution. An interesting question is then this: Given that $\mathbf{X}$ has an elliptically contoured distribution, what are the other necessary and sufficient conditions under which the underlying distribution of $\mathbf{X}$ is multivariate normal? This problem was considered by Kelker (1970), Cambanis, Huang, and Simons (1981), and others, a convenient reference is Fang and Zhang (1988, Sec. 2.7). We summarize two equivalent conditions in the following theorem.

Theorem 4.1.3. *Assume that* $\mathbf{X} = (\mathbf{X}_1, \mathbf{X}_2)'$ *has the density function* $f(\mathbf{x})$ *given in* (4.1.1), *where* $\mathbf{X}_1$ *is* $k \times 1$ *and* $\mathbf{X}_2$ *is* $(n - k) \times 1$. *Then the following statements are equivalent*:

(a) $\mathbf{X} \sim \mathcal{N}_n(\boldsymbol{\mu}, \boldsymbol{\Sigma}), \boldsymbol{\Sigma} > 0$.
(b) *The marginal distributions of* $\mathbf{X}_1$ *and* $\mathbf{X}_2$ *are multivariate normal for all* k, $1 \leq k \leq n - 1$.
(c) *The conditional distribution of* $\mathbf{X}_1$, *given* $\mathbf{X}_2 = \mathbf{x}_2$, *is multivariate normal for all* k, $1 \leq k \leq n - 1$, *and all* $\mathbf{x}_2$ *except perhaps on a set of probability zero.*

These conditions are stated in terms of the marginal and conditional distributions, and are different from those in Theorem 4.1.1.

Other related characterization results for the multivariate normal distribution can be found in Kagan, Linnik, and Rao (1973, pp. 475–477), Fang and Zhang (1988, Sec. 2.7), and some of the references given in Johnson and Kotz (1972, Chaps. 35 and 36).

4.2. Log-Concavity and Unimodality Properties

4.2.1. Log-Concavity and Prékopa's Theorem

Log-concave density functions have many nice analytical properties, and play an important role in statistics. To describe a useful result for this class of density functions we first observe the following definition:

Definition 4.2.1. A density function $f\colon \Re^n \to [0, \infty)$ is said to be log-concave if

$$f(\alpha\mathbf{x} + (1 - \alpha)\mathbf{y}) \geq [f(\mathbf{x})]^{\alpha}[f(\mathbf{y})]^{1-\alpha} \tag{4.2.1}$$

holds for all $\mathbf{x}, \mathbf{y} \in \Re^n$ and all $\alpha \in [0, 1]$. [If $f(\mathbf{x}) > 0$ holds for all $\mathbf{x} \in \Re^n$, then an equivalent condition is

$$\log f(\alpha \mathbf{x} + (1 - \alpha)\mathbf{y}) \geq \alpha \log f(\mathbf{x}) + (1 - \alpha)\log f(\mathbf{y}).] \tag{4.2.2}$$

In the univariate case, the normal density function with mean μ and variance σ^2 is log-concave. In the following theorem we show that the density of an n-dimensional normal variable with an arbitrary mean vector $\boldsymbol{\mu}$ and positive definite covariance matrix $\boldsymbol{\Sigma}$ is also log-concave.

Theorem 4.2.1. *Let $f(\mathbf{x}; \boldsymbol{\mu}, \boldsymbol{\Sigma})$ be the density function of an $\mathcal{N}_n(\boldsymbol{\mu}, \boldsymbol{\Sigma})$ distribution, $\boldsymbol{\Sigma} > 0$, given in* (3.2.1). *Then f is a log-concave function of $\mathbf{x} \in \Re^n$.*

PROOF. For arbitrary but fixed $\mathbf{x}, \mathbf{y} \in \Re^n$ and $\alpha \in [0, 1]$ we have, by the fact that $\boldsymbol{\Sigma}^{-1}$ is a positive definite matrix,

$$\begin{aligned}
&\log f(\alpha \mathbf{x} + (1 - \alpha)\mathbf{y}; \boldsymbol{\mu}, \boldsymbol{\Sigma}) - [\alpha \log f(\mathbf{x}; \boldsymbol{\mu}, \boldsymbol{\Sigma}) + (1 - \alpha)\log f(\mathbf{y}; \boldsymbol{\mu}, \boldsymbol{\Sigma})] \\
&\qquad = \tfrac{1}{2}\alpha(1 - \alpha)[(\mathbf{x} - \boldsymbol{\mu})'\boldsymbol{\Sigma}^{-1}(\mathbf{x} - \boldsymbol{\mu}) + (\mathbf{y} - \boldsymbol{\mu})'\boldsymbol{\Sigma}^{-1}(\mathbf{y} - \boldsymbol{\mu}) \\
&\qquad\qquad - 2(\mathbf{x} - \boldsymbol{\mu})'\boldsymbol{\Sigma}^{-1}(\mathbf{y} - \boldsymbol{\mu})] \\
&\qquad = \tfrac{1}{2}\alpha(1 - \alpha)[(\mathbf{x} - \mathbf{y})'\boldsymbol{\Sigma}^{-1}(\mathbf{x} - \mathbf{y})] \geq 0.
\end{aligned}$$

□

One of the important properties of log-concave density functions is described below: Let A, B be two sets in $\Re^n$. For arbitrary but fixed $\alpha \in [0, 1]$ we define a new set which is a convex combination of A and B:

$$\alpha A + (1 - \alpha)B = \{\mathbf{z}\colon \mathbf{z} \in \Re^n,\ \mathbf{z} = \alpha \mathbf{x} + (1 - \alpha)\mathbf{y} \text{ for some } \mathbf{x} \in A \text{ and } \mathbf{y} \in B\}.$$

(For $k > 2$ and real numbers $\alpha_1, \ldots, \alpha_k$ such that $\alpha_i \geq 0$, $\sum_{i=1}^k \alpha_i = 1$, the set $\sum_{i=1}^k \alpha_i A_i$ can be defined similarly for given $A_1, \ldots, A_k$ in $\Re^n$.) Prékopa (1971) showed that

Proposition 4.2.1. *Let $\mathbf{X} = (X_1, \ldots, X_n)'$ have density function $f(\mathbf{x})$ and let A, B be any sets*[1] *in $\Re^n$. If $f(\mathbf{x})$ is log-concave, then*

$$P[\mathbf{X} \in (\alpha A + (1 - \alpha)B)] \geq \{P[\mathbf{X} \in A]\}^{\alpha}\{P[\mathbf{X} \in B]\}^{1-\alpha} \tag{4.2.3}$$

holds for all $\alpha \in [0, 1]$. If the probability contents are all positive, then

$$\log P[\mathbf{X} \in (\alpha A + (1 - \alpha)B)] \geq \alpha \log P[\mathbf{X} \in A] + (1 - \alpha)\log P[\mathbf{X} \in B]$$

holds for all $\alpha \in [0, 1]$.

[1] More precisely, A and B are sets in $\Re^n$ such that A and B and $\alpha A + (1 - \alpha)B$ are all Borel-measurable so that the probabilities are properly defined. It should be noted that, as pointed out by Karlin (1983), the measurability of A and B does not guarantee the measurability of $\alpha A + (1 - \alpha)B$ for all $\alpha \in [0, 1]$.

The reader is referred to Prékopa (1971) for the proof of this result.

When combining Theorem 4.2.1 and Proposition 4.2.1, we obtain the following result for the multivariate normal distribution.

Theorem 4.2.2. *Let* $\mathbf{X}$ *have an* $\mathcal{N}_n(\boldsymbol{\mu}, \boldsymbol{\Sigma})$ *distribution,* $\boldsymbol{\Sigma} > 0$. *Then for any finite* k, *any sets* $A_1, \ldots, A_k$ *in* $\mathfrak{R}^n$, *and any real numbers* $\alpha_1, \ldots, \alpha_k$ *such that* $\alpha_i \geq 0$ *and* $\sum_{i=1}^n \alpha_i = 1$, *we have*

$$P\left[\mathbf{X} \in \sum_{i=1}^{k} \alpha_i A_i\right] \geq \prod_{i=1}^{k} \{P[\mathbf{X} \in A_i]\}^{\alpha_i}. \tag{4.2.4}$$

Proof. Without loss of generality assume that $0 < \alpha_i < 1$ $(i = 1, \ldots, k)$. Then we have

$$\begin{aligned}
&P\left[\mathbf{X} \in \sum_{i=1}^{k} \alpha_i A_i\right] \\
&= P\left[\mathbf{X} \in \alpha_1 A_1 + (1-\alpha_1)\sum_{i=2}^{k}\left(\frac{\alpha_i}{1-\alpha_1}\right)A_i\right] \\
&\geq \{P[\mathbf{X} \in A_1]\}^{\alpha_1}\left\{P\left[\mathbf{X} \in \sum_{i=2}^{k}\left(\frac{\alpha_i}{1-\alpha_1}\right)A_i\right]\right\}^{1-\alpha_1} \\
&\geq \{P[\mathbf{X} \in A_1]\}^{\alpha_1}\{P[\mathbf{X} \in A_2]\}^{\alpha_2} P\left[\mathbf{X} \in \sum_{i=3}^{k}\left(\frac{\alpha_i}{1-\alpha_1-\alpha_2}\right)A_i\right]^{1-\alpha_1-\alpha_2} \\
&\geq \cdots \\
&\geq \prod_{i=1}^{k} \{P[\mathbf{X} \in A_i]\}^{\alpha_i}.
\end{aligned}$$

□

Theorem 4.2.2 has many important applications in deriving bounds for multivariate normal probabilities. For the purpose of illustration we consider two simple examples given below.

Example 4.2.1. Let $\mathbf{X} = (X_1, X_2)'$ have an $\mathcal{N}_2(\boldsymbol{\mu}, \boldsymbol{\Sigma})$ distribution such that $\mu_1 = \mu_2$, $\sigma_1^2 = \sigma_2^2$, and $|\rho| < 1$. Then for every given $(a_1, a_2)' \in \mathfrak{R}^2$, the distribution function of $\mathbf{X}$ satisfies

$$F(a_1, a_2) = p[X_1 \leq a_1, X_2 \leq a_2] \leq P[X_1 \leq \bar{a}, X_2 \leq \bar{a}] = F(\bar{a}, \bar{a}),$$

where $\bar{a} = \frac{1}{2}(a_1 + a_2)$ is the arithmetic mean.

Proof. For $k = 2$ define

$$A_1 = \{(u_1, u_2)\colon u_1 \leq a_1, u_2 \leq a_2\}, \qquad A_2 = \{(u_1, u_2)\colon u_1 \leq a_2, u_2 \leq a_1\}.$$

Since the distribution of $\mathbf{X}$ is permutation symmetric, clearly we have

$$F(a_1, a_2) = P[\mathbf{X} \in A_1] = P[\mathbf{X} \in A_2] = F(a_2, a_1).$$

But

$$\tfrac{1}{2}A_1 + \tfrac{1}{2}A_2 = \{(u_1, u_2): u_1 \le \bar{a}, u_2 \le \bar{a}\}. \tag{4.2.5}$$

Hence

$$F(\bar{a}, \bar{a}) \ge \{F(a_1, a_2)\}^{1/2}\{F(a_2, a_1)\}^{1/2} = F(a_1, a_2). \qquad \square$$

To illustrate why a similar result holds for the multivariate case, in the next example we consider the case $n = 3$.

Example 4.2.2. Let $\mathbf{X}$ have an $\mathcal{N}_3(\boldsymbol{\mu}, \boldsymbol{\Sigma})$ distribution such that

$$\mu_1 = \mu_2 = \mu_3, \qquad \sigma_1^2 = \sigma_2^2 = \sigma_3^2, \qquad \text{and} \qquad \rho_{12} = \rho_{13} = \rho_{23} = \rho \in (-\tfrac{1}{2}, 1).$$

Then $F(a_1, a_2, a_3) \le F(\bar{a}, \bar{a}, \bar{a})$ holds for all $(a_1, a_2, a_3)' \in \Re^3$, where $\bar{a} = \frac{1}{3}(a_1 + a_2 + a_3)$.

Proof. For $i = 1, 2, \ldots, 6$ define

$$A_i = \{\mathbf{u}: \mathbf{u} \in \Re^3, \mathbf{u} \le \pi_i(\mathbf{a})\},$$

where $\mathbf{a} = (a_1, a_2, a_3)'$ and $\{\pi_i(\mathbf{a})\}_1^6$ is the set of the 3! permutations of the components of $\mathbf{a}$. The proof follows from Theorem 4.2.2 and the identity

$$\sum_{i=1}^{6} \tfrac{1}{6}A_i = \{\mathbf{u} | \mathbf{u} \in \Re^3, \mathbf{u} \le (\bar{a}, \bar{a}, \bar{a})'\}. \tag{4.2.6}$$

The details are left to the reader. $\square$

The results in Examples 4.2.1 and 4.2.2 are special cases of a more general theorem due to Marshall and Olkin (1974). That theorem and its related results follow by applying a convolution theorem in their paper, and will be treated in Sections 4.4 and 7.4.

4.2.2. Unimodality and Anderson's Theorem

The notion of unimodality of a density function is closely related to convexity, and serves as a mathematical tool for deriving useful results. There exist several different definitions of unimodality in the literature, and the reader is referred to Dharmadhikari and Joag-Dev (1988) for a comprehensive treatment of this topic. The following definition, known as A-unimodality, is due to Anderson (1955).

Definition 4.2.2. A density function $f(\mathbf{x})$: $\Re^n \to [0, \infty)$ is said to be A-unimodal if the set

$$A_\lambda = \{\mathbf{x}: f(\mathbf{x}) \ge \lambda\} \tag{4.2.7}$$

is convex for all $\lambda > 0$.

A known result concerning log-concave density functions and A-unimodal density functions is

Proposition 4.2.2. *All log-concave density functions are A-unimodal.*

Proof. For every fixed $\lambda > 0$ let $\mathbf{x}$, $\mathbf{y}$ be in A_λ. Then for any fixed $\alpha \in [0, 1]$ we have (by (4.2.1))

$$f(\alpha\mathbf{x} + (1-\alpha)\mathbf{y}) \geq [f(\mathbf{x})]^\alpha[f(\mathbf{y})]^{1-\alpha} \geq \lambda^\alpha(\lambda)^{1-\alpha} = \lambda.$$

Thus $\alpha\mathbf{x} + (1-\alpha)\mathbf{y} \in A_\lambda$. □

Combining Theorem 4.2.1 and Proposition 4.2.2 we immediately obtain the fact that a multivariate normal density function is A-unimodal. But this also follows by a direct verification.

Theorem 4.2.3. *Let $f(\mathbf{x}; \boldsymbol{\mu}, \boldsymbol{\Sigma})$ be the density function of an $\mathcal{N}_n(\boldsymbol{\mu}, \boldsymbol{\Sigma})$ distribution, $\boldsymbol{\Sigma} > 0$. Then the set*

$$\begin{aligned} A_\lambda &= \{\mathbf{x}\colon f(\mathbf{x}; \boldsymbol{\mu}, \boldsymbol{\Sigma}) \geq \lambda\} \\ &= \{\mathbf{x}\colon (\mathbf{x}-\boldsymbol{\mu})'\boldsymbol{\Sigma}^{-1}(\mathbf{x}-\boldsymbol{\mu}) \leq -2\log(\lambda(2\pi)^{n/2}|\boldsymbol{\Sigma}|^{1/2})\} \end{aligned}$$

is an ellipsoid centered at $\boldsymbol{\mu}$. Consequently, f is A-unimodal.

Anderson's theorem (Anderson, 1955) deals with a monotonicity property of the integral of a symmetric and A-unimodal density function over a symmetric and convex set. A function f (a set B) is said to be symmetric about the origin if $f(\mathbf{x}) = f(-\mathbf{x})$ (if $\mathbf{x} \in B$ implies $-\mathbf{x} \in B$) for all $\mathbf{x} \in \mathfrak{R}^n$. The theorem states:

Proposition 4.2.3. *Let $\mathbf{X}$ be an n-dimensional random variable with continuous density function $f(\mathbf{x})$. For $B \subset \mathfrak{R}^n$ and an arbitrary but fixed nonzero vector $\mathbf{u} \in \mathfrak{R}^n$ denote*

$$B + c\mathbf{u} = \{\mathbf{x}\colon \mathbf{x} = \mathbf{y} + c\mathbf{u} \text{ for } \mathbf{y} \in B\}, \qquad c \in \mathfrak{R}.$$

If $f(\mathbf{x})$ is symmetric about the origin and is A-unimodal, and B is symmetric about the origin and convex, then the probability integral $\int_{B+c\mathbf{u}} f(\mathbf{x})\,d\mathbf{x}$ is nonincreasing in $|c|$. Furthermore, it is strictly decreasing unless there exists an $\mathbf{v} \in \mathfrak{R}^n$ such that

$$(B + \mathbf{u}) \cap A_\lambda = (B \cap A_\lambda) + \mathbf{v} \qquad \text{holds for all } \lambda > 0, \tag{4.2.8}$$

where A_λ is defined in (4.2.7).

The proof of Proposition 4.2.3 was given by Anderson (1955). A more convenient reference for the proof is Tong (1980, pp. 52–54). Note that (4.2.8) is different from the original condition in Anderson (1955). The statement under the original condition is in error, a counterexample was found by A.P. Soms (Anderson, 1988).

Next we consider some applications of Proposition 4.2.3 to the multivariate normal distribution. For Q_n defined in (3.2.2) we have

$$Q_n(\mathbf{x}; \mathbf{0}, \mathbf{\Sigma}) = Q_n(-\mathbf{x}; \mathbf{0}, \mathbf{\Sigma}),$$

thus the multivariate normal density function satisfies $f(\mathbf{x}; \mathbf{0}, \mathbf{\Sigma}) = f(-\mathbf{x}; \mathbf{0}, \mathbf{\Sigma})$ for all $\mathbf{\Sigma} > 0$. Consequently, we obtain

Theorem 4.2.4. *Let* $\mathbf{X}$ *have an* $\mathcal{N}_n(\mathbf{0}, \mathbf{\Sigma})$ *distribution,* $\mathbf{\Sigma} > 0$. *Let* $B \subset \mathfrak{R}^n$ *be a set that is symmetric about the origin and convex. Then* $P[\mathbf{X} \in B + c\mathbf{u}]$ *is a nonincreasing function of* $|c|$ *for all fixed nonzero vectors* $\mathbf{u} \in \mathfrak{R}^n$.

A special application of Proposition 4.2.3 yields a result for the peakedness of the multivariate normal distribution via a partial ordering of the covariance matrices. (Peakedness will be treated formally in Section 7.5.) Let $\mathbf{X}, \mathbf{Y}$ be two n-dimensional normal random variables ($n \geq 1$), in certain applications we are interested in necessary and/or sufficient conditions for the inequality $P[\mathbf{X} \in B] \geq P[\mathbf{Y} \in B]$ to hold for all symmetric (about the origin) and convex sets $B \subset \mathfrak{R}^n$. For the univariate case in which $X \sim \mathcal{N}(0, \sigma_1^2)$ and $Y \sim \mathcal{N}(0, \sigma_2^2)$, it is clear that the inequality holds if and only if $P[|X| \leq \lambda] \geq P[|Y| \leq \lambda]$ holds for all $\lambda > 0$, or equivalently, $\sigma_2^2 - \sigma_1^2 \geq 0$ holds. An application of Proposition 4.2.3 yields the following n-dimensional analogy:

Theorem 4.2.5. *Let* $\mathbf{X} \sim \mathcal{N}_n(\mathbf{0}, \mathbf{\Sigma}_1)$ *and let* $\mathbf{Y} \sim \mathcal{N}_n(\mathbf{0}, \mathbf{\Sigma}_2)$, *where* $\mathbf{\Sigma}_i > 0$ ($i = 1, 2$). *If* $\mathbf{\Sigma}_2 - \mathbf{\Sigma}_1$ *is a positive definite or a positive semidefinite matrix, then* $P[\mathbf{X} \in B] \geq P[\mathbf{Y} \in B]$ *holds for all symmetric (about the origin) and convex sets* $B \subset \mathfrak{R}^n$.

Proof. Let $\mathbf{U} \sim \mathcal{N}_n(\mathbf{0}, \mathbf{\Sigma}_2 - \mathbf{\Sigma}_1)$ be independent of $\mathbf{X}$. Then $\mathbf{Y}$ and $\mathbf{X} + \mathbf{U}$ are identically distributed. Thus

$$\begin{aligned} P[\mathbf{Y} \in B] &= P[\mathbf{X} \in B - \mathbf{U}] \\ &= EP[\mathbf{X} \in B - \mathbf{u} | \mathbf{U} = \mathbf{u}] \\ &\leq EP[\mathbf{X} \in B | \mathbf{U} = \mathbf{u}] \\ &= P[\mathbf{X} \in B]. \end{aligned}$$ □

This result, due to Anderson (1955), has some important applications in multivariate analysis.

4.3. MTP_2 and MRR_2 Properties

The MTP_2 and MRR_2 properties of an n-dimensional multivariate normal density function are closely related to the TP_2 property of a bivariate normal density. Therefore we first describe some known results for the bivariate case.

4.3.1. The TP_2 and MLR Properties of Bivariate Normal Densities with Nonnegative Correlation Coefficients

Definition 4.3.1 (Karlin (1968, p. 11)). The density function $f(x_1, x_2)$ of a bivariate random variable $\mathbf{X} = (X_1, X_2)'$ is said to be totally positive of order 2 (TP_2) if the inequality

$$f(y_1 y_2) f(y_1^*, y_2^*) \leq f(x_1, x_2) f(x_1^*, x_2^*) \tag{4.3.1}$$

holds for all $(y_1, y_2)'$, $(y_1^*, y_2^*)'$ in the domain of f where $x_i = \max(y_i, y_i^*)$, $x_i^* = \min(y_i, y_i^*)$ $(i = 1, 2)$.

This notion provides a useful tool for studying the stochastic dependence of the components of bivariate random variables and yields important results. One of the results is that if $f(x_1, x_2)$ has the TP_2 property, then $\text{Cov}(g_1(X_1, X_2), g_2(X_1, X_2)) \geq 0$ holds for all nondecreasing functions g_1 and g_2. Intuitively speaking, if (4.3.1) holds, then a larger (a smaller) value of X_1 is more likely to be associated with a larger (a smaller) value of X_2. Consequently, $g_1(X_1, X_2)$ and $g_2(X_1, X_2)$ tend to "hang together," and thus are nonnegatively correlated.

We recall that a family of conditional density functions $\{f_{1|2}(x_1|x_2): x_2 \in \Lambda\}$ is said to have the monotone likelihood ratio (MLR) property if for all $x_2^*, x_2 \in \Lambda$, such that $x_2^* \leq x_2$, the likelihood ratio $f_{1|2}(x_1|x_2)/f_{1|2}(x_1|x_2^*)$ is a nondecreasing function of x_1. A result in Lehmann (1986, p. 115) states that if the family of conditional densities of X_1 has the MLR property, then $Eg(X_1|X_2 = x_2)$ is a nondecreasing function of x_2 for all nondecreasing functions g such that the conditional expectations exist. The following fact explains how the TP_2 property and the MLR property are related.

Fact 4.3.1. *The density function $f(x_1, x_2)$ of a bivariate random variable $\mathbf{X} = (X_1, X_2)'$ is TP_2 if and only if the family of conditional density functions*

$$\left\{f_{1|2}(x_1|x_2) = \frac{f(x_1, x_2)}{f_2(x_2)}: x_2 \in \Lambda\right\}$$

has the MLR property, where $\Lambda = \{x_2: x_2 \in \Re, f_2(x_2) > 0\}$ and f_2 is the marginal density of X_2.

Proof. Without loss of generality assume that y_2 and y_2^* in Λ satisfy $y_2^* < y_2$ (i.e., $x_2^* = y_2^*$ and $x_2 = y_2$). Then we have

$$\delta = \frac{f(y_1, y_2) f(y_1^*, y_2^*)}{f(x_1, x_2) f(x_1^*, x_2^*)}$$

$$= \frac{f_{1|2}(y_1|x_2) f_{1|2}(y_1^*|x_2^*)}{f_{1|2}(x_1|x_2) f_{1|2}(x_1^*|x_2^*)}.$$

Clearly, $\delta = 1$ for $y_1^* \le y_1$. For $x_1^* = y_1 < y_1^* = x_1$, $\delta \le 1$ holds if and only if

$$\frac{f_{1|2}(x_1^*|x_2)}{f_{1|2}(x_1^*|x_2^*)} \le \frac{f_{1|2}(x_1|x_2)}{f_{1|2}(x_1|x_2^*)}$$

holds. □

Note that Fact 4.3.1 was stated in Section 2.3 without proof. Now an application of this fact and the identity in (2.3.5) immediately yields

Theorem 4.3.1. *Let $(X_1, X_2)'$ have an $\mathcal{N}_2(\boldsymbol{\mu}, \boldsymbol{\Sigma})$ distribution with correlation coefficient $\rho \in (-1, 1)$.*

(a) *If $\rho \ge 0$, then the joint density function of $(X_1, X_2)'$ is TP_2.*
(b) *If $\rho < 0$, then the joint density of $(X_1, -X_2)'$ is TP_2.*

4.3.2. The MTP_2 Property

For $n > 2$, let $\mathbf{X} = (X_1, \ldots, X_n)'$ have density function $f(\mathbf{x})$. The following definition is a natural generalization of Definition 4.3.1.

Definition 4.3.2 (Karlin and Rinott (1980a)). $f(\mathbf{x})$: $\mathfrak{R}^n \to [0, \infty)$ is said to be multivariate-totally-positive-of-order-2 (MTP_2) if the inequality

$$f(\mathbf{y})f(\mathbf{y}^*) \le f(\mathbf{x})f(\mathbf{x}^*) \tag{4.3.2}$$

holds for all $\mathbf{y}$, $\mathbf{y}^*$ in the domain of f, where

$$x_i = \max\{y_i, y_i^*\}, \qquad x_i^* = \min\{y_i, y_i^*\}, \qquad i = 1, \ldots, n.$$

A definition which is closely related to MTP_2 is

Definition 4.3.3. A density function $f(\mathbf{x})$: $\mathfrak{R}^n \to [0, \infty)$ is said to be totally-positive-of-order-2-in-pairs (TP_2 in pairs) if $f(x_1, \ldots, x_i, \ldots, x_j, \ldots, x_n)$ is TP_2 in (x_i, x_j) for all $i \ne j$ and all fixed values of the remaining arguments.

This definition is equivalent to saying that the conditional density function of $(X_i, X_j)'$, given the values of the other variables, is TP_2. It is known that

Fact 4.3.2 (Kemperman (1977)).

(a) *If* (i) *$f(\mathbf{x})$ is TP_2 in pairs, and* (ii) *$f(\mathbf{y})f(\mathbf{y}^*) > 0$ implies $f(\mathbf{u}) > 0$ for all $\mathbf{u} = (u_1, \ldots, u_n)'$ satisfying*

$$\min\{y_i, y_i^*\} \le u_i \le \max\{y_i, y_i^*\}, \qquad i = 1, \ldots, n,$$

then $f(\mathbf{x})$ is MTP_2.
(b) *If the joint density function of $\mathbf{X} = (X_1, \ldots, X_n)'$ is MTP_2, then the marginal density of $(X_1, \ldots, X_k)'$ is MTP_2 for all $k < n$.*

Furthermore, it is known that the statement in Fact 4.3.2(a) is false without the condition in (a)(ii) (Kemperman, 1977). However, for the multivariate normal distribution this condition is immediately satisfied. For the proof of Fact 4.3.2 and additional discussions, see Kemperman (1977), Karlin and Rinott (1980a), Perlman and Olkin (1980), and Eaton (1987, Sec. 5.4).

EXAMPLE 4.3.1. To help understand the motivation for studying MTP_2 density functions, suppose that two students are selected independently from an infinite population, and their scores on n subjects (such as math, physics, biology, etc.), $X_1, \ldots, X_n$, are observed. Furthermore, suppose that the individual scores $y_1, y_1^*, y_2, y_2^*, \ldots, y_n, y_n^*$ are given, but the original record is lost so that it is not known which set of scores came from the same individual. If the desity function of $(X_1, \ldots, X_n)'$ has the MTP_2 property, then it is *most likely* that all of the n smaller scores came from one individual and all of the n larger scores came from the other individual. □

A critical application of the MTP_2 property of the density function of $\mathbf{X}$ is the corresponding association property of the components of $\mathbf{X}$. The notion of association of a set of random variables is due to Esary, Proschan, and Walkup (1967):

Definition 4.3.4. A set of random variables $\{X_1, \ldots, X_n\}$ is said to be (positively) associated if

$$\mathrm{Cov}(g_1(X_1, \ldots, X_n), g_2(X_1, \ldots, X_n)) \geq 0 \tag{4.3.3}$$

holds, or equivalently,

$$Eg_1(X_1, \ldots, X_n)g_2(X_1, \ldots, X_n) \geq Eg_1(X_1, \ldots, X_n)Eg_2(X_1, \ldots, X_n) \tag{4.3.4}$$

holds, for all g_1, g_2 which are nondecreasing in each coordinate when the other coordinates are held fixed (provided that the expectations in (4.3.4) exist).

If the components of an n-dimensional random variable $\mathbf{X} = (X_1, \ldots, X_n)'$ form a set of associated random variables, then we immediately obtain many useful inequalities. For example, we immediately have

$$P[g_1(\mathbf{X}) \geq \lambda_1, g_2(\mathbf{X}) \geq \lambda_2] \geq \prod_{i=1}^{2} P[g_i(\mathbf{X}) \geq \lambda_i] \tag{4.3.5}$$

for all nonnegative and nondecreasing functions g_1, g_2. Thus we have

$$P\left[\bigcap_{i=1}^{n} \{X_i \geq \lambda_i\}\right] \geq \prod_{i=1}^{n} P[X_i \geq \lambda_i]. \tag{4.3.6}$$

A key result in this area is the following theorem due to Fortuin, Kastelyn, and Ginibre (1971).

Proposition 4.3.1. *If the density function $f(\mathbf{x})$ of $\mathbf{X} = (X_1, \ldots, X_n)'$ is MTP_2, then $\{X_1, \ldots, X_n\}$ is a set of associated random variables.*

This proposition is known as the FKG inequality. Consequently, the condition on $f(\mathbf{x})$ given in (4.3.2) is also known as the FKG condition.

When applying these results to the multivariate normal distribution, an important problem is the verification of the FKG condition (hence the MTP_2 property) of the normal density function in terms of the parameters of the distribution. For the bivariate case, by the identity

$$\begin{pmatrix} \sigma_1^2 & \rho\sigma_1\sigma_2 \\ \rho\sigma_1\sigma_2 & \sigma_2^2 \end{pmatrix}^{-1} = \frac{1}{\sigma_1^2\sigma_2^2(1-\rho^2)} \begin{pmatrix} \sigma_2^2 & -\rho\sigma_1\sigma_2 \\ -\rho\sigma_1\sigma_2 & \sigma_1^2 \end{pmatrix} \equiv (\tau_{ij}),$$

we immediately have

$$\frac{f(x_1, x_2^*; \boldsymbol{\mu}, \boldsymbol{\Sigma}) f(x_1^*, x_2; \boldsymbol{\mu}, \boldsymbol{\Sigma})}{f(x_1, x_2; \boldsymbol{\mu}, \boldsymbol{\Sigma}) f(x_1^*, x_2^*; \boldsymbol{\mu}, \boldsymbol{\Sigma})} = \exp\left[\frac{-\rho(x_1 - x_1^*)(x_2 - x_2^*)}{\sigma_1\sigma_2(1-\rho^2)}\right].$$

Thus f is TP_2 if and only if $\tau_{12} \le 0$ (i.e., if an only if $\rho \ge 0$). This suggests that for the $\mathcal{N}_n(\boldsymbol{\mu}, \boldsymbol{\Sigma})$ distribution, $\boldsymbol{\Sigma} > 0$, all the off-diagonal elements of $\mathbf{T} = \boldsymbol{\Sigma}^{-1}$ should be nonpositive. Such a result was given by Barlow and Proschan (1975, pp. 149–150).

Theorem 4.3.2. *Let $\mathbf{X} = (X_1, \ldots, X_n)'$ have an $\mathcal{N}_n(\boldsymbol{\mu}, \boldsymbol{\Sigma})$ distribution, $\boldsymbol{\Sigma} > 0$, and let $\mathbf{T} = (\tau_{ij}) = \boldsymbol{\Sigma}^{-1}$. Then its density function $f(\mathbf{x}; \boldsymbol{\mu}, \boldsymbol{\Sigma})$ is MTP_2 if and only if $\tau_{ij} \le 0$ holds for all $i \ne j$.*

PROOF. (a)

(i) We first show that if $\tau_{12} \le 0$, then $f(x_1, x_2, \mathbf{x}_3; \boldsymbol{\mu}, \boldsymbol{\Sigma})$ is TP_2 in $(x_1, x_2)'$ for every fixed $\mathbf{x}_3 = (x_3, \ldots, x_n)'$. For arbitrary but fixed $\mathbf{y}_1 = (y_1, y_2)'$, $\mathbf{y}_1^* = (y_1^*, y_2^*)'$ in $\Re^2$ let $\mathbf{x}_1 = (x_1, x_2)'$ and $\mathbf{x}_1^* = (x_1^*, x_2^*)'$, where

$$x_i = \max\{y_i, y_i^*\}, \qquad x_i^* = \min\{y_i, y_i^*\}, \qquad i = 1, 2,$$

and define

$$\delta_{12} = \log\left[\frac{f(\mathbf{y}_1, \mathbf{x}_3; \boldsymbol{\mu}, \boldsymbol{\Sigma}) f(\mathbf{y}_1^*, \mathbf{x}_3; \boldsymbol{\mu}, \boldsymbol{\Sigma})}{f(\mathbf{x}_1, \mathbf{x}_3; \boldsymbol{\mu}, \boldsymbol{\Sigma}) f(\mathbf{x}_1^*, \mathbf{x}_3; \boldsymbol{\mu}, \boldsymbol{\Sigma})}\right].$$

Then it follows that

$$\begin{aligned} \delta_{12} &= -\tau_{12}[(y_1 y_2 + y_1^* y_2^*) - (x_1 x_2 + x_1^* x_2^*)] \\ &= \begin{cases} -\tau_{12}(y_1 - y_1^*)(y_2 - y_2^*) & \text{if } (y_1 - y_1^*)(y_2 - y_2^*) \le 0, \\ 0 & \text{otherwise.} \end{cases} \end{aligned} \tag{4.3.7}$$

Thus $\tau_{12} \le 0$ implies $\delta_{12} \le 0$.

(ii) By the same argument in (i) it follows that if $\tau_{ij} \le 0$ holds for all $i \ne j$, then $f(\mathbf{x}; \boldsymbol{\mu}, \boldsymbol{\Sigma})$ is TP_2 in pairs. Thus, by Fact 4.3.2(a), it is MTP_2.

(b) If $\tau_{ij} > 0$ for some pair (i, j), then δ_{ij} defined in (a) is ≥ 0 for every fixed $\mathbf{x}_3$. Thus $f(\mathbf{x})$ is not TP_2 in $(x_i, x_j)'$. By Fact 4.3.2(b), $f(\mathbf{x})$ is not MTP_2. □

Remark 4.3.1. If $f(\mathbf{x}; \boldsymbol{\mu}, \boldsymbol{\Sigma})$ is MTP_2, then the off-diagonal elements of the covariance matrix $\boldsymbol{\Sigma}$ must be all nonnegative. To see this, suppose that $\sigma_{ij} < 0$

for some $i \neq j$. Then (by Theorem 3.3.1) the marginal distribution of $(X_i, X_j)'$ is bivariate normal with correlation coefficient $\rho_{ij} < 0$, and (by Theorem 4.3.1) the marginal density function of $(X_i, X_j)'$ is not TP_2. But if $f(\mathbf{x}; \boldsymbol{\mu}, \boldsymbol{\Sigma})$ has the MTP_2 property then, by Fact 4.3.2(b), the marginal density of $(X_i, X_j)'$ must be TP_2. Contradiction.

Remark 4.3.1 states that a necessary condition for normal variables to have an MTP_2 density function is that all the correlation coefficients are nonnegative. But this condition is not sufficient. To see this fact we consider the following example.

EXAMPLE 4.3.2. Let $\mathbf{X}$ have an $\mathcal{N}_3(\boldsymbol{\mu}, \boldsymbol{\Sigma})$ distribution where $\boldsymbol{\Sigma} = (\sigma_{ij})$ is the covariance matrix given in Example 3.4.1. That is,

$$\sigma_{ij} = 1 \quad (i = 1, 2, 3) \qquad \text{and} \qquad \sigma_{12} = 1 - 2\varepsilon, \qquad \sigma_{13} = \sigma_{23} = 1 - \varepsilon,$$

for $0 < \varepsilon < \frac{1}{2}$. Elementary calculation shows that $\tau_{12} = (\varepsilon^2/|\boldsymbol{\Sigma}|) > 0$, thus the density function of $\mathbf{X}$ is not MTP_2. □

In view of this example and Remark 4.3.1, Theorem 4.3.2 actually yields the association property for only *a proper subclass* of nonnegatively correlated normal variables. The question of great interest is whether *all* nonnegatively correlated normal variables are associated. This problem has a long history, and the question was finally answered in the affirmative by Pitt (1982). Pitt's result asserts that, as stated in the title of his paper, "Positively Correlated Normal Variables are Associated." (This result was later extended to the elliptically contoured distributions by Joag-Dev, Perlman, and Pitt (1983).) The result will be stated in Chapter 5 (Theorem 5.1.1) and a sketch of the proof will be given there.

4.3.3. M-Matrices and MTP_2, MRR_2 Properties

The important role the covariance matrix plays in a multivariate normal distribution leads to the consideration of M-matrices.

Definition 4.3.5 (see Karlin and Rinott (1983a)). An $n \times n$ matrix $\mathbf{T} = (\tau_{ij})$ is called an M-matrix if it is of the form $\mathbf{T} = \lambda \mathbf{I}_n - \mathbf{C}$, where $\mathbf{C}$ has nonnegative elements and $\lambda > 0$ exceeds the absolute value of every characteristic root of $\mathbf{C}$.

Karlin and Rinott (1983a) provided a comprehensive treatment on M-matrices as covariance matrices of multivariate distributions. It is known that (Fan, 1958)

Fact 4.3.3. $\mathbf{T} = (\tau_{ij})$ *such that* $\tau_{ij} \leq 0$ *for all* $i \neq j$ *is an* M*-matrix if and only if* $\mathbf{T}^{-1} \equiv \boldsymbol{\Sigma} = (\sigma_{ij})$ *exists and* $\sigma_{ij} \geq 0$ *for all* $i \neq j$.

For other equivalent conditions due to Fan (1958), see Fact 1 of Karlin and Rinott (1983a).

In view of Fact 4.3.3, we can restate Theorem 4.3.2 in terms of M-matrices.

Theorem 4.3.2′. *Let* $\mathbf{X} = (X_1, \ldots, X_n)'$ *have an* $\mathcal{N}_n(\boldsymbol{\mu}, \boldsymbol{\Sigma})$ *distribution,* $\boldsymbol{\Sigma} = (\sigma_{ij}) > 0$ *(i.e.,* $\boldsymbol{\Sigma}$ *is positive definite). Then the density function of* $\mathbf{X}$ *is* MTP_2 *if and only if* $\mathbf{T} = \boldsymbol{\Sigma}^{-1}$ *is an M-matrix.*

Other useful results concerning M-matrices given in Karlin and Rinott (1983a) yield a partial ordering of positive dependence of normal variables. We summarize one of the results in the following theorem.

Theorem 4.3.3. *Assume that* $\mathbf{X} = (X_1, \ldots, X_n)'$ *have an* $\mathcal{N}_n(\boldsymbol{\mu}, \boldsymbol{\Sigma})$ *distribution,* $\boldsymbol{\Sigma} > 0$.

(a) *The partial correlation coefficient* $\rho_{ij\cdot k+1,\ldots,n}$ *is nonnegative for all pairs* (i, j) *and all* $k \geq \max\{i, j\}$ *if and only if* $\boldsymbol{\Sigma}^{-1}$ *is an M-matrix.*
(b) *If* $\boldsymbol{\Sigma}^{-1}$ *is an M-matrix, then the simple and multiple correlation coefficients and the linear regression coefficients are all nonnegative.*

Remark 4.3.2. It is easy to verify (by Proposition 4.3.1) that the partial correlation coefficient $\rho_{ij\cdot k+1,\ldots,n}$ is nonnegative for all pairs (i, j) and all subsets of the components of $(X_{k+1}, \ldots, X_n)'$ if and only if the joint density function $f(\mathbf{x}; \boldsymbol{\mu}, \boldsymbol{\Sigma})$ is TP_2 in pairs. By Fact 4.3.2(a), this is equivalent to saying that $f(\mathbf{x}; \boldsymbol{\mu}, \boldsymbol{\Sigma})$ is MTP_2. Thus this argument provides another proof for Theorem 4.3.2.

The result in Theorem 4.3.3(a) is due to Bølviken (1982). For the proof of Theorem 4.3.3 and a discussion on partial ordering of positive dependence via inequalities for M-matrices, see Karlin and Rinott (1983a).

A different problem of interest, treated by Karlin and Rinott (1980b), is when the covariance matrix itself (instead of its inverse) is an M-matrix. (In this case all random variables are nonpositively correlated.) Karlin and Rinott (1980b) gave definitions of the multivariate-reverse-rule-of-order-2 (MRR_2) density functions and strongly MRR_2 (S-MRR_2) density functions, and then proved some related results. In particular, they showed that if $\mathbf{X} \sim \mathcal{N}_3(\boldsymbol{\mu}, \boldsymbol{\Sigma})$ and if $\boldsymbol{\Sigma}$ is an M-matrix, then $f(\mathbf{x}; \boldsymbol{\mu}, \boldsymbol{\Sigma})$ is S-MRR_2. For $n \geq 4$, however, the problem remains open.

4.4. Schur-Concavity Property

4.4.1. Majorization and Some Basic Facts

The notion of majorization concerns the diversity of the components of a vector. For fixed $n \geq 2$ let

$$\mathbf{a} = (a_1, \ldots, a_n)', \qquad \mathbf{b} = (b_1, \ldots, b_n)', \tag{4.4.1}$$

denote two real vectors. Let

$$a_{[1]} \geq a_{[2]} \geq \cdots \geq a_{[n]}, \qquad b_{[1]} \geq b_{[2]} \geq \cdots \geq b_{[n]} \tag{4.4.2}$$

be their ordered components.

Definition 4.4.1. **a** is said to majorize **b**, in symbols $\mathbf{a} \succ \mathbf{b}$, if

$$\sum_{i=1}^{m} a_{[i]} \geq \sum_{i=1}^{m} b_{[i]} \qquad \text{holds for} \quad m = 1, 2, \ldots, n-1 \tag{4.4.3}$$

and $\sum_{i=1}^{n} a_i = \sum_{i=1}^{n} b_i$.

This definition provides a partial ordering, namely, $\mathbf{a} \succ \mathbf{b}$ implies that (for a fixed sum) the a_i's are more diverse than the b_i's. In particular, we immediately have:

Fact 4.4.1. $\mathbf{a} \succ (\bar{a}, \ldots, \bar{a})'$ *holds for all* **a** *where* $\bar{a} = (1/n)\sum_{i=1}^{n} a_i$.

Fact 4.4.2. *If* $a_i \geq 0$ $(i = 1, \ldots, n)$, *then* $(\sum_{i=1}^{n} a_i, 0, \ldots, 0)' \succ \mathbf{a}$ *holds.*

The following facts are less trivial but play an important role in majorization inequalities.

Fact 4.4.3. $\mathbf{a} \succ \mathbf{b}$ *holds if and only if there exists a finite number of real vectors* $\mathbf{c}_1, \mathbf{c}_2, \ldots, \mathbf{c}_N$ *such that*

$$\mathbf{a} = \mathbf{c}_1 \succ \mathbf{c}_2 \succ \cdots \succ \mathbf{c}_{N-1} \succ \mathbf{c}_N = \mathbf{b},$$

and such that for all j, $\mathbf{c}_j$ *and* $\mathbf{c}_{j+1}$ *differ in two coordinates only.*

The next fact deals with majorization and convex (concave) functions. Let $\psi\colon \mathfrak{R} \to \mathfrak{R}$ denote any continuous convex (concave) function and let a_1, a_2, b_1, b_2 be real numbers. Then it is easy to see that

$$(a_1, a_2)' \succ (b_1, b_2)' \quad \Leftrightarrow \quad \frac{a_1 + a_2}{2} = \frac{b_1 + b_2}{2} \quad \text{and} \quad |a_1 - a_2| \geq |b_1 - b_2|$$

$$\Rightarrow \quad \psi(a_1) + \psi(a_2) \geq (\leq) \psi(b_1) + \psi(b_2).$$

This observation together with Fact 4.4.3 and a similar argument yields

Fact 4.4.4. $\mathbf{a} \succ \mathbf{b}$ *holds if and only if* $\sum_{i=1}^{n} \psi(a_i) \geq (\leq) \sum_{i=1}^{n} \psi(b_i)$ *holds for all continuous convex (concave) functions* $\psi\colon \mathfrak{R} \to \mathfrak{R}$.

By choosing $\psi(t) = t^2$ we have

Fact 4.4.4′. *If* $\mathbf{a} \succ \mathbf{b}$ *holds, then* $(n-1)^{-1}\sum_{i=1}^{n} (a_i - \bar{a})^2 \geq (n-1)^{-1}\sum_{i=1}^{n} (b_i - \bar{b})^2$ *holds. Thus majorization is stronger than the variance concept in measuring the diversity of the components of a vector.*

From a geometric viewpoint, the notion of majorization is also closely related to the convex combinations of permutations of a vector. Let $\pi_1(\mathbf{a})$, $\pi_2(\mathbf{a}), \ldots, \pi_{n!}(\mathbf{a})$ denote the $n!$ permutations of $\mathbf{a}$, then it is known that

Fact 4.4.5. $\mathbf{a} \succ \mathbf{b}$ *holds if and only if* $\mathbf{b} = \sum_{j=1}^{n!} \alpha_j \pi_j(\mathbf{a})$ *holds for a set of real numbes* $\alpha_1, \ldots, \alpha_{n!}$ *such that* $\alpha_j \geq 0$ *and* $\sum_{j=1}^{n!} \alpha_j = 1$.

Let $\Pi = \{\mathbf{P}_1, \ldots, \mathbf{P}_{n!}\}$ denote the group of permutation matrices. Then $\mathbf{b}$ is of the form $\sum_{j=1}^{n!} \alpha_j \pi_j(\mathbf{a})$ if and only if

$$\mathbf{b} = \sum_{\mathbf{P}_j \in \Pi} \alpha_j \mathbf{a} \mathbf{P}_j = \mathbf{a}\mathbf{Q},$$

where $\mathbf{Q} = \sum_{\mathbf{P}_j \in \Pi} \alpha_j \mathbf{P}_j$. But Birkhoff's theorem (see, e.g., Marshall and Olkin (1979, p. 19)) says that a square matrix $\mathbf{Q}$ is a convex combination of the permutation matrices if and only if it is a doubly stochastic matrix (i.e., a matrix with nonnegative elements such that the row sums and column sums are one). Thus we have

Fact 4.4.6. $\mathbf{a} \succ \mathbf{b}$ *holds if and only if there exists a doubly stochastic matrix* $\mathbf{Q}$ *such that* $\mathbf{b} = \mathbf{a}\mathbf{Q}$.

In view of Facts 4.4.5 and 4.4.6, we may regard the linear transformation $\mathbf{b} = \mathbf{a}\mathbf{Q}$ as an averaging process when the sum of the vector components is kept fixed. It is in this sense that we say that if $\mathbf{a} \succ \mathbf{b}$, then $\mathbf{b}$ is an "average" of $\mathbf{a}$ (Hardy, Littlewood, and Pólya (1934, 1952, p. 49)).

For a comprehensive treatment of majorization and related inequalities, see Marshall and Olkin (1979).

4.4.2. Schur-Concavity Property of Permutation-Symmetric Normal Densities

A fruitful application of the notion of majorization concerns inequalities via Schur-concave (and Schur-convex) functions.

Definition 4.4.2. A function $f(\mathbf{x})$: $\mathfrak{R}^n \to \mathfrak{R}$ is said to be a Schur-concave function if $\mathbf{x} \succ \mathbf{y}$ implies $f(\mathbf{x}) \leq f(\mathbf{y})$ for all $\mathbf{x}, \mathbf{y} \in \mathfrak{R}^n$.

That is, $f(\mathbf{x})$ is a Schur-concave function if the functional value becomes larger when the components of $\mathbf{x}$ are less diverse in the sense of majorization.

There are many known results concerning Schur-concave functions. We summarize some of the results in the following statements as special applications to the multivariate normal distribution. For more details, see Marshall and Olkin (1979).

Fact 4.4.7. *If $f(\mathbf{x})$ is a Schur-concave function of $\mathbf{x}$, then it is a permutation symmetric function of $\mathbf{x}$; i.e., $f(\mathbf{x}) = f(\pi(\mathbf{x}))$ holds for all $\mathbf{x} \in \Re^n$ where $\pi(\mathbf{x})$ is any permutation of the components of $\mathbf{x}$.*

PROOF. Clearly we have $\mathbf{x} \succ \pi(\mathbf{x})$ and $\pi(\mathbf{x}) \succ \mathbf{x}$ for all π and all $\mathbf{x} \in \Re^n$. By Definition 4.4.2 we then have $f(\mathbf{x}) \leq f(\pi(\mathbf{x}))$ and $f(\pi(\mathbf{x})) \geq f(\mathbf{x})$. Thus $f(\mathbf{x}) = f(\pi(\mathbf{x}))$ holds for all $\mathbf{x}$ and all permutations π. □

The next result establishes the Schur-concavity property of a permutation-symmetric A-unimodal density function. Recall that (Definition 4.2.2) a density function $f(\mathbf{x})$ is said to be A-unimodal if $A_\lambda = \{\mathbf{x}\colon f(\mathbf{x}) \geq \lambda\}$ is a convex set for all $\lambda > 0$.

Proposition 4.4.1. *If the density function $f(\mathbf{x})\colon \Re^n \to [0, \infty)$ of $\mathbf{X}$ is permutation-symmetric and A-unimodal, then it is a Schur-concave function of $\mathbf{x}$.*

PROOF. It suffices to show that $\mathbf{x} \succ \mathbf{y}$ implies $f(\mathbf{x}) \leq f(\mathbf{y})$. By Fact 4.4.3 we may, without loss of generality, assume that $\mathbf{x}, \mathbf{y}$ differ in two coordinates only. Since f is permutation symmetric, we may further assume (for notational convenience) that $\mathbf{x}, \mathbf{y}$ are of the form

$$\mathbf{x} = (x_1, x_2, x_3, \ldots, x_n)', \qquad \mathbf{y} = (y_1, y_2, x_3, \ldots, x_n)',$$

where $(x_3, \ldots, x_n)'$ is arbitrary but fixed and $(x_1, x_2)' \succ (y_1, y_2)'$; that is,

$$(y_1, y_2)' = \alpha(x_1, x_2)' + (1 - \alpha)(x_2, x_1)' \qquad \text{for some} \quad \alpha \in [0, 1].$$

This implies $\mathbf{y} = \alpha\mathbf{x} + (1 - \alpha)\pi(\mathbf{x})$ where $\pi(\mathbf{x})$ is the vector obtained by interchanging x_1, x_2 in $\mathbf{x}$. Now for any given $\lambda > 0$ if $f(\mathbf{x}) = f(\pi(\mathbf{x})) = \lambda$, then by the A-unimodality condition we have

$$f(\mathbf{y}) = f(\alpha\mathbf{x} + (1 - \alpha)\pi(\mathbf{x})) \geq \lambda.$$ □

Proposition 4.4.1 yields results for certain important special cases:

Fact 4.4.8. *If the density function $f(\mathbf{x})$ of $\mathbf{X}$ is permutation-symmetric and log-concave, then it is a Schur-concave function of $\mathbf{x}$.*

PROOF. Immediate from Propositions 4.2.2 and 4.4.1. □

When applying Fact 4.4.8 to i.i.d. random variables, a special result follows:

Fact 4.4.9. *Assume that $X_1, \ldots, X_n$ are i.i.d. random variables with a continuous common marginal density $h(x)\colon \Re \to [0, \infty)$ such that the support of h is an interval I. If $h(x)$ is a log-concave function of x for $x \in I$, then the joint density function $f(\mathbf{x}) = \prod_{i=1}^n h(x_i)$ is a Schur-concave function of $\mathbf{x}$ for $\mathbf{x} \in I \times I \times \cdots \times I$.*

This statement holds because the log-concavity of h implies the log-concavity of f. In fact, the converse of Fact 4.4.9 is also true. A precise argument can be given along the lines of Fact 4.4.4 with $h(x) = \log \psi(x)$, and can be found in Marshall and Olkin (1979, p. 11).

If $\mathbf{X} = (X_1, \ldots, X_n)'$ has independent components with a common $\mathcal{N}(\mu, \sigma^2)$ marginal distribution then, since the marginal density function is log-concave in $\mathfrak{R}$, by Fact 4.4.9 the joint density if log-concave in $\mathfrak{R}^n$. In the following proposition we see that even if the X_i's are not independent but are equally correlated, the same conclusion follows.

Theorem 4.4.1. *Let $f(\mathbf{x}; \boldsymbol{\mu}, \Sigma)$ be the density function of an $\mathcal{N}_n(\boldsymbol{\mu}, \Sigma)$ distribution, $\Sigma > 0$. If f is permutation symmetric, i.e., if*

$$\mu_1 = \cdots = \mu_n, \quad \sigma_1^2 = \cdots = \sigma_n^2, \quad \text{and} \quad \rho_{ij} = \rho \in \left(-\frac{1}{n-1}, 1\right) \quad \text{for all} \quad i \neq j,$$

then it is a Schur-concave function of $\mathbf{x}$.

PROOF. By Theorem 4.2.1, $f(\mathbf{x}; \boldsymbol{\mu}, \Sigma)$ is a log-concave function of $\mathbf{x} \in \mathfrak{R}^n$. Thus it is A-unimodal (Proposition 4.2.2). Since it is also permutation symmetric, by Proposition 4.4.1 it is a Schur-concave function of $\mathbf{x}$. □

Once this Schur-concavity property is obtained, all of the existing results concerning log-concave functions immediately apply to permutation-symmetric multivariate normal density functions. In particular, the following convolution result due to Marshall and Olkin (1974 or 1979, p. 100) is of special interest.

Proposition 4.4.2. *If f and g are Schur-concave functions defined on $\mathfrak{R}^n$, then the function ψ defined on $\mathfrak{R}^n$ by*

$$\psi(\boldsymbol{\theta}) = \int_{\mathfrak{R}^n} g(\boldsymbol{\theta} - \mathbf{x}) f(\mathbf{x})\, d\mathbf{x}$$

is Schur-concave (whenever the integral exists).

As an illustration of an application of this result to the multivariate normal distribution, first note that the distribution function $F(\mathbf{a})$ of an n-dimensional random variable $\mathbf{X}$ can be expressed in the form

$$F(\mathbf{a}) = \int_{-\infty}^{a_1} \cdots \int_{-\infty}^{a_n} f(\mathbf{x})\, dx = \int_{\mathfrak{R}^n} \left\{ \prod_{i=1}^{n} I_{(-\infty, a_i]} \right\} f(\mathbf{x})\, d\mathbf{x},$$

where

$$I_{(-\infty, a_i]} = \begin{cases} 1 & \text{if} \quad a_i - x_i \geq 0, \\ 0 & \text{otherwise} \end{cases}$$

is the indicator function of $\{x_i: x_i \le a_i\}$. Since the indicator function $g(\mathbf{x})$ of the set

$$A = \{\mathbf{x}: \mathbf{x} \in \mathfrak{R}^n, x_i \ge 0, i = 1, \ldots, n\}$$

is a Schur-concave function of $\mathbf{x}$ and (by $g(\mathbf{a} - \mathbf{x}) = \prod_{i=1}^n I_{(-\infty, a_i)}$) $F(\mathbf{a})$ can be written as

$$F(\mathbf{a}) = \int_{\mathfrak{R}^n} g(\mathbf{a} - \mathbf{x}) f(\mathbf{x})\, d\mathbf{x},$$

it follows that (Marshall and Olkin, 1974)

Proposition 4.4.3. *If* $\mathbf{X} = (X_1, \ldots, X_n)'$ *has a Schur-concave density function, then its distribution function* $F(\mathbf{a})$ *is a Schur-concave function of* $\mathbf{a}$ *for* $\mathbf{a} \in \mathfrak{R}^n$.

As an immediate consequence, we observe

Theorem 4.4.2. *If* $\mathbf{X} = (X_1, \ldots, X_n)'$ *has a multivariate normal distribution with a common mean, a common variance, and a common correlation coefficient* $\rho \in [-1/(n-1), 1]$, *then its distribution function* $F(\mathbf{a})$ *is a Schur-concave function of* $\mathbf{a}$.

PROOF. If the covariance matrix $\boldsymbol{\Sigma}$ is positive definite (i.e., if $-1/(n-1) < \rho < 1$), then the statement follows immediately from Theorem 4.4.1 and Proposition 4.4.3. If $\boldsymbol{\Sigma}$ is positive semidefinite, then there exists a sequence of positive definite covariance matrices $\{\boldsymbol{\Sigma}_t\}$ such that $\boldsymbol{\Sigma}_t \to \boldsymbol{\Sigma}$ as $t \to \infty$. Since for $\mathbf{a} \succ \mathbf{b}$ we have

$$F_{\boldsymbol{\Sigma}_t}(\mathbf{a}) \le F_{\boldsymbol{\Sigma}_t}(\mathbf{b}), \qquad t = 1, 2, \ldots,$$

the inequality is preserved when passing to the limit. □

We note in passing that when $n = 2$, 3, and $\mathbf{b} = (\bar{a}, \ldots, \bar{a})'$, the corresponding results are already given in Examples 4.2.1 and 4.2.2 by applying Prékopa's theorem. That theorem can be applied even if the underlying multivariate normal density function is not permutation symmetric. However, when it *is* permutation symmetric, then an application of majorization inequalities yields deeper results. Some additional applications will be treated more comprehensively in Chapter 7.

4.5. Arrangement-Increasing Property

Let $\mathbf{x} = (x_1, \ldots, x_n)'$ and $\boldsymbol{\mu} = (\mu_1, \ldots, \mu_n)'$ be two real vectors in $\mathfrak{R}^n$. Let $\boldsymbol{\pi} = (\pi_1, \ldots, \pi_n)$ be a permutation of the set of integers $\{1, 2, \ldots, n\}$, and denote

$$\boldsymbol{\pi}(\mathbf{x}) = (x_{\pi_1}, \ldots, x_{\pi_n})', \qquad \boldsymbol{\pi}(\boldsymbol{\mu}) = (\mu_{\pi_1}, \ldots, \mu_{\pi_n})'$$

as the corresponding vectors obtained by permuting the elements of $\mathbf{x}$ and $\boldsymbol{\mu}$. Let us consider a function of $2n$ variables of the form

$$f(\mathbf{x}; \boldsymbol{\mu}): \mathfrak{R}^n \times \mathfrak{R}^n \to \mathfrak{R}.$$

Such a function is said to be an arrangement permutation-symmetric function of $(\mathbf{x}, \boldsymbol{\mu})$ if for every permutation π we have

$$f(\pi(\mathbf{x}), \pi(\boldsymbol{\mu})) = f(\mathbf{x}, \boldsymbol{\mu}) \qquad \text{for all} \quad \mathbf{x}, \boldsymbol{\mu} \in \mathfrak{R}^n.$$

Fact 4.5.1. *Let $f = f(\mathbf{x}; \boldsymbol{\mu}, \boldsymbol{\Sigma})$ be the density function of an $\mathcal{N}_n(\boldsymbol{\mu}, \boldsymbol{\Sigma})$ distribution. If $\boldsymbol{\Sigma} = \sigma^2\mathbf{R}$, where $\mathbf{R}$ is a correlation matrix such that*

$$\rho_{ij} = \rho \in \left(-\frac{1}{n-1}, 1\right) \qquad \textit{for all} \quad i \neq j,$$

and $\sigma^2 > 0$ is arbitrary but fixed, then f is an arrangement permutation-symmetric function of $(\mathbf{x}, \boldsymbol{\mu})$.

Proof. Immediate from the identity

$$(\mathbf{x} - \boldsymbol{\mu})'\boldsymbol{\Sigma}^{-1}(\mathbf{x} - \boldsymbol{\mu}) = (\pi(\mathbf{x}) - \pi(\boldsymbol{\mu}))'\boldsymbol{\Sigma}^{-1}(\pi(\mathbf{x}) - \pi(\boldsymbol{\mu}))$$

for all π and all $\mathbf{x}, \boldsymbol{\mu} \in \mathfrak{R}^n$. □

If f is an arrangement permutation-symmetric function, then for notational convenience we may assume that the components of $\mathbf{x}$ are already arranged in ascending order (i.e., $x_1 \leq x_2 \leq \cdots \leq x_n$), in symbols $\mathbf{x}\uparrow$. Consequently, the problem of interest is how the function behaves when the components of $\boldsymbol{\mu}$ are rearranged. More precisely, we are interested in a certain "monotonicity" property in the sense that the functional value increases when the components of $\boldsymbol{\mu}$ are similarly ordered.

To observe a more general result, a notion of the partial ordering of permutations is needed. Let $\boldsymbol{\mu}$ and $\mathbf{v}$ be two real vectors. We define "$\boldsymbol{\mu} \overset{p}{<} \mathbf{v}$" to mean that for some indices i, j, $1 \leq i < j \leq n$,

$$\mu_j = v_i < v_j = \mu_i \qquad \text{and} \qquad \mu_k = v_k \qquad \text{for all} \quad k \neq i, k \neq j.$$

That is, $\mathbf{v}$ can be obtained from $\boldsymbol{\mu}$ by interchanging μ_i and μ_j such that μ_i and μ_j are now rearranged in ascending order while all other components in $\boldsymbol{\mu}$ are held fixed. Furthermore, we define that "$\boldsymbol{\mu} \overset{b}{<} \mathbf{v}$" (Sobel, 1954; Savage, 1957; Lehmann, 1966; and Hollander, Proschan, and Sethuraman, 1977; see Marshal and Olkin (1979, p. 159)) stating that there exists a finite number of vectors $\mathbf{v}_1, \ldots, \mathbf{v}_N$ such that

$$\boldsymbol{\mu} = \mathbf{v}_1 \overset{p}{<} \mathbf{v}_2 \overset{p}{<} \cdots \overset{p}{<} \mathbf{v}_{N-1} \overset{p}{<} \mathbf{v}_N = \mathbf{v}. \tag{4.5.1}$$

This is to say that $\mathbf{v}$ can be obtained from $\boldsymbol{\mu}$ by rearranging two components at a time in this fashion in a finite number of operations.

EXAMPLE 4.5.1. For $n = 3$ it is easy to see that

$$(3, 2, 1)' \overset{p}{<} (3, 1, 2)' \overset{p}{<} (1, 3, 2)' \overset{p}{<} (1, 2, 3)',$$
$$(3, 2, 1)' \overset{p}{<} (2, 3, 1)' \overset{p}{<} (2, 1, 3)' \overset{p}{<} (1, 2, 3)'.$$

Thus $(3, 2, 1)' \overset{b}{<} (1, 2, 3)'$ holds and, by interchanging 1 and 3 directly, $(3, 2, 1)' \overset{p}{<} (1, 2, 3)'$ also holds. But we have neither $(3, 1, 2)' \overset{b}{<} (2, 3, 1)'$ nor $(2, 3, 1)' \overset{b}{<} (3, 1, 2)'$. □

The definition of arrangment-increasing functions follows from this notion of partial ordering of vectors.

Definition 4.5.1. $f(\mathbf{x}, \boldsymbol{\mu})$: $\mathfrak{R}^n \times \mathfrak{R}^n \to \mathfrak{R}$ is said to be an arrangement-increasing (AI) function of $(\mathbf{x}, \boldsymbol{\mu})$ if f is arrangement permutation-symmetric and if

$f(\mathbf{x}\uparrow, \boldsymbol{\mu}) \le f(\mathbf{x}\uparrow, \mathbf{v})$ holds for all $\mathbf{x}$ and all $\boldsymbol{\mu}$, $\mathbf{v}$ in $\mathfrak{R}^n$ such that $\boldsymbol{\mu} \overset{b}{<} \mathbf{v}$.

Many useful functions are known to be arrangement-increasing (see Hollander, Proschan, and Sethuraman (1977) and Marshall and Olkin (1979, Sec. 6.F)). One of them is the inner product of two vectors.

EXAMPLE 4.5.2. Let $\mathbf{a} = (a_1, \ldots, a_n)'$, $\mathbf{b} = (b_1, \ldots, b_n)'$, be two real vectors in $\mathfrak{R}^n$. Then the function $f(\mathbf{a}, \mathbf{b}) = \sum_{k=1}^n a_k b_k$ is an arrangement-increasing function of $(\mathbf{a}, \mathbf{b})$ (Sobel, 1954). In particular, for $a_{(1)} \le a_{(2)} \le \cdots \le a_{(n)}$ and $b_{(1)} \le b_{(2)} \le \cdots \le b_{(n)}$, we have

$$\sum_{k=1}^n a_{(k)} b_{(n-k+1)} \le \sum_{k=1}^n a_k b_k \le \sum_{k=1}^n a_{(k)} b_{(k)}$$

(Hardy, Littlewood, and Pólya, 1934, 1952, Chap. 10).

PROOF. Let $\mathbf{b}^{(1)} \overset{b}{<} \mathbf{b}^{(2)}$, and without loss of generality we may assume that $\mathbf{b}^{(1)} \overset{p}{<} \mathbf{b}^{(2)}$. Then

$$\sum_{k=1}^n a_{(k)} b_k^{(1)} - \sum_{k=1}^n a_{(k)} b_k^{(2)} = (a_{(j)} - a_{(i)})(b_i^{(1)} - b_j^{(1)}) \le 0$$

holds for some $1 \le i < j \le n$ and $b_i^{(1)} < b_j^{(1)}$. □

Our main aim in this section is to show that

Theorem 4.5.1. *Let $f(\mathbf{x}; \boldsymbol{\mu}, \boldsymbol{\Sigma})$ be the density function of an $\mathcal{N}_n(\boldsymbol{\mu}, \boldsymbol{\Sigma})$ distribution. If $\boldsymbol{\Sigma}$ is of the form $\sigma^2\mathbf{R}$ where $\mathbf{R}$ is a correlation matrix such that*

$$\rho_{ij} = \rho \in \left(-\frac{1}{n-1}, 1\right) \qquad \text{for all} \quad i \ne j \tag{4.5.2}$$

for arbitrary but fixed $\sigma^2 > 0$, then f is an arrangement-increasing function of

$(\mathbf{x}, \boldsymbol{\mu})$. *Consequently, we have*

$$f(\mathbf{x}; \boldsymbol{\mu}, \boldsymbol{\Sigma}) \le f(\mathbf{x}\uparrow; \boldsymbol{\mu}\uparrow, \boldsymbol{\Sigma}) \qquad \textit{for all} \quad \mathbf{x}, \boldsymbol{\mu} \in \Re^n.$$

We provide two different proofs below. The first proof involves a more general theorem concerning log-concave densities and arrangement-increasing functions, the second proof depends on a direct verification.

First Proof. Lemmma 2.2(a) of Hollander, Proschan, and Sethuraman (1977) states that if $f(\mathbf{x}; \boldsymbol{\mu}, \boldsymbol{\Sigma}) = g(\mathbf{x} - \boldsymbol{\mu})$ (for fixed $\boldsymbol{\Sigma}$) for some function $g: \Re^n \to \Re$ and is arrangement permutation-symmetric, then f is an arrangement-increasing function of $(\mathbf{x}, \boldsymbol{\mu})$ if and only if g is a Schur-concave function. The proof follows from this lemma, the details are left to the reader. □

Second Proof. If $\mathbf{R}$ is of the form given in (4.5.2), then $\mathbf{R}^{-1} = (\tau_{ij})$ is of the form

$$\tau_{ij} = \begin{cases} \dfrac{1 + (n-2)\rho}{\Delta_n(\rho)} & \text{for} \quad i = j, \\[2ex] \dfrac{-\rho}{\Delta_n(\rho)} & \text{for} \quad i \ne j, \end{cases}$$

where $\Delta_n(\rho) = (1 - \rho)[1 + (n-1)\rho] > 0$ (see Proposition 5.2.3 for the derivation of this result). To prove the proposition we may, without loss of generality, assume that $\boldsymbol{\mu} \overset{p}{<} \mathbf{v}$ and show that $f(\mathbf{x}\uparrow; \boldsymbol{\mu}, \boldsymbol{\Sigma}) \le f(\mathbf{x}\uparrow; \mathbf{v}, \boldsymbol{\Sigma})$. Furthermore, for notational convenience it may be assumed that

$$\boldsymbol{\mu} = (\mu_2, \mu_1, \mu_3, \ldots, \mu_n)', \qquad \mathbf{v} = (\mu_1, \mu_2, \mu_3, \ldots, \mu_n)',$$

where $\mu_1 < \mu_2$ and $\mu_3, \ldots, \mu_n$ are arbitrary but fixed. By the identity

$$(\mathbf{x} - \boldsymbol{\mu})'\boldsymbol{\Sigma}^{-1}(\mathbf{x} - \boldsymbol{\mu}) = \mathbf{x}'\boldsymbol{\Sigma}^{-1}\mathbf{x} + \boldsymbol{\mu}'\boldsymbol{\Sigma}^{-1}\boldsymbol{\mu} - 2\boldsymbol{\mu}'\boldsymbol{\Sigma}^{-1}\mathbf{x},$$

it follows that

$$(\mathbf{x}\uparrow - \boldsymbol{\mu})'\boldsymbol{\Sigma}^{-1}(\mathbf{x}\uparrow - \boldsymbol{\mu}) - (\mathbf{x}\uparrow - \mathbf{v})'\boldsymbol{\Sigma}^{-1}(\mathbf{x}\uparrow - \mathbf{v}) = \frac{2(\mu_2 - \mu_1)(x_2 - x_1)}{\sigma^2(1-\rho)} > 0 \tag{4.5.3}$$

for all $x_1 \le x_2$. Thus $f(\mathbf{x}\uparrow; \boldsymbol{\mu}, \boldsymbol{\Sigma}) \le f(\mathbf{x}\uparrow; \mathbf{v}, \boldsymbol{\Sigma})$ holds. □

The arrangement-increasing property established in Theorem 4.5.1 yields many interesting results for the multivariate normal distribution, and has useful applications in certain statistical inference problems. One of the applications is illustrated in the following example:

Example 4.5.3. Suppose that observations $X_1, X_2, \ldots, X_n$ are taken from n independent normal populations such that $X_i \sim \mathcal{N}(\mu_i, \sigma^2)$, $i = 1, \ldots, n$, where σ^2 is known. Suppose further that the values of $\mu_1, \ldots, \mu_n$ are known but it is not known which mean belongs to which population, and the statistical problem is to make a decision concerning the correct identification. Then an application of Theorem 4.5.1 implies that, according to the maximum likelihood principle, we should assert that the mean of the population associated with $X_{(i)}$ is $\mu_{(i)}$, where

$$X_{(1)} \leq \cdots \leq X_{(n)}, \qquad \mu_{(1)} \leq \cdots \leq \mu_{(n)}$$

are the ordered values of $X_1, \ldots, X_n$ and of $\mu_1, \ldots, \mu_n$, respectively. When the values of the μ_i's are unknown and we are interested in correctly ranking the means of the X_i's, a similar result follows. In Bechhofer, Kiefer, and Sobel (1968) this principle was applied extensively for ranking the parameters in an exponential family (including the normal means) in a sequential setting. □

Theorem 4.5.1 has another application that is similar but different from the one given in Example 4.5.3: Let $(X_1, \ldots, X_n)'$ have an $\mathcal{N}_n(\boldsymbol{\mu}, \boldsymbol{\Sigma})$ distribution where $\boldsymbol{\Sigma}$ has the form described in (4.5.2) and, without loss of generality, assume that $\mu_1 \leq \mu_2 \leq \cdots \leq \mu_n$. Let $\mathbf{T} = (T_1, \ldots, T_n)'$ denote the rank vector of the coomponents of $\mathbf{X}$, that is, $\mathbf{T} = (t_1, \ldots, t_n)' \equiv \mathbf{t}$ means that X_1 is the t_1th smallest, X_2 is the t_2th smallest, etc., among $X_1, \ldots, X_n$. Then Theorem 4.5.1 implies that among all the possible $\mathbf{t}$ vectors which are permutations of $(1, 2, \ldots, n)'$, the probability function $P_{\boldsymbol{\mu}\uparrow}[\mathbf{T} = \mathbf{t}]$ is maximized when $\mathbf{t} = \mathbf{t}_0 \equiv (1, 2, \ldots, n)'$.

This observation leads to an interesting question: Is a stronger result possible such that this probability can be partially ordered? The answer to this question is in the affirmative, as stated in the following theorem (which is a special case of a result in Hollander, Proschan, and Sethuraman (1977)).

Theorem 4.5.2. *Let* $\mathbf{X} = (X_1, \ldots, X_n)'$ *have an* $\mathcal{N}_n(\boldsymbol{\mu}, \sigma^2\mathbf{R})$ *distribution where* $\mathbf{R}$ *is a correlation matrix. If all the correlation coefficients* ρ_{ij} *are equal to* ρ *for* $i \neq j$ *for some* $\rho \in (-1/(n-1), 1)$, *then* $P_{\boldsymbol{\mu}}[\mathbf{T} = \mathbf{t}]$ *is an arrangement-increasing function of* $(\boldsymbol{\mu}, \mathbf{t})$. *Consequently, we have*

$$P_{\boldsymbol{\mu}\uparrow}[\mathbf{T} = \mathbf{t}_1] \leq P_{\boldsymbol{\mu}\uparrow}[\mathbf{T} = \mathbf{t}_2] \leq P_{\boldsymbol{\mu}\uparrow}[\mathbf{T} = \mathbf{t}_0]$$

for all $\mathbf{t}_1 \overset{b}{<} \mathbf{t}_2$ *which are permutations of* $(1, 2, \ldots, n)' \equiv \mathbf{t}_0$.

PROOF. Immediate from Theorem 4.4 of Hollander, Proschan, and Sethuraman (1977). □

In the following, we consider an example for the purpose of illustration.

EXAMPLE 4.5.4. Suppose that $\mathbf{X} \sim \mathcal{N}_3(\boldsymbol{\mu}, \boldsymbol{\Sigma})$ where the X_i's have a common variance σ^2 and are either equally correlated or are independent. Furthermore, suppose that $\mu_1 \leq \mu_2 \leq \mu_3$. Then by Example 4.5.1 we have

$$P_{\boldsymbol{\mu}}[\mathbf{T} = (3, 2, 1)'](= P_{\boldsymbol{\mu}}[X_3 \leq X_2 \leq X_1])$$
$$\leq P_{\boldsymbol{\mu}}[\mathbf{T} = (3, 1, 2)'] \leq P_{\boldsymbol{\mu}}[\mathbf{T} = (1, 3, 2)'] \leq P_{\boldsymbol{\mu}}[\mathbf{T} = (1, 2, 3)']. \quad \square$$

Problems

4.1. Verify the identity in (4.1.4).

4.2. Verify the identity in (4.1.5).

4.3. Show that for $n = 2$, the result in Theorem 4.1.1 is equivalent to the Box–Muller result given in Theorem 2.1.3.

4.4. Show that if $\mathbf{\Sigma}$ is an $n \times n$ positive definite matrix, then $g(\mathbf{x}) = \mathbf{x}'\mathbf{\Sigma}\mathbf{x}$ is a convex function of $\mathbf{x}$ for $\mathbf{x} \in \mathfrak{R}^n$.

4.5. Show that if $A_1, \ldots, A_k$ are symmetric (about the origin) and convex sets in $\mathfrak{R}^n$, then $\sum_{i=1}^k \alpha_i A_i$ is a symmetric and convex set in $\mathfrak{R}^n$ for all $\alpha_1, \ldots, \alpha_k$.

4.6. Show that if $\mathbf{X} \sim \mathcal{N}_n(\boldsymbol{\mu}, \mathbf{\Sigma})$, $\mathbf{\Sigma} > 0$, and if B contains a single point in $\mathfrak{R}^n$, then the inequality in (4.2.3) is trivial.

4.7. Verify the identities in (4.2.5) and (4.2.6).

4.8. Let $A_1 = \{\mathbf{u}\colon \mathbf{u} \in \mathfrak{R}^2, |u_1| \le a_1, |u_2| \le a_2\}$ and let $A_2 = \{\mathbf{u}\colon \mathbf{u} \in \mathfrak{R}^2, |u_1| \le a_2, |u_2| \le a_1\}$. Show that

$$\tfrac{1}{2}A_1 + \tfrac{1}{2}A_2 = \{\mathbf{u}\colon \mathbf{u} \in \mathfrak{R}^2, |u_1| \le \bar{a}, |u_2| \le \bar{a}\},$$

where $\bar{a} = \frac{1}{2}(a_1 + a_2)$.

4.9. Show that if $(X_1, X_2)'$ has a bivariate normal distribution with means 0, variances σ^2, and correlation coefficient $\rho \in (-1, 1)$, then

$$P[|X_1| \le a_1, |X_1| \le a_2] \le P[|X_1| \le \bar{a}, |X_1| \le \bar{a}],$$

for $\bar{a} = \frac{1}{2}(a_1 + a_2)$ (Tong, 1982a).

4.10. Let $\mathbf{X} \sim \mathcal{N}_n(\boldsymbol{\mu}, \mathbf{\Sigma})$, $\mathbf{\Sigma} > 0$, and let $A \subset \mathfrak{R}^n$ be symmetric (about the origin) and convex. Show that

$$P_{\boldsymbol{\mu}=\boldsymbol{\mu}_0}[\mathbf{X} \in A] = P_{\boldsymbol{\mu}=-\boldsymbol{\mu}_0}[\mathbf{X} \in A]$$

holds for all $\boldsymbol{\mu}_0 \in \mathfrak{R}^n$.

4.11. For $n \ge 2$ let $f(\mathbf{x}; \boldsymbol{\mu}, \mathbf{\Sigma})$ be the density function of an $\mathcal{N}_n(\boldsymbol{\mu}, \mathbf{\Sigma})$ distribution, $\mathbf{\Sigma} > 0$. Show that the condition in (4.2.8) is satisfied for $B = \{\mathbf{x}\colon \mathbf{x} \in \mathfrak{R}^n, |x_1| \le a\}$ and $\mathbf{u} = (1, 0, \ldots, 0)'$ where $a > 0$ is arbitrary but fixed (Anderson, 1988).

4.12. Verify the details in the proof of Example 4.2.2.

4.13. Consider the bivariate Cauchy density function

$$f(x_1, x_2) = c(1 + x_1^2 + x_2^2)^{-3/2} \qquad \text{for} \quad (x_1, x_2)' \in \mathfrak{R}^2,$$

where c is a positive real number. Show that f is A-unimodal but is not log-concave.

4.14. Let $f(x_1, x_2; \boldsymbol{\mu}, \mathbf{\Sigma})$ be the density function of an $\mathcal{N}_2(\boldsymbol{\mu}, \mathbf{\Sigma})$ distribution with correlation coefficient $\rho \in (-1, 1)$. Show directly by definition that if $\rho < 0$, then the family of conditional densities of X_1, given $-X_2 = y$, has the monotone likelihood ratio property. Consequently, all the inequalities in (b), (d), and (e) of Section 2.3 are reversed.

4.15. Let $f(\mathbf{x}; \boldsymbol{\mu}, \boldsymbol{\Sigma})$ be the density function of an $\mathcal{N}_3(\boldsymbol{\mu}, \boldsymbol{\Sigma})$ distribution where $\boldsymbol{\Sigma}$ is given in Example 4.3.2. Show that for every fixed $X_3 = x_3$, the conditional density function of $(X_1, X_2)'$ is not TP_2.

4.16. Verify (4.3.7).

4.17. Show that $\mathbf{a} \succ \mathbf{b}$ holds if and only if $-\mathbf{a} \succ -\mathbf{b}$ holds.

4.18. Show that $f(\mathbf{x})$ is a Schur-concave function of $\mathbf{x}$ if and only if $f(-\mathbf{x})$ is a Schur-concave function of $\mathbf{x}$ for $\mathbf{x} \in \mathfrak{R}^n$.

4.19. Show that a permutation-symmetric two-variable function $f(x_1, x_2)$ is Schur-concave if and only if

$$a_1 + a_2 = b_1 + b_2 \qquad \text{and} \qquad |a_1 - a_2| > |b_1 - b_2|,$$

implies $f(a_1, a_2) \leq f(b_1, b_2)$.

4.20. Let $f(x_1, x_2; \boldsymbol{\mu}, \boldsymbol{\Sigma})$ be the density function of an $\mathcal{N}_2(\boldsymbol{\mu}, \boldsymbol{\Sigma})$ distribution, where $\mu_1 = \mu_2, \sigma_1^2 = \sigma_2^2$, and $\rho \in (-1, 1)$. Use the statement in Problem 4.19 and a direct verification to show that f is a Schur-concave function of $(x_1, x_2)'$.

4.21. It is known (Tong, 1978) that $\Phi((x - \mu)/\sigma)$ is a log-concave function of x where $\Phi(z)$ is the $\mathcal{N}(0, 1)$ distribution function. Use this result and Fact 4.4.4 to show that if $X_1, \ldots, X_n$ are i.i.d. $\mathcal{N}(\mu, \sigma^2)$ variables, then $P[\bigcap_{i=1}^n \{X_i \leq a_i\}]$ is a Schur-concave function of $(a_1, \ldots, a_n)'$.

4.22. Let $X_1, \ldots, X_n$ be i.i.d. $\mathcal{N}(\mu, \sigma^2)$ variables and let $\mathbf{a} = (a_1, \ldots, a_n)'$, $\mathbf{b} = (b_1, \ldots, b_n)'$ be real vectors. Show that $\mathrm{Corr}(\sum_{i=1}^n a_i X_i, \sum_{i=1}^n b_i X_i)$ is an arrangement-increasing function of $(\mathbf{a}, \mathbf{b})$.

4.23. Verify the identity in (4.5.3).

CHAPTER 5

Positively Dependent and Exchangeable Normal Variables

The study of concepts of positive dependence of random variables, started in the late 1960s, has yielded numerous useful results in both statistical theory and applications. The results are generally given for large classes of distributions and are not just for the normal family. However, when the underlying distribution is multivariate normal, then many special results follow and most of them involve only the covariance matrix of the distribution.

In Section 5.1 we provide a survey of various notions of positive dependence of random variables and discuss their applications to the multivariate normal distribution. We show that, according to the most familar definitions of positive dependence (which we will describe), positively dependent normal variables are just nonnegatively correlated normal variables. Thus useful results can be obtained for such normal variables from the general theory of positive dependence.

Section 5.2 concerns certain basic distribution properties of permutation-symmetric normal variables; i.e., random variables whose joint distributions are multivariate normal with equal means, equal variances, and equal correlation coefficients. Those random variables are not necessarily positively dependent. If the common correlation coefficient is nonnegative, then they are exchangeable normal variables and are known to be positively dependent according to all of the definitions described in Section 5.1.

According to de Finetti's theorem, exchangeable random variables must be a mixture of conditionally independent and identically distributed random variables. The implications of this result for the multivariate normal distribution will be carefully examined in Section 5.3. Consequently, a characterization result for exchangeable normal variables will be discussed, and expressions for the joint density function and distribution function of exchangeable normal variables will be given. Furthermore, some partial orderings of the "strength" of positive dependence of exchangeable normal variables will be treated, and monotonicity results (as functions of the common correlation coefficient) will be proved.

5.1. Positively Dependent Normal Variables

Let $(X_1, \ldots, X_n)'$ be an n-dimensional random variable with density function $f(\mathbf{x})$. In this section we first discuss some notions of the positive dependence of $X_1, \ldots, X_n$ in general, and then give specific results for the multivariate normal distribution. The treatment is to be compared with that in Section 2.3 in the following sense: Section 2.3 contains positive dependence results for the bivariate normal distribution only, here we are concerned with corresponding results for the multivariate normal distribution.

5.1.1. Notions of Positive Dependence

We first observe the definition of MTP_2 density functions. This was already given in Section 4.3, for the purpose of completeness it is restated below:

Definition 5.1.1. The density function $f(\mathbf{x})$ of an n-dimensional random variable $\mathbf{X} = (X_1, \ldots, X_n)'$ is said to be multivariate-totally-positive-of-order-2 (MTP_2) if the inequality

$$f(\mathbf{y})f(\mathbf{y}^*) \leq f(\mathbf{x})f(\mathbf{x}^*)$$

holds for all $\mathbf{y} = (y_1, \ldots, y_n)'$ and $\mathbf{y}^* = (y_1^*, \ldots, y_n^*)'$ in the domain of f where

$$x_i^* = \min\{y_i, y_i^*\}, \qquad x_i = \max\{y_i, y_i^*\},$$

for $i = 1, \ldots, n$ and $\mathbf{x} = (x_1, \ldots, x_n)'$, $\mathbf{x}^* = (x_1^*, \ldots, x_n^*)'$.

The next definition, first considered by Veinott (1965) then treated more comprehensively by Barlow and Proschan (1975, pp. 146–149), concerns the monotonicity property of a sequence of conditional distributions.

Definition 5.1.2. The random variables $X_1, \ldots, X_n$ are said to be conditionally increasing in sequence (CIS) if the conditional probability

$$\alpha_{k,t} \equiv P[X_{k+1} > t \mid (X_1, \ldots, X_k)' = (x_1, \ldots, x_k)']$$

is a nondecreasing function of x_j for all t, all $1 \leq j \leq k$, all fixed $(x_1, \ldots, x_{j-1}, x_{j+1}, \ldots, x_k)'$, and all $k \leq n - 1$.

This definition provides a notion of positive dependence because when $X_1, \ldots, X_k$ take larger values, then X_{k+1} is more likely to take a larger value.

The next definition was previously stated in Section 4.3 and is restated below.

Definition 5.1.3. The random variables $X_1, \ldots, X_n$ are said to be (positively) associated (A) if

$$Eg_1(X_1, \ldots, X_n)g_2(X_1, \ldots, X_n) \geq Eg_1(X_1, \ldots, X_n)Eg_2(X_1, \ldots, X_n) \quad (5.1.1)$$

holds for all functions g_1, g_2 which are nondecreasing in each component, provided that the expectations exist.

Note that the inequality in (5.1.1) is equivalent to saying that

$$\operatorname{Cov}(g_1(X_1, \ldots, X_n), g_2(X_1, \ldots, X_n)) \geq 0 \quad (5.1.2)$$

holds, or equivalently,

$$\operatorname{Corr}(g_1(X_1, \ldots, X_n), g_2(X_1, \ldots, X_n)) \geq 0 \quad (5.1.3)$$

holds, for all nondecreasing functions g_1 and g_2.

An open set $A \subset \mathfrak{R}^n$ is said to be increasing if, for $\mathbf{x}^* = (x_1^*, \ldots, x_n^*)'$ and $\mathbf{x} = (x_1, \ldots, x_n)'$ in $\mathfrak{R}^n$, $\mathbf{x}^* \in A$ and $x_i^* \leq x_i$ $(i = 1, \ldots, n)$ imply $\mathbf{x} \in A$. Let A_1 and A_2 be two increasing sets. By choosing g_j to be the indicator function of A_j in (5.1.1) it is immediate that if $X_1, \ldots, X_n$ are associated, then

$$P[\mathbf{X} \in A_1 \cap A_2] \geq P[\mathbf{X} \in A_1]P[\mathbf{X} \in A_2] \quad (5.1.4)$$

holds. This consideration leads to the next definition of positive dependence.

Definition 5.1.4. The components of $\mathbf{X} = (X_1, \ldots, X_n)'$ are said to be positively dependent in increasing sets (PDIS) if (5.1.4) holds for all open and increasing sets A_1 and A_2 in $\mathfrak{R}^n$.

By choosing

$$A_1 = \{\mathbf{x}: x_k > a_k\}, \qquad A_2 = \{\mathbf{x}: x_i > a_i,\ i = k+1, \ldots, n\},$$

in (5.1.4) for $k = 1, \ldots, n-1$ it can be verified that if $X_1, \ldots, X_n$ are PDIS, then

$$P\left[\bigcap_{i=1}^{n} \{X_i > a_i\}\right] \geq \prod_{i=1}^{n} P[X_i > a_i] \quad (5.1.5)$$

holds for all $\mathbf{a} = (a_1, \ldots, a_n)'$. Similarly, it can be shown that if $X_1, \ldots, X_n$ are associated, then $-X_1, \ldots, -X_n$ are associated (Esary, Proschan, and Walkup, 1967). Thus association also implies that

$$P\left[\bigcap_{i=1}^{n} \{X_i \leq a_i\}\right] \geq \prod_{i=1}^{n} P[X_i \leq a_i] \quad (5.1.6)$$

holds for all $\mathbf{a}$. This fact leads to definitions of positive orthant dependence.

Definition 5.1.5. The random variables $X_1, \ldots, X_n$ are said to be positively upper orthant-dependent (PUOD) if (5.1.5) holds for all $\mathbf{a} \in \mathfrak{R}^n$.

Definition 5.1.6. The random variables $X_1, \ldots, X_n$ are said to be positively lower orthant-dependent (PLOD) if (5.1.6) holds for all $\mathbf{a} \in \mathfrak{R}^n$.

If $n = 2$ and X_1, X_2 satisfy (5.1.6), then they are also said to be positively quadrant-dependent (PQD) (see Lehmann, 1966). It is known that X_1, X_2 are PQD if and only if

$$\mathrm{Corr}(g_1(X_1), g_2(X_2)) \geq 0 \tag{5.1.7}$$

holds for all nondecreasing functions g_1 and g_2 such that g_i is a function of x_i only for $i = 1, 2$ (Esary, Proschan, and Walkup, 1967). It is also known that X_1, X_2 are PUOD if and only if they are PLOD (Lehmann, 1966); however, for $n > 2$ such statements are no longer true. Note that for any $n \geq 2$ the right-hand side of (5.1.5) and the right-hand side of (5.1.6) are just the joint probabilities when $X_1, \ldots, X_n$ are independent. Thus if $X_1, \ldots, X_n$ are PUOD or PLOD, then the random variables are more likely to take larger values together or smaller values together. Finally, a simple measure of dependence is the correlation coefficients. So we observe the trivial definition.

Definition 5.1.7. The random variable $X_1, \ldots, X_n$ are said to be nonnegatively correlated (NC) if $\mathrm{Corr}(X_i, X_j) \geq 0$, or equivalently, $\mathrm{Cov}(X_i, X_j) \geq 0$ holds, for all $i \neq j$.

We now proceed to study the implications of the concepts of positive dependence stated in Definitions 5.1.1–5.1.7. First we observe a simple but useful fact.

Proposition 5.1.1. *Let $\{X_1, \ldots, X_n\}$ be a set of random variables and let $\{X_{j_1}, \ldots, X_{j_k}\}$ be any given proper subset, where $k < n$.*

(a) *If the density function of $(X_1, \ldots, X_n)'$ is* MTP_2, *then the density function of $(X_{j_1}, \ldots, X_{j_k})'$ is* MTP_2.
(b) *If $X_1, \ldots, X_n$ are associated, then $X_{j_1}, \ldots, X_{j_k}$ are associated.*
(c) *If $X_1, \ldots, X_n$ are* PDIS, *then $X_{j_1}, \ldots, X_{j_k}$ are* PDIS.
(d) *If $X_1, \ldots, X_n$ are* PUOD *(or* PLOD*), then $X_{j_1}, \ldots, X_{j_k}$ are* PUOD *(or* PLOD*).*
(e) *If $X_1, \ldots, X_n$ are* NC, *then $X_{j_1}, \ldots, X_{j_k}$ are* NC.

PROOF. The proof of (a) can be found in Kemperman (1977). The proofs of (b)–(e) are easy and are left to the reader. □

Remark 5.1.1. We note that all of the notions of positive dependence stated in Definitions 5.1.1, 5.1.3–5.1.7 are permutation invariant in that: If $X_1, \ldots, X_n$ are positively dependent in the sense of Definition 5.1.m, then $X_{j_1}, \ldots, X_{j_n}$ are also positively dependent in the sense of Definition 5.1.m for all permutation $\{j_1, \ldots, j_n\}$ of $\{1, \ldots, n\}$ and for $m = 1, 3, 4, 5, 6, 7$.

Definition 5.1.2 depends on a particular sequence of conditional probabilities, and is *not* permutation invariant. To see this point let us consider the following example.

EXAMPLE 5.1.1. Let $(X_1, X_2, X_3)'$ have an $\mathcal{N}_3(\mathbf{0}, \mathbf{\Sigma})$ distribution given in Example 3.4.1 where

$$\sigma_{ii} = 1 \quad (i = 1, 2, 3), \qquad \sigma_{12} = 1 - 2\varepsilon, \qquad \sigma_{13} = \sigma_{23} = 1 - \varepsilon,$$

and $0 < \varepsilon < \frac{1}{2}$. Then it is easy to verify that:

(a) The conditional distribution of X_2 given $X_1 = x_1$ is

$$\mathcal{N}((1 - 2\varepsilon)x_1, 4\varepsilon(1 - \varepsilon)),$$

and the conditional distribution of X_3 given $(X_1, X_2)' = (x_1, x_2)'$ is

$$\mathcal{N}\left(\frac{x_1 + x_2}{2}, \varepsilon\right).$$

Thus X_1, X_2, X_3 are conditionally increasing in sequence.

(b) Now consider the sequence of random variables $\{X_3, X_2, X_1\}$. The conditional distribution of X_2, given $X_3 = x_3$, is

$$\mathcal{N}((1 - \varepsilon)x_3, \varepsilon(2 - \varepsilon)),$$

and the conditional distribution of X_1, given $(X_3, X_2)' = (x_3, x_2)'$, is

$$\mathcal{N}\left(\frac{-\varepsilon x_2 + 2(1 - \varepsilon)x_3}{2 - \varepsilon}, \sigma_{1 \cdot 32}^2\right),$$

where $\sigma_{1 \cdot 32}^2 = 1 - (2 - 5\varepsilon + 4\varepsilon^2)/(2 - \varepsilon)$. Consider the conditional probability

$$P[X_1 > t | (X_3, X_2)' = (x_3, x_2)'] = 1 - \Phi\left(\frac{t + \varepsilon x_2 - 2(1 - \varepsilon)x_3}{\sigma_{1 \cdot 32}}\right),$$

where Φ is the $\mathcal{N}(0, 1)$ distribution function. Since it is a decreasing function of x_2 for fixed t and x_3, the random variables X_3, X_2, X_1 are *not* conditionally increasing sequence. □

In the following proposition we summarize the implications of the definitions of positive dependence.

Proposition 5.1.2. *The following implications are true:*

$$\text{MTP}_2 \overset{(a)}{\Rightarrow} \text{CIS} \overset{(b)}{\Rightarrow} \text{A} \overset{(c)}{\Leftrightarrow} \text{PDIS}, \tag{5.1.8}$$

$$\text{A} \overset{(c)}{\Leftrightarrow} \text{PDIS} \begin{array}{l} \overset{(d)}{\Rightarrow} \text{PUOD} \overset{(f)}{\Rightarrow} \\ \underset{(e)}{\Rightarrow} \text{PLOD} \underset{(g)}{\Rightarrow} \end{array} \text{NC}. \tag{5.1.9}$$

Furthermore, all implications in (a), (b), (d), (e), (f), *and* (g) *are strict and, for* $n > 2$,

$$\text{PUOD} \overset{(h)}{\not\Rightarrow} \text{PLOD} \quad \textit{and} \quad \text{PLOD} \overset{(i)}{\not\Rightarrow} \text{PUOD}.$$

OUTLINE OF THE PROOF. The proof for implications (a) and (b) can be found in Barlow and Proschan (1975, pp. 149, 147). The equivalence statement in (c) was given by Esary, Proschan, and Walkup (1967). Implications (d) and (e) are immediate. The proof for implications (f) and (g) can be given by considering the bivariate distributions of all possible pairs $(X_i, X_j)'$ and then, for each pair, applying the argument given in Lehmann (1966).

To show that all implications are strict, it suffices to give a counterexample for each case.

(a) For the random variables X_1, X_2, X_3 with a joint distribution as given in Example 5.1.1, X_1, X_2, X_3 are CIS (Example 5.1.1 a), but the joint density function of $(X_1, X_2, X_3)'$ is not MTP_2 (Example 4.3.2).

(b) For the random variables X_1, X_2, X_3 given in Example 5.1.1, X_3, X_2, X_1 are associated (because X_1, X_2, X_3 are associated), but they are not CIS (Example 5.1.1(b)).

(d) and (e) An example for a bivariate random variable exists such that (5.1.7) holds for all nondecreasing one-variable functions $g_1(x_1)$ and $g_2(x_2)$, but (5.1.3) does not hold for all nondecreasing two-variable functions $g_1(x_1, x_2)$ and $g_2(x_1, x_2)$. The details are left to the reader.

(f) and (g) An example can be found in Lehmann (1966). □

Remark 5.1.2. The implication (b) should be interpreted as follows: Let $X_1, \ldots, X_n$ be random variables. If there exists a permutation $\{j_1, \ldots, j_n\}$ of $\{1, \ldots, n\}$ such *that* $X_{j_1}, \ldots, X_{j_n}$ are CIS, then $X_1, \ldots, X_n$ are associated.

Remark 5.1.3. As noted in Section 4.3, the implication $\text{MTP}_2 \Rightarrow \text{A}$ is due to Fortuin, Kastelyn, and Ginibre (1971) and is known in the literature as the FKG inequality. Thus the MTP_2 condition is also known as the FKG condition.

Remark 5.1.4. The statement in Proposition 5.1.2 is to be compared with Theorem 5.1.1 in Tong (1980, p. 80) in that: Proposition 5.1.2 concerns the positive dependence of n $(n \geq 2)$ variables, and the other theorem deals with the positive dependence of two variables only.

We note in passing that certain other notions of positive dependence have been introduced. For example, Shaked (1982) provided a notion of positive dependence that is weaker than the association of random variables, and Kimeldorf and Sampson (1987) have studied similar positive dependence orderings. Other results include Rinott and Pollak (1980) (for the bivariate case), Karlin and Rinott (1980a, b, 1983a), Shaked and Tong (1985), and Tong (1989). Those results especially concern the multivariate normal distribution and some of them will be treated further in this chapter.

5.1.2. Positively Dependent Normal Variables and the Correlation Matrix

If $\mathbf{X} = (X_1, \ldots, X_n)'$ has a multivariate normal distribution, then much more can be said about the positive dependence of $X_1, \ldots, X_n$, according to the notions defined in Definitions 5.1.1–5.1.7. For example, it is easy to verify that in this case, PUOD and PLOD are equivalent. Moreover, by an inequality of Slepian (1962) (see Theorem 5.1.7) we know that if $\mathbf{X}$ has an $\mathcal{N}_n(\boldsymbol{\mu}, \boldsymbol{\Sigma})$ distribution, then the probabilities on the left-hand side of (5.1.5) and the left-hand side of (5.1.6) are monotonically increasing in the correlation coefficients. Thus if the components of $\mathbf{X}$ are nonnegatively correlated, then they are both PUOD and PLOD.

A stronger result is the association theorem due to Pitt (1982). This result is stated below.

Theorem 5.1.1. *Let $\mathbf{X} = (X_1, \ldots, X_n)'$ have an $\mathcal{N}_n(\boldsymbol{\mu}, \boldsymbol{\Sigma} = (\sigma_{ij}))$ distribution. Then $X_1, \ldots, X_n$ are associated random variables if and only if*

$$\sigma_{ij} \geq 0 \qquad \text{for all} \quad i \neq j. \tag{5.1.10}$$

Consequently, if (5.1.10) *holds, then:*

(i) (5.1.1) *(and hence* (5.1.2) *and* (5.1.3)) *holds for all nondecreasing functions g_1 and g_2;*
(ii) (5.1.4) *holds for all increasing sets* A_1 *and* A_2; *and*
(iii) (5.1.5) *and* (5.1.6) *hold for all real vectors* $\mathbf{a} = (a_1, \ldots, a_n)'$.

OUTLINE OF PROOF. Without loss of generality assume $\boldsymbol{\mu} = \mathbf{0}$. Let $\mathbf{X}$ and $\mathbf{Z}$ be independent and identically distributed, and for $\lambda \in [0, 1]$ define

$$\mathbf{Y}_\lambda = \lambda \mathbf{X} + \sqrt{1 - \lambda^2}\,\mathbf{Z}.$$

Then it is easy to verify that

$$\begin{pmatrix} \mathbf{X} \\ \mathbf{Y}_\lambda \end{pmatrix} \sim \mathcal{N}_{2n}\left(\mathbf{0}, \begin{pmatrix} \boldsymbol{\Sigma} & \lambda\boldsymbol{\Sigma} \\ \lambda\boldsymbol{\Sigma} & \boldsymbol{\Sigma} \end{pmatrix}\right).$$

Let $g_1, g_2\colon \Re^n \to \Re$ be nondecreasing in each component and define

$$\psi(\lambda) = Eg_1(\mathbf{X})g_2(\mathbf{Y}_\lambda), \qquad \lambda \in [0, 1],$$

it suffices to show that if $\sigma_{ij} \geq 0$ holds for all $i \neq j$, then $\psi(1) \geq \psi(0)$.

(a) If $\boldsymbol{\Sigma}$ is positive definite and g_1, g_2 are both continuously differentiable with bounded partial derivatives, then $\psi(\lambda)$ can be written as

$$\psi(\lambda) = \int_{\Re^n} g_1(\mathbf{x}) f_1(\mathbf{x}) \left[\int_{\Re^n} g_2(\mathbf{y}) f_{\lambda,2|1}(\mathbf{y}|\mathbf{x})\, d\mathbf{y}\right] d\mathbf{x},$$

where $f_1(\mathbf{x})$ is the density function of $\mathbf{X}$ and $f_{\lambda,2|1}(\mathbf{y}|\mathbf{x})$ is the conditional density of $\mathbf{Y}_\lambda$, given $\mathbf{X} = \mathbf{x}$. Straightforward calculation shows that $f_{\lambda,2|1}(\mathbf{y}|\mathbf{x})$ is just the density of an $\mathcal{N}_n(\lambda\mathbf{x}, (1 - \lambda^2)\boldsymbol{\Sigma})$ distribution. Thus if g_2 is a nondecreasing function, then

$$\eta_j(\lambda, \mathbf{x}, \boldsymbol{\Sigma}) \equiv \frac{\partial}{\partial x_j} \int_{\Re^n} g_2(\mathbf{y}) f_{\lambda,2|1}(\mathbf{y}|\mathbf{x})\, d\mathbf{y} \geq 0 \qquad \text{for} \quad j = 1, \ldots, n. \tag{5.1.11}$$

An application of Plackett's (1954) identity yields

$$\frac{\partial}{\partial \lambda} f_{\lambda,2|1}(\mathbf{y}|\mathbf{x}) = -\frac{1}{\lambda}\left\{\sum_{i=1}^n \sum_{j=1}^n \sigma_{ij} \frac{\partial^2}{\partial x_i\, \partial x_j} f_{\lambda,2|1}(\mathbf{y}|\mathbf{x}) - \sum_{i=1}^n x_i \frac{\partial}{\partial x_i} f_{\lambda,2|1}(\mathbf{y}|\mathbf{x})\right\}.$$

Thus

$$\psi'(\lambda) = -\frac{1}{\lambda}\int_{\mathfrak{R}^n} f(\mathbf{x})g_1(\mathbf{x})\left\{\sum_{i=1}^n\sum_{j=1}^n \sigma_{ij}\frac{\partial}{\partial x_i}\eta_j(\lambda, \mathbf{x}, \boldsymbol{\Sigma}) - \sum_{i=1}^n x_i\eta_i(\lambda, \mathbf{x}, \boldsymbol{\Sigma})\right\} d\mathbf{x}$$

holds. Integrating by parts and applying the monotonicity property of g_1 and (5.1.10) yield

$$\psi'(\lambda) = \frac{1}{\lambda}\int_{\mathfrak{R}^n} f_1(\mathbf{x})\left\{\sum_{i=1}^n\sum_{j=1}^n \sigma_{ij}\frac{\partial}{\partial x_i} g_1(\mathbf{x})\eta_j(\lambda, \mathbf{x}, \boldsymbol{\Sigma})\right\} d\mathbf{x} \geq 0,$$

which implies $\psi(1) \geq \psi(0)$.

(b) The rest of the proof deals with removing the conditions that $\boldsymbol{\Sigma}$ is positive definite and that g_1, g_2 are continuously differentiable with bounded partial derivatives. The case in which $\boldsymbol{\Sigma}$ is positive semidefinite is easy because if $\boldsymbol{\Sigma}$ is singular, then there exists a sequence of positive definite matrices that converges to $\boldsymbol{\Sigma}$, and the inequality is preserved when passing to the limit. The problem of removing the differentiability condition on g_1 and g_2 is more difficult. The proof given by Pitt (1982) involves an almost sure approximation of a monotone continuous function by bounded monotone functions. For technical details, see Pitt (1982). □

Remark 5.1.5. Note that the density function of a normal variable $\mathbf{X} = (X_1, \ldots, X_n)'$ is not necessarily MTP_2 when (5.1.10) holds, because the inverse of $\boldsymbol{\Sigma}$ is not necessarily an M-matrix (see Theorem 4.3.2′ and Example 4.3.2). Thus the set of normal variables with MTP_2 densities is a proper subset of the set of normal variables whose components are associated.

Other results on the positive dependence of normal variables can be found in Gutmann (1978) and Perlman and Olkin (1980), and the related references. Perlman and Olkin considered the multivariate analysis-of-variance model and showed the unbiasedness properties of some invariant tests. Gutmann showed that if $(\mathbf{X}, \mathbf{Z})'$ has an $\mathcal{N}_{2n}(\boldsymbol{\mu}, \boldsymbol{\Sigma})$ distribution such that:

(a) $\mathbf{X}$ is $n \times 1$ and $\mathbf{Z}$ is $n \times 1$;
(b) the marginal distributions of $\mathbf{X}$ and $\mathbf{Z}$ are the same; and
(c) the covariance matrix between $\mathbf{X}$ and $\mathbf{Z}$ is positive definite;

then $\mathrm{Corr}(g(\mathbf{X}), g(\mathbf{Z})) \geq 0$ holds for all real-valued functions $g\colon \mathfrak{R}^n \to \mathfrak{R}$ such that the expectations exist.

5.1.3. Positive Dependence of Absolute Values of Normal Variables

In certain statistical applications (such as the estimation of the mean vector and multiple comparisons), we are interested in the positive dependence of the *absolute values* of normal variables. Specifically, let $\mathbf{X} = (X_1, \ldots, X_n)'$ have an

$\mathcal{N}_n(\boldsymbol{\mu}, \boldsymbol{\Sigma})$ distribution and define $|\mathbf{X}| = (|X_1|, \ldots, |X_n|)'$, the problem of interest is whether the positive dependence of $|X_1|, \ldots, |X_n|$ can also be characterized in terms of $\boldsymbol{\mu}$ and $\boldsymbol{\Sigma}$. If the answer is in the affirmative, then similar results for $(|X_1|, \ldots, |X_n|)'$ can be obtained without verifying conditions concerning the distribution of $|\mathbf{X}|$.

An earlier result in this area follows from an inequality of Šidák (1968). A precise statement of Šidák's inequality will be given in Chapter 7 (see Theorem 7.2.1), and a special consequence is:

Theorem 5.1.2. *If* $\mathbf{X} = (X_1, \ldots, X_n)'$ *has an* $\mathcal{N}_n(\mathbf{0}, \boldsymbol{\Sigma})$ *distribution, then*

$$P\left[\bigcap_{i=1}^{n} \left\{|X_i| \leq a_i\right\}\right] \geq \prod_{i=1}^{n} P[|X_i| \leq a_i]$$

holds for all $\mathbf{a} = (a_1, \ldots, a_n)'$, $a_i > 0$ $(i = 1, \ldots, n)$. *(In other words,* $|X_1|, \ldots, |X_n|$ *are* PLOD *for all* $\boldsymbol{\Sigma}$.)

Note that the only condition on the distribution of $\mathbf{X}$ is normality with zero means.

A related question of interest is whether $|X_1|, \ldots, |X_n|$ are also PUOD. The following counterexample given by Šidák (1968) shows that this is not true. (It also provides a counterexample showing that PLOD does not imply PUOD.)

Example 5.1.2. Let $(X_1, X_2, X_3)' = (Z_1, Z_2, (Z_1 + Z_2)/\sqrt{2})'$ where Z_1, Z_2 are i.i.d. $\mathcal{N}(0, \sigma^2)$ variables. Then for any given $a_1 = a_2 > 0$ and for sufficiently small $a_3 > 0$ we have

$$P\left[\bigcap_{i=1}^{3} \{|X_i| > a_i\}\right] < \prod_{i=1}^{3} P[|X_i| > a_i]. \tag{5.1.12}$$

□

A convenient reference for the proof of this result is Tong (1980, p. 27). Note that in this example the covariance matrix is positive semidefinite. A different example with a positive definite covariance matrix can be obtained by modifying Example 5.1.2, the details are left to the reader.

Since the association property is stronger than the PUOD property, Example 5.1.2 shows that $|X_1|, \ldots, |X_n|$ are not *always* associated random variables. Thus the question of interest concerns sufficient conditions on $\boldsymbol{\Sigma}$ under which the association property holds. A result for providing an answer to this question, due to Jogdeo (1977), is the following proposition (a convenient reference for its proof is Dharmadhikari and Joag-Dev (1988, p. 156)).

Proposition 5.1.3. *Let* $\mathbf{Y} = (Y_1, \ldots, Y_n)'$ *have independent components, each having a symmetric unimodal density function, and let* $\mathbf{X} = \mathbf{Y} + \mathbf{Z}$ *where* $\mathbf{Z} =$

$(Z_1, \ldots, Z_n)'$ is independent of $\mathbf{Y}$. If $|Z_1|, \ldots, |Z_n|$ are associated, then the components of $|\mathbf{X}| = (|X_1|, \ldots, |X_n|)'$ are associated.

Useful results for the association of absolute values of normal variables can be obtained by applying this proposition. One such result is:

Theorem 5.1.3. *For $n \geq 2$, let $\mathbf{X} = (X_1, \ldots, X_n)'$ have an $\mathcal{N}_n(\mathbf{0}, \mathbf{\Sigma} = (\sigma_{ij}))$ distribution. If there exist real numbers $\lambda_i \in [-1, 1]$ $(i = 1, \ldots, n)$, such that*

$$\sigma_{ij} = \begin{cases} \sigma_i^2 & \text{for} \quad i = j, \\ \lambda_i \lambda_j \sigma_i \sigma_j & \text{for} \quad i \neq j, \end{cases} \tag{5.1.13}$$

then $|X_1|, \ldots, |X_n|$ are associated.

Proof. Let $Y_1, \ldots, Y_n$ and Z_0 be independent $\mathcal{N}(0, 1)$ variables. Denote $\mathbf{Y} = (Y_1, \ldots, Y_n)'$ and, for given $\lambda_1, \ldots, \lambda_n$, denote $\mathbf{Z} = (\lambda_1 Z_0, \ldots, \lambda_n Z_0)'$. Then it is easy to verify that, (i) the components of $|\mathbf{Z}|$ are associated, and (ii) the n-dimensional random variable

$$(\sqrt{1 - \lambda_1^2}\, Y_1 + \lambda_1 Z_0, \ldots, \sqrt{1 - \lambda_n^2}\, Y_n + \lambda_n Z_0)',$$

and $\mathbf{X}/\boldsymbol{\sigma} \equiv (X_1/\sigma_1, \ldots, X_n/\sigma_n)'$ are identically distributed. Thus (by Proposition 5.1.3) the components of $|\mathbf{X}|/\boldsymbol{\sigma}$ are associated. Consequently, the components of $|\mathbf{X}|$ are associated. □

Theorem 5.1.3 implies that if $(X_1, \ldots, X_n)'$ has a multivariate normal distribution with mean vector $\mathbf{0}$ and covariance matrix satisfying (5.1.13), then $|X_1|, \ldots, |X_n|$ are PLOD. This PLOD result was first obtained by Dunn (1958), and was the motivating force for Šidák (1968) to obtain a proof for the result given in Theorem 5.1.2 (by removing the condition on $\mathbf{\Sigma}$ stated in (5.1.13)).

A problem of equal importance concerns conditions under which the joint density function of the absolute values of normal variables has the MTP_2 property. For $n = 2$ and $n = 3$, this problem was considered by Abdel-Hameed and Sampson (1978). They obtained the following result.

Theorem 5.1.4. *Let $\mathbf{X} = (X_1, \ldots, X_n)'$ have an $\mathcal{N}_n(\mathbf{0}, \mathbf{\Sigma})$ distribution, $\mathbf{\Sigma} > 0$. Then:*

(a) *for $n = 2$, the joint density function of $(|X_1|, |X_2|)'$ is TP_2;*
(b) *for $n = 3$, the joint density of $(|X_1|, |X_2|, |X_3|)'$ is MTP_2 if and only if $\prod_{i<j} \tau_{ij} \leq 0$, where $\mathbf{T} = (\tau_{ij}) = \mathbf{\Sigma}^{-1}$.*

Outline of the Proof. (a) For every given correlation coefficient ρ and variances σ_1^2, σ_2^2, the joint density of $|\mathbf{X}| = (|X_1|, |X_2|)'$ is of the form

$$f_{|\mathbf{X}|}(y_1, y_2) = k_1(y_1) k_2(y_2) h(y_1 y_2), \qquad y_i \geq 0, \quad i = 1, 2;$$

where $k_i(y_i)$ depends only on y_i and

$$h(z) = \cosh\left(\frac{\rho z}{2(1-\rho^2)\sigma_1\sigma_2}\right)$$

is nondecreasing and log-convex. Thus for arbitrary but fixed $0 \le s_1^* \le s_1$ and $0 \le s_2^* \le s_2$, we have

$$\frac{f_{|\mathbf{X}|}(s_1^*, s_2^*)f_{|\mathbf{X}|}(s_1, s_2)}{f_{|\mathbf{X}|}(s_1^*, s_2)f_{|\mathbf{X}|}(s_1, s_2^*)} = \frac{h(s_1^* s_2^*)h(s_1 s_2)}{h(s_1^* s_2)h(s_1 s_2^*)} \ge 1$$

by $s_1^* s_2^* + s_1 s_2 \ge s_1^* s_2 + s_1 s_2^*$ and $s_1 s_2 - s_1^* s_2^* \ge |s_1^* s_2 - s_1 s_2^*|$.

(b) For $n = 3$, the joint density function of $|\mathbf{X}| = (|X_1|, |X_2|, |X_3|)'$ can be written as

$$f_{|\mathbf{X}|}(y_1, y_2, y_3) = c \cdot \exp\left(-\frac{1}{2}\sum_{i=1}^{3} c_{ii} y_i^2\right) g(y_1, y_2, y_3), \quad y_i \ge 0 \ (i = 1, 2, 3),$$

where

$$g(y_1, y_2, y_3) = \sum_{i=0}^{1}\sum_{j=0}^{1} \exp[(-1)^i \tau_{11} y_1 y_2 + (-1)^j \tau_{13} y_1 y_3 + (-1)^{i+j+1} \tau_{23} y_2 y_3].$$

(i) If $\tau_{12}\tau_{13}\tau_{23} < 0$, then we may assume that $\tau_{ij} < 0$ for all $i \ne j$ (because $|\mathbf{X}|$ and $(|d_1 X_1|, |d_2 X_2|, |d_3 X_3|)'$ are identically distributed for all $d_i = 1$ or -1). Consequently, by the definition of TP_2 functions (Karlin, 1968, p. 49), it can be shown that $g(y_1, y_2, y_3)$ is TP_2 in pairs. Since $f_{|\mathbf{X}|}(\mathbf{y}) > 0$ for all $y_i > 0$ $(i = 1, 2, 3)$, clearly $f_{|\mathbf{X}|}(\mathbf{y})$ is an MTP_2 function. If at least one of the τ_{ij}'s $(i \ne j)$ is zero, then either the problem can be reduced to the bivariate case or an easy modification can be made. Thus $\tau_{12}\tau_{13}\tau_{23} \le 0$ implies that $f_{|\mathbf{X}|}(\mathbf{y})$ is MTP_2.

(ii) If $\tau_{12}\tau_{13}\tau_{23} > 0$, then we may assume that $\tau_{ij} > 0$ for all $i \ne j$. Consequently, it can be shown that for $y_3 = (\tau_{12}/\tau_{13}\tau_{23})^{1/2}$ there exists an open subset of $[0, \infty) \times [0, \infty)$ such that, for $(y_1, y_2)'$ in this subset, $f_{|\mathbf{X}|}(y_1, y_2, y_3)$ is not MTP_2. □

After proving Theorem 5.1.4 Adbel-Hameed and Sampson (1978) proposed a conjecture concerning the case for $n > 3$. Their conjecture was shown to be true in a subsequent paper by Karlin and Rinott (1981). A main result in Karlin and Rinott (1981) is that:

Theorem 5.1.5. *Let* $\mathbf{X} = (X_1, \ldots, X_n)'$ *have an* $\mathcal{N}_n(\mathbf{0}, \mathbf{\Sigma})$ *distribution. Then the joint density of* $(|X_1|, \ldots, |X_n|)'$ *is* MTP_2 *if and only if there exists a diagonal matrix* $\mathbf{D}$ *with diagonal elements either* 1 *or* -1, *such that the off-diagonal elements of* $\mathbf{D\Sigma}^{-1}\mathbf{D}$ *are all nonpositive.*

The proof for sufficiency depends on a similar but more general argument given in the proof of Theorem 5.1.4(a). The proof for necessity depends on a process for determining the matrix $\mathbf{D}$ uniquely. The reader is referred to Karlin and Rinott (1981) for details.

5.1.4. Comparisons of Positive Dependence

The notions of positive dependence introduced in Definitions 5.1.1–5.1.7 mainly concern comparison of positively dependent random variables with independent random variables. Since independent random variables represent the extreme case among the class of positively dependent random variables, a problem of great interest is the comparison of the "strength" of positive dependence of two sets of random variables when their marginal distributions are kept fixed. Specifically, let $\mathbf{X} = (X_1, \ldots, X_n)'$ and $\mathbf{Y} = (Y_1, \ldots, Y_n)'$ be n-dimensional random variables with joint density functions $f_{\mathbf{X}}(\mathbf{x})$ and $f_{\mathbf{Y}}(\mathbf{y})$, respectively. For comparing the positive dependence of the components of $\mathbf{X}$ with respect to that of the components of $\mathbf{Y}$ we assume that X_i and Y_i have the same marginal distribution for each i, in symbols,

$$X_i \stackrel{d}{=} Y_i, \qquad i = 1, \ldots, n. \tag{5.1.14}$$

The following two definitions are natural extensions of Definitions 5.1.5 and 5.1.6.

Definition 5.1.8. $\mathbf{X}$ is said to be more PUOD than $\mathbf{Y}$ if (5.1.14) holds and if

$$P\left[\bigcap_{i=1}^{n} \{X_i > a_i\}\right] \geq P\left[\bigcap_{i=1}^{n} \{Y_i > a_i\}\right]$$

holds for all $\mathbf{a} = (a_1, \ldots, a_n)'$.

Definition 5.1.9. $\mathbf{X}$ is said to be more PLOD than $\mathbf{Y}$ if (5.1.14) holds and if

$$P\left[\bigcap_{i=1}^{n} \{X_i \leq a_i\}\right] \geq P\left[\bigcap_{i=1}^{n} \{Y_i \leq a_i\}\right]$$

holds for all $\mathbf{a} = (a_1, \ldots, a_n)'$.

Finally, the weakest notion seems to be the comparison of the correlation coefficients between that of the X_i's and that of the Y_i's.

Definition 5.1.10. Let $\mathbf{X}$, $\mathbf{Y}$ have covariance matrices $\mathbf{\Sigma} = (\sigma_{ij})$ and $\mathbf{\Gamma} = (\gamma_{ij})$, respectively. $\mathbf{X}$ is said to be more correlated than $\mathbf{Y}$ ($\mathbf{X} \stackrel{\text{m.c.}}{>} \mathbf{Y}$) if (5.1.14) holds and if

$$\sigma_{ij} \geq \gamma_{ij} \qquad \text{for} \quad 1 \leq i < j \leq n \tag{5.1.15}$$

holds (in symbols $\mathbf{\Sigma} \geq \mathbf{\Gamma}$).

Note that in Definition 5.1.10 we do not require $\sigma_{ij} \geq 0$ and $\gamma_{ij} \geq 0$ for $i \neq j$. If $\mathbf{X}$ and $\mathbf{Y}$ are both multivariate normal variables, then the condition in

(5.1.14) is just that X_i and Y_i have the same mean and the same variance. In this case the comparison of positive dependence amounts to the comparison of the correlation matrices. In the following we summarize some of the important results for both the normal variables and the absolute of the normal variables.

Bølviken and Jogdeo (1982) proved a result for the distribution function of the absolute values of normal variables.

Theorem 5.1.6. *Let* $\mathbf{X} \sim \mathcal{N}_n(\mathbf{0}, \mathbf{\Sigma} = (\sigma_{ij}))$ *and* $\mathbf{Y} \sim \mathcal{N}_n(\mathbf{0}, \mathbf{\Gamma} = (\gamma_{ij}))$ *be such that* $\mathbf{\Sigma} > 0, \mathbf{\Gamma} > 0$, *and* $\sigma_{ii} = \gamma_{ii}\ (1 = 1, \ldots, n)$. *If* $\sigma_{ij} \geq \gamma_{ij}$ *for all* $i \neq j$ *and if* $\mathbf{\Sigma}^{-1}, \mathbf{\Gamma}^{-1}$ are *M-matrices, then*:

(a) $|\mathbf{X}|$ *is more* POUD *than* $|\mathbf{Y}|$; *and*
(b) $|\mathbf{X}|$ *is more* PLOD *than* $|\mathbf{Y}|$.

Theorem 5.1.6 essentially says that if $\mathbf{X}$ and $\mathbf{Y}$ are multivariate normal variables with mean vectors $\mathbf{0}$ and $\sigma_{ii} = \gamma_{ii}$ $(i = 1, \ldots, n)$, then (i) $X \overset{\text{m.c.}}{>} \mathbf{Y}$ *and* (ii) $\mathbf{\Sigma}^{-1}, \mathbf{\Gamma}^{-1}$ being *M-matrices jointly* imply that $|\mathbf{X}|$ is more PUOD (PLOD) than $|\mathbf{Y}|$. The following theorem, known as Slepian's (1962) inequality, states that the condition on the inverses of $\mathbf{\Sigma}$ and $\mathbf{\Gamma}$ in (ii) can be removed for the same partial orderings of $\mathbf{X}$ and $\mathbf{Y}$.

Theorem 5.1.7. *Let* $\mathbf{X} \sim \mathcal{N}_n(\boldsymbol{\mu}, \mathbf{\Sigma} = (\sigma_{ij}))$ and $\mathbf{Y} \sim \mathcal{N}_n(\boldsymbol{\mu}, \mathbf{\Gamma} = (\gamma_{ij}))$ *be such that* $\sigma_{ii} = \gamma_{ii}$ $(i = 1, \ldots, n)$. *If* $\sigma_{ij} \geq \gamma_{ij}$ *for all* $i \neq j$ *(that is, if* $\mathbf{X} \overset{\text{m.c.}}{>} \mathbf{Y}$), *then* $\mathbf{X}$ *is more* POUD *and more* PLOD *than* $\mathbf{Y}$.

A convenient reference for the proof of this result is Tong (1980, pp. 10–11).

We note that the result in Theorem 5.1.7 applies without any conditions on the signs of σ_{ij}'s and γ_{ij}'s. In addition to this result, there are certain more general results for positively and negatively correlated normal variables. One such result, due to Joag-Dev, Perlman, and Pitt (1983) and Joag-Dev and Proschan (1983), is

Theorem 5.1.8. *Let* $\mathbf{X} \sim \mathcal{N}_n(\boldsymbol{\mu}, \mathbf{\Sigma})$. *For* $k < n$ *let*

$$\mathbf{X}_1 = (X_1, \ldots, X_k)', \qquad \mathbf{X}_2 = (X_{k+1}, \ldots, X_n)',$$

and let $\mathbf{\Sigma}_{12}$ *be the covariance matrix of* $\mathbf{X}_1$ *and* $\mathbf{X}_2$.

(a) *If all elements of* $\mathbf{\Sigma}_{12}$ *are nonnegative, then*

$$Eg_1(\mathbf{X}_1)g_2(\mathbf{X}_2) \geq Eg_1(\mathbf{X}_1)Eg_2(\mathbf{X}_2) \tag{5.1.16}$$

holds for all nondecreasing functions g_1 *and* g_2 *such that the expectations exist.*

(b) *If all elements of* $\mathbf{\Sigma}_{12}$ *are nonpositive, then the inequality in* (5.1.16) *is reversed.*

Other notions of comparisons of dependence involved permutation-symmetric and exchangeable normal variables and normal variables with a common marginal distribution. This will be treated further in Section 5.3.

5.2. Permutation-Symmetric Normal Variables

For fixed n, let $\mathbf{X} = (X_1, \ldots, X_n)'$ be an n-dimensional random variable with distribution function $F(\mathbf{x})$ and density function $f(\mathbf{x})$. F and f are said to be permutation-symmetric if for every permutation $\boldsymbol{\pi} = \{j_1, \ldots, j_n\}$ of $\{1, \ldots, n\}$ and every $\mathbf{x} = (x_1, \ldots, x_n)' \in \mathfrak{R}^n$ we have

$$F(\boldsymbol{\pi}(\mathbf{x})) = F(\mathbf{x}), \qquad f(\boldsymbol{\pi}(\mathbf{x})) = f(\mathbf{x}), \tag{5.2.1}$$

where $\boldsymbol{\pi}(\mathbf{x}) = (x_{\pi_1}, \ldots, x_{\pi_n})'$.

If $\mathbf{X}$ has an $\mathcal{N}_n(\boldsymbol{\mu}, \boldsymbol{\Sigma})$ distribution, then clearly (5.2.1) holds if and only if the components of $\mathbf{X}$ have a common mean, a common variance, and a common correlation coefficient.

Definition 5.2.1. $X_1, \ldots, X_n$ are said to be permutation-symmetric normal variables, or $\mathbf{X} = (X_1, \ldots, X_n)'$ is said to have a permutation-symmetric multivariate normal distribution, if $\mathbf{X} \sim \mathcal{N}_n(\boldsymbol{\mu}, \boldsymbol{\Sigma} = (\sigma_{ij}))$ where

$$\boldsymbol{\mu} = (\mu, \ldots, \mu)' \qquad \text{for some} \quad \mu \in \mathfrak{R}, \tag{5.2.2}$$

and

$$\sigma_{ij} = \begin{cases} \sigma^2 > 0 & \text{for} \quad i = j, \\ \rho\sigma^2 & \text{for} \quad i \neq j. \end{cases} \tag{5.2.3}$$

The covariance matrix of permutation-symmetric normal variables given in (5.2.3) has certain interesting properties. One of them is:

Proposition 5.2.1. *Let* $\boldsymbol{\Sigma} = (\sigma_{ij})$ *be an* $n \times n$ *matrix satisfying* (5.2.3). *Then its determinant is*

$$|\boldsymbol{\Sigma}| = \sigma^{2n}[1 + (n-1)\rho](1-\rho)^{n-1}. \tag{5.2.4}$$

PROOF (Scheffé (1959, p. 403)). After subtracting the first row from each of the others, and then adding to the first column the sum of the other columns, we have

$$|\boldsymbol{\Sigma}| = \sigma^{2n} \begin{vmatrix} 1 + (n-1)\rho & \rho & \rho & \cdots & \rho \\ 0 & 1-\rho & 0 & \cdots & 0 \\ 0 & 0 & 1-\rho & \cdots & 0 \\ & & \cdots & & \\ 0 & 0 & 0 & \cdots & 1-\rho \end{vmatrix}$$

$$= \sigma^{2n}[1 + (n-1)\rho](1-\rho)^{n-1}.$$ □

By (5.2.4), it is immediate that $|\mathbf{\Sigma}| < 0$ holds for $\rho < -1/(n-1)$ and $|\mathbf{\Sigma}| > 0$ holds for $0 \le \rho < 1$. In the following proposition we state a necessary and sufficient condition under which $\mathbf{\Sigma}$ is a covariance matrix.

Proposition 5.2.2. *Let* $\mathbf{\Sigma} = (\sigma_{ij})$ *be an* $n \times n$ *matrix satisfying* (5.2.3). *Then*:

(a) $\mathbf{\Sigma}$ *is a positive definite matrix if and only if* $\rho \in (-1/(n-1), 1)$;
(b) $\mathbf{\Sigma}$ *is a positive semidefinite matrix if and only if* $\rho = -1/(n-1)$ *or* $\rho = 1$.

PROOF. (a) For every given real vector $\mathbf{c} = (c_1, \ldots, c_n)' \neq \mathbf{0}$ we have

$$\begin{aligned}\mathbf{c}'\mathbf{\Sigma}\mathbf{c} &= \sigma^{2n}\left[\rho \sum_{i \neq j} c_i c_j + \sum_{i=1}^{n} c_i^2\right] \\ &= \sigma^{2n}\left[\rho\left(\sum_{i=1}^{n} c_i\right)^2 + (1-\rho)\sum_{i=1}^{n} c_i^2\right].\end{aligned}$$

Clearly, $\mathbf{c}'\mathbf{\Sigma}\mathbf{c} > 0$ for all $\rho \in [0, 1)$. For $\rho \in (-1/(n-1), 0)$ we have

$$\rho \sum_{i \neq j} c_i c_j + \sum_{i=1}^{n} c_i^2 > 0 \qquad \text{if} \quad \sum_{i \neq j} c_i c_j \le 0;$$

$$\begin{aligned}\rho \sum_{i \neq j} c_i c_j + \sum_{i=1}^{n} c_i^2 &> \frac{1}{(n-1)}\left[(n-1)\sum_{i=1}^{n} c_i^2 - \sum_{i \neq j} c_i c_j\right] \\ &= \frac{1}{(n-1)}\left[\sum_{i<j} (c_i - c_j)^2\right] \ge 0 \qquad \text{if} \quad \sum_{i \neq j} c_i c_j > 0.\end{aligned}$$

Thus $\mathbf{c}'\mathbf{\Sigma}\mathbf{c} > 0$ for $\rho \in (-1/(n-1), 1)$.

(b) For $\rho = -1/(n-1)$, $\mathbf{\Sigma}$ is singular and is the limit of $\{\mathbf{\Sigma}(t)\}$ as $t \to 0^+$, where (for $t > 0$) $\mathbf{\Sigma}(t)$ is the positive definite matrix with $\rho = t - 1/(n-1)$ in (5.2.3). Since for every $\mathbf{c} \in \mathfrak{R}^n$ we have

$$\mathbf{c}'\mathbf{\Sigma}\mathbf{c} = \lim_{t \to 0^+} \mathbf{c}'\mathbf{\Sigma}(t)\mathbf{c} \ge 0,$$

$\mathbf{\Sigma}$ must be positive semidefinite. Similarly, $\mathbf{\Sigma}$ is positive semidefinite when $\rho = 1$.

(c) For $\rho < -1/(n-1)$, the determinant of $\mathbf{\Sigma}$ is negative. Thus $\mathbf{\Sigma}$ is neither positive definite nor positive semidefinite. □

Since we are primarily interested in the case in which $\mathbf{\Sigma}$ is positive definite, in the rest of this section we shall assume that $\rho \in (-1/(n-1), 1)$.

Proposition 5.2.3. *Let* $\mathbf{\Sigma} = (\sigma_{ij})$ *be a covariance matrix satisfying* (5.2.3), *where* $\rho \in (-1/(n-1), 1)$. *Then* $\mathbf{\Sigma}^{-1} = \mathbf{T} = (\tau_{ij})$ *is such that*

$$\tau_{ij} = \begin{cases} \dfrac{1+(n-2)\rho}{\sigma^2 \Delta_n(\rho)} & \textit{for} \quad i = j, \\[2ex] \dfrac{-\rho}{\sigma^2 \Delta_n(\rho)} & \textit{for} \quad i \neq j, \end{cases} \tag{5.2.5}$$

where

$$\Delta_n(\rho) = (1-\rho)[1+(n-1)\rho] > 0. \tag{5.2.6}$$

PROOF. Suppose that $\tau_{ii} = a$ and $\tau_{ij} = b$ for all i and all $i \neq j$. Then $\mathbf{T\Sigma} = \mathbf{I}_n$ yields

$$\begin{cases} a + (n-1)\rho b = \sigma^{-2}, \\ \rho a + [1+(n-2)\rho]b = 0. \end{cases}$$

Solving the two linear equations simultaneously yields (5.2.5). Since the inverse of $\mathbf{\Sigma}$ is unique, the solution is also unique. □

Proposition 5.2.3 can be applied to obtain the marginal and conditional distributions of permutation symmetric normal variables.

Theorem 5.2.1. *Let* $\mathbf{X} \sim \mathcal{N}_n(\boldsymbol{\mu}, \mathbf{\Sigma} = (\sigma_{ij}))$ *where* $\mu_i = \mu$, $\sigma_{ii} = \sigma^2$, $\sigma_{ij} = \rho\sigma^2$ *for all i and all $j \neq i$, and* $\rho \in (-1/(n-1), 1)$. *For fixed $k < n$ consider the partition*

$$\mathbf{X}_1 = (X_1, \ldots, X_k)', \qquad \mathbf{X}_2 = (X_{k+1}, \ldots, X_n)'. \tag{5.2.7}$$

Then:

(a) *the marginal distribution of* $\mathbf{X}_1$ *is* $\mathcal{N}_k(\boldsymbol{\mu}_1, \mathbf{\Sigma}_{11})$; *and*
(b) *the conditional distribution of* $\mathbf{X}_1$, *given* $\mathbf{X}_2 = \mathbf{x}_2$, *is* $\mathcal{N}_k(\boldsymbol{\mu}_{1\cdot 2}(\mathbf{x}_2), \mathbf{\Sigma}_{11\cdot 2})$, *where*

$$\boldsymbol{\mu} = (\mu, \ldots, \mu)', \qquad \mathbf{\Sigma}_{11}^{k\times k} = (\sigma_{ij}),$$

$$\boldsymbol{\mu}_{1\cdot 2}(\mathbf{x}_2) = (\nu, \ldots, \nu), \quad \nu = \nu(\mathbf{x}_2) = \mu + \frac{\rho}{1+(n-k-1)\rho}\sum_{i=k+1}^{n}(x_i - \mu),$$

and $\mathbf{\Sigma}_{11\cdot 2} = (\sigma_{ij\cdot k+1,\ldots,n})$ *is such that*

$$\sigma_{ij\cdot k+1,\ldots,n} = \begin{cases} \sigma^2(1-\rho)[1+(n-k)\rho]/[1+(n-k-1)\rho] & \text{for } i = j, \\ \sigma^2\rho(1-\rho)/[1+(n-k-1)\rho] & \text{for } i \neq j. \end{cases} \tag{5.2.8}$$

Consequently, the best predictor of X_i given $\mathbf{X}_2 = \mathbf{x}_2$ is ν for $i = 1, \ldots, k$.

PROOF. The proof follows from Theorems 3.3.1 and 3.3.4, Proposition 5.2.3, and Theorem 3.4.1, and by elementary calculation. □

Note that both the marginal density function and the conditional density function are also permutation-symmetric.

Theorem 5.2.2. *Let* $\mathbf{X} \sim \mathcal{N}_n(\boldsymbol{\mu}, \mathbf{\Sigma} = (\sigma_{ij}))$ *where* $\sigma_{ii} = \sigma^2$, $\sigma_{ij} = \rho\sigma^2$ *for all $i \neq j$ and* $\rho \in (-1/(n-1), 1)$. *Let* $\mathbf{X}_1, \mathbf{X}_2$ *be defined as in* (5.2.7). *Then:*

(a) *the multiple correlation coefficient between X_i and $\mathbf{X}_2$ is*

$$R_{i\cdot k+1,\ldots,n} = |\rho|\left[\frac{n-k}{1+(n-k-1)\rho}\right]^{1/2}, \qquad i = 1, \ldots, k; \tag{5.2.9}$$

(b) *the partial correlation coefficient between X_i and X_j, given $\mathbf{X}_2 = \mathbf{x}_2$, is*

$$\rho_{ij\cdot k+1,\ldots,n} = \frac{\rho}{1+(n-k)\rho}, \qquad 1 \le i < j \le k. \tag{5.2.10}$$

PROOF. Equation (5.2.9) follows from Theorem 3.4.2 and Proposition 5.2.3, (5.2.10) follows from Theorem 3.4.3 and (5.2.8). □

Note that the multiple correlation coefficient given in (5.2.9) is just the correlation between X_i and $\delta_\rho \sum_{j=k+1}^{n} X_j$ where

$$\delta_\rho = \begin{cases} 1 & \text{if} \quad \rho \ge 0, \\ -1 & \text{if} \quad \rho < 0. \end{cases} \tag{5.2.11}$$

When the normal variables are equally correlated and have a common variance σ^2, then the $k \times k$ matrix $\boldsymbol{\Sigma}_{12}\boldsymbol{\Sigma}_{22}^{-1}\boldsymbol{\Sigma}_{21}$ is just $\sigma^2\omega_k \cdot \mathbf{1}_k$, where $\mathbf{1}_k$ is the $k \times k$ matrix with elements one and

$$\omega_k = \frac{(n-k)\rho^2}{1+(n-k-1)\rho}.$$

Thus the matrix $-\lambda\boldsymbol{\Sigma}_{11} + \boldsymbol{\Sigma}_{12}\boldsymbol{\Sigma}_{22}^{-1}\boldsymbol{\Sigma}_{21} \equiv \sigma^2(\gamma_{ij})$ is such that

$$\gamma_{ij} = \begin{cases} d_1(\lambda) \equiv -\lambda + \omega_k & \text{for} \quad i = j, \\ d_2(\lambda) \equiv -\rho\lambda + \omega_k & \text{for} \quad i \ne j. \end{cases}$$

Applying a similar argument used in the proof of Proposition 5.2.1 we have

$$\begin{aligned} h_1(\lambda) &= |-\lambda\boldsymbol{\Sigma}_{11} + \boldsymbol{\Sigma}_{12}\boldsymbol{\Sigma}_{22}^{-1}\boldsymbol{\Sigma}_{21}| \\ &= \sigma^2(d_1(\lambda) + (k-1)d_2(\lambda))(d_1(\lambda) - d_2(\lambda))^{k-1}. \end{aligned}$$

Thus $h_1(\lambda) = 0$ has real roots

$$\begin{aligned} \lambda_1 &= \frac{k\omega_k}{1+(k-1)\rho} \\ &= \frac{k(n-k)\rho^2}{(1+(k-1)\rho)(1+(n-k-1)\rho)} \end{aligned}$$

and $\lambda_2 = \cdots = \lambda_k = 0$. Similarly, the determinant of $-\lambda\boldsymbol{\Sigma}_{22} + \boldsymbol{\Sigma}_{21}\boldsymbol{\Sigma}_{11}^{-1}\boldsymbol{\Sigma}_{12}$ can be obtained by interchanging $(n-k)$ and k in $h_1(\lambda)$; that is,

$$h_2(\lambda) = |-\lambda\boldsymbol{\Sigma}_{22} + \boldsymbol{\Sigma}_{21}\boldsymbol{\Sigma}_{11}^{-1}\boldsymbol{\Sigma}_{12}| = 0$$

has real roots $\lambda_{k+1} = \lambda_1$ and $\lambda_{k+2} = \cdots = \lambda_n = 0$. Combining, we have the following theorem.

Theorem 5.2.3. *Let $\mathbf{X}$ have an $\mathcal{N}_n(\boldsymbol{\mu}, \boldsymbol{\Sigma} = (\sigma_{ij}))$ distribution where $\sigma_{ii} = \sigma^2$ and $\sigma_{ij} = \rho\sigma^2$ for all $i \ne j$ and $\rho \in (-1/(n-1), 1)$. For fixed k let the components of $\mathbf{X}$ be partitioned as in (5.2.7). Then the only positive canonical correlation* *coefficient is*

$$\tau_1 = |\rho| \left[\frac{k(n-k)}{(1+(k-1)\rho)(1+(n-k-1)\rho)} \right]^{1/2}, \tag{5.2.12}$$

and it is the correlation coefficient between $c_1 \sum_{i=1}^{k} X_i$ *and* $\delta_\rho c_2 \sum_{j=k+1}^{n} X_i$ *where*

$$c_1 = \sigma^{-1}[k(1+(k-1)\rho)]^{-1/2}, \qquad c_2 = \sigma^{-1}[(n-k)(1+(n-k-1)\rho)]^{-1/2}, \tag{5.2.13}$$

and δ_ρ *is defined in* (5.2.11).

Finally, we note a result for the principal components of permutation-symmetric normal variables.

Theorem 5.2.4. *Let* $\mathbf{X}$ *have an* $\mathcal{N}_n(\boldsymbol{\mu}, \boldsymbol{\Sigma} = (\sigma_{ij}))$ *distribution where* $\sigma_{ii} = \sigma^2$ *and* $\sigma_{ij} = \rho\sigma^2$ *for all* $i \neq j$ *and* $\rho \in (-1/(n-1), 1)$. *Then the first principal component is given by*

$$Y_1 = \sum_{i=1}^{n} \frac{X_i}{\sqrt{n}} = \frac{1}{\sqrt{n}}(1, 1, \ldots, 1)\mathbf{X},$$

with variance $\lambda_1 = [1 + (n-1)\rho]\sigma^2$. *For* $r = 2, \ldots, n$ *the rth principal component is*

$$Y_r = \frac{1}{\sqrt{(n-r+2)(n-r+1)}}(0, \ldots, 0, -(n-r+1), 1, \ldots, 1)\mathbf{X}.$$

(That is, all the coefficients of the variables $X_1, \ldots, X_{r-2}$ *are zero, the coefficient of* X_{r-1} *is* $-[(n-r+1)/(n-r+2)]^{1/2}$, *and the coefficients of* $X_r, \ldots, X_n$ *are* $[(n-r+2)(n-r+1)]^{-1/2}$.) *The variance of* Y_r *is* $(1-\rho)\sigma^2$.

Proof. The determinant of the matrix $\boldsymbol{\Sigma} - \lambda\mathbf{I}_n$ is

$$h(\lambda) = |\boldsymbol{\Sigma} - \lambda\mathbf{I}_n| = [(\sigma^2 - \lambda) + (n-1)\rho\sigma^2][(\sigma^2 - \lambda) - \rho\sigma^2]^{n-1}.$$

Thus the eigenvalues of $\boldsymbol{\Sigma}$ are

$$\lambda_1 = [1 + (n-1)\rho]\sigma^2, \qquad \lambda_2 = \cdots = \lambda_n = (1-\rho)\sigma^2.$$

It is easy to verify that the principal components of $\mathbf{X}$ are $Y_1, \ldots, Y_n$, that λ_r is just the variance of Y_r $(r = 1, \ldots, n)$, and that the Y_r's are independent. □

5.3. Exchangeable Normal Variables

An important subclass of permutation-symmetric normal variables is the class of exchangeable normal variables. In this section we study exchangeable normal variables in greater detail. We first introduce the definition of exchangeability, and then examine the special consequence of de Finetti's theorem for exchangeable random variables when applied to the multivariate normal distribution. It is shown that when using a simple linear transformation, the density function and distribution function of exchangeable normal variables can be expressed in the forms of a single integral. Finally, we study some partial orderings of positive dependence of exchangeable normal variables and observe a few examples of their applications.

It should be noted that by "exchangeable random variables" we mean *infinitely* exchangeable random variables (see Definition 5.3.2 below). If the joint distribution of $(X_1, \dots, X_n)'$ is permutation-symmetric, then $X_1, \dots, X_n$ are sometimes said to be *finitely* exchangeable in the literature. To avoid possible confusion we call all finitely exchangeable random variables "permutatation-symmetric random variables" in this volume.

5.3.1. Exchangeable Random Variables and de Finetti's Theorem

Exchangeable random variables involve exchangeability of *an infinite sequence* of random variables. The following definition can be found in Loève (1963, p. 364).

Definition 5.3.1. Let $\{Y_i\}_{i=1}^{\infty}$ be an infinite sequence of univariate random variables. It is said to be a sequence of exchangeable random variables if, for every finite n and every permutation $\{\pi_1, \dots, \pi_n\}$ of $\{1, \dots, n\}$, $(Y_1, \dots, Y_n)'$ and $(Y_{\pi_1}, \dots, Y_{\pi_n})'$ are identically distributed.

For a finite n let $\mathbf{X} = (X_1, \dots, X_n)'$ be an n-dimensional random variable with density function $f(\mathbf{x})$ and distribution function $F(\mathbf{x})$.

Definition 5.3.2. $X_1, \dots, X_n$ are said to be exchangeable random variables if there exists a sequence of exchangeable random variables $\{X_i^*\}_{i=1}^{\infty}$ such that $(X_1, \dots, X_n)'$ and $(X_1^*, \dots, X_n^*)'$ are identically distributed.

It is obvious that the joint density function and distribution function of exchangeable random variables must be permutation-symmetric. However, it is not true that random variables with a permutation-symmetric density function are always exchangeable. To illustrate this point we consider an example given below.

EXAMPLE 5.3.1. Let $\mathbf{X} = (X_1, X_2, X_3)' \sim \mathcal{N}_3(\mathbf{0}, \mathbf{\Sigma} = (\sigma_{ij}))$ where $\sigma_{ii} = 1$ and $\sigma_{ij} = -0.1$ for $1 \le i < j \le 3$. Then the components of $\mathbf{X}$ are not exchangeable for the following reason: Suppose that there did exist an infinite sequence $\{X_i^*\}_{i=1}^{\infty}$ such that $(X_1^*, X_2^*, X_3^*)'$ and $\mathbf{X}$ have the same distribution. Then we would have $\mathrm{Var}(X_i^*) = 1$ and $\mathrm{Corr}(X_i^*, X_j^*) = -0.1$ for all $i \neq j$. But this is impossible because for any $n > 12$ the determinant of such an $n \times n$ matrix (with diagonal matrix one and off-diagonal elements -0.1) is negative (see Proposition 5.2.1), and hence it cannot be a covariance matrix. □

An important question is then: For a given n-dimensional random variable $\mathbf{X} = (X_1, \ldots, X_n)'$ with permutation-symmetric distribution, when are $X_1, \ldots, X_n$ exchangeable? The answer to this question is provided by de Finetti's theorem (see, e.g., Loève (1963, p. 365)).

Proposition 5.3.1. *Let the distribution of $\mathbf{X} = (X_1, \ldots, X_n)'$ be permutation-symmetric. Then $X_1, \ldots, X_n$ are exchangeable if and only if $X_1, \ldots, X_n$ are conditionally independent and identically distributed random variables; that is, if and only if there exists an r-dimensional ($r \geq 1$) random variable Z_0 such that the conditional distribution function of $\mathbf{X}$, given $Z_0 = z$, is $\prod_{i=1}^n G_z(x_i)$, where*

$$G_z(x) = P[X_1 \leq x | Z = z]. \tag{5.3.1}$$

Now let Z_0 have a distribution function $H(z)$, let Λ be the support of the density function of Z_0, and let $\{G_z(x)\colon z \in \Lambda\}$ denote the family of conditional distribution functions. If $X_1, \ldots, X_n$ are exchangeable, then the joint distribution of $\mathbf{X}$ can be expressed as a mixture of distributions.

Proposition 5.3.2. *$X_1, \ldots, X_n$ are exchangeable random variables if and only if there exist a family of distribution functions $\{G_z(x)\colon z \in \Lambda\}$ and a distribution $H(z)$, $z \in \Lambda$, such that the joint distribution of $X_1, \ldots, X_n$ is*

$$F(\mathbf{x}) = \int_\Lambda \prod_{i=1}^n G_z(x_i)\, dH(z). \tag{5.3.2}$$

If the density functions exist, then the joint density of $X_1, \ldots, X_n$ can be expressed as

$$f(\mathbf{x}) = \int_\Lambda \prod_{i=1}^n g_z(x_i) h(z)\, dz, \tag{5.3.3}$$

where $g_z(x) = (d/dx)G_z(x)$ and $h(z)$ is the density of Z_0.

The result in Proposition 5.3.2 suggests a direction of extension from a finite number of exchangeable random variables to an infinite sequence of exchangeable variables. To find a process of extension of (or construction for) such an infinite sequence, first note that if

(i) $\{Z_i\}_{i=1}^n$ is a sequence of i.i.d. random variables, (5.3.4)

(ii) Z_0(an $r \geq 1$ dimensional random variable) is independent of $\{Z_i\}_{i=1}^n$, (5.3.5)

and

(iii) $\psi\colon \mathfrak{R}^{r+1} \to \mathfrak{R}$ is any measurable function, (5.3.6) then the joint distribution of $\psi(Z_1, Z_0), \ldots, \psi(Z_n, Z_0)$ is of the form given in (5.3.2) with $G_z(x) = P[\psi(Z_1, Z_0) \leq x | Z_0 = z]$, thus they are exchangeable. To construct such an infinite sequence of exchangeable variables $\{X_i^*\}_{i=1}^{\infty}$, we can simply extend the finite sequence $\{Z_i\}_{i=1}^{n}$ to an infinite sequence of i.i.d. random variables $\{Z_i\}_{i=1}^{\infty}$ and then define

$$X_i^* = \psi(Z_i, Z_0), \qquad i = 1, 2, \ldots. \tag{5.3.7}$$

This shows that $X_1, \ldots, X_n$ are exchangeable if there exist random variables $\{Z_i\}_{i=1}^{n}$, Z_0, and a function ψ satisfying (5.3.4)–(5.3.6), such that $(X_1, \ldots, X_n)'$ and $(\psi(Z_1, Z_0), \ldots, \psi(Z_n, Z_0))'$ are identically distributed. It can be shown that (see, e.g., Shaked (1977)) the converse is also true. Thus we observe another characterization of a finite number of exchangeable random variables.

Proposition 5.3.3. *Random variables $X_1, \ldots, X_n$ are exchangeable if and only if there exist i.i.d. random variables $\{Z_i\}_{i=1}^{n}$, an r-dimensional $(r \geq 1)$ random variable Z_0, and a function ψ satisfying* (5.3.4)–(5.3.6), *such that $(X_1, \ldots, X_n)'$ and $(\psi(Z_1, Z_0), \ldots, \psi(Z_n, Z_0))'$ are identically distributed.*

Both Proposition 5.3.2 and 5.3.3 state that exchangeable random variables can be obtained by mixing i.i.d. random variables with another common random variable Z_0. Consequently, many important results concerning exchangeable variables can be obtained by first conditioning on $Z_0 = z$, and then unconditioning. Such results have been given in the literature under different labels, such as (random variables or) events which are almost independent (Dykstra, Hewett, and Thompson, 1973), random variables which are positively dependent by mixture (PDM, Shaked, 1977), and random variables which are conditionally i.i.d. (Tong, 1977). The following is an elementary result on the common correlation coefficient of exchangeable variables (Tong, 1980, p. 100).

Proposition 5.3.4. *If $X_1, \ldots, X_n$ are exchangeable random variables, then* $\mathrm{Corr}(X_i, X_j) = \rho \geq 0$ *for all* $i \neq j$.

The proof of this result is easy, and is left to the reader.

5.3.2. Characterization of Exchangeable Normal Variables

To study properties of exchangeable normal variables we first observe the obvious definition.

Definition 5.3.3. $X_1, \ldots, X_n$ are said to be exchangeable normal variables if they are exchangeable and their joint distribution is $\mathcal{N}_n(\boldsymbol{\mu}, \boldsymbol{\Sigma})$.

Since all exchangeable random variables must be permutation-symmetric, it is obvious that if $X_1, \ldots, X_n$ are exchangeable normal variables, then

$$\boldsymbol{\mu} = (\mu, \ldots, \mu)' \qquad \text{for some} \quad \mu \in \mathscr{R},$$

and $\boldsymbol{\Sigma} = (\sigma_{ij})$ is such that

$$\sigma_{ii} = \sigma^2, \qquad \sigma_{ij} = \rho\sigma^2 \qquad \text{for} \quad 1 \le i < j \le n.$$

In the following theorem we observe a characterization result for exchangeable normal variables.

Theorem 5.3.1. *The following statements are equivalent:*

(a) $X_1, \ldots, X_n$ *are exchangeable normal variables.*
(b) $\mathbf{X} = (X_1, \ldots, X_n)'$ *has an* $\mathscr{N}_n(\boldsymbol{\mu}, \boldsymbol{\Sigma})$ *distribution such that* $X_1, \ldots, X_n$ *have a common mean* μ, *a common variance* σ^2, *and a common correlation coefficient* $\rho \in [0, 1]$.
(c) *For* $\rho = 1$, $\mathbf{X}$ *and* $(\sigma Z_0 + \mu, \ldots, \sigma Z_0 + \mu)'$ *are identically distributed where* Z_0 *is an* $\mathscr{N}(0, 1)$ *variable; for* $\rho \in [0, 1)$, *the joint density function of* $\mathbf{X}$ *is a mixture given by*

$$f(\mathbf{x}) = \int_{-\infty}^{\infty} \left[(\sigma\sqrt{1-\rho})^{-n} \prod_{i=1}^{n} \phi(u_i + \lambda z) \right] \phi(z)\, dz, \tag{5.3.8}$$

where ϕ *is the* $\mathscr{N}(0, 1)$ *density function and*

$$\lambda = \sqrt{\frac{\rho}{1-\rho}}, \qquad u_i = \frac{x_i - \mu}{\sigma\sqrt{1-\rho}} \qquad (i = 1, \ldots, n).$$

(c′) *For* $\rho \in [0, 1)$, *the joint density function of* $\mathbf{X}$ *is given by*

$$f(\mathbf{x}) = c_n(\rho) \exp\left\{ -\frac{1}{2}\left[\sum_{i=1}^{n} \frac{(x_i - \mu)^2}{\sigma^2(1-\rho)} - \frac{\rho\left(\sum_{i=1}^{n} (x_i - \mu)/\sigma\right)^2}{1 + (n-1)\rho} \right] \right\}, \tag{5.3.8.$'$}$$

where

$$c_n(\rho) = (\sqrt{2\pi}\sigma)^{-n}(1-\rho)^{-(n-1)/2}[1 + (n-1)\rho]^{-1/2}.$$

(d) $\mathbf{X}$ *and*

$$(\sigma(\sqrt{1-\rho}Z_1 + \sqrt{\rho}Z_0) + \mu, \ldots, \sigma(\sqrt{1-\rho}Z_n + \sqrt{\rho}Z_0) + \mu)' \tag{5.3.9}$$

are identically distributed where $Z_0, Z_1, \ldots, Z_n$ *are i.i.d.* $\mathscr{N}(0, 1)$ *variables,* $\mu \in \mathfrak{R}$, $\sigma > 0$, *and* $\rho \in [0, 1]$.

PROOF. The proof for $\rho = 1$ is immediate. Thus it will be assumed that $\rho \in [0, 1)$ and the proof will be centered at the representation in (5.3.9).

(a)$\Leftrightarrow$(d). It is immediate to verify that (d)$\Rightarrow$(a) by choosing $\psi(z_i, z_0) = \sigma(\sqrt{1-\rho}z_i + \sqrt{\rho}z_0) + \mu$ in Proposition 5.3.3. On the other hand, suppose that $X_1, \ldots, X_n$ are exchangeable normal variables with a common mean μ, a common variance σ^2, and a common correlation coefficient ρ, then ρ must be nonnegative (Proposition 5.3.4). It is straightforward to verify that for all $\rho \in [0, 1)$, both $\mathbf{X}$ and the random variable in (5.3.9) have an $\mathcal{N}_n(\boldsymbol{\mu}, \boldsymbol{\Sigma})$ distribution. Thus (a) $\Rightarrow$ (d).

(c) $\Leftrightarrow$ (c)′. After integrating out the right-hand side of (5.3.8) we obtain (5.3.8)′.

(b) $\Leftrightarrow$ (c)′. For given $\rho \in [0, 1\}$, μ, and σ^2 we have, by simple algebraic calculation,

$$(2\pi)^{-n/2}|\boldsymbol{\Sigma}|^{-1/2}\exp(-\tfrac{1}{2}(\mathbf{x}-\boldsymbol{\mu})'\boldsymbol{\Sigma}^{-1}(\mathbf{x}-\boldsymbol{\mu})) = f(\mathbf{x}),$$

where $f(\mathbf{x})$ is given in (5.3.8)′.

(c) $\Leftrightarrow$ (d). By conditioning on $Z_0 = z$ then unconditioning, it follows that the density function given in (5.3.8) is that of the random variable defined in (5.3.9). □

Theorem 5.3.1 simply says that normal variables with a common mean μ, a common variance σ^2, and a common correlation coefficient ρ, are exchangeable normal variables if and only if $\rho \geq 0$ or, equivalently, if and only if it is a mixture of the means of conditionally i.i.d. univariate normal variables as defined in (5.3.9). This observation leads to another characterization result.

Theorem 5.3.2. *Random variables $X_1, \ldots, X_n$ are exchangeable normal variables with a common mean μ, a common variance σ^2, and a common correlation coefficient $\rho \geq 0$ if and only if there are the observations corresponding to the following experiment.*

(a) *generate an observation $\sigma\sqrt{\rho}Z_0 + \mu$ from the $\mathcal{N}(\mu, \rho\sigma^2)$ distribution, i.e., generate a Z_0 from the $\mathcal{N}(0, 1)$ distribution and then observe $Y = \sigma\sqrt{\rho}Z_0 + \mu$;*
(b) *for given $Y = y$, generate independent observations $X_1, \ldots, X_n$ from the $\mathcal{N}(y, \sigma^2(1-\rho))$ distribution.*

A related question is whether a mixture of the variance of the univariate normal variables also yields exchangeable normal variables. That is, if $\mathbf{X} = (X_1, \ldots, X_n)'$ has a joint density of the form

$$f(\mathbf{x}) = \int_0^\infty \prod_{i=1}^n \frac{1}{\sqrt{2\pi\theta^2}} \exp\left(-\frac{1}{2\theta^2}x_i^2\right) h(\theta)\, d\theta$$

for some density function $h(\theta)$ on $[0, \infty)$, are $X_1, \ldots, X_n$ exchangeable normal variables? The answer to this question is, of course, in the negative because $\mathbf{X}$ does not always have a multivariate normal distribution (although $X_1, \ldots, X_n$ are exchangeable). For example, if $h(\theta)$ is chosen to be the density function of $(V/\nu)^{-1/2}$ where V has a chi-square distribution with ν degrees of freedom, then $\mathbf{X}$ has a multivariate t distribution (see Chapter 9).

5.3.3. Some Examples of Applications of Exchangeable Normal Variables

Exchangeable normal variables make their appearance in many statistical applications. Here we discuss some examples of the applications. The examples are given for illustrative purposes only and, of course, are not exhaustive.

Application 5.3.1 (Random-Effects Models in the Analysis of Variance). The random-effects models in ANOVA problems are also called variance-components models. In the one-way ANOVA model we assume that

$$Y_{ij} = \mu + a_i + e_{ij} \qquad \text{for} \quad i = 1, \ldots, I; \quad j = 1, \ldots, J, \tag{5.3.10}$$

where the a_i's and e_{ij}'s are completely independent, the a_i's are $\mathcal{N}(0, \alpha^2)$ variables, and the e_{ij}'s are $\mathcal{N}(0, \beta^2)$ variables (see, e.g., Schéffe (1959, Sec. 7.2)). Simple algebra shows that, for each $i = 1, \ldots, I$, the components of $\mathbf{Y}_i = (Y_{i1}, \ldots, Y_{iJ})'$ are exchangeable normal variables with a common mean μ, a common variance $\sigma^2 = \alpha^2 + \beta^2$, and a common correlation coefficient $\rho = \alpha^2/(\alpha^2 + \beta^2)$. Thus in testing the hypotheses

$$H_0\colon \alpha^2 = \alpha_0^2 \quad \text{versus} \quad H_1\colon \alpha^2 \neq \alpha_0^2,$$

the sum square of errors (SSE) involves the sum of independent sum squares of the residuals of J exchangeable normal variables.

Applications 5.3.2 (The Distribution of a Data Variable in the Bayes Theory). In the Bayes theory concerning normal observations, it is generally assumed that the prior distribution of θ, the population mean, has an $\mathcal{N}(\mu, \omega^2)$ distribution for some μ and $\omega^2 > 0$. Thus, for given θ, if the random variables are (conditionally) i.i.d. normal variables, then the marginal distribution of the data variable $\mathbf{X} = (X_1, \ldots, X_n)'$ is a mixture. In this case the density function of $\mathbf{X}$ is known to be of the form (5.3.8) or, equivalently, (5.3.8)', and $X_1, \ldots, X_n$ are exchangeable normal variables.

Applications 5.3.3 (Simultaneous Comparisons of Normal Means with a Control). In the area of multiple comparisons it is often of interest to compare the means of several populations simultaneously with that of a control population. In symbols, let $\Pi_0, \Pi_1, \ldots, \Pi_n$ denote $n + 1$ normal populations with means θ_i and variances ω_i^2 $(i = 0, 1, \ldots, n)$. Suppose that N_i observations are taken from Π_i, and that $\bar{Y}_i$ denotes the sample mean. Furthermore, suppose that each of the Π_i's is to be compared with Π_0 simultaneously. Then the parameters

$$\mu_i = \theta_i - \theta_0, \qquad i = 1, \ldots, n,$$

are of interest and the natural estimates of μ_i's are $\bar{Y}_i - \bar{Y}_0$ $(i = 1, \ldots, n)$. If the

N_i's are chosen to satisfy

$$\frac{\omega_1^2}{N_1} = \cdots = \frac{\omega_n^2}{N_n} = \alpha^2,$$

then the components of

$$\mathbf{X} = (\bar{Y}_1 - \bar{Y}_0 - \mu_1, \ldots, \bar{Y}_n - \bar{Y}_0 - \mu_n)'$$

are exchangeable normal variables with a common mean 0, a common variance $\sigma^2 = \alpha^2 + \omega_0^2/N_0$, and a common correlation coefficient $\rho = \omega_0^2/(\omega_0^2 + N_0\alpha^2)$. Consequently, the confidence probability for $\boldsymbol{\mu} = (\mu_1, \ldots, \mu_n)'$ based on $(\bar{Y}_1 - \bar{Y}_0, \ldots, \bar{Y}_n - \bar{Y}_n)'$ is a joint probability of exchangeable normal variables.

5.3.4. Distribution Functions of Exchangeable Normal Variables and of Their Absolute Values

The density function of a multivariate normal variable can be found in (3.2.1), and the distribution function is just the integral of the density function over the set $\mathsf{X}_{i=1}^n (-\infty, x_i]$ in $\mathfrak{R}^n$. But if $X_1, \ldots, X_n$ are exchangeable normal variables, then a simpler expression is possible, and the distribution function can be expressed as a single integral instead of a multiple integral. The expression depends on the transformation given in (5.3.9), and the probability integrals are easier to evaluate numerically using this expression.

Theorem 5.3.3. *If $X_1, \ldots, X_n$ are exchangeable normal variables with a common means μ, a common variance σ^2, and a common correlation coefficient $\rho \in [0, 1)$, then their joint distribution function is*

$$F(\mathbf{x}) = \int_{-\infty}^{\infty} \prod_{i=1}^{n} \Phi\left(\frac{a_i + \sqrt{\rho}z}{\sqrt{1-\rho}}\right) \phi(z)\, dz, \tag{5.3.11}$$

where $a_i = (x_i - \mu)/\sigma$ $(i = 1, \ldots, n)$, and

$$\phi(z) = \frac{1}{\sqrt{2\pi}} e^{-z^2/2}, \qquad -\infty < z < \infty, \tag{5.3.12}$$

$$\Phi(z) = \int_{-\infty}^{z} \frac{1}{\sqrt{2\pi}} e^{-t^2/2}\, dt \tag{5.3.13}$$

are the $\mathcal{N}(0, 1)$ density function and distribution function, respectively.

Proof. By (5.3.9) we have

$$F(\mathbf{x}) = P\left[\bigcap_{i=1}^{n} \{\sigma(\sqrt{1-\rho}Z_i + \sqrt{\rho}Z_0) + \mu \le x_i\}\right],$$

where $Z_0, Z_1, \ldots, Z_n$ are i.i.d. $\mathcal{N}(0, 1)$ variables. Conditioning on $Z_0 = z$, then unconditioning, we have

$$\begin{aligned} F(\mathbf{x}) &= \int_{-\infty}^{\infty} P\left[\bigcap_{i=1}^{n} \left\{Z_i \le \frac{a_i - \sqrt{\rho} z}{\sqrt{1-\rho}}\right\} \middle| Z_0 = z\right] \phi(z)\, dz \\ &= \int_{-\infty}^{\infty} \prod_{i=1}^{n} \Phi\left(\frac{a_i - \sqrt{\rho} z}{\sqrt{1-\rho}}\right) \phi(z)\, dz, \end{aligned} \tag{5.3.14}$$

and, by $\phi(z) = \phi(-z)$, the right-hand side of (5.3.14) and the right-hand side of (5.3.11) are identical. □

Note that for $n = 2$ this result was already given in Section 2.2 (see (2.2.3)). Also note that the density function given in (5.3.8) may be directly obtained from (5.3.14) by differentiation.

In certain applications we are interested in the distribution function of the absolute values of exchangeable normal variables. In the following theorem we give an expression for the special case when their means are zero. (When the common mean is not zero, a similar expression can be obtained.)

Theorem 5.3.4. *If $X_1, \ldots, X_n$ are exchangeable normal variables with a common mean* 0, *a common variance σ^2, and a common correlation coefficient $\rho \in [0, 1)$, then the joint distribution function of $|\mathbf{X}| = (|X_1|, \ldots, |X_n|)'$ is*

$$\begin{aligned} F_{|\mathbf{X}|}(\mathbf{x}) = \int_{-\infty}^{\infty} \prod_{i=1}^{n} \Bigg[&\Phi\left(\left(\frac{x_i}{\sigma} + \sqrt{\rho} z\right) \Big/ \sqrt{1-\rho}\right) \\ &- \Phi\left(\left(-\frac{x_i}{\sigma} + \sqrt{\rho} z\right) \Big/ \sqrt{1-\rho}\right)\Bigg] \phi(z)\, dz, \end{aligned} \tag{5.3.15}$$

where ϕ and Φ *are given in* (5.3.12) *and* (5.3.13), *respectively.*

PROOF.
$$\begin{aligned} F_{|\mathbf{X}|}(\mathbf{x}) &= P\left[\bigcap_{i=1}^{n} \{-x_i \le \sigma(\sqrt{1-\rho} Z_i + \sqrt{\rho} Z_0) \le x_i\}\right] \\ &= \int_{-\infty}^{\infty} P\left[\bigcap_{i=1}^{n} \left\{-\frac{x_i}{\sigma} - \sqrt{\rho} z \le \sqrt{1-\rho}\, Z_0 \le \frac{x_i}{\sigma} - \sqrt{\rho} z\right\} \middle| Z_0 = z\right] \phi(z)\, dz \\ &= \int_{-\infty}^{\infty} \prod_{i=1}^{n} \left[\Phi\left(\left(\frac{x_i}{\sigma} - \sqrt{\rho} z\right) \Big/ \sqrt{1-\rho}\right) - \Phi\left(\left(-\frac{x_i}{\sigma} - \sqrt{\rho} z\right) \Big/ \sqrt{1-\rho}\right)\right] \phi(z)\, dz \\ &= \text{the right-hand side of (5.3.15).} \end{aligned}$$
□

Note that the distribution function of $|\mathbf{X}|$ given in (5.3.15) is obtained *without* deriving the density of $|\mathbf{X}|$.

5.3.5. Positive Dependence of Exchangeable Normal Variables and of Their Absolute Values

Intuitively speaking, exchangeable normal variables are positively dependent because their common mean depends on the value of another normal variable (Theorem 5.3.2), thus they tend to hang together. In the following we first observe the MTP_2 property of their joint density function.

Theorem 5.3.5. *Let* $\mathbf{X}$ *have an* $\mathcal{N}_n(\boldsymbol{\mu}, \boldsymbol{\Sigma})$ *distribution,* $\boldsymbol{\Sigma} > 0$, *with a common mean* μ, *a common variance* σ^2, *and a common correlation coefficient* ρ. *Then the joint density function of* $\mathbf{X}$ *is* MTP_2 *if and only if* $\rho \in [0, 1)$.

Proof. If $\rho \in [0, 1)$, then by Proposition 5.2.3 the off-diagonal elements of $\boldsymbol{\Sigma}^{-1}$ are all nonpositive. Thus by Theorem 4.3.2 the density of $\mathbf{X}$ is MTP_2. If $\rho \in (-1/(n-1), 0)$, then the off-diagonal elements of $\boldsymbol{\Sigma}^{-1}$ are all positive. Again by Theorem 4.3.2 the density of $\mathbf{X}$ is not MTP_2. □

The next theorem concerns the MTP_2 property of the joint density of the absolute values of X_i's when $\boldsymbol{\mu} = \mathbf{0}$.

Theorem 5.3.6. *Let* $\mathbf{X}$ *have an* $\mathcal{N}_n(\mathbf{0}, \boldsymbol{\Sigma})$ *distribution,* $n \geq 3$, *with a common variance* σ^2 *and a common correlation coefficient* ρ. *Then the joint density function of* $|\mathbf{X}| = (|X_1|, \ldots, |X_n|)'$ *is* MTP_2 *if and only if* $\rho \in [0, 1)$.

Proof. The proof is similar by applying Proposition 5.2.3 and Theorem 5.1.5. □

Theorems 5.3.5 and 5.3.6 can be applied to yield useful moment and probability inequalities. In particular, all the inequalities in (5.1.1)–(5.1.6) hold true for $\mathbf{X}$ (for $|\mathbf{X}|$) when the components of $\mathbf{X}$ are exchangeable normal variables (are exchangeable normal variables with zero means).

In certain applications, inequalities for $|\mathbf{X}|$ may be of interest when the common mean μ is not zero. The following theorem shows that even when $\mu \neq 0$ the components of $|\mathbf{X}|$ are also associated. Thus all the inequalities in (5.1.1)–(5.1.6) also hold true.

Theorem 5.3.7. *Let* $\mathbf{X} = (X_1, \ldots, X_n)'$ *have an* $\mathcal{N}_n(\boldsymbol{\mu}, \boldsymbol{\Sigma})$ *distribution with a common mean* μ, *a common variance* σ^2, *and a common correlation coefficient* ρ. *If* $\rho \in [0, 1)$, *then* $|X_1|, \ldots, |X_n|$ *are associated random variables.*

Proof. Let $Z_0, Z_1, \ldots, Z_n$ be i.i.d. $\mathcal{N}(0, 1)$ variables and define

$$\mathbf{Y} = \sigma\sqrt{1-\rho}(Z_1, \ldots, Z_n)', \qquad \mathbf{Z} = (\sigma\sqrt{\rho}Z_0 + \mu, \ldots, \sigma\sqrt{\rho}Z_0 + \mu)',$$

then:

(i) $\mathbf{X}$ and $\mathbf{Y} + \mathbf{Z}$ are identically distributed;
(ii) $\mathbf{Y}$ has independent components, each having a symmetric unimodal marginal density function; and
(iii) $|\sigma\sqrt{\rho}Z_0 + \mu|, \ldots, |\sigma\sqrt{\rho}Z_0 + \mu|$ are associated because a single random variable forms a set of associated random variables (Esary, Proschan, and Walkup, 1967). Thus by Proposition 5.1.3 the components of $|\mathbf{Y} + \mathbf{Z}|$, and hence that of $|\mathbf{X}|$, are associated. □

We note in passing that Theorem 5.3.7 also follows from the main result in Bølviken and Jogdev (1982).

5.3.6. Partial Orderings of Exchangeable Normal Variables by Positive Dependence

If $X_1, \ldots, X_n$ are exchangeable normal variables with a common correlation coefficient ρ then, intuitively speaking, the larger ρ is the more positively dependent they are. A question of interest is whether useful monotonicity results can be obtained as a function of ρ. In the following we discuss some of the known results along this direction.

The first result concerns a monotonicity property of the conditional variance, the multiple and partial correlations, and the canonical correlations.

Theorem 5.3.8. *Let* $\mathbf{X}$ *have an* $\mathcal{N}_n(\boldsymbol{\mu}, \boldsymbol{\Sigma})$ *distribution with a common mean* μ, *a common variance* σ^2, *and a common correlation coefficient* $\rho \in [0, 1)$. *For given* $k < n$, *let* $\mathbf{X}_1 = (X_1, \ldots, X_k)'$ and $\mathbf{X}_2 = (X_{k+1}, \ldots, X_n)'$. *Then:*

(a) *the conditional variance of* X_i, *given* $\mathbf{X}_2 = \mathbf{x}_2$, *is a decreasing function of* ρ *for* $1 \le i \le k$;
(b) *the multiple correlation coefficient between* X_i *and* $\mathbf{X}_2$ *is an increasing function of* ρ *for* $1 \le i \le k$;
(c) *the partial correlation coefficient between* X_i *and* X_j, *given* $\mathbf{X}_2 = \mathbf{x}_2$, *is an increasing function of* ρ *for* $1 \le i < j \le k$;
(d) *the only positive canonical correlation coefficient between* $\mathbf{X}_1$ *and* $\mathbf{X}_2$ *is an increasing function of* ρ.

Proof. Immediate from (5.2.8)–(5.2.10) and (5.2.12). □

Another monotonicity result, given in Shaked and Tong (1985), can be obtained via a partial ordering of the distribution function of a linear combination of random variables. Consider the random variable $U = \sum_{i=1}^n c_i X_i$, where the c_i's are real numbers such that $\sum_{i=1}^n c_i = 0$. If the X_i's are more positively dependent, then they tend to hang together more, thus U tends to take a smaller value. For exchangeable normal variables such a result can easily be obtained.

Theorem 5.3.9. *Let* $\mathbf{X}$ *have an* $\mathcal{N}_n(\boldsymbol{\mu}, \boldsymbol{\Sigma})$ *distribution with a common mean* μ, *a common variance* σ^2, *and a common correlation coefficient* $\rho \in [0, 1)$. *Then for arbitrary but fixed* $\lambda > 0$ *and real numbers* $c_1, \ldots, c_n$, *such that* $\sum_{i=1}^n c_i = 0$, *the probability* $P_\rho[|\sum_{i=1}^n c_i X_i| \le \lambda]$ *is an increasing function of* ρ.

PROOF. Clearly, $\sum_{i=1}^n c_i X_i$ has a normal distribution with mean 0 and variance ω^2, where

$$\begin{aligned}\omega^2 &= \sigma^2\left[\sum_{i=1}^n c_i^2 + 2\rho \sum_{i<j} c_i c_j\right]\\ &= \sigma^2\left[(1-\rho)\sum_{i=1}^n c_i^2 + \rho\left(\sum_{i=1}^n c_i\right)^2\right]\\ &= \sigma^2(1-\rho)\sum_{i=1}^n c_i^2,\end{aligned}$$

is a decreasing function of ρ. □

A different type of result concerns an ordering for the expectations of functions of the form $\prod_{i=1}^n g(X_i)$ where g is any (not necessarily monotonic) measurable function. The motivation is that if $X_1, \ldots, X_n$ tend to hang together more, then $g(X_1), \ldots, g(X_n)$ tend to hang together more for all nonnegative functions g. Thus the expected value of $\prod_{i=1}^n g(X_i)$ becomes larger. For exchangeable normal variables the following result was given by Rinott and Pollak (1980) (for $n = 2$) and Shaked and Tong (1985) (for general n):

Theorem 5.3.10. *Let* $\mathbf{X}$ *have an* $\mathcal{N}_n(\boldsymbol{\mu}, \boldsymbol{\Sigma})$ *distribution with a common mean* μ, *a common variance* σ^2, *and a common correlation coefficient* $\rho \in [0, 1)$. *Then* $E_\rho \prod_{i=1}^n g(X_i)$ *is a nondecreasing function of* ρ *for all* g *when* n *is an even integer, and for all* $g \ge 0$ *when* n *is any positive integer, provided that the expectations exist. Consequently, by letting* g *be the indicator function of a set* A *the probability* $P_\rho[\bigcap_{i=1}^n \{X_i \in A\}]$ *is a nondecreasing function of* ρ *for all* $A \subset \Re$ *and all* n.

PROOF. The proof given here is a special case of the proof for a more general result given in Tong (1989). Suppose that, for arbitrary but fixed $0 \le \rho_1 < \rho_2 < 1$, $\{X_1, \ldots, X_n\}$ and $\{Y_1, \ldots, Y_n\}$ are two sets of exchangeable normal variables with means μ, variances σ^2, and correlation coefficients ρ_2 (for the X_i's) and ρ_1 (for the Y_i's), respectively. We show that $E \prod_{i=1}^n g(X_i) \ge E \prod_{i=1}^n g(Y_i)$ holds.

Let $\{U_i\}_{i=1}^n$, $\{V_i\}_{i=1}^n$, and W be i.i.d. $\mathcal{N}(0, 1)$ variables. Then $(X_1, \ldots, X_n)'$ and

$$(\sigma(\sqrt{1-\rho_2}\,U_1 + \sqrt{\rho_2 - \rho_1}\,V_1 + \sqrt{\rho_1}\,W) + \mu, \ldots,$$
$$\sigma(\sqrt{1-\rho_2}\,U_n + \sqrt{\rho_2 - \rho_1}\,V_1 + \sqrt{\rho_1}\,W) + \mu)' \quad (5.3.16)$$

are identically distributed; similarly, $(Y_1, \ldots, Y_n)'$ and

$$(\sigma(\sqrt{1-\rho_2}\,U_1 + \sqrt{\rho_2 - \rho_1}\,V_1 + \sqrt{\rho_1}\,W) + \mu, \ldots,$$
$$\sigma(\sqrt{1-\rho_2}\,U_n + \sqrt{\rho_2 - \rho_1}\,V_n + \sqrt{\rho_1}\,W) + \mu)' \quad (5.3.17)$$

are identically distributed. (Note that the elements in (5.3.17) depend on different V_i variables and the elements in (5.3.16) depend on the common variable V_1.) For any n and $g \geq 0$ we can write

$$E \prod_{i=1}^n g(X_i) = E\left[E\left\{E\left(\prod_{i=1}^n g(\sigma(\sqrt{1-\rho_2}\,U_i + \sqrt{\rho_2 - \rho_1}\,V_1 + \sqrt{\rho_1}\,W) + \mu) | (V_1, W)' = (v_1, w)'\right) | W = w\right\}\right]$$
$$= E[E\{\psi^n(V_1, W) | W = w\}],$$

where

$$\psi(v_1, w) = E(g(\sigma(\sqrt{1-\rho_2}\,U_i + \sqrt{\rho_2 - \rho_1}\,V_1 + \sqrt{\rho_1}\,W) + \mu) | (V_1, W)' = (v_1, w)'\}]$$

is the conditional expectation. Since $\psi(V_1, w), \ldots, \psi(V_n, w)$ are nonnegative i.i.d. random variables for every fixed $W = w$, by Jensen's inequality we have

$$E\{\psi^n(V_1, W) | W = w\} \geq E\left\{\prod_{j=1}^n \psi(V_j, W) | W = w\right\}$$

for every fixed w. Thus, after unconditioning,

$$E \prod_{i=1}^n g(X_i) = E[E\{\psi^n(V_1, W) | W = w\}]$$
$$\geq E\left[E\left\{\prod_{j=1}^n \psi(V_j, W) | W = w\right\}\right] = E \prod_{i=1}^n g(Y_i)$$

holds. If n is an even integer, then the condition $g \geq 0$ can be removed. The argument is similar and is left to the reader. □

Note that for $n = 2$ the statement in Theorem 5.3.10 is equivalent to saying that $\mathrm{Corr}(g(X_1), g(X_2))$ is nondecreasing in ρ for all g; this was the motivation given by Rinott and Pollak (1980) for studying such a partial ordering.

Problems

5.1. Show that the joint density function of $(X_1, \ldots, X_n)'$ is MTP_2 if and only if the joint density function of $(c_1 X_1 + b_1, \ldots, c_n X_n + b_n)'$ is MTP_2 for all $c_i \in (0, \infty)$ and all $b_i \in (-\infty, \infty)$ $(i = 1, \ldots, n)$.

5.2. Show that $X_1, \ldots, X_n$ are associated if and only if $-X_1, \ldots, -X_n$ are associated (Esary, Proschan, and Walkup, 1967).

5.3. Show that all the definitions of MTP_2, association, PDIS, PUOD, PLOD, and NC stated in Definitions 5.1.1 and 5.1.3–5.1.7 are permutation invariant.

5.4. Show, by giving a counterexample for $n = 2$, that the inequality in (5.1.7) does not imply the inequality in (5.1.1).

5.5. Show directly by definition that if $\mathbf{X}$ has an $\mathcal{N}_n(\boldsymbol{\mu}, \boldsymbol{\Sigma})$ distribution, then PUOD and PLOD are equivalent.

5.6. Let $\mathbf{X}$ have an $\mathcal{N}_2(\mathbf{0}, \boldsymbol{\Sigma})$ distribution. Derive the density function of $(|X_1|, |X_2|)'$, and then show that it remains unchanged when the correlation coefficient between X_1 and X_2 is changed from ρ to $-\rho$.

5.7. Show directly that, for $\mathbf{X}$ defined in Problem 5.6, $\mathrm{Cov}(|X_1|, |X_2|) \geq 0$ holds for all $\rho \in (-1, 1)$.

5.8. Show that the density function of $|\mathbf{X}|$ given in Problem 5.6 is TP_2 for all $\rho \in (-1, 1)$.

5.9. Verify the statement in Example 5.1.1.

5.10. Show that if $g_2(\mathbf{y})$ is a nondecreasing function, then the right-hand side of (5.1.11) is nonnegative. (*Hint*: Use the fact that if U has an $\mathcal{N}(\mu, \sigma^2)$ distribution, then $Eg(U)$ is nondecreasing in μ for all nondecreasing functions g.)

5.11. Show that there exists an $\mathbf{X}$ with an $\mathcal{N}_3(\mathbf{0}, \boldsymbol{\Sigma})$ distribution such that $\boldsymbol{\Sigma}$ is positive definite and $|\mathbf{X}|$ is not PUOD.

5.12. Let $\mathbf{X}$ have an $\mathcal{N}_n(\mathbf{0}, \boldsymbol{\Sigma})$ distribution, and let $\mathbf{D}$ be a diagonal matrix with diagonal elements 1 or -1. Show that $|\mathbf{X}|$ and $|\mathbf{DX}|$ are identically distributed.

5.13. Show that if $\mathbf{X}$ is more positively dependent than $\mathbf{Y}$, in the sense of Definition 5.18 or 5.19 or 5.1.10, then any subset of the components of $\mathbf{X}$ is more positively dependent (in the same sense) than the corresponding subset of the components of $\mathbf{Y}$.

5.14. Let $\{\mathbf{X}_t\}_{t=1}^{\infty}$, $\{\mathbf{Y}_t\}_{t=1}^{\infty}$ be two sequences of n-dimensional random variables such that $\mathbf{X}_t \xrightarrow{d} \mathbf{X}$ and $\mathbf{Y}_t \xrightarrow{d} \mathbf{Y}$ ("$\xrightarrow{d}$" means convergence in distribution). Show that if $\mathbf{X}_t$ is more positively dependent than $\mathbf{Y}_t$, in the sense of Definition 5.1.8 or 5.1.9, then $\mathbf{X}$ is more positively dependent (in the same sense) than $\mathbf{Y}$.

5.15. Use the statement in Theorem 5.1.8(a) to prove Theorem 5.1.8(b). (*Hint*: Consider the random variable $(X_1, \ldots, X_k, -X_{k+1}, \ldots, -X_n)'$.)

5.16. Verify the conditional mean vector and the conditional covariance matrix given in Theorem 5.2.1.

5.17. Verify that the multiple correlation coefficient given in (5.2.9) is the correlation coefficient between X_i and $\delta_\rho \sum_{j=k+1}^{n} X_j$.

5.18. Verify (5.2.13).

5.19. Let $\boldsymbol{\Sigma} = (\sigma_{ij})$ be an $n \times n$ matrix such that $\sigma_{ii} = \sigma^2$ and $\sigma_{ij} = \rho\sigma^2$ for $1 \leq i < j \leq n$, $\rho \in (-1/(n-1), 1)$. Find an orthogonal matrix $\mathbf{C}$ such that $\mathbf{C\Sigma C}'$ is a diagonal matrix with positive diagonal elements.

5.20. Show that if $X_1, \ldots, X_n$ are exchangeable random variables, then their common correlation coefficient is nonnegative.

5.21. Let $X_1, \ldots, X_n$ be independent $\mathcal{N}(0, \sigma^2)$ variables. Let V be independent of the X_i's such that V/σ^2 has an $\chi^2(v)$ distribution. Denoting $t_i = X_i/\sqrt{V/v}$ $(i = 1, \ldots, n)$, show that $t_1, \ldots, t_n$ are exchangeable random variables.

5.22. (Continuation.) Show that $|t_1|, \ldots, |t_n|$ are exchangeable random variables.

5.23. In Problem 5.21, let $(X_1, \ldots, X_n)'$ have an $\mathcal{N}_n(\mathbf{0}, \boldsymbol{\Sigma})$ distribution with a common variance σ^2 and a common correlation coefficient ρ. Show that $t_1, \ldots, t_n$ are exchangeable random variables if and only if $\rho \in [0, 1]$. ($(t_1, \ldots, t_n)'$ has a multivariate t distribution with parameters ρ and v.)

5.24. Show that the right-hand side of (5.3.8)′ is the joint density function of an $\mathcal{N}_n(\boldsymbol{\mu}, \boldsymbol{\Sigma})$ variable with a common mean μ, a common variance σ^2, and a common correlation coefficient $\rho \in [0, 1)$.

5.25. Show that the right-hand side of (5.3.8) and the right-hand side of (5.3.8)′ are identical.

5.26. Show that the right-hand side of (5.3.11) and the right-hand side of (5.3.14) are identical.

5.27. Let $X_1, \ldots, X_n$ be exchangeable normal variables with a common mean $\mu \neq 0$. Find an expression for the joint distribution function of $(|X_1|, \ldots, |X_n|)'$ that is similar to the right-hand side of (5.3.15).

5.28. Let $\boldsymbol{\Sigma}$ be the covariance matrix of n exchangeable random variables and let $\mathbf{c}' = (c_1, \ldots, c_n)$ be such that $\sum_{i=1}^n c_i = 0$. Show that $\mathbf{c}'\boldsymbol{\Sigma}\mathbf{c}$ is a Schur-convex function of $\mathbf{c}$.

5.29. Show that the random variables in (5.3.16) (in (5.3.17)) have a common mean μ, a common variance σ^2, and a common correlation coefficient $\rho_2(\rho_1)$.

5.30. Use Theorem 5.3.10 to show that if X_1, X_2 are two exchangeable normal variables with correlation coefficient $\rho \in [0, 1)$, then $\mathrm{Corr}(g(X_1), g(X_2))$ is a nondecreasing function of ρ for all g such that the expectations exist.

5.31. Complete the proof of Theorem 5.3.10 for the case in which n is an even integer and g is not necessarily nonnegative.

CHAPTER 6

Order Statistics of Normal Variables

The theory and applications of order statistics have been studied extensively in the literature, a convenient reference is David (1981). In this chapter we present some results concerning the distributions and moments of order statistics when the parent distribution is multivariate normal.

Let $\mathbf{X} = (X_1, \ldots, X_n)'$ have an $\mathcal{N}_n(\boldsymbol{\mu}, \boldsymbol{\Sigma})$ distribution and let

$$X_{(1)} \leq X_{(2)} \leq \cdots \leq X_{(n)} \tag{6.0.1}$$

denote the order statistics. In Section 6.1 we give expressions for the marginal and joint density functions of $X_{(i)}$'s when $X_1, \ldots, X_n$ are either i.i.d. normal variables or exchangeable normal variables. (In the latter case the density functions can be expressed as a mixture.) The moments of order statistics of exchangeable normal variables will be given in terms of the corresponding moments of order statistics of i.i.d. normal variables. Section 6.2 concerns some partial orderings of positive dependence of order statistics of exchangeable normal variables. The general results state that when the X_i's are more positively dependent in a certain sense, then their order statistics are more positively dependent. In Section 6.3 we discuss a method for expressing the distribution of a certain partial sum or linear combination of order statistics of normal variables in the form of a multivariate normal probability, and the result has been found useful in certain applications. Section 6.4 contains some miscellaneous results on bounds for order statistics when the mean vector and the covariance matrix possess certain structures.

6.1. Order Statistics of Exchangeable Normal Variables

We first observe some well-known results concerning the density functions of order statistics of i.i.d. normal variables.

6.1.1. Density Functions of Order Statistics of i.i.d. $\mathcal{N}(0, 1)$ Variables

Let $Z_1, \ldots, Z_n$ denote i.i.d. $\mathcal{N}(0, 1)$ variables and let $Z_{(1)} \le \cdots \le Z_{(n)}$ be the corresponding order statistics. Let ϕ and Φ denote, respectively, the $\mathcal{N}(0, 1)$ density function and distribution function.

Theorem 6.1.1.

(a) *For every fixed* $1 \le i \le n$, *the marginal density function and distribution function of* $Z_{(i)}$ *are, respectively,*

$$f_{(i)}(z) = \frac{n!}{(i-1)!\,(n-i)!}\Phi^{i-1}(z)\Phi^{n-i}(-z)\phi(z), \tag{6.1.1}$$

$$F_{(i)}(z) = \sum_{t=i}^{n}\binom{n}{t}\Phi^{t}(z)\Phi^{n-t}(-z), \tag{6.1.2}$$

for $z \in (-\infty, \infty)$.

(b) *For every fixed* $1 \le i < j \le n$ *the joint density function of* $(Z_{(i)}, Z_{(j)})'$ *is*

$$f_{(i,j)}(z_i, z_j) = \frac{n!}{(i-1)!\,(j-i-1)!\,(n-j)!}\Phi^{i-1}(z_i)[\Phi(z_j) - \Phi(z_i)]^{j-i-1}$$
$$\times \Phi^{n-j}(-z_j)\phi(z_i)\phi(z_j) \tag{6.1.3}$$

for $-\infty < z_i \le z_j < \infty$.

(c) *In general, for every fixed* $1 \le r_1 < r_2 < \cdots < r_s \le n$, *the joint density function of* $(Z_{(r_1)}, \ldots, Z_{(r_s)})'$ *is*

$$f_{(r_1,\ldots,r_s)}(z_{r_1},\ldots,z_{r_s}) = c_n\left(\prod_{t=1}^{s}(\Phi(z_{r_t}) - \Phi(z_{r_{t-1}})\right)^{r_t - r_{t-1} - 1}$$
$$\times \Phi^{n-r_s}(-z_{r_s})\prod_{t=1}^{s}\phi(z_{r_t}), \tag{6.1.4}$$

where $-\infty < z_{r_1} \le \cdots \le z_{r_s} < \infty$, $\Phi(z_{r_0}) \equiv 0$, *and*

$$c_n = \frac{n!}{(r_1 - 1)!\left(\prod_{t=2}^{s}(r_t - r_{t-1} - 1)!\right)(n - r_s)!}. \tag{6.1.5}$$

PROOF. The proof follows immediately from existing results on density functions of order statstics of i.i.d. random variables (see, e.g., David (1981, pp. 8–10)). □

A related result depends on the following algebraic identity: For given real numbers $z_1, \ldots, z_n$ let $z_{(1)} \le \cdots \le z_{(n)}$ denote their ordered values. Let $u_i = -z_i$ $(i = 1, \ldots, n)$ and $u_{(1)} \le \cdots \le u_{(n)}$ be the corresponding ordered values of the u_i's. Then we always have

$$(z_{(1)}, \ldots, z_{(n)})' = (-u_{(n)}, \ldots, -u_{(1)})'.$$

If $Z_1, \ldots, Z_n$ are i.i.d. $\mathcal{N}(0, 1)$ variables and $U_i = -Z_i$ $(i = 1, \ldots, n)$, then

$(Z_{(1)}, \ldots, Z_{(n)})'$ and $(-U_{(n)}, \ldots, -U_{(1)})'$ are identically distributed. But $(U_1, \ldots, U_n)'$ and $(Z_1, \ldots, Z_n)'$ are also identically distributed. Thus we have

Theorem 6.1.2. *Let $Z_1, \ldots, Z_n$ be i.i.d. $\mathcal{N}(0, 1)$ variables and let $Z_{(1)} \le \cdots \le Z_{(n)}$ be their order statistics. Then*

$$(Z_{(1)}, \ldots, Z_{(n)})' \stackrel{d}{=} (-Z_{(n)}, \ldots, -Z_{(1)})', \tag{6.1.6}$$

where "$\stackrel{d}{=}$" means identity in distributions. Consequently,

$$(Z_{(r_1)}, \ldots, Z_{(r_s)})' \stackrel{d}{=} (-Z_{(n-r_1+1)}, \ldots, -Z_{(n-r_s+1)})' \tag{6.1.7}$$

holds for all $1 \le r_1 < \cdots < r_s \le n$. As a special case,

$$(Z_{(i)}, Z_{(j)})' \stackrel{d}{=} (-Z_{(n-i+1)}, -Z_{(n-j+1)})', \qquad Z_{(i)} \stackrel{d}{=} -Z_{(n-i+1)} \tag{6.1.8}$$

holds for all $i < j$.

In the following we give density functions of order statistics of exchangeable normal variables, thus confining ourselves to the case $\rho \ge 0$. We may also obtain related results for $\rho < 0$ as outlined in Section 5.6 of David (1981).

6.1.2. Density Functions of Order Statistics of Exchangeable Normal Variables

Let $\mathbf{X} = (X_1, \ldots, X_n)'$ have an $\mathcal{N}_n(\boldsymbol{\mu}, \boldsymbol{\Sigma})$ distribution such that

$$\mu_1 = \cdots = \mu_n = \mu, \quad \sigma_1^2 = \cdots = \sigma_n^2 = \sigma^2, \quad \rho_{ij} = \rho \in [0, 1) \quad (1 \le i < j \le n). \tag{6.1.9}$$

Then, by (5.3.9), $\mathbf{X}$ and

$$(\sigma(\sqrt{1-\rho}\,Z_1 + \sqrt{\rho}\,Z_0) + \mu, \ldots, \sigma(\sqrt{1-\rho}\,Z_n + \sqrt{\rho}\,Z_0) + \mu)' \equiv \mathbf{X}^* \tag{6.1.10}$$

are identically distributed where $Z_0, Z_1, \ldots, Z_n$ are i.i.d $\mathcal{N}(0, 1)$ variables. Since the order statistics of the components of $\mathbf{X}^*$ are the components of

$$\begin{aligned}(\sigma(\sqrt{1-\rho}Z_{(1)} + \sqrt{\rho}\,Z_0) + \mu, \ldots, \sigma(\sqrt{1-\rho}\,Z_{(n)} + \sqrt{\rho}\,Z_0) + \mu)' \\ \equiv (U_1, \ldots, U_n)' = \mathbf{U},\end{aligned} \tag{6.1.11}$$

where $Z_{(1)} \le \cdots \le Z_{(n)}$ are the order statistics of n i.i.d. $\mathcal{N}(0, 1)$ variables, we have

Theorem 6.1.3. *Let $X_1, \ldots, X_n$ be exchangeable normal variables satisfying (6.1.9). Then, for fixed integers $1 \le r_1 < \cdots < r_s \le n$, $(X_{(r_1)}, \ldots, X_{(r_s)})'$ and $(U_{r_1}, \ldots, U_{r_s})'$ are identically distributed.*

A special application of Theorem 6.1.3 is that

Corollary 6.1.1. *Let $X_1, \ldots, X_n$ be exchangeable normal variables satisfying (6.1.9), and let $f_{(i)}, F_{(i)}, f_{(i,j)}, f_{(r_1,\ldots,r_s)}$ be defined as in (6.1.1)–(6.1.4), respectively. Then:*

(a) *The density function and distribution function of* $X_{(i)}$ $(1 \le i \le n)$ *are, respectively,*

$$g_{(i)}(x) = \int_{-\infty}^{\infty} (\sigma\sqrt{1-\rho})^{-1} f_{(i)}\left(\frac{(x-\mu)/\sigma + \sqrt{\rho}\,z}{\sqrt{1-\rho}}\right)\phi(z)\,dz, \quad (6.1.12)$$

$$G_{(i)}(x) = \int_{-\infty}^{\infty} F_{(i)}\left(\frac{(x-\mu)/\sigma + \sqrt{\rho}\,z}{\sqrt{1-\rho}}\right)\phi(z)\,dz, \quad (6.1.13)$$

for $x \in (-\infty, \infty)$.

(b) *The joint density function of* $(X_{(i)}, X_{(j)})'$ $(1 \le i < j \le n)$ *is*

$$g_{(i,j)}(x_i, x_j) = \int_{-\infty}^{\infty} (\sigma^2(1-\rho))^{-1} f_{(i,j)}(v_i, v_j)\phi(z)\,dz \quad (6.1.14)$$

for $-\infty < x_i \le x_j < \infty$, *where* $v_t = ((x_t - \mu)/\sigma + \sqrt{\rho}\,z)/\sqrt{1-\rho}$, $t = i, j$.

(c) *In general, for fixed* $1 \le r_1 < \cdots < r_s \le n$, *the joint density function of* $(X_{(r_1)}, \ldots, X_{(r_s)})'$ *is*

$$g_{(r_1,\ldots,r_s)}(x_{r_1}, \ldots, x_{r_s}) = \int_{-\infty}^{\infty} (\sigma\sqrt{1-\rho})^{-s} f_{(r_1,\ldots,r_s)}(v_1, \ldots, v_s)\phi(z)\,dz \quad (6.1.15)$$

for $-\infty < x_{r_1} \le \cdots \le x_{r_s} < \infty$, *where* $v_t = ((x_{r_t} - \mu)/\sigma + \sqrt{\rho}\,z)/\sqrt{1-\rho}$ *for* $t = 1, \ldots, s$.

(d) *The joint density of* $(X_{(1)}, \ldots, X_{(n)})'$ *is*

$$g_{(1,\ldots,n)}(x_1, \ldots, x_n) = n! \int_{-\infty}^{\infty} (\sigma\sqrt{1-\rho})^{-n} \times \prod_{t=1}^{n} \phi\left(\frac{(x_i-\mu)/\sigma + \sqrt{\rho}\,z}{\sqrt{1-\rho}}\right)\phi(z)\,dz \quad (6.1.16)$$

for $-\infty < x_1 \le \cdots \le x_n < \infty$ *which, by Theorem 5.3.1, is just*

$$g_{(1,\ldots,n)}(x_1, \ldots, x_n) = \begin{cases} n!\, f(\mathbf{x}; \boldsymbol{\mu}, \boldsymbol{\Sigma}) & \text{for } -\infty < x_1 \le \cdots \le x_n < \infty, \\ 0 & \text{otherwise,} \end{cases} \quad (6.1.17)$$

where $f(\mathbf{x}; \boldsymbol{\mu}, \boldsymbol{\Sigma})$ *is the multivariate normal density function defined in* (3.2.1) *with a common mean* μ, *a common variance* σ^2, *and a common correlation coefficient* $\rho \in [0, 1)$.

PROOF. (a) By Theorem 6.1.3 and (6.1.11) we have

$$\begin{aligned} G_{(i)}(x) &= P[\sigma(\sqrt{1-\rho}\,Z_{(i)} + \sqrt{\rho}\,Z_0) + \mu \le x] \\ &= P\left[Z_{(i)} \le \frac{(x-\mu)/\sigma - \sqrt{\rho}\,Z_0}{\sqrt{1-\rho}}\right] \\ &= \int_{-\infty}^{\infty} F_{(i)}\left(\frac{(x-\mu)/\sigma + \sqrt{\rho}\,z}{\sqrt{1-\rho}}\right)\phi(z)\,dz, \end{aligned}$$

where $\phi(z)$ is the density function of $-Z_0$ and $F_{(i)}$ is given in (6.1.2). This yields (6.1.13). Equation (6.1.12) follows by differentiating the right-hand side of (6.1.13) under the integral sign (which is permissible).

(b), (c), and (d). Similar. □

We note in passing that the (joint) distribution of order statistics of exchangeable normal variables is a *mixture* of the (joint) distributions of order statistics of i.i.d. normal variables. In particular, the marginal distribution of the ith order statistic given in (6.1.13) is just a mixture of binomial probabilities.

If the common mean is zero, then the result given in Theorem 6.1.2 can be generalized to exchangeable normal variables.

Theorem 6.1.4. *Let $(X_1, \ldots, X_n)'$ have an $\mathcal{N}_n(\mathbf{0}, \Sigma)$ distribution with a common variance σ^2 and a common correlation coefficient $\rho \in [0, 1)$. Let $X_{(1)} \leq \cdots \leq X_{(n)}$ denote the order statistics. Then*

$$(X_{(r_1)}, \ldots, X_{(r_s)})' \stackrel{d}{=} (-X_{(n-r_1+1)}, \ldots, -X_{(n-r_s+1)})' \tag{6.1.18}$$

holds for all $1 \leq r_1 < \cdots < r_s \leq n$. Consequently, we have

$$(X_{(1)}, \ldots, X_{(n)})' \stackrel{d}{=} (-X_{(n)}, \ldots, -X_{(1)})'. \tag{6.1.19}$$

Proof. By (6.1.4) and Theorem 6.1.2,

$$f_{(r_1,\ldots,r_s)}\left(\frac{x_{r_1}/\sigma + \sqrt{\rho} z}{\sqrt{1-\rho}}, \ldots, \frac{x_{r_s}/\sigma + \sqrt{\rho} z}{\sqrt{1-\rho}}\right)$$
$$= f_{(n-r_1+1,\ldots,n-r_s+1)}\left(\frac{-x_{n-r_1+1}/\sigma - \sqrt{\rho} z}{\sqrt{1-\rho}}, \ldots, \frac{-x_{n-r_s+1}/\sigma - \sqrt{\rho} z}{\sqrt{1-\rho}}\right)$$

holds for all $x_{r_1} \leq \cdots \leq x_{r_s}$ and all z. Thus by (6.1.15) and the identity $\phi(z) = \phi(-z)$ we have

$$(\sigma\sqrt{1-\rho})^s g_{(r_1,\ldots,r_s)}(x_{r_1}, \ldots, x_{r_s})$$
$$= \int_{-\infty}^{\infty} f_{(n-r_1+1,\ldots,n-r_s+1)}(u_1, \ldots, u_s)\phi(z)\, dz$$
$$= \int_{-\infty}^{\infty} f_{(n-r_1+1,\ldots,n-r_s+1)}(v_1, \ldots, v_s)\phi(z)\, dz$$
$$= (\sigma\sqrt{1-\rho})^s g_{(n-r_1+1,\ldots,n-r_s+1)}(-x_{n-r_1+1}, \ldots, -x_{n-r_s+1}),$$

where for $i = 1, \ldots, s$

$$u_i = \frac{-x_{n-r_i+1}/\sigma - \sqrt{\rho} z}{\sqrt{1-\rho}}, \qquad v_i = \frac{-x_{n-r_i+1}/\sigma + \sqrt{\rho} z}{\sqrt{1-\rho}}.$$

Since $g_{(n-r_1+1,\ldots,n-r_s+1)}(-x_{n-r_1+1},\ldots,-x_{n-r_s+1})$ is the joint density function of $(-X_{n-r_1+1},\ldots,-X_{n-r_s+1})'$, the proof is complete. □

6.1.3. Moments

The kth moment of the order statistics of the i.i.d. $\mathcal{N}(0, 1)$ variables can be expressed in the following integral form:

$$EZ_{(i)}^k = \frac{n!}{(i-1)!\,(n-i)!}\int_{-\infty}^{\infty} z^k\Phi^{i-1}(z)\Phi^{n-i}(-z)\phi(z)\,dz \tag{6.1.20}$$

for all k and all $1 \le i \le n$. Furthermore, for $f_{(i,j)}$ defined in (6.1.3) the product moments of $(Z_{(i)}, Z_{(j)})'$ are given by

$$E(Z_{(i)}^k Z_{(j)}^m) = \int_{-\infty}^{\infty}\int_{-\infty}^{z_j} z_i^k z_j^m f_{(i,j)}(z_i, z_j)\,dz_i\,dz_j \tag{6.1.21}$$

for all k, m, and $1 \le i < j \le n$. Numerical methods for approximating this type of integrals on a computer are available, and the means, variances, and covariances of order statistics have been calculated. For example, Pearson and Hartley (1970, p. 190), Harter (1961), Sarhan and Greenberg (1962), and other related references contain tables of the values of the means

$$\nu_i = EZ_{(i)}, \qquad i = 1, \ldots, n; \tag{6.1.22}$$

Teichroew (1956) and Tietjen, Kahaner, and Beckman (1977) tabulated the variance and covariances

$$\lambda_i^2 = \mathrm{Var}(Z_{(i)}), \qquad \lambda_{ij} = \mathrm{Cov}(Z_{(i)}, Z_{(j)}). \tag{6.1.23}$$

Similar tables can be found in David, Kennedy, and Knight (1977) for the special case where the outlier mean is zero.

For exchangeable normal variables $X_1, \ldots, X_n$, the moments of their order statistics can be obtained by the expression given in (6.1.11). In the following theorem we show how the means, variances, and covariances are related to that of the order statistics of i.i.d. normal variables.

Theorem 6.1.5. *Let $(X_1, \ldots, X_n)'$ have an $\mathcal{N}_n(\boldsymbol{\mu}, \boldsymbol{\Sigma})$ distribution with a common mean μ, a common variance σ^2, and a common correlation coefficient $\rho \in [0, 1)$. Let $X_{(1)} \le \cdots \le X_{(n)}$ be their order statistics. Then:*

(a) $$EX_{(i)}^k = \sum_{(j_1,j_2)\in B}\binom{k}{j_1, j_2}(1-\rho)^{j_1/2}\rho^{j_2/2}\sigma^{j_1+j_2}EZ_{(i)}^{j_1}EZ_0^{j_2}\mu^{k-j_1-j_2} \tag{6.1.24}$$

holds for all k and all $1 \le i \le n$, where $B = \{(j_1, j_2): j_1 \ge 0, j_2 \ge 0, j_1 + j_2 \le k\}$, Z_0 is an $\mathcal{N}(0, 1)$ variable, and $Z_{(1)} \le \cdots \le Z_{(n)}$ are the order statistics of i.i.d. $\mathcal{N}(0, 1)$ variables. Consequently,

$$EX_{(i)} = \sigma\sqrt{1-\rho}\,EZ_{(i)} + \mu \tag{6.1.25}$$

and

$$\mathrm{Var}(X_{(i)}) = \mathrm{Var}(X_{(n-i+1)}) = \sigma^2[(1-\rho)\,\mathrm{Var}(Z_{(i)}) + \rho] \tag{6.1.26}$$

hold for all $1 \leq i \leq n$. *If* $\mu = 0$, *then*

$$EX_{(i)}^k = (-1)^k EX_{(n-i+1)}^k \tag{6.1.27}$$

holds for all i *and all* $k = 1, 2, \ldots$.

(b)
$$\begin{aligned}\mathrm{Cov}(X_{(i)}, X_{(j)}) &= \mathrm{Cov}(X_{(n-i+1)}, X_{(n-j+1)}) \\ &= \sigma^2[(1-\rho)\,\mathrm{Cov}(Z_{(i)}, Z_{(j)}) + \rho]\end{aligned} \tag{6.1.28}$$

holds for all $1 \leq i < j \leq n$.

PROOF. Equations (6.1.24), (6.1.25), and (6.1.27) follow immediately from Theorem 6.1.3. Equations (6.1.26) and (6.1.28) follow from Theorem 6.1.3 and the identities

$$E(X_{(i)} - EX_{(i)})^2 = \sigma^2[(1-\rho)E(Z_{(i)} - EZ_{(i)})^2 + \rho EZ_0^2],$$

$$E(X_{(i)} - EX_{(i)})(X_{(j)} - EX_{(j)}) = \sigma^2[(1-\rho)E(Z_{(i)} - EZ_{(i)})(Z_{(j)} - EZ_{(j)}) + \rho EZ_0^2].$$

□

The result in (6.1.25) was first given by Owen and Steck (1962). They considered only the special case $\mu = 0$, but for $\mu \neq 0$ an extension of their result, as shown here, is immediate.

6.1.4. An Example of Application

A simple but important application of the order statistics of exchangeable normal variables exists in the area of animal genetic selection in agricultural research. Here we discuss this application for the purpose of illustration.

Suppose that an agricultural genetic selection project involves n animals, and the top performers are to be selected for breeding. In symbols, let $X_1, \ldots, X_n$ denote the measurements of a certain biological or physical character of the n animals (such as the body weights or back fats of n pigs). Let $X_{(1)} \leq \cdots \leq X_{(n)}$ be the order statistics. For fixed $k < n$ suppose that the k animals with scores $X_{(n-k+1)}, \ldots, X_{(n)}$ are to be selected. If the common mean of the X_i's is μ then, under the additive model, the common mean of the observations of off-springs of the animal with score $X_{(i)}$ is $EX_{(i)}$ ($i = n-k+1, \ldots, n$). Thus if this animal is used for breeding, then the expected gain in one generation is $EX_{(i)} - \mu$.

An important question of concern is how the expected gain, $EX_{(i)} - \mu$, behaves when the n animals are genetically related. This is the case, for example, when they are from the same family and have the same parents. In this situation, a variance-components model of the form (6.1.10) (where Z_0 represents the common influence of their parents) is generally assumed by geneticists (see Rawlings (1976) or Hill (1976)). Under the assumption of normality, $X_1, \ldots, X_n$ are exchangeable normal variables with a common mean μ, a common variance σ^2, and a common correlation coefficient $\rho \in [0, 1)$, and the correlation coefficient ρ is an increasing function of the heritability coefficient. Thus, if the parents have a stronger influence on the animals, then the heritability coefficient is larger, consequently ρ is larger.

It has been well known to geneticists that if the animals are genetically related, then the condition of independence of $X_1, \ldots, X_n$ is not satisfied (Rawlings, 1976). Since by (6.1.25) the mean of $X_{(i)}$ is a decreasing function of $\rho \in [0, 1)$ for $i > n/2$, the performance of the best animals is less outstanding, thus the expected gain of the genetic selection project is less significant, when the heritability coefficient in question is larger.

For other related applications of the moments of order statistics of i.i.d. and exchangeable normal variables, see Tietjen, Kahaner, and Beckman (1977) and David (1981).

6.2. Positive Dependence of Order Statistics of Normal Variables

The moment result given in Theorem 6.1.5 (particularly (6.1.25)) suggests that order statistics of exchangeable normal variables tend to hang tother, and that they tend to hang together more when the correlation coefficient ρ is larger. In this section we study such results by investigating their positive dependence properties. Certain results will be given for the more general case, and the results for exchangeable normal variables then follow as special consequences. The reader is referred to Section 5.1 for notions of the positive dependence of random variables.

6.2.1. Association and MTP_2 Properties

The first result, given below, concerns only extreme order statistics. The theorem states that when the normal variables are more correlated, then they tend to hang together more. Thus their maximum tends to be stochastically smaller and their minimum tends to be stochastically larger.

Theorem 6.2.1. *Let* $\mathbf{X} = (X_1, \ldots, X_n)'$ *and* $\mathbf{Y} = (Y_1, \ldots, Y_n)'$ *be two multivariate normal variables with a common mean vector* $\boldsymbol{\mu}$ *and covariance matrices* $\boldsymbol{\Sigma}_1 = (\sigma_{ij})$ *and* $\boldsymbol{\Sigma}_2 = (\tau_{ij})$, *respectively. Let* $X_{(1)} \leq \cdots \leq X_{(n)}$, $Y_{(1)} \leq \cdots \leq Y_{(n)}$ *denote the corresponding order statistics. If*

$$\sigma_{ii} = \tau_{ii} \qquad \text{for} \quad i = 1, \ldots, n,$$

and

$$\sigma_{ij} \geq \tau_{ij} \qquad \text{for all} \quad 1 \leq i < j \leq n,$$

then

$$X_{(1)} \overset{st}{\geq} Y_{(1)}, \qquad X_{(n)} \overset{st}{\leq} Y_{(n)}$$

holds. Equivalently, the inequalities $Eg(X_{(1)}) \geq Eg(Y_{(1)})$ *and* $Eg(Y_{(n)}) \leq Eg(Y_{(n)})$ *hold for all nondecreasing functions* g *such that the expectations exist.*

Proof. The proof follows immediately from Slepian's inequality (Theorem 5.1.7) and the identities

$$P[X_{(n)} \leq x] = P\left[\bigcap_{i=1}^{n} \{X_i \leq x\}\right], \quad P[X_{(1)} > x] = P\left[\bigcap_{i=1}^{n} \{X_i > x\}\right]. \quad \square$$

Note that the correlation coefficients in Theorem 6.2.1 are not necessarily nonnegative.

To study the positive dependence of the order statistics of normal variables we recall (see Section 5.1) that: The condition concerning the correlation coefficients is the weakest, the association property is stronger, and the MTP_2 property is the strongest. The following fact, due to Bickel (1967), concerns the order statistics of independent observations only, but is not just for the normal distribution.

Fact 6.2.1. *Let* $X_1, \ldots, X_n$ *be i.i.d. random variables and let* $X_{(1)} \leq \cdots \leq X_{(n)}$ *be their order statistics. Then*

$$\mathrm{Corr}(X_{(i)}, X_{(j)}) \geq 0 \qquad \textit{holds for all} \quad 1 \leq i < j \leq n. \tag{6.2.1}$$

After introducing the notion of the association of random variables Esary, Proschan, and Walkup (1967) noted that nondecreasing functions of order statistics are nondecreasing functions of the original observations. Thus, by applying a main theorem in their association paper, they noted that

Fact 6.2.2. *If* $X_1, \ldots, X_n$ *are associated random variables, then their order statistics are associated random variables. Thus if* $X_1, \ldots, X_n$ *are independent (but not necessarily identically distributed), then their order statistics are associated. Consequently* (6.2.1) *holds.*

Combining Fact 6.2.2 and Theorem 5.1.1 we immediately have the following result for the order statistics of nonnegatively correlated normal variables.

Theorem 6.2.2. *Let* $\mathbf{X} = (X_1, \ldots, X_n)'$ *have an* $\mathcal{N}_n(\boldsymbol{\mu}, \boldsymbol{\Sigma} = (\sigma_{ij}))$ *distribution and let* $X_{(1)} \leq \cdots \leq X_{(n)}$ *be the order statistics. If* $\sigma_{ij} \geq 0$ *holds for all* $i \neq j$, *then* $X_{(1)}, \ldots, X_{(n)}$ *are associated random variables.*

This theorem asserts that the association property is inherited by the order statistics. A related question is whether the strongest notion of positive dependence, the MTP_2 property, can also be inherited. We provide a partial answer to this question by first observing the following result.

Proposition 6.2.1. *Let* $\mathbf{X} = (X_1, \ldots, X_n)'$ *have a continuous density function* $f(\mathbf{x})$ *such that* $A = \{\mathbf{x}: f(\mathbf{x}) > 0\}$, *the support of f, is a permutation-symmetric and convex set in* $\mathfrak{R}^n$. *Let* $X_{(1)} \le \cdots \le X_{(n)}$ *denote the order statistics. If* $f(\mathbf{x})$ *is* MTP_2, *then the joint density function of* $(X_{(1)}, \ldots, X_{(n)})'$ *is also* MTP_2.

PROOF. We adopt the core of the argument used in the proof of Proposition 3.11 in Karlin and Rinott (1980a) (which is for i.i.d. random variables instead of permutation-symmetric random variables). Express the joint density function of the order statistics as

$$g(\mathbf{x}) = \delta(x_1, \ldots, x_n) f(\mathbf{x}) \qquad \text{for} \quad \mathbf{x} \in A,$$

and zero otherwise, where

$$\delta(x_1, \ldots, x_n) = \begin{cases} n! & \text{for } x_1 \le x_2 \le \cdots \le x_n, \\ 0 & \text{otherwise.} \end{cases} \tag{6.2.2}$$

Since δ and f are both MTP_2, by Proposition 3.3 of Karlin and Rinott (1980a), $g(\mathbf{x})$ is MTP_2. □

A simple application of Theorem 4.3.2 and Proposition 6.2.1 yields the following result for the order statistics of exchangeable normal variables.

Theorem 6.2.3. *If* $X_1, \ldots, X_n$ *are exchangeable normal variables (i.e., if they have a common mean* μ, *a common variance* σ^2, *and a common correlation coefficient* $\rho \in [0, 1)$), *then the joint density function of their order statistics is* MTP_2. *Consequently, all the inequalities in* (5.1.1)–(5.1.7) *apply to their order statistics.*

Similarly, let $h(y_1, \ldots, y_n)$ be the joint density function of the order statistics of $|X_1|, \ldots, |X_n|$. By Theorem 5.1.5 and Proposition 6.2.1 we have

Theorem 6.2.4. *If* $X_1, \ldots, X_n$ *are exchangeable normal variables with means* 0, *then* $h(y_1, \ldots, y_n)$ *is* MTP_2.

Note that Theorems 6.2.3 and 6.2.4 yield results which are stronger than that in David (1981, p. 113).

6.2.2. Comparisons of Positive Dependence

Theorem 6.2.3 states that the order statistics of exchangeable normal variables possess all the positive dependence properties in Section 5.1. A related question is whether the "strength" of their positive dependence can be partial ordered via a partial ordering of the "strength" of the original normal variables. Shaked and Tong (1985) showed that the answer to this question is in the affirmative.

The results in Shaked and Tong (1985) are for a large class of exchangeable random variables and are not just for the normal variables. However, if the underlying distribution is multivariate normal, then the proof becomes much easier. To compare the positive dependence of the components of two n-dimensional random variables let us consider

$$\mathbf{X} = (X_1, \ldots, X_n)', \qquad \mathbf{Y} = (Y_1, \ldots, Y_n)',$$

such that $X_1, \ldots, X_n$ are exchangeable, $Y_1, \ldots, Y_n$ are exchangeable, and X_1 and Y_1 have a common marginal distribution. Let

$$X_{(1)} \leq \cdots \leq X_{(n)}, \qquad Y_{(1)} \leq \cdots \leq Y_{(n)}$$

denote the corresponding order statistics. Shaked and Tong (1985) studied the following partial orderings of positive dependence of the components of $\mathbf{X}$ and of $\mathbf{Y}$ (and of their order statistics).

Definition 6.2.1.

(a) We write $\mathbf{X} \overset{a}{>} \mathbf{Y}$ (that is, the X_i's are more positively dependent than the Y_i's in the sense of "a") if

$$\left|\sum_{i=1}^{n} c_i X_{(i)}\right| \overset{st}{\leq} \left|\sum_{i=1}^{n} c_i Y_{(i)}\right| \qquad \text{holds whenever} \quad \sum_{i=1}^{n} c_i = 0,$$

which is equivalent to saying that

$$P\left[\left|\sum_{i=1}^{n} c_i X_{(i)}\right| > \lambda\right] \leq P\left[\left|\sum_{i=1}^{n} c_i Y_{(i)}\right| > \lambda\right]$$

$$\text{holds for all} \quad \lambda > 0 \text{ whenever} \quad \sum_{i=1}^{n} c_i = 0.$$

(b) We write $\mathbf{X} \overset{b}{>} \mathbf{Y}$ if

$$\left|\sum_{i=1}^{n} c_i X_i\right| \overset{st}{\leq} \left|\sum_{i=1}^{n} c_i Y_i\right| \qquad \text{holds whenever} \quad \sum_{i=1}^{n} c_i = 0.$$

(c) We write $\mathbf{X} \overset{c}{>} \mathbf{Y}$ if

$$(F_{\mathbf{Y}_{(1)}}(t), \ldots, F_{\mathbf{Y}_{(n)}}(t)) \succ (F_{\mathbf{X}_{(1)}}(t), \ldots, F_{\mathbf{X}_{(n)}}(t))$$

holds for all t where "$\succ$" denotes majorization and $F_{\mathbf{X}_{(i)}}$, $F_{\mathbf{Y}_{(i)}}$ are the distribution functions of $X_{(i)}$ and $Y_{(i)}$, respectively.

(d) We write $\mathbf{X} \overset{d}{>} \mathbf{Y}$ if

$$(EY_{(1)}, \ldots, EY_{(n)})' \succ (EX_{(1)}, \ldots, EX_{(n)})'$$

holds.

The partial ordering "$\overset{a}{>}$" and "$\overset{b}{>}$" imply that if the components of $\mathbf{X}$ are more positively dependent, then they (and their order statistics) tend to hang together more, thus their linear combinations subject to

$\sum_{i=1}^{n} c_i = 0$ are stochasticially smaller. Similarly, the vectors of the distribution functions and of the means of their order statistics are less diverse in the sense of majorization.

It is known that (see Marshall and Olkin (1979, p. 350))

Fact 6.2.3. $\mathbf{X} \overset{c}{>} \mathbf{Y}$ *holds if and only if*

$$(Eg(Y_{(1)}), \ldots, Eg(Y_{(n)}))' \succ (Eg(X_{(1)}), \ldots, Eg(X_{(n)}))'$$

holds for all monotonic functions g such that the expectations exist.

Thus, obviously, $\mathbf{X} \overset{c}{>} \mathbf{Y}$ implies $\mathbf{X} \overset{d}{>} \mathbf{Y}$. Shaked and Tong (1985) showed that

Proposition 6.2.2.

$$\mathbf{X} \overset{a}{>} \mathbf{Y} \overset{\text{(i)}}{\Rightarrow} \mathbf{X} \overset{b}{>} \mathbf{Y}, \qquad \mathbf{X} \overset{a}{>} \mathbf{Y} \overset{\text{(ii)}}{\Rightarrow} \mathbf{X} \overset{d}{>} \mathbf{Y},$$

$$\mathbf{X} \overset{c}{>} \mathbf{Y} \overset{\text{(iii)}}{\Rightarrow} \mathbf{X} \overset{d}{>} \mathbf{Y}.$$

PROOF. (i) Let $\boldsymbol{\pi} = \{\pi_1, \ldots, \pi_n\}$ denote any given permutation of $\{1, \ldots, n\}$. Then for all $\lambda > 0$ and $c_1, \ldots, c_n$ satisfying $\sum_{i=1}^{n} c_i = 0$ we have

$$P\left[\left|\sum_{i=1}^{n} c_i X_i\right| > \lambda | X_{\pi_1} \le \cdots \le X_{\pi_n}\right] = P\left[\left|\sum_{i=1}^{n} c_{\pi_i} X_{(i)}\right| > \lambda | X_{\pi_1} \le \cdots \le X_{\pi_n}\right]$$
$$= P\left[\left|\sum_{i=1}^{n} c_{\pi_i} X_{(i)}\right| > \lambda\right].$$

Similarly,

$$P\left[\left|\sum_{i=1}^{n} c_i Y_i\right| > \lambda \middle| Y_{\pi_1} \le \cdots \le Y_{\pi_n}\right] = P\left[\left|\sum_{i=1}^{n} c_{\pi_i} Y_{(i)}\right| > \lambda\right].$$

Thus, letting $\sum_{\pi}$ denote the summation over all permutations of $\{1, \ldots, n\}$, $\mathbf{X} \overset{a}{>} \mathbf{Y}$ implies

$$P\left[\left|\sum_{i=1}^{n} c_i X_i\right| > \lambda\right] = \sum_{\pi} \frac{1}{n!} P\left[\left|\sum_{i=1}^{n} c_i X_i\right| > \lambda | X_{\pi_1} \le \cdots \le X_{\pi_n}\right]$$
$$= \sum_{\pi} \frac{1}{n!} P\left[\left|\sum_{i=1}^{n} c_{\pi_i} X_{(i)}\right| > \lambda\right]$$
$$\le \sum_{\pi} \frac{1}{n!} P\left[\left|\sum_{i=1}^{n} c_{\pi_i} Y_i\right| > \lambda | Y_{\pi_1} \le \cdots \le Y_{\pi_n}\right]$$
$$= P\left[\left|\sum_{i=1}^{n} c_i Y_i\right| > \lambda\right].$$

(ii) By choosing $c_i = 1$ and $c_{i-1} = -1$ we have

$$EX_{(i)} - EX_{(i-1)} \le EY_{(i)} - EY_{(i-1)}, \qquad i = 1, \ldots, n-1.$$

The proof follows from this inequality and the obvious fact that $\sum_{i=1}^{n} EX_{(i)} = \sum_{i=1}^{n} EY_{(i)}$. The details are left to the reader.

(iii) Immediate from Fact 6.2.3. □

For exchangeable normal variables, the partial orderings of positive dependence can be completely determined by the correlation coefficient (Shaked and Tong, 1985).

Theorem 6.2.5. *Let $X_1, \ldots, X_n$ be exchangeable normal variables with means μ, variances σ^2, and correlation coefficients ρ_2; let $Y_1, \ldots, Y_n$ be exchangeable normal variables with means μ, variances σ^2, and correlation coefficients ρ_1. If $\rho_2 > \rho_1 \geq 0$, then $\mathbf{X} \overset{*}{>} \mathbf{Y}$ holds for $* = a, b, c, d$.*

Proof. (a) $\mathbf{X} \overset{a}{>} \mathbf{Y}$. Let $U_1, \ldots, U_n$ be the order statistics of exchangeable normal variables such that the population means are μ, the population variances are σ^2, and the correlation coefficients are ρ. Then by the expression in (6.1.11) we have

$$P\left[\left|\sum_{i=1}^{n} c_i U_i\right| > \lambda\right] = P\left[\left|\sum_{i=1}^{n} c_i Z_{(i)}\right| > \lambda/\sqrt{1-\rho}\right]$$

$$\text{whenever} \quad \sum_{i=1}^{n} c_i = 0.$$

This yields $\mathbf{X} \overset{a}{>} \mathbf{Y}$.

(c) $\mathbf{X} \overset{c}{>} \mathbf{Y}$. By a result of Shaked (1977), for every fixed integer k $(1 \leq k \leq n)$ the function

$$h_{k,n}(p) = \sum_{i=1}^{k} \sum_{j=i}^{n} \binom{n}{j} p^j (1-p)^{n-j}$$

is concave on $[0, 1]$. Clearly, $\mathbf{X}$ and $\mathbf{Y}$ are distributed as, respectively,

$$(\sigma(\sqrt{1-\rho_2}\, Z_1 + \sqrt{\rho_2 - \rho_1}\, V_0 + \sqrt{\rho_1}\, Z_0) + \mu, \ldots,$$
$$\sigma(\sqrt{1-\rho_2}\, Z_n + \sqrt{\rho_2 - \rho_1}\, V_0 + \sqrt{\rho_1}\, Z_0) + \mu)',$$
$$(\sigma(\sqrt{1-\rho_2}\, Z_1 + \sqrt{\rho_2 - \rho_1}\, V_1 + \sqrt{\rho_1}\, Z_0) + \mu, \ldots,$$
$$\sigma(\sqrt{1-\rho_2}\, Z_n + \sqrt{\rho_2 - \rho_1}\, V_n + \sqrt{\rho_1}\, Z_0) + \mu)',$$

where $Z_0, Z_1, \ldots, Z_n, V_0, V_1, \ldots, V_n$ are i.i.d. $\mathcal{N}(0, 1)$ variables. The conditional distribution of X_i, given $(V_0, Z_0)' = (v, z)'$, is

$$P[X_i \leq t \mid (V_0, Z_0)' = (v, z)'] = \Phi\left(\frac{(t-\mu)/\sigma - \sqrt{\rho_2 - \rho_1}\, v - \sqrt{\rho_1}\, z}{\sqrt{1-\rho_2}}\right)$$
$$\equiv p(t, v, z),$$

where Φ is the $\mathcal{N}(0, 1)$ distribution function. Thus, letting ϕ be the $\mathcal{N}(0, 1)$

density function we have

$$\sum_{i=1}^{k} F_{x_{(i)}}(t) = \int_{-\infty}^{\infty} \left[\int_{-\infty}^{\infty} h_{k,n}(p(t, v, z))\phi(v)\, dv \right] \phi(z)\, dz$$

$$= \int_{-\infty}^{\infty} \left[\int_{-\infty}^{\infty} \sum_{i=1}^{k} \sum_{j=i}^{n} \binom{n}{j} (p(t, v, z))^{j} (1 - p(t, v, z))^{n-j} \phi(v)\, dv \right] \phi(z)\, dz.$$

Let

$$p^*(t, z) = \int_{-\infty}^{\infty} p(t, v, z)\phi(v)\, dv$$

denote the conditional expectation of $p(t, v, z)$ given $Z_0 = z$. Then straightforward calculation shows that

$$p^*(t, z) = \Phi\left(\frac{(t - \mu)/\sigma - \sqrt{\rho_1}\, z}{\sqrt{1 - \rho_1}}\right) = P[Y_i \leq t | Z_0 = z].$$

Since $h_{k,n}(p)$ is a concave function, by Jensen's inequality we have

$$\int_{-\infty}^{\infty} h_{k,n}(p(t, v, z))\phi(v)\, dv \leq h_{k,n}(p^*(t, z))$$

for every given $Z_0 = z$. The proof follows by unconditioning and applying the identity $\sum_{i=1}^{n} F_{x_{(i)}}(t) = \sum_{i=1}^{n} F_{y_{(i)}}(t)$.

The rest of the proof follows from Proposition 6.2.2. In fact, $\mathbf{X} \overset{d}{>} \mathbf{Y}$ follows directly from (6.1.25) and $\sum_{i=1}^{n} EX_{(i)} = \sum_{i=1}^{n} EY_{(i)}$. □

A consequence of Theorem 6.2.5 is that

Corollary 6.2.1. *Let $X_1, \ldots, X_n$ and $Y_1, \ldots, Y_n$ be defined as in Theorem* 6.2.5. *If $\rho_2 > \rho_1 \geq 0$, then the range of the Y_i's is stochastically larger than the range of the X_i's.*

Note that this result follows immediately without applying Theorem 6.2.5 (see Problem 6.17).

6.3. Distributions of Certain Partial Sums and Linear Combinations of Order Statistics

Let $\mathbf{X} = (X_1, \ldots, X_n)'$ have an $\mathcal{N}_n(\boldsymbol{\mu}, \boldsymbol{\Sigma})$ distribution and let $X_{(1)} \leq \cdots \leq X_{(n)}$ be the order statistics. In certain statistical applications we are interested in the partial sums of the $X_{(i)}$'s of the form $\sum_{i=n-k+1}^{n} X_{(i)}$ or $\sum_{i=1}^{k} X_{(i)}$. For example, in the agricultural genetic selection problem described in Section 6.1.4 such partial sums are of great interest, and the first partial sum is called the selection differential (David, 1981, p. 37). The expectations of these partial sums can be obtained by finding $EX_{(i)}$ for each i, but their distributions are much more complicated. In this section we discuss a representation result for the distributions of such partial sums and, more generally, for certain linear combinations of order statistics. This approach appears to be first adopted by Liang (1987).

The representation depends on an algebraic identity which can be found in Marshall and Olkin (1979, p. 349).

Proposition 6.3.1. *For fixed* $1 \leq k \leq n$, *let* Π^* *be the set of all* $\binom{n}{k}$ *vectors such that each* $\mathbf{d}_r = (d_{r_1}, \ldots, d_{r_n})' \in \Pi^*$ *contains* k 1's *and* $(n-k)$ 0's. *Then for all given real numbers* $x_1, \ldots, x_n$ *and their ordered values* $x_{(1)} \leq \cdots \leq x_{(n)}$ *the identity*

$$\sum_{i=n-k+1}^{n} x_{(i)} = \sup_{\mathbf{d}_r \in \Pi^*} \sum_{s=1}^{n} d_{r_s} x_s = \sup_{\mathbf{d}_r \in \Pi^*} \mathbf{d}_r'\mathbf{x} \tag{6.3.1}$$

holds, where $\mathbf{x} = (x_1, \ldots, x_n)'$.

For arbitrary but fixed real numbers $0 \leq c_1 \leq \cdots \leq c_n$, let Π denote the $n!$ vectors of permutations of $\mathbf{c}_0 = (c_1, \ldots, c_n)'$. That is, $\mathbf{c}_r = (c_{r_1}, \ldots, c_{r_n})' \in \Pi$ is a permutation of $\mathbf{c}_0$ for $r = 1, 2, \ldots, n!$. By a similar argument it can be shown that

Proposition 6.3.2. *For all real vectors* $\mathbf{x} = (x_1, \ldots, x_n)'$ *and all given real numbers* $0 \leq c_1 \leq \cdots \leq c_n$ *we have*

$$\sum_{i=1}^{n} c_i x_{(i)} = \sup_{\mathbf{c}_r \in \Pi} \mathbf{c}_r'\mathbf{x}. \tag{6.3.2}$$

Proposition 6.3.2 implies that the random variables $\sum_{i=1}^{n} c_i X_{(i)}$ and $\sup_{\mathbf{c}_r \in \Pi} \mathbf{c}_r'\mathbf{X}$ are identically distributed. Now let us consider the linear transformation $\mathbf{Y} = \mathbf{C}\mathbf{X}$ where

$$\mathbf{C}' = (\mathbf{c}_1, \ldots, \mathbf{c}_m), \qquad \mathbf{c}_r = (c_{r_1}, \ldots, c_{r_n})', \tag{6.3.3}$$

and $\mathbf{C}$ is an $m \times n$ matrix ($m = n!$) such that $\mathbf{c}_r$ is a permutation of $(c_1, \ldots, c_n)'$. If $\mathbf{X}$ has an $\mathcal{N}_n(\boldsymbol{\mu}, \boldsymbol{\Sigma})$ distribution, then $\mathbf{Y}$ also has a multivariate normal distribution. Thus we obtain:

Theorem 6.3.1. *Let* $\mathbf{X}$ *have an* $\mathcal{N}_n(\boldsymbol{\mu}, \boldsymbol{\Sigma})$ *distribution and let* $X_{(1)} \leq \cdots \leq X_{(n)}$ *be the order statistics. Then for all fixed real numbers* $0 \leq c_1 \leq \cdots \leq c_n$ *we have*

$$P\left[\sum_{i=1}^{n} c_i X_{(i)} \leq x\right] = P\left[\bigcap_{j=1}^{m} \{Y_j \leq x\}\right], \tag{6.3.4}$$

where $\mathbf{Y} = (Y_1, \ldots, Y_m)'$ *has an* $\mathcal{N}_m(\mathbf{C}\boldsymbol{\mu}, \mathbf{C}\boldsymbol{\Sigma}\mathbf{C}')$ *distribution* ($m = n!$) *and* $\mathbf{C}$ *is the* $m \times n$ *matrix defined in* (6.3.3).

If the sequence of real numbers $\{c_1, \ldots, c_n\}$ is monotonically decreasing (instead of increasing), then a similar result can be obtained.

Theorem 6.3.1′. *Let* $\mathbf{X}$ *have an* $\mathcal{N}_n(\boldsymbol{\mu}, \boldsymbol{\Sigma})$ *distribution and let* $X_{(1)} \leq \cdots \leq X_{(n)}$ *be the order statistics. Then for all fixed real numbers* $c_1 \geq \cdots \geq c_n \geq 0$ *we have*

$$P\left[\sum_{i=1}^{n} c_i X_{(i)} \leq x\right] = 1 - P\left[\bigcap_{j=1}^{m} \{Y_j > x\}\right], \tag{6.3.5}$$

where $\mathbf{Y}$ *is defined as in Theorem* 6.3.1.

Proof. Let $\mathbf{X}^* = -\mathbf{X}$, then $\mathbf{X}^*$ has an $\mathcal{N}_n(-\boldsymbol{\mu}, \boldsymbol{\Sigma})$ distribution. Since

$$P\left[\sum_{i=1}^{n} c_i X_{(i)} \leq x\right] = 1 - P\left[\sum_{i=1}^{n} c_i(-X_{(i)}) \leq -x\right]$$

$$= 1 - P\left[\sum_{i=1}^{n} c_{n-i+1} X_{(i)}^* \leq -x\right],$$

where $X_{(1)}^* \leq \cdots \leq X_{(n)}^*$ are the order statistics of the components of $-\mathbf{X}$, the statement follows from Theorem 6.3.1. □

Remark 6.3.1. By choosing

(i) $c_n = 1$ and $c_{n-1} = \cdots = c_1 = 0$, and
(ii) $c_1 = 1$ and $c_2 = \cdots = c_n = 0$,

equations (6.3.4) and (6.3.5) yield the well-known result concerning the distribution functions of the maximum and the minimum

$$P[X_{(n)} \leq x] = P\left[\bigcap_{i=1}^{n} \{X_i \leq x\}\right],$$

$$P[X_{(1)} \leq x] = 1 - P\left[\bigcap_{i=1}^{n} \{X_i > x\}\right].$$

When the distribution of $\mathbf{X}$ is permutation-symmetric, then the results in Theorems 6.3.1 and 6.3.1′ can be simplified, especially when n is not very large. We consider such an example given below.

Example 6.3.1. Let $\mathbf{X} = (X_1, X_2, X_3)'$ have an $\mathcal{N}_3(\boldsymbol{\mu}, \boldsymbol{\Sigma})$ distribution with a common mean μ, a common variance σ^2, and a common correlation coefficient $\rho \in (-\frac{1}{2}, 1)$.

(a) For given real numbers $0 \leq c_1 \leq c_2 \leq c_3$ we have

$$P\left[\sum_{i=1}^{3} c_i X_{(i)} \leq x\right] = P\left[\bigcap_{j=1}^{6} \{Y_j \leq x\}\right],$$

where $(Y_1, \ldots, Y_6)'$ has a multivariate normal distribution with means and variances, respectively,

$$EY_r = \mu \sum_{i=1}^{3} c_i, \quad \operatorname{Var}(Y_r) = \sigma^2\left((1-\rho)\sum_{i=1}^{3} c_i^2 + \rho\left(\sum_{i=1}^{3} c_i\right)^2\right), \tag{6.3.6}$$

and correlation coefficients

$$\operatorname{Corr}(Y_r, Y_s) = \sigma^2\left((1-\rho)\sum_{j=1}^{3} c_{r_j}c_{s_j} + \rho\left(\sum_{j=1}^{3} c_{r_j}\right)\left(\sum_{j=1}^{3} c_{s_j}\right)\right)/(\operatorname{Var}(Y_r)). \tag{6.3.7}$$

(b) For given real numbers $c_1 \geq c_2 \geq c_3 \geq 0$ we have

$$P\left[\sum_{i=1}^{3} c_i X_{(i)} \leq x\right] = 1 - P\left[\bigcap_{j=1}^{6} \{Y_j > x\}\right],$$

where $(Y_1, \ldots, Y_6)'$ is defined as in (a).

(c) By choosing $c_2 = c_3 = 1$ and $c_1 = 0$ we have

$$\begin{aligned} P[X_{(2)} + X_{(3)} \leq x] &= P[X_1 + X_2 \leq x, X_2 + X_1 \leq x, X_1 + X_3 \leq x, X_3 + X_1 \leq x, \\ &\qquad X_2 + X_3 \leq x, X_3 + X_2 \leq x] \\ &= P[X_1 + X_2 \leq x, X_1 + X_3 \leq x, X_2 + X_3 \leq x] \\ &= P\left[\bigcap_{j=1}^{3} \{Y_j \leq x\}\right], \end{aligned}$$

where $(Y_1, Y_2, Y_3)'$ is a multivariate normal variable with means 2μ, variances $2\sigma^2(1+\rho)$, and correlation coefficients $(1+3\rho)/2(1+\rho)$. In this case, the joint distribution of the Y_j's is also permutation-symmetric.

(d) Similarly, by choosing $c_1 = c_2 = 1$ and $c_3 = 0$, we obtain

$$P[X_{(1)} + X_{(2)} \leq x] = 1 - P\left[\bigcap_{j=1}^{3} \{Y_j > x\}\right],$$

where $(Y_1, Y_2, Y_3)'$ is defined as in (c). □

It should be noted that in most cases the distribution of $\mathbf{Y} = (Y_1, \ldots, Y_m)'$ is singular and is not permutation-symmetric. For example, if $n = 4$ and we are interested in the distribution of $X_{(3)} + X_{(4)}$ then, when applying Theorem 6.3.1, it involves a six-dimensional normal variable $\mathbf{Y} = (Y_1, \ldots, Y_6)'$ given by

$$Y_1 = X_1 + X_2, \qquad Y_2 = X_1 + X_3, \qquad Y_3 = X_1 + X_4, \qquad Y_4 = X_2 + X_3,$$
$$Y_5 = X_2 + X_4, \qquad Y_6 = X_3 + X_4,$$

In this case, the distribution of $\mathbf{Y}$ is singular with unequal correlation coefficients.

Although the representations given in Theorems 6.3.1 and 6.3.1′ might be complicated for evaluating the probability integrals for linear combinations of order statistics, it has been found useful in proving certain analytical results. For example, it was conjectured in Tong (1982b) that

Conjecture 6.3.1. *Let $X_1, \ldots, X_n$ be exchangeable normal variables with a common mean μ, a common variance σ^2, and a common correlation coefficient*

$\rho \in [0, 1)$. Let $X_{(1)} \leq \cdots \leq X_{(n)}$ be the order statistics. Then $P_\rho[\sum_{i=1}^n c_i X_{(i)} \leq x]$ is a nondecreasing function of ρ for all $0 \leq c_1 \leq \cdots \leq c_n$ and all x. (In other words, $\sum_{i=1}^n c_i X_{(i)}$ is stochastically larger when ρ is smaller.)

This conjecture was motivated by the fact that the maximum, $X_{(n)}$, is stochastically larger when ρ is smaller (Theorem 6.2.1).

In a recent thesis Liang (1987) showed that the statement of this conjecture is not completely true. He first showed that the probability $P_\rho[\sum_{i=1}^n c_i X_{(i)} \leq x]$ is an increasing function of ρ for all $x \leq 0$; and then showed that the statement is not true, at least when $x > 0$ and n is sufficiently large. The proof depends on an application of the representation in Theorem 6.3.1 and on Slepian's inequality (Theorem 5.1.7), and his result has recently been extended to elliptically contoured distributions by Fang and Liang (1989).

6.4. Miscellaneous Results

Let $\mathbf{X} = (X_1, \ldots, X_n)'$ have an $\mathcal{N}_n(\boldsymbol{\mu}, \boldsymbol{\Sigma})$ distribution and let $X_{(1)} \leq \cdots \leq X_{(n)}$ be the order statistics. When the joint distribution of the X_i's is permutation-symmetric, then results for the order statistics are relatively easy to obtain. Otherwise, the problem becomes complicated due to the lack of symmetry, thus bounds and inequalities on their distribution functions and moments are useful. In this section we state such results under weaker (or no) conditions on the mean vector and the covariance matrix.

6.4.1. Moment Inequalities Via Algebraic Inequalities

Several distribution-free moment inequalities can be obtained by applying known algebraic inequalities. One such result is due to Samuelson (1968).

Proposition 6.4.1. *Let $x_1, \ldots, x_n$ be real numbers. Let $\bar{x} = (1/n)\sum_{i=1}^n x_i$, $s^2 = (1/n)\sum_{i=1}^n (x_i - \bar{x})^2$, and let $x_{(1)} \leq \cdots \leq x_{(n)}$ be their ordered values. Then*

$$\max_{1 \leq i \leq n} |x_i - \bar{x}| = \max\{|x_{(1)} - \bar{x}|, |x_{(n)} - \bar{x}|\} \leq \sqrt{n-1}\, s. \tag{6.4.1}$$

Furthermore, the inequality is sharp.

When applying this result to the multivariate normal distribution we immediately have

Theorem 6.4.1. *Let $\mathbf{X}$ have an $\mathcal{N}_n(\boldsymbol{\mu}, \boldsymbol{\Sigma})$ distribution and let $X_{(1)} \leq \cdots \leq X_{(n)}$ be the order statistics. Let $S^2 = (1/n)\sum_{i=1}^n (X_i - \bar{X})^2$ where $\bar{X} = (1/n)\sum_{i=1}^n X_i$.*

Then

$$P\left[\frac{1}{\sqrt{n-1}}\max\{|X_{(1)}-\bar{X}|, |X_{(n)}-\bar{X}|\} \le S\right] = 1. \tag{6.4.2}$$

Note that here S is different from that in (3.5.4), and (6.4.2) implies

$$P[R = X_{(n)} - X_{(1)} \le 2\sqrt{n-1}S] = 1, \tag{6.4.3}$$

hence

$$ER \le 2\sqrt{n-1}ES. \tag{6.4.4}$$

However, (6.4.4) is not as sharp as the result

$$ER \le \sqrt{2n}ES, \tag{6.4.5}$$

which was given previously by Thomson (1955).

The result of Samuelson (1968) was generalized by Wolkowicz and Styan (1979) and by Fahmy and Proschan (1981). Fahmy and Proschan considered upper bounds on the differences of pairs of ordered values. Their algebraic inequality states

Proposition 6.4.2. *Let* x_i*'s,* $x_{(i)}$*'s,* $\bar{x}$*, and* s^2 *be defined as in Proposition* 6.4.1. *Then for all* $1 \le i < j \le n$ *we have*

$$x_{(j)} - x_{(i)} \le c_{n,i,j}s, \tag{6.4.6}$$

where

$$c_{n,i,j} = \left[\frac{n(n-j+i+1)}{i(n-j+1)}\right]^{1/2}. \tag{6.4.7}$$

When applying this result to the multivariate normal distribution we have

Theorem 6.4.2. *Let* $\mathbf{X}$*,* $X_{(i)}$*'s,* $\bar{X}$*, and* S *be defined as in Theorem* 6.4.1. *Then*

$$P[X_{(j)} - X_{(i)} \le c_{n,i,j}S] = 1 \tag{6.4.8}$$

holds for all $1 \le i < j \le n$*. In particular, for all* $i < n/2$, we have

$$P\left[X_{(n-i+1)} - X_{(i)} \le \left(\frac{\sqrt{2n}}{\sqrt{i}}\right)S\right] = 1, \tag{6.4.9}$$

$$P\left[X_{(i+1)} - X_{(i)} \le \left(\frac{n}{\sqrt{i(n-1)}}\right)S\right] = 1, \tag{6.4.10}$$

and the inequality in (6.4.5).

A distribution-free result for the means of the linear combinations of order statistics, given by Arnold and Groeneveld (1979), has a special application to the multivariate normal distribution. In the following theorem we state the multivariate normal version of their result and adopt their original proof (which does not require normality).

Theorem 6.4.3. *Let* $\mathbf{X}$ *have an* $\mathcal{N}_n(\boldsymbol{\mu}, \boldsymbol{\Sigma})$ *distribution and let* $X_{(1)} \le \cdots \le X_{(n)}$ *be the order statistics. Then for all fixed real numbers* $c_1, \ldots, c_n$ *we have*

$$\left| E \sum_{i=1}^{n} c_i (X_{(i)} - \bar{\mu}) \right| \le \left[\sum_{i=1}^{n} (c_i - \bar{c})^2 \right]^{1/2} \left[\sum_{i=1}^{n} ((\mu_i - \bar{\mu})^2 + \sigma_i^2) \right]^{1/2},$$

where $\bar{c} = (1/n) \sum_{i=1}^{n} c_i$ *and* $\bar{\mu} = (1/n) \sum_{i=1}^{n} \mu_i$.

PROOF. Let $\bar{X} = (1/n) \sum_{i=1}^{n} X_i$. By the Cauchy–Schwarz inequality we have

$$\begin{aligned}\left| \sum_{i=1}^{n} (c_i - \bar{c})(X_{(i)} - \bar{X}) \right| &\le \left[\sum_{i=1}^{n} (c_i - \bar{c})^2 \right]^{1/2} \left[\sum_{i=1}^{n} (X_i - \bar{X})^2 \right]^{1/2} \\ &\le \left[\sum_{i=1}^{n} (c_i - \bar{c})^2 \right]^{1/2} \left[\sum_{i=1}^{n} (X_i - \bar{\mu})^2 \right]^{1/2}.\end{aligned}$$

Since (by Jensen's inequality) $E|V| \ge |EV|$ and $E\sqrt{W} \le \sqrt{EW}$ hold for all $W \ge 0$, we have

$$\begin{aligned}\left| E \sum_{i=1}^{n} c_i (X_{(i)} - \bar{\mu}) \right| &= \left| E \sum_{i=1}^{n} (c_i - \bar{c})((X_{(i)} - \bar{X}) + (\bar{X} - \bar{\mu})) \right| \\ &= \left| E \sum_{i=1}^{n} (c_i - \bar{c})(X_{(i)} - \bar{X}) \right| \\ &\le \left[\sum_{i=1}^{n} (c_i - \bar{c})^2 \right]^{1/2} \left[E \sum_{i=1}^{n} (X_i - \bar{X})^2 \right]^{1/2} \\ &\le \left[\sum_{i=1}^{n} (c_i - \bar{c})^2 \right]^{1/2} \left[E \sum_{i=1}^{n} (X_i - \bar{\mu})^2 \right]^{1/2} \\ &= \left[\sum_{i=1}^{n} (c_i - \bar{c})^2 \right]^{1/2} \left[\sum_{i=1}^{n} ((\mu_i - \bar{\mu})^2 + \sigma_i^2) \right]^{1/2}. \quad \square\end{aligned}$$

As a special consequence, Theorem 6.4.3 yields the following result for permutation-symmetric normal variables.

Corollary 6.4.1. *Let* $X_1, \ldots, X_n$ *be permutation-symmetric normal variables with a common mean* μ, *a common variance* σ^2, *and a common correlation coefficient* $\rho \in (1/(n-1), 1)$. *Let* $X_{(1)} \le \cdots \le X_{(n)}$ *be their order statistics. Then*

$$\left| \sum_{i=n-k+1}^{n} E(X_{(i)} - \mu) \right| \le \sqrt{n}\sigma \left[k\left(1 - \frac{k}{n}\right)^2 + (n-k)\left(\frac{k}{n}\right)^2 \right]^{1/2} \qquad (6.4.11)$$

holds for all ρ.

There exist other distribution-free results concerning the moments of order statistics. For example, when $X_1, \ldots, X_n$ are i.i.d. random variables, Hartley and David (1954) gave upper bounds on the mean of $X_{(n)}$ and lower bounds on the mean of $X_{(1)}$ in terms of the population mean and the population variance. Combining, this yields an upper bound on the mean of the range. Related results that apply to multivariate normal distribution can also be found in the recent review paper by David (1988).

6.4.2. Bounds When the Covariance Matrix Has Certain Structures

The results stated in Theorems 6.4.1–6.4.3 are distribution-free, thus they apply to a multivariate normal distribution with an arbitrary mean vector and covariance matrix. If the covariance matrix has a certain structure, then some special results exist. In the following, we first give a result for the case of equal variances and equal correlation coefficients, and show how the order statistics depend on the mean vector of the multivariate normal distribution.

Let $\mathbf{X}$ have an $\mathcal{N}_n(\boldsymbol{\mu}, \boldsymbol{\Sigma})$ distribution where $\boldsymbol{\Sigma}$ is such that

$$\sigma_{ij} = \begin{cases} \sigma^2 & \text{for } i = j, \\ \rho\sigma^2 & \text{for } i \neq j, \end{cases} \tag{6.4.12}$$

for some fixed $\rho \in (-1/(n-1), 1)$. Let $X_{(1)} \leq \cdots \leq X_{(n)}$ denote the order statistics. Consider the additive model

$$\mathbf{X} = \mathbf{Y} + \boldsymbol{\mu}, \tag{6.4.13}$$

where $\mathbf{Y}$ has an $\mathcal{N}_n(\mathbf{0}, \boldsymbol{\Sigma})$ distribution, and let

$$Y_{(1)} \leq \cdots \leq Y_{(n)}, \qquad \mu_{(1)} \leq \cdots \leq \mu_{(n)}, \tag{6.4.14}$$

denote, respectively, the order statistics of the Y_i's and the order values of the components of $\boldsymbol{\mu}$.

Smith and Tong (1983) studied probability and moment inequalities for the convex functions of order statistics under the model (6.4.13), and gave results which are not just for the multivariate normal distribution. If $\mathbf{X}$ and $\mathbf{Y}$ are normally distributed, then the result given below follows as a special case. To describe the result let us consider the functions $g_1, \ldots, g_n$ that satisfy the following condition.

Condition 6.4.1. For $i = 1, \ldots, n$:

(a) $g_i(x)$: $\Re \to \Re$ is monotonically nondecreasing both in x and in i; and
(b) $(d/dx)g_i(x) \equiv g_i'(x)$ exists for all $x \in \Re$ and is monotonically nondecreasing in i for each x.

It follows that

Theorem 6.4.4. *Let* $\mathbf{X}$ *have an* $\mathcal{N}_n(\boldsymbol{\mu}, \boldsymbol{\Sigma})$ *distribution when* $\boldsymbol{\Sigma}$ *satisfies* (6.4.12), *and define* $\alpha(\boldsymbol{\mu}) = P_{\boldsymbol{\mu}}[\sum_{i=1}^n c_i g_i(X_{(i)}) \leq \lambda]$ *where* $\lambda \in \Re$ *is arbitrary but fixed.*

(a) *If Condition* 6.4.1 *is satisfied, then* $\alpha(\boldsymbol{\mu})$ *is a Schur-concave function of* $\boldsymbol{\mu}$ *for all* c_i*'s such that* $0 \leq c_1 \leq \cdots \leq c_n$.

(b) *If Condition* 6.4.1 *is satisfied and if* $g_i(x) = ax + b, a \geq 0\,(i = 1, \ldots, n)$, *then* $\alpha(\boldsymbol{\mu})$ *is a Schur-concave function of* $\boldsymbol{\mu}$ *for all* c_i*'s satisfying* $c_1 \leq \cdots \leq c_n$.

(*For the definition of Schur-concave functions, see Definition* 4.4.2.)

PROOF. Let $A = \{\mathbf{x}: \mathbf{x} \in \mathfrak{R}^n, \sum_{i=1}^n c_i g_i(x_{(i)}) > \lambda\}$ and let $\chi_A(\mathbf{x})$ be the indicator function of A. Since $h(\mathbf{x}) = -\sum_{i=1}^n c_i g_i(x_{(i)})$ is a Schur-concave function of $\mathbf{x}$, it follows that $1 - \chi_A(\mathbf{x})$ is a Schur-concave function of $\mathbf{x}$. On the other hand, the density function of $\mathbf{Y}$ (which has an $\mathcal{N}_n(\mathbf{0}, \boldsymbol{\Sigma})$ distribution) is also Schur-concave (Theorem 4.4.1). Thus by the convolution theorem of Marshall and Olkin (see Marshall and Olkin (1979, p. 100) or Proposition 4.4.2) the probability

$$P_{\boldsymbol{\mu}}[(\mathbf{Y} - \boldsymbol{\mu}) \notin A] = E_{\boldsymbol{\mu}}[1 - \chi_A(\mathbf{X})]$$

is a Schur-concave function of $\boldsymbol{\mu}$. But $\boldsymbol{\mu}_1 \succ \boldsymbol{\mu}_2$ holds if and only if $-\boldsymbol{\mu}_1 \succ -\boldsymbol{\mu}_2$ holds. Thus

$$\alpha(\boldsymbol{\mu}) = P_{\boldsymbol{\mu}}[\mathbf{X} = (\mathbf{Y} + \boldsymbol{\mu}) \notin A] = P_{\boldsymbol{\mu}}\left[\sum_{i=1}^n c_i g_i(X_{(i)}) \leq \lambda\right]$$

is a Schur-concave function of $\boldsymbol{\mu}$. This completes the proof of (a).

The proof of (b) is similar. □

An immediate consequence of Theorem 6.4.4 is

Corollary 6.4.2. *Let* $\mathbf{X}$ *have an* $\mathcal{N}_n(\boldsymbol{\mu}, \boldsymbol{\Sigma})$ *distribution such that* $\boldsymbol{\Sigma}$ *satisfies* (6.4.12), *and let* $g: \mathfrak{R} \to \mathfrak{R}$ *be a convex and nondecreasing function such that* $g'(x)$ *exists. Then* $P_{\boldsymbol{\mu}}[\sum_{i=1}^n c_i g(X_{(i)}) \leq \lambda]$ *is a Schur-concave function of* $\boldsymbol{\mu}$ *and* $-E_{\boldsymbol{\mu}} \sum_{i=1}^n c_i g(X_{(i)})$ *is a Schur-concave function of* $\boldsymbol{\mu}$ *for all* λ *and all* $0 \leq c_1 \leq \cdots \leq c_n$.

When g is a linear function, then the condition concerning the sign of c_i's can be removed. Thus we have

Corollary 6.4.3. *Let* $\mathbf{X}$ *have an* $\mathcal{N}_n(\boldsymbol{\mu}, \boldsymbol{\Sigma})$ *distribution such that* $\boldsymbol{\Sigma}$ *satisfies* (6.4.12). *Then* $P_{\boldsymbol{\mu}}[\sum_{i=1}^n c_i X_{(i)} \leq \lambda]$ *is a Schur-concave function of* $\boldsymbol{\mu}$ *and* $-E_{\boldsymbol{\mu}} \sum_{i=1}^n c_i X_{(i)}$ *is a Schur-concave function of* μ *for all* λ *and all* $c_1 \leq \cdots \leq c_n$. *Consequently,* $P_{\boldsymbol{\mu}}[\sum_{i=1}^n c_i X_{(i)} \leq \lambda]$ *is maximized and* $E_{\boldsymbol{\mu}} \sum_{i=1}^n c_i X_{(i)}$ *is minimized when* $\mu_1 = \cdots = \mu_n$, *given their sum.*

Smith and Tong (1983) also gave a distribution-free inequality under the model in (6.4.13). The inequality depends on the fact that

$$(Y_{(n)} + \mu_{(n)}, \ldots, Y_{(1)} + \mu_{(1)})' \succ (X_{(n)}, \ldots, X_{(1)})' \succ (Y_{(n)} + \mu_{(1)}, \ldots, Y_{(1)} + \mu_{(n)})' \tag{6.4.15}$$

holds pointwise, where "$\succ$" denotes majorization. Their result was recently strengthened by David (1986). David's result holds for order statistics of any rank and has applications to outlier problems when sampling from normal populations.

The result in Theorem 6.4.4 is for the order statistics of normal variables with a common variance, a common correlation coefficient, and different means. In the following we describe a corresponding result when their means are equal but their cavariance matrix has a certain block structure.

Let $k_1, \ldots, k_n$ be nonnegative integers such that $\sum_{i=1}^n k_i = n$, and denote $\mathbf{k} = (k_1, \ldots, k_n)'$. Without loss of generality, it may be assumed that

$$k_1 \geq \cdots \geq k_r > 0, \qquad k_{r+1} = \cdots = k_n = 0,$$

for some $r \leq n$. Let us define r square matrices such that $\boldsymbol{\Sigma}_{jj}(k)$ satisfies (6.4.12) for $j = 1, \ldots, r$, and then define an $n \times n$ matrix $\boldsymbol{\Sigma}(\mathbf{k})$ given by

$$\boldsymbol{\Sigma}(\mathbf{k}) = \begin{pmatrix} \boldsymbol{\Sigma}_{11} & \mathbf{0} & \cdots & \mathbf{0} \\ \mathbf{0} & \boldsymbol{\Sigma}_{22} & \cdots & \mathbf{0} \\ & \cdots & & \\ \mathbf{0} & \mathbf{0} & \cdots & \boldsymbol{\Sigma}_{rr} \end{pmatrix}. \tag{6.4.16}$$

Let $\mathbf{X} = (X_1, \ldots, X_n)'$ have an $\mathcal{N}_n(\boldsymbol{\mu}, \boldsymbol{\Sigma}(\mathbf{k}))$ distribution. For fixed block sizes $k_1, \ldots, k_r$, X_i and X_j are correlated with a common correlation coefficient ρ if they are in the same block, and are independent if they belong to different blocks. The problem of interest is how the distributions and moments of the extreme order statistics $X_{(1)}$ and $X_{(n)}$ depend on the block size vector $\mathbf{k}$.

This problem is motivated by an application in agricultural genetic selection, and is illustrated in the following example.

EXAMPLE 6.4.1. Referring to the example discussed in Section 6.1.4, suppose that there are $n = 4$ animals available, and the best one is to be selected for breeding. Furthermore, suppose that the animals are from two families and the family sizes are either 3 or 1 or 2 and 2. Since individual animals from the same family are genetically related, it follows that for the scores X_1, X_2, X_3, X_4 (with family sizes 3 and 1), X_1, X_2, X_3 are equally correlated and are independent of X_4. Similarly, for the scores X_1^*, X_2^*, X_3^*, X_4^* (with family sizes 2 and 2), X_1^* and X_2^* are correlated, X_3^* and X_4^* are correlated, and $(X_1^*, X_2^*)'$ and $(X_3^*, X_4^*)'$ are independent. The random variable of concern is either $X_{(4)} = \max_{1 \leq i \leq 4} X_i$ (when the family size vector is $(3, 1)'$) or $X_{(4)}^* = \max_{1 \leq i \leq 4} X_i^*$ (when the family size vector is $(2, 2)'$). Under the variance-components model described in Section 6.1.4, $\mathbf{X}$ has an $\mathcal{N}_4(\boldsymbol{\mu}, \boldsymbol{\Sigma})$ distribution and $\mathbf{X}^*$ has an $\mathcal{N}_4(\boldsymbol{\mu}, \boldsymbol{\Sigma}^*)$ distribution, where $\mu_1 = \cdots = \mu_4 = \mu$ and

$$\boldsymbol{\Sigma} = \sigma^2 \begin{pmatrix} 1 & \rho & \rho & 0 \\ \rho & 1 & \rho & 0 \\ \rho & \rho & 1 & 0 \\ 0 & 0 & 0 & 1 \end{pmatrix} = \begin{pmatrix} \boldsymbol{\Sigma}_{33} & \mathbf{0} \\ \mathbf{0} & \boldsymbol{\Sigma}_{11} \end{pmatrix}, \tag{6.4.17}$$

$$\boldsymbol{\Sigma}^* = \begin{pmatrix} 1 & \rho & 0 & 0 \\ \rho & 1 & 0 & 0 \\ 0 & 0 & 1 & \rho \\ 0 & 0 & \rho & 1 \end{pmatrix} = \begin{pmatrix} \boldsymbol{\Sigma}_{22} & \mathbf{0} \\ \mathbf{0} & \boldsymbol{\Sigma}_{22} \end{pmatrix}. \tag{6.4.18}$$

The question of interest is which family vector (or equivalently, which covariance matrix) is to the geneticist's advantage in the sense that the expected gain is larger. □

If $n = mr$ holds for some positive integers m and r, then there are r families with m animals in each family. In this special case the problem possesses a symmetry property; the marginal density functions of the order statistics were derived, and the means computed numerically, by Rawlings (1976) and Hill (1976). To extend the applications of their results from the equal family-size case to the general case, Tong (1982b) gave an inequality for the extreme order statistics when the family sizes are $k_1, \ldots, k_r$ (unequal). The result was obtained via the diversity of $k_1, \ldots, k_r$ in the sense of majorization.

To describe this result let $\mathbf{k} = (k_1, \ldots, k_n)'$ and $\mathbf{k}^* = (k_1^*, \ldots, k_n^*)'$ denote the two vectors of nonnegative integers such that

$$k_1 \geq \cdots \geq k_r > 0, \qquad k_{r+1} = \cdots = k_n = 0;$$

$$k_1^* \geq \cdots \geq k_{r^*}^* > 0, \qquad k_{r^*+1}^* = \cdots = k_n^* = 0;$$

and $\sum_{i=1}^{r} k_i = \sum_{i=1}^{r^*} k_i^* = n$. Let $\mathbf{\Sigma} = \mathbf{\Sigma}(\mathbf{k})$, $\mathbf{\Sigma}^* = \mathbf{\Sigma}(\mathbf{k}^*)$ denote the two $n \times n$ matrices given in (6.4.16).

Theorem 6.4.5. *Let $(X_1, \ldots, X_n)'$ have an $\mathcal{N}_n(\boldsymbol{\mu}, \mathbf{\Sigma})$ distribution, let $(X_1^*, \ldots, X_n^*)'$ have an $\mathcal{N}_n(\boldsymbol{\mu}, \mathbf{\Sigma}^*)$ distribution, and let*

$$X_{(1)} \leq \cdots \leq X_{(n)}, \qquad X_{(1)}^* \leq \cdots \leq X_{(n)}^*$$

denote the corresponding order statistics. If $\mu_1 = \cdots = \mu_n$ and $\mathbf{k} \succ \mathbf{k}^*$, then:

(a) $$P[X_{(n)} \leq \lambda] \geq P[X_{(n)}^* \leq \lambda] \qquad \text{holds for all } \lambda$$

and $Eg(X_{(n)}) \leq Eg(X_{(n)}^*)$ holds for all nondecreasing functions g, thus $EX_{(n)} \leq EX_{(n)}^*$;

(b) $$P[X_{(1)} \leq \lambda] \leq P[X_{(1)}^* \leq \lambda] \qquad \text{holds for all } \lambda$$

and $Eg(X_{(1)}) \geq Eg(X_{(1)}^*)$ holds for all nondecreasing functions g.

Proof. The proof follows as a special case of the main result in Tong (1989). That result, when applied to the multivariate normal distribution, is stated and proved as Theorem 7.3.4. □

Remark 6.4.1. If $n = mr$ for positive integers m and r, then

$$(k_1, \ldots, k_r, 0, \ldots, 0)' \succ (m, \ldots, m, 0, \ldots, 0)' \succ (1, 1, \ldots, 1)'$$

holds. Thus by Theorem 6.4.5 the numerical value of the mean of the largest order statistics given in Rawlings (1976) and Hill (1976) provides an upper bound when the family sizes are unequal. Furthermore, it will be most advantageous to the geneticist if all the n animals are from different families (that is, $k_1 = \cdots = k_n = 1$).

Problems

6.1. Let X_1 and X_2 be two independent normal variables with means μ_1, μ_2 and variances σ_1^2, σ_2^2, respectively. Show that the marginal distribution functions of their order statistics $X_{(1)}$, $X_{(2)}$ are, respectively,

$$F_{(1)}(x) = \Phi\left(\frac{x-\mu_1}{\sigma_1}\right) + \Phi\left(\frac{x-\mu_2}{\sigma_2}\right) - \Phi\left(\frac{x-\mu_1}{\sigma_1}\right)\Phi\left(\frac{x-\mu_2}{\sigma_2}\right),$$

$$F_{(2)}(x) = \Phi\left(\frac{x-\mu_1}{\sigma_1}\right)\Phi\left(\frac{x-\mu_2}{\sigma_2}\right),$$

where Φ is the $\mathcal{N}(0, 1)$ distribution function.

6.2. (Continuation.) Find the density functions of $X_{(1)}$ and $X_{(2)}$ by differentiation.

6.3. (Continuation.) Find the density function of the range $R = X_{(2)} - X_{(1)}$.

6.4. (Continuation.) Show algebraically that the inequalities

$$P[X_{(1)} \le x_1, X_{(2)} \le x_2] > P[X_{(1)} \le x_1]P[X_{(2)} \le x_2],$$

$$P[X_{(1)} > x_1, X_{(2)} > x_2] > P[X_{(1)} > x_1]P[X_{(2)} > x_2]$$

hold for all $x_1 < x_2$.

In Problems 6.5–6.7, $X_1, \ldots, X_n$ are assumed to be i.i.d. $\mathcal{N}(\mu, \sigma^2)$ variables and that $X_{(1)} \le \cdots \le X_{(n)}$ denotes their order statistics.

6.5. Find the density function and distribution function of $X_{(i)}$ for fixed $1 \le i \le n$.

6.6. Find the joint density function of $(X_{(i)}, X_{(j)})'$ for fixed $1 \le i < j \le n$.

6.7. Find the joint density function of $(X_{(r_1)}, \ldots, X_{(r_s)})'$ for fixed $1 \le r_1 < \cdots < r_s \le n$.

6.8. Complete the proof of (b), (c), (d) in Corollary 6.1.1.

In Problems 6.9–6.13, $Z_1, \ldots, Z_n$ are assumed to be i.i.d. $\mathcal{N}(0, 1)$ variables and that $Z_{(1)} \le \cdots \le Z_{(n)}$ donotes their order statistics. Show directly by applying (6.1.1) and (6.1.3) that

6.9. $EZ_{(i)}^k = (-1)^k EZ_{(n-i+1)}^k$ for all $1 \le i \le n$ and all positive integers k.

6.10. $EZ_{(i)} < 0$ holds for all $i < n/2$, $EZ_{(i)} > 0$ holds for all $i > n/2$, and $EZ_{((n+1)/2)} = 0$ holds when n is an odd integer.

6.11. $\text{Var}(Z_{(i)}) = \text{Var}(Z_{(n-i+1)})$ for all $1 \le i \le n$.

6.12. $\text{Cov}(Z_{(i)}, Z_{(j)}) = \text{Cov}(Z_{(n-i+1)}, Z_{(n-j+1)})$ for all $1 \le i < j \le n$.

6.13. $\text{Corr}(Z_{(i)}, Z_{(j)}) = \text{Corr}(Z_{(n-i+1)}, Z_{(n-j+1)})$ for all $1 \le i < j \le n$.

6.14. Show that the two density functions given in (6.1.16) and (6.1.17) are identical. (*Hint*: see Theorem 5.3.1.)

6.15. Verify that the function $\delta(x_1, \ldots, x_n)$ defined in (6.2.2) is MTP_2.

6.16. Verify the proof of Proposition 6.2.2(ii) by showing that if $a_{(1)} \le \cdots \le a_{(n)}$, $b_{(1)} \le \cdots \le b_{(n)}$, $\sum_{i=1}^n a_{(i)} = \sum_{i=1}^n b_{(i)}$, and

$$a_{(i)} - a_{(i-1)} \ge b_{(i)} - b_{(i-1)} \qquad \text{for} \quad i = 2, \ldots, n,$$

then $(a_{(1)}, \ldots, a_{(n)})' \succ (b_{(1)}, \ldots, b_{(n)})'$.

6.17. Let $X_1, \ldots, X_n$ be exchangeable normal variables with a common mean μ, a common variance σ^2, and a common correlation coefficient $\rho \in [0, 1)$. Use (6.1.14) to derive the density function of the range $R = X_{(n)} - X_{(1)}$, then show that R and $\sqrt{1-\rho}\,(Z_{(n)} - Z_{(1)})$ are identically distributed where $Z_{(1)}, \ldots, Z_{(n)}$ are the order statistics of n $\mathcal{N}(0, 1)$ variables.

6.18. Denote $\mathbf{x} = (x_1, \ldots, x_n)'$ and let $x_{(1)} \le \cdots \le x_{(n)}$ be their ordered values. Show that $g(\mathbf{x}) = \sum_{i=1}^n c_i x_{(i)}$ is a convex function of $\mathbf{x}$ for all $0 \le c_1 \le \cdots \le c_n$.

6.19. (Continuation.) Show that $g(\mathbf{x})$ is a concave function of $\mathbf{x}$ for all $c_1 \ge \cdots \ge c_n \ge 0$.

6.20. Let $(X_1, \ldots, X_n)'$ be an n-dimensional random variable with mean vector $\boldsymbol{\mu} = (\mu_1, \ldots, \mu_n)'$. Let $X_{(1)} \le \cdots \le X_{(n)}$ and $\mu_{(1)} \le \cdots \le \mu_{(n)}$ be the ordered values of the means. Show that (Marshall and Olkin, 1979, p. 348)

$$(EX_{(1)}, \ldots, EX_{(n)})' \succ (\mu_{(1)}, \ldots, \mu_{(n)})'.$$

6.21. Verify the statement in Proposition 6.3.2.

6.22. Let $\mathbf{X} = (X_1, \ldots, X_n)'$ have an $\mathcal{N}_n(\boldsymbol{\mu}, \boldsymbol{\Sigma})$ distribution and let $X_{(1)}$, $X_{(n)}$ be the extreme order statistics. Show that if $\mathrm{Corr}(X_i, X_j) \ge 0$ for all $i \ne j$, then the inequalities

$$P[X_{(n)} \le x] \ge \prod_{i=1}^n \Phi\left(\frac{x - \mu_i}{\sigma_i}\right),$$

and

$$P[X_{(1)} \le x] \le 1 - \prod_{i=1}^n \Phi\left(\frac{-x + \mu_i}{\sigma_i}\right),$$

hold for all x, where Φ is the $\mathcal{N}(0, 1)$ distribution function.

6.23. Let $X_1, \ldots, X_n$ be i.i.d. $\mathcal{N}(\mu, \sigma^2)$ variables and let $X_{(1)} \le \cdots \le X_{(n)}$ be their order statistics. Show that

$$P[X_{(j)} - X_{(i)} \le c_{n,i,j}\lambda] \ge \int_0^{n\lambda^2} g(u)\, du$$

holds for all λ where g is the density function of a $\chi^2(n-1)$ distribution and $c_{n,i,j}$ is defined in (6.4.7).

6.24. Show that the coefficient of the upper bound on $X_{(i+1)} - X_{(i)}$ given in (6.4.10) is minimized when $|i - (n/2)| \le \frac{1}{2}$ for every fixed n.

6.25. Let $(X_1, \ldots, X_n)'$ be an n-dimensional random variable with means $\mu_1, \ldots, \mu_n$, variances $\sigma_1^2, \ldots, \sigma_n^2$ and correlation coefficients ρ_{ij}'s. Let $\bar{X} = (1/n)\sum_{i=1}^n X_i$ and $\bar{\mu} = (1/n)\sum_{i=1}^n \mu_i$. Show that $E\sum_{i=1}^n (X_i - \bar{X})^2 \le E\sum_{i=1}^n (X_i - \bar{\mu})^2$.

6.26. Show that the right-hand side of (6.4.11) also provides an upper bound for $|\sum_{i=1}^{k} E(X_{(i)} - \mu)|$.

6.27. Verify (6.4.15).

6.28. Show that if $g: \mathfrak{R} \to \mathfrak{R}$ is convex and increasing and if $\mathbf{X}$ has an $\mathcal{N}_n(\boldsymbol{\mu}, \boldsymbol{\Sigma})$ distribution, then

$$\sum_{i=1}^{n} Eg(Y_{(i)} + \mu_{(n-i+1)}) \leq \sum_{i=1}^{n} Eg(X_{(i)}) \leq \sum_{i=1}^{n} Eg(Y_{(i)} + \mu_{(i)})$$

holds, where $\mathbf{Y}$ has an $\mathcal{N}_n(\mathbf{0}, \boldsymbol{\Sigma})$ distribution and the $X_{(i)}$'s, $Y_{(i)}$'s are order statistics.

CHAPTER 7

Related Inequalities

7.1. Introduction

As noted by Pólya (1967), "Inequalities play a role in most branches of mathematics and have widely different applications." This is certainly true in statistics and probability. From the viewpoint of applications, inequalities have become a useful tool in estimation and hypothesis-testing problems (such as for yielding bounds on the variances of estimators and on the probability contents of confidence regions, and for establishing monotonicity properties of the power functions of certain tests), in multivariate analysis, in reliability theory, and so forth. Perhaps the usefulness of inequalities in multivariate analysis can be best illustrated by the following situation: Suppose that in an applied problem the confidence probability of a given confidence region for the mean vector is difficult to evaluate. If an inequality in the form of a lower bound on the confidence probability can easily be obtained, and if the lower bound already meets the required level of specification, then we know for sure that the true confidence probability meets or exceeds the required level.

The general study of the theory of inequalities in statistics and probability is, of course, closely related to the developments of inequalities in mathematics. As Mitrinović (1970, p. v) pointed out, although "the theory of inequalities (in mathematics) began its development from (the days of) C.F. Gauss, A.L. Cauchy, and P.L. Cebysev," it is "the classical work *Inequalities* by G.H. Hardy, J.E. Littlewood, and G. Pólya (1934, 1952) ... which transformed the field of inequalities from a collection of isolated formulas into a systematic discipline." After the publication of the second edition of their book in 1952, there have been several other volumes on mathematical inequalities; such as Beckenbach and Bellman (1965) and Mitrinović (1970). The book by Marshall and Olkin (1979) contains an up-to-date treatment of the theory of majorization inequalities and its applications in linear algebra, geometry, as well as in statistics and probability, and is highly influenced by Hardy, Littlewood, and Pólya (1934, 1952). Among the conference proceedings, there have been three volumes edited by Shisha (1967, 1970, 1972).

Among the books and monographs related to inequalities in statistics and probability, some chapters in the volumes by Karlin and Studden (1966) and Karlin (1968) involve such inequalities, mainly for totally positive density functions. The book by Barlow and Proschan (1975) contains probability inequalities and their applications in reliability theory. The monograph by Marshall and Olkin (1979) mainly concerns inequalities in statistics and probability, and partial orderings for probability distributions, via the theory of majorization. The book by Tong (1980) deals with probability inequalities in multivariate distributions via dependence, association, and mixture of random variables and distributions, via monotonicity and diversity of the parameter vectors, and other related concepts, and also includes statistical applications. The monograph by Eaton (1987) involves inequalities via majorization, log-concavity, and group-induced orderings; the recent book by Dharmadhikari and Joag-Dev (1988) contains inequalities for random variables with unimodal density functions. The proceedings volume edited by Tong (1984) with the cooperation of Olkin, Perlman, Proschan, and Rao contains 30 papers on inequalities written by leaders in the field. The forthcoming proceedings volume edited by Block, Sampson, and Savits (1989) contains inequalities via dependence of random variables.

In addition to those books and monographs, inequalities-related results include the contributions of many research workers in the form of research papers. And, during the early stages of the development, most of the published research results concerned the multivariate normal distribution. This is partially due to the mathematical simplicity of its density function, and partially due to the fact that normality has been assumed in most applications. Then more powerful mathematical tools have become available, and more general results have been obtained for larger families of distributions. Consequently, those results apply to the multivariate normal distribution.

In this chapter we present a survey of some of the useful inequalities for the multivariate normal distribution that exist in the literature. Section 7.2 contains results via dependence and the correlation structure of the normal variables. Attempts will be made to limit the overlaps with other reference sources (such as Chapter 2 of Tong (1980)) to a minimum. Section 7.3 contains inequalities concerning exchangeable normal variables, and the results depend on the dimension of the random variables. In Section 7.4 we present a comprehensive treatment of some of the majorization inequalities for the probability contents of geometric regions in a certain class under a multivariate normal density function. Most of the results have become available only recently (i.e., after the publication of the Marshall–Olkin (1979) book), and yield useful bounds in statistical applications. Finally, Section 7.5 deals with some miscellaneous results.

7.2. Dependence-Related Inequalities

Most of the results for dependence and correlation-related inequalities for the multivariate normal distribution have already been presented in Chapters 4 and 5 of this book. In this section we, for the purpose of completeness, briefly review some of them with the addition of a few new ones.

We begin with Slepian's inequality which was stated in Theorem 5.1.7 in a more general form. We first note that if $\mathbf{\Sigma} = (\sigma_i \sigma_j \rho_{ij})$ is a covariance matrix then, for all fixed ρ_{rs} such that $(r, s) \neq (i, j)$, the set of points

$$I_{(i,j)} = \{\rho_{ij}: \mathbf{\Sigma} \text{ is positive definite}\} \tag{7.2.1}$$

must be an interval. Based on this fact we observe a special version of Slepian's inequality:

Result 7.2.1. *If* $\mathbf{X} = (X_1, \ldots, X_n)'$ *has an* $\mathcal{N}_n(\boldsymbol{\mu}, \mathbf{\Sigma})$ *distribution where* $\mathbf{\Sigma} = (\sigma_i \sigma_j \rho_{ij})$ *then, for all fixed* ρ_{rs} $((r, s) \neq (i, j))$ *and all* $\mathbf{a} = (a_1, \ldots, a_n)'$, *the probability contents*

$$P_{\boldsymbol{\mu},\mathbf{\Sigma}}\left[\bigcap_{i=1}^{n} \{X_i \le a_i\}\right], \qquad P_{\boldsymbol{\mu},\mathbf{\Sigma}}\left[\bigcap_{i=1}^{n} \{X_i > a_i\}\right], \tag{7.2.2}$$

are strictly increasing in $\rho_{ij} \in I_{(i,j)}$.

This result was first obtained by Plackett (1954) and put in a more general form (as stated in Theorem 5.1.7) by Slepian (1962). A convenient reference for its proof is Tong (1980, pp. 9–11).

The probability contents in (7.2.2) are for regions of the form

$$A_1 = \{\mathbf{x}: \mathbf{x} \in \Re^n, x_i \le a_i, i = 1, \ldots, n\},$$

$$A_2 = \{\mathbf{x}: \mathbf{x} \in \Re^n, x_i > a_i, i = 1, \ldots, n\}.$$

Thus an interesting question is whether there are other geometric regions A such that $P_{\boldsymbol{\mu},\mathbf{\Sigma}}[\mathbf{X} \in A]$ is also an increasing function of the correlation coefficients. This question leads to the problem of the characterization of Slepian regions. Dharmadhikari and Joag-Dev (1984) studied this problem for the bivariate normal distribution, their main result states

Result 7.2.2. *Let* $\mathbf{X}$ *have a bivariate normal distribution with means* μ_1, μ_2, *variances* σ_1^2, σ_2^2, *and correlation coefficient* $\rho \in (-1, 1)$. *Let* A *be a subset of* $\Re^2$. *Then* $P_\rho[\mathbf{X} \in A]$ *is a nondecreasing function of* ρ *if and only if* A *is of the form* $A = Q_1 \cup Q_3 \cup B$, *where*

$$Q_1 = \{(x_1, x_2)': x_1 \ge a_1, x_2 \ge a_2\}, \qquad Q_3 = \{(x_1, x_2)': x_1 \le b_1, x_2 \le b_2\},$$

B is a finite disjoint union of horizontal (or vertical) infinite strips, and the interiors of Q_1, Q_3, and B are disjoint, and one or more of Q_1, Q_3, and B may be empty.

Note that a horizontal infinite strip is a set of points given by $\{(x_1, x_2)'\colon |x_2 - c| \le a\}$ for some real numbers c and $a > 0$, a vertical infinite strip is defined similarly. Obviously, the probability content of such a strip depends only on the marginal distribution and does not involve ρ.

When the random variables are nonnegatively correlated, then an association result due to Pitt (1982) is that:

Result 7.2.3. *Let* $\mathbf{X}$ *have an* $\mathcal{N}_n(\boldsymbol{\mu}, \boldsymbol{\Sigma} = (\sigma_{ij}))$ *distribution. Then*

$$Eg_1(\mathbf{X})g_2(\mathbf{X}) \ge Eg_1(\mathbf{X})Eg_2(\mathbf{X}) \tag{7.2.3}$$

holds for all nondecreasing functions g_1 *and* g_2 *such that the expectations exist if and only if* $\sigma_{ij} \ge 0$ *holds for all* $i \ne j$.

This result was stated and proved in Theorem 5.1.1. It implies that if $\sigma_{ij} \ge 0$ holds for all $i \ne j$, then

$$P[\mathbf{X} \in (A_1 \cap A_2)] \ge P[\mathbf{X} \in A_1]P[\mathbf{X} \in A_2] \tag{7.2.4}$$

holds for all nondecreasing sets A_1, A_2 in $\mathfrak{R}^n$, thus in particular

$$P\left[\bigcap_{i=1}^{n} \{X_i \ge a_i\}\right] \ge \prod_{i=1}^{n} P[X_i \ge a_i] \tag{7.2.5}$$

holds for all $a_1, \ldots, a_n$ (which also follows from Slepian's inequality).

A stronger condition on the positive dependence of the components of $\mathbf{X}$ is that the density function of $\mathbf{X}$ has an MTP_2 property. Barlow and Proschan (1975, pp. 149–150) proved that if $\mathbf{X}$ has a multivariate normal distribution with covariance matrix $\boldsymbol{\Sigma}$, then its density function is MTP_2 if and only if the off-diagonal elements of $\boldsymbol{\Sigma}^{-1}$ are all nonpositive. For details, see Section 4.3 (particularly Theorem 4.3.2). As a special case, if all the correlation coefficients are $\rho \in [0, 1)$, then this condition is satisfied. Consequently, the inequalities in (7.2.3)–(7.2.5) hold true.

For the absolute value of normal variables with mean vector $\mathbf{0}$ a key result is the following theorem due to Šidák (1968):

Theorem 7.2.1. *Let* $\boldsymbol{\Sigma} = (\sigma_{ij})$ *be a positive definite matrix, and for arbitrary but fixed* $\boldsymbol{\lambda} = (\lambda_1, \ldots, \lambda_n)'$, $\lambda_j \in [-1, 1]$ $(j = 1, \ldots, n)$, *let* $\boldsymbol{\Sigma}(\boldsymbol{\lambda}) = (\omega_{ij}(\boldsymbol{\lambda}))$ *be such that*

$$\omega_{ij}(\boldsymbol{\lambda}) = \begin{cases} \sigma_{ii} & \text{for } \ i = j, \\ \lambda_i \lambda_j \sigma_{ij} & \text{for } \ i \ne j. \end{cases} \tag{7.2.6}$$

Let $\mathbf{X}$ *have an* $\mathcal{N}_n(\mathbf{0}, \boldsymbol{\Sigma}(\boldsymbol{\lambda}))$ *distribution. Then* $P_{\boldsymbol{\Sigma}(\boldsymbol{\lambda})}[\bigcap_{i=1}^n \{|X_i| \le a_i\}]$ *is a nondecreasing function of* $|\lambda_j| \in [0, 1]$ *when the values of* $\lambda_{j'}$ $(j' \ne j, j' = 1, \ldots, n)$ *are kept fixed.*

A convenient reference for the proof of this theorem is Tong (1980, pp. 22–23). Note that we have

$$P_{\Sigma(\boldsymbol{\lambda})}\left[\bigcap_{i=1}^{n}\{|X_i| \le a_i\}\right] = P_{\Sigma(\lambda_1,\ldots,\lambda_{j-1},-\lambda_j,\lambda_{j+1},\ldots,\lambda_n)}\left[\bigcap_{i=1}^{n}\{|X_i| \le a_i\}\right] \quad (7.2.7)$$

for each j. Consequently, by choosing $\lambda_1 = \cdots = \lambda_n = 0$, we have

Corollary 7.2.1. *If* $\mathbf{X} = (X_1, \ldots, X_n)'$ *has an* $\mathcal{N}_n(\mathbf{0}, \Sigma)$ *distribution, then*

$$P_{\Sigma}\left[\bigcap_{i=1}^{n}\{|X_i| \le a_i\}\right] \ge \prod_{i=1}^{n} P|X_i| \le a_i] \quad (7.2.8)$$

holds for all $\mathbf{a} = (a_1, \ldots, a_n)'$, $a_i > 0$ $(i = 1, \ldots, n)$.

This result was previously stated in Theorem 5.1.2. Note that the right-hand side of (7.2.8) represents the true probability content when $X_1, \ldots, X_n$ are independent. It has been found useful in many inference problems concerning the mean vector, and obviously it is a better result to use than the Bonferroni inequality. The result in Theorem 7.2.1 was later generalized by Das Gupta, Eaton, Olkin, Perlman, Savage, and Sobel (1972) to the class of elliptically contoured distributions.

For other related results on the positive dependence of $|X_1|, \ldots, |X_n|$, see Section 5.1.

7.3. Dimension-Related Inequalities

7.3.1. Exchangeable Normal Variables

Let $\mathbf{X} = (X_1, \ldots, X_n)'$ have an $\mathcal{N}_n(\boldsymbol{\mu}, \Sigma)$ distribution. If

$$\mu_1 = \cdots = \mu_n = \mu, \qquad \sigma_1^2 = \cdots = \sigma_n^2 = \sigma^2, \qquad \text{and} \qquad \rho_{ij} = \rho \in [0, 1) \quad (i \ne j), \quad (7.3.1)$$

then $X_1, \ldots, X_n$ are exchangeable normal variables and their distribution properties and related results can be found in Sections 5.2 and 5.3.

In a number of statistical applications, we are interested in probabilities of the form

$$\beta_1(n) = P\left[\bigcap_{i=1}^{n}\{X_i \le a\}\right], \quad (7.3.2)$$

$$\beta_2(n) = P\left[\bigcap_{i=1}^{n}\{|X_i| \le a\}\right]. \quad (7.3.3)$$

These types of probabilities can be computed numerically and have been tabulated for selected values of n (see Sections 8.3, 8.4, and the Appendix). Then the question of interest is: For $k < n$, if the values of $\beta_1(k)$, $\beta_2(k)$ are already tabulated but $\beta_1(n)$ and $\beta_2(n)$ are not available, can we use the table values to obtain bounds for $\beta_1(n)$ and $\beta_2(n)$? The answer to this question was provided in Tong (1970):

Theorem 7.3.1. *Let $X_1, \ldots, X_n$ be exchangeable normal variables satisfying* (7.3.1). *Let $\beta_1(n)$, $\beta_2(n)$ denote the multivariate normal probabilities defined in* (7.3.2) *and* (7.3.3), *respectively. Then the inequalities*

$$[\beta_j(k)]^{n/k} \leq \beta_j(n), \qquad j = 1, 2, \tag{7.3.4}$$

$$\beta_j(k)\beta_j(n-k) \leq \beta_j(n) \qquad j = 1, 2 \tag{7.3.5}$$

hold for all integers $1 \leq k < n$. Furthermore, the inequalities become equalities if and only if $\rho = 0$.

PROOF. By (5.3.9) we have $\beta_1(n) = E(U(Z))^{n/k}$ where

$$U(Z) = \Phi^k\left(\frac{(a-\mu)/\sigma + \sqrt{\rho}Z}{\sqrt{1-\rho}}\right)$$

is a nonnegative random variable, Φ is the $\mathcal{N}(0, 1)$ distribution function, and Z is the $\mathcal{N}(0, 1)$ random variable. Since $g(u) = u^{n/k}$ is a convex function for $u \geq 0$ for all positive integers $1 \leq k < n$, by Jensen's inequality we have

$$\beta_1(n) = E(U(Z))^{n/k} \geq (EU(Z))^{n/k} = [\beta_1(k)]^{n/k},$$

and the inequality is strict unless the distribution of $U(Z)$ is singular (i.e., $\rho = 0$). This completes the proof of (7.3.4) for $j = 1$. Since (7.3.4) implies

$$[\beta_1(k)]^n \leq [\beta_1(n)]^k, \qquad [\beta_1(n-k)]^n \leq [\beta_1(n)]^{n-k},$$

we have

$$[\beta_1(k)\beta_1(n-k)]^n \leq [\beta_1(n)]^n,$$

which is (7.3.5) for $j = 1$. The proof for $j = 2$ is similar and is left to the reader. □

Remark 7.3.1. The result give in Tong (1970) is for the special case $\mu = 0$. But the original proof can be modified easily, as shown above, for the general case.

Remark 7.3.2. Note that the numerical value of a lower bound for $\beta_j(n)$ is simply the (n/k)th power of $\beta_j(k)$. Combining this fact with the trivial upper bound we have

$$[\beta_j(k)]^{n/k} \leq \beta_j(n) \leq \beta_j(k), \qquad j = 1, 2 \tag{7.3.6}$$

for all $1 \leq k < n$, and the bounds are close to the true value if the ratio n/k is close to one. Note that for $j = 1$ and $k = 1$, the lower bound in (7.3.6) also follows from Slepian's inequality (Theorem 5.1.7).

In a subsequent paper, Šidák (1973) used the core of the argument in the proof of Theorem 7.3.1 to obtain a more general result. His generalization is for all exchangeable random variables. In the following theorem we give a modified version of his result when the underlying distribution is multivariate normal.

Theorem 7.3.2. *Let $X_1, \ldots, X_n$ be exchangeable normal variables and, for an arbitrary but fixed Borel-measurable set $A \subset \mathfrak{R}$, define*

$$\gamma(n) \equiv P\left[\bigcap_{i=1}^{n} \{X_i \in A\}\right], \qquad n = 1, 2, \ldots. \tag{7.3.7}$$

Then the inequalities

$$[\gamma(k)]^{n/k} \le \gamma(n), \qquad \gamma(k)\gamma(n-k) \le \gamma(n) \tag{7.3.8}$$

hold for all positive integers $k < n$.

Proof. By the proof of Theorem 5.3.1 we can write

$$\gamma(n) = \int_{-\infty}^{\infty} \prod_{i=1}^{n} P[(\sigma(\sqrt{1-\rho}\, Z_i + \sqrt{\rho} z) + \mu) \in A]\phi(z)\, dz = E(U(Z))^{n/k}, \tag{7.3.9}$$

where

$$U(z) = \{P[(\sigma(\sqrt{1-\rho}\, Z_1 + \sqrt{\rho} z) + \mu) \in A | Z = z]\}^k \tag{7.3.10}$$

is the conditional probability. The rest of the argument follows similarly. □

In a paper concerning a majorization inequality for all exchangeable random variables Tong (1977) obtained a generalization of Theorem 7.3.2. The multivariate normal version of his result states:

Theorem 7.3.3. *Assume that $X_1, \ldots, X_n$ are exchangeable normal variables. Let $\mathbf{k} = (k_1, \ldots, k_r)'$ and $\mathbf{k}^* = (k_1^*, \ldots, k_r^*)'$ be two real vectors of nonnegative integers such that $\sum_{i=1}^{r} k_i = \sum_{i=1}^{r} k_i^* = n$. Let $\gamma(0) = 1$; and for $k_t > 0$ let $\gamma(k_t)$ be defined as in (7.3.7) for an arbitrary but fixed Borel-measurable set $A \subset \mathfrak{R}$. If $\mathbf{k} \succ \mathbf{k}^*$, then*

$$\prod_{t=1}^{r} \gamma(k_t) \ge \prod_{t=1}^{r} \gamma(k_t^*). \tag{7.3.11}$$

Proof. The proof depends on a moment inequality for all nonnegative random variables U: If the nth moment of U exists and

$$\text{if } \mathbf{k} \succ \mathbf{k}^*, \qquad \text{then } \prod_{t=1}^{r} EU^{k_t} \ge \prod_{t=1}^{r} EU^{k_t^*} \tag{7.3.12}$$

(see (1.3) of Tong (1977)). The proof of the theorem follows by letting $U = U(Z)$ where $U(Z)$ is defined in (7.3.10). The details are left to the reader. □

Remark 7.3.3. It can be verified easily that Theorem 7.3.2 is a special case of Theorem 7.3.3. To see that they are not equivalent, simply consider $\mathbf{k} = (n-1, 1)'$ and $\mathbf{k}^* = (n-2, 2)'$. Then Theorem 7.3.3 implies that

$$P\left[\bigcap_{i=1}^{n-2}\{X_i \in A\}\right]P\left[\bigcap_{i=1}^{2}\{X_i \in A\}\right] \leq P\left[\bigcap_{i=1}^{n-1}\{X_i \in A\}\right]P[X_1 \in A],$$

but Theorem 7.3.2 fails to apply.

7.3.2. A Class of Positively Dependent Normal Variables

The results given in Theorems 7.3.1–7.3.3 are for exchangeable normal variables only, thus the random variables have a common nonnegative correlation coefficient. In the following, we present a more general result when the correlation matrix possesses a certain structure. For fixed $r \leq n$ let $k_1, \ldots, k_r$ be positive integers such that $\sum_{t=1}^{r} k_t = n$, and let $\mathbf{k} = (k_1, \ldots, k_r, 0, \ldots, 0)'$ be the corresponding n-dimensional vector. Let the components of $\mathbf{X} = (X_1, \ldots, X_n)'$ be partitioned into r blocks with block sizes $k_1, \ldots, k_r$, respectively, i.e.,

$$\begin{aligned}(X_1, \ldots, X_n)' &\\ = (X_1, \ldots, X_{k_1}, X_{k_1+1}, \ldots, X_{k_1+k_2}, \ldots, X_{\sum_{t=1}^{r-1}k_t+1}, \ldots, X_n)' &\\ \equiv (\mathbf{X}^{(1)}, \mathbf{X}^{(2)}, \ldots, \mathbf{X}^{(r)})'. & \qquad (7.3.13)\end{aligned}$$

For arbitrary but fixed $\rho_2 > \rho_1 \geq 0$ we define a covariance matrix $\mathbf{\Sigma}(\mathbf{k}) = (\sigma_{ij}(\mathbf{k}))$ given by

$$\sigma_{ij}(k) = \begin{cases} \sigma^2\rho_2 & \text{for} \quad 1 \leq i < j \leq k_1 \ldots \quad \text{or} \quad \sum_{t=1}^{r-1} k_t + 1 \leq i < j \leq n, \\ \sigma^2\rho_1 & \text{otherwise;} \end{cases} \qquad (7.3.14)$$

that is, the correlation coefficient of X_i and X_j is ρ_2 if they belong to the same block, and is ρ_1 otherwise. Similarly, let $\mathbf{k}^* = (k_1^*, \ldots, k_{r^*}^*, 0, \ldots, 0)'$ be another vector of positive integers in which r^* plays the role played by r in $\mathbf{k}$, and let $\mathbf{\Sigma}(\mathbf{k}^*)$ be defined similarly.

Now let

$$\mathbf{X} = (X_1, \ldots, X_n)' \sim \mathcal{N}_n(\boldsymbol{\mu}, \mathbf{\Sigma}(\mathbf{k})), \quad \mathbf{Y} = (Y_1, \ldots, Y_n)' \sim \mathcal{N}_n(\boldsymbol{\mu}, \mathbf{\Sigma}(\mathbf{k}^*)) \qquad (7.3.15)$$

be such that

$$\mu_1 = \cdots = \mu_n = \mu. \qquad (7.3.16)$$

Then the marginal distributions of $X_1, \ldots, X_n$ and $Y_1, \ldots, Y_n$ are $\mathcal{N}(\mu, \sigma^2)$. If we choose $\mathbf{k} = (n, 0, \ldots, 0)'$ and $\mathbf{k}^* = (1, 1, \ldots, 1)'$, then $X_1, \ldots, X_n$ $(Y_1, \ldots, Y_n)$ are exchangeable normal variables with a common correlation coefficient ρ_2

(ρ_1). Thus by Theorem 5.3.10, $X_1, \ldots, X_n$ are more positively dependent than $Y_1, \ldots, Y_n$ in the sense that $E\prod_{i=1}^n g(X_i) \geq E\prod_{i=1}^n g(Y_i)$ holds for all nonnegative real-valued functions g. A question of interest is whether the same inequality holds for all $\mathbf{k}, \mathbf{k}'$ such that $\mathbf{k} \succ \mathbf{k}'$. The answer to this question is in the affirmative, as shown by Tong (1989).

Theorem 7.3.4. *Let* $\mathbf{X}, \mathbf{Y}$ *satisfy* (7.3.15) *and* (7.3.16) *where* $\rho_2 > \rho_1 \geq 0$.

(a) *If* $\mathbf{k} \succ \mathbf{k}^*$, *then*

$$E\prod_{i=1}^n g(X_i) \geq E\prod_{i=1}^n g(Y_i) \tag{7.3.17}$$

holds for all $g: \Re \to [0, \infty)$ *such that the expectations exist.*

(b) *If* $\mathbf{k} \succ \mathbf{k}^*$ *and* k_t, k_t^* *are all even integers* (*including* 0) *for* $t = 1, \ldots, n$, *then* (7.3.17) *holds for all* $g: \Re \to \Re$ *such that the expectations exist.*

The result in Tong (1989) is for a large class of positively dependent random variables, and is not just for the normal variables. In the following proof we modify the original proof for the special case when the underlying distribution is multivariate normal.

Proof of Theorem 7.3.4. Let $\{U_i\}_1^n$, $\{V_i\}_1^n$, and W be i.i.d. $\mathcal{N}(0, 1)$ variables, and define

$$\begin{aligned}
\mathbf{X}^{(1)} &= (\sigma(\sqrt{1-\rho_2}U_1 + \sqrt{\rho_2-\rho_1}\,V_1 + \sqrt{\rho_1}\,W) + \mu, \ldots, \\
&\qquad \sigma(\sqrt{1-\rho_2}\,U_{k_1} + \sqrt{\rho_2-\rho_1}\,V_1 + \sqrt{\rho_1}\,W) + \mu)', \\
\mathbf{X}^{(2)} &= (\sigma(\sqrt{1-\rho_2}U_{k_1+1} + \sqrt{\rho_2-\rho_1}\,V_2 + \sqrt{\rho_1}\,W) + \mu, \ldots, \\
&\qquad \sigma(\sqrt{1-\rho_2}\,U_{k_1+k_2} + \sqrt{\rho_2-\rho_1}\,V_2 + \sqrt{\rho_1}\,W) + \mu)', \\
&\cdots \\
\mathbf{X}^{(r)} &= (\sigma(\sqrt{1-\rho_2}\,U_{\sum_{t=1}^{r-1}k_t+1} + \sqrt{\rho_2-\rho_1}\,V_r + \sqrt{\rho_1}\,W) + \mu, \ldots, \\
&\qquad \sigma(\sqrt{1-\rho_2}\,U_n + \sqrt{\rho_2-\rho_1}\,V_r + \sqrt{\rho_1}\,W) + \mu)'.
\end{aligned}$$

Then $(\mathbf{X}^{(1)}, \ldots, \mathbf{X}^{(r)})'$ and $\mathbf{X}$ are identically distributed. Thus for all $g \geq 0$ and all positive integers n we have

$$\begin{aligned}
E\prod_{i=1}^n g(X_i) &= E\prod_{t=1}^r E\Bigg[E\Bigg\{\prod_{i=1}^{k_t} g(\sigma(\sqrt{1-\rho_2}\,U_i + \sqrt{\rho_2-\rho_1}\,V_t \\
&\qquad + \sqrt{\rho_1}\,W) + \mu)|(V_t, W)' = (v_t, w)'\Bigg\}|W = w\Bigg] \\
&= E\prod_{t=1}^r E[\psi^{k_t}(V_t, W)|W = w],
\end{aligned}$$

where

$$\psi(v_t, w) = E\{g(\sigma(\sqrt{1-\rho_2}\,U_1 + \sqrt{\rho_2 - \rho_1}\,V_t + \sqrt{\rho_1}\,W) + \mu) | (V_t, W)' = (v_t, w)'\}$$

denotes the conditional expectation. Since ψ is nonnegative, by the moment inequality in (7.3.12) we have, after unconditioning,

$$E \prod_{i=1}^{n} g(X_i) = E \prod_{t=1}^{r} E[\psi^{k_t}(V_t, W) | W = w]$$

$$\geq E \prod_{t=1}^{r^*} E[\psi^{k_t^*}(V_t, W) | W = w] = E \prod_{i=1}^{n} g(Y_i).$$

This completes the proof for $g \geq 0$ for all $\mathbf{k} \succ \mathbf{k}^*$. If the elements of $\mathbf{k}$ and $\mathbf{k}^*$ are all even integers and if g is not necessarily nonnegative, a similar argument follows. The details are left to the reader. □

When letting g be the indicator function of a set, we immediately have

Corollary 7.3.1. *Let* $\mathbf{X}$, $\mathbf{Y}$ *satisfy* (7.3.15) *and* (7.3.16) *where* $\rho_2 > \rho_1 \geq 0$. *If* $\mathbf{k} \succ \mathbf{k}^*$, *then*

$$P\left[\bigcap_{i=1}^{n} \{X_i \in A\}\right] \geq P\left[\bigcap_{i=1}^{n} \{Y_i \in A\}\right] \tag{7.3.18}$$

holds for all Borel-measurable sets $A \subset \mathfrak{R}$.

Remark 7.3.4. We note that:

(a) Theorem 7.3.4 is a generalization of Theorem 5.3.10 (by choosing $\mathbf{k} = (n, 0, \ldots, 0)'$ and $\mathbf{k}^* = (1, 1, \ldots, 1)'$); and
(b) Corollary 7.3.1 is a generalization of Theorem 7.3.3 (by choosing $\rho_2 = \rho$ and $\rho_1 = 0$).

Also note that by choosing $\rho_2 = \rho, \rho_1 = 0$, and $A = \{x: x \leq \lambda\}$, Corollary 7.3.1 yields a proof for Theorem 6.4.5. In real-life applications, experiments with a covariance matrix $\boldsymbol{\Sigma}(\mathbf{k})$ can be found in the example given in Section 6.1.4 or in similar situations.

If $\mathbf{k}$ contains only even integers and $\mathbf{k}^* = (1, 1, \ldots, 1)'$, then the condition $g \geq 0$ is not required (Tong, 1989). This result is stated below. Its proof is similar and is omitted.

Corollary 7.3.2. *Let* $\mathbf{X}$ *satisfy* (7.3.15) *and* (7.3.16) *where* $\rho_2 > \rho_1 \geq 0$. *If all the elements of* $\mathbf{k}$ *are even integers* (*including* 0), *then*

$$E \prod_{i=1}^{n} g(X_i) \geq \prod_{i=1}^{n} Eg(X_i).$$

In certain applications the covariance matrix $\boldsymbol{\Sigma}(s) = (\sigma_{ij}(s))$ of $\mathbf{X}$ may depend on an integer s such that

$$\sigma_{ij}(s) = \begin{cases} \sigma^2\rho_2 & \text{for } 1 \le i < j \le s, \\ \sigma^2\rho_1 & \text{otherwise.} \end{cases} \tag{7.3.19}$$

That is, the correlation coefficient of any pair of the first s variables is ρ_2, and the correlation coefficients of all other pairs are ρ_1 ($\rho_2 > \rho_2 \ge 0$). A simple application of Theorem 7.3.4 and Corollary 7.3.1 yields the following monotonicity property:

Corollary 7.3.3. *Let* $\mathbf{X} \sim \mathcal{N}_n(\boldsymbol{\mu}, \boldsymbol{\Sigma}(s))$ *where* $\mu_1 = \cdots = \mu_n$. *Then:*

(a) $E_{\boldsymbol{\Sigma}(s)} \prod_{i=1}^n g(X_i)$ *is a nondecreasing function of* s *for* $s = 1, 2, \ldots, n$ *for all* $g \ge 0$;
(b) $E_{\boldsymbol{\Sigma}(s)} \prod_{i=1}^n g(X_i)$ *is a nondecreasing function of* s *for even integers* $s = 0, 2, \ldots, n$ *and for all* g, *provided that the expectations exist; and*
(c) $P_{\boldsymbol{\Sigma}(s)}[\bigcap_{i=1}^n \{X_i \in A\}]$ *is a nondecreasing function of* s *for* $s = 1, 2, \ldots, n$ *for all Borel-measurable sets* $A \subset \mathfrak{R}$ *and all* n.

PROOF. (a) follows from Theorem 7.3.4 by taking $\mathbf{k} = (s + 1, 1, \ldots, 1, 0)'$ and $\mathbf{k}^* = (s, 1, \ldots, 1)'$.

(b) follows similarly by $\frac{1}{2}\mathbf{k} \succ \frac{1}{2}\mathbf{k}^*$.

(c) also follows similarly. □

To illustrate the applications of Theorem 7.3.4 and Corollaries 7.3.1–7.3.3 we consider the following example:

EXAMPLE 7.3.1. Suppose that $(X_1, X_2, X_3, X_4)'$ has an $\mathcal{N}_4(\boldsymbol{\mu}, \boldsymbol{\Sigma})$ distribution with $\mu_1 = \cdots = \mu_4$. Denote

$$\mathbf{k}_4 = (4, 0, 0, 0)', \quad \mathbf{k}_3 = (3, 1, 0, 0)', \quad \mathbf{k}_2 = (2, 2, 0, 0)', \quad \mathbf{k}_1 = (1, 1, 1, 1)';$$

define

$$\boldsymbol{\Sigma}(\mathbf{k}_3) = \sigma^2 \begin{pmatrix} 1 & \rho_2 & \rho_2 & \rho_1 \\ \rho_2 & 1 & \rho_2 & \rho_1 \\ \rho_2 & \rho_2 & 1 & \rho_1 \\ \rho_1 & \rho_1 & \rho_1 & 1 \end{pmatrix},$$

$$\boldsymbol{\Sigma}(\mathbf{k}_2) = \sigma^2 \begin{pmatrix} 1 & \rho_2 & \rho_1 & \rho_1 \\ \rho_2 & 1 & \rho_1 & \rho_1 \\ \rho_1 & \rho_1 & 1 & \rho_2 \\ \rho_1 & \rho_1 & \rho_2 & 1 \end{pmatrix},$$

and let $\boldsymbol{\Sigma}(\mathbf{k}_4)$ ($\boldsymbol{\Sigma}(\mathbf{k}_1)$) be the corresponding covariance matrix with variances σ^2 and covariances $\sigma^2\rho_2$ ($\sigma^2\rho_1$). Since $\mathbf{k}_{j+1} \succ \mathbf{k}_j$ holds for $j = 1, 2, 3$, we have

$$E_{\boldsymbol{\Sigma}(\mathbf{k}_{j+1})} \prod_{i=1}^4 g(X_i) \ge E_{\boldsymbol{\Sigma}(\mathbf{k}_j)} \prod_{i=1}^4 g(X_i)$$

for all $g \geq 0$ such that the expectations exist, and

$$P_{\Sigma(\mathbf{k}_{j+1})}\left[\bigcap_{i=1}^{4} \{X_i \in A\}\right] \geq P_{\Sigma(\mathbf{k}_j)}\left[\bigcap_{i=1}^{4} \{X_i \in A\}\right] \tag{7.3.20}$$

for all Borel-measurable sets $A \subset \mathfrak{R}$. Note that if $A = \{x: x \leq a\}$, then the inequality in (7.3.20) follows from Slepian's inequality for $j = 3$ but not for $j = 2$. □

7.4. Probability Inequalities for Asymmetric Geometric Regions

In this section we present inequalities for the probability contents of geometric regions in a certain class, using majorization as a tool. We shall focus our attention on the multivariate normal distribution. Similar results for larger classes of distributions can be found in the recent review article by Tong (1988).

As an example, consider the probability contents of rectangles when the underlying distribution of $\mathbf{X} = (X_1, X_2)'$ is bivariate normal with a common mean and a common variance. Let

$$A(a_1, a_2) = \{(x_1, x_2)': |x_1| \leq a_1, |x_2| \leq a_2\}$$

denote a rectangle in $\mathfrak{R}^2$ centered at the origin and with perimeter $4(a_1 + a_2)$. Since $(a_1, a_2)' \succ (b_1, b_2)'$ if and only if $a_1 + a_2 = b_1 + b_2$ and $|a_1 - a_2| \geq |b_1 - b_2|$ hold, the two rectangles $A(a_1, a_2)$ and $A(b_1, b_2)$ have the same perimeter, but $A(a_1, a_2)$ is more asymmetric (or $A(b_1, b_2)$ is closer to being the square $A(\bar{a}, \bar{a})$, $\bar{a} = \frac{1}{2}(a_1 + a_2)$). Since the joint density function of $\mathbf{X}$ is permutation-symmetric and unimodal, we may expect that $A(b_1, b_2)$ has a larger probability content. By Theorem 7.4.1 stated below we see that this is indeed true.

In addition to rectangles, majorization will be used for providing a partial ordering of the degree of asymmetry of a large class of geometric regions. For example, a region

$$A(a_1, a_2) = \left\{(x_1, x_2)': \left(\frac{x_1}{a_1}\right)^2 + \left(\frac{x_2}{a_2}\right)^2 \leq \lambda\right\}$$

defines an ellipse in $\mathfrak{R}^2$. If $(a_1^2, a_2^2)' \succ (b_1^2, b_2^2)'$ then, for fixed $c = a_1^2 + a_2^2 = b_1^2 + b_1^2$, $A(b_1, b_2)$ is closer to being a circle. Thus it seems reasonable to expect that the probability content of $A(b_1, b_2)$ is larger under a permutation-symmetric bivariate normal density function. This again is true, as we shall see in Theorem 7.4.2 below.

The geometric regions considered in this section include (one-sided and two-sided) n-dimensional rectangles, ellipsoids, and a large class of convex sets. The condition imposed on the density function of $\mathbf{X}$ is just Schur-concavity. Since a permutation-symmetric multivariate normal density function is a

Schur-concave function (Theorem 4.4.1), the results hold for the multivariate normal distribution. For convenience we state the following condition:

Condition 7.4.1. $\mathbf{X} = (X_1, \ldots, X_n)'$ have an $\mathcal{N}_n(\boldsymbol{\mu}, \boldsymbol{\Sigma})$ distribution where

$$\mu_1 = \cdots = \mu_n = \mu, \qquad \sigma_1^2 = \cdots = \sigma_n^2 = \sigma^2, \qquad \text{and} \qquad \rho_{ij} = \rho \in \left[-\frac{1}{n-1}, 1\right]. \tag{7.4.1}$$

This condition requires permutation symmetry instead of exchangeability. Thus the common correlation coefficient is not necessarily nonnegative as imposed in Section 7.3. Furthermore, it also includes the special case in which the distribution is singular with $\rho = -1/(n-1)$ and $\rho = 1$. In the results given below inequalities will be established for the nonsingular case only. Once this is accomplished, then they can be preserved when passing to the limit (as $\rho \to -1/(n-1)$ or $\rho \to 1$).

7.4.1. A Schur-Concavity Property of the Distribution Function

In one of the earlier papers on majorization inequalities in multivariate analysis, Marshall and Olkin (1974) considered the probability contents of one-sided n-dimensional rectangles

$$A_0(\mathbf{a}) \equiv \{\mathbf{x}: \mathbf{x} \in \Re^n, x_i \leq a_i, i = 1, \ldots, n\}, \tag{7.4.2}$$

where $\mathbf{a} = (a_1, \ldots, a_n)'$. They first proved a fundamental convolution theorem (Marshall and Olkin (1974 or 1979, p. 100), see Proposition 4.4.2), then used the theorem to obtain results given in Proposition 4.4.3 and Theorem 4.4.2. For the purpose of completeness the result in Theorem 4.4.2 is restated below:

Fact 7.4.1. *Under Condition* 7.4.1, $F_{\mathbf{x}}(\mathbf{a}) = P[\mathbf{X} \in A_0(\mathbf{a})]$ *(the distribution function of* $\mathbf{X}$*) is a Schur-concave function of* $\mathbf{a}$; *that is,* $\mathbf{a} \succ \mathbf{b}$ *implies* $F_{\mathbf{X}}(\mathbf{a}) \leq F_{\mathbf{X}}(\mathbf{b})$. *As a special case,*

$$F_{\mathbf{X}}(\mathbf{a}) \leq F_{\mathbf{X}}(\bar{\mathbf{a}}) \qquad \textit{holds for all} \quad \mathbf{a} \in \Re^n, \tag{7.4.3}$$

where $\bar{\mathbf{a}} = (\bar{a}, \ldots, \bar{a})'$, $\bar{a} = (1/n)\sum_{i=1}^n a_i$.

Fact 7.4.1 immediately yields the following result:

Corollary 7.4.1. *Let* $\mathbf{X}$ *have an* $\mathcal{N}_n(\boldsymbol{\mu}, \boldsymbol{\Sigma})$ *distribution such that* $\sigma_1^2 = \cdots = \sigma_n^2$ *and* $\rho_{ij} = \rho \in [-1/(n-1), 1]$. *Then* $P_{\boldsymbol{\mu}}[\bigcap_{i=1}^n \{X_i \leq a\}]$ *is a Schur-concave function of* $\boldsymbol{\mu}$ *for all* $a \in \Re$.

7.4.2. A Class of Geometric Regions Centered at the Origin

Motivated by the result in Proposition 4.4.3, Tong (1982a) considered the probability contents of two-sided rectangles of the form

$$A_{\infty}(\mathbf{a}) = \{\mathbf{x}\colon \mathbf{x} \in \Re^n, |x_i| \le a_i, i = 1, \ldots, n\}, \tag{7.4.4}$$

and proved that

Proposition 7.4.1. *If $f(\mathbf{x})$ (the density function of $\mathbf{X}$) is a Schur-concave function of $\mathbf{x}$, then $P[\mathbf{X} \in A_{\infty}(\mathbf{a})]$ is a Schur-concave function of $\mathbf{a}$.*

The proof of Proposition 7.4.1 does not follow by a modification of the proof of Proposition 4.4.3, thus a different argument is needed. For details, see Tong (1982a, Lemma 2.1).

An application of Proposition 7.4.1 immediately yields a Schur-concavity property for the absolute values of permutation-symmetric normal variables.

Theorem 7.4.1. *Under Condition 7.4.1, $F_{|\mathbf{X}|}(\mathbf{a}) = P[\mathbf{X} \in A_{\infty}(\mathbf{a})]$ is a Schur-concave function of $\mathbf{a}$. Consequently,*

$$P\left[\bigcap_{i=1}^{n} \{|X_i| \le a_i\}\right] \le P\left[\bigcap_{i=1}^{n} \{|X_i| \le \bar{a}\}\right] \tag{7.4.5}$$

holds for all $\mathbf{a} \in \Re^n$.

Note that the probability content on the left-hand side of (7.4.5) is for an n-dimensional rectangle and the probability on the right-hand side of (7.4.5) is for an n-dimensional cube, both centered at the origin, when the perimeter is kept fixed.

In addition to the results for rectangles, a similar application of Lemma 2.1 in Tong (1982a) also yields an inequality for ellipsoids: For given $\mathbf{a} = (a_1, \ldots, a_n)'$, $a_i > 0$ $(i = 1, \ldots, n)$, consider an ellipsoid defined by

$$A_2(\mathbf{a}) = \left\{\mathbf{x}\colon \mathbf{x} \in \Re^n, \sum_{i=1}^{n} \left(\frac{x_i}{a_i}\right)^2 \le \lambda\right\}, \qquad \lambda > 0 \text{ fixed.} \tag{7.4.6}$$

Proposition 7.4.2. *If $f(\mathbf{x})$ (the density function of $\mathbf{X}$) is a Schur-concave function of $\mathbf{x}$, then $P[\mathbf{X} \in A_2(\mathbf{a})]$ is a Schur-concave function of $\mathbf{a}^2 = (a_1^2, \ldots, a_n^2)'$.*

This result implies:

Theorem 7.4.2. *Under Condition 7.4.1, $P[\mathbf{X} \in A_2(\mathbf{a})] = P[\sum_{i=1}^{n} (X_i/a_i)^2 \le \lambda]$ is a Schur-concave function of $\mathbf{a}^2$ for all fixed $\lambda > 0$. Consequently,*

$$P\left[\sum_{i=1}^{n} \left(\frac{X_i}{a_i}\right)^2 \le \lambda\right] \le P\left[\sum_{i=1}^{n} X_i^2 \le \lambda \overline{a^2}\right] \tag{7.4.7}$$

holds for all $\mathbf{a}^2 \in \Re^n$ and all $\lambda > 0$ where $\overline{a^2} = (1/n)\sum_{i=1}^{n} a_i^2$.

Note that the probability content on the left-hand side of (7.4.7) is for an ellipsoid, and that on the right-hand side of (7.4.7) is for a sphere in $\mathfrak{R}^n$. Also note that the normal variables $X_1, \ldots, X_n$ are not necessarily independent and their common mean is not necessarily 0. But when these two additional conditions are met, then a different result is possible. That result, due to Okamoto (1960) and Marshall and Olkin (1979), states

Theorem 7.4.3. *Assume that Condition 7.4.1 is satisfied. If $\mu = 0$ and $\rho = 0$, then $P[\sum_{i=1}^n (X_i/a_i)^2 \le \lambda]$ is a Schur-concave function of $(\log a_1, \ldots, \log a_n)'$ for all fixed $\lambda > 0$.*

The reader is referred to Marshall and Olkin (1979, p. 303) for the proof of this result.

When applying Theorems 7.4.2 and 7.4.3 to the multivariate normal distribution with unequal variances, we immediately have

Corollary 7.4.2. *Let $(Y_1, \ldots, Y_n)'$ have an $\mathcal{N}_n(\boldsymbol{\mu}, \boldsymbol{\Sigma})$ distribution with a common mean μ, a common correlation coefficient $\rho \in [-1/(n-1), 1]$, and variances $\sigma_1^2, \ldots, \sigma_n^2$. Then $P[\sum_{i=1}^n Y_i^2 \le \lambda]$ is a Schur-concave function of $(\sigma_1^{-2}, \ldots, \sigma_n^{-2})$ for all $\lambda > 0$. Thus*

$$P\left[\sum_{i=1}^{n} Y_i^2 \le \lambda\right] \le P\left[\sum_{i=1}^{n} Z_i^2 \le \frac{\lambda}{n} \sum_{i=1}^{n} \sigma_i^{-2}\right] \tag{7.4.8}$$

holds for all $\lambda > 0$ where $(Z_1, \ldots, Z_n)'$ has a multivariate normal distribution with a common mean μ, a common variance one, and a common correlation coefficient ρ. If in addition $\mu = 0$ and $\rho = 0$, then $P[\sum_{i=1}^n Y_i^2 \le \lambda]$ is a Schur-concave function of $(\log \sigma_1, \ldots, \log \sigma_n)'$; thus

$$P\left[\sum_{i=1}^{n} Y_i^2 \le \lambda\right] \le P\left[\chi^2_{(n)} \le \lambda\left(\prod_{i=1}^{n} \sigma_i^2\right)^{-1/n}\right] \tag{7.4.9}$$

holds for all $\lambda > 0$, where $\chi^2(n)$ is a chi-squared variable with n degrees of freedom.

Note that when $\mu = 0$ and $\rho = 0$, the bound in (7.4.9) is sharper than that in (7.4.8).

After proving Propositions 7.4.1 and 7.4.2, Tong (1982a) considered a larger class of geometric regions defined by

$$A_m(\mathbf{a}) = \left\{\mathbf{x}\colon \mathbf{x} \in \mathfrak{R}^n, \sum_{i=1}^{n} \left(\frac{x_i}{a_i}\right)^m \le \lambda\right\}, \qquad \lambda > 0 \text{ fixed}, \tag{7.4.10}$$

for $m = 2, 4, 6, \ldots, \infty$, and conjectured that the probability content of $A_m(\mathbf{a})$ is a Schur-concave function of $(a_1^{m/(m-1)}, \ldots, a_n^{m/(m-1)})'$. This conjecture seems reasonable because it was already known that the statement is true for $m = 2$ (Proposition 7.4.2) and $m = \infty$ (Proposition 7.4.1). In a subsequent paper,

Karlin and Rinott (1983b) provided an answer to this conjecture by proving the following proposition.

Proposition 7.4.3. *If* $\mathbf{X} = (X_1, \ldots, X_n)'$ *is a nonnegative n-dimensional random variable with a joint density that is Schur-concave, then*

$$P\left[\sum_1^n \left(\frac{X_i^\alpha}{c_i^\beta}\right) \leq \lambda\right], \quad \lambda > 0, \quad \alpha \geq 1, \quad 0 \leq \beta \leq \alpha - 1, \quad c_i > 0 \quad (i = 1, \ldots, n) \tag{7.4.11}$$

is a Schur-concave function of $\mathbf{c} = (c_1, \ldots, c_n)'$.

The condition that $\mathbf{X}$ is nonnegative is only used to assure the convexity of the function $u(x, c) = (x^\alpha/c^\beta)$ in their proof. Thus when applying it to the multivariate normal distribution, it follows by a similar argument given in their proof and by passing to the limit as $(m \to \infty)$ that

Theorem 7.4.4. *Under Condition* 7.4.1, $P[\sum_{i=1}^n (X_i^m/c_i^{m-1}) \leq \lambda]$ *is a Schur-concave function of* $(c_1, \ldots, c_n)'$ *for all* $c_i > 0$ *and for* $m = 2, 4, 6, \ldots, \infty$. *Consequently*, $P[\sum_{i=1}^n (X_i/a_i)^m \leq \lambda]$ *is a Schur-concave function of* $(a_1^{m/(m-1)}, \ldots, a_n^{m/(m-1)})'$ *for* $m = 2, 4, 6, \ldots, \infty$ *and for all* $\lambda > 0$.

This theorem applies to a large class of geometric regions centered at the origin, and implies both Theorems 7.4.1 and 7.4.2 as special cases.

7.4.3. n-Dimensional Rectangles with Fixed Perimeter

The majorization inequality in Theorem 7.4.1 deals with n-dimensional rectangles centered at the origin. To consider rectangles not necessarily centered at the origin, for a given $2 \times n$ matrix

$$\mathbf{A} = \begin{pmatrix} a_{11} & a_{12} & \cdots & a_{1n} \\ a_{21} & a_{22} & \cdots & a_{2n} \end{pmatrix} \equiv \begin{pmatrix} \mathbf{a}_1' \\ \mathbf{a}_2' \end{pmatrix}, \tag{7.4.12}$$

such that $a_{1j} < a_{2j}$ $(j = 1, \ldots, n)$ we define a rectangle

$$S(\mathbf{A}) = \{\mathbf{x}: \mathbf{x} \in \Re^n, a_{1i} \leq x_i \leq a_{2i} \text{ for } i = 1, \ldots, n\}. \tag{7.4.13}$$

Let $\mathbf{B} = \begin{pmatrix} \mathbf{b}_1' \\ \mathbf{b}_2' \end{pmatrix}$ denote another $2 \times n$ matrix. If the $\mathbf{b}_j$'s are less diverse than the $\mathbf{a}_j$'s $(j = 1, 2)$ in a certain fashion, then we may expect that the probability content of $S(\mathbf{A})$ is smaller than that of $S(\mathbf{B})$. To obtain such a result we need the following definition of multivariate majorization (Marshall and Olkin, 1979, Chap. 15).

Definition 7.4.1.

(a) $\mathbf{A}$ is said to row-wise majorize $\mathbf{B}$ (in symbols $\mathbf{A} \overset{r}{\succ} \mathbf{B}$) if $\mathbf{a}_1 \succ \mathbf{b}_1$ and $\mathbf{a}_2 \succ \mathbf{b}_2$.
(b) $\mathbf{A}$ is said to majorize $\mathbf{B}$ in a multivariate sense ($\mathbf{A} \overset{m}{\succ} \mathbf{B}$) if there exists a doubly stochastic matrix $\mathbf{Q}$ such that $\mathbf{B} = \mathbf{AQ}$.
(c) For arbitrary but fixed $r \neq s$ the T-transform matrix $\mathbf{T}_{rs}$ is of the form

$$\mathbf{T}_{rs} = \alpha \mathbf{I} + (1 - \alpha)\mathbf{I}_{rs},$$

where $\mathbf{I}$ is the identical matrix, $\mathbf{I}_{rs}$ is the matrix obtained by interchanging the rth and the sth columns of $\mathbf{I}$, and $\alpha \in [0, 1]$. $\mathbf{A}$ is said to chain majorize $\mathbf{B}$ ($\mathrm{A} \overset{c}{\succ} \mathbf{B}$) if there exists an $n \times n$ matrix $\mathbf{T}$ which is the product of a finite number of T-transform matrices such that $\mathbf{B} = \mathbf{AT}$.

Note that

$$\mathbf{A} \overset{c}{\succ} \mathbf{B} \overset{\text{(i)}}{\Rightarrow} \mathbf{A} \overset{m}{\succ} \mathbf{B} \overset{\text{(ii)}}{\Rightarrow} \mathbf{A} \overset{r}{\succ} \mathbf{B} \tag{7.4.14}$$

and that the implications are strict. This is true because:

(i) there exists a doubly stochastic matrix that is not the product of a finite number of T-transform matrices, and
(ii) $\mathbf{A} \overset{r}{\succ} \mathbf{B}$ if and only if there exist doubly stochastic matrices $\mathbf{Q}_1$ and $\mathbf{Q}_2$ (not necessarily the same one) such that $\mathbf{b}_i = \mathbf{a}_i \mathbf{Q}_i$ $(i = 1, 2)$.

It is easy to see that if $\mathbf{A} \overset{c}{\succ} \mathbf{B}$ or $\mathbf{A} \overset{m}{\succ} \mathbf{B}$, then

$$(a_{21} - a_{11}, \ldots, a_{2n} - a_{1n})' \succ (b_{21} - b_{11}, \ldots, b_{2n} - b_{1n})'.$$

Thus, for the rectangles $S(\mathbf{A})$ and $S(\mathbf{B})$ defined in (7.4.13), their perimeters are the same but $S(\mathbf{B})$ is closer to being a cube. Consequently, we may expect that the probability content of $S(\mathbf{B})$ is larger under suitable conditions on the density function $f(\mathbf{x})$. In the following we state two such results obtained independently by Karlin and Rinott (1983b) and Tong (1983, 1989). The first result requires a stronger condition on multivariate majorization but applies to a larger class of density functions.

Proposition 7.4.4. *If $f(\mathbf{x})$ (the density function of $\mathbf{X}$) is a Schur-concave function, and $\mathbf{A} \overset{c}{\succ} \mathbf{B}$, then*

$$P[\mathbf{X} \in S(\mathbf{A})] \leq P[\mathbf{X} \in S(\mathbf{B})]. \tag{7.4.15}$$

Proposition 7.4.5. *If $f(\mathbf{x})$ is a permutation symmetric and log-concave function of $\mathbf{x}$, and $\mathbf{A} \overset{m}{\succ} \mathbf{B}$, then* (7.4.15) *holds.*

The proofs of Propositions 7.4.4 and 7.4.5 depend on the fact that a convex combination of two n-dimensional rectangles is again an n-dimensional rectangle. As a consequence, Proposition 7.4.5 follows by an application of Prékopa's theorem (Proposition 4.2.1). For details, see Karlin adn Rinott (1983b) or Tong (1983, 1989).

The density function of a permutation-symmetric multivariate normal variable is a permutation-symmetric log-concave function, and hence a Schur-concave function (Theorems 4.2.1 and 4.4.1). Consequently, an application of Proposition 7.4.5 yields

Theorem 7.4.5. *Under Condition* 7.4.1, $\mathbf{A} \overset{m}{\succ} \mathbf{B}$ *implies* $P[\mathbf{X} \in S(\mathbf{A})] \leq P[\mathbf{X} \in S(\mathbf{B})]$. *Thus*

$$P\left[\bigcap_{i=1}^{n} \{a_{1i} \leq X_i \leq a_{2i}\}\right] \leq P\left[\bigcap_{i=1}^{n} \{\bar{a}_1 \leq X_i \leq \bar{a}_2\}\right]$$

holds for all $\mathbf{a}_1 = (a_{11}, \ldots, a_{1n})'$ *and* $\mathbf{a}_2 = (a_{21}, \ldots, a_{2n})'$, *where* $\bar{a}_j = (1/n)\sum_{i=1}^{n} a_{ji}$ $(j = 1, 2)$.

We note in passing that when choosing $a_{1i} = -a_{2i}$ $(i = 1, \ldots, n)$, Theorem 7.4.5 reduces to Theorem 7.4.1 as a special case. Furthermore, note that the notion of row-wise majorization is too general to be useful for deriving this type of inequality, because a counterexample shows that $P[\mathbf{X} \in S(\mathbf{A})] > P[\mathbf{X} \in S(\mathbf{B})]$ may hold even if we have $\mathbf{A} \overset{r}{\succ} \mathbf{B}$ (Tong, 1983, 1989).

7.4.4. Geometric Regions with Fixed Volume

For the rectangular and elliptical regions defined in (7.4.4) and (7.4.6), their volumes (Vol) are multiples of $\prod_{i=1}^{n} a_i$. Thus if $(a_1, \ldots, a_n)' \succ (b_1, \ldots, b_n)'$ or $(a_1^2, \ldots, a_n^2)' \succ (b_1^2, \ldots, b_n^2)'$ holds, then we have

$$\mathrm{Vol}(A_\infty(\mathbf{a})) \leq \mathrm{Vol}(A_\infty(\mathbf{b})) \qquad \text{or} \qquad \mathrm{Vol}(A_2(\mathbf{a})) \leq \mathrm{Vol}(A_2(\mathbf{b})),$$

with strict inequality if $\mathbf{a}$ is not a permutation of $\mathbf{b}$. Consequently, in the inequalities stated in Theorems 7.4.1 and 7.4.2, the difference in probability contents might be partially due to the difference in the volumes of the sets. In view of this fact, a corresponding result will be of interest if *the volumes* of the sets are kept fixed. This can be accomplished by considering inequalities via the majorization

$$(\log a_1, \ldots, \log a_n)' \succ (\log b_1, \ldots, \log b_n)'.$$

Such majorization inequalities depend on the diversity of the elements of $\mathbf{a}$ when the *geometric mean* (instead of the arithmetic mean) is kept fixed.

Shaked and Tong (1983, 1988) studied this problem for a class of geometric regions. They first showed in a counterexample that a corresponding result is impossible under the sole assumption of the Schur-concavity of $f(\mathbf{x})$. For a positive result, the following definition of monotone unimodality, given by Dharmadhikari and Jogdeo (1976), is needed.

Definition 7.4.2. An n-dimensional random variable $\mathbf{X}$ (or its density $f(\mathbf{x})$) is said to be monotone unimodal if, for every symmetric (about the origin) and convex set $A \subset \mathfrak{R}^n$ and for every $\mathbf{u} \neq \mathbf{0}$, the probability $P[\mathbf{X} \in A + c\mathbf{u}]$ is nonincreasing in c for $c \geq 0$.

Using this property and certain properties of the arrangement-increasing functions given in Hollander, Proschan, and Sethuraman (1977), Shaked and Tong (1983, 1988) obtained the following theorem for the bivariate case.

Proposition 7.4.6. *If $(X_1, X_2)'$ has a density function $f(x_1, x_2)$ that is Schur-concave and monotone unimodal, and $f(x_1, -x_2)$ is Schur-concave, then $P[(X_1/a_1, X_2/a_2)' \in A]$ is a Schur-concave function of* $(\log a_1, \log a_2)'$ *for all measurable sets $A \subset \mathfrak{R}^2$ which are convex, permutation-symmetric, and symmetric about the origin.*

An immediate application of this result to the bivariate normal distribution is

Theorem 7.4.6. *If $(X_1, X_2)'$ has a bivariate normal distribution with a common mean* 0, *a common variance σ^2, and correlation coefficient $\rho \in [-1, 1]$, then $P[(X_1/a_1, X_2/a_2)' \in A]$ is a Schur-concave function of* $(\log a_1, \log a_2)'$ *for all measurable sets $A \subset \mathfrak{R}^2$ which are convex, permutation-symmetric, and symmetric about the origin.*

An equivalent result is

Theorem 7.4.6′. *If $(Y_1, Y_2)'$has a bivariate normal distribution with a common mean* 0, *variances σ_1^2 and σ_2^2, and a correlation coefficient $\rho \in [-1, 1]$, then $P[(Y_1, Y_2)' \in A]$ is a Schur-concave function of* $(\log \sigma_1, \log \sigma_2)'$ *for all measurable sets $A \subset \mathfrak{R}^2$ which are convex, permutation-symmetric, and symmetric about the origin. Consequently, for fixed $\prod_{i=1}^2 \sigma_i$ this probability content is maximized when $\sigma_1 = \sigma_2$.*

A special case of Theorem 7.4.6, in which A is a rectangle in $\mathfrak{R}^2$, was obtained independently by Kunte and Rattihalli (1984). Das Gupta and Rattihalli (1984) also gave a result for the multivariate normal distribution when the components are independent. Their result asserts that when the volume of the n-dimensional rectangle is kept fixed, then the probability content is maximized when the rectangle becomes a cube. The result is stated below.

Theorem 7.4.7. *Let* **X** *have an $\mathcal{N}_n(\mathbf{0}, \mathbf{\Sigma})$ distribution such that $\sigma_i^2 = \sigma^2$ and $\rho_{ij} = 0$ $(1 \leq i < j \leq n)$. Then, subject to a fixed $\prod_{i=1}^n a_i$, $P[\bigcap_{i=1}^n \{|X_i| \leq a_i\}]$ is maximized when $a_1 = \cdots = a_n = (\prod_{i=1}^n a_i)^{1/n}$.*

After finding a proof for Proposition 7.4.6, Shaked and Tong (1983, 1988) conjectured that an n-dimensional version of that result is also true.

Conjecture 7.4.1. *For $n > 2$, if $f(\mathbf{x})$ (the density of $\mathbf{X} = (X_1, \ldots, X_n)'$) is permutation-symmetric and monotone unimodal, and if $A \subset \mathfrak{R}^n$ is Borel-measurable, permutation-symmetric, convex, and symmetric (about the origin), then $P[(X_1/a_1, \ldots, X_n/a_n)' \in A]$ is a Schur-concave function of $(\log a_1, \ldots, \log a_n)'$.*

To our knowledge, it is not yet known whether this conjecture is true.

7.5. Other Related Inequalities

In this section we give related results on inequalities via the peakedness of distributions and the arrangement-increasing property of the multivariate normal distribution. We also discuss Mills' ratio, and present some miscellaneous results.

7.5.1. Peakedness-Related Inequalities

Peakedness is a descriptive index of a distribution that provides an indication of concentration. Although the notion is intuitive, a formal definition for the univariate case was first introduced by Birnbaum (1948):

Definition 7.5.1. A (univariate) random variable X is said to be more peaked about μ than a random variable Y about ν if

$$P\{|X - \mu| < \lambda\} \geq P\{|Y - \nu| < \lambda\} \qquad \text{for all } \lambda.$$

When $\mu = \nu = 0$ we say that X is more peaked than Y.

The following definition, due to Sherman (1955), is a multivariate analogy of Definition 7.5.1.

Definition 7.5.2. An n-dimensional random variable $\mathbf{X}$ is said to be more peaked than $\mathbf{Y}$ if their density functions exist and if

$$P\{\mathbf{X} \in A\} \geq P\{\mathbf{Y} \in A\}$$

holds for all $A \in \mathscr{A}_n$, the class of compact, convex, symmetric (about the origin) sets in $\mathfrak{R}^n$.

Note that if inequalities can be obtained for all compact, convex, symmetric sets in $\mathfrak{R}^n$, then they can be obtained for all convex and symmetric sets in $\mathfrak{R}^n$. This is so because a convex and symmetric set can be expressed as the limit of an increasing sequence of compact, convex, and symmetric sets.

The studies of peakedness, for certain specific multivariate distributions and geometric regions, have played an important role in the development of the theory of inequalities in statistics (see, e.g., Tong (1980, Chap. 2–4)). In the following we describe peakedness-related inequalities which directly concern the multivariate normal distribution.

One class of inequalities can be obtained via an application of Anderson's theorem (Anderson 1955, see Proposition 4.2.3). When applying to the multivariate normal distribution, an immediate consequence is

Fact 7.5.1. *Let $\boldsymbol{\mu}_0 \neq \mathbf{0}$ be an arbitrary but fixed real vector in $\mathfrak{R}^n$. If $\mathbf{X}$ has an $\mathcal{N}_n(\boldsymbol{\mu}, \boldsymbol{\Sigma})$ distribution, then $P_{\boldsymbol{\mu}=c\boldsymbol{\mu}_0}[\mathbf{X} \in A]$ is a nonincreasing function of $|c| \in [0, \infty)$ for all $A \in \mathscr{A}_n$.*

This result shows how the probability content depends on the mean vector $\boldsymbol{\mu}$ when it moves away from the origin along a given direction. The next result, due to Anderson (1955), shows how it depends on the covariance matrix. The result was already stated and proved in Theorem 4.2.5, it is restated here for the purpose of completeness.

Fact 7.5.2. *Let $\boldsymbol{\Sigma}_1, \boldsymbol{\Sigma}_2$ be two covariance matrices, and let $\mathbf{X}$ have an $\mathcal{N}_n(\mathbf{0}, \boldsymbol{\Sigma})$ distribution. If $\boldsymbol{\Sigma}_2 - \boldsymbol{\Sigma}_1$ is either positive definite or positive semidefinite, then $P_{\boldsymbol{\Sigma}=\boldsymbol{\Sigma}_1}[\mathbf{X} \in A] \geq P_{\boldsymbol{\Sigma}=\boldsymbol{\Sigma}_2}[\mathbf{X} \in A]$ holds for all $A \in \mathscr{A}_n$.*

Another class of inequalities depends on linear combinations of random variables via majorization. To motivate this approach, consider independent univariate normal variables $X_1, \ldots, X_n$ with means μ and variances σ^2. Let $\mathbf{a} = (a_1, \ldots, a_n)'$ and $\mathbf{b} = (b_1, \ldots, b_n)'$ denote two real vectors, and define

$$U = \sum_{i=1}^{n} a_i X_i, \qquad V = \sum_{i=1}^{n} b_i X_i.$$

Then U, V are normal variables with means $\mu \sum_{i=1}^n a_i$, $\mu \sum_{i=1}^n b_i$ and variances $\sigma^2 \sum_{i=1}^n a_i^2$, $\sigma^2 \sum_{i=1}^n b_i^2$, respectively. If $\mathbf{a} \succ \mathbf{b}$, then the means of U, V are the same ($= \nu$, say) and, by $\sum_{i=1}^n a_i^2 \geq \sum_{i=1}^n b_i^2$, $\mathrm{Var}(U) \geq \mathrm{Var}(V)$ holds. Thus according to Definition 7.5.1, $V - \nu$ is more peaked than $U - \nu$. When choosing $\mathbf{a} = (1/(n-1), \ldots, 1/(n-1), 0)'$ and $\mathbf{b} = (1/n, \ldots, 1/n)'$ and defining $\bar{X}_n = (1/n)\sum_{i=1}^n X_i$ $(n = 1, 2, \ldots)$, an immediate consequence is that $P[|\bar{X}_n - \mu| \leq \lambda]$ converges to one *monotonically* in n for all $\lambda > 0$.

The problem for the univariate normal variables discussed above is easy to solve, because in this case it suffices to just compare the variances of U and V. For the general case such a result is, of course, more difficult to obtain. A theorem of Proschan (1965) provides a solution for all univariate random variables with symmetric and log-concave density functions:

Proposition 7.5.1. *Let $Z_1, \ldots, Z_n$ be i.i.d. random variables with a continuous density function $f(z)$ such that $f(z) = f(-z)$ and that $\log f(z)$ is a concave function of z. Let $\mathbf{a}, \mathbf{b}$ be two n-dimensional real vectors. If $\mathbf{a} \succ \mathbf{b}$, then $\sum_{i=1}^n b_i Z_i$*

is more peaked than $\sum_{i=1}^n a_i Z_i$. *Consequently,* $P[|\bar{Z}_n| \le \lambda]$ *converges to one monotonically in n for all* $\lambda > 0$.

Motivated by this result, Olkin and Tong (1988) obtained two generalizations for the multivariate distributions. The first generalization deals with k-dimensional i.i.d. random variables, and the second one concerns linear combinations of permutation-symmetric (instead of i.i.d.) univariate random variables.

Proposition 7.5.2. *Let* $\mathbf{Z}_1, \ldots, \mathbf{Z}_n$ *be i.i.d. k-dimensional random variables* ($k \ge 1$) *with a continuous density function* $f(\mathbf{z})$ *such that* $f(\mathbf{z}) = f(-\mathbf{z})$ *and that* $\log f(\mathbf{z})$ *is a concave function of* $\mathbf{z}$ *for* $\mathbf{z} \in \Re^n$. *If* $\mathbf{a} \succ \mathbf{b}$, *then* $\sum_{i=1}^n b_i \mathbf{Z}_i$ *is more peaked than* $\sum_{i=1}^n a_i \mathbf{Z}_i$ *(in the sense of Definition* 7.5.2).

Proposition 7.5.3. *Let* $(Z_1, \ldots, Z_n)'$ *have a continuous density function* $f(\mathbf{z})$ *that is permutation-symmetric. If the conditional density of*

$$\left\{c(Z_1 + Z_2) + \sum_{i=3}^{n} a_i Z_i\right\} \Bigg| (Z_1 - Z_2) = v$$

is symmetric about the origin and unimodal for all fixed c, v and $a_3, \ldots, a_n$, *then* $\mathbf{a} \succ \mathbf{b}$ *implies that* $\sum_{i=1}^n b_i Z_i$ *is more peaked than* $\sum_{i=1}^n b_i Z_i$ *(in the sense of Definition* 7.5.1).

The proofs of Propositions 7.5.2 and 7.5.3 depend on an application of Anderson's theorem and is different in spirit from Proschan's proof of Proposition 7.5.1. For details, see Olkin and Tong (1988).

Since a multivariate normal density function is log-concave (Theorem 4.2.1), Proposition 7.5.2 immediately yields

Theorem 7.5.1. *Let* $\mathbf{X}_1, \ldots, \mathbf{X}_n$ *be i.i.d.* $\mathcal{N}_k(\boldsymbol{\mu}, \boldsymbol{\Sigma})$ *variables* ($k \ge 1$) *and let* $\mathbf{a}, \mathbf{b}$ *be two n-dimensional real vectors. If* $\mathbf{a} \succ \mathbf{b}$, *then* $\sum_{i=1}^n b_i(\mathbf{X}_i - \boldsymbol{\mu})$ *is more peaked than* $\sum_{i=1}^n a_i(\mathbf{X}_i - \boldsymbol{\mu})$. *Thus* $P[(\bar{\mathbf{X}}_n - \boldsymbol{\mu}) \in A]$ *converges to one monotonically in n for all symmetric (about the origin) and convex sets* $A \in \Re^k$.

Furthermore, it is easy to verify that if $(X_1, \ldots, X_n)'$ has a permutation-symmetric multivariate normal density function with means 0, then the conditions in Proposition 7.5.3 are satisfied. Thus we also have

Theorem 7.5.2. *Let* $(X_1, \ldots, X_n)'$ *have an* $\mathcal{N}_n(\mathbf{0}, \boldsymbol{\Sigma})$ *distribution with a common variance* σ^2 *and a common correlation coefficient* $\rho \in (-1/(n-1), 1)$. *If* $\mathbf{a} \succ \mathbf{b}$, *then* $\sum_{i=1}^n b_i X_i$ *is more peaked than* $\sum_{i=1}^n a_i X_i$.

Note that Theorem 7.5.2 also follows by a direct comparison of the variances of $\sum_{i=1}^n a_i X_i$ and $\sum_{i=1}^n b_i X_i$. The calculation of the variances is easy and is left to the reader.

7.5.2. Inequalities via the Arrangement-Increasing Property

As discussed in Section 4.5, the notion of arrangement-increasing (AI) functions leads to a variety of inequalities (see Definition 4.5.1 for the definition of AI functions), and many of them directly apply to the multivariate normal distribution.

A recent result of Boland, Proschan, and Tong (1988), which depends on an application of the convolution theorem of Hollander, Proschan, and Sethuraman (1977), states

Proposition 7.5.4. *Let* $\{f_{\boldsymbol{\theta}}(\mathbf{x}): \boldsymbol{\theta} \in \Omega \subset \mathfrak{R}^n\}$ *be a family of multivariate density functions, and assume that* $\mathbf{X}$ *has density* $f_{\boldsymbol{\theta}}(\mathbf{x})$ *which is an AI function of* $(\mathbf{x}, \boldsymbol{\theta})$. *If* $g(\mathbf{a}, \mathbf{x})$ *is an AI function of* $(\mathbf{a}, \mathbf{x})$, *then* $P_{\boldsymbol{\theta},\mathbf{a}}[g(\mathbf{a}, \mathbf{X}) \geq \lambda]$ *is an AI function of* $(\boldsymbol{\theta}, \mathbf{a})$ *for all* λ.

Now consider the family of multivariate normal density functions $\{f_{\boldsymbol{\mu}}(\mathbf{x}): \boldsymbol{\mu} \in \mathfrak{R}^n\}$ with mean vector $\boldsymbol{\mu}$, a common variance σ^2, and a common correlation coefficient $\rho \in (-1/(n-1), 1)$. Since it was already established that $f_{\boldsymbol{\mu}}(\mathbf{x})$ is an AI function of $(\mathbf{x}, \boldsymbol{\mu})$ (Theorem 4.5.1), useful inequalities for the multivariate normal distribution can be obtained by suitably choosing $g(\mathbf{a}, \mathbf{x})$ in Proposition 7.5.4. The fact stated below contains some useful applications.

Fact 7.5.3. *If* $\mathbf{X}$ *has an* $\mathcal{N}_n(\boldsymbol{\mu}, \Sigma)$ *distribution such that* $\sigma_{ii} = \sigma^2$ *and* $\rho_{ij} = \rho \in (-1/(n-1), 1)$ *for all* $i \neq j$, *then the following probabilities are AI functions of* $(\boldsymbol{\mu}, \mathbf{a})$ (Hollander, Proschan, and Sethuraman (1977) and Boland, Proschan, and Tong (1988)):

(i) *univariate probabilites*

$$P_{\boldsymbol{\mu}}\left[\sum_{i=1}^{n} a_i X_i \geq \lambda\right], \qquad P_{\boldsymbol{\mu}}\left[\sum_{i=1}^{n} |X_i - a_i| \leq \lambda\right], \qquad P_{\boldsymbol{\mu}}\left[\sum_{i=1}^{n} (X_i - a_i)^2 \leq \lambda\right],$$

(ii) *multivariate probabilities*

$$P_{\boldsymbol{\mu}}\left[\bigcap_{i=1}^{n} \{X_i \leq a_i\}\right], \qquad P_{\boldsymbol{\mu}}\left[\bigcap_{i=1}^{n} \{X_i \geq a_i\}\right], \qquad P_{\boldsymbol{\mu}}\left[\bigcap_{i=1}^{n} \{|X_i - a_i| \leq \lambda\}\right],$$

where λ *is arbitrary but fixed. Consequently, these probabilities are maximized when*

$$\boldsymbol{\mu} = (\mu_{(1)}, \ldots, \mu_{(n)})', \qquad \mathbf{a} = (a_{(1)}, \ldots, a_{(n)})',$$

and are minimized when

$$\boldsymbol{\mu} = (\mu_{(1)}, \ldots, \mu_{(n)})', \qquad \mathbf{a} = (a_{(n)}, a_{(n-1)}, \ldots, a_{(1)})',$$

where $\mu_{(i)} \leq \mu_{(i+1)}$ *and* $a_{(i)} \leq a_{(i+1)}$ $(i = 1, \ldots, n-1)$ *are the ordered values of the* μ_i*'s and of the* a_i*'s, respectively.*

A different type of inequality, given in Boland, Proschan, and Tong (1988), can be obtained by applying the convolution theorem in Hollander, Proschan, and Sethuraman (1977).

Proposition 7.5.5. *Let* $g_1, g_2 \colon \Re^n \times \Re^n \to \Re$ *be AI functions, and let* $h_1, h_2 \colon \Re \to \Re$ *be nondecreasing. If* $\mathbf{X}$ *has a permutation-symmetric density function, then*

$$\psi(\mathbf{a}, \mathbf{b}) = E[h_1(g_1(\mathbf{a}, \mathbf{X}))h_2(g_2(\mathbf{b}, \mathbf{X}))]$$

is an AI function of $(\mathbf{a}, \mathbf{b})$.

When applying to the multivariate normal distribution we have (Boland, Proschan, and Tong, 1988)

Fact 7.5.4. *If* $\mathbf{X}$ *has an* $\mathcal{N}_n(\boldsymbol{\mu}, \boldsymbol{\Sigma})$ *distribution such that* $\mu_i = \mu$, $\sigma_{ii} = \sigma^2$, *and* $\rho_{ij} = \rho \in (-1/(n-1), 1)$ *for all* $i \neq j$, *then the following probabilities are AI functions of* $(\mathbf{a}, \mathbf{b})$:

(i) $$\psi_1(\mathbf{a}, \mathbf{b}) = P\left[\bigcap_{i=1}^{n} \{a_i \le X_i \le b_i\}\right], \qquad a_i < b_i \ (i = 1, \ldots, n),$$

(ii) $$\psi_2(\mathbf{a}, \mathbf{b}) = P\left[\sum_{i=1}^{n} a_i X_i \ge \lambda_1, \sum_{i=1}^{n} b_i X_i \ge \lambda_2\right],$$

(iii) $$\psi_3(\mathbf{a}, \mathbf{b}) = P\left[\bigcap_{i=1}^{n} \{X_i \ge a_i\} \text{ and } \sum_{i=1}^{n} |X_i - b_i| \le \lambda_0\right],$$

(iv) $$\psi_4(\mathbf{a}, \mathbf{b}) = P\left[\bigcap_{i=1}^{n} \{X_i \ge a_i\} \text{ and } \max_{1 \le i \le n} |X_i - b_i| \le \lambda_0\right],$$

where $\lambda_0, \lambda_1, \lambda_2$ *are arbitrary but fixed. Consequently, these probabilities are maximized when*

$$\mathbf{a} = (a_{(1)}, \ldots, a_{(n)})', \qquad \mathbf{b} = (b_{(1)}, \ldots, b_{(n)})',$$

and are minimized when

$$\mathbf{a} = (a_{(1)}, \ldots, a_{(n)})', \qquad \mathbf{b} = (b_{(n)}, b_{(n-1)}, \ldots, b_{(1)})',$$

where $a_{(i)} \le a_{(i+1)}$ *and* $b_{(i)} \le b_{(i+1)}$ $(i = 1, \ldots, n-1)$ *are the ordered values of the components of* $\mathbf{a}$ *and* $\mathbf{b}$, *respectively.*

The result in Fact 7.5.4(i) was first obtained by Boland (1985) using a different proof. Note that the result in Fact 7.5.4(ii) also follows from Slepian's inequality; the details are left to the reader.

In a recent paper Boland and Proschan (1988) considered the multivariate version of AI functions and obtained some useful results, thus many of the results given above can be extended. The reader is referred to their paper for further discussions.

7.5.3. Laplace–Feller Inequality and Mills' Ratio

Mills' ratio concerns the ratio of the tail probability to the density function of a random variable. When the underlying distribution is normal, some special results follow.

For the univariate case, let Z be an $\mathcal{N}(0, 1)$ variable with distribution function $\Phi(z)$ and density function $\phi(z)$. The problem of interest is to find the function $R(z)$ such that

$$\frac{1-\Phi(z)}{\phi(z)} = R(z), \qquad z > 0, \tag{7.5.1}$$

then find bounds on $R(z)$ that are easy to evaluate numerically. By the identity $\Phi(-z) = 1 - \Phi(z)$ we can write

$$\Phi(-z) = \int_z^\infty \phi(t)\,dt = \int_0^\infty \phi(y+z)\,dy = \phi(z)\int_0^\infty e^{-zy}e^{-y^2/2}\,dy,$$

and

$$R(z) = \int_0^\infty e^{-zy}e^{-y^2/2}\,dy.$$

By the inequalities

$$\sum_{k=0}^{2r+1} \frac{1}{k!}(-c)^k < e^{-c} < \sum_{k=0}^{2r} \frac{1}{k!}(-c)^k, \qquad r = 0, 1, 2, \ldots \tag{7.5.2}$$

for all $c > 0$, we has

$$\sum_{k=0}^{2r+1} \frac{1}{k!}\int_0^\infty (-\tfrac{1}{2}y^2)^k e^{-zy}\,dy < R(z) < \sum_{k=0}^{2r} \frac{1}{k!}\int_0^\infty (-\tfrac{1}{2}y^2)^k e^{-zy}\,dy$$

for all r. Then by

$$\int_0^\infty e^{-zy}\,dy = z^{-1} \quad \text{and} \quad \int_0^\infty y^{2k}e^{-zy}\,dy = (2k!)z^{-(2k+1)} \quad \text{for} \quad k = 1, 2, \ldots,$$

we immediately obtain the following result which is known as the Laplace–Feller inequality (Feller, 1957, p. 179):

Fact 7.5.5. *Let $\Phi(z)$ and $\phi(z)$ be the $\mathcal{N}(0, 1)$ distribution function and density function, respectively. Then for all $z > 0$ we have*

$$\frac{1-\Phi(z)}{\phi(z)} \doteq \frac{1}{z}\left[1 - \frac{1}{z^2} + \frac{1\cdot 3}{z^4} - \frac{1\cdot 3\cdot 5}{z^6} + \cdots + (-1)^m \frac{1\cdot 3\cdot 5\cdots(2m-1)}{z^{2m}}\right]. \tag{7.5.3}$$

Furthermore, the right-hand side of (7.5.3) *provides an upper bound on the ratio when m is even, and a lower bound when m is odd. In particular, we have*

$$(z^{-1} - z^{-3}) < \frac{1 - \Phi(z)}{\phi(z)} < z^{-1} \qquad \text{for all} \quad z > 0. \tag{7.5.4}$$

For the general case in which X has an $\mathcal{N}(\mu, \sigma^2)$ distribution, the density function $f(x)$ of X is $(1/\sigma)\phi(z)$ where $z = (x - \mu)/\sigma$. Furthermore, the tail probability $P[X > x]$ is $1 - \Phi(z)$. Thus the Mills ratio $P[X > x]/f(x)$ is just $\sigma(1 - \Phi(z))/\phi(z)$. Consequently, we observe

Fact 7.5.6. *If X has an $\mathcal{N}(\mu, \sigma^2)$ distribution with density function $f(x)$, then for $z = (x - \mu)/\sigma > 0$ the Mills ratio satisfies*

$$\sigma(z^{-1} - z^{-3}) < \frac{P[X > x]}{f(x)} < \frac{\sigma}{z}. \tag{7.5.5}$$

Savage (1962) used the inequality in (7.5.2) to obtain a Mills ratio and bounds for the multivariate normal distribution. To describe his result let $\mathbf{\Sigma}$ be any positive definite matrix. Let $\mathbf{Z}$ have an $\mathcal{N}_n(\mathbf{0}, \mathbf{\Sigma})$ distribution, and let f be the corresponding density function of $\mathbf{Z}$. Then for every given real vector $\mathbf{z} = (z_1, \ldots, z_n)'$ we can write

$$P\left[\bigcap_{i=1}^{n} \{Z_i > z_i\}\right] = P\left[\bigcap_{i=1}^{n} \{Z_i - z_i > 0\}\right]$$
$$= \int_{\mathfrak{R}_+^n} f(\mathbf{z}) \exp[-\mathbf{z}\mathbf{\Sigma}^{-1}\mathbf{y} - \tfrac{1}{2}\mathbf{y}'\mathbf{\Sigma}^{-1}\mathbf{y}]\, d\mathbf{y},$$

where $\mathfrak{R}_+^n = \{\mathbf{y}: \mathbf{y} \in \mathfrak{R}^n, y_i \geq 0, i = 1, \ldots, n\}$. Consequently, the Mills ratio is

$$R(\mathbf{z}) = \frac{P\left[\bigcap_{i=1}^{n} \{Z_i > z_i\}\right]}{f(\mathbf{z})} = \int_{\mathfrak{R}_+^n} \exp[-\mathbf{z}'\mathbf{\Sigma}^{-1}\mathbf{y} - \tfrac{1}{2}\mathbf{y}'\mathbf{\Sigma}^{-1}\mathbf{y}]\, d\mathbf{y}. \tag{7.5.6}$$

Let us denote

$$\boldsymbol{\lambda}(\mathbf{z}) = (\lambda_1(\mathbf{z}), \ldots, \lambda_n(\mathbf{z}))' = \mathbf{z}'\mathbf{\Sigma}^{-1}. \tag{7.5.7}$$

If $\mathbf{z}$ satisfies $\lambda_i(\mathbf{z}) > 0$ $(i = 1, \ldots, n)$ then, by letting $\frac{1}{2}\mathbf{y}'\mathbf{\Sigma}^{-1}\mathbf{y}$ play the role of c in (7.5.2), we observe (Savage, 1962)

Theorem 7.5.3. *Let $\mathbf{Z}$ have an $\mathcal{N}_n(\mathbf{0}, \mathbf{\Sigma})$ distribution, $\mathbf{\Sigma} > 0$. If $\lambda_i(\mathbf{z}) > 0$ for $i = 1, \ldots, n$, then the Mills ratio given in (7.5.6) satisfies*

$$\sum_{k=0}^{2r+1} \frac{1}{k!} \int_{\mathfrak{R}_+^n} (-\tfrac{1}{2}\mathbf{y}'\mathbf{\Sigma}^{-1}\mathbf{y})^k \exp\left[-\sum_{i=1}^{n} \lambda_i(\mathbf{z}) y_i\right] \prod_{i=1}^{n} dy_i < R(\mathbf{z})$$
$$< \sum_{k=0}^{2r} \frac{1}{k!} \int_{\mathfrak{R}_+^n} (-\tfrac{1}{2}\mathbf{y}'\mathbf{\Sigma}^{-1}\mathbf{y})^k \exp\left[-\sum_{i=1}^{n} \lambda_i(\mathbf{z}) y_i\right] \prod_{i=1}^{n} dy_i \tag{7.5.8}$$

for $r = 0, 1, 2, \ldots$. *By choosing* $r = 0$ *and integrating out both sides we have*

$$\left(\prod_{i=1}^{n} \lambda_i(\mathbf{z})\right)^{-1} \left[1 - \frac{1}{2}\sum_{i=1}^{n}\sum_{j=1}^{n} \frac{\tau_{ij}(1+\delta_{ij})}{\lambda_i(\mathbf{z})\lambda_j(\mathbf{z})}\right] < R(\mathbf{z}) < \left(\prod_{i=1}^{n} \lambda_i(\mathbf{z})\right)^{-1}, \quad (7.5.9)$$

where $\mathbf{\Sigma}^{-1} = (\tau_{ij})$ *and* $\delta_{ij} = 1$ *for* $i = j$ *and* $= 0$ *otherwise.*

To illustrate the application of Theorem 7.5.3, Savage (1962) provided the following example:

EXAMPLE 7.5.1. For $n = 2$, let $(Z_1, Z_2)'$ have an $\mathcal{N}_2(\mathbf{0}, \mathbf{\Sigma})$ distribution with $\sigma_1^2 = \sigma_2^2 = 1$ and $\rho = \frac{1}{2}$. Let $z_1 = z_2 = 3$. Then lower and upper bounds on $P[\bigcap_{i=1}^{2} \{Z_i \geq 3\}]$ can be obtained numerically from (7.5.9), and the numerical values of the bounds are, respectively, 0.000057 and 0.000114. The true value of this probability is 0.000082. □

Other contributions to results on Mills' ratio for the multivariate normal distribution include Ruben (1964), Steck (1979), Iyengar (1986), and others. Ruben's (1964) result deals with an asymptotic expansion of the multivariate normal probability integral, Steck (1979) derived lower bounds on $R(z)$ by expressing it as the expectation of a convex function using Jensen's inequality, and Iyengar (1986) gave simple sufficient conditions for an approximation in Steck (1979) to be a lower bound on $R(z)$.

7.5.4. Some Miscellaneous Results

There exist many other inequalities for the multivariate normal distribution, and some of them were obtained in connection with certain statistical applications. In the following we describe two such results which are useful in the area of ranking and selection problems.

A result of Rinott and Santner (1977) deals with the probability content of normal variables when the covariance matrix has a certain structure. Let $\mathbf{\Sigma}_1 = \mathbf{I}_n$ (the identity matrix) and let $\mathbf{\Sigma}_2 = (\sigma_{ij})$ be such that

$$\sigma_{ij} = \begin{cases} 1 + \alpha^2 & \text{for} \quad i = j, \\ \alpha^2 & \text{for} \quad i \neq j, \end{cases}$$

where $\alpha \in \mathfrak{R}$. Let $\mathbf{X}$ have an $\mathcal{N}_n(\mathbf{0}, \mathbf{\Sigma})$ distribution. They considered the function

$$h_\alpha(a) = P_{\mathbf{\Sigma}=\mathbf{\Sigma}_2}\left[\bigcap_{i=1}^{n} \{X_i \leq a\}\right] - P_{\mathbf{\Sigma}=\mathbf{\Sigma}_1}\left[\bigcap_{i=1}^{n} \{X_i \leq a\}\right], \qquad a \in \mathfrak{R}, \quad (7.5.10)$$

and proved

Theorem 7.5.4. *For every given* $\alpha \in \mathfrak{R}$, $h_\alpha(a)$ *has exactly one sign change; i.e., there exists an* $a_0 \in \mathfrak{R}$ *such that* $h_\alpha(a) \geq 0$ (≤ 0) *for all* $a \leq a_0$ *(for all* $a \geq a_0$*).*

The proof of this theorem depends on the application of a total positivity result in Karlin (1968) and the identity

$$h_\alpha(a) = \int_{-\infty}^{\infty} \Phi^n(a + \alpha y)\phi(y)\,dy - \Phi^n(a). \tag{7.5.11}$$

Note that, by Slepian's inequality, $h_\alpha(a) > 0$ holds for all $a \le 0$, and thus the value of a_0 must be positive. This result yields a solution for comparing the probability of a correct decision to select the best treatment in an analysis of covariance model.

Another result, given by Olkin, Sobel, and Tong (1982), concerns the probability of correctly ranking normal populations. Let $X_1, \ldots, X_n$ be independent univariate normal variables with means $\mu_1, \ldots, \mu_n$ and a common variance σ^2. Assuming that $\mu_1 < \mu_2 < \cdots < \mu_n$, a ranking of the populations (based on the observations) is said to be correct if $X_1 < X_2 < \cdots < X_n$ holds. Thus the probability of correctly ranking the n populations is

$$P_{(\mu_1,\ldots,\mu_n)}[X_1 < X_2 < \cdots < X_n] \equiv h(\mu_1, \ldots, \mu_n),$$

which is a multivariate normal probability. Let $\theta_i = \mu_i - \mu_{i-1}$ $(i = 2, \ldots, n)$ denote the spacings. The question of interest is how the probability function h depends on the θ_i's. Olkin, Sobel, and Tong (1982) showed

Theorem 7.5.5. *For $n = 3$, the function*

$$h(\mu_1, \mu_2, \mu_3) = h(\mu_1, \mu_1 + \theta_1, \mu_1 + \theta_1 + \theta_2)$$

is a Schur-concave function of $(\theta_1, \theta_2)'$ for every given μ_1. Thus it is maximized (for given $\mu_3 - \mu_1$) when $\mu_2 = \frac{1}{2}(\mu_1 + \mu_3)$ holds.

The proof of this result specifically depends on the functional form for the normal density function. For $n > 3$, a corresponding result has not yet been obtained.

Problems

7.1. Show that $I_{(i,j)}$ in (7.2.1) is an interval. [*Hint*: See Problem 3.6.]

7.2. Let $\mathbf{X}$ have an $\mathcal{N}_n(\boldsymbol{\mu}, \boldsymbol{\Sigma})$ distribution with correlation coefficients ρ_{ij}. Let $\rho_* = \min_{i \ne j} \rho_{ij}$ and $\rho^* = \max_{i \ne j} \rho_{ij}$. Show that

$$P_{\boldsymbol{\mu},\boldsymbol{\Sigma}_*}\left[\bigcap_{i=1}^n \{X_i \le a_i\}\right] \le P_{\boldsymbol{\mu},\boldsymbol{\Sigma}}\left[\bigcap_{i=1}^n \{X_i \le a_i\}\right] \le P_{\boldsymbol{\mu},\boldsymbol{\Sigma}^*}\left[\bigcap_{i=1}^n \{X_i \le a_i\}\right],$$

$$P_{\boldsymbol{\mu},\boldsymbol{\Sigma}_*}\left[\bigcap_{i=1}^n \{X_i > a_i\}\right] \le P_{\boldsymbol{\mu},\boldsymbol{\Sigma}}\left[\bigcap_{i=1}^n \{X_i > a_i\}\right] \le P_{\boldsymbol{\mu},\boldsymbol{\Sigma}^*}\left[\bigcap_{i=1}^n \{X_i > a_i\}\right],$$

where $\boldsymbol{\Sigma}_*$ $(\boldsymbol{\Sigma}^*)$ is the covariance matrix obtained by substituting ρ_* (ρ^*) for ρ_{ij} in $\boldsymbol{\Sigma}$.

7.3. Show that in Problem 7.2 if $\rho_* \geq 0$, then

$$P_{\boldsymbol{\mu},\boldsymbol{\Sigma}}\left[\bigcap_{i=1}^{n}\{X_i \leq a_i\}\right] \geq \prod_{i=1}^{n}\Phi\left(\frac{a_i-\mu_i}{\sigma_i}\right),$$

$$P_{\boldsymbol{\mu},\boldsymbol{\Sigma}}\left[\bigcap_{i=1}^{n}\{X_i > a_i\}\right] \geq \prod_{i=1}^{n}\Phi\left(\frac{-a_i+\mu_i}{\sigma_i}\right),$$

where Φ is the $\mathcal{N}(0, 1)$ distribution function.

7.4. Show that in Problem 7.2 if $\rho^* \leq 0$, then

$$P_{\boldsymbol{\mu},\boldsymbol{\Sigma}}\left[\bigcap_{i=1}^{n}\{X_i \leq a_i\}\right] \leq \prod_{i=1}^{n}\Phi\left(\frac{a_i-\mu_i}{\sigma_i}\right),$$

$$P_{\boldsymbol{\mu},\boldsymbol{\Sigma}}\left[\bigcap_{i=1}^{n}\{X_i > a_i\}\right] \leq \prod_{i=1}^{n}\Phi\left(\frac{-a_i+\mu_i}{\sigma_i}\right),$$

7.5. Show that in Problem 7.4 if in addition $\sigma_i = \sigma$ $(i = 1, \ldots, n)$, then

$$P_{\boldsymbol{\mu},\boldsymbol{\Sigma}}\left[\bigcap_{i=1}^{n}\{X_i \leq a_i\}\right] \leq \left[\Phi\left(\frac{\bar{a}-\bar{\mu}}{\sigma}\right)\right]^n,$$

$$P_{\boldsymbol{\mu},\boldsymbol{\Sigma}}\left[\bigcap_{i=1}^{n}\{X_i > a_i\}\right] \leq \left[\Phi\left(\frac{-\bar{a}+\bar{\mu}}{\sigma}\right)\right]^n,$$

where $\bar{\mu} = (1/n)\sum_{i=1}^{n}\mu_i$ and $\bar{a} = (1/n)\sum_{i=1}^{n}a_i$.

7.6. Show that in Problem 7.4 if in addition the σ_i's are not necessarily equal but are bounded below by σ_*, and if $a_i - \mu_i \geq 0$ for all i, then

$$P_{\boldsymbol{\mu},\boldsymbol{\Sigma}}\left[\bigcap_{i=1}^{n}\{X_i \leq a_i\}\right] \leq \left[\Phi\left(\frac{\bar{a}-\bar{\mu}}{\sigma_*}\right)\right]^n.$$

7.7. Verify (7.2.7).

7.8. Complete the proof of Theorem 7.3.1 for $j = 2$.

7.9. Show that Theorem 7.3.3 implies Theorem 7.3.2 by identifying the vectors $\mathbf{k}$ and $\mathbf{k}^*$ needed to yield (7.3.8).

7.10. Show that Corollary 7.3.1 is a generalization of Theorem 7.3.3.

7.11. Show that if $X_1, \ldots, X_n$ are exchangeable normal variables and if n is an even integer, then $E\prod_{i=1}^{n} g(X_i) \geq \prod_{i=1}^{n} Eg(X_i)$ holds for all g such that the expectations exist. (*Hint*: see Theorem 5.3.10.)

7.12. Use the result in Problem 7.11 to prove Corollary 7.3.2 for the special case $\rho_1 = 0$.

7.13. Prove Corollary 7.3.2 for the general case when ρ_1 is not necessarily zero.

7.14. Use the result in Fact 7.4.1 to prove Corollary 7.4.1.

7.15. Let Vol(A) denote the volume of a region $A \subset \Re^n$. Show that for $A_\infty(\mathbf{a})$ defined in (7.4.4), $\mathbf{a} \succ \mathbf{b}$ implies Vol$(A_\infty(\mathbf{a})) \leq$ Vol$(A_\infty(\mathbf{b}))$.

7.16. (Continuation.) Show that for $A_2(\mathbf{a})$ defined in (7.4.6)

$$\mathbf{a}^2 = (a_1^2, \ldots, a_n^2)' \succ \mathbf{b}^2 = (b_1^2, \ldots, b_n^2)'$$

implies $\text{Vol}(A_2(\mathbf{a})) \leq \text{Vol}(A_2(\mathbf{b}))$.

7.17. Let $\chi_1^2, \ldots, \chi_n^2$ be independent chi-squared variables with one degree of freedom. Show that $P[\sum_{i=1}^n c_i\chi_i^2 \leq \lambda]$ is a Schur-concave function of $(c_1^{-1}, \ldots, c_n^{-1})'$ for all $c_i > 0$ $(i = 1, \ldots, n)$ and all λ.

7.18. (Continuation.) Show that $P[\sum_{i=1}^n c_i\chi_i^2 \leq \lambda]$ is a Schur-concave function of $(\log c_1, \ldots, \log c_n)'$ for all λ.

7.19. (Continuation.) Obtain a corresponding result when $\chi_1^2, \ldots, \chi_n^2$ are independent chi-squared variables with degrees of freedom $\nu_1, \ldots, \nu_n$, respectively, then show that

$$P\left[\sum_{i=1}^n c_i\chi_i^2 \leq \lambda\right] \leq P\left[\chi^2(N) \leq \lambda\left(\prod_{i=1}^n c_i^{-\nu_i}\right)^{1/N}\right],$$

where $\chi^2(N)$ is the chi-squared variable with N degrees of freedom and $N = \sum_{i=1}^n \nu_i$.

7.20. Let χ_1^2, χ_2^2 be two independent chi-squared variables with two degrees of freedom each. Show that $P[c_1\chi_1^2 + c_2\chi_2^2 \leq \lambda]$ is a Schur-convex function of $(c_1, c_2)'$ for $\lambda \leq 2(c_1 + c_2)$ and is also a Schur-concave function of $(c_1, c_2)'$ for $\lambda \geq 3(c_1 + c_2)$ (Diaconis, 1976, see Marshall and Olkin, 1979, p. 377).

7.21. Show that if $\mathbf{X}$ has a continuous density function then, for $A_m(\mathbf{a})$ and $A_\infty(\mathbf{a})$ defined in (7.4.10) and (7.4.4), respectively,

$$\lim_{m\to\infty} P[\mathbf{X} \in A_m(\mathbf{a})] = P[\mathbf{X} \in A_\infty(\mathbf{a})]$$

holds for all $\mathbf{a}$ such that $a_i > 0$ $(i = 1, \ldots, n)$.

7.22. Let A, A^* be two two-dimensional rectangles given by

$$A = \{(x_1, x_2)': a_{11} \leq x_1 \leq a_{21}, a_{12} \leq x_2 \leq a_{22}\},$$
$$A^* = \{((x_1, x_2)': a_{12} \leq x_1 \leq a_{22}, a_{11} \leq x_2 \leq a_{21}\}.$$

Show that $\alpha A + (1 - \alpha)A^*$ is a two-dimensional rectangle for all $0 \leq \alpha \leq 1$.

7.23. (Continuation.) Show that if $\mathbf{X}$ has a permutation-symmetric bivariate normal distribution, then $P[\mathbf{X} \in (\alpha A + (1 - \alpha)A^*)]$ is an increasing function of $\alpha \in (0, 0.5)$.

7.24. Show that Theorem 7.4.5 implies Theorem 7.4.1 by establishing the following fact: Let $\mathbf{a}, \mathbf{b}$ two n-dimensional real vector with positive components, then $\mathbf{a} \succ \mathbf{b}$ if and only if $\begin{pmatrix} \mathbf{a}' \\ -\mathbf{a}' \end{pmatrix} \overset{m}{\succ} \begin{pmatrix} \mathbf{b}' \\ -\mathbf{b}' \end{pmatrix}$.

7.25. Assume that $\mathbf{X}$ is an n-dimensional permutation-symmetric multivariate normal variable. Let

$$\mathbf{a}_1 = (c_1 + \varepsilon, c_1 - \varepsilon, a_{13}, \ldots, a_{1n})', \qquad \mathbf{a}_2 = (c_2 + \varepsilon, c_2 - \varepsilon, a_{23}, \ldots, a_{2n})',$$
$$\mathbf{b}_1 = (c_1, c_1, a_{13}, \ldots, a_{1n})'$$

and $\mathbf{b}_2 = \mathbf{a}_2$. Let

$$\mathbf{A} = \begin{pmatrix} \mathbf{a}'_1 \\ \mathbf{a}'_2 \end{pmatrix}, \qquad \mathbf{B} = \begin{pmatrix} \mathbf{b}'_1 \\ \mathbf{b}'_2 \end{pmatrix}.$$

Show that for $\varepsilon = c_2 - c_1 > 0$ and $a_{2i} > a_{1i}$ $(i = 3, \ldots, n)$ we have $\mathbf{A} \overset{r}{\succ} \mathbf{B}$ and $P[\mathbf{X} \in S(\mathbf{A})] > P[\mathbf{X} \in S(\mathbf{B})]$, where $S(\mathbf{A})$ is defined in (7.4.13) (Tong, 1983, 1989).

7.26. Let $f(x_1, x_2)$ be the density function of a bivariate normal variable with means 0. Show that f is monotone unimodal according to Definition 7.4.2.

7.27. Let X and Y be two univariate normal variables with means 0 and variances σ_1^2, σ_2^2, respectively. Show that X is more peaked than Y if and only if $\sigma_1^2 \leq \sigma_2^2$.

7.28. (Continuation.) Show that $Eg(|X|) \leq Eg(|Y|)$ holds for all nondecreasing functions g (such that the expectations exist) if and only if $EX^2 \leq EY^2$.

7.29. Show that if $(X_1, \ldots, X_n)'$ has a permutation-symmetric $\mathcal{N}_n(\mathbf{0}, \boldsymbol{\Sigma})$ distribution, then the conditions in Proposition 7.5.3 are satisfied.

7.30. Use Proposition 7.5.4 to prove Fact 7.5.3 by showing that all the functions $g(\mathbf{a}, \mathbf{x})$ involved are AI functions.

7.31. Use Proposition 7.5.5 to prove Fact 7.5.4 by showing that the following functions are AI:

(i) $g_1(\mathbf{u}, \mathbf{v}) = I_{\{u_i \leq v_i, i=1,\ldots,n\}}$ where I is the indicator function;
(ii) $g_2(\mathbf{u}, \mathbf{v}) = \sum_{i=1}^n u_i v_i$;
(iii) $g_3(\mathbf{u}, \mathbf{v}) = -\max_{1 \leq i \leq n} |u_i - v_i|$; and
(iv) $g_4(\mathbf{u}, \mathbf{v}) = -\sum_{i=1}^n |u_i - v_i|$.

7.32. Verify Fact 7.5.4(ii) directly by using Slepian's inequality and the result in Problem 7.31 (ii).

7.33. Verify the bounds in (7.5.9).

7.34. Verify the identity in (7.5.11).

7.35. Show that the value of a_0 in Theorem 7.5.4 is positive.

CHAPTER 8

Statistical Computing Related to the Multivariate Normal Distribution

In this chapter we discuss some useful methods concerning statistical computing related to the multivariate normal distribution. Section 8.1 deals with methods for generating random variates from a multivariate normal distribution in simulation studies. The methods involve linear transformations of i.i.d. univariate normal variables, and the linear transformation used in a given application depends on the covariance matrix of the distribution. In Sections 8.2 and 8.3 we discuss numerical methods for evaluating probability integrals under a multivariate normal density function. Special attention will be focused on the computation of the distribution functions of normal variables and of their absolute values (called one-sided and two-sided probability integrals). Equi-coordinate percentage points and probability integrals for exchangeable normal variables and for their absolute values have been tabulated numerically, and the tables are given in the Appendix of this volume. The accuracy and uses of the tables are discussed in Section 8.4.

8.1. Generation of Multivariate Normal Variates

Simulation studies constitute an integral part of statistical computing, and may be applied to yield empirical results when analytical results are difficult to obtain. There exist several books in this area, one of the classical references is Hammersley and Handscomb (1964).

In most simulation studies we begin with the generation of "random numbers." A sequence of (pseudo) independent uniform [0, 1] variables U_1, $U_2, \ldots$ is usually called a sequence of random numbers. The generation of such a sequence on a computer involves an algorithm for generating a sequence of real numbers *deterministically*, given the seed number, and the development of the algorithm involves number theory and the capacity of the computer. Since this is a well-researched area, we will assume that there already exists a built-in random number generator on the computer that can generate enough random numbers $U_1, U_2, \ldots$ needed in a study.

8.1.1. Generation of i.i.d. $\mathcal{N}(\mu, \sigma^2)$ Variates

There are several useful methods for generating a sequence of (pseudo) independent univariate normal variates, see, e.g., Kennedy and Gentle (1980, Sec. 6.5.1), Johnson (1987, Sec. 2.2), and other related references.

One of the methods is due to Box and Muller (1958). It follows from Theorem 2.1.3 that if N is an even integer and if $U_1, \ldots, U_N$ are independent uniform [0, 1] variables, then for $k = 1, \ldots, N/2$

$$Z_{2k-1} = \sqrt{-2 \ln U_{2k-1}}\, \sin(2\pi U_{2k}), \qquad Z_{2k} = \sqrt{-2 \ln U_{2k-1}}\, \cos(2\pi U_{2k}) \tag{8.1.1}$$

are i.i.d. $\mathcal{N}(0, 1)$ variables. Consequently, to generate (an even or odd number of) N independent $\mathcal{N}(\mu, \sigma^2)$ variables the following algorithm may be used:

Algorithm 8.1.1.

(a) Input μ, σ^2, and $M = [(N + 1)/2]$ where $[x]$ is the largest integer $\leq x$.
(b) For $k = 1, \ldots, M$, obtain random numbers U_{2k-1} and U_{2k}, and then compute

$$X_{2k-1} = \mu + \sigma\sqrt{-2 \ln U_{2k-1}}\, \sin(2\pi U_{2k}), \tag{8.1.2}$$

$$X_{2k} = \mu + \sigma\sqrt{-2 \ln U_{2k-1}}\, \cos(2\pi U_{2k}). \tag{8.1.3}$$

This algorithm transforms $2M$ random numbers into $2M$ $\mathcal{N}(\mu, \sigma^2)$ variates. If an odd number of normal variates are needed (i.e., if $N = 2M - 1$), then X_{2M} should be discarded.

Algorithm 8.1.1 requires the evaluations of both the logarithmic and trigonometric functions. An alternative method, due to Marsaglia and Bray (1964), needs only the logarithmic function but, on average, requires more random numbers. The method depends on the following fact which can be justified by applying Theorem 4.1.1.

Fact 8.1.1. *Let U_1, U_2 be independent uniform* [0, 1] *variables and let $V = \sum_{i=1}^{2} (2U_i - 1)^2$. Denote*

$$Z_i = \sqrt{(-2 \ln V)/V}\,(2U_i - 1), \qquad i = 1, 2.$$

Then the conditional distribution of $(Z_1, Z_2)'$, given $V \leq 1$, is $\mathcal{N}_2(0, \mathbf{I}_2)$.

Using this result, an algorithm for generating i.i.d. $\mathcal{N}(\mu, \sigma^2)$ variates can be obtained easily, the details are left to the reader. When this method is used, the expected number of random numbers needed to generate $2M$ normal variates is $2M\{P[\sum_{i=1}^{2}(2U_i - 1)^2 \le 1]\}^{-1}$, which is $8M/\pi$.

Other normal generators include those proposed by Marsaglia (1964) (for truncated normal variates), Marsaglia, MacLaren, and Bray (1964), Kinderman and Ramage (1976), Marsaglia and Tsang (1984), and others.

We note in passing that tables of simulated values of $\mathcal{N}(0, 1)$ variates are also available. For example, the extensive tables published by the RAND Corporation (1955) include one hundred thousand such values. To obtain $\mathcal{N}(\mu, \sigma^2)$ variates we simply multiply the table values by σ then add a constant μ. The same source also contains one million random digits which can be used for producing random numbers.

8.1.2. Generation of Exchangeable Normal Variates

Consider the situation in which we are interested in generating N (pseudo) independent n-dimensional normal variates $\mathbf{X}_1, \ldots, \mathbf{X}_N$, such that $\mathbf{X}_t = (X_{1t}, \ldots, X_{nt})'$ $(t = 1, \ldots, N)$ has an $\mathcal{N}_n(\boldsymbol{\mu}, \boldsymbol{\Sigma})$ distribution with a common mean μ, a common variance σ^2, and a common correlation coefficient $\rho \in [0, 1)$. One such method is to generate $N(n + 1)$ i.i.d. $\mathcal{N}(0, 1)$ variates first, using one of the methods described above, and then applying the linear transformation given in (5.3.9). For notational convenience, let us use double subscriptions and let us denote by $\{Z_{0t}, Z_{1t}, \ldots, Z_{nt}\}_{t=1}^{N}$ the $N(n + 1)$ $\mathcal{N}(0, 1)$ variates generated. Then a corresponding algorithm for generating $\mathbf{X}_1, \ldots, \mathbf{X}_N$ is

Algorithm 8.1.2.

(a) Input μ, σ^2, ρ, n, and N.
(b) For $t = 1, \ldots, N$ compute

$$X_{it} = \mu + \sigma(\sqrt{1 - \rho}Z_{it} + \sqrt{\rho}Z_{0t}), \qquad i = 1, \ldots, n, \tag{8.1.4}$$

and form $\mathbf{X}_t = (X_{1t}, \ldots, X_{nt})'$.

This algorithm requires $n + 1$ $\mathcal{N}(0, 1)$ variates to produce an n-dimensional multivariate normal variate, and one of them is "wasted" in the process. However, the transformation is easy to perform and the calculation is relatively simple, thus it is quite efficient when the ratio N/n is not too large.

8.1.3. Generation of Multivariate Normal Variates with a Special Correlation Structure

In certain statistical applications the covariance matrix $\boldsymbol{\Sigma} = (\sigma_{ij})$ may be of the form

$$\sigma_{ij} = \begin{cases} \sigma_i^2 & \text{for} \quad i = j, \\ \sigma_i\sigma_j\lambda_i\lambda_j & \text{for} \quad i \ne j, \end{cases} \tag{8.1.5}$$

where $\lambda_i \in [-1, 1]$ $(i = 1, \ldots, n)$. In this case, the correlation coefficients are

$\rho_{ij} = \lambda_i \lambda_j$ for all $i \neq j$. To generate $\mathbf{X}_1, \ldots, \mathbf{X}_N$ according to an $\mathcal{N}_n(\boldsymbol{\mu}, \boldsymbol{\Sigma})$, when $\boldsymbol{\Sigma}$ has such a structure and $\boldsymbol{\mu} = (\mu_1, \ldots, \mu_n)'$, we modify Algorithm 8.1.2 to read

Algorithm 8.1.3. Same as in Algorithm 8.1.2 except that (8.1.4) is replaced by

$$X_{it} = \mu_i + \sigma_i(\sqrt{1 - \lambda_i^2} Z_{it} + \lambda_i Z_{0t}). \tag{8.1.6}$$

Note that here the μ_i's are not necessarily the same and the correlation coefficients are not necessarily all nonnegative. If $\mu_i = \mu$, $\sigma_i = \sigma$, and $\lambda_i = \sqrt{\rho} \geq 0$ $(i = 1, \ldots, n)$, then Algorithm 8.1.3 reduces to Algorithm 8.1.2 as a special case.

8.1.4. Generation of Random Variates with an Arbitrary Nonsingular Multivariate Normal Distribution

Next we consider the most general case: Suppose that in a study we are interested in generating $\mathbf{X}_1, \ldots, \mathbf{X}_N$ from an $\mathcal{N}_n(\boldsymbol{\mu}, \boldsymbol{\Sigma})$ distribution with arbitrary but fixed $\boldsymbol{\mu}$ and $\boldsymbol{\Sigma}$ (which is positive definite). The method described below depends on the following result: For every $n \times n$ positive definite matrix $\boldsymbol{\Sigma} = (\sigma_{ij})$ there exists an $n \times n$ matrix $\mathbf{T} = (\tau_{ij})$ such that $\mathbf{T}\mathbf{T}' = \boldsymbol{\Sigma}$ (Proposition 3.2.1). In general, the matrix $\mathbf{T}$ is not unique. However, if we restrict our attention to the subclass of all lower triangular matrices, then it is unique and can be obained easily.

Proposition 8.1.1. *If* $\boldsymbol{\Sigma} = (\sigma_{ij})$ *is an* $n \times n$ *positive definite matrix, then there exists a unique lower triangular matrix* $\mathbf{T} = (\tau_{ij})$ *satisfying* $\mathbf{T}\mathbf{T}' = \boldsymbol{\Sigma}$. *Furthermore, the elements of* $\mathbf{T}$ *are given by*

$$\tau_{ij} = 0 \qquad \textit{for all} \quad 1 \leq i < j \leq n,$$

$$\tau_{11} = \sqrt{\sigma_{11}},$$

$$\tau_{i1} = \frac{\sigma_{i1}}{\sqrt{\sigma_{11}}} \qquad \textit{for} \quad i = 2, \ldots, n$$

$$\tau_{jj} = \left(\sigma_{jj} - \sum_{r=1}^{j-1} \tau_{jr}^2\right)^{1/2} \qquad \textit{for} \quad j = 2, \ldots, n,$$

$$\tau_{ij} = \frac{1}{\tau_{jj}}\left(\sigma_{ij} - \sum_{r=1}^{j-1} \tau_{ir}\tau_{jr}\right) \qquad \textit{for} \quad j < i \textit{ and } i = 2, \ldots, n-1.$$

Proof (See, e.g., Graybill (1976, p. 232)). By $\tau_{ij} = 0$ for $i < j$, simple calculation yields (from $\mathbf{T}\mathbf{T}' = \boldsymbol{\Sigma}$)

$$\tau_{11}^2 = \sigma_{11}, \qquad \tau_{i1}\tau_{11} = \sigma_{i1} \qquad (i = 2, \ldots, n), \tag{8.1.7}$$

$$\sum_{r=1}^{2} \tau_{2r}^2 = \sigma_{22}, \qquad \sum_{r=1}^{2} \tau_{ir}\tau_{2r} = \sigma_{i2} \qquad (i = 3, \ldots, n), \tag{8.1.8}$$

$$\sum_{r=1}^{j} \tau_{jr}^2 = \sigma_{jj}, \qquad \sum_{r=1}^{j} \tau_{ir}\tau_{jr} = \sigma_{ij} \qquad (3 \leq j < i \leq n). \tag{8.1.9}$$

The statement follows by first solving τ_{11} and τ_{i1} in (8.1.7), then solving τ_{22}, τ_{i2} in (8.1.8) in terms of τ_{11} and τ_{i1}, and then, for $j = 3, \ldots, n-1$, solving τ_{jj} and τ_{ij} in (8.1.9) in terms of $\tau_{ij'}$, for $1 \leq j' < j$ and $i = 1, \ldots, n$. □

The result in Proposition 8.1.1 is known as the Cholesky decomposition. If $\mathbf{Z} \sim \mathcal{N}_n(\mathbf{0}, \mathbf{I}_n)$ and $\mathbf{T}$ is the matrix obtained by applying Proposition 8.1.1, then $\mathbf{X} = \mathbf{TZ} + \boldsymbol{\mu}$ has an $\mathcal{N}_n(\boldsymbol{\mu}, \boldsymbol{\Sigma})$ distribution. Consequently, to generate independent random variates $\mathbf{X}_1, \ldots, \mathbf{X}_N$ according to this distribution, the following algorithm may be used.

Algorithm 8.1.4.

(a) Compute $\mathbf{T} = (\tau_{ij})$.
(b) Input $N, n, \boldsymbol{\mu} = (\mu_1, \ldots, \mu_n)'$, and $\mathbf{T} = (\tau_{ij})$.
(c) Generate $Z_{1t}, \ldots, Z_{nt}$ (which are (pseudo) independent $\mathcal{N}(0, 1)$ variates) and apply the transformation $\mathbf{X}_t = \mathbf{TZ}_t + \boldsymbol{\mu}$, i.e., compute

$$X_{it} = \sum_{j=1}^{i} \tau_{ij} Z_j + \mu_i \qquad \text{for} \quad i = 1, \ldots, n, \tag{8.1.10}$$

and then form $\mathbf{X}_t = (X_{1t}, \ldots, X_{nt})'$.
(d) Repeat Step (c) for $t = 1, \ldots, N$.

In Algorithm 8.1.4 it requires only n univariate normal variates to produce an n-dimensional multivariate normal variate, but the computation involved in (8.1.10) is more complicated than that in (8.1.4) or (8.1.6).

8.1.5. An Example

Suppose that we are interested in generating N multivariate normal variates which are distributed according to an $\mathcal{N}_3(\boldsymbol{\mu}, \boldsymbol{\Sigma})$ distribution where

$$\mu_1 = 0, \qquad \mu_2 = \mu_3 = 1,$$

$$\rho_{12} = \tfrac{1}{4}, \qquad \rho_{13} = \rho_{23} = -\tfrac{1}{8},$$

$$\sigma_1^2 = 1, \qquad \sigma_2^2 = \sigma_3^2 = 4.$$

(a) Clearly the covariance matrix is of the form (8.1.5) with $\lambda_1 = \lambda_2 = \frac{1}{2}$ and $\lambda_3 = -\frac{1}{4}$. By Algorithm 8.1.3 we may generate $\mathbf{Z}_t = (Z_{0t}, Z_{1t}, Z_{2t}, Z_{3t})'$ and then obtain $\mathbf{X}_t = (X_{1t}, X_{2t}, X_{3t})'$, where

$$X_{1t} = 0 + 1\left(\frac{\sqrt{3}}{2} Z_{1t} + \tfrac{1}{2} Z_{0t}\right),$$

$$X_{2t} = 1 + 2\left(\frac{\sqrt{3}}{2} Z_{2t} + \tfrac{1}{2} Z_{0t}\right),$$

$$X_{3t} = 1 + 2\left(\frac{\sqrt{15}}{4} Z_{3t} - \tfrac{1}{4} Z_{0t}\right),$$

for $t = 1, \ldots, N$. In this case it takes four $\mathcal{N}(0, 1)$ deviates to produce one $\mathbf{X}_t$.

(b) If Algorithm 8.1.4 is to be used, then simple calculation shows

$$\mathbf{T} = \begin{pmatrix} 1 & 0 & 0 \\ \frac{1}{2} & \frac{\sqrt{15}}{2} & 0 \\ -\frac{1}{4} & -\frac{3}{4\sqrt{15}} & \frac{\sqrt{78}}{2\sqrt{5}} \end{pmatrix}.$$

Thus, for $t = 1, \ldots, N$ we obtain

$$X_{1t} = 0 + 1 \cdot Z_{1t},$$

$$X_{2t} = 1 + \left(\tfrac{1}{2}Z_{1t} + \frac{\sqrt{15}}{2}Z_{2t}\right),$$

and

$$X_{3t} = 1 + \left(-\tfrac{1}{4}Z_{1t} - \frac{3}{4\sqrt{15}}Z_{2t} + \frac{\sqrt{78}}{2\sqrt{5}}Z_{3t}\right).$$

8.1.6. Other Related Results

In addition to the transformation methods described above, other methods have been proposed in the literature. (For example, Deak (1979, 1980) considered an ellipsoid method for generating multivariate normal variables and then discussed the efficiencies of those methods.) The generation of multivariate normal variates also leads to the solutions of other related problems in multivariate analysis. One such problem concerns the value of a multivariate normal probability integral over a given geometric region. The numerical evaluation of the true value of an integral is not always feasible, especially when the region is of an irregular shape. In this case, a Monte Carlo study (which involves the generation of multivariate normal variates) becomes useful, and the basic idea of this method will be described in the next section.

In some other applications, the generation of multivariate normal variates constitutes a first step toward more complicated simulation studies. For example, in generating correlation matrices with a given mean matrix or with given eigenvalues (Marsaglia and Olkin, 1984), we need to first generate multivariate normal variates and then use a specified transformation. Similarly, for generating random orthogonal matrices, we also need to generate multivariate normal variates first (see Anderson, Olkin, and Underhill (1987)). For sources of other related applications, see the references in Johnson (1987).

8.2. Evaluation and Approximations of Multivariate Normal Probability Integrals

Let $\mathbf{X}$ have an $\mathcal{N}_n(\boldsymbol{\mu}, \boldsymbol{\Sigma})$ distribution, $\boldsymbol{\Sigma} > 0$, and let $f(\mathbf{x}; \boldsymbol{\mu}, \boldsymbol{\Sigma})$ be the density function of $\mathbf{X}$ defined in (3.2.1). Let $A \subset \Re^n$ be a given Borel-measurable set. The problem of concern is to find methods for evaluating or approximating the probability integral

$$I(\boldsymbol{\mu}, \boldsymbol{\Sigma}, A) = P[\mathbf{X} \in A] = \int_A f(\mathbf{x}; \boldsymbol{\mu}, \boldsymbol{\Sigma})\, d\mathbf{x}. \tag{8.2.1}$$

From an applied viewpoint this is an important problem, because the numerical value of $I(\boldsymbol{\mu}, \boldsymbol{\Sigma}, A)$ is often needed in parameter estimation, hypothesis-testing, classification and discriminant analysis, and other related problems in multivariate analysis.

In this section we review some of the methods that exist in the literature, with emphasis on the special case in which A is a (one-sided or two-sided) n-dimensional rectangle.

8.2.1. An Application of Monte Carlo Methods

It is well known that Monte Carlo methods may be used to approximate the numerical value of an integral when analytical results are not available. To describe a method that applies to the multivariate normal distribution, we first assume that a computer subroutine for generating n-dimensional random variates $\mathbf{X}_1, \mathbf{X}_2, \ldots$, with an $\mathcal{N}_n(\boldsymbol{\mu}, \boldsymbol{\Sigma})$ distribution, is already available (see, e.g., Algorithms 8.1.2–8.1.4), and then consider a simple algorithm.

Algorithm 8.2.1.

(a) Input n, $\boldsymbol{\mu}$, $\boldsymbol{\Sigma}$, and N (the number of replications).
(b) Set $c_0 = 0$.
(c) Repeat the following process for $t = 1$ to N: Generate $\mathbf{X}_t$ and observe c_t where

$$c_t = \begin{cases} c_{t-1} & \text{if } \mathbf{X}_t \notin A, \\ c_{t-1} + 1 & \text{if } \mathbf{X}_t \in A. \end{cases}$$

(d) Compute $\hat{I} = c_N/N$, the estimated value of $I(\boldsymbol{\mu}, \boldsymbol{\Sigma}, A)$.

The value of $\hat{I}$ is, of course, (pseudo) random. To determine N for a preassigned accuracy such that

$$P[|\hat{I} - I(\boldsymbol{\mu}, \boldsymbol{\Sigma}, A)| \leq \varepsilon] \geq 1 - \alpha \tag{8.2.2}$$

holds for given $\varepsilon > 0$ and $\alpha > 0$, we may use the binominal approximation to the $\mathcal{N}(0, 1)$ distribution. Since this is a well-known fact the details are omitted.

The algorithm described above is just for the crude Monte Carlo method. It is given here to illustrate the idea of using Monte Carlo methods in statistical computing. It is not recommended for use in practice, because there already exist more efficient procedures with the application of error-reduction principles (see, e.g., Hammersley and Handscomb (1964, Chap. 5)). The evaluation of multivariate normal probability integrals via Monte Carlo methods have been studied by Abbe (1964), Dunn, Kronmal, and Yee (1968), Deak (1978),

Moran (1984), and others. In particular, Dunn, Kronmal, and Yee (1968) provided extensive tables for the multivariate t distribution, thus multivariate normal probability integrals can be obtained from their tables by letting the number of degrees of freedom be infinity.

8.2.2. Infinite-Series Approach for Approximating Orthant Probabilities

The problem of approximating orthant probabilities for a multivariate normal distribution has a rich history, and constitutes an integral part of statistical computing in multivariate analysis. The general problem concerns numerical methods for approximating

$$P_{\boldsymbol{\mu},\boldsymbol{\Sigma}}\left[\bigcap_{i=1}^{n}\{X_i \le a_i\}\right] \quad \text{or} \quad P_{\boldsymbol{\mu},\boldsymbol{\Sigma}}\left[\bigcap_{i=1}^{n}\{X_i \ge b_i\}\right], \tag{8.2.3}$$

where $a_1, \ldots, a_n, b_1, \ldots, b_n$, are arbitrary but fixed real numbers and $\mathbf{X} = (X_1, \ldots, X_n)'$ has an $\mathcal{N}_n(\boldsymbol{\mu}, \boldsymbol{\Sigma})$ distribution. Since we can write

$$P_{\boldsymbol{\mu},\boldsymbol{\Sigma}}\left[\bigcap_{i=1}^{n}\{X_i \le a_i\}\right] = P_{\mathbf{R}}\left[\bigcap_{i=1}^{n}\left\{Z_i \le \frac{a_i - \mu_i}{\sigma_i}\right\}\right],$$

where $Z_i = (X_i - \mu_i)/\sigma_i$ $(i = 1, \ldots, n)$ and $\mathbf{R} = (\rho_{ij})$ is the corresponding correlation matrix, without loss of generality it may be assumed that the mean vector of $\mathbf{X}$ is already $\mathbf{0}$ and the covariance matrix is $\mathbf{R} = (\rho_{ij})$. Thus the problem of interest is the evaluation of the probability

$$g(\rho_{12}, \ldots, \rho_{n-1,n}; a_1, \ldots, a_n) = P_{\mathbf{R}}\left[\bigcap_{i=1}^{n}\{X_i \le a_i\}\right] \tag{8.2.4}$$

as a function of the a_i's and ρ_{ij}'s.

Most existing results in this area concern asymptotic expansions for the multivariate normal density function, and thus the function g itself, in the form of an infinite series. After this is accomplished, approximations to g can then be obtained by computing a finite number of terms. For example, in one of the earliest papers, Pearson (1901) gave a method for evaluating bivariate normal probability integrals using the tetrachoric series. Kendall (1941) considered a generalization of the tetrachoric series to several variables (which was also studied by Aitken (unpublished)), and investigated the asymptotic expansion of the orthant probability for three-dimensional normal variables. Moran (1948) adopted a similar approach, and the usefulness of this method was subsequently discussed in David (1953). David (1953) gave expressions for the orthant probabilities using a geometric approach. She compared the results with the Aitken–Kendall–Moran method, and declared it inefficient due to the slow convergence of the infinite series used in the asymptotic expansions. More recently, Harris and Soms (1980) studied the convergence of the tetrachoric series, and discovered that the assertion concerning the convergence of the series for all $n \geq 2$ and all $n \times n$ covariance matrices is false.

In addition to the references cited above, there have been quite a few other results for certain special cases. These include Mehler (1866), Kibble (1945), Ruben (1954, 1961, 1962, 1964), Das (1956), McFadden (1956, 1960), Henery (1981), and others. For additional references see Gupta (1963b) and Johnson and Kotz (1972, Chap. 35). Related references that appear in Russian can be found in the review article by Martynov (1981).

Mehler (1866) obtained an asymptotic expansion for the ratio of two bivariate normal densities $f(\mathbf{x}; \mathbf{0}, \mathbf{\Sigma})/f(\mathbf{x}; \mathbf{0}, \mathbf{I}_2)$ when the variances are one, and then used it to obtain an approximation for the orthant probability. His approach was later generalized by Kibble (1945) to the multivariate case. Ruben (1954) discussed the geometric significance of the moments of order statistics from a correlated multivariate normal population, and gave results in the form of an asymptotic expansion for orthant probabilities. The methods in Ruben (1961, 1962) depend on a similar expansion, and he (Ruben, 1964) also gave related results concerning Mills' ratio of the multivariate normal distribution. Das (1956) considered an asymptotic expression of the orthant probability via a change-of-variable process and a conditioning argument. McFadden (1956) gave results for the special case of $n = 4$ and $\rho_{ij} = \rho \in (-\frac{1}{3}, 1)$ and, subsequently he (McFadden, 1960) gave two infinite series expansions which are, for $n = 4$, under weaker conditions on the ρ_{ij}'s. The approach in Henery (1981) is to find an asymptotic expression conditioned on the other variables that are truncated. The conditional distribution of the remaining variables can be described by an expansion, which is similar to the tetrachoric series in the bivariate case but has faster convergence under certain conditions. This approach was previously considered by Mendell and Elston (1974) and Rice, Reich, and Cloninger (1979) in applications to multifactorial qualitative traits in biometry. In addition to those results, Owen (1956) and Steck (1958) computed tables which are needed for evaluating the bivariate and trivariate normal probability integrals.

Most of the papers cited above focus on the special case $a_1 = \cdots = a_n = 0$. That is, letting

$$p_n = P_{\mathbf{R}}\left[\bigcap_{i=1}^{n} \{X_i \leq 0\}\right], \tag{8.2.5}$$

the problem of interest is to find expressions for the orthant probability p_n (in closed forms if possible), in terms of the correlation coefficients. David (1953) used the inclusion–exclusion formula to study this problem; she pointed out the immediate result

$$p_2 = \frac{1}{4} + \frac{1}{2\pi} \operatorname{arc\,sin} \rho, \tag{8.2.6}$$

where ρ is the correlation coefficient of the bivariate normal distribution (see

Problem 2.8), and then showed that

$$p_3 = \frac{1}{8} + \frac{1}{4\pi}(\arcsin \rho_{12} + \arcsin \rho_{13} + \arcsin \rho_{23}) \tag{8.2.7}$$

holds for $n = 3$. If $n \geq 4$, then a closed-form representation for p_n is not possible. Abrahamson (1964) studied this problem for $n = 4$ and obtained an integral representation for p_4. Under the additional condition that $\rho_{ij} = \rho$ for all $i \neq j$, some special results can be found in Steck (1962), Bacon (1963), and others. For example, it is known that

$$p_4 = \frac{1}{16} + \frac{3}{4\pi}\arcsin \rho + \frac{3}{2\pi^2}\int_0^\rho (1 - y^2)^{-1/2} \arcsin\left(\frac{y}{1 + 2y}\right) dy, \tag{8.2.8}$$

and a similar expression exists for p_5. Furthermore, if $\rho = \frac{1}{2}$, then (by (5.3.9)) it can be verified that

$$p_n = \frac{1}{n + 1} \quad \text{for all } n. \tag{8.2.9}$$

8.2.3. Other Methods of Approximations

Other methods for approximating a multivariate normal probability integral include change-of-variables methods, quadrature methods in numerical analysis, and conditioning. Some of those methods are not limited to the approximations of orthant probabilities, and are also applicable to the probability integrals over other geometric regions.

Cadwell (1951) applied linear transformations to find a method for obtaining the integral of a bivariate normal density function over any polygon. Later John (1966) studied the evaluation of probability integrals over convex polyhedra. Milton (1972), by means of a modification of a multidimensional adaptive Simpson quadrature with error control, provided a computer algorithm for evaluating the probability integral of a multivariate normal distribution over any geometric region. Genz and Kahaner (1986) described a method for the special case in which $\mathbf{\Sigma}^{-1} = (\tau_{ij})$ satisfies $\tau_{ij} = 0$ for all $|i - j| > 1$. Iyengar (1982, 1988) considered an approximation to the probability itegral $I(\mathbf{0}, \mathbf{R}, A)$ in (8.2.1) by using $I(\mathbf{0}, \mathbf{R}(\bar{\rho}), A)$, where $A \in \mathfrak{R}^n$ is permutation-symmetric and $\mathbf{R}(\bar{\rho})$ is the correlation matrix obtained by substituting all ρ_{ij}'s in $\mathbf{R}$ for their arithmetic mean. This method is useful because the value of $I(\boldsymbol{\mu}, \mathbf{\Sigma}(\bar{\rho}), A)$ is easier to evaluate, especially when $\bar{\rho}$ is nonnegative.

Another approach is conditioning. John (1959) considered the evaluation of orthant probabilities of an n-dimensional normal variable by conditioning on $X_1 = x_1$, thus reducing the dimension from n to $n - 1$. Ihm (1959) and Marsaglia (1963) studied the evaluation of multivariate normal probability integrals when the covariance matrix is of the form $\mathbf{\Sigma} = \mathbf{D} + \mathbf{B}$, where $\mathbf{D}$ is a diagonal matrix. If $\mathbf{X}$ is a multivariate normal variable with mean vector $\boldsymbol{\mu}$ and covariance matrix $\mathbf{D} + \mathbf{B}$, then $\mathbf{X}$ and $\mathbf{Y} + \mathbf{Z}$ are identically distributed where $\mathbf{Y}$, $\mathbf{Z}$ are independent and are distributed according to $\mathcal{N}_n(\mathbf{0}, \mathbf{D})$ and $\mathcal{N}_n(\boldsymbol{\mu}, \mathbf{B})$, respectively. Since the components of $\mathbf{Y}$ are independent, the evaluation of a probability integral may be made easier by first computing the conditional probability, given $\mathbf{Z} = \mathbf{z}$.

8.2.4. Dimension-Reduction Methods

A significant result on dimension reduction for evaluating multivariate normal probability integrals is due to Plackett (1954). He proved the identity

$$\frac{\partial}{\partial \rho_{ij}} f(\mathbf{x}; \mathbf{0}, \boldsymbol{\Sigma}) = \frac{\partial^2}{\partial x_i\, \partial x_j} f(\mathbf{x}; \mathbf{0}, \boldsymbol{\Sigma}), \qquad i \neq j, \tag{8.2.10}$$

where $f(\mathbf{x}; \mathbf{0}, \boldsymbol{\Sigma})$ is the multivariate normal density function with mean vector $\mathbf{0}$ and covariance matrix $\boldsymbol{\Sigma} > 0$. Since the distribution function is of the form

$$F(\mathbf{a}; \mathbf{0}, \boldsymbol{\Sigma}) = \int_{-\infty}^{a_1} \int_{-\infty}^{a_2} \int_{-\infty}^{a_3} \cdots \int_{-\infty}^{a_n} f(\mathbf{x}; \mathbf{0}, \boldsymbol{\Sigma}) \prod_{i=1}^{n} dx_i, \tag{8.2.11}$$

and interchanging differentiation and integration is permissible, this identity yields

$$\begin{aligned}
&\frac{\partial}{\partial \rho_{12}} F(\mathbf{a}; \mathbf{0}, \boldsymbol{\Sigma}) \\
&\quad = \int_{-\infty}^{a_3} \cdots \int_{-\infty}^{a_n} f(a_1, a_2, x_3, \ldots, x_n; \mathbf{0}, \boldsymbol{\Sigma}) \prod_{i=3}^{n} dx_i \\
&\quad = f_1(a_1, a_2; \mathbf{0}, \boldsymbol{\Sigma}_{11}) \int_{-\infty}^{a_3} \cdots \int_{-\infty}^{a_n} f_{2|1}(\mathbf{x}_2; \boldsymbol{\mu}_{2|1}, \boldsymbol{\Sigma}_{22\cdot 1}) \prod_{i=3}^{n} dx_i,
\end{aligned} \tag{8.2.12}$$

where f_1 is the marginal density function of $(X_1, X_2)'$ evaluated at $(a_1, a_2)'$ and $f_{2|1}$ is the conditional density of $(X_3, \ldots, X_n)'$ given $(X_1, X_2)' = (a_1, a_2)'$. Using (8.2.12), the probability integral $F(\mathbf{a}, \mathbf{0}, \boldsymbol{\Sigma})$ can be expressed in the form of a single integral over ρ_{12}, and the integrand involves f_1 and a probability integral of the remaining $n - 2$ variables $X_3, \ldots, X_n$.

This method has been found useful by several authors. In particular, Steck (1962) and Bacon (1963) both used this identity to obtain dimension-reduction methods for evaluating orthant probabilities for equally correlated normal variables for small n. An important by-product of the identity in (8.2.10) is the inequality known as Slepian's inequality (Theorem 5.1.7) which, generally speaking, says that $F(\mathbf{a}, \mathbf{0}, \boldsymbol{\Sigma})$ is an increasing function of the correlation coefficients. This result follows from the fact that the right-hand side of (8.2.12) is always positive.

8.2.5. An Integral Representation When the Correlation Matrix Has a Special Structure

A special problem of interest concerns the covariance matrix of an n-dimensional normal variable with the structure described in (8.1.5); that is, the correlation coefficients are such that $\rho_{ij} = \lambda_i \lambda_j$ for $\lambda_i \in [-1, 1]$ $(i = 1, \ldots, n)$ for all $i \neq j$. If $\mathbf{X}$ is distributed according to $\mathcal{N}_n(\boldsymbol{\mu}, \boldsymbol{\Sigma})$ and (8.1.5) is satisfied, then clearly $\mathbf{X}$ and

$$(\sigma_1(\sqrt{1 - \lambda_1^2}Z_1 + \lambda_1 Z_0) + \mu_1, \ldots, \sigma_n(\sqrt{1 - \lambda_n^2}Z_n + \lambda_n Z_0) + \mu_n)'$$

are identically distributed, where $Z_0, Z_1, \ldots, Z_n$ are i.i.d. $\mathcal{N}(0, 1)$ variables. Thus if A is an n-dimensional rectangle given by

$$A = \{\mathbf{x} \colon \mathbf{x} \in \mathfrak{R}^n, b_i \le x_i \le a_i, 1 = 1, \ldots, n\},$$

where $-\infty \le b_i < a_i \le \infty$ $(i = 1, \ldots, n)$, then the probability integral can be expressed as (by conditioning on $Z_0 = z$ then unconditioning)

$$\begin{aligned} P[\mathbf{X} \in A] &= \int_{-\infty}^{\infty} \prod_{i=1}^{n} P[b_i \le \sigma_i(\sqrt{1 - \lambda_i^2}Z_i + \lambda_i z) + \mu_i \le a_i]\phi(z)\,dz \\ &= \int_{-\infty}^{\infty} \prod_{i=1}^{n} \left[\Phi\left(\frac{(a_i - \mu_i)/\sigma_i + \lambda_i z}{\sqrt{1 - \lambda_i^2}}\right)\right. \\ &\qquad \left. - \Phi\left(\frac{(b_i - \mu_i)/\sigma_i + \lambda_i z}{\sqrt{1 - \lambda_i^2}}\right)\right]\phi(z)\,dz, \end{aligned} \tag{8.2.13}$$

where Φ and ϕ are the $\mathcal{N}(0, 1)$ distribution function and the density function, respectively. The right-hand side of (8.2.13) is a *single* integral instead of a multiple integral over $\mathfrak{R}^n$. In the special case in which $\lambda_i = \sqrt{\rho} \ge 0$ for all i, (8.2.13) reduces to

$$\begin{aligned} &P[\mathbf{X} \in A] \\ &= \int_{-\infty}^{\infty} \prod_{i=1}^{n} \left[\Phi\left(\frac{(a_i - \mu_i)/\sigma_i + \sqrt{\rho}z}{\sqrt{1 - \rho}}\right) - \Phi\left(\frac{(b_i - \mu_i)/\sigma_i + \sqrt{\rho}z}{\sqrt{1 - \rho}}\right)\right]\phi(z)\,dz. \end{aligned} \tag{8.2.14}$$

The expressions in (8.2.13) and (8.2.14) were used by Bechhofer (1954), Dunnett and Sobel (1955), Moran (1956), Stuart (1958), Curnow and Dunnett (1962), Steck and Owen (1962), Steck (1962), Gupta (1963a), and others, to evaluate multivariate normal probability integrals. Since it involves the integral of only one variable, it is easier to evaluate numerically on a computer. This method will be discussed further in the next section for computing the probability integrals of exchangeable normal variables.

8.3. Computation of One-Sided and Two-Sided Multivariate Normal Probability Integrals

If $\mathbf{X} = (X_1, \ldots, X_n)'$ have an $\mathcal{N}_n(\mathbf{0}, \mathbf{\Sigma})$ distribution with variances $\sigma_1^2, \ldots, \sigma_n^2$ and correlation coefficients $\rho \in [0, 1)$, then the expressions in (8.2.14) can be simplified further. In particular, the distribution functions of $\mathbf{X}$ and $|\mathbf{X}|$ are, respectively,

$$F_{\mathbf{X}}(\mathbf{a}) = P\left[\bigcap_{i=1}^{n} \{X_i \leq a_i\}\right]$$

$$= \int_{-\infty}^{\infty} \prod_{i=1}^{n} \Phi\left(\left(\frac{a_i}{\sigma_i} + \sqrt{\rho} z\right) \Big/ \sqrt{1-\rho}\right) \phi(z)\, dz, \tag{8.3.1}$$

$$F_{|\mathbf{X}|}(\mathbf{a}) = P\left[\bigcap_{i=1}^{n} \{|X_i| \leq a_i\}\right]$$

$$= \int_{-\infty}^{\infty} \prod_{i=1}^{n} \left[\Phi\left(\left(\frac{a_i}{\sigma_i} + \sqrt{\rho} z\right) \Big/ \sqrt{1-\rho}\right) - \Phi\left(\left(\frac{-a_i}{\sigma_i} + \sqrt{\rho} z\right) \Big/ \sqrt{1-\rho}\right)\right] \phi(z)\, dz. \tag{8.3.2}$$

A change of variable in (8.3.1) and (8.3.2) yields

$$F_{\mathbf{X}}(\mathbf{a}) = \int_{-\infty}^{\infty} g_{1,\mathbf{a}}(u) e^{-u^2}\, du, \tag{8.3.3}$$

$$F_{|\mathbf{X}|}(\mathbf{a}) = \int_{-\infty}^{\infty} g_{2,\mathbf{a}}(u) e^{-u^2}\, du, \tag{8.3.4}$$

where

$$g_{1,\mathbf{a}}(u) = \frac{1}{\sqrt{\pi}} \prod_{i=1}^{n} \Phi\left(\left(\frac{a_i}{\sigma_i} + \sqrt{2\rho} u\right) \Big/ \sqrt{1-\rho}\right), \tag{8.3.5}$$

$$g_{2,\mathbf{a}}(u) = \frac{1}{\sqrt{\pi}} \prod_{i=1}^{n} \left[\Phi\left(\left(\frac{a_i}{\sigma_i} + \sqrt{2\rho} u\right) \Big/ \sqrt{1-\rho}\right) - \Phi\left(\left(\frac{-a_i}{\sigma_i} + \sqrt{2\rho} u\right) \Big/ \sqrt{1-\rho}\right)\right]. \tag{8.3.6}$$

Since there already exist numerical methods for approximating integrals of the form $\int_{-\infty}^{\infty} g(u) e^{-u^2}\, du$ when g is well-behaved, the values of the integrals on the right-hand side of (8.3.3) and the right-hand side of (8.3.4) can be approximated on a computer. For a discussion of such methods in statistical computing, see, e.g., Thisted (1988, Sec. 5.3).

When the Gaussian quadrature method is used, computing formulas have already been developed. For example, Stroud and Secrest (1966) contains values of (d_i, u_i) $(i = 1, \ldots, M)$, with 30 significant digits, such that $\int_{-\infty}^{\infty} g(u)e^{-u^2}\,du$ can be approximated by $\sum_{i=1}^{M} d_i g(u_i)$. Thus the right-hand side of (8.3.1) and the right-hand side of (8.3.2) can be computed using a linear combination of the functional values of $g_{j,\mathbf{a}}(u)$ $(j = 1, 2)$ at selected points $u_1, \ldots, u_M$.

We note in passing that, for the bivariate normal distribution, it is always possible to have expressions of the forms in (8.3.3) and (8.3.4) (even if the correlation coefficient ρ is negative). Thus if $n = 2$, then the distribution functions of $\mathbf{X}$ and $|\mathbf{X}|$ can be evaluated numerically for all $\rho \in (-1, 1)$ using the Gaussian quadrature method. This statement follows from the result in (2.1.12) (or (2.2.3)); the details are left to the reader.

8.4. The Tables

Using the formulas in Stroud and Secrest (1966) with $M = 120$, the numerical values of the probability integrals in (8.3.1), (8.3.2), and the corresponding percentage points have been tabulated for the special case

$$\sigma_1^2 = \cdots = \sigma_n^2 = 1 \qquad \text{and} \qquad a_1 = \cdots = a_n = a. \tag{8.4.1}$$

The tables were computed in 1986 on a Cyber 205 Supercomputer at Georgia Tech Computing Network using double precision. The subroutine used to evaluate $\Phi(z)$ is the one in the IMSL Library, which is known to have good accuracy.

The tables have been classified into four groups. Tables for $\mathbf{X}$ are called one-sided tables and tables for $|\mathbf{X}|$ are called two-sided tables:

(a) Table A. One-Sided Percentage Points
The table contains values of c satisfying

$$P\left[\bigcap_{i=1}^{n} \{X_i \le c\}\right] = \gamma \tag{8.4.2}$$

for $n = 2(1)20$, $\rho = 0.0(0.1)0.9$, $\frac{1}{3}$, $\frac{2}{3}$, $\frac{1}{4}$, and $\frac{3}{4}$, and $\gamma = 0.90, 0.95, 0.99$; where $(X_1, \ldots, X_n)'$ has an $\mathcal{N}_n(\mathbf{0}, \mathbf{\Sigma})$ distribution with variances one and correlation coefficients ρ.

(b) Table B. Two-Sided Percentage Points
The table contains values of c satisfying

$$P\left[\bigcap_{i=1}^{n} \{|X_i| \le c\}\right] = \gamma \tag{8.4.3}$$

for the same set of n, ρ, and γ values described in (a).

(c) Table C-J ($J = 0, 1, \ldots, 13$). One-Sided Probability Integral

The tables contain values of $P[\bigcap_{i=1}^{n}\{X_i \le a\}]$ for $n = 2(1)10(2)20$, $a = -2.0(0.1)4.0$, and $\rho = 0.0, 0.1(0.1)0.9$ (for $J = 0, 1, \ldots, 9$), $\frac{1}{3}, \frac{2}{3}, \frac{1}{4}$, and $\frac{3}{4}$ (for $J = 10, 11, 12, 13$).

(d) Table D-J ($J = 0, 1, \ldots, 13$). Two-Sided Probability Integral

The tables contain values of $P[\bigcap_{i=1}^{n}\{|X_i| \le a\}]$ for $a = 0.1(0.1)5.0$ and for the same set of n, ρ values described in (c).

The table values in (a) and (b) contain four decimal places, and the table values in (c) and (d) contain five decimal places. The tables can be found in the Appendix of this book.

8.4.1. Accuracy of the Tables

To compare the accuracy of the tables we first present a survey of some existing tables.

(a) *Tables of one-sided percentage points*

[a1] Bechhofer (1954) gave values of $\sqrt{2}c$ (where c is the percentage point) for $n = 1(1)9$, $\rho = 0.5$, and $\gamma = 0.05(0.05)0.80(0.02)0.90(0.01)0.99, 0.995, 0.999$, and 0.9995. The entries have four decimal places.

[a2] Gupta (1963a) gave tables of percentage points for $n = 1(1)50$, $\rho = 0.5$, $\gamma = 0.75, 0.90, 0.95, 0.975$, and 0.99; three decimal places.

[a3] Milton (1963) computed values of percentage points for $n = 2(1)9(5)24$, $\rho = 0.00(0.05)1.00, \frac{21}{41}, \frac{11}{21}, \frac{5}{9}, \frac{2}{3}$, and $\gamma = 0.50, 0.75, 0.90, 0.95, 0.975, 0.99, 0.995, 0.999, 0.9995, 0.9999$; six decimal places.

[a4] Gupta, Nagel, and Panchapakesan (1973) tabulated percentage points for $n = 1(1)10(2)50$, $\rho = 0.1(0.1)0.9, \frac{1}{3}, \frac{2}{3}, \frac{1}{4}, \frac{3}{4}, \frac{1}{8}, \frac{3}{8}, \frac{5}{8}, \frac{7}{8}$, and $\gamma = 0.75, 0.90, 0.95, 0.975, 0.99$; four decimal places.

[a5] Gibbons, Olkin, and Sobel (1977) gave percentage points for $n = 1(1)9$, $\rho = 0.0(0.1)1.0$, and $\gamma = 0.75, 0.90, 0.95, 0.975, 0.99$; three decimal places.

[a6] For the case of unequal correlation coefficients, Tong (1969) published a set of tables of multivariate normal percentage points for the following correlation structure:

$$\rho_{ij} = \begin{cases} \frac{1}{2} & \text{for} \quad i, j \le q \text{ or } i, j \ge q + 1, \\ -\frac{1}{2} & \text{for} \quad i \le q \text{ and } j \ge q + 1, \end{cases}$$

where q is the largest integer $\le (n + 1)/2$. The tables give values for $n = 2(1)10(2)20$, and $\gamma = 0.50, 0.75, 0.90, 0.95, 0.975, 0.99$; five decimal places.

[a7] Other tables were given by several authors (e.g., Dunnett, 1955; Steffens, 1969; Gibbons, Olkin, and Sobel, 1977) in connection with the multivariate t distribution when the number of degrees of freedom is infinity.

(b) *Tables of two-sided percentage points*

[b1] Odeh (1982) published tables in this category for $n = 2(1)40(2)50$, $\rho = 0.1(0.1)0.9, \frac{1}{3}, \frac{2}{3}, \frac{1}{4}, \frac{3}{4}, \frac{1}{8}, \frac{3}{8}, \frac{5}{8}, \frac{7}{8}$, and $1/(1+\sqrt{n})$, $\gamma = 0.75, 0.90, 0.95, 0.975, 0.99, 0.995$, and 0.999; four decimal places.

[b2] The multivariate t tables of Pillai and Ramachandran (1954) and Dunnett (1964) yield two-sided percentage points when the number of degrees of freedom is infinity.

(c) *Tables of one-sided probability integrals*

[c1] Owen (1956) provided tables which can be used to obtain bivariate normal probabilities; six decimal places are given.

[c2] Steck (1958) gave tables to compute the trivariate normal probability integral; seven decimal places.

[c3] The National Bureau of Standards (1959) published a set of tables for the bivariate normal distribution for $a = -4.0(0.1)0.0$ and $\pm\rho = 0.0(0.05)0.95(0.01)1.0$; six decimal places.

[c4] Gupta (1963a) gave table values for $n = 1(1)12$, $a = -3.50(0.10)3.50$, and $\rho = 0.1(0.1)0.9, \frac{1}{3}, \frac{2}{3}, \frac{1}{4}, \frac{3}{4}, \frac{1}{8}, \frac{3}{8}, \frac{5}{8}, \frac{7}{8}$, five decimal places.

[c5] Milton (1963) gave tables for $n = 2(1)9(5)24$, $a = 0.0(0.2)5.0$, and $\rho = 0.00(0.05)1.00, \frac{21}{41}, \frac{11}{21}, \frac{5}{9}, \frac{2}{3}$; eight decimal places.

[c6] Table values for the multivariate normal probability integral $P[\bigcap_{i=1}^{n}\{X_i \le ia\}]$, where $(X_1, \ldots, X_n)'$ is distributed according to a multivariate normal distribution with means 0, variances 1, and correlation coefficients 0.5, were given by Olkin, Sobel, and Tong (1982) for $n = 2(1)10$, 12, 15, 20, and $a = 0.00(0.02)0.20(0.10)1.60$; four decimal places.

(d) *Tables of two-sided probability integrals*

There appears to be no separate tables in this category, and the multivariate t tables of Dunn, Kronmal, and Yee (1968) seem to be the only existing source which yield values for the multivariate normal distribution when the number of degrees of freedom is infinity.

A large number of entries in our tables have been selected for comparison with existing table values. The following is a summary of the results.

(1) For most of the numbers checked, the table values either agree completely or differ by only one unit in the last digit given (due to the rounding-off of the numbers) from entries in the following tables: Bechhofer (1954), Milton (1963), Gupta, Nagel, and Panchapakesan (1973), Gibbons, Olkin, and Sobel (1977), Dunnett (1955), Odeh (1982), and the National Bureau of Standards (1959).

(2) Table A agrees mostly with Gupta's (1963a) Table 1 except that for a few entries the difference is at least 0.002. But then the table in Gupta, Nagel, and Panchapakesan (1973) is an improved version of Gupta (1963a), and Table A does agree with the latter in most cases.

(3) Table D-J ($J = 0, 1, \ldots, 13$) does not agree with that of Dunn, Kronmal, and Yee (1968) in most cases, and the difference is usually in the third decimal place. This is obviously caused by the "random errors" in their tables since those tables were constructed using the Monte Carlo method.

Overall, it is safe to say that the errors of the table values are at most 10^{-4} for the entries in Tables A and B, and at most 10^{-5} for the entries in Tables C-J and D-J ($J = 0, \ldots, 13$).

8.4.2. Uses of the Tables

The tables given in the Appendix can be used for many purposes. In the following we discuss some of the related applications.

(a) *Confidence probabilities and sample size determination.* In finding a rectangular-type (one-sided or two-sided) confidence region for the mean vector of a multivariate normal distribution, the confidence probability is of the form given in (8.3.1) or (8.3.2). If the sample size is preassigned, then the numerical value of the confidence probability can be found in Table C-J or D-J. On the other hand, if the sample size is to be determined with a given level of confidence γ, then the entries in Tables A and B can be used for this purpose.

(b) *Test of hypotheses for means.* In testing hypotheses for the mean vector of a multivariate normal distribution using the union–intersection test, the acceptance region is an n-dimensional rectangle. Thus the type I error of the test can be obtained from Table C-J or D-J when the sample size is preassigned. Similarly, if the significant level of the test is given, then the sample size required can be determined by using Table A or B.

(c) If in (a) and (b) the correlation coefficients are unequal, then the inequalities given in Chapter 7 can be applied to obtain bounds, and the numerical values of the bounds can be found in Table C-J or D-J. An example is given below for the purpose of illustration:

EXAMPLE 8.4.1. (i) Suppose that in a given application we are interested in the value of $P[\bigcap_{i=1}^{8} \{X_i \le 2\}]$ where $(X_1, \ldots, X_8)'$ has an $\mathcal{N}_8(\mathbf{0}, \Sigma)$ distribution with variance one and correlation coefficient ρ_{ij}. If $\max_{i \neq j} \rho_{ij} = 0.3$ then, by Theorem 5.1.7 and Table C-3, the underlying probability is bounded above by 0.86013.

(ii) (Continuation.) Suppose that we are interested in $P[\bigcap_{i=1}^{8} \{|X_i| \le 2\}]$, then by Corollary 7.2.1 this probability is bounded below by $[\Phi(2) - \Phi(-2)]^8$, *no matter what the true correlation coefficients are.* Furthermore, the numerical value of this lower bound is 0.68898 (Table D-0). □

(d) If the correlation coefficients are the same but the end points are unequal, then an application of Theorems 4.4.2 and 7.4.1 yields upper bounds, and the numerical values of the upper bounds can be found in Table C-J or D-J.

EXAMPLE 8.4.2. Suppose that $(X_1, \ldots, X_4)'$ has an $\mathcal{N}_4(\mathbf{0}, \Sigma)$ distribution with variance one, and correlation coefficient $\rho = 0.5$. If the probability of concern is

$$F_{\mathbf{X}}(\mathbf{a}) = P\left[\bigcap_{i=1}^{4} \{X_i \le a_i\}\right] \quad \text{or} \quad F_{|\mathbf{X}|}(\mathbf{a}) = P\left[\bigcap_{i=1}^{4} \{|X_i| \le a_i\}\right], \tag{8.4.4}$$

where $\mathbf{a} = (2.5, 2.5, 1.5, 1.5)'$, then we have

$$F_{\mathbf{X}}(\mathbf{a}) \le P\left[\bigcap_{i=1}^{4} \{X_i \le 2\}\right], \qquad F_{|\mathbf{X}|}(\mathbf{a}) \le P\left[\bigcap_{i=1}^{4} \{|X_i| \le 2\}\right]. \tag{8.4.5}$$

The numerical values on the right-hand side of (8.4.4) and the right-hand side of (8.4.5) are, respectively, 0.92845 and 0.85694 (from Tables C-5 and D-5, in fact, the probability $F_{|\mathbf{X}|}(\mathbf{a})$ is known to be 0.7613 (Tong, 1982a)). When each of the a_i values is closer to their arithmetic mean $\bar{a} = 2.0$ then, of course, the true value of the probability is closer to its upper bound. □

(e) The table values in Tables C-J and D-J are for $n \le 20$. In a given real-life applicaion if the value of n is larger than 20, then by Theorem 7.3.1 (or 7.3.2 or 7.3.3) lower and upper bounds can be obtained, and the numerical values of the bounds can be obtained from the tables.

EXAMPLE 8.4.3. If we are interested in

$$\gamma_1 = P\left[\bigcap_{i=1}^{30} \{X_i \le 2.6\}\right] \quad \text{or} \quad \gamma_2 = P\left[\bigcap_{i=1}^{30} \{|X_i| \le 2.6\}\right],$$

where $(X_1, \ldots, X_{30})'$ has an $\mathcal{N}_{30}(\mathbf{0}, \Sigma)$ distribution with variance one and correlation coefficient $\rho = 0.7$, then by Theorem 7.3.1, Tables C-7 and D-7 we have

$$0.94381 = 0.96218^{30/20} < \gamma_1 < P\left[\bigcap_{i=1}^{20} \{X_i \le 2.6\}\right] = 0.96218, \tag{8.4.6}$$

$$0.88870 = 0.92435^{30/20} < \gamma_2 < P\left[\bigcap_{i=1}^{20} \{|X_i| \le 2.6\}\right] = 0.92435. \tag{8.4.7}$$

□

(f) The table values in Tables C-J and D-J are given for $\rho = 0.0, 0.1, \ldots, 0.9$ (for $J = 0, 1, \ldots, 9$), $\frac{1}{3}, \frac{2}{3}, \frac{1}{4}$ and $\frac{3}{4}$ (for $J = 10, 11, 12,$ and 13) only. In certain applications other values of ρ may be of interest. If the true value of

$$\gamma_1(\rho) = P_\rho\left[\bigcap_{i=1}^{n} \{X_i \le a\}\right] \tag{8.4.8}$$

is needed where $(X_1, \ldots, X_n)'$ has an $\mathcal{N}_n(\mathbf{0}, \Sigma)$ distribution with variances one and correlation coefficients ρ, and if the values of $\gamma_1(\rho_1)$ and $\gamma_1(\rho_2)$ are already tabulated for $\rho_1 < \rho < \rho_2$, then it seems natural to approximate $\gamma_1(\rho)$ by a linear interpolation, which is

$$\gamma_1(\rho) \doteq \gamma_1(\rho_1) + \frac{\rho - \rho_1}{\rho_2 - \rho_1}(\gamma_1(\rho_2) - \gamma_1(\rho_1)). \qquad (8.4.9)$$

A question of concern is whether the right-hand side of (8.4.9) is also a bound. This question can be partially answered by the following result (Iyengar and Tong, 1989):

Fact 8.4.1. *If $a \le 0$, then $\gamma_1(\rho)$, defined in* (8.4.8), *is a convex function of ρ for $\rho \in [0, 1]$. Consequently, the right-hand side of* (8.4.9) *provides an upper bound on $\gamma_1(\rho)$ for all $a \le 0$ and $0 \le \rho_1 < \rho < \rho_2$.*

To sum up, the tables given in the Appendix are not just for the equicoordinate probabilities of equally correlated normal variables. When combining with related results on inequalities, the tables also provide numerical values for the upper and lower bounds in the more general case.

Problems

8.1. Consider an algorithm for generating (pseudo) random integers between 0 and 63 given by

$$V_{i+1} = 3V_i + 1 \ (\mathrm{mod}\ 63), \qquad i = 0, 1, 2, \ldots.$$

If the seed number is $V_0 = 5$, compute $V_1, \ldots, V_8$. (*Note*. For a given nonnegative integer v, $v^* = v \ (\mathrm{mod}\ 63)$ is the integer satisfying $0 \le v^* < 63$ and $v = 63j + v^*$ for some nonnegative integer j.)

8.2. (Continuation.) Use $V_1, \ldots, V_8$ to generate random numbers in [0, 1] given by

$$U_i = \frac{V_i}{63}, \qquad i = 1, \ldots, 8.$$

Carry four decimal places.

8.3. (Continuation.) Use Algorithm 8.1.1 and the values of U_i ($i = 1, \ldots, 8$) obtained in Problem 8.2 to generate eight random variates $Z_1, \ldots, Z_8$ which are distributed according to an $\mathcal{N}(0, 1)$ distribution.

8.4. Use Algorithm 8.1.2 (or 8.1.3) and the value sof $Z_1, \ldots, Z_8$ obtained in Problem 8.3 to generate $\mathbf{X}_1, \mathbf{X}_2$ which are distributed according to an $\mathcal{N}_3(\boldsymbol{\mu}, \boldsymbol{\Sigma})$ distribution with means 1, variances 4, and correlation coefficients $\frac{1}{2}$.

8.5. Let $\boldsymbol{\Sigma}$ be the 3×3 covariance matrix given in Problem 8.4. Find the lower triangular matrix $\mathbf{T}$ such that $\mathbf{TT}' = \boldsymbol{\Sigma}$.

8.6. Use Algorithm 8.1.4 and the values of $Z_1, \ldots, Z_6$ obtained in Problem 8.3 to generate $\mathbf{X}_1, \mathbf{X}_2$ described in Problem 8.4.

8.7. Let $\boldsymbol{\Sigma}$ be an 3×3 matrix with $\sigma_{ii} = 1$ and $\sigma_{ij} = \rho \in (0, 1)$ for $i \ne j$. Find a 3×3 matrix $\mathbf{B} = (b_{ij})$ such that $b_{ii} = b$ and $b_{ij} = c$ for $i \ne j$, and then find a 3×3 lower triangular matrix $\mathbf{T}$ such that $\mathbf{BB}' = \mathbf{TT}' = \boldsymbol{\Sigma}$.

8.8. (Continuation.) Develop an algorithm for generating three-dimensional normal variates with a mean vector $\boldsymbol{\mu}$ and covariance $\boldsymbol{\Sigma}$ given in Problem 8.7 using the transformation $\mathbf{X} = \mathbf{BZ} + \boldsymbol{\mu}$, where $\mathbf{Z}$ is an $\mathcal{N}_3(\mathbf{0}, \mathbf{I}_3)$ variable.

8.9. Justify the statement in Fact 8.1.1.

8.10. Show that when using the result in Fact 8.1.1 to generate $2M$ univariate normal variates, the expected number of random numbers needed is $8M/\pi$.

8.11. Suppose that the crude Monte Carlo method is to be used and that in (8.2.2) ε and α are chosen to be 2×10^{-2} and 10^{-2}, respectively. If it is known that $I(\boldsymbol{\mu}, \boldsymbol{\Sigma}, A)$ is less than 0.3, find the value of N.

8.12. Let $(X_1, X_2, X_3)'$ have an $\mathcal{N}_3(\mathbf{0}, \boldsymbol{\Sigma})$ distribution with variances σ_i^2 and correlation coefficients ρ_{ij}. Show that $P[X_i \geq 0, X_j \geq 0] = \frac{1}{4} + (1/2\pi) \text{ arc sin } \rho_{ij}$ for all $i \neq j$.

8.13. (Continuation.) Show that if $\rho_{ij} \geq 0$ for all $i \neq j$, then

$$P\left[\bigcap_{i=1}^{3} \{X_i \leq 0\}\right] = P\left[\bigcap_{i=1}^{3} \{X_i \geq 0\}\right] \geq \frac{1}{8} + \frac{3}{4\pi} \text{ arc sin } \bar{\rho},$$

where $\bar{\rho} = \frac{1}{3}(\rho_{12} + \rho_{13} + \rho_{23})$. (*Hint*: First show that arc sin ρ is a convex function of ρ for $\rho \in [0, 1]$.)

8.14. (Continuation.) Show that if $\rho_{ij} \leq 0$ for all $i \neq j$, then the inequality in Problem 8.13 is reversed.

8.15. Prove the result in (8.2.9).

8.16. Show that the right-hand side of (8.3.1) and the right-hand side of (8.3.3) (the right-hand side of (8.3.2) and the right-hand side of (8.3.4)) are identical.

8.17. Let $(X_1, X_2)'$ have an $\mathcal{N}_2(\mathbf{0}, \boldsymbol{\Sigma})$ distribution with variances σ_1^2, σ_2^2 and correlation coefficient $\rho \in (-1, 0)$. Find the function $g_{\mathbf{a}}(u)$ such that

$$P\left[\bigcap_{i=1}^{2} \{X_i \leq a_i\}\right] = \int_{-\infty}^{\infty} g_{\mathbf{a}}(u) e^{-u^2}\, du.$$

(*Hint*: See (2.2.3) in Chapter 2.)

8.18. Let $(X_1, \ldots, X_{16})'$ be an $\mathcal{N}_{16}(\mathbf{0}, \boldsymbol{\Sigma})$ variable with variances 4 and unknown correlaton matrix $\mathbf{R} = (\rho_{ij})$. Use Table D-0 to find the numerical value of a lower bound (which does not depend on $\mathbf{R}$) for $P[\bigcap_{i=1}^{16} \{|X_i| \leq 5\}]$.

8.19. Let $X = (X_1, X_2, X_3)'$ be an $\mathcal{N}_3(\mathbf{0}, \boldsymbol{\Sigma})$ variable with variances 9 and correlation coefficients

$$\rho_{12} = 0.2, \qquad \rho_{13} = -0.1, \qquad \rho_{23} = 0.25.$$

Use Table C-12 to find the numerical value of an upper bound for $P[\bigcap_{i=1}^{3} \{X_i \leq -0.6\}]$.

8.20. (Continuation.) Find the numerical value of an upper bound for the probability $P[\bigcap_{i=1}^{3} \{X_i \leq 0\}]$, then compare it with the true value calculated from (8.2.7).

8.21. For the random variable $\mathbf{X}$ defined in Problem 8.19 use Table C-12 to find the numerical value of an upper bound for $P[\bigcap_{i=1}^{3} \{X_i \geq -1.8\}]$.

8.22. For the random variable $\mathbf{X}$ defined in Problem 8.19 find the numerical value of an upper bound for $P[X_1 \le 3.2, X_2 \le 2.0, X_3 \le 2.9]$.

8.23. Show that the left-hand side of (8.4.6) (of (8.4.7)) is larger than $(P[\bigcap_{i=1}^{k}\{X_i \le 2.6\}])^{30/k}$ (larger than $(P[\bigcap_{i=1}^{k}\{|X_i| \le 2.6\}])^{30/k}$) for all $k < 20$.

8.24. Let $(X_1, \ldots, X_{10})'$ have an $\mathcal{N}_{10}(\mathbf{0}, \mathbf{\Sigma})$ distribution with variances one and correlation coefficients $\rho = 0.68$. Use Tables C-6 and C-7 to calculate the numerical value of an upper bound for $P[\bigcap_{i=1}^{10}\{X_i \le -0.5\}]$.

CHAPTER 9

The Multivariate t Distribution

If Z is an $\mathcal{N}(0, 1)$ variable and independent of S, where νS^2 has a chi-square distribution with ν degrees of freedom, then the random variable $t = Z/S$ is called a Student's t variable with ν degrees of freedom. The distribution of t can be found in elementary textbooks, and it plays a central role in statistical inference problems concerning the mean of a univariate normal distribution with unknown variance. The multivariate t distribution, defined below and studied in this chapter, is a multivariate generalization of Student's t distribution.

Let $\mathbf{R} = (\rho_{ij})$ be an $n \times n$ symmetric matrix such that it is either positive definite or positive semidefinite and $\rho_{ii} = 1$ $(i = 1, \ldots, n)$. Let $\mathbf{Z} = (Z_1, \ldots, Z_n)'$ have an $\mathcal{N}(\mathbf{0}, \mathbf{R})$ distribution, and let the univariate random variable S be such that (i) S is independent of $\mathbf{Z}$, and (ii) νS^2 has a $\chi^2(\nu)$ distribution. Then a natural generalization of the Student's t variable is

$$\mathbf{t} = (t_1, \ldots, t_n)' \equiv \left(\frac{Z_1}{S}, \ldots, \frac{Z_n}{S}\right)'. \tag{9.0.1}$$

It is clear that the distribution of $\mathbf{t}$ involves only $\mathbf{R}$ and ν. Furthermore, it follows that for $\nu \geq 3$ the correlation coefficient between t_i and t_j is just ρ_{ij} (see Remark 9.1.1). Thus the matrix $\mathbf{R}$ is the correlation matrix of $\mathbf{t}$.

Remark 9.0.1. It should be pointed out that in addition to the random variable $\mathbf{t}$ defined in (9.0.1), these are other multivariate t variables studied in the literature for both theoretical and applied purposes. For example, another commonly used multivariate t variable is the one given in the following: For $j = 1, \ldots, N$, let $\mathbf{X}_j = (X_{1j}, \ldots, X_{nj})'$ be independent $\mathcal{N}_n(\mathbf{0}, \mathbf{\Sigma})$ variables. For

$i = 1, \ldots, n$, let $\bar{X}_i$ and V_i^2 be given by

$$\bar{X}_i = \frac{1}{N}\sum_{j=1}^{N} X_{ij}, \qquad V_i^2 = \frac{1}{N-1}\sum_{j=1}^{N}(X_{ij} - \bar{X}_i)^2, \tag{9.0.2}$$

then define

$$\mathbf{t}^* = \left(\frac{\sqrt{N}\bar{X}_1}{V_1}, \ldots, \frac{\sqrt{N}\bar{X}_n}{V_n}\right)'. \tag{9.0.3}$$

This random variable is also called a multivariate t variable in the literature, and the marginal distribution of $\sqrt{N}\bar{X}_i/V_i$ is Student's t with $N - 1$ degrees of freedom ($i = 1, \ldots, n$). To avoid possible confusion, only a random variable of the form in (9.0.1) will be called a multivariate t variable in this chapter, and its distribution will be called a multivariate t distribution.

Definition 9.0.1. The n-dimensional random variable $\mathbf{t}$ defined in (9.0.1) is called a multivariate t variable, and its distribution is called a multivariate t distribution with parameters $\mathbf{R}$ and ν, where $\mathbf{R}$ is the correlation matrix and ν is the number of degrees of freedom of the distribution; in symbols, $\mathbf{t} \sim t(\mathbf{R}, \nu)$.

The multivariate t distribution has been found useful in inference problems concerning the mean vector of a multivariate normal distribution. An example of application, dealing with simultaneous comparisons of n treatments with a control (Dunnett, 1955), is given below.

EXAMPLE 9.0.1. For $i = 0, 1, \ldots, n$ and $j = 1, \ldots, N$, let X_{ij} denote the jth observation from the ith population (the zeroth population denotes the control population). Under the assumption that the X_{ij}'s are independent $\mathcal{N}(\theta_i, \sigma^2)$ variables, where the θ_i's and σ^2 are unknown, we are interested in comparing the parameters

$$\mu_i = \theta_i - \theta_0 \qquad (i = 1, \ldots, n),$$

simultaneously based on the sample means $\bar{X}_i$ and the sample variances V_i^2 ($i = 0, 1, \ldots, n$) given in (9.0.2). Denote $\nu = (n + 1)(N - 1)$,

$$Y_i = \bar{X}_i - \bar{X}_0 \quad (i = 1, \ldots, n), \qquad S_0^2 = \sum_{i=0}^{n} \frac{V_i^2}{n+1}, \tag{9.0.4}$$

and consider the n-dimensional random variable

$$\mathbf{Z} = \frac{\sqrt{N}}{\sqrt{2}\sigma}(Y_1 - \mu_1, \ldots, Y_n - \mu_n)',$$

which has an $\mathcal{N}_n(\mathbf{0}, \mathbf{R})$ distribution with $\rho_{ij} = \frac{1}{2}$ ($i \neq j$). Let

$$A_1 = \{\mathbf{y}\colon \mathbf{y} \in \Re^n,\ y_i \geq Y_i - dS_0 \text{ for } i = 1, \ldots, n\}, \tag{9.0.5}$$

$$A_2 = \{\mathbf{y}\colon \mathbf{y} \in \Re^n,\ |Y_i - y_i| \leq dS_0 \text{ for } i = 1, \ldots, n\} \tag{9.0.6}$$

be the one-sided and two-sided confidence regions for $\boldsymbol{\mu} = (\mu_1, \ldots, \mu_n)'$. Then the corresponding confidence probabilities are

$$\gamma_1 = P[\boldsymbol{\mu} \in A_1] = P\left[\bigcap_{i=1}^{n} \{t_i \le a\}\right], \tag{9.0.7}$$

$$\gamma_2 = P[\boldsymbol{\mu} \in A_2] = P\left[\bigcap_{i=1}^{n} \{|t_i| \le a\}\right], \tag{9.0.8}$$

respectively, where $a = \sqrt{N}d/\sqrt{2}$ and $\mathbf{t} = (t_1, \ldots, t_n)'$ is the multivariate t variable with correlation coefficients $\frac{1}{2}$ and degrees of freedom ν.

9.1. Distribution Properties

In this section we give results concerning properties of the multivariate t distribution.

Proposition 9.1.1. *The distribution of* $\mathbf{t}$ *is nonsingular* (*i.e., the density function of* $\mathbf{t}$ *exists*) *if and only if* $\mathbf{R}$ *is positive definite.*

PROOF. Immediate. □

For the nonsingular case the density function of $\mathbf{t}$ was derived by Dunnett and Sobel (1954).

Proposition 9.1.2. *If* $\mathbf{R}$ *is positive definite, then the density function of* $\mathbf{t}$ (*with correlation matrix* $\mathbf{R}$ *and degrees of freedom* ν) *is*

$$h(\mathbf{t}; \mathbf{R}, \nu) = \frac{\Gamma((n+\nu)/2)}{(\nu\pi)^{n/2}\Gamma(\nu/2)|\mathbf{R}|^{1/2}}\left(1 + \frac{1}{\nu}\mathbf{t}'\mathbf{R}^{-1}\mathbf{t}\right)^{-(n+\nu)/2}, \qquad \mathbf{t} \in \mathfrak{R}^n. \tag{9.1.1}$$

PROOF. Let $\mathbf{T} = (\tau_{ij}) \equiv \mathbf{R}^{-1}$. Then the joint density function of $(\mathbf{Z}, S)'$ is

$$2\left[(\nu\pi)^{n/2}\Gamma\left(\frac{\nu}{2}\right)|\mathbf{R}|^{1/2}\right]^{-1}\left(\frac{\nu}{2}\right)^{(n+\nu)/2} s^{\nu-1}\exp\left[-\frac{1}{2}\left\{\sum_{i=1}^{n}\sum_{j=1}^{n}\tau_{ij}z_iz_j + \nu s^2\right\}\right],$$

$$\mathbf{z} \in \mathfrak{R}^n, \quad s > 0.$$

Letting $t_i = z_i/s$ $(i = 1, \ldots, n)$ and integrating out s yield (9.1.1). □

Next we give the first two moments of the components of $\mathbf{t}$. The result is obtained by conditioning and applying a well-known identity concerning the expectations of conditional variances and covariances.

Proposition 9.1.3. *Let* $\mathbf{t} = (t_1, \ldots, t_n)'$ *have a multivariate t distribution with correlation matrix* $\mathbf{R} = (\rho_{ij})$ *and degrees of freedom* ν. *Then for* $\nu \geq 3$:

(a) $Et_i = 0$ *for* $i = 1, \ldots, n$;
(b) $\operatorname{Var} t_i = \nu/(\nu - 2)$ *for* $i = 1, \ldots, n$; *and*
(c) $\operatorname{Cov}(t_i, t_j) = \nu\rho_{ij}/(\nu - 2)$ *for* $1 \leq i < j \leq n$.

Proof. Since $\mathbf{Z}$ and S are independent, the conditional distribution of $(t_i, t_j)'$, given $S = s$, is bivariate normal with means 0, variances s^{-2}, and correlation coefficient ρ_{ij}. Thus

$$Et_i = E(E(t_i|S = s)) = E(0) = 0.$$

To find the second moments, consider the well-known identity

$$\operatorname{Cov}(t_i, t_j) = E[\operatorname{Cov}(t_i, t_j)|S = s] + \operatorname{Cov}[E(t_i|S = s), E(t_j|S = s)]$$

for all $i, j = 1, \ldots, n$. Clearly, we have

$$E[\operatorname{Cov}(t_i, t_j)|S = s] = \rho_{ij} ES^{-2},$$
$$\operatorname{Cov}[E(t_i|S = s), E(t_j|S = s)] = 0.$$

If $\nu \geq 3$, then ES^{-2} exists and is equal to $\nu/(\nu - 2)$. Thus, by choosing $i = j$ and $i < j$, respectively, (b) and (c) hold. □

Remark 9.1.1. It follows from Proposition 9.1.3 that, for $\nu \geq 3$,

$$\operatorname{Corr}(t_i, t_j) = \rho_{ij} \qquad \text{for} \quad 1 \leq i < j \leq n. \tag{9.1.2}$$

Thus the matrix $\mathbf{R}$ in (9.1.1) is the correlation matrix of $\mathbf{t}$ as stated in Definition 9.0.1.

Some distribution properties of the family of elliptically contoured distributions can be found in Section 4.1. Since $h(\mathbf{t}; \mathbf{R}, \nu)$ given in (9.1.1) is an elliptically contoured density function with $\boldsymbol{\Sigma} = \mathbf{R}$ and $\boldsymbol{\mu} = \mathbf{0}$, all results stated in Section 4.1 apply to the multivariate t distribution. Consequently, the marginal and conditional distributions can be obtained easily. For this purpose we consider the partition of the components of $\mathbf{t}$ and $\mathbf{R}$ given by

$$\mathbf{t} = \begin{pmatrix} \mathbf{t}^{(1)} \\ \mathbf{t}^{(2)} \end{pmatrix}, \qquad \mathbf{R} = \begin{pmatrix} \mathbf{R}_{11} & \mathbf{R}_{12} \\ \mathbf{R}_{21} & \mathbf{R}_{22} \end{pmatrix}, \tag{9.1.3}$$

where $\mathbf{t}^{(1)}$ is $k \times 1$, $\mathbf{t}^{(2)}$ is $(n - k) \times 1$, $\mathbf{R}_{11}$ is $k \times k$, $\mathbf{R}_{22}$ is $(n - k) \times (n - k)$, and $\mathbf{R}_{12}$ is the covariance matrix between $\mathbf{t}^{(1)}$ and $\mathbf{t}^{(2)}$. Then it follows from (4.1.5), Proposition 4.1.1, and by elementary calculations that

Proposition 9.1.4. *If* $\mathbf{t}$ *has the multivariate t distribution with density function* $h(\mathbf{t}; \mathbf{R}, \nu)$ *given in* (9.1.1), *then*:

(a) *the marginal density functions of* $\mathbf{t}^{(1)}$ *and* $\mathbf{t}^{(2)}$ *are, respectively,*

$$h_1(\mathbf{t}_1; \mathbf{R}_{11}, \nu) = \frac{\Gamma((k+\nu)/2)}{(\nu\pi)^{k/2}\Gamma(\nu/2)|\mathbf{R}_{11}|^{1/2}} \times \left(1 + \frac{1}{\nu}\mathbf{t}_1'\mathbf{R}_{11}^{-1}\mathbf{t}_1\right)^{-(k+\nu)/2}, \qquad \mathbf{t}_1 \in \Re^k,$$

$$h_2(\mathbf{t}_2; \mathbf{R}_{22}, \nu) = \frac{\Gamma((n-k+\nu)/2)}{(\nu\pi)^{(n-k)/2}\Gamma(\nu/2)|\mathbf{R}_{22}|^{1/2}} \times \left(1 + \frac{1}{\nu}\mathbf{t}_2'\mathbf{R}_{22}^{-1}\mathbf{t}_2\right)^{-(n-k+v)/2}, \qquad \mathbf{t}_2 \in \Re^{n-k};$$

(b) *the conditional density function of* $\mathbf{t}^{(1)}$ *given* $\mathbf{t}^{(2)} = \mathbf{t}_2$ *is*

$$h_{1|2}(\mathbf{t}_1|\mathbf{t}_2) = c(\mathbf{R}, \nu, n, k)\left[1 + \frac{1}{\nu}\mathbf{t}_2'\mathbf{R}_{22}^{-1}\mathbf{t}_2\right]^{(n-k+\nu)/2} \times \left[1 + \frac{1}{\nu}(\mathbf{t}_2'\mathbf{R}_{22}^{-1}\mathbf{t}_2 + u_{1\cdot 2}(\mathbf{t}_1, \mathbf{t}_2; \mathbf{R}))\right]^{-(n+\nu)/2}, \qquad \mathbf{t}_1 \in \Re^k,$$

where

$$\mathbf{R}_{11\cdot 2} = \mathbf{R}_{11} - \mathbf{R}_{12}\mathbf{R}_{22}^{-1}\mathbf{R}_{21},$$

$$c(\mathbf{R}, \nu, n, k) = \frac{\Gamma((n+\nu)/2)}{\Gamma((n-k+\nu)/2)(\nu\pi)^{k/2}|\mathbf{R}_{11\cdot 2}|^{1/2}},$$

and

$$u_{1\cdot 2}(\mathbf{t}_1, \mathbf{t}_2; \mathbf{R}) = (\mathbf{t}_1 - \mathbf{R}_{12}\mathbf{R}_{22}^{-1}\mathbf{t}_2)'\mathbf{R}_{11\cdot 2}^{-1}(\mathbf{t}_1 - \mathbf{R}_{12}\mathbf{R}_{22}^{-1}\mathbf{t}_2).$$

Note that as a consequence of Proposition 9.1.4, the marginal distribution of t_i is Student's t with ν degrees of freedom for each $i = 1, \ldots, n$.

Since $h(\mathbf{t}; \mathbf{R}, \nu)$ depends on $\mathbf{t}$ only through the quadratic form $Q(\mathbf{t}, \mathbf{R}) = \mathbf{t}'\mathbf{R}^{-1}\mathbf{t}$, and is a decreasing function of $Q(\mathbf{t}, \mathbf{R})$, for all fixed ν and $\mathbf{R}$, by Proposition 4.2.2 it is A-unimodal. If, in addition, all correlation coefficients are equal to $\rho \in (-1/(n-1), 1)$, then $h(\mathbf{t}; \mathbf{R}, \nu)$ is permutation-symmetric; thus by Proposition 4.4.1 it is a Schur-concave function of $\mathbf{t}$. Summarizing these results we have

Proposition 9.1.5.

(a) *The density function* $h(\mathbf{t}; \mathbf{R}, \nu)$ *given in* (9.1.1) *is* A*-unimodal.*

(b) *If* $\mathbf{R} = (\rho_{ij})$ *is such that*

$$\rho_{ij} = \begin{cases} 1 & \text{for } i = j, \\ \rho & \text{for } i \neq j, \end{cases}$$

where $\rho \in (-1/(n-1), 1)$ *is arbitrary but fixed, then* $h(\mathbf{t}; \mathbf{R}, \nu)$ *is a Schur-concave function of* $\mathbf{t}$.

As a consequence of Proposition 9.1.5 all the results concerning A-unimodal and Schur-concave density functions given in Chapter 4 apply to the multivariate t distribution. This includes results in Propositions 4.2.3, 4.4.3, 7.4.1, 7.4.2, and others.

9.2. Probability Inequalities

In this section we summarize some of the results concerning probability inequalities for the multivariate t distribution. The results are classified into two groups: The dependence-related inequalities and inequalities that can be derived via majorization.

9.2.1. Dependence-Related Inequalities

By the independence of $\mathbf{Z}$ and S, the conditional distribution of $\mathbf{t} = (Z_1/S, \ldots, Z_n/S)'$, given $S = s$, is $\mathcal{N}_n(\mathbf{0}, (1/s)^2\mathbf{R})$. Thus, by conditioning and then unconditioning,

$$Eg(\mathbf{t}) = E\left\{E\left[g\left(\frac{1}{s}\mathbf{Z}\right)\middle| S = s\right]\right\} \tag{9.2.1}$$

holds for all $g\colon \Re^n \to \Re$. In particular, we have

$$P[\mathbf{t} \in A] = EP\left[\left(\frac{1}{s}\mathbf{Z}\right) \in A | S = s\right] \tag{9.2.2}$$

for all $A \subset \Re^n$. This fact can be applied to extend most of the dependence-related inequalities from the multivariate normal distribution to the multivariate t distribution. We summarize some of the results below; the reader is referred to Definitions 5.1.1–5.1.7 for notions of positive dependence.

Proposition 9.2.1. *If $\mathbf{t} = (t_1, \ldots, t_n)' \sim t(\mathbf{R}, \nu)$ where $\mathbf{R} = (\rho_{ij})$ is a correlation matrix, then $P_{\mathbf{R}}[\bigcap_{i=1}^n \{t_i \le a_i\}]$ is an increasing function of ρ_{ij} for all $i \ne j$ while the other correlation coefficients are held fixed.*

PROOF. Immediate from Theorem 5.1.7. □

Proposition 9.2.2. *Assume that $\mathbf{t} \sim t(\mathbf{R}, \nu)$. Then $t_1, \ldots, t_n$ are associated random variables if and only if $\rho_{ij} \ge 0$ for all $i \ne j$.*

PROOF. Although this can be shown independently using (9.2.1) and Theorem 5.1.1, it also follows immediately from a more general result of Joag-Dev, Perlman, and Pitt (1983) for the association of elliptically contoured random variables. □

Let $\mathbf{t}$ and $\mathbf{R}$ be partitioned as in (9.1.3).

Corollary 9.2.1. *Assume that* $\mathbf{t} = (\mathbf{t}^{(1)}, \mathbf{t}^{(2)})' \sim t(\mathbf{R}, \nu)$. *If all of the elements in* $\mathbf{R}_{12}$ *are nonnegative, then*

$$P[\mathbf{t}^{(1)} \in A_1, \mathbf{t}^{(2)} \in A_2] \geq P[\mathbf{t}^{(1)} \in A_1]P[\mathbf{t}^{(2)} \in A_2] \tag{9.2.3}$$

holds for all nondecreasing sets $A_1 \in \mathfrak{R}^k$ *and* $A_2 \in \mathfrak{R}^{n-k}$.

Combining this result with a monotonicity argument (see, e.g., Tong (1980, p. 38), which yields the inequalities on the right-hand sides in (9.2.4) and (9.2.5)), we have

Corollary 9.2.2. *Assume that* $\mathbf{t} \sim t(\mathbf{R}, \nu)$. *If* $\rho_{ij} \geq 0$ *for all* $i \neq j$, *then the inequalities*

$$P\left[\bigcap_{i=1}^{n} \{t_i \leq a_i\}\right] \geq P_{\mathbf{R}=\mathbf{I}_n}\left[\bigcap_{i=1}^{n} \{t_i \leq a_i\}\right] \geq \prod_{i=1}^{n} P[t_i \leq a_i], \tag{9.2.4}$$

$$P\left[\bigcap_{i=1}^{n} \{t_i > a_i\}\right] \geq P_{\mathbf{R}=\mathbf{I}_n}\left[\bigcap_{i=1}^{n} \{t_i > a_i\}\right] \geq \prod_{i=1}^{n} P[t_i > a_i] \tag{9.2.5}$$

hold for all $\mathbf{a} = (\mathbf{a}_1, \ldots, a_n)' \in \mathfrak{R}^n$, *where* $\mathbf{I}_n$ *is the identity matrix.*

Note that the lower bounds on the right-hand side of (9.2.4) and the right-hand side of (9.2.5) can be obtained from Student's t distribution.

Corollary 9.2.2 states that if all the ρ_{ij}'s are nonnegative, then $t_1, \ldots, t_n$ are both PUOD and PLOD. An important result of Šidák (1968) concerns the PLOD property of the random variable $(|t_1|, \ldots, |t_n|)'$ without any conditions on $\mathbf{R}$. Thus, by a similar monotonicity argument, we have

Proposition 9.2.3. *If* $\mathbf{t} \sim t(\mathbf{R}, \nu)$, *then*

$$P\left[\bigcap_{i=1}^{n} \{|t_i| \leq a_i\}\right] \geq P_{\mathbf{R}=\mathbf{I}_n}\left[\bigcap_{i=1}^{n} \{|t_i| \leq a_i\}\right] \geq \prod_{i=1}^{n} P[|t_i| \leq a_i] \tag{9.2.6}$$

holds for all $\mathbf{a}$ *such that* $a_i > 0$ $(i = 1, \ldots, n)$.

The inequality on the left in Proposition 9.2.3 follows immediately by combining (9.2.2) and Corollary 7.2.1, and was generalized to the family of elliptically contoured distributions by Das Gupta, Eaton, Olkin, Perlman, Savage, and Sobel (1972).

Other dependence-related inequalities can be obtained for exchangeable t variables. As discussed in Section 5.3, the notion of exchangeability is equivalent to positive dependence by mixture (Proposition 5.3.2). Therefore an analogy of Theorem 5.3.1 is

Proposition 9.2.4. *Assume that* $\mathbf{t} \sim t(\mathbf{R}, \nu)$. *Then* $t_1, \ldots, t_n$ *are exchangeable random variables (according to Definition 5.3.1) if and only if* $\rho_{ij} = \rho \in [0, 1]$ *for all* $i \neq j$.

PROOF. The proof of this result is easy, and is left to the reader. □

If $t_1, \ldots, t_n$ are exchangeable t variables with a common correlation coefficient ρ and fixed degrees of freedom ν, then partial orderings of their positive dependence can be obtained by the corresponding results for exchangeable normal variables. In particular, it is easy to see that

Proposition 9.2.5. *Assume that* $\mathbf{t} \sim t(\mathbf{R}, \nu)$ *where* $\rho_{ij} = \rho \in [0, 1)$ *for all* $i \neq j$. *Then for all* $\lambda > 0$ *and all real numbers* $c_1, \ldots, c_n$ *such that* $\sum_{i=1}^{n} c_i = 0$, *the probability* $P_\rho[|\sum_{i=1}^{n} c_i t_i| \leq \lambda]$ *is an increasing function of* ρ.

This result is similar to Theorem 5.3.9. A result that is similar to Theorem 5.3.10 is

Proposition 9.2.6. *Assume that* $\mathbf{t} \sim t(\mathbf{R}, \nu)$ *where* $\rho_{ij} = \rho \in [0, 1)$ *for all* $i \neq j$. *Then* $E_\rho \prod_{i=1}^{n} g(t_i)$ *is a nondecreasing function of* ρ *for all* $g: \mathfrak{R} \to \mathfrak{R}$ *when* n *is an even integer, and for all* $g \geq 0$ *when* n *is any positive integer, such that the expectations exist. Consequently,* $P_\rho[\bigcap_{i=1}^{n} \{t_i \in A\}]$ *is a nondecreasing function of* ρ *for all* $A \subset \mathfrak{R}$ *and all* n.

PROOF. The proof follows from (9.2.2) and Theorem 5.3.10. □

9.2.2. Majorization Inequalities

Most of the majorization inequalities for the multivariate normal distribution can be modified for the multivariate t distribution by conditioning on $S = s$ and then unconditioning. The reader is referred to Section 4.4 and Chapter 7 for definitions of majorization and Schur-concave functions and related results concerning the multivariate normal distribution.

The first result, given below, is a dimension-related inequality for exchangeable t variables. Let $\mathbf{t} = (t_1, \ldots, t_n)'$ have an $t(\mathbf{R}, \nu)$ distribution. Let $A \subset \mathfrak{R}$ denote any measurable set and define

$$\gamma(\mathbf{k}) = P\left[\bigcap_{i=1}^{k} \{t_i \in A\}\right], \qquad k = 1, 2, \ldots, n.$$

A result of Tong (1977) implies that

Proposition 9.2.7. *Assume that* $\mathbf{t} \sim t(\mathbf{R}, \nu)$, *and let*

$$\mathbf{k} = (k_1, \ldots, k_r, 0, \ldots, 0)', \qquad \mathbf{k}^* = (k_1^*, \ldots, k_{r^*}^*, 0, \ldots, 0)',$$

be two n-dimensional vectors whose elements are nonnegative integers. If $\mathbf{k} \succ \mathbf{k}^*$ *and* $\rho_{ij} = \rho$ *for all* $i \neq j$ *for some* $\rho \in [0, 1]$, *then*

$$\prod_{j=1}^{r} \gamma(k_j) \geq \prod_{j=1}^{r^*} \gamma(k_j^*). \tag{9.2.7}$$

This result is similar to Theorem 7.3.3. As a special case, we have

Corollary 9.2.3. *Assume that* $\mathbf{t} \sim t(\mathbf{R}, \nu)$. *If* $\rho_{ij} = \rho$ *for all* $i \neq j$ *for some* $\rho \in [0, 1]$, *then the inequalities*

$$P\left[\bigcap_{i=1}^{n} \{t_i \in A\}\right] \geq \left(P\left[\bigcap_{i=1}^{k} \{t_i \in A\}\right]\right)^{n/k}, \tag{9.2.8}$$

$$P\left[\bigcap_{i=1}^{n} \{t_i \in A\}\right] \geq P\left[\bigcap_{i=1}^{k} \{t_i \in A\}\right] P\left[\bigcap_{i=1}^{n-k} \{t_i \in A\}\right] \tag{9.2.9}$$

hold for all $A \subset \Re$ *and all* $1 \leq k < n$.

Tong (1970) proved (9.2.8) and (9.2.9) for the special cases $A = \{x: x \leq a\}$ and $A = \{x: |x| \leq a\}$. Inequalities in (9.2.8) and (9.2.9) were given by Šidák (1973) for an arbitrary $A \subset \Re$.

Probability bounds for the distribution functions of $\mathbf{t}$ and $|\mathbf{t}|$ can be obtained via majorization inequalities when the variables are equally correlated but not necessarily exchangeable. Proposition 9.1.5 asserts that if $\rho_{ij} = \rho$ for all $i \neq j$, then the density function of $\mathbf{t}$ is a Schur-concave function. Thus straightforward applications of Propositions 4.4.3 and 7.4.1 yield

Proposition 9.2.8. *Assume that* $\mathbf{t} \sim t(\mathbf{R}, \nu)$. *If* $\rho_{ij} = \rho$ *for all* $i \neq j$ *for some* $\rho \in (-1/(n-1), 1)$, *then* $P[\bigcap_{i=1}^{n} \{t_i \leq a_i\}]$ *and* $P[\bigcap_{i=1}^{n} \{|t_i| \leq a_i\}]$ *are Schur-concave functions of* $\mathbf{a} = (a_1, \ldots, a_n)'$. *Consequently, we have*

$$P\left[\bigcap_{i=1}^{n} \{t_i \leq a_i\}\right] \leq P\left[\bigcap_{i=1}^{n} \{t_i \leq \bar{a}\}\right], \tag{9.2.10}$$

$$P\left[\bigcap_{i=1}^{n} \{|t_i| \leq a_i\}\right] \leq P\left[\bigcap_{i=1}^{n} \{|t_i| \leq \bar{a}\}\right], \tag{9.2.11}$$

where $\bar{a} = (1/n) \sum_{i=1}^{n} a_i$.

Most of the other majorization inequalities for the multivariate normal distribution given in Chapter 7 also apply to the multivariate t distribution via obvious modifications. For example, results similar to Theorems 7.4.2 and 7.4.3 are

Proposition 9.2.9. *Assume that* $\mathbf{t} \sim t(\mathbf{R}, \nu)$. *If* $\rho_{ij} = \rho$ *for all* $i \neq j$ *for some* $\rho \in [-1/(n-1), 1]$, *then* $P[\sum_{i=1}^{n} (t_i/a_i)^2 \leq \lambda]$ *is a Schur-concave function of* $(a_1^2, \ldots, a_n^2)'$ *for all* $\lambda > 0$.

Proposition 9.2.10. *Assume that* $\mathbf{t} \sim t(\mathbf{R}, \nu)$. *If* $\rho_{ij} = 0$ *for all* $i \neq j$, *then* $P[\sum_{i=1}^{n} (t_i/a_i)^2 \leq \lambda]$ *is a Schur-concave function of* $(\log a_1, \ldots, \log a_n)'$, $a_i > 0$ $(i = 1, \ldots, n)$, *for all* $\lambda > 0$. *Thus we have*

$$P\left[\sum_{i=1}^{n} \left(\frac{t_i}{a_i}\right)^2 \leq \lambda\right] \leq P\left[\sum_{i=1}^{n} t_i^2 \leq \lambda \left(\prod_{i=1}^{n} a_i\right)^{2/n}\right].$$

Other useful results can be obtained by modifying Theorem 7.4.4, Propositions 7.4.4 and 7.4.6, and other related theorems given in Section 7.4. For example, a direct application of Proposition 7.4.4 yields

Proposition 9.2.11. *Assume that* $\mathbf{t} \sim t(\mathbf{R}, \nu)$. *If* $\rho_{ij} = \rho$ *for all* $i \neq j$ *for some* $\rho \in (-1/(n-1), 1)$, *then*

$$P\left[\bigcap_{i=1}^{n} \{a_{1i} \leq t_i \leq a_{2i}\}\right] \leq P\left[\bigcap_{i=1}^{n} \{\bar{a}_1 \leq t_i \leq \bar{a}_2\}\right],$$

where $\bar{a}_j = (1/n)\sum_{i=1}^{n} a_{ji}$ $(j = 1, 2)$.

This result, of course, is a generalization of (9.2.11).

9.3. Convergence to the Multivariate Normal Distribution

In the univariate case, the density function of a Student's t variable converges to that of an $\mathcal{N}(0, 1)$ variable as $\nu \to \infty$. The following result is a multivariate analogy.

Proposition 9.3.1. *Let* $h(\mathbf{t}; \mathbf{R}, \nu)$ *be given as in* (9.1.1). *Let* $f(\mathbf{t}; \mathbf{0}, \mathbf{R})$ *denote the density function of an* $\mathcal{N}_n(\mathbf{0}, \mathbf{R})$ *variable defined in* (3.2.1). *Then*

$$\lim_{\nu \to \infty} h(\mathbf{t}, \mathbf{R}, \nu) = f(\mathbf{t}; \mathbf{0}, \mathbf{R}) \qquad \text{for all} \quad \mathbf{t} \in \Re^n. \tag{9.3.1}$$

PROOF. It is immediate that

$$\left(1 + \frac{1}{\nu}\mathbf{t}'\mathbf{R}^{-1}\mathbf{t}\right)^{-(n+\nu)/2} \to \exp(-\tfrac{1}{2}\mathbf{t}'\mathbf{R}^{-1}\mathbf{t}) \qquad \text{as} \quad \nu \to \infty.$$

Thus it suffices to show that

$$\frac{\Gamma((n+\nu)/2}{(\nu\pi)^{n/2}\Gamma(\nu/2)|\mathbf{R}|^{1/2}} \to \frac{1}{(2\pi)^{n/2}|\mathbf{R}|^{1/2}} \qquad \text{as} \quad \nu \to \infty. \tag{9.3.2}$$

The statement in (9.3.2) is obvious when n is an even integer. If n is odd, then it follows similarly from the fact that

$$\frac{\sqrt{2}\Gamma((\nu+1)/2)}{\sqrt{\nu}\Gamma(\nu/2)} \to 1 \qquad \text{as} \quad \nu \to \infty. \qquad \square$$

A convergence theorem of Scheffé (1947) implies that if $\{f_\nu(\mathbf{t})\}_{\nu=1}^{\infty}$ and $f(\mathbf{t})$ are density functions, that are absolutely continuous with respect to Lebesgue measure, and if $f_\nu(\mathbf{t}) \to f(\mathbf{t})$ pointwise as $\nu \to \infty$, then $\int_A f_\nu(\mathbf{t})\, d\mathbf{t}$ converges to $\int_A f(\mathbf{t})\, d\mathbf{t}$ for all measurable sets $A \subset \Re^n$. Combining this result with Proposition 9.3.1 we immediately have

Corollary 9.3.1. *Let* $\mathbf{t}$ *be the multivariate* t *variable defined in* (9.0.1) *with a positive definite correlation matrix* $\mathbf{R}$ and degrees of freedom v, *and let* $\mathbf{Z}$ *have an* $\mathcal{N}_n(\mathbf{0}, \mathbf{R})$ *distribution. Then*

$$\lim_{v \to \infty} P[\mathbf{t} \in A] = P[\mathbf{Z} \in A] \tag{9.3.3}$$

holds for all Borel-measurable sets $A \subset \Re^n$.

As a special case, we note that (i) $\mathbf{t}$ converges to $\mathbf{Z}$ in distribution and (ii) $|\mathbf{t}| = (|t_1|, \ldots, |t_n|)'$ converges to $|\mathbf{Z}| = (|Z_1|, \ldots, |Z_n|)'$ in distribution as $v \to \infty$.

This convergence-in-distribution result leads to the following result concerning the convergence of percentage points. To describe this result we first note a known fact:

Fact 9.3.1. *Let* $\{F_v(x)\}_{v=1}^{\infty}$ *be a sequence of distribution functions of univariate random variables and let* $F(x)$ *be another distribution function. For arbitrary but fixed* $\gamma \in (0, 1)$ *let*

$$c_{v,\gamma} = \inf_x \{x: F_v(x) \geq \gamma\}, \qquad v = 1, 2, \ldots,$$

denote the sequence of percentage points. If

(i) $F(x)$ *is continuous and strictly increasing in an interval* $[a, b]$ *such that* $F(a) < \gamma < F(b)$; *and*
(ii) $F_v(x) \to F(x)$ *at every continuity point of* $F(x)$ *as* $v \to \infty$,

then $c_{v,\gamma} \to c_\gamma$ *as* $v \to \infty$, *where* $c_\gamma = F^{-1}(\gamma)$ *is the* γ*th percentage point of* $F(x)$.

Now let us consider the equicoordinate percentage points given by

$$P\left[\bigcap_{i=1}^{n} \{t_i \leq c_{v,\gamma}\}\right] = \gamma, \qquad v = 1, 2, \ldots, \tag{9.3.4}$$

$$P\left[\bigcap_{i=1}^{n} \{Z_i \leq c_\gamma\}\right] = \gamma, \tag{9.3.5}$$

where $(t_1, \ldots, t_n)' \sim t(\mathbf{R}, v)$ and $(Z_1, \ldots, Z_n)' \sim \mathcal{N}_n(\mathbf{0}, \mathbf{R})$. Since the left-hand side of (9.3.4) and the left-hand side of (9.3.5) are just the univariate probabilities

$$P\left[\max_{1 \leq i \leq n} t_i \leq c_{v,\gamma}\right] \quad \text{and} \quad P\left[\max_{1 \leq i \leq n} Z_i \leq c_\gamma\right],$$

respectively, we have

Proposition 9.3.2. *Let* $\{c_{v,\gamma}\}_{v=1}^{\infty}$ *and* c_γ *satisfy* (9.3.4) *and* (9.3.5), *respectively, where* $\mathbf{R}$ *is positive definite and* $\gamma \in (0, 1)$ *is arbitrary but fixed. Then*

$$\lim_{v \to \infty} c_{v,\gamma} = c_\gamma. \tag{9.3.6}$$

Similarly, let us consider the equicoordinate percentage points of the distributions of the absolute values of $\mathbf{t}$, and define

$$P\left[\bigcap_{i=1}^{n} \{|t_i| \le c_{\nu,\gamma}^*\}\right] = \gamma, \tag{9.3.7}$$

$$P\left[\bigcap_{i=1}^{n} \{|Z_i| \le c_{\gamma}^*\}\right] = \gamma. \tag{9.3.8}$$

By a similar argument we have

Proposition 9.3.3. *Let* $\{c_{\nu,\gamma}^*\}_{\nu=1}^{\infty}$ *and* c_γ^* *satisfy* (9.3.7) *and* (9.3.8), *respectively, where* $\mathbf{R}$ *is positive definite and* $\gamma \in (0, 1)$ *is arbitrary but fixed. Then*

$$\lim_{\nu\to\infty} c_{\nu,\gamma}^* = c_\gamma^*. \tag{9.3.9}$$

It is known that if $t(\nu)$ is a Student's t variable with ν degrees of freedom, then $P[|t(\nu)| \le \lambda]$, hence $P[t(\nu) \le \lambda]$, is an increasing function of ν for all $\lambda > 0$. Thus for $\gamma > 0.5$ the sequence of percentage points of Student's t distributions is decreasing as ν increases. A reasonable question is whether a similar statement holds for the multivariate t distribution. A result of Dunn (1965) shows that the answer to this question is in the negative at least for the case $\rho_{ij} = 0$ $(i \ne j)$.

Proposition 9.3.4. *Let* $\mathbf{t} \sim t(\mathbf{I}_n, \nu)$ *when* $\mathbf{I}_n$ *is the* $n \times n$ *identity matrix. Then for arbitrary but fixed* $\lambda > 0$ *and* $\nu_1 < \nu_2$ *there exists an* $M = M(\lambda, \nu_1, \nu_2)$ *such that the inequalities*

$$P_{\nu=\nu_1}\left[\bigcap_{i=1}^{n} \{t_i \le \lambda\}\right] > P_{\nu=\nu_2}\left[\bigcap_{i=1}^{n} \{t_i \le \lambda\}\right],$$

$$P_{\nu=\nu_1}\left[\bigcap_{i=1}^{n} \{|t_i| \le \lambda\}\right] > P_{\nu=\nu_2}\left[\bigcap_{i=1}^{n} \{|t_i| \le \lambda\}\right]$$

hold for all $n > M$.

Her proof depends on a property of the density function of a chi variable with ν degrees of freedom. For details, see Dunn (1965).

9.4. Tables for Exchangeable t Variables

If $t_1, \ldots, t_n$ are exchangeable t variables, i.e., if $\mathbf{t} = (t_1, \ldots, t_n)' \sim t(\mathbf{R}, \nu)$ such that $\rho_{ij} = \rho \ge 0$ for all $i \ne j$, then, by (9.0.1) and Theorem 5.3.1, $\mathbf{t}$ and

$$\left(\frac{\sqrt{1-\rho}\,Z_1 + \sqrt{\rho}\,Z_0}{S}, \ldots, \frac{\sqrt{1-\rho}\,Z_n + \sqrt{\rho}\,Z_0}{S}\right)'$$

are identically distributed, where $Z_0, Z_1, \ldots, Z_n$ are i.i.d. $\mathcal{N}(0, 1)$ variables and νS^2 has a $\chi^2(\nu)$ distribution and is independent of $(Z_0, Z_1, \ldots, Z_n)'$. Consequently, we can write

$$\begin{aligned}
\gamma_1(\nu, a) &\equiv P\left[\bigcap_{i=1}^{n} \{t_i \le a\}\right] \\
&= EP\left[\bigcap_{i=1}^{n} \left\{Z_i \le \frac{as - \sqrt{\rho} Z_0}{\sqrt{1-\rho}}\right\} \middle| S = s\right] \\
&= E\left[E \prod_{i=1}^{n} P\left[Z_i \le \frac{as - \sqrt{\rho} z}{\sqrt{1-\rho}} \middle| (S, Z_0)' = (s, z)'\right] \middle| S = s\right] \\
&= \int_0^\infty \left[\int_{-\infty}^{\infty} \Phi^n\left(\frac{as + \sqrt{\rho} z}{\sqrt{1-\rho}}\right) \phi(z)\, dz\right] \psi_\nu(s)\, ds, \qquad (9.4.1)
\end{aligned}$$

where ϕ and Φ are the $\mathcal{N}(0, 1)$ density function and distribution function, respectively, and ψ_ν is the density function of S. Similarly, we have

$$\begin{aligned}
\gamma_2(\nu, a) &\equiv P\left[\bigcap_{i=1}^{n} \{|t_i| \le a\}\right] \\
&= \int_0^\infty \left[\int_{-\infty}^{\infty} \left[\Phi\left(\frac{as + \sqrt{\rho} z}{\sqrt{1-\rho}}\right) - \Phi\left(\frac{-as + \sqrt{\rho} z}{\sqrt{1-\rho}}\right)\right]^n \phi(z)\, dz\right] \psi_\nu(s)\, ds. \qquad (9.4.2)
\end{aligned}$$

A change of variable in the integrals yields

$$\gamma_1(\nu, a) = \int_0^\infty \left[\int_{-\infty}^{\infty} g_1(u, w) e^{-u^2}\, du\right] e^{-w}\, dw, \qquad (9.4.3)$$

$$\gamma_2(\nu, a) = \int_0^\infty \left[\int_{-\infty}^{\infty} g_2(u, w) e^{-u^2}\, du\right] e^{-w}\, dw, \qquad (9.4.4)$$

where

$$g_1(u, w) = \frac{1}{\sqrt{\pi}\, \Gamma(\nu/2)} \Phi^n\left(\sqrt{\frac{2\rho}{1-\rho}} u + a \sqrt{\frac{2w}{\nu(1-\rho)}}\right) w^{\nu/2-1},$$

$$g_2(u, w) = \frac{1}{\sqrt{\pi}\, \Gamma(\nu/2)} \left[\Phi\left(\sqrt{\frac{2\rho}{1-\rho}} u + a \sqrt{\frac{2w}{\nu(1-\rho)}}\right) - \Phi\left(\sqrt{\frac{2\rho}{1-\rho}} u - a \sqrt{\frac{2w}{\nu(1-\rho)}}\right)\right]^n w^{\nu/2-1}.$$

The numerical values of $\gamma_1(\nu, a)$ and $\gamma_2(\nu, a)$ can be approximated using existing methods. For example, Stroud and Secrest (1966) contains values of (d_i, u_i) $(i = 1, \ldots, N)$ and (b_j, w_j) $(j = 1, \ldots, M)$ such that, when g is well behaved,

$$\int_{-\infty}^{\infty} g(u, w) e^{-u^2}\, du \doteq \sum_{i=1}^{N} d_i g(u_i, w)$$

and

$$\int_{-\infty}^{\infty} g(w)e^{-w}\,dw \doteq \sum_{j=1}^{M} b_j g(w_j)$$

hold. Thus a method for approximating $\gamma_1(v, a)$ and $\gamma_2(v, a)$ is to approximate the integrals in (9.4.3) and (9.4.4) by evaluating the sum of NM terms. The percentage points can be computed similarly.

Tables of one-sided and two-sided equicoordinate percentage points for exchangeable t variables have been computed, using this and other related methods, by Dunnett and Sobel (1954), Pillai and Ramachandran (1954), Dunnett (1955), Halperin, Greenhouse, Cornfield, and Zalokar (1955), Krishnaiah and Armitage (1966), Dunn, Kronmal, and Yee (1968), Hahn and Hendrickson (1971), and others (for additional references, see Johnson and Kotz (1972, Chap. 37)). Recently Tong (1986) and Bechhofer and Dunnett (1988) gave more detailed tables. Tong's (1986) tables also include one-sided and two-sided probability integrals.

It should be noted that although the tables are given only for exchangeable t variables with equal coordinates, the results given in Section 9.2 extend the domain of the usefulness of the tables. For illustration we consider the following examples. The table values used here are taken from Tong (1986).

EXAMPLE 9.4.1. Suppose that $n = 8$, $v = 30$, and the elements of $\mathbf{R}$ are such that $\max_{i<j} \rho_{ij} \leq 0.3$. If $a = 2.0$, then by Proposition 9.2.1 we have

$$P_{\mathbf{R}}\left[\bigcap_{i=1}^{8} \{t_i \leq 2.0\}\right] \leq P_{\rho_{ij}=0.3}\left[\bigcap_{i=1}^{8} \{t_i \leq 2.0\}\right] = 0.84230. \qquad \square$$

EXAMPLE 9.4.2. Suppose that $n = 8$, $v = 30$, and the values of ρ_{ij} are unknown. Then by Proposition 9.2.3

$$P_{\mathbf{R}}\left[\bigcap_{i=1}^{8} \{|t_i| \leq 2.0\}\right] \geq P_{\rho_{ij}=0}\left[\bigcap_{i=1}^{8} \{|t_i| \leq 2.0\}\right] = 0.65708$$

holds no matter what the true values of ρ_{ij}'s are. □

EXAMPLE 9.4.3. Suppose that $n = 30$, $v = 18$, $a = 2.0$, and $\rho_{ij} = 0.3$ for all $i \neq j$. Since the true value of $\gamma_1(18, 2.0)$ is not tabulated for $n = 30$ but is tabulated for $n = 20$ in Tong (1986), by (9.2.8) we have

$$0.59229 = (0.70527)^{30/20} < P\left[\bigcap_{i=1}^{30} \{t_i \leq 2.0\}\right]$$

$$< P\left[\bigcap_{i=1}^{20} \{t_i \leq 2.0\}\right] = 0.70527.$$

A similar example can be given for $|\mathbf{t}|$ and for other values of n and ρ. □

EXAMPLE 9.4.4. Suppose that $n = 3$, $v = 20$, and $\rho_{ij} = 0.5$ for all $i \neq j$. In a given application if we are interested in the true value of

$$P[t_1 \leq 2.2, t_2 \leq 1.8, t_3 \leq 2.0],$$

which is not tabulated, then by (9.2.10) this probability is bounded above by $P[\bigcap_{i=1}^{3}\{t_i \le 2.0\}]$, which is 0.92831. A similar example can also be given for $|\mathbf{t}|$. □

These examples, of course, are very similar to those given in Section 8.4 concerning the multivariate normal tables. Additional examples of applications can be given using the results in Section 9.2; the details are left to the reader.

Problems

9.1. Show that the confidence probabilities γ_1, γ_2 of the confidence regions A_1, A_2 defined in (9.0.5) and (9.0.6) are those given in (9.0.7) and (9.0.8), respectively.

9.2. Show that if νS^2 has a $\chi^2(\nu)$ distribution, then $ES^{-2} = \nu/(\nu - 2)$ for $\nu \ge 3$.

9.3. Simplify the result concerning the marginal distribution and conditional distribution of a multivariate t variable when $\mathbf{R} = (\rho_{ij})$ is such that $\rho_{ij} = \rho \in (-1/(n-1), 1)$ for all $i \ne j$.

9.4. It is known that if $f(\mathbf{z})$ is a Schur-concave function of $\mathbf{z} \in \Re^n$, then $\int_0^\infty f(u\mathbf{z})\, dH(u)$ is a Schur-concave function of $\mathbf{z} \in \Re^n$ where $H(u)$ is the distribution function of a nonnegative random variable. Use this result to show directly that the multivariate t density function with common correlation coefficient is Schur-concave.

9.5. Give a direct proof for Proposition 9.2.2.

9.6. Let $\mathbf{t} = (t_1, \ldots, t_n)' \sim t(\mathbf{R}, \nu)$ such that $\rho_{ij} = \rho \ge 0$ for all $i \ne j$. Show that $\mathrm{Corr}_\rho(g(t_i), g(t_j))$ is a nondecreasing function of ρ for all $g\colon \Re \to \Re$ such that the expectations exist.

9.7. Find a direct proof for the inequality in (9.2.8) without using Proposition 9.2.7. (*Hint*: See proof of Theorem 7.3.1.)

9.8. Assuming that (9.2.8) holds, prove the inequality in (9.2.9).

9.9. Use the result in Theorem 7.4.2 to find a direct proof for Proposition 9.2.9.

9.10. Verify (9.3.2).

9.11. It is known that if $F(x)$ is a continuous distribution function of x for $x \in \Re$ and if $F_\nu(x) \to F(x)$ pointwise as $\nu \to \infty$, then the convergence is uniform in x. Use this result to show that

$$P\left[\bigcap_{i=1}^{n}\{t_i \le a\}\right] \to P\left[\bigcap_{i=1}^{n}\{Z_i \le a\}\right] \quad \text{uniformly in } a,$$

$$P\left[\bigcap_{i=1}^{n}\{|t_i| \le a\}\right] \to P\left[\bigcap_{i=1}^{n}\{|Z_i| \le a\}\right] \quad \text{uniformly in } a$$

as $\nu \to \infty$, where $\mathbf{t} \sim t(\mathbf{R}, \nu)$ and $\mathbf{Z}$ has an $\mathcal{N}_n(\mathbf{0}, \mathbf{R})$ distribution.

9.12. Let $\mathbf{t} \sim t(\mathbf{R}, \nu)$ where $\rho_{ij} = \rho \ge 0$ for all $i \ne j$. Find the function $g(u, w)$ such that

$$P\left[\bigcap_{i=1}^{n}\{t_i \le a_i\}\right] = \int_0^\infty \left[\int_{-\infty}^{\infty} g(u, w)e^{-u^2}\, du\right] e^{-w}\, dw.$$

9.13. (Continuation.) Find the function $g(u, w)$ such that

$$P\left[\bigcap_{i=1}^{n} \{|t_i| \leq a_i\}\right] = \int_0^{\infty} \left[\int_{-\infty}^{\infty} g(u, w)e^{-u^2}\, du\right] e^{-w}\, dw.$$

9.14. Prove a convexity result that is similar to Fact 8.4.1 for the multivariate t distribution.

9.15. Let $\mathbf{t} \sim t(\mathbf{R}, v)$ where $n = 25$, $v = 30$, and $\rho_{ij} = 0.2$ for all $i \neq j$. Given $P[\bigcap_{i=1}^{20} \{|t_i| \leq 2.2\}] = 0.57180$, find the numerical values of the upper and lower bounds for $P[\bigcap_{i=1}^{25} \{|t_i| \leq 2.2\}]$.

References

Abbe, E.N. (1964). Experimental comparison of Monte Carlo sampling techniques to evaluate the multivariate normal integral. *Technical Research Note, No. 28*, U.S. Army Behavioral Science Research Laboratory, Alexandria, VA.

Abdel-Hameed, M. and Sampson, A.R. (1978). Positive dependence of the bivariate and trivariate absolute normal, t, χ^2 and F distributions. *Ann. Statist.*, **6**, 1360–1368.

Abrahamson, I.G. (1964). Orthant probabilities for the quadrivariate normal distribution. *Ann. Math. Statist.*, **35**, 1685–1703.

Aitken, A.C. (unpublished work on the tetrachoric series).

Anderson, T.W. (1955). The integral of a symmetric unimodal function over a symmetric convex set and some probability inequalities. *Proc. Amer. Math. Soc.*, **6**, 170–176.

Anderson, T.W. (1984). *An Introduction to Multivariate Statistical Analysis*, 2nd ed. Wiley, New York.

Anderson, T.W. (1988). Personal communication.

Anderson, T.W. and Fang, K.T. (1984). Cochran's theorem for elliptically contoured distributions. *Proc. China–Japan Symp. Statist.*, Beijing University Press, Beijing, China, pp. 4–7. Also published in full in *Sankhyā, A*, **49** (1987), 305–315.

Anderson, T.W., Fang, K.T., and Hsu, H. (1986). Maximum likelihood estimates and likelihood-ratio criteria for multivariance elliptically contoured distributions. *Canad. J. Statist.*, **14**, 55–59.

Anderson, T.W., Olkin, I., and Underhill, L.G. (1987). Generation of random orthogonal matrices. *SIAM J. Sci. Statist. Comput.*, **8**, 625–629.

Anderson, T.W. and Styan, G.P.H. (1982). Cochran's theorem, rank additivity and tripotent matrices. In *Statistics and Probability: Essays in Honor of C.R. Rao*, G. Kallianpur, P.R. Krishnaiah, and J.K. Ghosh, eds. North-Holland, Amsterdam and New York, pp. 1–23.

Arnold, B.C. and Groeneveld, R.A. (1979). Bounds on expectations of linear systematic statistics based on dependent samples. *Ann. Statist.*, **7**, 220–223.

Bacon, R.H. (1963). Approximations to multivariate normal orthant probabilities. *Ann. Math. Statist.*, **34**, 191–198.

Barlow, R.E. and Proschan, F. (1975). *Statistical Theory of Reliability and Life Testing.* Holt, Rinehart and Winston, New York.

Bechhofer, R.E. (1954). A single-stage multiple decision procedure for ranking means of normal populations with known variances. *Ann. Math. Statist.*, **25**, 16–39.

Bechhofer, R.E. and Dunnett, C.W. (1988). Percentage points of multivariate Student's t distributions. In *Selected Tables in Mathematical Statistics*, Vol. 11, Institute of Mathematical Statistics, ed. American Mathematical Society, Providence, RI, pp. 1–343.

Bechhofer, R.E., Kiefer, J., and Sobel, M. (1968). *Sequential Identification and Ranking Procedures.* University of Chicago Press, Chicago, IL.

Beckenbach, E.F. and Bellman, R. (1965). *Inequalities.* Springer-Verlag, Berlin and New York.

Bickel, P.J. (1967). Some contributions to the theory of order statistics. *Proc. Fifth Berkeley Symp. Math. Statist. Probab.*, Vol. 1, L.M. LeCam and J. Neyman, eds. University of California Press, Berkeley, CA, pp. 575–591.

Birnbaum, Z.W. (1948). On random variables with comparable peakedness. *Ann. Math. Statist.*, **19**, 76–81.

Block, H.W., Sampson, A.R., and Savits, T.H., eds. (1989). *Topics in Statistical Dependence.* To be published by the Institute of Mathematical Statistics, Hayward, CA.

Boland, P.J. (1985). Integrating Schur-concave densities on rectangles. Unpublished manuscript.

Boland P.J. and Proschan, F. (1988). Multivariate arrangement increasing functions with applications in probability and statistics. *J. Multivariate Anal.*, **25**, 286–298.

Boland, P.J., Proschan, F., and Tong, Y.L. (1988). Moment and geometric probability inequalities arising from arrangement increasing functions. *Ann. Probab.*, **16**, 407–413.

Bølviken, E. (1982). Probability inequalities for the multivariate normal with non-negative partial correlations. *Scand. J. Statist.*, **9**, 49–58.

Bølviken, E. and Jogdev, K. (1982). Monotonicity of the probability of a rectangular region under a multivariate normal distribution. *Scand. J. Statist.*, **9**, 171–174.

Bose, R.C. and Roy, S.N. (1938). The exact distribution of Studentized D^2-statistic. *Sankhyā*, **4**, 10–38.

Bowker, A.H. (1960). A representation of Hotelling's T^2 and Anderson's classification statistic W in terms of simple statistics. In *Contributions to Probability and Statistics: Essays in Honor of Harold Hotelling*, I. Olkin, S.G. Ghurye, W. Hoeffding, W.G. Madow, and H.B. Mann, eds. Stanford University Press, Stanford, CA, pp. 142–149.

Box, G.E.P. and Muller, M.E. (1958). A note on the generation of random normal deviates. *Ann. Math. Statist.*, **29**, 610–611.

Cadwell, J.H. (1951). The bivariate normal integral. *Biometrika*, **38**, 475–481.

Cambanis, S., Huang, S., and Simons, G. (1981). On the theory of elliptically contoured distributions. *J. Multivariate Anal.*, **11**, 368–385.

Craig, A.T. (1943). Note on the independence of certain quadratic forms. *Ann. Math. Statist.*, **14**, 195–197.

Curnow, R.N. and Dunnett, C.W. (1962). The numerical evaluation of certain multivariate normal integrals. *Ann. Math. Statist.*, **33**, 571–579.

Das, S.C. (1956). The numerical evaluation of a class of integrals, II. *Proc. Cambridge Philos. Soc.*, **52**, 442–448.

Das Gupta, S., Eaton, M.L., Olkin, I., Perlman, M.D., Savage, L.J., and Sobel, M. (1972). Inequalities on the probability content of convex regions for elliptically contoured distributions. *Proc. Sixth Berkeley Symp. Math. Statist. Probab.*, Vol. 2, L.M. LeCam, J. Neyman, and E.L. Scott, eds. University of California Press, Berkeley, CA, pp. 241–265.

Das Gupta, S. and Rattihalli, R.N. (1984). Probability content of a rectangle under normal distribution: Some inequalities. *Sankhyā, A*, **46**, 454–457.

David, F.N. (1938). *Tables of the Ordinates and Probability Integral of the Distribution of the Correlation Coefficient in Small Samples*, Cambridge University Press, Cambridge, England.

David, F.N. (1953). A note on the evaluation of the multivariate normal integral. *Biometrika*, **40**, 458–459.

David, H.A. (1981). *Order Statistics*, 2nd ed. Wiley, New York.

David, H.A. (1986). Inequalities for ordered sums. *Ann. Inst. Statist. Math., A*, **38**, 551–555.

David, H.A. (1988). General bounds and inequalities in order statistics. *Commun. Statist.—Theory Meth.*, **17**, 2119–2134.

David, H.A., Kennedy, W.J., and Knight, R.D. (1977). Means, variances, and covariances of normal order statistics in the presence of an outlier. In *Selected Tables in Mathematical Statistics*, Vol. 5, Institute of Mathematical Statistics, ed. American Mathematical Society, Providence, RI, pp. 75–204.

Deak, I. (1978). Monte Carlo evaluation of the multidimensional normal distribution function by the ellipsoid method. *Probl. Contr. Infor. Theory*, **7**, 203–212.

Deak, I. (1979). The ellipsoid method for generating normally distributed random vectors. *Zastosowania Mat.*, **17**, 95–107.

Deak, I. (1980). Fast procedures for generating stationary normal vectors. *J. Statist. Comput. Simul.*, **16**, 225–242.

Dharmadhikari, S.W. and Joag-Dev, K. (1984). Regions whose probabilities increase with the correlation coefficient and Slepian's theorem. In *Inequalities in Statistics and Probability*, Y.L. Tong, ed. Institute of Mathematical Statistics, Hayward, CA, pp. 156–164.

Dharmadhikari, S.W. and Joag-Dev, K. (1988). *Unimodality, Convexity and Applications*. Academic Press, New York.

Dharmadhikari, S.W. and Jogdeo, K. (1976). Multivariate unimodality. *Ann. Statist.*, **4**, 607–613.

Diaconis, P. (1976). Unpublished manuscript.

Dunn, O.J. (1958). Estimation of the means of dependent variables. *Ann. Math. Statist.*, **29**, 1095–1111.

Dunn, O.J. (1965). A property of the multivariate t distribution. *Ann. Math. Statist.*, **36**, 712–714.

Dunn, O.J., Kronmal, R.A., and Yee, W.J. (1968). Tables of the multivariate t distribution. *Technical Report*, School of Public Health, UCLA, Los Angeles, CA.

Dunnett, C.W. (1955). A multiple comparison procedure for comparing several treatments with a control. *J. Amer. Statist. Assoc.*, **50**, 1096–1121.

Dunnett, C.W. (1964). New tables for multiple comparisons with a control. *Biometrics*, **20**, 482–491.

Dunnett, C.W. and Sobel, M. (1954). A bivariate generalization of Student's t distribution with tables for certain special cases. *Biometrika*, **41**, 153–169.

Dunnett. C.W. and Sobel, M. (1955). Approximations to the probability integral and certain percentage points of a multivariate analogue of Student's t-distribution. *Biometrika*, **42**, 258–260.

Dykstra, R.L. (1970). Establishing the positive definiteness of the sample covariance matrix. *Ann. Math. Statist.*, **41**, 2153–2154.

Dykstra, R.L., Hewett, J.E., and Thompson, W.A. (1973). Events which are almost independent. *Ann. Statist.*, **1**, 674–681.

Eaton, M.L. (1987). *Lectures on Topics in Probability Inequalities.* Centre for Mathematics and Computer Science, Amsterdam, The Netherlands.

Edgeworth, F.Y. (1892). Correlated averages. *Philos. Mag., Ser.* 5, **34**, 190–204.

Esary, J.D., Proschan, F., and Walkup, D.W. (1967). Association of random variables, with applications. *Ann. Math. Statist.*, **38**, 1466–1474.

Fahmy, S. and Proschan, F. (1981). Bounds on differences of order statistics. *Amer. Statist.*, **35**, 46–47.

Fan, K. (1958). Topological proofs for certain theorems on matrices with non-negative elements. *Monatsh. Math.*, **62**, 219–237.

Fang, K.T. (1988). Personal communication.

Fang, K.T. and Liang, J.J. (1989). Inequalities for partial sums of normal and elliptical order statistics and implications in genetic selection. To appear in *Canad. J. Statist.*

Fang, K.T. and Zhang, Y.T. (1988). *Generalized Multivariate Analysis.* Science Press, Beijing and Springer-Verlag, Berlin and New York.

Feller, W. (1957). *An Introduction to Probability Theory and Its Applications*, 2nd ed. Wiley, New York.

Fisher, R.A. (1915). Frequency distribution of the values of the correlation coefficient in samples from an indefinitely large population. *Biometrika*, **10**, 507–521.

Fisher, R.A. (1924). The distribution of the partial correlation coefficient. *Metron*, **3**, 329–332.

Fisher, R.A. (1928). The general sampling distribution of the multiple correlation coefficient. *Proc. Roy. Soc. London, A*, **121**, 654–673.

Fortuin, C.M., Kastelyn, P.W., and Ginibre, J. (1971). Correlation inequalities on some partially ordered sets. *Commun. Math. Phys.*, **22**, 89–103.

Galton, F. (1888). Co-relations and their measurement, chiefly from anthropometric data. *Proc. Roy. Soc. London*, **45**, 135–145.

Genz, A. and Kahaner, D.K. (1986). The numerical evaluation of certain multivariate normal integrals. *J. Comput. Appl. Math.*, **16**, 255–258.

Gibbons, J.D., Olkin, I., and Sobel, M. (1977). *Selecting and Ordering Populations: A New Statistical Methodology.* Wiley, New York.

Graybill, F.A. (1976). *Theory and Application of the Linear Model.* Duxbury Press, North Scituate, MA.

Gupta, S.S. (1963a). Probability integrals of multivariate normal and multivariate t. *Ann. Math. Statist.*, **34**, 792–828.

Gupta, S.S. (1963b). Bibliography on the multivariate normal integrals and related topics. *Ann. Math. Statist.*, **34**, 829–838.

Gupta, S.S., Nagel, K., and Panchapakesan, S. (1973). On the order statistics from equally correlated normal random variables. *Biometrika*, **60**, 403–413.

Gutmann, S. (1978). Correlations of functions of normal variables. *J. Multivariate Anal.*, **8**, 573–578.

Hahn, G.J. and Hendrickson, R.W. (1971). A table of percentage points of the distribution of the largest absolute value of k Student variates and its applications. *Biometrika*, **58**, 323–332.

Halperin, M., Greenhouse, S.W., Cornfield, J., and Zalokar, J. (1955). Tables of percentage points for the studentized maximum absolute deviate in normal samples. *J. Amer. Statist. Assoc.*, **50**, 185–195.

Hammersley, J.M. and Handscomb, D.C. (1964). *Monte Carlo Methods.* Methuen, London.

Hardy, G.H., Littlewood, J.E., and Pólya, G. (1934, 1952). *Inequalities.* 1st and 2nd eds. Cambridge University Press, Cambridge, England.

Harris, B. and Soms, A.P. (1980). The use of the tetrachoric series for evaluating multivariate normal probabilities. *J. Multivariate Anal.*, **10**, 252–267.
Harter, H.L. (1961). Expected values of normal order statistics. *Biometrika*, **48**, 151–165. Erratum, *Biometrika*, **48**, 476.
Hartley, H.O. and David, H.A. (1954). Universal bounds for mean range and extreme observation. *Ann. Math. Statist.*, **25**, 85–89.
Henery, R.J. (1981). An approximation to certain multivariate normal probabilities. *J. Roy. Statist. Soc.*, *B*, **43**, 81–85.
Hill, W.G. (1976). Order statistics of correlated variables and implications in genetic selection. *Biometrics*, **32**, 889–902.
Hollander, M., Proschan, F., and Sethuraman, J. (1977). Functions decreasing in transposition and their applications in ranking problems. *Ann. Statist.*, **5**, 722–733.
Hotelling, H. (1931). The generalization of Student's ratio. *Ann. Math. Statist.*, **2**, 360–378.
Hotelling, H. (1933). Analysis of a complex of statistical variables into principal components. *J. Educ. Psych.*, **24**, 417–441, 498–520.
Hotelling, H. (1936). Relations between two sets of variates. *Biometrika*, **28**, 321–377.
Hotelling, H. (1953). New light on the correlation coefficient and its transforms. *J. Roy. Statist. Soc.*, *B*, **15**, 193–225.
Hsu, P.L. (1938), Notes on Hotelling's generalized T^2. *Ann. Math. Statist.*, **9**, 231–243.
Hsu, P.L. (1939). On the distribution of the roots of certain determinantal equations. *Ann. Eugen.*, **9**, 250–258.

Ihm, P. (1959). Numerical evaluation of certain multivariate normal integrals. *Sankhyā*, **21**, 363–366.
Iyanaga, S. and Kawada, Y., eds. (1980). *Encyclopedic Dictionary of Mathematics.* MIT Press, Cambridge, MA and Mathematical Society of Japan.
Iyengar, S. (1982). On the evaluation of certain multivariate normal probabilities. *Technical Report, No.* 322, Department of Statistics, Stanford University, Stanford, CA.
Iyengar, S. (1986). On a lower bound for the multivariate normal Mills' ratio. *Ann. Probab.*, **14**, 1399–1403.
Iyengar, S. (1988). Evaluation of normal probabilities of symmetric regions. *SIAM J. Sci. Statist. Comput.*, **9**, 418–423.
Iyengar, S. and Tong, Y.L. (1989). Convexity properties of elliptically contoured distributions with applications. *Sankhyā*, *A*, **51**, 13–29.

Joag-Dev, K., Perlman, M.D., and Pitt, L.D. (1983). Association of normal random variables and Slepian's inequality. *Ann. Probab.*, **11**, 451–455.
Joag-Dev, K. and Proschan, F. (1983). Negative association of random variables. *Ann. Statist.*, **11**, 286–296.
Jogdev, K. (1977). Association and probability inequalities. *Ann. Statist.*, **5**, 495–504.
John, S. (1959). On the evaluation of the probability integral of a multivariate normal distribution. *Sankhyā*, **21**, 367–370.
John, S. (1966). On the evaluation of probabilities of convex polyhedra under multivariate normal and *t*-distributions. *J. Roy. Statist. Soc.*, *B*, **28**, 366–369.
Johnson, M.E. (1987). *Multivariate Statistical Simulation.* Wiley, New York.
Johnson, N.L. and Kotz, S. (1972). *Distributions in Statistics: Continuous Multivariate Distributions.* Wiley, New York.

Kagan, A.M., Linnik, Y.V., and Rao, C.R. (1973, translated by B. Ramachandran). *Characterization Problems in Mathematical Statistics.* Wiley, New York.

Karlin, S. (1968). *Total Positivity*, Vol. 1. Stanford University Press, Stanford, CA.

Karlin, S. (1983). Personal communication.

Karlin, S. and Rinott, Y. (1980a). Classes of orderings of measures and related correlation inequalities. I. Multivariate totally positive distributions. *J. Multivariate Anal.*, **10**, 467–498.

Karlin, S. and Rinott, Y. (1980b). Classes of orderings of measures and related correlation inequalities II. Multivariate reverse rule distributions. *J. Multivariate Anal.*, **10**, 499–516.

Karlin, S. and Rinott, Y. (1981). Total positivity properties of absolute value multinormal variables with applications to confidence interval estimates and related probabilistic inequalities. *Ann. Statist.*, **9**, 1035–1049.

Karlin, S. and Rinott, Y. (1983a). *M*-Matrices and covariance matrices of multinormal distributions. *Linear Algebra Appl.*, **52/53**, 419–438.

Karlin, S. and Rinott, Y. (1983b). Comparison of measures, multivariate majorization, and applications to statistics. In *Studies in Econometrics, Time Series and Multivariate Analysis*, S. Karlin, T. Amemiya, and L.A. Goodman, eds. Academic Press, New York, pp. 465–489.

Karlin, S. and Studden, W.J. (1966). *Tchebycheff Systems: With Applications in Analysis and Statistics.* Interscience, New York.

Kelker, D. (1970). Distribution theory of spherical distribution and a location-scale parameter generalization. *Sankhyā, A.*, **32**, 419–430.

Kemperman, J.H.B. (1977). On the FKG-inequality for measures on a partially ordered space. *Indag. Math.*, **39**, 313–331.

Kendall, M.G. (1941). Proof of relations connected with tetrachoric series and its generalization. *Biometrika*, **32**, 196–198.

Kennedy, W.J. and Gentle, J.E. (1980). *Statistical Computing.* Dekker, New York.

Khatri, C.G. and Mukerjee, R. (1987). Characterization of normality within the class of elliptical contoured distributions. *Statist. Probab. Letters*, **5**, 187–190. Erratum, **7**, 265.

Kibble, W.F. (1945). An extension of a theorem of Mehler on Hermite polynomials, *Proc. Cambridge Philos. Soc.*, **41**, 12–15.

Kimeldorf, G. and Sampson, A.R. (1987). Positive dependence orderings. *Ann. Inst. Statist. Math., A*, **39**, 113–118.

Kinderman, A.J. and Ramage, J.G. (1976). Computer generation of normal random variables. *J. Amer. Statst. Assoc.*, **71**, 893–896.

Krishnaiah, P.R. and Armitage, P.V. (1966). Tables for multivariate *t* distribution. *Sankhyā, B*, **28**, 31–56.

Kunte, S. and Rattihalli, R.N. (1984). Rectangular regions of maximum probability content. *Ann. Statist.*, **12**, 1106–1108.

Lehmann, E.L. (1966). Some concepts of dependence. *Ann. Math. Statist.*, **37**, 1137–1153.

Lehmann, E.L. (1986). *Testing Statistical Hypotheses*, 2nd ed. Wiley, New York.

Liang, J.J. (1987). *On a Probability Problem in Animal Genetic Selection.* M.S. Thesis, Institute of Mathematics, Nankai University, Tianjin, China.

Loève, M. (1963). *Probability Theory*, 3rd ed. D. Van Nostrand Co., Princeton, NJ.

Mahalanobis, P.C., Bose, R.C., and Roy, S.N. (1937). Normalization of statistical variates and the use of rectangular coordinates in the theory of sampling distribution. *Sankhyā*, **3**, 1–40.

Marsaglia, G. (1963). Expressing the normal distribution with covariance matrix $\mathbf{A} + \mathbf{B}$ in terms of one with covariance matrix $\mathbf{A}$. *Biometrika*, **50**, 535–538.

Marsaglia, G. (1964). Generating a variable from the tail of the normal distribution. *Technometrics*, **6**, 101–102.

Marsaglia, G. and Bray, T.A. (1964). A convenient method for generating normal random variables. *SIAM Review*, **6**, 260–264.
Marsaglia, G., MacLaren, M.D., and Bray, T.A. (1964). A fast procedure for generating normal random variables. *Commun. Assoc. Comput. Mach.*, **7**, 4–10.
Marsaglia, G. and Olkin, I. (1984). Generating correlation matrices. *SIAM J. Sci. Statist. Comput.*, **5**, 470–475.
Marsaglia, G. and Tsang, W.W. (1984). A fast, easily implemented method for sampling from decreasing or symmetric unimodal density functions. *SIAM J. Sci. Statist. Comput.*, **5**, 349–359.
Marshall, A.W. and Olkin, I. (1974). Majorization in multivariate distributions. *Ann. Statist.*, **2**, 1189–1200.
Marshall, A.W. and Olkin, I. (1979). *Inequalities: Theory of Majorization and Its Applications*. Academic Press, New York.
Martynov, G.V. (1981). Evaluation of the normal distribution function. *J. Soviet Math.*, **17**, 1857–1875.
McFadden, J.A. (1956). An approximation for the symmetric, quadrivariate normal integral. *Biometrika*, **43**, 206–207.
McFadden, J.A. (1960). Two expansions for the quadrivariate normal integral. *Biometrika*, **47**, 325–333.
Mehler, F.G. (1866). Über die Entwicklung einer Funktion von beliebig vielen Variablen nach Laplace'schen Funktionen höherer Ordnung. *J. Reine Angewandte Math.*, **66**, 161–176.
Mendell, N.L. and Elston, R.C. (1974). Multifactorial traits: Genetic analysis and prediction of recurrence risks. *Biometrics*, **30**, 41–57.
Milton, R.C. (1963). Tables of the equally correlated normal probability integral. *Technical Report, No.* 27, Department of Statistics, University of Minnesota, Minneapolis, MN.
Milton, R.C. (1972). Computer evaluation of the multivariate normal integral. *Technometrics*, **14**, 881–889.
Mitrinović, D.S. (1970). *Analytic Inequalities*. Springer-Verlag, Berlin and New York.
Moran, P.A.P. (1948). Rank correlation and product moment correlation. *Biometrika*, **35**, 203–206.
Moran, P.A.P. (1956). The numerical evaluation of a class of integrals. *Proc. Cambridge Philos. Soc.*, **52**, 230–233.
Moran, P.A.P. (1984). The Monte Carlo evaluation of orthant probabilities for multivariate normal distributions. *Austral. J. Statist.*, **26**, 39–44.

National Bureau of Standards (1959). *Tables of the Bivariate Normal Distribution Function and Related Functions*. Applied Mathematics Series, No. 50, U.S. Department of Commerce, Washington, DC.

Odeh, R.E. (1982). Tables of percentage points of the distribution of the maximum absolute value of equally correlated normal random variables. *Commun. Statist. Simula. Comp.*, **11**, 65–87.
Ogawa, J. (1949). On the independence of bilinear and quadratic forms of random sample from a normal population. *Ann. Inst. Statist. Math.*, **1**, 83–108.
Okamoto, M. (1960). An inequality for the weighted sum of χ^2 variates. *Bull. Math. Statist.*, **9**, 69–70.
Olkin, I. and Roy, S.N. (1954). On multivariate distribution theory. *Ann. Math. Statist.*, **25**, 329–339.
Olkin, I., Sobel, M., and Tong, Y.L. (1982). Bounds for a k-fold integral for location and scale parameter models with applications to statistical ranking and selection problems. In *Statistical Decision Theory and Related Topics III*, Vol. 2. S.S. Gupta and J.O. Berger, eds. Academic Press, New York, pp. 193–212.

Olkin, I. and Tong, Y.L. (1988). Peakedness in multivariate distributions. In *Statistical Decision Theory and Related Topics, IV*, Vol. 2. S.S. Gupta and J.O. Berger, eds. Springer-Verlag, Berlin and New York, pp. 373–383.

Owen, D.B. (1956). Tables for computing bivariate normal probabilities. *Ann Math. Statist.*, **27**, 1075–1090.

Owen, D.B. and Steck, G.P. (1962). Moments of order statistics from the equicorrelated multivariate normal distribution. *Ann. Math. Statist.*, **33**, 1286–1291.

Pearson, E.S. and Hartley, H.O. (1970). *Biometrika Tables for Statisticians*, Vol. **1**, 3rd ed. Cambridge University Press, Cambridge, England.

Pearson, E.S. and Kendall, M.G., eds. (1970). *Studies in the History of Statistics and Probability*. Griffin, London.

Pearson, K. (1896). Mathematical contributions to the theory of evolution.—III. Regression, heredity and panmixia. *Philos. Trans. Roy. Soc. London, A*, **187**, 253–318.

Pearson, K. (1901). Mathematical contributions to the theory of evolution.—VII. On the correlation of characters not quantitatively measurable. *Philos. Trans. Roy. Soc. London, A*, **195**, 1–47.

Pearson, K. (1920). Notes on the history of correlation. *Biometrika*, **13**, 25–45.

Perlman, M.D. and Olkin, I., (1980). Unbiasedness of invariant tests for MANOVA and other multivariate problems. *Ann. Statist.*, **8**, 1326–1341.

Pillai, K.C.S. and Ramachandran, K.V. (1954). On the distribution of the ith observation in an ordered sample from a normal population to an independent estimate of the standard deviation. *Ann. Math. Statist.*, **25**, 565–572.

Pitt, L.D. (1982). Positively correlated normal variables are associated. *Ann. Probab.*, **10**, 496–499.

Plackett, R.L. (1954). A reduction formula for normal multivariate integrals. *Biometrika*, **41**, 351–360.

Pólya, G. (1967). Inequalities and the principle of nonsufficient reason. In *Inequalities*. O. Shisha, ed. Academic Press, New York, pp. 1–15.

Prékopa, A. (1971). Logarithmic concave measures with applications. *Acta Sci. Math.*, **32**, 302–316.

Proschan, F. (1965). Peakedness of distributions of convex combinations. *Ann. Math. Statist.*, **36**, 1703–1706.

RAND Corporation (1955). *A Million Random Digits with* 100,000 *Normal Deviates*. The Free Press, Glencoe, IL.

Rao, C.R. (1973). *Linear Statistical Inference and Its Applications*, 2nd ed. Wiley, New York.

Rawlings, J.O. (1976). Order statistics for a special case of unequally correlated multinormal variates. *Biometrics*, **32**, 875–887.

Rice, J., Reich, T., and Cloninger, C.R. (1979). An approximation to the multivariate normal integral: Its application to multifactorial qualitative traits. *Biometrics*, **35**, 451–459.

Rinott, Y. and Pollak, M. (1980). A stochastic ordering induced by a concept of positive dependence and monotonicity of asymptotic test sizes. *Ann. Statist.*, **8**, 190–198.

Rinott, Y. and Santner, T.J. (1977). An inequality for multivariate normal probabilities with application to a design problem. *Ann. Statist.*, **5**, 1228–1234.

Ruben, H. (1954). On the moments of order statistics in samples from normal populations. *Biometrika*, **41**, 200–227.

Ruben, H. (1961). On the numerical evaluation of a class of multivariate normal integrals. *Proc. Roy. Soc. Edinburgh*, **65**, 272–281.

Ruben, H. (1962). An asymptotic expansion for a class of multivariate normal integrals. *J. Austral. Math. Soc.*, **2**, 253–264.

Ruben, H. (1964). An asymptotic expansion for the multivariate normal distribution and Mills' ratio. *J. Res. Nat. Bureau Standards—B*, **68B**, 3–11.

Samuelson, P.A. (1968). How deviant can you be? *J. Amer. Statist. Assoc.*, **63**, 1522–1525.

Sarhan, A.E. and Greenberg, B.G., eds. (1962). *Contributions to Order Statistics*. Wiley, New York.

Savage, I.R. (1957). Contributions to the theory of rank order statistics—the "trend" case. *Ann. Math. Statist.*, **28**, 968–977.

Savage, I.R. (1962). Mills' ratio for multivariate normal distributions. *J. Res. Nat. Bureau Standards—B*, **66B**, 93–96.

Scheffé, H. (1947). A useful convergence theorem for probability distributions. *Ann. Math. Statist.*, **18**, 434–438.

Scheffé, H. (1959). *The Analysis of Variance*. Wiley, New York.

Seal, H.L. (1967). The historical development of the Gauss linear model. *Biometrika*, **54**, 1–24.

Shaked, M. (1977). A concept of positive dependence for exchangeable random variables. *Ann. Statist.*, **5**, 505–515.

Shaked, M. (1982). A general theory of some positive dependence notions. *J. Multivariate Anal.*, **12**, 199–218.

Shaked, M. and Tong, Y.L. (1983, 1988). Inequalities for probability contents of convex sets via geometric average. *Technical Report* (1983). Revised version published in *J. Multivariate Anal.*, **24** (1988), 330–340.

Shaked, M. and Tong, Y.L. (1985). Some partial orderings of exchangeable random variables by positive dependence. *J. Multivariate Anal.*, **17**, 339–349.

Sherman, S. (1955). A theorem on convex sets with applications. *Ann. Math. Statist.*, **26**, 763–766.

Shisha, O., ed. (1967, 1970, 1972). *Inequalities, Inequalities II, III*. Academic Press, New York.

Šidák, Z. (1968). On multivariate normal probabilities of rectangles: Their dependence on the correlations. *Ann. Math. Statist.*, **39**, 1425–1434.

Šidák, Z. (1973). A chain of inequalities for some types of multivariate distributions with nine special cases. *Apl. Mat.*, **18**, 110–118.

Slepian, D. (1962). The one-sided barrier problem for Gaussian noise. *Bell System Tech. J.*, **41**, 463–501.

Smith, N.L. and Tong, Y.L. (1983). Inequalities for functions of order statistics under an additive model. *Ann. Inst. Statist. Math.*, *A*, **35**, 255–265.

Sobel, M. (1954). On a generalization of an inequality of Hardy, Littlewood and Pólya. *Proc. Amer. Math. Soc.*, **5**, 596–602.

Steck, G.P. (1958). A table for computing trivariate normal probabilities. *Ann. Math. Statist.*, **29**, 780–800.

Steck, G.P. (1962). Orthant probabilities for the equicorrelated multivariate normal distribution. *Biometrika*, **49**, 433–445.

Steck, G.P. (1979). Lower bounds for the multivariate normal Mills' ratio. *Ann. Probab.*, **7**, 547–551.

Steck, G.P. and Owen, D.B. (1962). A note on the equicorrelated multivariate normal distribution. *Biometrika*, **49**, 269–271.

Steffens, F.E. (1969). Critical values for bivariate Student t-tests. *J. Amer. Statist. Assoc.*, **64**, 637–646.

Stigler, S. (1986). *The History of Statistics: The Measurement of Uncertainty Before* 1900. Harvard University Press, Cambridge, MA.

Stroud, A.H. and Secrest, D. (1966). *Gaussian Quadrature Formulas*. Prentice-Hall, Englewood Cliffs, NJ.

Stuart, A. (1958). Equally correlated variates and the multinormal integral. *J. Roy. Statist. Soc. B*, **20**, 373–378.

Tamhankar, M.V. (1967). A characterization of normality. *Ann. Math. Statist.*, **38**, 1924–1927.

Teichroew, D. (1956). Tables of expected values of order statistics and products of order statistics for samples of size twenty and less from the normal distribution. *Ann. Math. Statist.*, **27**, 410–426.

Thisted, R.A. (1988). *Elements of Statistical Computing.* Chapman and Hall, London and New York.

Thomson, G.W. (1955). Bounds for the ratio of range in standard deviation. *Biometrika*, **42**, 268–269.

Tietjen, G.L., Kahaner, D.K., and Beckman, R.J. (1977). Variances and covariances of the normal order statistics for sample sizes 2 to 50. In *Selected Tables in Mathematical Statistics,* Vol. 5. Institute of Mathematical Statistics, ed. American Mathematical Society, Providence, RI, pp. 1–74.

Tong, Y.L. (1969). On partitioning a set of normal populations by their locations with respect to a control. *Ann. Math. Statist.*, **40**, 1300–1324,

Tong, Y.L. (1970). Some probability inequalities of multivariate normal and multivariate *t*. *J. Amer. Statist. Assoc.*, **65**, 1243–1247.

Tong, Y.L. (1977). An ordering theorem for conditionally independent and identically distributed random variables. *Ann. Statist.*, **5**, 274–277.

Tong, Y.L. (1978). An adaptive solution to ranking and selection problems. *Ann. Statist.*, **6**, 658–672.

Tong, Y.L. (1980). *Probability Inequalities in Multivariate Distributions.* Academic Press, New York.

Tong, Y.L. (1982a). Rectangular and elliptical probability inequalties for Schur-concave random variables. *Ann. Statist.*, **10**, 637–642.

Tong, Y.L. (1982b). Some applications of inequalities for extreme order statistics to a genetic selection problem. *Biometrics*, **38**, 333–339.

Tong, Y.L. (1983, 1989). Probability inequalities for *n*-dimensional rectangles via multivariate majorization. *Technical Report, No.* 189 (1983), Department of Statistics, Stanford University, Stanford, CA. Revised version in *Contributions to Probability and Statistics*: *Essays in Honor of Ingram Olkin*, L.J. Gleser, M.D. Perlman, S.J. Press, and A.R. Sampson, eds. Springer-Verlag, New York and Berlin, pp. 146–159.

Tong, Y.L., ed. (1984) (with the cooperation of I. Olkin, M.D. Perlman, F. Proschan and C.R. Rao). *Inequalities in Statistics and Probability.* The Institute of Mathematical Statistics, Hayward, CA.

Tong, Y.L. (1986). Tables of the multivariate *t* distribution. *Technical Report*, School of Mathematics, Georgia Institute of Technology, Atlanta, GA.

Tong, Y.L. (1988). Some majorization inequalities in multivariate statistical analysis. *SIAM Review*, **30**, 602–622.

Tong, Y.L. (1989). Inequalities for a class of positively dependent random variables with a common marginal. *Ann. Statist.*, **17**, 429–435.

Veinott, A.F. (1965). Optimal policy in a dynamic, single product, nonstationary model with several demand classes. *Operations Research*, **13**, 761–778.

Wishart, J. (1928). The generalized product moment distribution in samples from a normal multivariate population. *Biometrika*, **20A**, 32–52.

Walkowicz, H. and Styan, G.P.H. (1979). Extensions of Samuelson's inequality. *Amer. Statist.*, **33**, 143–144.

Yule, G.U. (1897a). On the significance of Bravais' formulae for regression in the case of skew correlation. *Proc. Roy. Soc. London*, **60**, 477–489.

Yule, G.U. (1897b). On the theory of correlation. *J. Roy. Statist. Soc.*, **60**, 812–854.

APPENDIX

Tables

In this appendix we give tables of equicoordinate one-sided and two-sided percentage points and probability integrals of the multivariate normal distribution with means 0, variances 1, and correlation coefficients $\rho \geq 0$. The tables are classified into four groups and are listed below:

(a) Table A. One-Sided Percentage Points
The table contains values of c satisfying

$$P\left[\bigcap_{i=1}^{n} \{X_i \leq c\}\right] = \gamma$$

for $n = 2(1)20$, $\rho = 0.0(0.1)0.9, \frac{1}{3}, \frac{2}{3}, \frac{1}{4}$, and $\frac{3}{4}$, and $\gamma = 0.90, 0.95, 0.99$; where $(X_1, \ldots, X_n)'$ has an $\mathcal{N}_n(\mathbf{0}, \boldsymbol{\Sigma})$ distribution with variances 1 and correlation coefficients ρ.

(b) Table B. Two-Sided Percentage Points
The table contains values of c satisfying

$$P\left[\bigcap_{i=1}^{n} \{|X_i| \leq c\}\right] = \gamma$$

for the same set of n, ρ, and γ values described in (a).

(c) Table C-J ($J = 0, 1, \ldots, 13$). One-Sided Probability Integral
The tables contain values of $P[\bigcap_{i=1}^{n} \{X_i \leq a\}]$ for $n = 2(1)10(2)20$, $a = -2.0(0.1)4.0$, and $\rho = 0.0, 0.1(0.1)0.9$ ($J = 0, 1, \ldots, 9$), $\frac{1}{3}, \frac{2}{3}, \frac{1}{4}$, and $\frac{3}{4}$ ($J = 10, 11, 12, 13$).

(d) Table D-J ($J = 0,1, \ldots, 13$). Two-Sided Probability Integral
The tables contain values of $P[\bigcap_{i=1}^{n} \{|X_i| \leq a\}]$ for $a = 0.1(0.1)5.0$ and for the same set of n, ρ values described in (c).

Table A. One-Sided Percentage Points

$\gamma = 0.90$

n \ ρ	0.0	0.1	0.2	0.3	0.4	0.5	0.6	0.7	0.8	0.9	1/3	2/3	1/4	3/4
2	1.6322	1.6258	1.6175	1.6069	1.5936	1.5770	1.5560	1.5291	1.4931	1.4397	1.6028	1.5389	1.6125	1.5126
3	1.8183	1.8089	1.7964	1.7801	1.7595	1.7335	1.7008	1.6589	1.6031	1.5209	1.7738	1.6741	1.7888	1.6332
4	1.9432	1.9320	1.9167	1.8965	1.8707	1.8383	1.7974	1.7452	1.6759	1.5744	1.8886	1.7641	1.9072	1.7132
5	2.0365	2.0240	2.0065	1.9834	1.9537	1.9162	1.8691	1.8091	1.7296	1.6137	1.9742	1.8308	1.9957	1.7724
6	2.1105	2.0970	2.0779	2.0523	2.0194	1.9779	1.9258	1.8595	1.7719	1.6446	2.0422	1.8835	2.0659	1.8191
7	2.1717	2.1574	2.1368	2.1092	2.0737	2.0288	1.9725	1.9009	1.8066	1.6699	2.0983	1.9268	2.1240	1.8574
8	2.2237	2.2087	2.1869	2.1576	2.1197	2.0719	2.0120	1.9360	1.8359	1.6912	2.1460	1.9634	2.1733	1.8897
9	2.2689	2.2533	2.2304	2.1995	2.1596	2.1092	2.0462	1.9662	1.8613	1.7096	2.1873	1.9951	2.2160	1.9177
10	2.3087	2.2926	2.2688	2.2365	2.1948	2.1421	2.0762	1.9929	1.8835	1.7257	2.2237	2.0230	2.2538	1.9423
11	2.3443	2.3277	2.3031	2.2695	2.2261	2.1714	2.1030	2.0166	1.9033	1.7401	2.2562	2.0478	2.2875	1.9642
12	2.3764	2.3594	2.3340	2.2993	2.2544	2.1979	2.1272	2.0379	1.9211	1.7530	2.2856	2.0702	2.3179	1.9838
13	2.4056	2.3883	2.3622	2.3265	2.2802	2.2219	2.1491	2.0573	1.9372	1.7647	2.3123	2.0905	2.3456	2.0017
14	2.4325	2.4148	2.3880	2.3513	2.3038	2.2439	2.1692	2.0751	1.9520	1.7754	2.3367	2.1091	2.3710	2.0181
15	2.4573	2.4393	2.4119	2.3743	2.3256	2.2643	2.1878	2.0914	1.9656	1.7853	2.3593	2.1262	2.3944	2.0332
16	2.4803	2.4620	2.4340	2.3956	2.3458	2.2831	2.2049	2.1066	1.9782	1.7944	2.3803	2.1421	2.4162	2.0471
17	2.5018	2.4832	2.4547	2.4155	2.3646	2.3006	2.2209	2.1207	1.9900	1.8029	2.3998	2.1568	2.4365	2.0601
18	2.5219	2.5031	2.4741	2.4341	2.3822	2.3170	2.2359	2.1339	2.0009	1.8108	2.4181	2.1707	2.4555	2.0723
19	2.5408	2.5217	2.4922	2.4515	2.3988	2.3325	2.2500	2.1463	2.0112	1.8183	2.4353	2.1836	2.4733	2.0837
20	2.5586	2.5393	2.5094	2.4680	2.4144	2.3470	2.2632	2.1579	2.0209	1.8253	2.4515	2.1959	2.4902	2.0944

$\gamma = 0.95$

n \ ρ	0.0	0.1	0.2	0.3	0.4	0.5	0.6	0.7	0.8	0.9	1/3	2/3	1/4	3/4
2	1.9545	1.9508	1.9456	1.9385	1.9289	1.9163	1.8997	1.8773	1.8460	1.7976	1.9356	1.8855	1.9423	1.8631
3	2.1212	2.1158	2.1080	2.0969	2.0820	2.0621	2.0358	2.0005	1.9516	1.8767	2.0924	2.0135	2.1029	1.9783
4	2.2340	2.2276	2.2180	2.2042	2.1854	2.1603	2.1272	2.0830	2.0219	1.9289	2.1985	2.0992	2.2116	2.0551
5	2.3187	2.3116	2.3006	2.2847	2.2629	2.2338	2.1954	2.1443	2.0740	1.9674	2.2782	2.1630	2.2933	2.1122
6	2.3862	2.3785	2.3664	2.3488	2.3246	2.2922	2.2495	2.1928	2.1150	1.9977	2.3415	2.2136	2.3584	2.1572
7	2.4421	2.4340	2.4210	2.4019	2.3756	2.3404	2.2941	2.2327	2.1488	2.0225	2.3940	2.2552	2.4123	2.1943
8	2.4898	2.4813	2.4675	2.4472	2.4190	2.3814	2.3320	2.2666	2.1773	2.0434	2.4387	2.2905	2.4582	2.2257
9	2.5312	2.5224	2.5079	2.4865	2.4568	2.4170	2.3648	2.2959	2.2020	2.0615	2.4776	2.3211	2.4982	2.2529
10	2.5679	2.5587	2.5437	2.5212	2.4900	2.4484	2.3937	2.3217	2.2237	2.0774	2.5119	2.3480	2.5334	2.2768
11	2.6007	2.5913	2.5756	2.5523	2.5198	2.4764	2.4195	2.3447	2.2431	2.0915	2.5425	2.3720	2.5650	2.2981
12	2.6303	2.6207	2.6046	2.5804	2.5467	2.5017	2.4428	2.3654	2.2605	2.1042	2.5703	2.3937	2.5935	2.3173
13	2.6574	2.6475	2.6309	2.6059	2.5711	2.5247	2.4640	2.3843	2.2763	2.1157	2.5955	2.4134	2.6196	2.3347
14	2.6822	2.6722	2.6551	2.6294	2.5936	2.5458	2.4834	2.4015	2.2908	2.1263	2.6187	2.4314	2.6434	2.3507
15	2.7051	2.6950	2.6775	2.6511	2.6144	2.5653	2.5013	2.4174	2.3041	2.1360	2.6401	2.4480	2.6655	2.3654
16	2.7265	2.7161	2.6983	2.6713	2.6336	2.5834	2.5179	2.4322	2.3164	2.1450	2.6600	2.4635	2.6860	2.3790
17	2.7464	2.7359	2.7177	2.6901	2.6516	2.6003	2.5334	2.4459	2.3280	2.1533	2.6785	2.4778	2.7052	2.3917
18	2.7651	2.7544	2.7359	2.7077	2.6684	2.6161	2.5479	2.4588	2.3387	2.1611	2.6959	2.4913	2.7231	2.4036
19	2.7826	2.7719	2.7530	2.7243	2.6842	2.6309	2.5615	2.4709	2.3488	2.1685	2.7123	2.5039	2.7400	2.4148
20	2.7992	2.7883	2.7691	2.7399	2.6991	2.6449	2.5743	2.4822	2.3583	2.1754	2.7277	2.5158	2.7559	2.4253

$\gamma = 0.99$

n \ ρ	0.0	0.1	0.2	0.3	0.4	0.5	0.6	0.7	0.8	0.9	1/3	2/3	1/4	3/4
2	2.5750	2.5739	2.5722	2.5692	2.5647	2.5578	2.5476	2.5324	2.5091	2.4694	2.5679	2.5382	2.5709	2.5221
3	2.7119	2.7105	2.7078	2.7032	2.6959	2.6849	2.6684	2.6440	2.6068	2.5444	2.7011	2.6532	2.7058	2.6274
4	2.8058	2.8041	2.8008	2.7950	2.7857	2.7716	2.7505	2.7194	2.6724	2.5943	2.7924	2.7312	2.7983	2.6985
5	2.8769	2.8750	2.8712	2.8645	2.8536	2.8370	2.8123	2.7759	2.7213	2.6313	2.8614	2.7896	2.8683	2.7515
6	2.9339	2.9318	2.9277	2.9202	2.9080	2.8893	2.8615	2.8209	2.7600	2.6604	2.9167	2.8362	2.9244	2.7937
7	2.9814	2.9792	2.9747	2.9666	2.9532	2.9327	2.9024	2.8580	2.7920	2.6844	2.9628	2.8747	2.9712	2.8285
8	3.0220	3.0197	3.0149	3.0062	2.9919	2.9698	2.9372	2.8897	2.8191	2.7046	3.0022	2.9075	3.0112	2.8581
9	3.0575	3.0551	3.0501	3.0408	3.0256	3.0021	2.9674	2.9171	2.8426	2.7222	3.0365	2.9360	3.0461	2.8837
10	3.0889	3.0864	3.0812	3.0715	3.0554	3.0306	2.9942	2.9413	2.8633	2.7376	3.0669	2.9612	3.0770	2.9063
11	3.1171	3.1146	3.1091	3.0990	3.0821	3.0562	3.0181	2.9630	2.8818	2.7513	3.0942	2.9836	3.1048	2.9265
12	3.1426	3.1401	3.1344	3.1239	3.1063	3.0793	3.0397	2.9825	2.8984	2.7636	3.1189	3.0039	3.1299	2.9447
13	3.1660	3.1634	3.1575	3.1466	3.1284	3.1004	3.0594	3.0003	2.9136	2.7748	3.1415	3.0224	3.1529	2.9613
14	3.1875	3.1848	3.1788	3.1675	3.1487	3.1198	3.0775	3.0166	2.9274	2.7851	3.1622	3.0394	3.1740	2.9765
15	3.2074	3.2046	3.1985	3.1869	3.1675	3.1377	3.0942	3.0316	2.9402	2.7946	3.1814	3.0551	3.1935	2.9905
16	3.2259	3.2231	3.2168	3.2049	3.1850	3.1544	3.1097	3.0456	2.9521	2.8033	3.1993	3.0696	3.2117	3.0035
17	3.2432	3.2404	3.2340	3.2218	3.2013	3.1699	3.1242	3.0587	2.9632	2.8115	3.2160	3.0832	3.2287	3.0157
18	3.2594	3.2566	3.2501	3.2376	3.2166	3.1845	3.1377	3.0709	2.9735	2.8191	3.2316	3.0959	3.2447	3.0270
19	3.2747	3.2718	3.2652	3.2524	3.2310	3.1982	3.1505	3.0823	2.9832	2.8263	3.2464	3.1078	3.2597	3.0377
20	3.2892	3.2863	3.2795	3.2665	3.2446	3.2112	3.1625	3.0931	2.9924	2.8330	3.2603	3.1191	3.2739	3.0477

Table B. Two-Sided Percentage Points

$\gamma = 0.90$

n \ ρ	0.0	0.1	0.2	0.3	0.4	0.5	0.6	0.7	0.8	0.9	1/3	2/3	1/4	3/4
2	1.9488	1.9476	1.9440	1.9378	1.9287	1.9163	1.8997	1.8773	1.8460	1.7976	1.9351	1.8855	1.9412	1.8631
3	2.1141	2.1121	2.1062	2.0962	2.0818	2.0620	2.0358	2.0005	1.9516	1.8767	2.0919	2.0135	2.1017	1.9783
4	2.2263	2.2237	2.2162	2.2035	2.1852	2.1603	2.1272	2.0830	2.0219	1.9289	2.1981	2.0992	2.2106	2.0551
5	2.3107	2.3077	2.2989	2.2841	2.2627	2.2338	2.1954	2.1443	2.0740	1.9674	2.2777	2.1630	2.2923	2.1122
6	2.3780	2.3747	2.3648	2.3483	2.3244	2.2922	2.2495	2.1928	2.1150	1.9977	2.3412	2.2136	2.3574	2.1572
7	2.4339	2.4302	2.4195	2.4014	2.3755	2.3404	2.2941	2.2327	2.1488	2.0225	2.3937	2.2552	2.4114	2.1943
8	2.4815	2.4776	2.4660	2.4467	2.4189	2.3814	2.3320	2.2666	2.1773	2.0434	2.4384	2.2905	2.4574	2.2257
9	2.5229	2.5188	2.5065	2.4861	2.4566	2.4170	2.3648	2.2959	2.2020	2.0615	2.4773	2.3211	2.4974	2.2529
10	2.5596	2.5552	2.5423	2.5208	2.4899	2.4484	2.3937	2.3217	2.2237	2.0774	2.5116	2.3480	2.5327	2.2768
11	2.5923	2.5878	2.5743	2.5519	2.5197	2.4764	2.4195	2.3447	2.2431	2.0915	2.5423	2.3720	2.5643	2.2981
12	2.6220	2.6173	2.6033	2.5800	2.5466	2.5017	2.4428	2.3654	2.2605	2.1042	2.5700	2.3937	2.5928	2.3173
13	2.6490	2.6441	2.6297	2.6056	2.5711	2.5247	2.4640	2.3843	2.2763	2.1157	2.5953	2.4134	2.6189	2.3347
14	2.6739	2.6688	2.6539	2.6291	2.5935	2.5458	2.4834	2.4015	2.2908	2.1263	2.6185	2.4314	2.6428	2.3507
15	2.6969	2.6917	2.6763	2.6508	2.6143	2.5653	2.5013	2.4174	2.3041	2.1360	2.6399	2.4480	2.6649	2.3654
16	2.7182	2.7129	2.6972	2.6710	2.6335	2.5834	2.5179	2.4322	2.3164	2.1450	2.6598	2.4635	2.6854	2.3790
17	2.7382	2.7327	2.7166	2.6898	2.6515	2.6003	2.5334	2.4459	2.3280	2.1533	2.6784	2.4778	2.7046	2.3917
18	2.7568	2.7512	2.7348	2.7074	2.6683	2.6161	2.5479	2.4588	2.3387	2.1611	2.6957	2.4913	2.7225	2.4036
19	2.7744	2.7687	2.7519	2.7240	2.6842	2.6309	2.5615	2.4709	2.3488	2.1685	2.7121	2.5039	2.7394	2.4148
20	2.7910	2.7852	2.7681	2.7396	2.6991	2.6449	2.5743	2.4822	2.3583	2.1754	2.7275	2.5158	2.7553	2.4253

$\gamma = 0.95$

n \ ρ	0.0	0.1	0.2	0.3	0.4	0.5	0.6	0.7	0.8	0.9	1/3	2/3	1/4	3/4
2	2.2365	2.2356	2.2330	2.2285	2.2217	2.2121	2.1987	2.1799	2.1524	2.1081	2.2265	2.1869	2.2310	2.1676
3	2.3877	2.3864	2.3823	2.3751	2.3643	2.3490	2.3276	2.2976	2.2543	2.1853	2.3720	2.3088	2.3791	2.2781
4	2.4909	2.4892	2.4841	2.4750	2.4613	2.4418	2.4146	2.3768	2.3224	2.2365	2.4710	2.3909	2.4801	2.3523
5	2.5688	2.5668	2.5608	2.5502	2.5343	2.5115	2.4798	2.4359	2.3730	2.2743	2.5456	2.4522	2.5561	2.4075
6	2.6310	2.6289	2.6222	2.6104	2.5925	2.5670	2.5317	2.4827	2.4130	2.3040	2.6052	2.5009	2.6170	2.4512
7	2.6828	2.6804	2.6732	2.6603	2.6408	2.6130	2.5745	2.5214	2.4460	2.3284	2.6546	2.5411	2.6675	2.4872
8	2.7270	2.7245	2.7167	2.7029	2.6820	2.6522	2.6110	2.5542	2.4739	2.3491	2.6968	2.5752	2.7106	2.5178
9	2.7655	2.7629	2.7546	2.7400	2.7178	2.6862	2.6426	2.5827	2.4980	2.3669	2.7336	2.6049	2.7482	2.5442
10	2.7996	2.7968	2.7882	2.7729	2.7495	2.7163	2.6705	2.6077	2.5192	2.3825	2.7660	2.6310	2.7814	2.5676
11	2.8302	2.8273	2.8183	2.8022	2.7778	2.7432	2.6955	2.6301	2.5382	2.3965	2.7951	2.6543	2.8112	2.5883
12	2.8578	2.8548	2.8455	2.8288	2.8035	2.7675	2.7180	2.6503	2.5552	2.4090	2.8214	2.6753	2.8381	2.6071
13	2.8831	2.8800	2.8703	2.8531	2.8268	2.7896	2.7385	2.6686	2.5707	2.4203	2.8454	2.6944	2.8627	2.6241
14	2.9063	2.9031	2.8932	2.8754	2.8483	2.8099	2.7573	2.6855	2.5849	2.4307	2.8675	2.7120	2.8853	2.6397
15	2.9278	2.9245	2.9143	2.8960	2.8682	2.8287	2.7746	2.7010	2.5980	2.4403	2.8879	2.7282	2.9062	2.6541
16	2.9478	2.9444	2.9339	2.9152	2.8866	2.8461	2.7907	2.7154	2.6102	2.4492	2.9068	2.7432	2.9257	2.6675
17	2.9664	2.9630	2.9523	2.9331	2.9038	2.8624	2.8058	2.7288	2.6215	2.4574	2.9245	2.7572	2.9438	2.6799
18	2.9839	2.9804	2.9695	2.9498	2.9199	2.8776	2.8198	2.7414	2.6320	2.4652	2.9411	2.7703	2.9608	2.6916
19	3.0004	2.9968	2.9857	2.9656	2.9351	2.8920	2.8331	2.7532	2.6419	2.4724	2.9567	2.7826	2.9768	2.7025
20	3.0160	3.0123	3.0010	2.9805	2.9494	2.9055	2.8455	2.7643	2.6513	2.4792	2.9715	2.7942	2.9920	2.7128

$\gamma = 0.99$

n \ ρ	0.0	0.1	0.2	0.3	0.4	0.5	0.6	0.7	0.8	0.9	1/3	2/3	1/4	3/4
2	2.8062	2.8059	2.8049	2.8029	2.7996	2.7943	2.7859	2.7730	2.7522	2.7154	2.8020	2.7780	2.8040	2.7639
3	2.9342	2.9337	2.9321	2.9290	2.9237	2.9150	2.9014	2.8804	2.8470	2.7890	2.9275	2.8885	2.9308	2.8657
4	3.0222	3.0216	3.0197	3.0157	3.0089	2.9977	2.9803	2.9533	2.9110	2.8380	3.0138	2.9636	3.0180	2.9347
5	3.0890	3.0884	3.0861	3.0816	3.0735	3.0603	3.0397	3.0081	2.9587	2.8744	3.0793	3.0202	3.0842	2.9863
6	3.1428	3.1420	3.1395	3.1344	3.1253	3.1105	3.0873	3.0518	2.9966	2.9032	3.1319	3.0653	3.1374	3.0274
7	3.1876	3.1868	3.1841	3.1785	3.1685	3.1522	3.1268	3.0880	3.0279	2.9268	3.1758	3.1027	3.1817	3.0614
8	3.2260	3.2251	3.2223	3.2163	3.2055	3.1879	3.1604	3.1188	3.0545	2.9468	3.2133	3.1346	3.2197	3.0903
9	3.2595	3.2586	3.2556	3.2492	3.2378	3.2190	3.1898	3.1455	3.0776	2.9641	3.2461	3.1623	3.2529	3.1153
10	3.2893	3.2883	3.2852	3.2784	3.2663	3.2465	3.2157	3.1691	3.0979	2.9794	3.2751	3.1868	3.2824	3.1375
11	3.3160	3.3150	3.3117	3.3047	3.2920	3.2711	3.2389	3.1903	3.1160	2.9929	3.3012	3.2087	3.3088	3.1572
12	3.3402	3.3392	3.3358	3.3285	3.3152	3.2935	3.2599	3.2093	3.1324	3.0051	3.3248	3.2285	3.3327	3.1751
13	3.3624	3.3614	3.3578	3.3502	3.3365	3.3139	3.2790	3.2267	3.1473	3.0162	3.3464	3.2466	3.3546	3.1913
14	3.3828	3.3817	3.3781	3.3702	3.3560	3.3326	3.2966	3.2427	3.1609	3.0264	3.3663	3.2631	3.3748	3.2063
15	3.4017	3.4006	3.3969	3.3888	3.3741	3.3500	3.3129	3.2574	3.1735	3.0357	3.3847	3.2784	3.3935	3.2200
16	3.4192	3.4182	3.4143	3.4060	3.3909	3.3661	3.3280	3.2711	3.1852	3.0444	3.4019	3.2927	3.4109	3.2328
17	3.4357	3.4346	3.4307	3.4222	3.4066	3.3812	3.3421	3.2839	3.1961	3.0525	3.4179	3.3059	3.4271	3.2447
18	3.4512	3.4500	3.4460	3.4373	3.4214	3.3953	3.3553	3.2959	3.2063	3.0600	3.4329	3.3183	3.4424	3.2559
19	3.4657	3.4646	3.4605	3.4516	3.4353	3.4086	3.3678	3.3071	3.2159	3.0671	3.4471	3.3300	3.4568	3.2663
20	3.4795	3.4783	3.4742	3.4650	3.4484	3.4212	3.3795	3.3177	3.2249	3.0738	3.4605	3.3411	3.4704	3.2762

Table C-0. One-Sided Probability Integral, $\rho = 0.0$

a \ n	2	3	4	5	6	7	8	9	10	12	14	16	18	20
-2.0	.00052	.00001	.00000	.00000	.00000	.00000	.00000	.00000	.00000	.00000	.00000	.00000	.00000	.00000
-1.9	.00082	.00002	.00000	.00000	.00000	.00000	.00000	.00000	.00000	.00000	.00000	.00000	.00000	.00000
-1.8	.00129	.00005	.00000	.00000	.00000	.00000	.00000	.00000	.00000	.00000	.00000	.00000	.00000	.00000
-1.7	.00199	.00009	.00000	.00000	.00000	.00000	.00000	.00000	.00000	.00000	.00000	.00000	.00000	.00000
-1.6	.00300	.00016	.00001	.00000	.00000	.00000	.00000	.00000	.00000	.00000	.00000	.00000	.00000	.00000
-1.5	.00446	.00030	.00002	.00000	.00000	.00000	.00000	.00000	.00000	.00000	.00000	.00000	.00000	.00000
-1.4	.00652	.00053	.00004	.00000	.00000	.00000	.00000	.00000	.00000	.00000	.00000	.00000	.00000	.00000
-1.3	.00937	.00091	.00009	.00001	.00000	.00000	.00000	.00000	.00000	.00000	.00000	.00000	.00000	.00000
-1.2	.01324	.00152	.00018	.00002	.00000	.00000	.00000	.00000	.00000	.00000	.00000	.00000	.00000	.00000
-1.1	.01841	.00250	.00034	.00005	.00001	.00000	.00000	.00000	.00000	.00000	.00000	.00000	.00000	.00000
-1.0	.02517	.00399	.00063	.00010	.00002	.00000	.00000	.00000	.00000	.00000	.00000	.00000	.00000	.00000
-0.9	.03388	.00624	.00115	.00021	.00004	.00001	.00000	.00000	.00000	.00000	.00000	.00000	.00000	.00000
-0.8	.04488	.00951	.00201	.00043	.00009	.00002	.00000	.00000	.00000	.00000	.00000	.00000	.00000	.00000
-0.7	.05855	.01417	.00343	.00083	.00020	.00005	.00001	.00000	.00000	.00000	.00000	.00000	.00000	.00000
-0.6	.07521	.02063	.00566	.00155	.00043	.00012	.00003	.00001	.00000	.00000	.00000	.00000	.00000	.00000
-0.5	.09520	.02937	.00906	.00280	.00086	.00027	.00008	.00003	.00001	.00000	.00000	.00000	.00000	.00000
-0.4	.11873	.04091	.01410	.00486	.00167	.00058	.00020	.00007	.00002	.00000	.00000	.00000	.00000	.00000
-0.3	.14599	.05578	.02131	.00814	.00311	.00119	.00045	.00017	.00007	.00001	.00000	.00000	.00000	.00000
-0.2	.17702	.07448	.03134	.01318	.00555	.00233	.00098	.00041	.00017	.00003	.00001	.00000	.00000	.00000
-0.1	.21176	.09745	.04484	.02063	.00950	.00437	.00201	.00093	.00043	.00009	.00002	.00000	.00000	.00000
0.0	.25000	.12500	.06250	.03125	.01562	.00781	.00391	.00195	.00098	.00024	.00006	.00002	.00000	.00000
0.1	.29141	.15731	.08492	.04584	.02475	.01336	.00721	.00389	.00210	.00061	.00018	.00005	.00002	.00000
0.2	.33554	.19437	.11259	.06522	.03778	.02188	.01268	.00734	.00425	.00143	.00048	.00016	.00005	.00002
0.3	.38181	.23593	.14578	.09008	.05566	.03439	.02125	.01313	.00811	.00310	.00118	.00045	.00017	.00007
0.4	.42958	.28155	.18454	.12095	.07927	.05196	.03405	.02232	.01463	.00628	.00270	.00116	.00050	.00021
0.5	.47812	.33060	.22860	.15807	.10930	.07558	.05226	.03613	.02499	.01195	.00571	.00273	.00131	.00062
0.6	.52671	.38226	.27742	.20134	.14612	.10605	.07696	.05586	.04054	.02135	.01125	.00592	.00312	.00164
0.7	.57462	.43558	.33019	.25029	.18973	.14382	.10902	.08264	.06265	.03600	.02069	.01189	.00683	.00392
0.8	.62117	.48957	.38585	.30411	.23968	.18890	.14888	.11734	.09248	.05745	.03568	.02217	.01377	.00855
0.9	.66576	.54322	.44323	.36165	.29509	.24077	.19646	.16030	.13079	.08708	.05797	.03859	.02569	.01711
1.0	.70786	.59556	.50107	.42157	.35469	.29841	.25107	.21124	.17772	.12580	.08905	.06304	.04462	.03158
1.1	.74707	.64572	.55812	.48240	.41696	.36039	.31150	.26924	.23271	.17385	.12988	.09703	.07249	.05415
1.2	.78310	.69299	.61325	.54268	.48024	.42498	.37607	.33280	.29450	.23063	.18060	.14143	.11076	.08673
1.3	.81577	.73680	.66548	.60106	.54288	.49033	.44286	.39999	.36127	.29472	.24042	.19613	.16000	.13052
1.4	.84501	.77677	.71404	.65638	.60337	.55464	.50985	.46868	.43083	.36405	.30763	.25995	.21966	.18561
1.5	.87085	.81267	.75838	.70771	.66043	.61631	.57514	.53671	.50086	.43617	.37984	.33078	.28806	.25086
1.6	.89340	.84445	.79817	.75443	.71309	.67401	.63708	.60217	.56917	.50850	.45429	.40587	.36260	.32395
1.7	.91286	.87217	.83330	.79617	.76069	.72679	.69440	.66345	.63388	.57864	.52822	.48219	.44017	.40181
1.8	.92943	.89604	.86384	.83280	.80288	.77403	.74622	.71941	.69356	.64462	.59913	.55685	.51755	.48103
1.9	.94339	.91630	.88999	.86443	.83961	.81550	.79208	.76933	.74724	.70494	.66503	.62739	.59187	.55837
2.0	.95502	.93329	.91206	.89131	.87103	.85122	.83185	.81293	.79443	.75870	.72457	.69197	.66085	.63112
2.1	.96459	.94736	.93043	.91381	.89749	.88145	.86571	.85024	.83505	.80548	.77696	.74945	.72291	.69731
2.2	.97239	.95887	.94554	.93239	.91943	.90664	.89404	.88161	.86935	.84534	.82200	.79930	.77723	.75577
2.3	.97867	.96817	.95779	.94752	.93736	.92730	.91736	.90752	.89779	.87864	.85989	.84155	.82359	.80602
2.4	.98367	.97561	.96761	.95968	.95181	.94401	.93627	.92860	.92098	.90595	.89115	.87660	.86229	.84821
2.5	.98762	.98149	.97539	.96933	.96332	.95733	.95139	.94548	.93961	.92798	.91649	.90514	.89393	.88287
2.6	.99070	.98608	.98149	.97691	.97236	.96782	.96331	.95882	.95435	.94548	.93668	.92797	.91934	.91079
2.7	.99308	.98964	.98620	.98278	.97938	.97598	.97260	.96923	.96587	.95918	.95254	.94595	.93940	.93290
2.8	.99490	.99235	.98982	.98729	.98477	.98225	.97974	.97724	.97474	.96977	.96482	.95989	.95499	.95012
2.9	.99627	.99441	.99256	.99071	.98886	.98701	.98517	.98333	.98150	.97784	.97419	.97056	.96694	.96334
3.0	.99730	.99596	.99461	.99327	.99193	.99059	.98925	.98792	.98658	.98392	.98127	.97862	.97598	.97335
3.1	.99807	.99710	.99614	.99517	.99421	.99325	.99229	.99133	.99037	.98845	.98654	.98463	.98273	.98082
3.2	.99863	.99794	.99725	.99657	.99588	.99520	.99452	.99383	.99315	.99179	.99042	.98906	.98770	.98635
3.3	.99903	.99855	.99807	.99759	.99710	.99662	.99614	.99566	.99518	.99421	.99325	.99229	.99133	.99038
3.4	.99933	.99899	.99865	.99832	.99798	.99764	.99731	.99697	.99664	.99596	.99529	.99462	.99395	.99328
3.5	.99953	.99930	.99907	.99884	.99861	.99837	.99814	.99791	.99768	.99721	.99675	.99628	.99582	.99536
3.6	.99968	.99952	.99936	.99920	.99905	.99889	.99873	.99857	.99841	.99809	.99777	.99746	.99714	.99682
3.7	.99978	.99968	.99957	.99946	.99935	.99925	.99914	.99903	.99892	.99871	.99849	.99828	.99806	.99785
3.8	.99986	.99978	.99971	.99964	.99957	.99949	.99942	.99935	.99928	.99913	.99899	.99884	.99870	.99855
3.9	.99990	.99986	.99981	.99976	.99971	.99966	.99962	.99957	.99952	.99942	.99933	.99923	.99913	.99904
4.0	.99994	.99990	.99987	.99984	.99981	.99978	.99975	.99971	.99968	.99962	.99956	.99949	.99943	.99937

Table C-1. One-Sided Probability Integral, $\rho = 0.1$

a \ n	2	3	4	5	6	7	8	9	10	12	14	16	18	20
-2.0	.00087	.00005	.00000	.00000	.00000	.00000	.00000	.00000	.00000	.00000	.00000	.00000	.00000	.00000
-1.9	.00134	.00009	.00001	.00000	.00000	.00000	.00000	.00000	.00000	.00000	.00000	.00000	.00000	.00000
-1.8	.00202	.00016	.00002	.00000	.00000	.00000	.00000	.00000	.00000	.00000	.00000	.00000	.00000	.00000
-1.7	.00300	.00028	.00003	.00001	.00000	.00000	.00000	.00000	.00000	.00000	.00000	.00000	.00000	.00000
-1.6	.00440	.00048	.00007	.00001	.00000	.00000	.00000	.00000	.00000	.00000	.00000	.00000	.00000	.00000
-1.5	.00633	.00079	.00012	.00002	.00000	.00000	.00000	.00000	.00000	.00000	.00000	.00000	.00000	.00000
-1.4	.00899	.00129	.00023	.00005	.00001	.00000	.00000	.00000	.00000	.00000	.00000	.00000	.00000	.00000
-1.3	.01256	.00205	.00040	.00009	.00002	.00001	.00000	.00000	.00000	.00000	.00000	.00000	.00000	.00000
-1.2	.01729	.00321	.00071	.00018	.00005	.00002	.00001	.00000	.00000	.00000	.00000	.00000	.00000	.00000
-1.1	.02344	.00491	.00120	.00033	.00010	.00004	.00001	.00001	.00000	.00000	.00000	.00000	.00000	.00000
-1.0	.03132	.00736	.00199	.00061	.00020	.00007	.00003	.00001	.00001	.00000	.00000	.00000	.00000	.00000
-0.9	.04125	.01082	.00322	.00107	.00039	.00015	.00006	.00003	.00001	.00000	.00000	.00000	.00000	.00000
-0.8	.05355	.01559	.00510	.00183	.00072	.00030	.00013	.00006	.00003	.00001	.00000	.00000	.00000	.00000
-0.7	.06854	.02204	.00786	.00306	.00128	.00057	.00027	.00013	.00007	.00002	.00001	.00000	.00000	.00000
-0.6	.08653	.03057	.01186	.00497	.00223	.00106	.00053	.00027	.00015	.00005	.00002	.00001	.00000	.00000
-0.5	.10776	.04162	.01746	.00786	.00375	.00189	.00099	.00054	.00031	.00011	.00004	.00002	.00001	.00000
-0.4	.13242	.05562	.02515	.01210	.00614	.00326	.00181	.00103	.00061	.00023	.00010	.00004	.00002	.00001
-0.3	.16062	.07301	.03543	.01816	.00976	.00547	.00317	.00190	.00117	.00048	.00021	.00010	.00005	.00003
-0.2	.19237	.09418	.04883	.02658	.01508	.00888	.00540	.00337	.00216	.00095	.00045	.00023	.00012	.00007
-0.1	.22755	.11942	.06588	.03794	.02266	.01398	.00887	.00577	.00384	.00180	.00091	.00048	.00027	.00015
0.0	.26594	.14891	.08709	.05286	.03314	.02137	.01413	.00955	.00659	.00330	.00175	.00098	.00057	.00034
0.1	.30721	.18272	.11283	.07196	.04720	.03173	.02180	.01528	.01089	.00580	.00325	.00191	.00116	.00073
0.2	.35089	.22070	.14336	.09574	.06551	.04580	.03263	.02365	.01741	.00982	.00580	.00356	.00226	.00148
0.3	.39645	.26259	.17875	.12461	.08870	.06431	.04741	.03547	.02689	.01601	.00993	.00637	.00421	.00286
0.4	.44327	.30791	.21889	.15877	.11724	.08795	.06692	.05157	.04020	.02519	.01635	.01094	.00752	.00528
0.5	.49068	.35605	.26340	.19820	.15141	.11722	.09186	.07277	.05823	.03827	.02594	.01805	.01285	.00933
0.6	.53802	.40625	.31173	.24261	.19122	.15244	.12276	.09979	.08180	.05622	.03968	.02864	.02109	.01580
0.7	.58461	.45769	.36310	.29145	.23642	.19360	.15990	.13310	.11159	.07995	.05858	.04377	.03326	.02566
0.8	.62984	.50948	.41659	.34393	.28641	.24039	.20320	.17289	.14799	.11019	.08361	.06450	.05049	.04003
0.9	.67313	.56074	.47120	.39906	.34035	.29216	.25226	.21899	.19105	.14738	.11552	.09181	.07387	.06008
1.0	.71401	.61064	.52586	.45570	.39715	.34794	.30628	.27080	.24041	.19159	.15471	.12639	.10432	.08690
1.1	.75211	.65841	.57955	.51267	.45557	.40653	.36416	.32738	.29528	.24241	.20118	.16856	.14244	.12130
1.2	.78715	.70344	.63131	.56879	.51430	.46657	.42456	.38744	.35451	.29898	.25438	.21812	.18835	.16368
1.3	.81896	.74522	.68034	.62298	.57205	.52664	.48600	.44951	.41664	.36002	.31329	.27435	.24163	.21390
1.4	.84747	.78340	.72597	.67430	.62764	.58538	.54698	.51200	.48004	.42393	.37647	.33600	.30125	.27122
1.5	.87272	.81779	.76774	.72199	.68007	.64155	.60608	.57335	.54307	.48895	.44215	.40140	.36573	.33432
1.6	.89480	.84831	.80534	.76552	.72855	.69415	.66209	.63215	.60415	.55331	.50844	.46863	.43316	.40140
1.7	.91387	.87504	.83868	.80458	.77255	.74241	.71402	.68723	.66193	.61534	.57347	.53570	.50148	.47039
1.8	.93016	.89811	.86777	.83902	.81174	.78583	.76118	.73772	.71535	.67365	.63558	.60070	.56865	.53912
1.9	.94390	.91777	.89281	.86893	.84607	.82417	.80317	.78302	.76367	.72718	.69338	.66200	.63280	.60557
2.0	.95537	.93431	.91403	.89449	.87563	.85743	.83986	.82288	.80646	.77520	.74589	.71835	.69242	.66798
2.1	.96483	.94806	.93179	.91601	.90069	.88580	.87135	.85729	.84362	.81738	.79250	.76888	.74643	.72506
2.2	.97255	.95933	.94645	.93387	.92160	.90961	.89791	.88647	.87529	.85367	.83298	.81317	.79417	.77593
2.3	.97877	.96848	.95839	.94850	.93880	.92929	.91995	.91079	.90180	.88431	.86744	.85115	.83541	.82020
2.4	.98374	.97581	.96800	.96031	.95275	.94530	.93797	.93074	.92363	.90971	.89620	.88306	.87029	.85787
2.5	.98766	.98161	.97564	.96974	.96391	.95816	.95248	.94686	.94131	.93042	.91977	.90937	.89920	.88926
2.6	.99073	.98616	.98164	.97716	.97273	.96834	.96399	.95969	.95543	.94702	.93877	.93067	.92272	.91491
2.7	.99309	.98968	.98630	.98294	.97960	.97630	.97301	.96976	.96653	.96013	.95383	.94763	.94151	.93548
2.8	.99491	.99238	.98987	.98738	.98490	.98244	.97999	.97756	.97514	.97034	.96560	.96091	.95628	.95170
2.9	.99628	.99443	.99259	.99076	.98894	.98712	.98532	.98352	.98173	.97818	.97466	.97117	.96771	.96428
3.0	.99731	.99596	.99463	.99330	.99197	.99065	.98934	.98802	.98672	.98412	.98153	.97897	.97642	.97389
3.1	.99807	.99711	.99615	.99519	.99423	.99328	.99233	.99139	.99044	.98856	.98669	.98483	.98298	.98114
3.2	.99863	.99794	.99726	.99658	.99590	.99522	.99454	.99387	.99319	.99185	.99051	.98917	.98784	.98652
3.3	.99903	.99855	.99807	.99759	.99711	.99663	.99615	.99568	.99520	.99425	.99330	.99235	.99141	.99047
3.4	.99933	.99899	.99865	.99832	.99798	.99765	.99732	.99698	.99665	.99598	.99532	.99465	.99399	.99333
3.5	.99953	.99930	.99907	.99884	.99861	.99838	.99814	.99791	.99768	.99722	.99676	.99630	.99584	.99538
3.6	.99968	.99952	.99936	.99921	.99905	.99889	.99873	.99857	.99841	.99810	.99778	.99747	.99715	.99684
3.7	.99978	.99968	.99957	.99946	.99935	.99925	.99914	.99903	.99892	.99871	.99850	.99828	.99807	.99785
3.8	.99986	.99978	.99971	.99964	.99957	.99949	.99942	.99935	.99928	.99913	.99899	.99885	.99870	.99856
3.9	.99990	.99986	.99981	.99976	.99971	.99966	.99962	.99957	.99952	.99942	.99933	.99923	.99914	.99904
4.0	.99994	.99991	.99987	.99984	.99981	.99978	.99975	.99972	.99968	.99962	.99956	.99949	.99943	.99937

Table C-2. One-Sided Probability Integral, $\rho = 0.2$

a \ n	2	3	4	5	6	7	8	9	10	12	14	16	18	20
-2.0	.00137	.00015	.00002	.00001	.00000	.00000	.00000	.00000	.00000	.00000	.00000	.00000	.00000	.00000
-1.9	.00204	.00025	.00005	.00001	.00000	.00000	.00000	.00000	.00000	.00000	.00000	.00000	.00000	.00000
-1.8	.00298	.00042	.00008	.00002	.00001	.00000	.00000	.00000	.00000	.00000	.00000	.00000	.00000	.00000
-1.7	.00431	.00067	.00015	.00004	.00001	.00000	.00000	.00000	.00000	.00000	.00000	.00000	.00000	.00000
-1.6	.00614	.00107	.00025	.00007	.00003	.00001	.00000	.00000	.00000	.00000	.00000	.00000	.00000	.00000
-1.5	.00861	.00168	.00043	.00014	.00005	.00002	.00001	.00000	.00000	.00000	.00000	.00000	.00000	.00000
-1.4	.01192	.00257	.00072	.00024	.00009	.00004	.00002	.00001	.00001	.00000	.00000	.00000	.00000	.00000
-1.3	.01626	.00387	.00117	.00042	.00017	.00008	.00004	.00002	.00001	.00000	.00000	.00000	.00000	.00000
-1.2	.02189	.00573	.00187	.00072	.00031	.00015	.00008	.00004	.00002	.00001	.00000	.00000	.00000	.00000
-1.1	.02906	.00834	.00293	.00119	.00054	.00027	.00014	.00008	.00005	.00002	.00001	.00000	.00000	.00000
-1.0	.03807	.01192	.00449	.00194	.00093	.00048	.00027	.00016	.00010	.00004	.00002	.00001	.00001	.00000
-0.9	.04921	.01676	.00676	.00308	.00155	.00084	.00048	.00029	.00018	.00008	.00004	.00002	.00001	.00001
-0.8	.06278	.02315	.00996	.00480	.00252	.00142	.00084	.00053	.00034	.00016	.00008	.00004	.00003	.00002
-0.7	.07906	.03146	.01439	.00730	.00401	.00234	.00144	.00093	.00062	.00030	.00016	.00009	.00005	.00003
-0.6	.09830	.04206	.02041	.01087	.00623	.00378	.00240	.00159	.00109	.00055	.00030	.00018	.00011	.00007
-0.5	.12072	.05533	.02840	.01586	.00946	.00595	.00390	.00265	.00186	.00098	.00056	.00034	.00022	.00015
-0.4	.14643	.07165	.03879	.02267	.01405	.00914	.00618	.00432	.00310	.00171	.00101	.00064	.00042	.00028
-0.3	.17552	.09135	.05204	.03174	.02042	.01372	.00954	.00684	.00503	.00289	.00177	.00115	.00077	.00054
-0.2	.20792	.11471	.06856	.04356	.02903	.02011	.01439	.01057	.00794	.00475	.00301	.00201	.00139	.00099
-0.1	.24351	.14192	.08878	.05863	.04041	.02883	.02117	.01593	.01223	.00759	.00498	.00341	.00242	.00177
0.0	.28205	.17307	.11301	.07741	.05508	.04043	.03044	.02343	.01836	.01182	.00799	.00563	.00409	.00305
0.1	.32317	.20810	.14149	.10033	.07358	.05546	.04277	.03363	.02689	.01791	.01248	.00902	.00671	.00511
0.2	.36644	.24684	.17430	.12769	.09634	.07448	.05876	.04716	.03842	.02646	.01897	.01405	.01069	.00831
0.3	.41134	.28893	.21138	.15966	.12375	.09797	.07897	.06463	.05360	.03810	.02808	.02130	.01655	.01311
0.4	.45728	.33392	.25248	.19624	.15599	.12631	.10390	.08662	.07305	.05351	.04048	.03142	.02491	.02011
0.5	.50364	.38120	.29720	.23725	.19309	.15970	.13389	.11358	.09734	.07336	.05688	.04513	.03650	.02999
0.6	.54980	.43008	.34496	.28229	.23486	.19813	.16912	.14584	.12689	.09824	.07799	.06318	.05205	.04350
0.7	.59513	.47982	.39502	.33077	.28089	.24137	.20952	.18348	.16191	.12859	.10437	.08624	.07232	.06143
0.8	.63907	.52961	.44658	.38194	.33054	.28895	.25477	.22633	.20240	.16462	.13645	.11488	.09798	.08449
0.9	.68109	.57869	.49874	.43491	.38301	.34016	.30431	.27398	.24806	.20632	.17442	.14944	.12950	.11331
1.0	.72076	.62632	.55059	.48871	.43733	.39411	.35733	.32572	.29832	.25334	.21815	.19003	.16716	.14827
1.1	.75773	.67185	.60127	.54234	.49246	.44975	.41283	.38063	.35234	.30505	.26723	.23640	.21089	.18948
1.2	.79175	.71472	.64999	.59484	.54732	.50597	.46968	.43760	.40905	.36052	.32088	.28798	.26028	.23669
1.3	.82266	.75451	.69605	.64532	.60088	.56162	.52669	.49542	.46726	.41861	.37809	.34386	.31459	.28930
1.4	.85040	.79091	.73891	.69302	.65221	.61565	.58270	.55285	.52568	.47802	.43760	.40288	.37274	.34635
1.5	.87500	.82373	.77816	.73733	.70051	.66710	.63663	.60872	.58305	.53740	.49801	.46365	.43342	.40659
1.6	.89654	.85293	.81357	.77782	.74515	.71517	.68753	.66196	.63821	.59543	.55793	.52474	.49514	.46857
1.7	.91518	.87856	.84504	.81421	.78572	.75929	.73468	.71170	.69017	.65093	.61600	.58469	.55641	.53074
1.8	.93112	.90074	.87260	.84641	.82197	.79906	.77755	.75728	.73814	.70287	.67106	.64217	.61579	.59159
1.9	.94460	.91971	.89639	.87448	.85382	.83431	.81582	.79827	.78159	.75051	.72213	.69607	.67202	.64973
2.0	.95587	.93571	.91664	.89856	.88138	.86502	.84940	.83448	.82019	.79334	.76854	.74552	.72407	.70402
2.1	.96518	.94904	.93365	.91894	.90486	.89135	.87838	.86590	.85388	.83111	.80986	.78994	.77122	.75357
2.2	.97279	.96002	.94775	.93594	.92456	.91358	.90297	.89271	.88278	.86381	.84594	.82904	.81303	.79783
2.3	.97893	.96894	.95928	.94993	.94086	.93207	.92352	.91522	.90714	.89161	.87685	.86279	.84938	.83654
2.4	.98385	.97612	.96860	.96128	.95416	.94721	.94043	.93381	.92734	.91484	.90287	.89138	.88035	.86973
2.5	.98773	.98182	.97604	.97038	.96485	.95944	.95413	.94893	.94384	.93393	.92438	.91517	.90626	.89764
2.6	.99077	.98629	.98190	.97758	.97334	.96918	.96509	.96106	.95710	.94938	.94188	.93461	.92754	.92067
2.7	.99312	.98977	.98646	.98321	.98000	.97684	.97372	.97065	.96762	.96168	.95589	.95024	.94473	.93934
2.8	.99492	.99243	.98998	.98755	.98515	.98278	.98044	.97812	.97583	.97133	.96692	.96260	.95837	.95422
2.9	.99629	.99446	.99265	.99086	.98909	.98733	.98560	.98387	.98217	.97880	.97549	.97224	.96904	.96589
3.0	.99731	.99598	.99467	.99336	.99207	.99078	.98951	.98824	.98698	.98450	.98205	.97963	.97725	.97490
3.1	.99807	.99712	.99617	.99523	.99429	.99336	.99243	.99152	.99060	.98879	.98700	.98523	.98348	.98175
3.2	.99863	.99795	.99727	.99660	.99593	.99526	.99460	.99394	.99329	.99198	.99069	.98941	.98814	.98689
3.3	.99904	.99856	.99808	.99760	.99713	.99666	.99619	.99572	.99525	.99433	.99341	.99249	.99159	.99069
3.4	.99933	.99899	.99866	.99833	.99799	.99766	.99733	.99701	.99668	.99603	.99538	.99473	.99409	.99346
3.5	.99954	.99930	.99907	.99884	.99861	.99838	.99816	.99793	.99770	.99725	.99679	.99635	.99590	.99545
3.6	.99968	.99952	.99937	.99921	.99905	.99889	.99874	.99858	.99842	.99811	.99780	.99749	.99718	.99687
3.7	.99978	.99968	.99957	.99946	.99936	.99925	.99914	.99904	.99893	.99872	.99851	.99829	.99808	.99787
3.8	.99986	.99978	.99971	.99964	.99957	.99950	.99942	.99935	.99928	.99914	.99899	.99885	.99871	.99857
3.9	.99990	.99986	.99981	.99976	.99971	.99966	.99962	.99957	.99952	.99943	.99933	.99924	.99914	.99905
4.0	.99994	.99991	.99987	.99984	.99981	.99978	.99975	.99972	.99968	.99962	.99956	.99950	.99943	.99937

Table C-3. One-Sided Probability Integral, $\rho = 0.3$

a \ n	2	3	4	5	6	7	8	9	10	12	14	16	18	20
-2.0	.00204	.00036	.00009	.00003	.00001	.00001	.00000	.00000	.00000	.00000	.00000	.00000	.00000	.00000
-1.9	.00295	.00057	.00016	.00006	.00002	.00001	.00001	.00000	.00000	.00000	.00000	.00000	.00000	.00000
-1.8	.00422	.00089	.00027	.00010	.00004	.00002	.00001	.00001	.00000	.00000	.00000	.00000	.00000	.00000
-1.7	.00594	.00137	.00044	.00017	.00008	.00004	.00002	.00001	.00001	.00000	.00000	.00000	.00000	.00000
-1.6	.00826	.00207	.00070	.00029	.00014	.00007	.00004	.00002	.00002	.00001	.00000	.00000	.00000	.00000
-1.5	.01133	.00308	.00111	.00048	.00024	.00013	.00008	.00005	.00003	.00001	.00001	.00000	.00000	.00000
-1.4	.01535	.00451	.00172	.00078	.00040	.00022	.00013	.00009	.00006	.00003	.00002	.00001	.00001	.00000
-1.3	.02052	.00650	.00262	.00124	.00066	.00038	.00024	.00015	.00010	.00005	.00003	.00002	.00001	.00001
-1.2	.02709	.00923	.00393	.00195	.00107	.00064	.00040	.00027	.00019	.00010	.00006	.00003	.00002	.00002
-1.1	.03531	.01290	.00580	.00299	.00170	.00104	.00068	.00046	.00032	.00018	.00010	.00007	.00004	.00003
-1.0	.04546	.01777	.00840	.00451	.00265	.00167	.00111	.00077	.00055	.00031	.00019	.00012	.00008	.00006
-0.9	.05781	.02410	.01196	.00668	.00406	.00263	.00179	.00126	.00092	.00053	.00033	.00022	.00015	.00011
-0.8	.07263	.03221	.01676	.00971	.00609	.00405	.00282	.00203	.00151	.00090	.00058	.00039	.00028	.00020
-0.7	.09017	.04243	.02309	.01388	.00896	.00611	.00434	.00320	.00242	.00148	.00097	.00067	.00048	.00036
-0.6	.11063	.05509	.03131	.01948	.01295	.00904	.00657	.00493	.00379	.00239	.00161	.00113	.00083	.00063
-0.5	.13418	.07052	.04177	.02687	.01836	.01314	.00974	.00744	.00582	.00377	.00259	.00186	.00139	.00106
-0.4	.16090	.08902	.05487	.03645	.02558	.01872	.01416	.01100	.00874	.00582	.00409	.00300	.00227	.00177
-0.3	.19082	.11085	.07096	.04861	.03500	.02618	.02019	.01596	.01287	.00879	.00632	.00472	.00363	.00287
-0.2	.22385	.13620	.09039	.06376	.04705	.03595	.02824	.02268	.01856	.01300	.00954	.00726	.00568	.00455
-0.1	.25983	.16516	.11344	.08229	.06217	.04847	.03875	.03162	.02624	.01883	.01411	.01092	.00868	.00705
0.0	.29849	.19774	.14031	.10453	.08077	.06421	.05221	.04325	.03638	.02673	.02043	.01609	.01298	.01068
0.1	.33949	.23381	.17109	.13073	.10321	.08358	.06907	.05805	.04948	.03718	.02896	.02319	.01898	.01582
0.2	.38237	.27314	.20575	.16104	.12975	.10694	.08977	.07650	.06602	.05070	.04022	.03273	.02717	.02293
0.3	.42664	.31534	.24413	.19547	.16056	.13458	.11466	.09901	.08647	.06781	.05476	.04524	.03807	.03253
0.4	.47175	.35996	.28591	.23387	.19565	.16662	.14397	.12590	.11122	.08898	.07309	.06129	.05225	.04516
0.5	.51710	.40641	.33064	.27594	.23487	.20306	.17782	.15738	.14055	.11461	.09568	.08138	.07026	.06142
0.6	.56213	.45405	.37774	.32124	.27789	.24370	.21613	.19348	.17458	.14496	.12293	.10598	.09262	.08184
0.7	.60624	.50219	.42653	.36916	.32423	.28817	.25863	.23403	.21325	.18015	.15505	.13543	.11972	.10690
0.8	.64892	.55011	.47627	.41898	.37325	.33592	.30488	.27869	.25630	.22008	.19211	.16989	.15185	.13693
0.9	.68969	.59715	.52617	.46991	.42417	.38623	.35424	.32690	.30327	.26446	.23394	.20933	.18907	.17212
1.0	.72815	.64264	.57545	.52111	.47615	.43829	.40593	.37795	.35349	.31275	.28016	.25349	.23125	.21242
1.1	.76398	.68602	.62337	.57172	.52828	.49117	.45905	.43095	.40613	.36423	.33015	.30187	.27798	.25753
1.2	.79695	.72682	.66925	.62093	.57967	.54394	.51264	.48495	.46026	.41801	.38312	.35375	.32865	.30693
1.3	.82692	.76465	.71252	.66803	.62949	.59568	.56573	.53895	.51484	.47308	.43808	.40822	.38242	.35985
1.4	.85383	.79926	.75273	.71240	.67698	.64554	.61737	.59195	.56886	.52838	.49396	.46424	.43826	.41531
1.5	.87772	.83049	.78954	.75354	.72151	.69276	.66674	.64304	.62132	.58283	.54965	.52067	.49505	.47221
1.6	.89866	.85831	.82277	.79110	.76260	.73674	.71311	.69140	.67135	.63544	.60408	.57637	.55163	.52938
1.7	.91681	.88275	.85234	.82489	.79991	.77703	.75594	.73640	.71822	.68532	.65624	.63027	.60687	.58562
1.8	.93236	.90397	.87828	.85483	.83328	.81335	.79483	.77755	.76135	.73175	.70530	.68143	.65972	.63985
1.9	.94552	.92214	.90073	.88099	.86267	.84558	.82958	.81454	.80035	.77420	.75058	.72905	.70931	.69109
2.0	.95654	.93751	.91990	.90350	.88816	.87373	.86013	.84726	.83504	.81234	.79161	.77256	.75494	.73857
2.1	.96566	.95036	.93606	.92262	.90995	.89796	.88657	.87572	.86538	.84600	.82814	.81158	.79616	.78172
2.2	.97313	.96096	.94949	.93863	.92831	.91848	.90910	.90011	.89148	.87521	.86009	.84596	.83270	.82020
2.3	.97917	.96961	.96052	.95186	.94357	.93563	.92801	.92067	.91359	.90015	.88756	.87571	.86452	.85390
2.4	.98401	.97658	.96947	.96264	.95608	.94975	.94365	.93774	.93203	.92111	.91080	.90103	.89174	.88288
2.5	.98784	.98213	.97663	.97132	.96619	.96122	.95640	.95172	.94717	.93843	.93012	.92220	.91462	.90736
2.6	.99084	.98650	.98230	.97822	.97426	.97040	.96665	.96300	.95943	.95254	.94595	.93963	.93355	.92770
2.7	.99317	.98990	.98673	.98363	.98061	.97766	.97478	.97196	.96920	.96385	.95870	.95374	.94895	.94431
2.8	.99495	.99252	.99015	.98783	.98555	.98333	.98114	.97900	.97690	.97280	.96884	.96500	.96127	.95765
2.9	.99631	.99452	.99276	.99104	.98935	.98769	.98605	.98445	.98286	.97977	.97676	.97384	.97099	.96821
3.0	.99732	.99602	.99474	.99348	.99223	.99101	.98980	.98861	.98743	.98513	.98288	.98068	.97853	.97643
3.1	.99808	.99714	.99621	.99530	.99439	.99350	.99262	.99175	.99089	.98919	.98753	.98590	.98431	.98274
3.2	.99863	.99796	.99730	.99664	.99599	.99535	.99472	.99409	.99346	.99223	.99102	.98983	.98867	.98752
3.3	.99904	.99856	.99809	.99763	.99717	.99671	.99626	.99581	.99536	.99448	.99361	.99275	.99191	.99108
3.4	.99933	.99900	.99867	.99834	.99802	.99770	.99738	.99706	.99674	.99612	.99550	.99489	.99429	.99369
3.5	.99954	.99931	.99908	.99885	.99863	.99840	.99818	.99796	.99774	.99730	.99687	.99644	.99601	.99559
3.6	.99968	.99953	.99937	.99921	.99906	.99890	.99875	.99860	.99844	.99814	.99784	.99754	.99725	.99696
3.7	.99978	.99968	.99957	.99947	.99936	.99925	.99915	.99905	.99894	.99873	.99853	.99833	.99812	.99792
3.8	.99986	.99978	.99971	.99964	.99957	.99950	.99943	.99936	.99929	.99915	.99901	.99887	.99873	.99860
3.9	.99990	.99986	.99981	.99976	.99971	.99967	.99962	.99957	.99952	.99943	.99934	.99924	.99915	.99906
4.0	.99994	.99991	.99987	.99984	.99981	.99978	.99975	.99972	.99969	.99962	.99956	.99950	.99944	.99938

Table C-4. One-Sided Probability Integral, $\rho = 0.4$

a \ n	2	3	4	5	6	7	8	9	10	12	14	16	18	20
-2.0	.00292	.00074	.00027	.00012	.00006	.00004	.00002	.00001	.00001	.00001	.00000	.00000	.00000	.00000
-1.9	.00413	.00112	.00043	.00020	.00011	.00006	.00004	.00003	.00002	.00001	.00001	.00000	.00000	.00000
-1.8	.00576	.00168	.00067	.00032	.00018	.00011	.00007	.00005	.00003	.00002	.00001	.00001	.00000	.00000
-1.7	.00794	.00247	.00103	.00052	.00029	.00018	.00012	.00008	.00006	.00003	.00002	.00001	.00001	.00001
-1.6	.01081	.00358	.00157	.00081	.00047	.00030	.00020	.00014	.00010	.00006	.00004	.00002	.00002	.00001
-1.5	.01454	.00513	.00234	.00125	.00075	.00048	.00033	.00023	.00017	.00010	.00007	.00005	.00003	.00002
-1.4	.01933	.00724	.00345	.00191	.00117	.00077	.00053	.00039	.00029	.00018	.00011	.00008	.00006	.00004
-1.3	.02538	.01007	.00500	.00285	.00179	.00120	.00085	.00062	.00047	.00029	.00020	.00014	.00010	.00008
-1.2	.03294	.01382	.00714	.00420	.00270	.00185	.00133	.00099	.00076	.00049	.00033	.00024	.00018	.00014
-1.1	.04225	.01872	.01006	.00610	.00401	.00281	.00205	.00155	.00121	.00079	.00054	.00040	.00030	.00023
-1.0	.05356	.02500	.01394	.00870	.00587	.00418	.00311	.00239	.00189	.00125	.00088	.00065	.00050	.00039
-0.9	.06714	.03295	.01906	.01223	.00843	.00612	.00463	.00361	.00288	.00195	.00140	.00105	.00081	.00065
-0.8	.08321	.04285	.02567	.01693	.01193	.00882	.00677	.00535	.00433	.00299	.00218	.00166	.00130	.00105
-0.7	.10199	.05501	.03409	.02308	.01661	.01251	.00975	.00780	.00638	.00450	.00334	.00257	.00205	.00166
-0.6	.12365	.06973	.04463	.03099	.02277	.01744	.01380	.01119	.00926	.00665	.00502	.00392	.00315	.00259
-0.5	.14831	.08726	.05763	.04100	.03074	.02394	.01921	.01577	.01320	.00966	.00740	.00586	.00477	.00396
-0.4	.17600	.10785	.07339	.05347	.04086	.03234	.02631	.02187	.01850	.01380	.01073	.00861	.00708	.00594
-0.3	.20672	.13168	.09222	.06872	.05350	.04302	.03547	.02983	.02550	.01936	.01528	.01242	.01033	.00875
-0.2	.24036	.15885	.11436	.08709	.06902	.05634	.04706	.04004	.03457	.02671	.02139	.01760	.01480	.01266
-0.1	.27671	.18940	.13998	.10884	.08775	.07268	.06148	.05288	.04611	.03623	.02942	.02451	.02082	.01798
0.0	.31549	.22324	.16917	.13419	.10998	.09238	.07909	.06876	.06053	.04833	.03980	.03354	.02879	.02508
0.1	.35636	.26020	.20193	.16325	.13592	.11570	.10022	.08803	.07821	.06344	.05293	.04512	.03911	.03437
0.2	.39888	.29999	.23812	.19603	.16569	.14287	.12514	.11100	.09949	.08194	.06925	.05968	.05224	.04630
0.3	.44255	.34223	.27750	.23241	.19928	.17396	.15401	.13791	.12466	.10419	.08914	.07764	.06860	.06130
0.4	.48685	.38643	.31971	.27216	.23657	.20894	.18689	.16887	.15390	.13044	.11294	.09939	.08860	.07982
0.5	.53123	.43205	.36428	.31491	.27730	.24765	.22368	.20388	.18725	.16087	.14088	.12521	.11260	.10223
0.6	.57515	.47847	.41064	.36017	.32105	.28977	.26416	.24277	.22463	.19550	.17309	.15531	.14083	.12882
0.7	.61807	.52508	.45814	.40734	.36731	.33484	.30794	.28523	.26579	.23419	.20954	.18973	.17344	.15979
0.8	.65950	.57122	.50612	.45575	.41543	.38229	.35450	.33080	.31033	.27666	.25002	.22837	.21038	.19517
0.9	.69902	.61629	.55387	.50468	.46470	.43141	.40319	.37888	.35770	.32245	.29419	.27095	.25145	.23482
1.0	.73625	.65973	.60071	.55339	.51436	.48147	.45327	.42876	.40721	.37095	.34151	.31703	.29628	.27843
1.1	.77091	.70102	.64600	.60115	.56364	.53165	.50394	.47963	.45808	.42144	.39131	.36598	.34431	.32551
1.2	.80280	.73978	.68919	.64730	.61179	.58117	.55438	.53067	.50949	.47309	.44280	.41706	.39484	.37541
1.3	.83178	.77567	.72979	.69122	.65813	.62927	.60379	.58104	.56056	.52502	.49509	.46941	.44704	.42732
1.4	.85781	.80847	.76743	.73244	.70205	.67527	.65141	.62994	.61047	.57636	.54730	.52212	.50000	.48035
1.5	.88093	.83808	.80185	.77055	.74305	.71859	.69660	.67666	.65845	.62625	.59852	.57426	.55278	.53355
1.6	.90121	.86445	.83290	.80529	.78078	.75876	.73881	.72058	.70383	.67394	.64792	.62496	.60446	.58598
1.7	.91881	.88765	.86053	.83652	.81498	.79547	.77764	.76124	.74607	.71877	.69478	.67341	.65419	.63674
1.8	.93390	.90781	.88480	.86420	.84554	.82850	.81281	.79829	.78476	.76024	.73848	.71894	.70122	.68504
1.9	.94669	.92511	.90583	.88840	.87247	.85780	.84420	.83153	.81967	.79798	.77857	.76099	.74494	.73019
2.0	.95742	.93977	.92383	.90927	.89585	.88341	.87180	.86091	.85066	.83180	.81475	.79920	.78491	.77169
2.1	.96631	.95205	.93903	.92703	.91589	.90548	.89571	.88650	.87777	.86161	.84689	.83336	.82084	.80919
2.2	.97360	.96221	.95170	.94194	.93282	.92423	.91613	.90844	.90113	.88750	.87498	.86340	.85262	.84252
2.3	.97951	.97051	.96214	.95431	.94693	.93995	.93332	.92700	.92097	.90964	.89916	.88940	.88026	.87166
2.4	.98425	.97722	.97064	.96442	.95853	.95293	.94759	.94247	.93756	.92829	.91965	.91155	.90393	.89672
2.5	.98801	.98258	.97746	.97259	.96796	.96352	.95927	.95518	.95124	.94376	.93675	.93014	.92388	.91794
2.6	.99096	.98682	.98288	.97911	.97551	.97204	.96871	.96548	.96237	.95642	.95082	.94550	.94044	.93561
2.7	.99325	.99012	.98712	.98425	.98148	.97881	.97623	.97372	.97129	.96663	.96221	.95800	.95397	.95011
2.8	.99501	.99267	.99042	.98825	.98615	.98412	.98214	.98022	.97835	.97475	.97132	.96803	.96487	.96183
2.9	.99634	.99461	.99294	.99132	.98975	.98822	.98673	.98528	.98386	.98112	.97848	.97595	.97351	.97115
3.0	.99735	.99608	.99485	.99366	.99250	.99136	.99025	.98917	.98810	.98604	.98405	.98213	.98027	.97847
3.1	.99809	.99718	.99629	.99542	.99457	.99373	.99292	.99211	.99133	.98980	.98831	.98688	.98548	.98413
3.2	.99864	.99799	.99735	.99672	.99610	.99550	.99491	.99432	.99375	.99263	.99154	.99048	.98944	.98844
3.3	.99904	.99858	.99812	.99768	.99724	.99680	.99638	.99596	.99554	.99473	.99394	.99317	.99241	.99168
3.4	.99933	.99901	.99869	.99837	.99806	.99775	.99745	.99715	.99686	.99628	.99571	.99516	.99461	.99408
3.5	.99954	.99931	.99909	.99887	.99865	.99844	.99823	.99802	.99781	.99740	.99700	.99660	.99622	.99584
3.6	.99968	.99953	.99938	.99922	.99907	.99892	.99878	.99863	.99849	.99820	.99792	.99765	.99737	.99711
3.7	.99979	.99968	.99958	.99947	.99937	.99927	.99917	.99907	.99897	.99877	.99858	.99839	.99820	.99801
3.8	.99986	.99978	.99971	.99964	.99957	.99951	.99944	.99937	.99930	.99917	.99904	.99891	.99878	.99865
3.9	.99990	.99986	.99981	.99976	.99972	.99967	.99962	.99958	.99953	.99944	.99935	.99927	.99918	.99909
4.0	.99994	.99991	.99987	.99984	.99981	.99978	.99975	.99972	.99969	.99963	.99957	.99951	.99945	.99940

Table C-5. One-Sided Probability Integral, $\rho = 0.5$

a \ n	2	3	4	5	6	7	8	9	10	12	14	16	18	20
-2.0	.00405	.00137	.00063	.00035	.00021	.00014	.00010	.00007	.00006	.00004	.00002	.00002	.00001	.00001
-1.9	.00561	.00201	.00096	.00054	.00034	.00023	.00016	.00012	.00009	.00006	.00004	.00003	.00002	.00002
-1.8	.00767	.00289	.00143	.00083	.00053	.00037	.00026	.00020	.00016	.00010	.00007	.00005	.00004	.00003
-1.7	.01037	.00411	.00210	.00125	.00082	.00057	.00042	.00032	.00025	.00017	.00012	.00009	.00007	.00005
-1.6	.01386	.00576	.00305	.00185	.00124	.00088	.00066	.00051	.00040	.00027	.00020	.00015	.00011	.00009
-1.5	.01832	.00799	.00436	.00272	.00185	.00133	.00101	.00079	.00063	.00043	.00032	.00024	.00019	.00015
-1.4	.02394	.01093	.00616	.00393	.00272	.00200	.00153	.00121	.00098	.00068	.00050	.00039	.00031	.00025
-1.3	.03094	.01476	.00858	.00560	.00395	.00294	.00228	.00182	.00149	.00105	.00079	.00061	.00049	.00041
-1.2	.03955	.01970	.01179	.00788	.00565	.00427	.00335	.00270	.00223	.00160	.00122	.00096	.00078	.00064
-1.1	.04999	.02596	.01600	.01092	.00797	.00611	.00485	.00395	.00329	.00241	.00185	.00147	.00120	.00101
-1.0	.06251	.03380	.02142	.01494	.01109	.00861	.00692	.00570	.00479	.00355	.00276	.00222	.00183	.00154
-0.9	.07734	.04347	.02832	.02015	.01521	.01197	.00973	.00809	.00686	.00516	.00406	.00330	.00275	.00233
-0.8	.09469	.05526	.03695	.02683	.02058	.01641	.01348	.01133	.00969	.00739	.00588	.00483	.00406	.00347
-0.7	.11472	.06941	.04762	.03525	.02746	.02218	.01842	.01562	.01348	.01043	.00840	.00696	.00589	.00508
-0.6	.13757	.08619	.06060	.04570	.03614	.02957	.02481	.02124	.01847	.01449	.01180	.00987	.00843	.00733
-0.5	.16332	.10580	.07617	.05850	.04694	.03887	.03296	.02847	.02495	.01984	.01634	.01380	.01188	.01040
-0.4	.19198	.12841	.09458	.07393	.06017	.05041	.04318	.03762	.03323	.02677	.02228	.01899	.01649	.01453
-0.3	.22349	.15414	.11606	.09227	.07612	.06451	.05579	.04902	.04363	.03561	.02995	.02575	.02254	.01999
-0.2	.25771	.18303	.14075	.11374	.09508	.08147	.07113	.06302	.05650	.04668	.03967	.03441	.03034	.02710
-0.1	.29442	.21503	.16873	.13850	.11727	.10156	.08948	.07991	.07215	.06034	.05179	.04532	.04025	.03619
0.0	.33333	.25000	.20000	.16667	.14286	.12500	.11111	.10000	.09091	.07692	.06667	.05882	.05263	.04762
0.1	.37408	.28772	.23446	.19823	.17192	.15193	.13620	.12350	.11302	.09673	.08463	.07528	.06783	.06175
0.2	.41623	.32788	.27192	.23308	.20445	.18240	.16487	.15058	.13869	.12000	.10596	.09499	.08619	.07894
0.3	.45931	.37006	.31206	.27104	.24032	.21637	.19713	.18129	.16801	.14692	.13088	.11824	.10799	.09950
0.4	.50282	.41379	.35450	.31177	.27930	.25368	.23287	.21559	.20099	.17757	.15955	.14520	.13347	.12368
0.5	.54624	.45855	.39874	.35486	.32104	.29403	.27187	.25332	.23750	.21190	.19198	.17596	.16276	.15166
0.6	.58906	.50376	.44425	.39981	.36509	.33704	.31380	.29417	.27732	.24977	.22809	.21050	.19588	.18350
0.7	.63079	.54885	.49041	.44605	.41091	.38220	.35820	.33775	.32006	.29089	.26767	.24865	.23273	.21915
0.8	.67098	.59323	.53661	.49293	.45788	.42894	.40451	.38353	.36526	.33483	.31036	.29014	.27307	.25841
0.9	.70922	.63638	.58224	.53983	.50536	.47660	.45211	.43090	.41231	.38107	.35568	.33452	.31652	.30096
1.0	.74520	.67778	.62670	.58608	.55267	.52450	.50030	.47920	.46056	.42898	.40306	.38126	.36258	.34633
1.1	.77866	.71701	.66944	.63107	.59913	.57195	.54839	.52770	.50930	.47786	.45180	.42970	.41063	.39392
1.2	.80941	.75373	.71000	.67424	.64414	.61828	.59568	.57569	.55780	.52698	.50119	.47913	.45996	.44307
1.3	.83734	.78766	.74799	.71510	.68713	.66287	.64151	.62248	.60535	.57559	.55045	.52879	.50982	.49301
1.4	.86243	.81864	.78309	.75327	.72763	.70519	.68529	.66744	.65127	.62297	.59885	.57789	.55943	.54296
1.5	.88471	.84656	.81513	.78843	.76525	.74480	.72652	.71001	.69498	.66847	.64567	.62572	.60801	.59214
1.6	.90427	.87143	.84398	.82040	.79973	.78134	.76479	.74975	.73598	.71151	.69029	.67158	.65487	.63980
1.7	.92124	.89331	.86964	.84908	.83090	.81459	.79982	.78631	.77388	.75163	.73217	.71489	.69937	.68529
1.8	.93581	.91233	.89218	.87449	.85870	.84444	.83144	.81948	.80841	.78848	.77090	.75519	.74098	.72803
1.9	.94818	.92867	.91172	.89669	.88317	.87087	.85958	.84914	.83943	.82183	.80619	.79211	.77931	.76758
2.0	.95855	.94253	.92845	.91585	.90442	.89395	.88429	.87531	.86691	.85159	.83787	.82545	.81409	.80363
2.1	.96717	.95416	.94260	.93217	.92264	.91385	.90569	.89806	.89090	.87776	.86591	.85510	.84517	.83598
2.2	.97424	.96380	.95443	.94590	.93805	.93077	.92397	.91758	.91156	.90045	.89035	.88110	.87255	.86459
2.3	.97998	.97170	.96419	.95730	.95092	.94497	.93938	.93411	.92911	.91984	.91137	.90356	.89630	.88952
2.4	.98459	.97809	.97215	.96665	.96153	.95673	.95220	.94790	.94382	.93620	.92918	.92268	.91661	.91092
2.5	.98825	.98321	.97856	.97423	.97017	.96635	.96272	.95927	.95597	.94979	.94407	.93874	.93373	.92902
2.6	.99113	.98726	.98367	.98030	.97712	.97411	.97125	.96851	.96589	.96094	.95634	.95202	.94796	.94411
2.7	.99337	.99043	.98768	.98509	.98264	.98030	.97807	.97592	.97386	.96996	.96631	.96287	.95961	.95652
2.8	.99509	.99288	.99081	.98884	.98697	.98517	.98345	.98180	.98020	.97716	.97430	.97160	.96903	.96658
2.9	.99640	.99476	.99321	.99173	.99032	.98896	.98765	.98639	.98517	.98283	.98063	.97853	.97653	.97461
3.0	.99738	.99618	.99504	.99394	.99289	.99187	.99089	.98994	.98901	.98724	.98556	.98396	.98242	.98094
3.1	.99812	.99724	.99641	.99560	.99483	.99408	.99335	.99264	.99195	.99063	.98936	.98815	.98699	.98587
3.2	.99866	.99803	.99743	.99684	.99628	.99573	.99520	.99468	.99417	.99319	.99225	.99135	.99048	.98964
3.3	.99905	.99861	.99818	.99776	.99735	.99695	.99657	.99619	.99582	.99511	.99442	.99376	.99312	.99249
3.4	.99934	.99902	.99872	.99842	.99813	.99785	.99758	.99730	.99704	.99653	.99603	.99555	.99508	.99463
3.5	.99954	.99932	.99911	.99890	.99870	.99850	.99830	.99811	.99793	.99756	.99720	.99686	.99652	.99620
3.6	.99969	.99954	.99939	.99924	.99910	.99896	.99883	.99869	.99856	.99830	.99805	.99781	.99757	.99734
3.7	.99979	.99968	.99958	.99948	.99939	.99929	.99920	.99910	.99901	.99883	.99866	.99849	.99832	.99816
3.8	.99986	.99979	.99972	.99965	.99959	.99952	.99946	.99939	.99933	.99921	.99909	.99897	.99885	.99874
3.9	.99990	.99986	.99981	.99977	.99972	.99968	.99964	.99959	.99955	.99947	.99939	.99931	.99923	.99915
4.0	.99994	.99991	.99988	.99985	.99982	.99979	.99976	.99973	.99970	.99965	.99959	.99954	.99948	.99943

Table C-6. One-Sided Probability Integral, $\rho = 0.6$

a \ n	2	3	4	5	6	7	8	9	10	12	14	16	18	20
-2.0	.00550	.00237	.00132	.00084	.00059	.00044	.00034	.00027	.00022	.00016	.00012	.00010	.00008	.00006
-1.9	.00747	.00335	.00191	.00124	.00088	.00066	.00052	.00042	.00035	.00025	.00019	.00015	.00013	.00010
-1.8	.01003	.00468	.00274	.00182	.00131	.00099	.00078	.00064	.00053	.00039	.00030	.00024	.00020	.00017
-1.7	.01333	.00645	.00387	.00262	.00191	.00147	.00117	.00096	.00081	.00060	.00047	.00038	.00031	.00027
-1.6	.01753	.00880	.00541	.00372	.00275	.00214	.00172	.00143	.00121	.00091	.00071	.00058	.00049	.00042
-1.5	.02279	.01186	.00747	.00523	.00392	.00308	.00251	.00209	.00178	.00135	.00108	.00088	.00075	.00064
-1.4	.02933	.01581	.01018	.00725	.00551	.00438	.00359	.00302	.00259	.00199	.00160	.00133	.00112	.00097
-1.3	.03736	.02082	.01372	.00994	.00765	.00614	.00509	.00431	.00372	.00290	.00235	.00196	.00167	.00145
-1.2	.04708	.02711	.01826	.01345	.01049	.00851	.00711	.00607	.00528	.00415	.00339	.00285	.00245	.00214
-1.1	.05873	.03492	.02403	.01798	.01420	.01164	.00981	.00844	.00738	.00587	.00484	.00410	.00355	.00312
-1.0	.07253	.04447	.03125	.02375	.01898	.01572	.01336	.01158	.01019	.00819	.00681	.00582	.00506	.00448
-0.9	.08866	.05601	.04017	.03099	.02507	.02096	.01796	.01568	.01389	.01128	.00947	.00814	.00713	.00634
-0.8	.10731	.06978	.05104	.03996	.03271	.02761	.02385	.02097	.01869	.01533	.01298	.01124	.00991	.00885
-0.7	.12863	.08600	.06412	.05093	.04216	.03593	.03128	.02769	.02483	.02057	.01755	.01531	.01358	.01220
-0.6	.15270	.10488	.07965	.06416	.05370	.04618	.04052	.03610	.03256	.02724	.02344	.02059	.01837	.01659
-0.5	.17956	.12657	.09786	.07989	.06759	.05864	.05184	.04649	.04217	.03563	.03090	.02732	.02452	.02226
-0.4	.20919	.15118	.11893	.09837	.08410	.07360	.06553	.05915	.05395	.04602	.04022	.03580	.03231	.02947
-0.3	.24150	.17876	.14299	.11978	.10344	.09128	.08187	.07434	.06819	.05869	.05169	.04631	.04202	.03853
-0.2	.27631	.20927	.17012	.14425	.12580	.11192	.10107	.09233	.08514	.07395	.06561	.05915	.05397	.04972
-0.1	.31338	.24262	.20030	.17186	.15130	.13567	.12334	.11334	.10505	.09204	.08226	.07461	.06845	.06336
0.0	.35242	.27862	.23345	.20259	.17999	.16263	.14882	.13753	.12810	.11320	.10189	.09297	.08574	.07973
0.1	.39304	.31701	.26941	.23636	.21185	.19282	.17756	.16499	.15442	.13759	.12470	.11445	.10608	.09909
0.2	.43482	.35742	.30790	.27297	.24674	.22618	.20954	.19573	.18407	.16532	.15083	.13923	.12968	.12167
0.3	.47732	.39946	.34859	.31214	.28445	.26252	.24463	.22969	.21698	.19639	.18034	.16739	.15667	.14761
0.4	.52003	.44266	.39105	.35352	.32466	.30160	.28263	.26668	.25302	.23073	.21320	.19895	.18708	.17699
0.5	.56249	.48650	.43480	.39665	.36699	.34305	.32321	.30641	.29194	.26815	.24927	.23381	.22085	.20978
0.6	.60419	.53046	.47931	.44104	.41094	.38644	.36596	.34851	.33339	.30835	.28831	.27178	.25784	.24586
0.7	.64470	.57400	.52403	.48612	.45599	.43123	.41039	.39251	.37693	.35095	.32997	.31255	.29776	.28499
0.8	.68360	.61660	.56840	.53133	.50155	.47688	.45595	.43788	.42204	.39545	.37380	.35570	.34024	.32682
0.9	.72054	.65780	.61187	.57608	.54704	.52277	.50204	.48402	.46815	.44131	.41928	.40073	.38480	.37090
1.0	.75522	.69715	.65392	.61982	.59186	.56830	.54804	.53032	.51463	.48791	.46581	.44707	.43089	.41670
1.1	.78740	.73429	.69411	.66202	.63545	.61289	.59335	.57616	.56086	.53462	.51275	.49409	.47788	.46360
1.2	.81694	.76893	.73203	.70222	.67731	.65598	.63738	.62093	.60621	.58080	.55946	.54114	.52513	.51096
1.3	.84376	.80085	.76739	.74004	.71697	.69707	.67961	.66407	.65010	.62584	.60530	.58756	.57197	.55811
1.4	.86782	.82993	.79994	.77516	.75408	.73576	.71958	.70510	.69202	.66916	.64967	.63273	.61777	.60439
1.5	.88918	.85610	.82955	.80739	.78836	.77171	.75691	.74361	.73152	.71027	.69203	.67608	.66191	.64919
1.6	.90793	.87938	.85616	.83658	.81963	.80469	.79133	.77926	.76825	.74877	.73192	.71710	.70388	.69196
1.7	.92420	.89985	.87979	.86269	.84778	.83455	.82266	.81185	.80195	.78432	.76898	.75541	.74324	.73221
1.8	.93817	.91763	.90050	.88577	.87282	.86125	.85079	.84124	.83246	.81673	.80295	.79068	.77963	.76958
1.9	.95004	.93291	.91846	.90592	.89481	.88482	.87574	.86742	.85972	.84587	.83366	.82273	.81283	.80379
2.0	.96000	.94588	.93383	.92328	.91387	.90536	.89759	.89042	.88377	.87173	.86105	.85144	.84270	.83469
2.1	.96828	.95677	.94684	.93808	.93020	.92304	.91647	.91038	.90470	.89438	.88517	.87684	.86922	.86221
2.2	.97508	.96580	.95772	.95052	.94402	.93807	.93258	.92747	.92269	.91396	.90611	.89899	.89244	.88639
2.3	.98061	.97321	.96671	.96087	.95556	.95068	.94615	.94192	.93795	.93066	.92407	.91805	.91250	.90735
2.4	.98505	.97922	.97405	.96938	.96509	.96114	.95745	.95399	.95073	.94472	.93926	.93425	.92961	.92528
2.5	.98859	.98405	.97998	.97628	.97287	.96970	.96673	.96394	.96130	.95641	.95194	.94782	.94399	.94041
2.6	.99137	.98787	.98471	.98181	.97913	.97662	.97427	.97204	.96993	.96600	.96240	.95905	.95594	.95301
2.7	.99354	.99087	.98844	.98620	.98411	.98216	.98031	.97856	.97689	.97378	.97090	.96823	.96572	.96336
2.8	.99521	.99319	.99135	.98964	.98803	.98652	.98509	.98373	.98243	.97999	.97773	.97562	.97363	.97175
2.9	.99648	.99498	.99359	.99230	.99108	.98993	.98884	.98779	.98679	.98490	.98315	.98150	.97994	.97847
3.0	.99744	.99633	.99530	.99433	.99342	.99255	.99173	.99094	.99017	.98873	.98739	.98612	.98492	.98377
3.1	.99816	.99735	.99659	.99588	.99520	.99455	.99394	.99334	.99277	.99169	.99066	.98970	.98878	.98791
3.2	.99868	.99810	.99755	.99703	.99653	.99606	.99560	.99516	.99474	.99393	.99317	.99244	.99175	.99109
3.3	.99907	.99865	.99826	.99788	.99752	.99718	.99684	.99652	.99621	.99562	.99506	.99452	.99401	.99351
3.4	.99935	.99905	.99877	.99851	.99825	.99800	.99776	.99753	.99730	.99687	.99646	.99607	.99569	.99533
3.5	.99955	.99934	.99915	.99896	.99877	.99860	.99843	.99826	.99810	.99779	.99749	.99721	.99694	.99667
3.6	.99969	.99955	.99941	.99928	.99915	.99903	.99891	.99879	.99868	.99846	.99825	.99804	.99785	.99766
3.7	.99979	.99969	.99960	.99951	.99942	.99933	.99925	.99917	.99909	.99893	.99879	.99864	.99850	.99837
3.8	.99986	.99979	.99973	.99967	.99961	.99955	.99949	.99943	.99938	.99927	.99917	.99907	.99897	.99888
3.9	.99991	.99986	.99982	.99978	.99974	.99970	.99966	.99962	.99958	.99951	.99944	.99937	.99930	.99924
4.0	.99994	.99991	.99988	.99985	.99982	.99980	.99977	.99975	.99972	.99967	.99962	.99958	.999[illegible]3	.99949

Table C-7. One-Sided Probability Integral, $\rho = 0.7$

a \ n	2	3	4	5	6	7	8	9	10	12	14	16	18	20
-2.0	.00736	.00389	.00252	.00182	.00140	.00113	.00094	.00080	.00070	.00055	.00045	.00038	.00033	.00029
-1.9	.00983	.00535	.00353	.00258	.00201	.00163	.00137	.00117	.00102	.00081	.00067	.00057	.00050	.00044
-1.8	.01298	.00727	.00488	.00361	.00284	.00233	.00197	.00170	.00149	.00119	.00099	.00085	.00074	.00066
-1.7	.01698	.00977	.00668	.00501	.00398	.00329	.00279	.00243	.00214	.00173	.00145	.00125	.00109	.00097
-1.6	.02198	.01300	.00904	.00687	.00551	.00459	.00392	.00343	.00304	.00248	.00209	.00181	.00159	.00142
-1.5	.02817	.01710	.01210	.00930	.00754	.00633	.00545	.00478	.00426	.00350	.00297	.00259	.00229	.00206
-1.4	.03574	.02226	.01601	.01247	.01020	.00863	.00748	.00660	.00591	.00489	.00418	.00366	.00325	.00293
-1.3	.04490	.02867	.02097	.01652	.01364	.01163	.01014	.00900	.00810	.00676	.00582	.00511	.00457	.00414
-1.2	.05586	.03654	.02716	.02165	.01804	.01549	.01360	.01213	.01097	.00923	.00799	.00706	.00634	.00576
-1.1	.06882	.04610	.03480	.02806	.02359	.02041	.01802	.01616	.01468	.01245	.01084	.00964	.00869	.00793
-1.0	.08398	.05756	.04412	.03598	.03051	.02658	.02362	.02129	.01942	.01659	.01455	.01300	.01178	.01079
-0.9	.10151	.07114	.05534	.04563	.03903	.03424	.03060	.02773	.02541	.02187	.01929	.01732	.01577	.01450
-0.8	.12156	.08705	.06871	.05725	.04939	.04363	.03921	.03571	.03287	.02850	.02529	.02282	.02086	.01926
-0.7	.14423	.10547	.08442	.07109	.06182	.05498	.04969	.04548	.04203	.03671	.03277	.02972	.02728	.02529
-0.6	.16958	.12654	.10268	.08734	.07656	.06853	.06229	.05728	.05316	.04676	.04198	.03826	.03527	.03281
-0.5	.19760	.15037	.12364	.10621	.09383	.08453	.07725	.07136	.06650	.05889	.05318	.04870	.04508	.04209
-0.4	.22824	.17700	.14741	.12784	.11380	.10316	.09477	.08795	.08229	.07337	.06661	.06129	.05697	.05338
-0.3	.26137	.20641	.17405	.15235	.13662	.12460	.11505	.10725	.10073	.09040	.08253	.07629	.07119	.06694
-0.2	.29679	.23852	.20354	.17977	.16237	.14895	.13822	.12941	.12201	.11021	.10115	.09392	.08799	.08301
-0.1	.33425	.27316	.23581	.21009	.19106	.17628	.16438	.15455	.14625	.13293	.12263	.11437	.10756	.10182
0.0	.37341	.31011	.27069	.24319	.22265	.20656	.19353	.18269	.17351	.15868	.14712	.13780	.13008	.12354
0.1	.41390	.34906	.30794	.27891	.25700	.23971	.22561	.21382	.20378	.18747	.17468	.16430	.15565	.14830
0.2	.45531	.38964	.34727	.31697	.29389	.27554	.26048	.24782	.23698	.21927	.20529	.19387	.18432	.17616
0.3	.49720	.43144	.38828	.35705	.33304	.31380	.29790	.28448	.27293	.25395	.23885	.22647	.21604	.20711
0.4	.53909	.47400	.43056	.39875	.37407	.35414	.33758	.32352	.31137	.29128	.27520	.26192	.25070	.24105
0.5	.58053	.51682	.47362	.44161	.41655	.39617	.37913	.36458	.35196	.33096	.31405	.30000	.28808	.27778
0.6	.62107	.55943	.51696	.48513	.45999	.43941	.42209	.40724	.39428	.37261	.35505	.34039	.32788	.31702
0.7	.66030	.60133	.56006	.52880	.50389	.48335	.46598	.45099	.43786	.41579	.39777	.38266	.36971	.35842
0.8	.69785	.64206	.60244	.57210	.54772	.52747	.51025	.49532	.48218	.45997	.44174	.42636	.41311	.40153
0.9	.73339	.68121	.64362	.61451	.59093	.57122	.55436	.53967	.52669	.50463	.48640	.47095	.45758	.44584
1.0	.76667	.71842	.68315	.65557	.63304	.61409	.59778	.58350	.57084	.54920	.53121	.51588	.50256	.49082
1.1	.79749	.75336	.72067	.69484	.67358	.65557	.63999	.62629	.61409	.59313	.57559	.56057	.54747	.53588
1.2	.82572	.78582	.75586	.73196	.71213	.69523	.68053	.66755	.65593	.63588	.61901	.60448	.59176	.58046
1.3	.85130	.81563	.78849	.76663	.74836	.73269	.71899	.70684	.69592	.67698	.66095	.64708	.63487	.62400
1.4	.87422	.84269	.81839	.79863	.78200	.76765	.75504	.74380	.73367	.71599	.70095	.68787	.67632	.66598
1.5	.89455	.86698	.84547	.82783	.81287	.79988	.78841	.77815	.76885	.75257	.73863	.72646	.71566	.70596
1.6	.91238	.88854	.86972	.85415	.84085	.82924	.81894	.80968	.80126	.78644	.77369	.76250	.75253	.74355
1.7	.92785	.90746	.89119	.87760	.86592	.85567	.84652	.83827	.83074	.81743	.80590	.79574	.78666	.77844
1.8	.94112	.92389	.90997	.89826	.88812	.87917	.87115	.86388	.85723	.84541	.83513	.82602	.81785	.81043
1.9	.95239	.93798	.92622	.91624	.90754	.89982	.89288	.88656	.88075	.87039	.86133	.85326	.84600	.83938
2.0	.96186	.94994	.94011	.93170	.92433	.91776	.91181	.90638	.90138	.89240	.88451	.87747	.87109	.86527
2.1	.96973	.95998	.95186	.94486	.93868	.93315	.92812	.92351	.91925	.91157	.90479	.89870	.89318	.88811
2.2	.97620	.96831	.96167	.95591	.95080	.94620	.94200	.93813	.93454	.92806	.92230	.91711	.91238	.90803
2.3	.98146	.97515	.96979	.96510	.96092	.95713	.95367	.95046	.94748	.94207	.93724	.93287	.92887	.92518
2.4	.98569	.98070	.97642	.97265	.96927	.96619	.96336	.96074	.95829	.95383	.94982	.94619	.94285	.93977
2.5	.98907	.98515	.98177	.97878	.97608	.97361	.97132	.96920	.96722	.96358	.96030	.95732	.95457	.95202
2.6	.99172	.98869	.98605	.98370	.98156	.97960	.97779	.97609	.97450	.97157	.96892	.96650	.96426	.96218
2.7	.99379	.99147	.98943	.98760	.98594	.98440	.98297	.98163	.98037	.97804	.97593	.97398	.97218	.97050
2.8	.99539	.99363	.99208	.99067	.98938	.98819	.98708	.98603	.98505	.98322	.98155	.98001	.97858	.97724
2.9	.99661	.99529	.99412	.99305	.99207	.99115	.99030	.98949	.98873	.98731	.98601	.98480	.98368	.98263
3.0	.99753	.99655	.99567	.99487	.99413	.99344	.99279	.99217	.99159	.99050	.98950	.98857	.98770	.98688
3.1	.99822	.99750	.99685	.99626	.99570	.99519	.99470	.99423	.99379	.99297	.99221	.99150	.99083	.99020
3.2	.99873	.99821	.99773	.99729	.99689	.99650	.99614	.99580	.99547	.99485	.99428	.99374	.99324	.99276
3.3	.99910	.99872	.99838	.99807	.99777	.99749	.99722	.99697	.99672	.99627	.99584	.99544	.99507	.99471
3.4	.99937	.99910	.99886	.99863	.99842	.99821	.99802	.99784	.99766	.99732	.99701	.99672	.99644	.99617
3.5	.99956	.99937	.99920	.99904	.99889	.99874	.99860	.99847	.99834	.99810	.99788	.99766	.99746	.99726
3.6	.99970	.99957	.99945	.99933	.99923	.99912	.99903	.99893	.99884	.99867	.99851	.99835	.99821	.99807
3.7	.99980	.99971	.99962	.99954	.99947	.99940	.99933	.99926	.99920	.99907	.99896	.99885	.99875	.99865
3.8	.99986	.99980	.99974	.99969	.99964	.99959	.99954	.99949	.99945	.99936	.99928	.99921	.99913	.99906
3.9	.99991	.99987	.99983	.99979	.99976	.99972	.99969	.99966	.99963	.99957	.99951	.99946	.99941	.99936
4.0	.99994	.99991	.99989	.99986	.99984	.99981	.99979	.99977	.99975	.99971	.99967	.99963	.99960	.99957

Table C-8. One-Sided Probability Integral, $\rho = 0.8$

a \ n	2	3	4	5	6	7	8	9	10	12	14	16	18	20
-2.0	.00983	.00624	.00460	.00367	.00307	.00264	.00233	.00209	.00190	.00162	.00142	.00126	.00114	.00105
-1.9	.01290	.00836	.00624	.00502	.00423	.00367	.00325	.00293	.00267	.00228	.00201	.00180	.00163	.00150
-1.8	.01678	.01109	.00838	.00680	.00576	.00503	.00448	.00405	.00370	.00319	.00281	.00253	.00231	.00213
-1.7	.02162	.01455	.01114	.00912	.00778	.00682	.00610	.00554	.00509	.00440	.00390	.00353	.00323	.00298
-1.6	.02758	.01891	.01465	.01209	.01039	.00916	.00823	.00750	.00691	.00601	.00536	.00486	.00446	.00414
-1.5	.03486	.02434	.01907	.01588	.01373	.01217	.01098	.01005	.00929	.00813	.00728	.00662	.00610	.00567
-1.4	.04363	.03101	.02458	.02064	.01796	.01600	.01450	.01332	.01235	.01087	.00977	.00892	.00825	.00769
-1.3	.05411	.03913	.03136	.02655	.02325	.02082	.01896	.01747	.01626	.01438	.01298	.01190	.01104	.01032
-1.2	.06648	.04890	.03962	.03381	.02979	.02682	.02452	.02268	.02117	.01882	.01707	.01571	.01461	.01370
-1.1	.08093	.06052	.04957	.04263	.03779	.03419	.03139	.02914	.02728	.02439	.02221	.02051	.01914	.01799
-1.0	.09764	.07419	.06141	.05322	.04746	.04315	.03978	.03705	.03480	.03127	.02860	.02650	.02480	.02338
-0.9	.11673	.09010	.07535	.06580	.05902	.05391	.04990	.04664	.04394	.03968	.03645	.03389	.03181	.03007
-0.8	.13833	.10841	.09158	.08056	.07267	.06669	.06197	.05813	.05492	.04984	.04597	.04289	.04038	.03827
-0.7	.16250	.12925	.11025	.09768	.08862	.08170	.07621	.07172	.06796	.06198	.05739	.05373	.05073	.04820
-0.6	.18926	.15271	.13151	.11733	.10703	.09912	.09281	.08762	.08326	.07630	.07093	.06663	.06309	.06010
-0.5	.21856	.17883	.15543	.13962	.12804	.11910	.11193	.10601	.10102	.09301	.08680	.08180	.07767	.07417
-0.4	.25031	.20758	.18205	.16462	.15176	.14177	.13371	.12704	.12139	.11227	.10517	.09944	.09467	.09063
-0.3	.28434	.23890	.21134	.19234	.17822	.16718	.15824	.15079	.14447	.13423	.12621	.11970	.11427	.10965
-0.2	.32042	.27262	.24321	.22274	.20740	.19535	.18553	.17733	.17034	.15895	.15000	.14270	.13659	.13138
-0.1	.35828	.30854	.27750	.25569	.23923	.22621	.21556	.20663	.19898	.18649	.17660	.16851	.16172	.15590
0.0	.39758	.34638	.31399	.29100	.27354	.25965	.24823	.23861	.23034	.21678	.20600	.19714	.18967	.18326
0.1	.43794	.38580	.35238	.32844	.31011	.29545	.28335	.27311	.26428	.24973	.23811	.22851	.22040	.21341
0.2	.47894	.42643	.39232	.36766	.34866	.33337	.32068	.30990	.30059	.28516	.27277	.26251	.25380	.24627
0.3	.52016	.46785	.43342	.40831	.38882	.37305	.35990	.34870	.33898	.32281	.30976	.29891	.28967	.28166
0.4	.56115	.50960	.47524	.44995	.43019	.41411	.40065	.38913	.37910	.36235	.34878	.33743	.32774	.31931
0.5	.60149	.55124	.51732	.49214	.47233	.45613	.44250	.43079	.42057	.40342	.38945	.37773	.36768	.35892
0.6	.64075	.59230	.55920	.53440	.51477	.49862	.48498	.47322	.46292	.44556	.43135	.41939	.40910	.40010
0.7	.67858	.63237	.60040	.57626	.55702	.54112	.52763	.51595	.50568	.48831	.47403	.46196	.45155	.44241
0.8	.71462	.67102	.64051	.61727	.59863	.58314	.56994	.55847	.54836	.53119	.51700	.50496	.49454	.48537
0.9	.74861	.70792	.67911	.65698	.63913	.62421	.61145	.60032	.59047	.57369	.55976	.54789	.53759	.52849
1.0	.78033	.74275	.71585	.69502	.67811	.66391	.65171	.64103	.63156	.61534	.60182	.59026	.58018	.57127
1.1	.80960	.77529	.75044	.73105	.71521	.70185	.69032	.68019	.67117	.65568	.64271	.63158	.62185	.61321
1.2	.83634	.80534	.78264	.76480	.75012	.73769	.72692	.71742	.70894	.69432	.68202	.67142	.66213	.65386
1.3	.86051	.83279	.81229	.79605	.78262	.77118	.76122	.75242	.74454	.73089	.71936	.70939	.70062	.69280
1.4	.88212	.85761	.83930	.82468	.81251	.80211	.79302	.78495	.77771	.76511	.75443	.74516	.73698	.72966
1.5	.90124	.87981	.86362	.85060	.83971	.83035	.82215	.81484	.80826	.79677	.78699	.77847	.77093	.76416
1.6	.91798	.89944	.88529	.87383	.86419	.85587	.84854	.84199	.83608	.82573	.81687	.80913	.80225	.79607
1.7	.93249	.91661	.90438	.89440	.88597	.87865	.87218	.86638	.86113	.85191	.84398	.83703	.83083	.82525
1.8	.94492	.93147	.92102	.91243	.90512	.89876	.89312	.88804	.88343	.87530	.86829	.86212	.85661	.85162
1.9	.95547	.94420	.93536	.92805	.92179	.91632	.91145	.90706	.90306	.89598	.88985	.88443	.87958	.87518
2.0	.96432	.95498	.94759	.94143	.93614	.93149	.92733	.92357	.92014	.91404	.90874	.90404	.89982	.89598
2.1	.97168	.96402	.95790	.95277	.94834	.94443	.94093	.93775	.93483	.92964	.92511	.92108	.91745	.91415
2.2	.97772	.97151	.96650	.96227	.95861	.95536	.95244	.94978	.94733	.94296	.93914	.93572	.93264	.92982
2.3	.98264	.97765	.97359	.97015	.96715	.96448	.96207	.95987	.95785	.95421	.95101	.94815	.94556	.94319
2.4	.98660	.98263	.97939	.97661	.97418	.97201	.97005	.96825	.96659	.96360	.96096	.95859	.95643	.95446
2.5	.98975	.98663	.98406	.98185	.97991	.97816	.97658	.97512	.97378	.97135	.96919	.96725	.96548	.96386
2.6	.99223	.98981	.98780	.98605	.98451	.98313	.98187	.98070	.97962	.97767	.97593	.97436	.97292	.97160
2.7	.99417	.99231	.99075	.98939	.98818	.98709	.98610	.98518	.98432	.98277	.98138	.98012	.97897	.97791
2.8	.99567	.99425	.99305	.99200	.99107	.99022	.98945	.98873	.98806	.98684	.98574	.98475	.98383	.98299
2.9	.99681	.99574	.99483	.99403	.99332	.99267	.99207	.99151	.99099	.99005	.98919	.98841	.98770	.98703
3.0	.99767	.99688	.99619	.99559	.99505	.99456	.99410	.99368	.99328	.99255	.99189	.99129	.99073	.99022
3.1	.99832	.99773	.99723	.99678	.99637	.99600	.99565	.99533	.99503	.99448	.99398	.99352	.99309	.99269
3.2	.99880	.99837	.99800	.99767	.99736	.99709	.99683	.99659	.99637	.99595	.99557	.99522	.99490	.99460
3.3	.99915	.99884	.99857	.99833	.99811	.99790	.99771	.99754	.99737	.99706	.99678	.99652	.99628	.99605
3.4	.99940	.99918	.99899	.99881	.99865	.99850	.99837	.99824	.99811	.99789	.99768	.99749	.99731	.99714
3.5	.99958	.99943	.99929	.99917	.99905	.99894	.99884	.99875	.99866	.99850	.99835	.99821	.99807	.99795
3.6	.99971	.99960	.99951	.99942	.99934	.99926	.99919	.99912	.99906	.99894	.99883	.99873	.99864	.99855
3.7	.99980	.99973	.99966	.99960	.99954	.99949	.99944	.99939	.99935	.99926	.99919	.99911	.99905	.99898
3.8	.99987	.99982	.99977	.99973	.99969	.99965	.99962	.99958	.99955	.99949	.99944	.99939	.99934	.99929
3.9	.99991	.99988	.99985	.99982	.99979	.99976	.99974	.99972	.99969	.99965	.99962	.99958	.99955	.99951
4.0	.99994	.99992	.99990	.99988	.99986	.99984	.99982	.99981	.99979	.99977	.99974	.99972	.99969	.99967

Table C-9. One-Sided Probability Integral, $\rho = 0.9$

a \ n	2	3	4	5	6	7	8	9	10	12	14	16	18	20
-2.0	.01336	.01013	.00844	.00738	.00663	.00608	.00565	.00530	.00501	.00456	.00422	.00395	.00373	.00355
-1.9	.01727	.01325	.01111	.00976	.00882	.00811	.00755	.00710	.00673	.00614	.00570	.00535	.00507	.00483
-1.8	.02211	.01715	.01450	.01280	.01160	.01071	.01000	.00943	.00896	.00820	.00763	.00717	.00679	.00648
-1.7	.02806	.02201	.01873	.01662	.01513	.01400	.01311	.01239	.01179	.01084	.01011	.00954	.00906	.00866
-1.6	.03527	.02797	.02397	.02138	.01953	.01814	.01703	.01613	.01538	.01417	.01325	.01252	.01192	.01142
-1.5	.04395	.03522	.03039	.02724	.02498	.02327	.02191	.02080	.01987	.01838	.01724	.01632	.01555	.01491
-1.4	.05427	.04395	.03818	.03439	.03166	.02957	.02791	.02655	.02540	.02358	.02217	.02105	.02012	.01934
-1.3	.06641	.05434	.04752	.04300	.03974	.03723	.03524	.03359	.03221	.02998	.02825	.02686	.02570	.02473
-1.2	.08056	.06659	.05860	.05329	.04942	.04644	.04405	.04208	.04043	.03777	.03570	.03403	.03263	.03144
-1.1	.09687	.08086	.07162	.06543	.06090	.05740	.05458	.05225	.05027	.04709	.04460	.04260	.04095	.03955
-1.0	.11549	.09734	.08675	.07961	.07435	.07028	.06700	.06428	.06197	.05824	.05530	.05291	.05091	.04920
-0.9	.13652	.11615	.10415	.09600	.08998	.08528	.08148	.07832	.07564	.07129	.06789	.06513	.06282	.06083
-0.8	.16002	.13740	.12395	.11474	.10791	.10257	.09824	.09462	.09154	.08651	.08254	.07930	.07660	.07430
-0.7	.18602	.16116	.14624	.13595	.12828	.12226	.11736	.11326	.10977	.10407	.09957	.09587	.09274	.09005
-0.6	.21448	.18746	.17107	.15970	.15119	.14448	.13899	.13438	.13044	.12399	.11889	.11472	.11122	.10822
-0.5	.24533	.21624	.19844	.18601	.17665	.16925	.16319	.15809	.15372	.14654	.14080	.13606	.13206	.12863
-0.4	.27841	.24743	.22829	.21484	.20467	.19658	.18994	.18434	.17952	.17162	.16533	.16014	.15573	.15191
-0.3	.31352	.28088	.26051	.24612	.23518	.22646	.21927	.21318	.20793	.19926	.19231	.18658	.18174	.17757
-0.2	.35040	.31636	.29492	.27967	.26802	.25870	.25100	.24448	.23885	.22953	.22204	.21579	.21046	.20583
-0.1	.38875	.35361	.33129	.31531	.30305	.29319	.28502	.27807	.27205	.26207	.25406	.24742	.24177	.23686
0.0	.42822	.39233	.36931	.35274	.33996	.32967	.32111	.31382	.30749	.29693	.28837	.28122	.27513	.26985
0.1	.46841	.43213	.40866	.39165	.37848	.36782	.35893	.35134	.34474	.33376	.32486	.31740	.31100	.30540
0.2	.50892	.47263	.44894	.43168	.41825	.40735	.39822	.39040	.38358	.37215	.36287	.35512	.34849	.34273
0.3	.54934	.51341	.48976	.47241	.45886	.44782	.43856	.43061	.42367	.41202	.40249	.39445	.38753	.38147
0.4	.58925	.55405	.53068	.51344	.49991	.48884	.47951	.47149	.46447	.45268	.44306	.43497	.42799	.42187
0.5	.62825	.59412	.57127	.55431	.54095	.52999	.52073	.51274	.50573	.49388	.48414	.47592	.46883	.46264
0.6	.66597	.63323	.61112	.59461	.58155	.57079	.56168	.55381	.54690	.53522	.52559	.51742	.51032	.50406
0.7	.70209	.67099	.64982	.63394	.62130	.61086	.60199	.59430	.58752	.57603	.56655	.55854	.55161	.54551
0.8	.73631	.70708	.68703	.67189	.65980	.64978	.64125	.63384	.62730	.61617	.60692	.59903	.59217	.58612
0.9	.76840	.74122	.72242	.70814	.69670	.68717	.67904	.67195	.66569	.65503	.64619	.63865	.63208	.62624
1.0	.79818	.77317	.75572	.74241	.73169	.72275	.71508	.70839	.70245	.69229	.68383	.67660	.67031	.66476
1.1	.82554	.80276	.78674	.77445	.76452	.75620	.74905	.74281	.73726	.72776	.71981	.71297	.70697	.70164
1.2	.85042	.82988	.81534	.80411	.79500	.78734	.78074	.77496	.76981	.76096	.75357	.74723	.74168	.73675
1.3	.87281	.85449	.84141	.83127	.82300	.81603	.81002	.80473	.80001	.79188	.78502	.77911	.77393	.76932
1.4	.89275	.87658	.86494	.85587	.84845	.84217	.83673	.83194	.82767	.82030	.81409	.80872	.80398	.79974
1.5	.91033	.89620	.88596	.87794	.87134	.86575	.86089	.85660	.85275	.84609	.84047	.83561	.83134	.82754
1.6	.92568	.91345	.90453	.89751	.89171	.88678	.88249	.87869	.87528	.86937	.86435	.85998	.85612	.85265
1.7	.93893	.92847	.92078	.91469	.90965	.90534	.90158	.89825	.89526	.89005	.88564	.88180	.87841	.87536
1.8	.95025	.94139	.93483	.92962	.92528	.92156	.91831	.91542	.91282	.90827	.90440	.90101	.89802	.89534
1.9	.95984	.95241	.94687	.94245	.93875	.93558	.93279	.93032	.92808	.92418	.92084	.91792	.91531	.91296
2.0	.96786	.96170	.95708	.95336	.95025	.94757	.94521	.94310	.94119	.93786	.93500	.93250	.93029	.92829
2.1	.97451	.96946	.96563	.96255	.95995	.95771	.95573	.95397	.95237	.94955	.94713	.94500	.94309	.94138
2.2	.97997	.97586	.97273	.97020	.96806	.96620	.96456	.96309	.96176	.95941	.95739	.95562	.95403	.95259
2.3	.98440	.98110	.97857	.97650	.97476	.97324	.97189	.97068	.96958	.96764	.96596	.96448	.96316	.96197
2.4	.98796	.98533	.98331	.98165	.98024	.97901	.97791	.97693	.97604	.97445	.97308	.97186	.97077	.96978
2.5	.99080	.98873	.98712	.98580	.98467	.98368	.98281	.98201	.98129	.98001	.97890	.97792	.97704	.97623
2.6	.99303	.99142	.99015	.98911	.98822	.98744	.98674	.98611	.98553	.98451	.98361	.98282	.98211	.98146
2.7	.99477	.99352	.99254	.99173	.99103	.99042	.98987	.98937	.98892	.98811	.98740	.98678	.98621	.98569
2.8	.99611	.99516	.99441	.99378	.99324	.99276	.99234	.99195	.99159	.99096	.99040	.98991	.98946	.98906
2.9	.99714	.99642	.99585	.99537	.99495	.99459	.99426	.99396	.99368	.99319	.99276	.99237	.99202	.99170
3.0	.99791	.99737	.99694	.99658	.99627	.99599	.99574	.99551	.99530	.99492	.99459	.99430	.99403	.99378
3.1	.99849	.99809	.99777	.99750	.99727	.99706	.99687	.99669	.99654	.99625	.99600	.99577	.99557	.99538
3.2	.99892	.99863	.99839	.99819	.99802	.99786	.99772	.99759	.99747	.99726	.99707	.99690	.99674	.99660
3.3	.99923	.99902	.99885	.99870	.99857	.99846	.99836	.99826	.99817	.99801	.99787	.99775	.99763	.99752
3.4	.99946	.99931	.99919	.99908	.99899	.99890	.99883	.99876	.99869	.99858	.99847	.99838	.99829	.99821
3.5	.99963	.99952	.99943	.99935	.99929	.99923	.99917	.99912	.99907	.99899	.99891	.99884	.99878	.99872
3.6	.99974	.99967	.99960	.99955	.99950	.99946	.99942	.99938	.99935	.99929	.99923	.99918	.99914	.99910
3.7	.99982	.99977	.99973	.99969	.99966	.99963	.99960	.99957	.99955	.99950	.99947	.99943	.99940	.99937
3.8	.99988	.99984	.99981	.99979	.99976	.99974	.99972	.99971	.99969	.99966	.99963	.99961	.99958	.99956
3.9	.99992	.99990	.99987	.99986	.99984	.99983	.99981	.99980	.99979	.99977	.99975	.99973	.99971	.99970
4.0	.99995	.99993	.99992	.99990	.99989	.99988	.99987	.99987	.99986	.99984	.99983	.99982	.99981	.99980

Table C-10. One-Sided Probability Integral, $\rho = \frac{1}{3}$

a \ n	2	3	4	5	6	7	8	9	10	12	14	16	18	20
-2.0	.00231	.00046	.00014	.00005	.00002	.00001	.00001	.00000	.00000	.00000	.00000	.00000	.00000	.00000
-1.9	.00331	.00072	.00023	.00009	.00004	.00002	.00001	.00001	.00000	.00000	.00000	.00000	.00000	.00000
-1.8	.00469	.00111	.00037	.00015	.00007	.00004	.00002	.00001	.00001	.00000	.00000	.00000	.00000	.00000
-1.7	.00656	.00168	.00059	.00026	.00013	.00007	.00004	.00003	.00002	.00001	.00000	.00000	.00000	.00000
-1.6	.00906	.00251	.00093	.00042	.00022	.00012	.00007	.00005	.00003	.00002	.00001	.00001	.00000	.00000
-1.5	.01234	.00368	.00145	.00068	.00036	.00021	.00013	.00008	.00006	.00003	.00002	.00001	.00001	.00000
-1.4	.01661	.00532	.00220	.00108	.00059	.00035	.00022	.00015	.00010	.00006	.00003	.00002	.00001	.00001
-1.3	.02207	.00758	.00330	.00168	.00095	.00058	.00038	.00026	.00018	.00010	.00006	.00004	.00003	.00002
-1.2	.02896	.01063	.00486	.00257	.00150	.00094	.00063	.00043	.00031	.00018	.00011	.00007	.00005	.00004
-1.1	.03754	.01469	.00705	.00386	.00232	.00150	.00102	.00072	.00053	.00031	.00019	.00013	.00009	.00007
-1.0	.04807	.02002	.01005	.00571	.00353	.00233	.00162	.00117	.00087	.00052	.00033	.00023	.00016	.00012
-0.9	.06083	.02688	.01411	.00829	.00528	.00357	.00253	.00186	.00141	.00086	.00057	.00039	.00029	.00021
-0.8	.07607	.03558	.01948	.01185	.00776	.00537	.00388	.00290	.00223	.00140	.00094	.00067	.00049	.00037
-0.7	.09402	.04644	.02649	.01664	.01119	.00792	.00583	.00443	.00346	.00223	.00154	.00111	.00083	.00064
-0.6	.11489	.05978	.03547	.02298	.01586	.01147	.00860	.00665	.00526	.00349	.00245	.00180	.00136	.00106
-0.5	.13881	.07591	.04678	.03123	.02209	.01631	.01246	.00978	.00785	.00533	.00382	.00285	.00220	.00174
-0.4	.16586	.09512	.06076	.04176	.03024	.02280	.01772	.01413	.01150	.00799	.00584	.00443	.00347	.00278
-0.3	.19604	.11763	.07778	.05495	.04072	.03130	.02475	.02003	.01651	.01174	.00875	.00675	.00536	.00435
-0.2	.22928	.14360	.09813	.07119	.05393	.04224	.03395	.02787	.02328	.01692	.01284	.01007	.00810	.00666
-0.1	.26538	.17311	.12206	.09082	.07028	.05604	.04576	.03808	.03221	.02392	.01848	.01472	.01200	.00998
0.0	.30409	.20613	.14974	.11413	.09012	.07311	.06061	.05113	.04375	.03318	.02608	.02108	.01742	.01465
0.1	.34504	.24251	.18121	.14133	.11377	.09384	.07893	.06744	.05838	.04516	.03611	.02961	.02478	.02108
0.2	.38780	.28201	.21642	.17250	.14144	.11853	.10109	.08744	.07654	.06036	.04905	.04079	.03456	.02972
0.3	.43187	.32423	.25516	.20763	.17324	.14739	.12737	.11149	.09863	.07922	.06539	.05513	.04726	.04108
0.4	.47670	.36871	.29711	.24653	.20913	.18049	.15796	.13983	.12497	.10217	.08560	.07311	.06340	.05568
0.5	.52173	.41489	.34180	.28887	.24891	.21777	.19288	.17258	.15574	.12950	.11008	.09520	.08348	.07403
0.6	.56638	.46212	.38866	.33418	.29223	.25897	.23200	.20971	.19100	.16140	.13910	.12175	.10790	.09661
0.7	.61010	.50974	.43703	.38187	.33858	.30371	.27501	.25100	.23061	.19789	.17281	.15300	.13698	.12377
0.8	.65236	.55707	.48618	.43124	.38733	.35140	.32143	.29605	.27426	.23880	.21116	.18902	.17088	.15576
0.9	.69271	.60344	.53536	.48150	.43771	.40135	.37062	.34429	.32145	.28377	.25392	.22968	.20957	.19263
1.0	.73076	.64824	.58381	.53186	.48892	.45275	.42180	.39499	.37150	.33223	.30064	.27463	.25281	.23423
1.1	.76621	.69093	.63084	.58150	.54009	.50473	.47412	.44731	.42360	.38346	.35068	.32334	.30014	.28018
1.2	.79882	.73104	.67581	.62968	.59039	.55641	.52665	.50033	.47683	.43657	.40323	.37506	.35090	.32991
1.3	.82847	.76822	.71818	.67570	.63902	.60691	.57849	.55310	.53024	.49062	.45734	.42890	.40424	.38261
1.4	.85509	.80223	.75753	.71900	.68529	.65545	.62876	.60471	.58286	.54458	.51201	.48384	.45918	.43734
1.5	.87873	.83292	.79354	.75912	.72863	.70134	.67670	.65430	.63380	.59748	.56619	.53884	.51465	.49305
1.6	.89946	.86027	.82604	.79573	.76858	.74403	.72166	.70115	.68224	.64841	.61891	.59285	.56958	.54863
1.7	.91743	.88431	.85497	.82866	.80484	.78310	.76312	.74466	.72752	.69656	.66925	.64488	.62294	.60301
1.8	.93283	.90518	.88036	.85785	.83727	.81831	.80076	.78441	.76913	.74129	.71646	.69410	.67379	.65520
1.9	.94588	.92307	.90235	.88336	.86583	.84956	.83437	.82013	.80674	.78213	.75996	.73980	.72135	.70434
2.0	.95681	.93821	.92114	.90533	.89062	.87686	.86392	.85172	.84017	.81878	.79932	.78149	.76503	.74976
2.1	.96586	.95088	.93698	.92401	.91184	.90037	.88952	.87922	.86942	.85113	.83435	.81884	.80442	.79096
2.2	.97327	.96134	.95017	.93967	.92973	.92031	.91134	.90279	.89460	.87922	.86499	.85173	.83933	.82767
2.3	.97927	.96988	.96102	.95261	.94462	.93699	.92969	.92269	.91596	.90322	.89135	.88021	.86972	.85980
2.4	.98408	.97677	.96982	.96319	.95684	.95074	.94488	.93924	.93378	.92341	.91366	.90445	.89573	.88744
2.5	.98789	.98226	.97688	.97171	.96673	.96193	.95729	.95280	.94845	.94012	.93224	.92476	.91763	.91081
2.6	.99088	.98659	.98247	.97849	.97463	.97090	.96728	.96376	.96034	.95376	.94749	.94150	.93576	.93025
2.7	.99319	.98997	.98684	.98381	.98087	.97801	.97522	.97250	.96985	.96472	.95980	.95508	.95054	.94616
2.8	.99497	.99257	.99023	.98795	.98573	.98356	.98144	.97937	.97734	.97340	.96960	.96594	.96240	.95897
2.9	.99632	.99455	.99282	.99112	.98947	.98785	.98625	.98469	.98316	.98018	.97729	.97449	.97177	.96913
3.0	.99733	.99604	.99477	.99353	.99231	.99111	.98993	.98877	.98763	.98540	.98323	.98112	.97906	.97706
3.1	.99808	.99715	.99623	.99533	.99444	.99357	.99270	.99185	.99101	.98937	.98776	.98619	.98466	.98316
3.2	.99864	.99797	.99731	.99666	.99602	.99539	.99477	.99415	.99354	.99235	.99117	.99002	.98890	.98779
3.3	.99904	.99857	.99810	.99764	.99719	.99674	.99629	.99585	.99541	.99455	.99370	.99287	.99206	.99125
3.4	.99933	.99900	.99867	.99835	.99803	.99771	.99740	.99708	.99677	.99616	.99556	.99497	.99438	.99380
3.5	.99954	.99931	.99908	.99886	.99863	.99841	.99819	.99797	.99776	.99733	.99690	.99649	.99607	.99566
3.6	.99968	.99953	.99937	.99922	.99906	.99891	.99876	.99861	.99846	.99816	.99786	.99757	.99728	.99700
3.7	.99979	.99968	.99957	.99947	.99936	.99926	.99915	.99905	.99895	.99874	.99854	.99834	.99814	.99795
3.8	.99986	.99978	.99971	.99964	.99957	.99950	.99943	.99936	.99929	.99915	.99902	.99888	.99874	.99861
3.9	.99990	.99986	.99981	.99976	.99971	.99967	.99962	.99957	.99953	.99943	.99934	.99925	.99916	.99907
4.0	.99994	.99991	.99987	.99984	.99981	.99978	.99975	.99972	.99969	.99963	.99956	.99950	.99944	.99938

Table C-11. One-Sided Probability Integral, $\rho = \frac{2}{3}$

a \ n	2	3	4	5	6	7	8	9	10	12	14	16	18	20
-2.0	.00669	.00331	.00204	.00142	.00106	.00083	.00068	.00057	.00048	.00037	.00030	.00025	.00021	.00018
-1.9	.00897	.00459	.00289	.00204	.00154	.00122	.00100	.00085	.00073	.00056	.00045	.00038	.00032	.00028
-1.8	.01192	.00630	.00405	.00290	.00222	.00177	.00147	.00124	.00107	.00084	.00068	.00057	.00049	.00043
-1.7	.01567	.00854	.00560	.00407	.00315	.00254	.00212	.00181	.00157	.00124	.00101	.00086	.00074	.00065
-1.6	.02039	.01144	.00765	.00564	.00441	.00360	.00302	.00259	.00227	.00180	.00149	.00126	.00110	.00097
-1.5	.02626	.01517	.01035	.00773	.00611	.00503	.00425	.00368	.00323	.00259	.00216	.00184	.00161	.00142
-1.4	.03347	.01990	.01383	.01047	.00837	.00694	.00592	.00515	.00455	.00368	.00309	.00265	.00233	.00207
-1.3	.04224	.02581	.01827	.01402	.01133	.00948	.00813	.00712	.00632	.00516	.00436	.00377	.00333	.00297
-1.2	.05277	.03313	.02387	.01856	.01515	.01278	.01105	.00973	.00869	.00716	.00609	.00530	.00470	.00422
-1.1	.06528	.04208	.03085	.02430	.02003	.01704	.01483	.01313	.01179	.00980	.00840	.00735	.00655	.00591
-1.0	.07997	.05287	.03943	.03145	.02618	.02245	.01967	.01752	.01581	.01325	.01144	.01007	.00902	.00817
-0.9	.09702	.06575	.04985	.04025	.03383	.02924	.02579	.02310	.02095	.01771	.01539	.01363	.01226	.01116
-0.8	.11659	.08092	.06234	.05094	.04323	.03765	.03342	.03011	.02744	.02338	.02045	.01823	.01648	.01506
-0.7	.13880	.09859	.07715	.06378	.05462	.04793	.04282	.03878	.03551	.03051	.02686	.02407	.02187	.02007
-0.6	.16371	.11892	.09448	.07899	.06825	.06033	.05424	.04939	.04543	.03935	.03487	.03142	.02867	.02643
-0.5	.19134	.14203	.11451	.09679	.08436	.07510	.06793	.06218	.05746	.05015	.04472	.04052	.03715	.03439
-0.4	.22163	.16797	.13737	.11736	.10315	.09248	.08413	.07741	.07185	.06319	.05670	.05164	.04757	.04420
-0.3	.25448	.19677	.16314	.14082	.12479	.11264	.10307	.09530	.08885	.07871	.07107	.06506	.06019	.05616
-0.2	.28970	.22835	.19185	.16727	.14941	.13575	.12491	.11605	.10866	.09696	.08807	.08103	.07530	.07052
-0.1	.32702	.26257	.22343	.19669	.17705	.16189	.14977	.13981	.13145	.11812	.10791	.09978	.09312	.08754
0.0	.36614	.29921	.25775	.22902	.20769	.19109	.17771	.16665	.15732	.14234	.13077	.12150	.11387	.10744
0.1	.40668	.33798	.29459	.26412	.24124	.22328	.20871	.19659	.18630	.16969	.15676	.14633	.13770	.13040
0.2	.44822	.37852	.33366	.30173	.27751	.25833	.24266	.22955	.21837	.20018	.18592	.17434	.16471	.15652
0.3	.49031	.42041	.37459	.34154	.31622	.29601	.27937	.26537	.25336	.23372	.21820	.20552	.19491	.18585
0.4	.53248	.46319	.41696	.38317	.35703	.33599	.31856	.30380	.29108	.27014	.25346	.23976	.22824	.21835
0.5	.57426	.50637	.46027	.42616	.39950	.37788	.35985	.34449	.33119	.30916	.29149	.27688	.26452	.25388
0.6	.61520	.54944	.50403	.47001	.44317	.42123	.40281	.38704	.37331	.35043	.33194	.31657	.30350	.29219
0.7	.65487	.59190	.54770	.51418	.48750	.46552	.44695	.43095	.41697	.39351	.37443	.35847	.34483	.33298
0.8	.69288	.63328	.59076	.55815	.53194	.51020	.49171	.47570	.46164	.43790	.41846	.40211	.38806	.37580
0.9	.72890	.67313	.63272	.60137	.57596	.55471	.53654	.52072	.50676	.48305	.46351	.44697	.43270	.42019
1.0	.76266	.71106	.67311	.64335	.61900	.59851	.58087	.56544	.55175	.52839	.50899	.49249	.47817	.46557
1.1	.79394	.74676	.71154	.68362	.66059	.64106	.62416	.60929	.59605	.57332	.55432	.53806	.52390	.51138
1.2	.82263	.77996	.74766	.72179	.70027	.68189	.66590	.65176	.63912	.61728	.59891	.58311	.56928	.55700
1.3	.84863	.81049	.78122	.75753	.73766	.72059	.70565	.69237	.68045	.65974	.64221	.62705	.61372	.60184
1.4	.87196	.83824	.81202	.79059	.77248	.75681	.74302	.73072	.71961	.70023	.68372	.66936	.65668	.64534
1.5	.89264	.86318	.83997	.82081	.80450	.79030	.77774	.76647	.75626	.73835	.72300	.70958	.69768	.68698
1.6	.91079	.88533	.86502	.84811	.83359	.82088	.80958	.79939	.79012	.77378	.75969	.74731	.73628	.72634
1.7	.92654	.90478	.88722	.87246	.85971	.84847	.83842	.82933	.82102	.80630	.79353	.78226	.77217	.76304
1.8	.94006	.92168	.90667	.89394	.88287	.87305	.86423	.85621	.84886	.83577	.82435	.81421	.80511	.79683
1.9	.95154	.93618	.92350	.91266	.90316	.89469	.88704	.88006	.87364	.86213	.85205	.84306	.83494	.82754
2.0	.96119	.94849	.93791	.92877	.92072	.91350	.90695	.90095	.89541	.88543	.87664	.86876	.86163	.85509
2.1	.96920	.95883	.95009	.94249	.93574	.92967	.92413	.91903	.91430	.90576	.89819	.89138	.88518	.87949
2.2	.97579	.96741	.96027	.95402	.94844	.94339	.93876	.93448	.93051	.92328	.91685	.91103	.90572	.90082
2.3	.98115	.97445	.96869	.96361	.95905	.95489	.95107	.94753	.94422	.93819	.93279	.92789	.92339	.91923
2.4	.98546	.98016	.97557	.97149	.96780	.96443	.96131	.95841	.95570	.95073	.94625	.94217	.93841	.93492
2.5	.98889	.98475	.98113	.97789	.97494	.97224	.96973	.96738	.96518	.96113	.95746	.95411	.95101	.94813
2.6	.99159	.98839	.98557	.98302	.98070	.97855	.97656	.97468	.97292	.96966	.96670	.96397	.96145	.95909
2.7	.99370	.99125	.98907	.98710	.98529	.98361	.98203	.98056	.97916	.97657	.97421	.97202	.96999	.96809
2.8	.99532	.99347	.99181	.99030	.98890	.98760	.98638	.98522	.98413	.98210	.98023	.97851	.97689	.97538
2.9	.99656	.99517	.99392	.99277	.99171	.99071	.98978	.98889	.98805	.98647	.98502	.98367	.98240	.98121
3.0	.99750	.99647	.99554	.99468	.99387	.99312	.99241	.99173	.99109	.98988	.98877	.98772	.98674	.98582
3.1	.99819	.99744	.99675	.99612	.99552	.99496	.99442	.99392	.99343	.99252	.99167	.99087	.99012	.98941
3.2	.99871	.99817	.99766	.99720	.99676	.99634	.99595	.99557	.99521	.99452	.99389	.99329	.99272	.99218
3.3	.99909	.99870	.99834	.99800	.99768	.99737	.99708	.99681	.99654	.99604	.99556	.99512	.99469	.99429
3.4	.99936	.99908	.99883	.99858	.99835	.99813	.99792	.99772	.99753	.99716	.99681	.99649	.99618	.99588
3.5	.99956	.99936	.99918	.99901	.99884	.99869	.99854	.99839	.99825	.99799	.99774	.99750	.99727	.99706
3.6	.99970	.99956	.99943	.99931	.99920	.99909	.99898	.99888	.99878	.99859	.99841	.99824	.99808	.99792
3.7	.99979	.99970	.99961	.99953	.99945	.99937	.99930	.99923	.99916	.99902	.99890	.99878	.99866	.99855
3.8	.99986	.99980	.99974	.99968	.99963	.99957	.99952	.99947	.99942	.99933	.99924	.99916	.99908	.99900
3.9	.99991	.99986	.99982	.99979	.99975	.99971	.99968	.99964	.99961	.99955	.99948	.99943	.99937	.99931
4.0	.99994	.99991	.99988	.99986	.99983	.99981	.99978	.99976	.99974	.99969	.99965	.99961	.99957	.99954

Table C-12. One-Sided Probability Integral, $\rho = \frac{1}{4}$

a \ n	2	3	4	5	6	7	8	9	10	12	14	16	18	20
-2.0	.00168	.00024	.00005	.00001	.00000	.00000	.00000	.00000	.00000	.00000	.00000	.00000	.00000	.00000
-1.9	.00247	.00039	.00009	.00003	.00001	.00000	.00000	.00000	.00000	.00000	.00000	.00000	.00000	.00000
-1.8	.00356	.00062	.00015	.00005	.00002	.00001	.00000	.00000	.00000	.00000	.00000	.00000	.00000	.00000
-1.7	.00508	.00098	.00026	.00009	.00003	.00002	.00001	.00000	.00000	.00000	.00000	.00000	.00000	.00000
-1.6	.00715	.00151	.00044	.00015	.00006	.00003	.00002	.00001	.00000	.00000	.00000	.00000	.00000	.00000
-1.5	.00991	.00230	.00071	.00027	.00012	.00006	.00003	.00002	.00001	.00000	.00000	.00000	.00000	.00000
-1.4	.01357	.00345	.00114	.00045	.00021	.00010	.00006	.00003	.00002	.00001	.00000	.00000	.00000	.00000
-1.3	.01832	.00508	.00180	.00075	.00036	.00019	.00010	.00006	.00004	.00002	.00001	.00000	.00000	.00000
-1.2	.02441	.00735	.00278	.00123	.00061	.00033	.00019	.00012	.00007	.00003	.00002	.00001	.00001	.00000
-1.1	.03210	.01047	.00421	.00195	.00101	.00056	.00034	.00021	.00014	.00007	.00003	.00002	.00001	.00001
-1.0	.04168	.01468	.00626	.00305	.00164	.00095	.00058	.00038	.00025	.00012	.00007	.00004	.00002	.00002
-0.9	.05342	.02025	.00914	.00466	.00260	.00156	.00098	.00065	.00045	.00023	.00013	.00008	.00005	.00003
-0.8	.06762	.02749	.01310	.00699	.00405	.00250	.00163	.00110	.00077	.00041	.00024	.00015	.00010	.00007
-0.7	.08453	.03675	.01846	.01028	.00617	.00394	.00263	.00182	.00131	.00072	.00043	.00028	.00018	.00013
-0.6	.10439	.04838	.02556	.01483	.00922	.00606	.00415	.00295	.00216	.00124	.00076	.00050	.00034	.00024
-0.5	.12738	.06274	.03478	.02099	.01350	.00912	.00641	.00465	.00347	.00206	.00131	.00088	.00061	.00044
-0.4	.15360	.08016	.04653	.02916	.01936	.01344	.00968	.00718	.00546	.00335	.00219	.00150	.00107	.00079
-0.3	.18311	.10095	.06121	.03977	.02722	.01941	.01431	.01084	.00839	.00532	.00358	.00251	.00183	.00137
-0.2	.21583	.12532	.07922	.05327	.03755	.02746	.02070	.01599	.01261	.00825	.00569	.00409	.00304	.00232
-0.1	.25162	.15344	.10089	.07010	.05081	.03808	.02932	.02308	.01852	.01248	.00883	.00649	.00491	.00381
0.0	.29022	.18532	.12648	.09066	.06748	.05176	.04067	.03262	.02660	.01845	.01338	.01004	.00775	.00612
0.1	.33127	.22090	.15615	.11528	.08800	.06900	.05530	.04513	.03739	.02666	.01979	.01516	.01191	.00956
0.2	.37435	.25994	.18994	.14418	.11274	.09027	.07370	.06116	.05145	.03768	.02861	.02235	.01787	.01457
0.3	.41893	.30210	.22771	.17745	.14193	.11593	.09634	.08123	.06933	.05208	.04041	.03218	.02617	.02165
0.4	.46445	.34691	.26918	.21500	.17569	.14623	.12358	.10578	.09154	.07045	.05582	.04526	.03740	.03140
0.5	.51030	.39377	.31393	.25660	.21393	.18125	.15563	.13514	.11849	.09331	.07542	.06223	.05223	.04446
0.6	.55588	.44203	.36137	.30181	.25641	.22089	.19253	.16946	.15044	.12109	.09974	.08369	.07129	.06149
0.7	.60060	.49095	.41080	.35003	.30265	.26484	.23410	.20870	.18745	.15405	.12919	.11013	.09514	.08313
0.8	.64391	.53980	.46144	.40054	.35202	.31256	.27994	.25259	.22938	.19223	.16398	.14191	.12426	.10990
0.9	.68530	.58784	.51245	.45248	.40372	.36337	.32946	.30062	.27582	.23545	.20411	.17916	.15890	.14217
1.0	.72437	.63439	.56299	.50495	.45686	.41638	.38185	.35208	.32616	.28326	.24929	.22177	.19908	.18009
1.1	.76077	.67884	.61227	.55704	.51046	.47063	.43617	.40607	.37954	.33497	.29899	.26936	.24457	.22353
1.2	.79427	.72067	.65954	.60787	.56355	.52509	.49137	.46155	.43498	.38965	.35241	.32126	.29482	.27209
1.3	.82472	.75947	.70419	.65663	.61520	.57874	.54637	.51742	.49135	.44625	.40855	.37654	.34901	.32505
1.4	.85205	.79498	.74571	.70263	.66457	.63063	.60014	.57258	.54751	.50357	.46625	.43410	.40608	.38143
1.5	.87630	.82701	.78374	.74533	.71094	.67991	.65173	.62599	.60236	.56042	.52426	.49268	.46483	.44006
1.6	.89755	.85552	.81806	.78434	.75378	.72590	.70031	.67672	.65489	.61566	.58135	.55101	.52394	.49961
1.7	.91595	.88057	.84858	.81943	.79270	.76807	.74525	.72403	.70422	.66826	.63637	.60784	.58211	.55874
1.8	.93170	.90228	.87533	.85050	.82750	.80609	.78609	.76734	.74971	.71737	.68833	.66205	.63811	.61617
1.9	.94503	.92086	.89847	.87762	.85812	.83982	.82258	.80630	.79089	.76234	.73641	.71270	.69089	.67073
2.0	.95618	.93656	.91819	.90093	.88465	.86925	.85464	.84074	.82750	.80276	.78005	.75908	.73962	.72148
2.1	.96540	.94966	.93478	.92069	.90729	.89453	.88234	.87068	.85950	.83844	.81892	.80073	.78370	.76772
2.2	.97294	.96046	.94856	.93721	.92634	.91592	.90591	.89628	.88700	.86938	.85290	.83741	.82281	.80900
2.3	.97904	.96925	.95986	.95083	.94214	.93375	.92565	.91782	.91024	.89575	.88208	.86913	.85684	.84514
2.4	.98392	.97633	.96900	.96191	.95505	.94840	.94194	.93567	.92957	.91784	.90670	.89607	.88592	.87619
2.5	.98778	.98196	.97631	.97081	.96547	.96026	.95519	.95024	.94541	.93607	.92713	.91855	.91031	.90237
2.6	.99080	.98639	.98208	.97787	.97376	.96974	.96581	.96196	.95819	.95086	.94380	.93700	.93042	.92405
2.7	.99314	.98983	.98658	.98340	.98028	.97721	.97421	.97125	.96835	.96269	.95720	.95189	.94672	.94170
2.8	.99494	.99247	.99005	.98767	.98533	.98303	.98076	.97852	.97632	.97200	.96780	.96371	.95973	.95583
2.9	.99630	.99449	.99270	.99094	.98921	.98749	.98580	.98413	.98248	.97924	.97607	.97297	.96994	.96697
3.0	.99732	.99600	.99470	.99341	.99214	.99088	.98963	.98840	.98718	.98478	.98242	.98011	.97783	.97560
3.1	.99807	.99713	.99619	.99526	.99433	.99342	.99251	.99162	.99073	.98897	.98724	.98553	.98385	.98220
3.2	.99863	.99796	.99728	.99662	.99596	.99530	.99465	.99400	.99336	.99209	.99084	.98960	.98837	.98717
3.3	.99904	.99856	.99808	.99761	.99715	.99668	.99622	.99576	.99530	.99439	.99349	.99260	.99173	.99086
3.4	.99933	.99899	.99866	.99833	.99800	.99768	.99735	.99703	.99671	.99607	.99543	.99480	.99418	.99356
3.5	.99954	.99930	.99908	.99885	.99862	.99839	.99816	.99794	.99771	.99727	.99682	.99638	.99595	.99551
3.6	.99968	.99952	.99937	.99921	.99905	.99890	.99874	.99859	.99843	.99812	.99782	.99751	.99721	.99691
3.7	.99978	.99968	.99957	.99946	.99936	.99925	.99915	.99904	.99893	.99872	.99851	.99831	.99810	.99789
3.8	.99986	.99978	.99971	.99964	.99957	.99950	.99943	.99935	.99928	.99914	.99900	.99886	.99872	.99858
3.9	.99990	.99986	.99981	.99976	.99971	.99966	.99962	.99957	.99952	.99943	.99933	.99924	.99915	.99905
4.0	.99994	.99991	.99987	.99984	.99981	.99978	.99975	.99972	.99968	.99962	.99956	.99950	.99944	.99937

Table C-13. One-Sided Probability Integral, $\rho = \frac{3}{4}$

a \ n	2	3	4	5	6	7	8	9	10	12	14	16	18	20
-2.0	.00850	.00494	.00342	.00259	.00209	.00174	.00149	.00131	.00116	.00095	.00081	.00070	.00062	.00056
-1.9	.01125	.00670	.00471	.00361	.00293	.00246	.00213	.00187	.00167	.00138	.00118	.00103	.00091	.00082
-1.8	.01475	.00899	.00641	.00498	.00407	.00345	.00299	.00264	.00237	.00197	.00169	.00149	.00133	.00120
-1.7	.01914	.01193	.00864	.00678	.00559	.00477	.00416	.00370	.00333	.00279	.00241	.00212	.00190	.00173
-1.6	.02460	.01569	.01153	.00914	.00760	.00652	.00572	.00511	.00462	.00390	.00338	.00300	.00270	.00246
-1.5	.03130	.02041	.01521	.01219	.01021	.00882	.00778	.00698	.00634	.00538	.00470	.00418	.00378	.00346
-1.4	.03945	.02627	.01987	.01608	.01358	.01180	.01047	.00943	.00860	.00735	.00645	.00577	.00524	.00481
-1.3	.04924	.03349	.02567	.02099	.01786	.01562	.01393	.01261	.01155	.00993	.00877	.00788	.00718	.00661
-1.2	.06088	.04226	.03283	.02711	.02325	.02046	.01834	.01667	.01533	.01327	.01177	.01063	.00972	.00898
-1.1	.07455	.05280	.04156	.03464	.02993	.02650	.02388	.02180	.02012	.01753	.01564	.01418	.01301	.01206
-1.0	.09046	.06532	.05207	.04382	.03814	.03396	.03076	.02821	.02612	.02291	.02054	.01870	.01723	.01603
-0.9	.10874	.08002	.06459	.05485	.04808	.04307	.03920	.03610	.03356	.02962	.02668	.02440	.02257	.02106
-0.8	.12954	.09709	.07933	.06797	.06000	.05406	.04943	.04571	.04265	.03787	.03429	.03149	.02923	.02736
-0.7	.15293	.11668	.09647	.08338	.07411	.06715	.06169	.05728	.05363	.04790	.04359	.04019	.03744	.03516
-0.6	.17896	.13891	.11618	.10127	.09062	.08255	.07620	.07103	.06674	.05996	.05482	.05076	.04745	.04469
-0.5	.20761	.16386	.13859	.12181	.10970	.10047	.09315	.08718	.08218	.07427	.06822	.06342	.05949	.05620
-0.4	.23878	.19153	.16375	.14509	.13150	.12107	.11274	.10591	.10018	.09104	.08401	.07841	.07380	.06992
-0.3	.27235	.22187	.19170	.17118	.15611	.14445	.13510	.12738	.12088	.11046	.10240	.09593	.09059	.08609
-0.2	.30809	.25478	.22237	.20008	.18356	.17069	.16031	.15170	.14441	.13267	.12354	.11617	.11006	.10488
-0.1	.34575	.29006	.25565	.23172	.21382	.19979	.18840	.17891	.17084	.15777	.14755	.13925	.13235	.12648
0.0	.38497	.32746	.29135	.26594	.24679	.23167	.21932	.20899	.20017	.18580	.17449	.16527	.15756	.15099
0.1	.42540	.36666	.32920	.30254	.28229	.26618	.25296	.24184	.23231	.21671	.20435	.19423	.18573	.17846
0.2	.46661	.40728	.36886	.34123	.32005	.30310	.28912	.27730	.26712	.25038	.23704	.22607	.21682	.20887
0.3	.50817	.44891	.40995	.38164	.35976	.34214	.32751	.31510	.30437	.28663	.27241	.26066	.25070	.24212
0.4	.54963	.49109	.45204	.42336	.40103	.38292	.36781	.35493	.34375	.32517	.31020	.29776	.28719	.27804
0.5	.59053	.53335	.49465	.46594	.44341	.42502	.40960	.39639	.38489	.36567	.35009	.33709	.32599	.31636
0.6	.63046	.57522	.53730	.50890	.48642	.46798	.45242	.43904	.42734	.40770	.39169	.37827	.36677	.35674
0.7	.66901	.61623	.57951	.55172	.52958	.51129	.49579	.48239	.47063	.45080	.43455	.42086	.40908	.39878
0.8	.70583	.65597	.62080	.59394	.57236	.55444	.53918	.52593	.51426	.49447	.47817	.46438	.45247	.44201
0.9	.74062	.69403	.66074	.63506	.61430	.59694	.58208	.56914	.55769	.53819	.52204	.50831	.49641	.48593
1.0	.77315	.73009	.69892	.67467	.65491	.63830	.62401	.61151	.60041	.58143	.56562	.55212	.54037	.52999
1.1	.80322	.76387	.73503	.71237	.69379	.67808	.66451	.65258	.64195	.62369	.60840	.59528	.58383	.57368
1.2	.83074	.79516	.76877	.74786	.73059	.71590	.70315	.69190	.68185	.66449	.64988	.63730	.62626	.61645
1.3	.85564	.82383	.79995	.78087	.76500	.75144	.73961	.72912	.71972	.70342	.68963	.67770	.66720	.65784
1.4	.87794	.84981	.82845	.81123	.79682	.78444	.77359	.76393	.75525	.74012	.72726	.71609	.70622	.69739
1.5	.89769	.87309	.85419	.83884	.82591	.81473	.80489	.79611	.78818	.77431	.76246	.75212	.74296	.73473
1.6	.91500	.89372	.87719	.86366	.85218	.84221	.83340	.82550	.81835	.80578	.79499	.78554	.77713	.76956
1.7	.93001	.91180	.89751	.88571	.87564	.86685	.85905	.85204	.84566	.83440	.82470	.81616	.80855	.80166
1.8	.94289	.92748	.91525	.90508	.89636	.88870	.88187	.87571	.87009	.86014	.85151	.84389	.83707	.83089
1.9	.95382	.94092	.93058	.92191	.91443	.90784	.90194	.89659	.89169	.88299	.87542	.86870	.86267	.85718
2.0	.96300	.95231	.94367	.93637	.93003	.92442	.91937	.91478	.91057	.90306	.89648	.89063	.88536	.88055
2.1	.97063	.96187	.95472	.94864	.94334	.93861	.93435	.93046	.92688	.92046	.91483	.90979	.90524	.90107
2.2	.97690	.96980	.96396	.95895	.95456	.95063	.94707	.94381	.94080	.93538	.93061	.92633	.92244	.91888
2.3	.98200	.97631	.97158	.96751	.96391	.96068	.95774	.95504	.95254	.94803	.94403	.94043	.93715	.93414
2.4	.98611	.98160	.97781	.97453	.97162	.96899	.96660	.96439	.96233	.95862	.95531	.95232	.94959	.94707
2.5	.98938	.98584	.98285	.98023	.97790	.97579	.97386	.97207	.97041	.96738	.96467	.96222	.95997	.95790
2.6	.99195	.98921	.98687	.98481	.98297	.98129	.97975	.97832	.97698	.97455	.97236	.97037	.96855	.96685
2.7	.99396	.99185	.99004	.98844	.98700	.98568	.98447	.98334	.98228	.98034	.97860	.97700	.97553	.97417
2.8	.99551	.99391	.99253	.99129	.99018	.98916	.98821	.98733	.98650	.98497	.98360	.98233	.98117	.98008
2.9	.99670	.99550	.99445	.99351	.99265	.99187	.99114	.99046	.98982	.98863	.98756	.98657	.98566	.98480
3.0	.99759	.99670	.99591	.99521	.99456	.99397	.99341	.99289	.99240	.99149	.99066	.98990	.98919	.98852
3.1	.99826	.99760	.99702	.99650	.99601	.99557	.99515	.99476	.99438	.99369	.99306	.99248	.99194	.99142
3.2	.99876	.99828	.99785	.99747	.99711	.99678	.99647	.99617	.99589	.99538	.99490	.99446	.99405	.99366
3.3	.99912	.99878	.99847	.99818	.99792	.99768	.99745	.99723	.99703	.99665	.99629	.99596	.99565	.99536
3.4	.99938	.99914	.99892	.99871	.99852	.99835	.99818	.99802	.99787	.99759	.99733	.99709	.99686	.99664
3.5	.99957	.99940	.99924	.99910	.99896	.99884	.99872	.99860	.99849	.99829	.99810	.99792	.99776	.99760
3.6	.99971	.99958	.99947	.99937	.99928	.99919	.99910	.99902	.99894	.99880	.99866	.99853	.99841	.99830
3.7	.99980	.99972	.99964	.99957	.99950	.99944	.99938	.99932	.99927	.99916	.99907	.99898	.99889	.99881
3.8	.99986	.99981	.99976	.99971	.99966	.99962	.99957	.99953	.99950	.99942	.99936	.99929	.99923	.99917
3.9	.99991	.99987	.99984	.99980	.99977	.99974	.99971	.99968	.99966	.99961	.99956	.99952	.99947	.99943
4.0	.99994	.99991	.99989	.99987	.99985	.99983	.99981	.99979	.99977	.99974	.99970	.99967	.99964	.99961

Table D-0. Two-Sided Probability Integral, $\rho = 0.0$

a \ n	2	3	4	5	6	7	8	9	10	12	14	16	18	20
0.1	.00635	.00051	.00004	.00000	.00000	.00000	.00000	.00000	.00000	.00000	.00000	.00000	.00000	.00000
0.2	.02513	.00398	.00063	.00010	.00002	.00000	.00000	.00000	.00000	.00000	.00000	.00000	.00000	.00000
0.3	.05561	.01311	.00309	.00073	.00017	.00004	.00001	.00000	.00000	.00000	.00000	.00000	.00000	.00000
0.4	.09662	.03003	.00934	.00290	.00090	.00028	.00009	.00003	.00001	.00000	.00000	.00000	.00000	.00000
0.5	.14663	.05615	.02150	.00823	.00315	.00121	.00046	.00018	.00007	.00001	.00000	.00000	.00000	.00000
0.6	.20385	.09204	.04155	.01876	.00847	.00382	.00173	.00078	.00035	.00007	.00001	.00000	.00000	.00000
0.7	.26633	.13745	.07093	.03661	.01889	.00975	.00503	.00260	.00134	.00036	.00010	.00003	.00001	.00000
0.8	.33211	.19139	.11030	.06356	.03663	.02111	.01217	.00701	.00404	.00134	.00045	.00015	.00005	.00002
0.9	.39927	.25229	.15942	.10073	.06365	.04022	.02541	.01606	.01015	.00405	.00162	.00065	.00026	.00010
1.0	.46606	.31818	.21722	.14829	.10124	.06911	.04718	.03221	.02199	.01025	.00478	.00223	.00104	.00048
1.1	.53096	.38689	.28192	.20542	.14968	.10907	.07948	.05791	.04220	.02241	.01190	.00632	.00335	.00178
1.2	.59269	.45629	.35128	.27043	.20820	.16028	.12339	.09500	.07313	.04335	.02569	.01523	.00902	.00535
1.3	.65028	.52438	.42286	.34100	.27498	.22174	.17881	.14419	.11628	.07561	.04917	.03197	.02079	.01352
1.4	.70306	.58951	.49429	.41446	.34752	.29139	.24433	.20486	.17178	.12077	.08491	.05970	.04197	.02951
1.5	.75062	.65033	.56344	.48815	.42293	.36642	.31746	.27504	.23829	.17887	.13426	.10078	.07565	.05678
1.6	.79281	.70592	.62856	.55967	.49833	.44371	.39508	.35178	.31323	.24833	.19688	.15609	.12375	.09811
1.7	.82968	.75573	.68837	.62702	.57113	.52023	.47386	.43162	.39315	.32619	.27063	.22454	.18630	.15457
1.8	.86144	.79954	.74208	.68876	.63926	.59332	.55069	.51112	.47439	.40866	.35203	.30326	.26124	.22504
1.9	.88843	.83741	.78931	.74398	.70125	.66098	.62301	.58723	.55351	.49175	.43689	.38815	.34484	.30637
2.0	.91107	.86962	.83005	.79228	.75623	.72182	.68898	.65763	.62771	.57189	.52103	.47469	.43248	.39402
2.1	.92982	.89660	.86456	.83367	.80389	.77517	.74747	.72076	.69501	.64623	.60088	.55871	.51950	.48304
2.2	.94516	.91888	.89333	.86849	.84434	.82086	.79803	.77584	.75427	.71290	.67381	.63686	.60193	.56892
2.3	.95756	.93703	.91693	.89726	.87802	.85918	.84076	.82272	.80508	.77091	.73820	.70687	.67688	.64815
2.4	.96748	.95162	.93601	.92067	.90557	.89073	.87612	.86176	.84763	.82007	.79340	.76759	.74263	.71848
2.5	.97532	.96320	.95124	.93943	.92776	.91624	.90486	.89362	.88252	.86074	.83949	.81877	.79856	.77885
2.6	.98144	.97229	.96323	.95425	.94535	.93654	.92781	.91916	.91059	.89369	.87711	.86083	.84486	.82918
2.7	.98618	.97934	.97255	.96581	.95911	.95246	.94586	.93930	.93278	.91989	.90718	.89464	.88228	.87009
2.8	.98981	.98475	.97972	.97471	.96973	.96477	.95984	.95494	.95006	.94037	.93078	.92130	.91190	.90261
2.9	.99255	.98885	.98516	.98148	.97782	.97417	.97053	.96691	.96330	.95613	.94901	.94194	.93492	.92795
3.0	.99461	.99192	.98924	.98657	.98391	.98125	.97860	.97596	.97333	.96808	.96286	.95767	.95250	.94737
3.1	.99613	.99421	.99228	.99036	.98844	.98653	.98462	.98272	.98082	.97702	.97325	.96948	.96573	.96200
3.2	.99725	.99588	.99451	.99315	.99178	.99042	.98906	.98770	.98634	.98363	.98093	.97824	.97555	.97287
3.3	.99807	.99710	.99614	.99518	.99421	.99325	.99229	.99133	.99037	.98846	.98655	.98464	.98274	.98084
3.4	.99865	.99798	.99731	.99664	.99596	.99529	.99462	.99395	.99328	.99194	.99061	.98927	.98794	.98661
3.5	.99907	.99860	.99814	.99768	.99721	.99675	.99628	.99582	.99536	.99443	.99351	.99258	.99166	.99074
3.6	.99936	.99905	.99873	.99841	.99809	.99777	.99746	.99714	.99682	.99619	.99555	.99492	.99429	.99365
3.7	.99957	.99935	.99914	.99892	.99871	.99849	.99828	.99806	.99785	.99742	.99699	.99656	.99613	.99570
3.8	.99971	.99957	.99942	.99928	.99913	.99899	.99884	.99870	.99855	.99827	.99798	.99769	.99740	.99711
3.9	.99981	.99971	.99962	.99952	.99942	.99933	.99923	.99913	.99904	.99885	.99865	.99846	.99827	.99808
4.0	.99987	.99981	.99975	.99968	.99962	.99956	.99949	.99943	.99937	.99924	.99911	.99899	.99886	.99873
4.1	.99992	.99988	.99983	.99979	.99975	.99971	.99967	.99963	.99959	.99950	.99942	.99934	.99926	.99917
4.2	.99995	.99992	.99989	.99987	.99984	.99981	.99979	.99976	.99973	.99968	.99963	.99957	.99952	.99947
4.3	.99997	.99995	.99993	.99991	.99990	.99988	.99986	.99985	.99983	.99980	.99976	.99973	.99969	.99966
4.4	.99998	.99997	.99996	.99995	.99994	.99992	.99991	.99990	.99989	.99987	.99985	.99983	.99981	.99978
4.5	.99999	.99998	.99997	.99997	.99996	.99995	.99995	.99994	.99993	.99992	.99990	.99989	.99988	.99986
4.6	.99999	.99999	.99998	.99998	.99997	.99997	.99997	.99996	.99996	.99995	.99994	.99993	.99992	.99992
4.7	.99999	.99999	.99999	.99999	.99998	.99998	.99998	.99998	.99997	.99997	.99996	.99996	.99995	.99995
4.8	.99999	.99999	.99999	.99999	.99999	.99999	.99999	.99999	.99998	.99998	.99998	.99997	.99997	.99997
4.9	.99999	.99999	.99999	.99999	.99999	.99999	.99999	.99999	.99999	.99999	.99999	.99998	.99998	.99998
5.0	.99999	.99999	.99999	.99999	.99999	.99999	.99999	.99999	.99999	.99999	.99999	.99999	.99999	.99999

Table D-1. Two-Sided Probability Integral, $\rho = 0.1$

$a \backslash n$	2	3	4	5	6	7	8	9	10	12	14	16	18	20
0.1	.00638	.00051	.00004	.00000	.00000	.00000	.00000	.00000	.00000	.00000	.00000	.00000	.00000	.00000
0.2	.02525	.00404	.00065	.00010	.00002	.00000	.00000	.00000	.00000	.00000	.00000	.00000	.00000	.00000
0.3	.05588	.01329	.00317	.00076	.00018	.00004	.00001	.00000	.00000	.00000	.00000	.00000	.00000	.00000
0.4	.09706	.03042	.00957	.00302	.00095	.00030	.00010	.00003	.00001	.00000	.00000	.00000	.00000	.00000
0.5	.14726	.05683	.02200	.00854	.00332	.00129	.00051	.00020	.00008	.00001	.00000	.00000	.00000	.00000
0.6	.20465	.09307	.04245	.01941	.00889	.00408	.00188	.00086	.00040	.00009	.00002	.00000	.00000	.00000
0.7	.26729	.13886	.07233	.03776	.01975	.01035	.00543	.00286	.00150	.00042	.00012	.00003	.00001	.00000
0.8	.33319	.19317	.11226	.06538	.03815	.02229	.01305	.00765	.00449	.00155	.00054	.00019	.00007	.00002
0.9	.40042	.25438	.16195	.10331	.06601	.04224	.02707	.01736	.01115	.00461	.00192	.00080	.00033	.00014
1.0	.46724	.32049	.22025	.15162	.10454	.07217	.04989	.03452	.02392	.01151	.00555	.00269	.00130	.00063
1.1	.53211	.38931	.28532	.20942	.15391	.11326	.08344	.06153	.04541	.02480	.01359	.00746	.00411	.00226
1.2	.59377	.45871	.35488	.27491	.21322	.16554	.12866	.10008	.07791	.04733	.02882	.01759	.01076	.00659
1.3	.65127	.52671	.42649	.34573	.28055	.22787	.18523	.15070	.12269	.08148	.05424	.03618	.02418	.01618
1.4	.70394	.59165	.49778	.41920	.35333	.29804	.25159	.21252	.17963	.12856	.09219	.06623	.04766	.03435
1.5	.75138	.65224	.56665	.49268	.42867	.37322	.32515	.28342	.24719	.18830	.14369	.10983	.08406	.06442
1.6	.79344	.70756	.63140	.56379	.50372	.45029	.40273	.36036	.32260	.25885	.20801	.16738	.13485	.10876
1.7	.83019	.75710	.69080	.63063	.57596	.52627	.48106	.43990	.40241	.33709	.28273	.23740	.19954	.16787
1.8	.86185	.80064	.74409	.69180	.64342	.59862	.55713	.51868	.48302	.41923	.36424	.31675	.27569	.24013
1.9	.88874	.83827	.79091	.74645	.70468	.66543	.62852	.59381	.56114	.50142	.44842	.40132	.35941	.32208
2.0	.91130	.87027	.83128	.79422	.75896	.72542	.69349	.66309	.63414	.58026	.53129	.48674	.44616	.40918
2.1	.92999	.89708	.86549	.83514	.80598	.77796	.75102	.72511	.70019	.65313	.60953	.56910	.53157	.49670
2.2	.94528	.91923	.89400	.86957	.84590	.82296	.80072	.77917	.75827	.71834	.68075	.64535	.61198	.58051
2.3	.95765	.93727	.91741	.89804	.87914	.86071	.84273	.82518	.80806	.77502	.74353	.71349	.68483	.65746
2.4	.96754	.95179	.93635	.92121	.90636	.89180	.87752	.86352	.84977	.82306	.79732	.77253	.74863	.72559
2.5	.97535	.96332	.95146	.93979	.92830	.91697	.90582	.89483	.88401	.86284	.84228	.82231	.80290	.78405
2.6	.98147	.97237	.96338	.95449	.94571	.93703	.92845	.91998	.91159	.89512	.87902	.86328	.84788	.83283
2.7	.98620	.97939	.97265	.96596	.95934	.95278	.94627	.93983	.93344	.92083	.90845	.89628	.88431	.87256
2.8	.98982	.98478	.97977	.97481	.96987	.96497	.96011	.95527	.95047	.94097	.93160	.92235	.91323	.90422
2.9	.99256	.98887	.98519	.98154	.97791	.97429	.97070	.96712	.96356	.95650	.94952	.94260	.93575	.92898
3.0	.99461	.99193	.98927	.98661	.98396	.98133	.97870	.97609	.97348	.96831	.96317	.95807	.95301	.94799
3.1	.99614	.99421	.99229	.99038	.98848	.98658	.98468	.98279	.98091	.97716	.97343	.96972	.96604	.96237
3.2	.99725	.99589	.99452	.99316	.99180	.99044	.98909	.98774	.98640	.98371	.98104	.97838	.97573	.97309
3.3	.99807	.99710	.99614	.99518	.99422	.99327	.99231	.99136	.99040	.98850	.98661	.98472	.98284	.98096
3.4	.99865	.99798	.99731	.99664	.99597	.99530	.99463	.99396	.99330	.99197	.99064	.98932	.98800	.98668
3.5	.99907	.99861	.99814	.99768	.99721	.99675	.99629	.99583	.99537	.99444	.99352	.99261	.99169	.99077
3.6	.99936	.99905	.99873	.99841	.99809	.99778	.99746	.99714	.99683	.99619	.99556	.99493	.99430	.99367
3.7	.99957	.99935	.99914	.99892	.99871	.99849	.99828	.99806	.99785	.99742	.99699	.99656	.99613	.99571
3.8	.99971	.99957	.99942	.99928	.99913	.99899	.99884	.99870	.99856	.99827	.99798	.99769	.99740	.99712
3.9	.99981	.99971	.99962	.99952	.99942	.99933	.99923	.99914	.99904	.99885	.99866	.99846	.99827	.99808
4.0	.99987	.99981	.99975	.99968	.99962	.99956	.99949	.99943	.99937	.99924	.99911	.99899	.99886	.99874
4.1	.99992	.99988	.99983	.99979	.99975	.99971	.99967	.99963	.99959	.99950	.99942	.99934	.99926	.99917
4.2	.99995	.99992	.99989	.99987	.99984	.99981	.99979	.99976	.99973	.99968	.99963	.99957	.99952	.99947
4.3	.99997	.99995	.99993	.99991	.99990	.99988	.99986	.99985	.99983	.99980	.99976	.99973	.99969	.99966
4.4	.99998	.99997	.99996	.99995	.99994	.99992	.99991	.99990	.99989	.99987	.99985	.99983	.99981	.99978
4.5	.99999	.99998	.99997	.99997	.99996	.99995	.99995	.99994	.99993	.99992	.99990	.99989	.99988	.99986
4.6	.99999	.99999	.99998	.99998	.99997	.99997	.99997	.99996	.99996	.99995	.99994	.99993	.99992	.99992
4.7	.99999	.99999	.99999	.99999	.99998	.99998	.99998	.99998	.99997	.99997	.99996	.99996	.99995	.99995
4.8	.99999	.99999	.99999	.99999	.99999	.99999	.99999	.99999	.99998	.99998	.99998	.99997	.99997	.99997
4.9	.99999	.99999	.99999	.99999	.99999	.99999	.99999	.99999	.99999	.99999	.99999	.99998	.99998	.99998
5.0	.99999	.99999	.99999	.99999	.99999	.99999	.99999	.99999	.99999	.99999	.99999	.99999	.99999	.99999

Table D-2. Two-Sided Probability Integral, $\rho = 0.2$

a \ n	2	3	4	5	6	7	8	9	10	12	14	16	18	20
0.1	.00647	.00053	.00004	.00000	.00000	.00000	.00000	.00000	.00000	.00000	.00000	.00000	.00000	.00000
0.2	.02563	.00420	.00070	.00012	.00002	.00000	.00000	.00000	.00000	.00000	.00000	.00000	.00000	.00000
0.3	.05669	.01381	.00340	.00084	.00021	.00005	.00001	.00000	.00000	.00000	.00000	.00000	.00000	.00000
0.4	.09841	.03156	.01022	.00333	.00109	.00036	.00012	.00004	.00001	.00000	.00000	.00000	.00000	.00000
0.5	.14917	.05883	.02341	.00938	.00378	.00153	.00062	.00025	.00010	.00002	.00000	.00000	.00000	.00000
0.6	.20712	.09611	.04498	.02120	.01004	.00478	.00228	.00109	.00053	.00012	.00003	.00001	.00000	.00000
0.7	.27024	.14301	.07629	.04096	.02210	.01198	.00651	.00355	.00194	.00058	.00018	.00005	.00002	.00001
0.8	.33649	.19838	.11783	.07040	.04226	.02547	.01540	.00934	.00568	.00211	.00079	.00030	.00011	.00004
0.9	.40393	.26047	.16911	.11038	.07237	.04763	.03144	.02081	.01381	.00611	.00272	.00122	.00055	.00025
1.0	.47081	.32721	.22879	.16076	.11342	.08030	.05701	.04058	.02895	.01481	.00762	.00394	.00205	.00107
1.1	.53560	.39635	.29489	.22037	.16528	.12435	.09381	.07093	.05374	.03100	.01799	.01049	.00614	.00360
1.2	.59706	.46575	.36502	.28719	.22669	.17943	.14237	.11320	.09017	.05749	.03685	.02372	.01532	.00993
1.3	.65427	.53345	.43670	.35870	.29547	.24399	.20191	.16740	.13902	.09630	.06702	.04684	.03284	.02309
1.4	.70659	.59787	.50760	.43220	.36891	.31556	.27043	.23214	.19956	.14806	.11032	.08250	.06189	.04655
1.5	.75365	.65777	.57571	.50509	.44407	.39113	.34506	.30486	.26968	.21176	.16692	.13200	.10468	.08321
1.6	.79534	.71232	.63943	.57514	.51821	.46764	.42257	.38232	.34629	.28492	.23522	.19474	.16163	.13443
1.7	.83173	.76106	.69768	.64059	.58901	.54227	.49980	.46113	.42585	.36409	.31218	.26834	.23114	.19948
1.8	.86306	.80385	.74977	.70022	.65468	.61273	.57400	.53816	.50495	.44548	.39396	.34913	.30997	.27565
1.9	.88968	.84079	.79546	.75332	.71404	.67736	.64303	.61086	.58065	.52553	.47659	.43297	.39394	.35891
2.0	.91201	.87220	.83483	.79965	.76647	.73513	.70547	.67737	.65071	.60131	.55654	.51584	.47871	.44476
2.1	.93051	.89852	.86817	.83930	.81181	.78559	.76055	.73661	.71369	.67067	.63105	.59442	.56049	.52898
2.2	.94565	.92027	.89597	.87266	.85028	.82876	.80804	.78809	.76885	.73235	.69826	.66633	.63637	.60819
2.3	.95791	.93801	.91882	.90027	.88234	.86498	.84817	.83187	.81606	.78579	.75720	.73012	.70444	.68004
2.4	.96772	.95230	.93733	.92278	.90863	.89486	.88145	.86837	.85562	.83104	.80759	.78519	.76374	.74320
2.5	.97547	.96366	.95214	.94087	.92987	.91910	.90857	.89826	.88816	.86856	.84972	.83158	.81410	.79722
2.6	.98155	.97260	.96382	.95522	.94677	.93847	.93033	.92232	.91445	.89910	.88424	.86985	.85588	.84232
2.7	.98625	.97954	.97294	.96644	.96004	.95373	.94752	.94139	.93535	.92352	.91201	.90078	.88984	.87916
2.8	.98985	.98487	.97996	.97511	.97032	.96559	.96091	.95629	.95172	.94274	.93395	.92535	.91693	.90868
2.9	.99258	.98892	.98531	.98173	.97819	.97468	.97121	.96777	.96436	.95764	.95103	.94454	.93817	.93189
3.0	.99462	.99197	.98934	.98673	.98414	.98157	.97902	.97649	.97398	.96901	.96412	.95930	.95454	.94985
3.1	.99614	.99423	.99234	.99045	.98858	.98672	.98487	.98303	.98121	.97759	.97401	.97048	.96698	.96352
3.2	.99726	.99590	.99455	.99320	.99186	.99053	.98920	.98789	.98657	.98397	.98139	.97883	.97630	.97378
3.3	.99807	.99711	.99616	.99521	.99426	.99332	.99238	.99144	.99051	.98865	.98681	.98499	.98317	.98137
3.4	.99865	.99799	.99732	.99665	.99599	.99533	.99467	.99401	.99336	.99205	.99076	.98947	.98819	.98691
3.5	.99907	.99861	.99815	.99769	.99723	.99677	.99631	.99585	.99540	.99449	.99359	.99269	.99180	.99091
3.6	.99936	.99905	.99873	.99842	.99810	.99779	.99747	.99716	.99685	.99622	.99560	.99498	.99436	.99375
3.7	.99957	.99935	.99914	.99893	.99871	.99850	.99828	.99807	.99786	.99743	.99701	.99659	.99617	.99575
3.8	.99971	.99957	.99942	.99928	.99913	.99899	.99885	.99870	.99856	.99827	.99799	.99770	.99742	.99714
3.9	.99981	.99971	.99962	.99952	.99942	.99933	.99923	.99914	.99904	.99885	.99866	.99847	.99828	.99809
4.0	.99987	.99981	.99975	.99968	.99962	.99956	.99949	.99943	.99937	.99924	.99912	.99899	.99887	.99874
4.1	.99992	.99988	.99983	.99979	.99975	.99971	.99967	.99963	.99959	.99951	.99942	.99934	.99926	.99918
4.2	.99995	.99992	.99989	.99987	.99984	.99981	.99979	.99976	.99973	.99968	.99963	.99957	.99952	.99947
4.3	.99997	.99995	.99993	.99991	.99990	.99988	.99986	.99985	.99983	.99980	.99976	.99973	.99969	.99966
4.4	.99998	.99997	.99996	.99995	.99994	.99992	.99991	.99990	.99989	.99987	.99985	.99983	.99981	.99978
4.5	.99999	.99998	.99997	.99997	.99996	.99995	.99995	.99994	.99993	.99992	.99990	.99989	.99988	.99986
4.6	.99999	.99999	.99998	.99998	.99997	.99997	.99997	.99996	.99996	.99995	.99994	.99993	.99992	.99992
4.7	.99999	.99999	.99999	.99999	.99998	.99998	.99998	.99998	.99997	.99997	.99996	.99996	.99995	.99995
4.8	.99999	.99999	.99999	.99999	.99999	.99999	.99999	.99999	.99998	.99998	.99998	.99997	.99997	.99997
4.9	.99999	.99999	.99999	.99999	.99999	.99999	.99999	.99999	.99999	.99999	.99999	.99998	.99998	.99998
5.0	.99999	.99999	.99999	.99999	.99999	.99999	.99999	.99999	.99999	.99999	.99999	.99999	.99999	.99999

Table D-3. Two-Sided Probability Integral, $\rho = 0.3$

a \ n	2	3	4	5	6	7	8	9	10	12	14	16	18	20
0.1	.00665	.00057	.00005	.00000	.00000	.00000	.00000	.00000	.00000	.00000	.00000	.00000	.00000	.00000
0.2	.02631	.00448	.00078	.00014	.00002	.00000	.00000	.00000	.00000	.00000	.00000	.00000	.00000	.00000
0.3	.05813	.01471	.00379	.00099	.00026	.00007	.00002	.00000	.00000	.00000	.00000	.00000	.00000	.00000
0.4	.10078	.03351	.01133	.00388	.00134	.00046	.00016	.00006	.00002	.00000	.00000	.00000	.00000	.00000
0.5	.15255	.06224	.02581	.01082	.00458	.00195	.00084	.00036	.00016	.00003	.00001	.00000	.00000	.00000
0.6	.21144	.10127	.04925	.02422	.01201	.00599	.00301	.00151	.00077	.00020	.00005	.00001	.00000	.00000
0.7	.27536	.15002	.08291	.04630	.02607	.01477	.00841	.00481	.00276	.00092	.00031	.00010	.00004	.00001
0.8	.34220	.20712	.12704	.07869	.04911	.03083	.01945	.01232	.00783	.00319	.00131	.00054	.00023	.00009
0.9	.40998	.27064	.18085	.12195	.08281	.05655	.03880	.02672	.01846	.00888	.00431	.00210	.00103	.00051
1.0	.47693	.33835	.24269	.17553	.12779	.09351	.06873	.05069	.03750	.02068	.01150	.00643	.00362	.00204
1.1	.54155	.40794	.31033	.23785	.18339	.14207	.11050	.08623	.06748	.04162	.02587	.01617	.01016	.00641
1.2	.60264	.47726	.38124	.30658	.24785	.20124	.16400	.13405	.10986	.07428	.05057	.03463	.02382	.01645
1.3	.65933	.54443	.45292	.37899	.31863	.26892	.22771	.19335	.16456	.11993	.08798	.06488	.04805	.03572
1.4	.71103	.60795	.52310	.45237	.39280	.34225	.29906	.26197	.22997	.17819	.13890	.10879	.08555	.06750
1.5	.75745	.66670	.58993	.52423	.46748	.41810	.37488	.33686	.30327	.24700	.20225	.16633	.13728	.11366
1.6	.79849	.71999	.65202	.59255	.54010	.49352	.45193	.41462	.38102	.32313	.27534	.23553	.20212	.17394
1.7	.83429	.76745	.70843	.65583	.60862	.56598	.52728	.49201	.45975	.40289	.35451	.31299	.27714	.24599
1.8	.86508	.80902	.75867	.71310	.67159	.63357	.59859	.56629	.53636	.48265	.43582	.39469	.35832	.32601
1.9	.89124	.84487	.80262	.76387	.72812	.69499	.66416	.63539	.60844	.55935	.51571	.47664	.44146	.40963
2.0	.91319	.87534	.84042	.80802	.77781	.74953	.72297	.69795	.67431	.63070	.59131	.55550	.52278	.49273
2.1	.93138	.90088	.87243	.84577	.82068	.79699	.77456	.75326	.73299	.69521	.66062	.62877	.59931	.57195
2.2	.94629	.92201	.89914	.87753	.85702	.83752	.81892	.80114	.78411	.75208	.72243	.69484	.66906	.64488
2.3	.95836	.93926	.92112	.90385	.88734	.87154	.85637	.84179	.82775	.80114	.77625	.75289	.73088	.71007
2.4	.96803	.95318	.93897	.92535	.91225	.89964	.88747	.87571	.86433	.84261	.82214	.80277	.78437	.76687
2.5	.97569	.96427	.95328	.94267	.93242	.92250	.91288	.90354	.89447	.87705	.86050	.84474	.82968	.81525
2.6	.98169	.97301	.96460	.95645	.94853	.94084	.93334	.92604	.91891	.90516	.89201	.87941	.86730	.85564
2.7	.98634	.97981	.97346	.96727	.96123	.95534	.94958	.94395	.93844	.92774	.91746	.90755	.89798	.88872
2.8	.98991	.98505	.98030	.97566	.97111	.96666	.96229	.95801	.95380	.94561	.93769	.93002	.92258	.91535
2.9	.99262	.98904	.98553	.98209	.97870	.97538	.97211	.96890	.96573	.95954	.95353	.94769	.94199	.93644
3.0	.99465	.99204	.98948	.98695	.98447	.98202	.97960	.97722	.97487	.97026	.96576	.96137	.95708	.95287
3.1	.99616	.99428	.99242	.99059	.98879	.98700	.98524	.98349	.98177	.97838	.97506	.97181	.96862	.96549
3.2	.99727	.99593	.99460	.99329	.99199	.99070	.98943	.98817	.98692	.98446	.98205	.97967	.97733	.97503
3.3	.99808	.99713	.99619	.99526	.99433	.99342	.99251	.99161	.99072	.98896	.98722	.98551	.98382	.98215
3.4	.99866	.99799	.99734	.99668	.99603	.99539	.99475	.99412	.99349	.99224	.99100	.98978	.98858	.98739
3.5	.99907	.99861	.99816	.99770	.99725	.99680	.99636	.99592	.99547	.99460	.99373	.99288	.99203	.99119
3.6	.99937	.99905	.99874	.99843	.99812	.99781	.99750	.99719	.99689	.99628	.99568	.99509	.99450	.99391
3.7	.99957	.99936	.99914	.99893	.99872	.99851	.99830	.99809	.99788	.99747	.99706	.99665	.99624	.99584
3.8	.99971	.99957	.99942	.99928	.99914	.99900	.99886	.99871	.99857	.99829	.99802	.99774	.99746	.99719
3.9	.99981	.99971	.99962	.99952	.99943	.99933	.99924	.99914	.99905	.99886	.99868	.99849	.99831	.99812
4.0	.99987	.99981	.99975	.99968	.99962	.99956	.99950	.99943	.99937	.99925	.99912	.99900	.99888	.99876
4.1	.99992	.99988	.99984	.99979	.99975	.99971	.99967	.99963	.99959	.99951	.99943	.99935	.99927	.99919
4.2	.99995	.99992	.99989	.99987	.99984	.99981	.99979	.99976	.99973	.99968	.99963	.99958	.99952	.99947
4.3	.99997	.99995	.99993	.99991	.99990	.99988	.99986	.99985	.99983	.99980	.99976	.99973	.99970	.99966
4.4	.99998	.99997	.99996	.99995	.99994	.99992	.99991	.99990	.99989	.99987	.99985	.99983	.99981	.99979
4.5	.99999	.99998	.99997	.99997	.99996	.99995	.99995	.99994	.99993	.99992	.99991	.99989	.99988	.99986
4.6	.99999	.99999	.99998	.99998	.99997	.99997	.99997	.99996	.99996	.99995	.99994	.99993	.99992	.99992
4.7	.99999	.99999	.99999	.99999	.99998	.99998	.99998	.99998	.99997	.99997	.99996	.99996	.99995	.99995
4.8	.99999	.99999	.99999	.99999	.99999	.99999	.99999	.99999	.99998	.99998	.99998	.99997	.99997	.99997
4.9	.99999	.99999	.99999	.99999	.99999	.99999	.99999	.99999	.99999	.99999	.99999	.99998	.99998	.99998
5.0	.99999	.99999	.99999	.99999	.99999	.99999	.99999	.99999	.99999	.99999	.99999	.99999	.99999	.99999

Table D-4. Two-Sided Probability Integral, $\rho = 0.4$

a \ n	2	3	4	5	6	7	8	9	10	12	14	16	18	20
0.1	.00692	.00063	.00006	.00001	.00000	.00000	.00000	.00000	.00000	.00000	.00000	.00000	.00000	.00000
0.2	.02735	.00492	.00091	.00017	.00003	.00001	.00000	.00000	.00000	.00000	.00000	.00000	.00000	.00000
0.3	.06034	.01608	.00439	.00122	.00034	.00010	.00003	.00001	.00000	.00000	.00000	.00000	.00000	.00000
0.4	.10442	.03648	.01305	.00474	.00174	.00065	.00024	.00009	.00003	.00000	.00000	.00000	.00000	.00000
0.5	.15767	.06740	.02948	.01309	.00588	.00266	.00121	.00056	.00026	.00005	.00001	.00000	.00000	.00000
0.6	.21796	.10900	.05571	.02890	.01516	.00801	.00426	.00228	.00123	.00036	.00011	.00003	.00001	.00000
0.7	.28303	.16040	.09279	.05445	.03228	.01929	.01160	.00701	.00425	.00158	.00059	.00023	.00009	.00003
0.8	.35068	.21991	.14059	.09108	.05959	.03928	.02605	.01736	.01161	.00525	.00240	.00110	.00051	.00024
0.9	.41888	.28534	.19784	.13889	.09841	.07022	.05040	.03634	.02630	.01390	.00742	.00399	.00216	.00117
1.0	.48585	.35426	.26249	.19672	.14870	.11316	.08657	.06652	.05130	.03078	.01864	.01137	.00697	.00430
1.1	.55014	.42430	.33197	.26244	.20910	.16762	.13505	.10925	.08868	.05892	.03949	.02665	.01809	.01233
1.2	.61063	.49334	.40363	.33330	.27718	.23180	.19473	.16421	.13891	.10018	.07285	.05332	.03923	.02899
1.3	.66653	.55960	.47499	.40646	.35000	.30290	.26321	.22951	.20071	.15460	.11999	.09370	.07352	.05792
1.4	.71733	.62175	.54395	.47923	.42452	.37773	.33732	.30216	.27138	.22032	.18012	.14808	.12228	.10136
1.5	.76280	.67886	.60888	.54937	.49801	.45319	.41372	.37870	.34745	.29418	.25064	.21462	.18453	.15920
1.6	.80294	.73038	.66865	.61518	.56824	.52659	.48934	.45578	.42538	.37240	.32784	.28990	.25730	.22907
1.7	.83789	.77609	.72258	.67551	.63358	.59587	.56171	.53055	.50199	.45135	.40778	.36985	.33654	.30708
1.8	.86794	.81602	.77038	.72968	.69297	.65960	.62902	.60086	.57479	.52793	.48687	.45052	.41806	.38886
1.9	.89346	.85042	.81206	.77744	.74589	.71691	.69013	.66525	.64203	.59982	.56231	.52863	.49815	.47039
2.0	.91487	.87964	.84785	.81885	.79217	.76746	.74445	.72290	.70266	.66551	.63209	.60175	.57401	.54848
2.1	.93264	.90414	.87815	.85421	.83200	.81127	.79182	.77350	.75618	.72414	.69502	.66834	.64372	.62088
2.2	.94721	.92443	.90345	.88396	.86573	.84861	.83244	.81712	.80256	.77542	.75054	.72755	.70618	.68621
2.3	.95903	.94103	.92430	.90864	.89390	.87995	.86671	.85411	.84206	.81946	.79857	.77914	.76095	.74385
2.4	.96850	.95445	.94128	.92886	.91709	.90589	.89521	.88498	.87517	.85665	.83941	.82325	.80805	.79367
2.5	.97602	.96517	.95492	.94519	.93592	.92706	.91855	.91038	.90251	.88756	.87355	.86034	.84784	.83597
2.6	.98192	.97363	.96575	.95823	.95102	.94409	.93742	.93098	.92475	.91286	.90165	.89102	.88091	.87126
2.7	.98650	.98024	.97425	.96850	.96296	.95762	.95245	.94745	.94259	.93327	.92443	.91601	.90796	.90024
2.8	.99001	.98534	.98084	.97650	.97230	.96823	.96428	.96044	.95670	.94950	.94263	.93606	.92974	.92366
2.9	.99268	.98923	.98589	.98265	.97950	.97644	.97346	.97056	.96772	.96223	.95697	.95191	.94703	.94231
3.0	.99469	.99216	.98971	.98732	.98499	.98272	.98050	.97833	.97620	.97208	.96810	.96426	.96054	.95694
3.1	.99619	.99436	.99257	.99083	.98913	.98746	.98583	.98423	.98266	.97959	.97663	.97376	.97097	.96825
3.2	.99729	.99598	.99469	.99344	.99221	.99100	.98981	.98865	.98750	.98525	.98307	.98095	.97889	.97687
3.3	.99809	.99716	.99625	.99535	.99447	.99361	.99276	.99192	.99109	.98946	.98788	.98634	.98483	.98335
3.4	.99866	.99801	.99737	.99674	.99612	.99551	.99490	.99431	.99372	.99256	.99142	.99031	.98923	.98816
3.5	.99908	.99862	.99818	.99774	.99730	.99688	.99645	.99603	.99562	.99480	.99400	.99321	.99244	.99167
3.6	.99937	.99906	.99875	.99845	.99815	.99785	.99755	.99726	.99697	.99640	.99584	.99529	.99475	.99421
3.7	.99957	.99936	.99915	.99894	.99874	.99853	.99833	.99813	.99793	.99754	.99715	.99677	.99640	.99602
3.8	.99971	.99957	.99943	.99929	.99915	.99901	.99888	.99874	.99860	.99834	.99807	.99781	.99755	.99730
3.9	.99981	.99971	.99962	.99953	.99943	.99934	.99925	.99916	.99907	.99889	.99871	.99853	.99836	.99818
4.0	.99987	.99981	.99975	.99969	.99963	.99956	.99950	.99944	.99938	.99926	.99914	.99903	.99891	.99879
4.1	.99992	.99988	.99984	.99980	.99976	.99971	.99967	.99964	.99960	.99952	.99944	.99936	.99928	.99921
4.2	.99995	.99992	.99989	.99987	.99984	.99982	.99979	.99976	.99974	.99969	.99964	.99958	.99953	.99948
4.3	.99997	.99995	.99993	.99992	.99990	.99988	.99986	.99985	.99983	.99980	.99977	.99973	.99970	.99967
4.4	.99998	.99997	.99996	.99995	.99994	.99992	.99991	.99990	.99989	.99987	.99985	.99983	.99981	.99979
4.5	.99999	.99998	.99997	.99997	.99996	.99995	.99995	.99994	.99993	.99992	.99991	.99989	.99988	.99987
4.6	.99999	.99999	.99998	.99998	.99997	.99997	.99997	.99996	.99996	.99995	.99994	.99993	.99993	.99992
4.7	.99999	.99999	.99999	.99999	.99998	.99998	.99998	.99998	.99997	.99997	.99996	.99996	.99995	.99995
4.8	.99999	.99999	.99999	.99999	.99999	.99999	.99999	.99999	.99998	.99998	.99998	.99997	.99997	.99997
4.9	.99999	.99999	.99999	.99999	.99999	.99999	.99999	.99999	.99999	.99999	.99999	.99998	.99998	.99998
5.0	.99999	.99999	.99999	.99999	.99999	.99999	.99999	.99999	.99999	.99999	.99999	.99999	.99999	.99999

Table D-5. Two-Sided Probability Integral, $\rho = 0.5$

a \ n	2	3	4	5	6	7	8	9	10	12	14	16	18	20
0.1	.00732	.00071	.00007	.00001	.00000	.00000	.00000	.00000	.00000	.00000	.00000	.00000	.00000	.00000
0.2	.02889	.00558	.00111	.00023	.00005	.00001	.00000	.00000	.00000	.00000	.00000	.00000	.00000	.00000
0.3	.06360	.01815	.00534	.00160	.00049	.00015	.00005	.00001	.00000	.00000	.00000	.00000	.00000	.00000
0.4	.10972	.04089	.01571	.00616	.00245	.00098	.00040	.00016	.00007	.00001	.00000	.00000	.00000	.00000
0.5	.16509	.07497	.03506	.01671	.00807	.00394	.00193	.00096	.00047	.00012	.00003	.00001	.00000	.00000
0.6	.22729	.12017	.06534	.03618	.02030	.01149	.00656	.00376	.00217	.00073	.00025	.00008	.00003	.00001
0.7	.29387	.17515	.10720	.06676	.04209	.02678	.01716	.01106	.00716	.00304	.00130	.00056	.00024	.00011
0.8	.36251	.23777	.15987	.10927	.07556	.05271	.03703	.02615	.01855	.00944	.00485	.00252	.00131	.00069
0.9	.43112	.30548	.22145	.16300	.12131	.09103	.06876	.05221	.03981	.02339	.01388	.00831	.00500	.00303
1.0	.49797	.37567	.28932	.22597	.17830	.14178	.11344	.09120	.07363	.04846	.03222	.02158	.01455	.00986
1.1	.56168	.44593	.36061	.29536	.24417	.20331	.17025	.14322	.12094	.08704	.06324	.04629	.03408	.02521
1.2	.62125	.51424	.43262	.36809	.31584	.27276	.23678	.20643	.18059	.13941	.10859	.08516	.06717	.05321
1.3	.67600	.57904	.50300	.44129	.39005	.34676	.30972	.27769	.24978	.20367	.16746	.13857	.11525	.09627
1.4	.72555	.63924	.56995	.51253	.46390	.42202	.38551	.35336	.32483	.27643	.23701	.20440	.17712	.15408
1.5	.76976	.69412	.63219	.57997	.53502	.49574	.46099	.42996	.40203	.35370	.31327	.27892	.24941	.22381
1.6	.80870	.74335	.68892	.64235	.60172	.56578	.53362	.50459	.47817	.43177	.39215	.35783	.32776	.30116
1.7	.84256	.78686	.73974	.69891	.66289	.63069	.60160	.57511	.55081	.50760	.47014	.43720	.40793	.38167
1.8	.87166	.82477	.78456	.74931	.71790	.68958	.66379	.64012	.61826	.57900	.54456	.51393	.48641	.46146
1.9	.89637	.85738	.82353	.79353	.76656	.74205	.71957	.69881	.67951	.64459	.61363	.58585	.56067	.53765
2.0	.91711	.88509	.85694	.83176	.80894	.78804	.76875	.75083	.73409	.70357	.67629	.65161	.62907	.60835
2.1	.93433	.90833	.88522	.86436	.84531	.82775	.81145	.79622	.78192	.75568	.73204	.71050	.69072	.67242
2.2	.94847	.92760	.90886	.89180	.87611	.86156	.84796	.83521	.82317	.80096	.78080	.76232	.74524	.72936
2.3	.95995	.94339	.92838	.91460	.90185	.88994	.87877	.86823	.85825	.83971	.82278	.80716	.79266	.77910
2.4	.96918	.95618	.94430	.93331	.92307	.91346	.90440	.89581	.88764	.87240	.85838	.84538	.83325	.82186
2.5	.97650	.96642	.95712	.94847	.94035	.93269	.92544	.91854	.91195	.89958	.88814	.87748	.86748	.85805
2.6	.98226	.97452	.96733	.96060	.95424	.94822	.94249	.93702	.93177	.92188	.91268	.90405	.89592	.88823
2.7	.98673	.98086	.97537	.97019	.96528	.96060	.95613	.95185	.94773	.93992	.93262	.92574	.91923	.91304
2.8	.99017	.98577	.98162	.97768	.97393	.97035	.96691	.96359	.96040	.95432	.94860	.94320	.93806	.93315
2.9	.99279	.98952	.98642	.98347	.98064	.97792	.97531	.97278	.97034	.96567	.96125	.95706	.95305	.94922
3.0	.99476	.99236	.99007	.98788	.98577	.98374	.98178	.97987	.97803	.97449	.97112	.96791	.96484	.96189
3.1	.99623	.99449	.99282	.99121	.98965	.98815	.98670	.98528	.98390	.98125	.97872	.97630	.97397	.97173
3.2	.99732	.99606	.99485	.99369	.99256	.99146	.99039	.98935	.98834	.98638	.98450	.98270	.98096	.97928
3.3	.99811	.99721	.99635	.99551	.99470	.99391	.99314	.99238	.99165	.99022	.98884	.98752	.98623	.98499
3.4	.99868	.99805	.99744	.99685	.99627	.99570	.99515	.99461	.99408	.99305	.99206	.99109	.99016	.98925
3.5	.99908	.99865	.99822	.99780	.99740	.99700	.99661	.99623	.99585	.99512	.99441	.99372	.99305	.99239
3.6	.99937	.99907	.99878	.99849	.99820	.99793	.99765	.99739	.99712	.99661	.99611	.99562	.99514	.99468
3.7	.99957	.99937	.99917	.99897	.99877	.99858	.99839	.99821	.99803	.99767	.99732	.99698	.99665	.99632
3.8	.99971	.99957	.99944	.99930	.99917	.99904	.99891	.99879	.99866	.99842	.99817	.99794	.99771	.99748
3.9	.99981	.99972	.99962	.99953	.99945	.99936	.99927	.99919	.99910	.99893	.99877	.99861	.99845	.99830
4.0	.99987	.99981	.99975	.99969	.99963	.99957	.99952	.99946	.99940	.99929	.99918	.99907	.99897	.99886
4.1	.99992	.99988	.99984	.99980	.99976	.99972	.99968	.99964	.99961	.99953	.99946	.99939	.99932	.99925
4.2	.99995	.99992	.99989	.99987	.99984	.99982	.99979	.99977	.99974	.99970	.99965	.99960	.99955	.99951
4.3	.99997	.99995	.99993	.99992	.99990	.99988	.99987	.99985	.99984	.99980	.99977	.99974	.99971	.99968
4.4	.99998	.99997	.99996	.99995	.99994	.99993	.99992	.99991	.99990	.99988	.99986	.99984	.99982	.99980
4.5	.99999	.99998	.99997	.99997	.99996	.99995	.99995	.99994	.99993	.99992	.99991	.99990	.99988	.99987
4.6	.99999	.99999	.99998	.99998	.99997	.99997	.99997	.99996	.99996	.99995	.99994	.99993	.99993	.99992
4.7	.99999	.99999	.99999	.99999	.99998	.99998	.99998	.99998	.99997	.99997	.99996	.99996	.99995	.99995
4.8	.99999	.99999	.99999	.99999	.99999	.99999	.99999	.99999	.99998	.99998	.99998	.99998	.99997	.99997
4.9	.99999	.99999	.99999	.99999	.99999	.99999	.99999	.99999	.99999	.99999	.99999	.99999	.99998	.99998
5.0	.99999	.99999	.99999	.99999	.99999	.99999	.99999	.99999	.99999	.99999	.99999	.99999	.99999	.99999

Table D-6. Two-Sided Probability Integral, $\rho = 0.6$

a \ n	2	3	4	5	6	7	8	9	10	12	14	16	18	20
0.1	.00792	.00085	.00009	.00001	.00000	.00000	.00000	.00000	.00000	.00000	.00000	.00000	.00000	.00000
0.2	.03118	.00661	.00145	.00033	.00007	.00002	.00000	.00000	.00000	.00000	.00000	.00000	.00000	.00000
0.3	.06840	.02133	.00691	.00229	.00077	.00026	.00009	.00003	.00001	.00000	.00000	.00000	.00000	.00000
0.4	.11744	.04760	.02001	.00860	.00376	.00166	.00074	.00033	.00015	.00003	.00001	.00000	.00000	.00000
0.5	.17572	.08622	.04383	.02277	.01201	.00640	.00344	.00186	.00101	.00030	.00009	.00003	.00001	.00000
0.6	.24045	.13639	.08002	.04795	.02915	.01791	.01109	.00691	.00433	.00172	.00069	.00028	.00011	.00005
0.7	.30889	.19604	.12844	.08586	.05820	.03985	.02750	.01910	.01332	.00656	.00327	.00165	.00083	.00042
0.8	.37859	.26239	.18733	.13629	.10047	.07479	.05609	.04231	.03207	.01864	.01096	.00650	.00388	.00233
0.9	.44747	.33251	.25389	.19729	.15521	.12323	.09853	.07922	.06399	.04220	.02815	.01893	.01281	.00872
1.0	.51387	.40365	.32493	.26579	.21990	.18348	.15411	.13012	.11035	.08017	.05886	.04357	.03245	.02430
1.1	.57658	.47351	.39741	.33838	.29110	.25238	.22014	.19296	.16981	.13279	.10487	.08345	.06680	.05374
1.2	.63477	.54034	.46877	.41189	.36526	.32617	.29287	.26414	.23910	.19765	.16490	.13855	.11706	.09935
1.3	.68793	.60290	.53706	.48374	.43924	.40131	.36844	.33961	.31407	.27076	.23538	.20594	.18112	.15996
1.4	.73583	.66040	.60094	.55204	.51066	.47493	.44358	.41576	.39081	.34778	.31179	.28116	.25472	.23164
1.5	.77844	.71244	.65958	.61553	.57784	.54496	.51583	.48974	.46615	.42494	.38992	.35962	.33304	.30948
1.6	.81589	.75886	.71252	.67347	.63973	.61003	.58353	.55961	.53784	.49945	.46643	.43753	.41190	.38893
1.7	.84841	.79973	.75965	.72551	.69576	.66937	.64566	.62414	.60444	.56943	.53904	.51221	.48822	.46655
1.8	.87635	.83528	.80104	.77159	.74571	.72261	.70172	.68266	.66513	.63376	.60631	.58191	.55995	.54000
1.9	.90007	.86582	.83693	.81185	.78964	.76968	.75154	.73490	.71952	.69185	.66747	.64566	.62592	.60790
2.0	.92000	.89176	.86767	.84657	.82776	.81074	.79519	.78086	.76756	.74350	.72216	.70296	.68550	.66948
2.1	.93655	.91353	.89368	.87616	.86041	.84609	.83294	.82076	.80941	.78877	.77035	.75369	.73847	.72445
2.2	.95016	.93160	.91544	.90105	.88804	.87614	.86515	.85494	.84538	.82792	.81223	.79798	.78489	.77279
2.3	.96121	.94642	.93342	.92175	.91113	.90136	.89231	.88385	.87591	.86132	.84814	.83611	.82501	.81471
2.4	.97011	.95845	.94810	.93875	.93019	.92227	.91490	.90799	.90147	.88944	.87852	.86850	.85922	.85057
2.5	.97718	.96809	.95996	.95255	.94573	.93940	.93347	.92789	.92261	.91282	.90389	.89565	.88799	.88082
2.6	.98275	.97574	.96942	.96362	.95826	.95325	.94854	.94409	.93987	.93201	.92479	.91811	.91187	.90602
2.7	.98708	.98174	.97688	.97240	.96822	.96431	.96062	.95712	.95379	.94755	.94180	.93645	.93144	.92672
2.8	.99042	.98639	.98270	.97927	.97607	.97305	.97019	.96747	.96487	.95999	.95546	.95123	.94726	.94350
2.9	.99296	.98996	.98718	.98459	.98216	.97986	.97767	.97558	.97358	.96981	.96629	.96300	.95988	.95693
3.0	.99488	.99266	.99060	.98867	.98684	.98511	.98346	.98187	.98035	.97747	.97477	.97224	.96983	.96755
3.1	.99631	.99469	.99318	.99175	.99040	.98911	.98787	.98669	.98554	.98337	.98133	.97940	.97757	.97582
3.2	.99737	.99620	.99510	.99406	.99307	.99212	.99121	.99033	.98948	.98786	.98634	.98489	.98351	.98219
3.3	.99814	.99730	.99652	.99576	.99504	.99435	.99369	.99305	.99243	.99124	.99011	.98904	.98801	.98703
3.4	.99870	.99811	.99755	.99701	.99650	.99600	.99552	.99506	.99461	.99374	.99292	.99214	.99138	.99066
3.5	.99910	.99869	.99829	.99791	.99755	.99720	.99685	.99652	.99620	.99558	.99499	.99442	.99388	.99335
3.6	.99938	.99910	.99882	.99856	.99830	.99805	.99781	.99758	.99735	.99691	.99649	.99609	.99570	.99532
3.7	.99958	.99938	.99919	.99901	.99884	.99866	.99850	.99833	.99818	.99787	.99757	.99729	.99701	.99674
3.8	.99972	.99958	.99946	.99933	.99921	.99909	.99898	.99887	.99876	.99854	.99834	.99814	.99795	.99776
3.9	.99981	.99972	.99964	.99955	.99947	.99939	.99931	.99924	.99916	.99901	.99887	.99874	.99860	.99847
4.0	.99988	.99982	.99976	.99970	.99965	.99959	.99954	.99949	.99944	.99934	.99925	.99915	.99906	.99897
4.1	.99992	.99988	.99984	.99980	.99977	.99973	.99970	.99966	.99963	.99956	.99950	.99944	.99938	.99932
4.2	.99995	.99992	.99990	.99987	.99985	.99983	.99980	.99978	.99976	.99971	.99967	.99963	.99959	.99955
4.3	.99997	.99995	.99993	.99992	.99990	.99989	.99987	.99986	.99984	.99982	.99979	.99976	.99973	.99971
4.4	.99998	.99997	.99996	.99995	.99994	.99993	.99992	.99991	.99990	.99988	.99986	.99985	.99983	.99981
4.5	.99999	.99998	.99997	.99997	.99996	.99995	.99995	.99994	.99994	.99992	.99991	.99990	.99989	.99988
4.6	.99999	.99999	.99998	.99998	.99998	.99997	.99997	.99996	.99996	.99995	.99995	.99994	.99993	.99992
4.7	.99999	.99999	.99999	.99999	.99998	.99998	.99998	.99998	.99998	.99997	.99997	.99996	.99996	.99995
4.8	.99999	.99999	.99999	.99999	.99999	.99999	.99999	.99999	.99998	.99998	.99998	.99998	.99997	.99997
4.9	.99999	.99999	.99999	.99999	.99999	.99999	.99999	.99999	.99999	.99999	.99999	.99999	.99998	.99998
5.0	.99999	.99999	.99999	.99999	.99999	.99999	.99999	.99999	.99999	.99999	.99999	.99999	.99999	.99999

Table D-7. Two-Sided Probability Integral, $\rho = 0.7$

a \ n	2	3	4	5	6	7	8	9	10	12	14	16	18	20
0.1	.00886	.00108	.00014	.00002	.00000	.00000	.00000	.00000	.00000	.00000	.00000	.00000	.00000	.00000
0.2	.03475	.00834	.00209	.00054	.00014	.00004	.00001	.00000	.00000	.00000	.00000	.00000	.00000	.00000
0.3	.07576	.02661	.00976	.00367	.00140	.00054	.00021	.00008	.00003	.00001	.00000	.00000	.00000	.00000
0.4	.12907	.05840	.02756	.01334	.00656	.00327	.00164	.00083	.00042	.00011	.00003	.00001	.00000	.00000
0.5	.19136	.10378	.05862	.03392	.01996	.01188	.00713	.00431	.00262	.00098	.00037	.00014	.00005	.00002
0.6	.25929	.16077	.10362	.06836	.04582	.03106	.02123	.01461	.01011	.00490	.00241	.00119	.00059	.00030
0.7	.32981	.22621	.16087	.11697	.08634	.06442	.04847	.03670	.02793	.01638	.00972	.00582	.00351	.00213
0.8	.40038	.29656	.22712	.17757	.14080	.11280	.09107	.07398	.06040	.04073	.02779	.01913	.01326	.00924
0.9	.46904	.36860	.29856	.24645	.20611	.17402	.14800	.12661	.10882	.08127	.06139	.04676	.03586	.02764
1.0	.53436	.43971	.37169	.31960	.27807	.24407	.21566	.19158	.17093	.13748	.11175	.09156	.07549	.06255
1.1	.59541	.50799	.44373	.39350	.35265	.31853	.28946	.26432	.24232	.20559	.17612	.15200	.13194	.11508
1.2	.65161	.57216	.51272	.46553	.42660	.39365	.36519	.34026	.31815	.28051	.24950	.22341	.20111	.18181
1.3	.70266	.63145	.57737	.53389	.49765	.46666	.43965	.41577	.39442	.35759	.32673	.30031	.27735	.25713
1.4	.74847	.68545	.63692	.59750	.56435	.53578	.51070	.48839	.46831	.43338	.40377	.37815	.35564	.33560
1.5	.78911	.73398	.69099	.65574	.62585	.59993	.57704	.55657	.53805	.50564	.47794	.45379	.43241	.41325
1.6	.82476	.77709	.73946	.70833	.68174	.65854	.63795	.61944	.60264	.57305	.54760	.52529	.50543	.48754
1.7	.85569	.81493	.78238	.75522	.73186	.71135	.69307	.67656	.66152	.63490	.61187	.59157	.57343	.55702
1.8	.88224	.84777	.81994	.79652	.77624	.75835	.74231	.72778	.71448	.69084	.67028	.65207	.63573	.62090
1.9	.90479	.87596	.85244	.83247	.81508	.79965	.78576	.77312	.76151	.74078	.72266	.70653	.69200	.67878
2.0	.92372	.89988	.88022	.86341	.84867	.83552	.82363	.81276	.80276	.78481	.76903	.75493	.74218	.73053
2.1	.93946	.91996	.90371	.88971	.87737	.86630	.85624	.84702	.83850	.82314	.80958	.79741	.78636	.77623
2.2	.95240	.93662	.92335	.91183	.90161	.89240	.88399	.87626	.86909	.85612	.84460	.83422	.82476	.81607
2.3	.96292	.95029	.93958	.93020	.92184	.91427	.90733	.90093	.89496	.88413	.87447	.86573	.85774	.85037
2.4	.97139	.96139	.95284	.94530	.93854	.93238	.92672	.92148	.91658	.90765	.89965	.89238	.88571	.87954
2.5	.97813	.97031	.96355	.95756	.95215	.94721	.94265	.93841	.93443	.92716	.92061	.91464	.90914	.90403
2.6	.98345	.97739	.97211	.96740	.96313	.95921	.95557	.95218	.94900	.94314	.93785	.93300	.92852	.92435
2.7	.98759	.98294	.97887	.97521	.97187	.96880	.96594	.96326	.96074	.95608	.95185	.94797	.94437	.94100
2.8	.99078	.98726	.98415	.98134	.97876	.97638	.97416	.97206	.97009	.96643	.96310	.96002	.95716	.95448
2.9	.99322	.99058	.98823	.98610	.98413	.98230	.98059	.97898	.97745	.97461	.97201	.96961	.96736	.96525
3.0	.99506	.99310	.99135	.98974	.98826	.98688	.98558	.98435	.98318	.98101	.97900	.97714	.97540	.97376
3.1	.99644	.99500	.99370	.99251	.99141	.99037	.98939	.98847	.98759	.98594	.98441	.98299	.98166	.98040
3.2	.99745	.99641	.99546	.99459	.99377	.99301	.99228	.99159	.99093	.98970	.98855	.98748	.98647	.98552
3.3	.99820	.99745	.99677	.99613	.99554	.99497	.99444	.99393	.99345	.99253	.99168	.99089	.99013	.98942
3.4	.99874	.99821	.99772	.99726	.99683	.99643	.99604	.99567	.99532	.99465	.99402	.99344	.99288	.99235
3.5	.99912	.99875	.99840	.99808	.99777	.99748	.99721	.99694	.99669	.99620	.99575	.99532	.99492	.99453
3.6	.99940	.99914	.99890	.99867	.99845	.99825	.99805	.99786	.99768	.99734	.99701	.99670	.99641	.99613
3.7	.99959	.99941	.99924	.99909	.99894	.99879	.99865	.99852	.99839	.99815	.99792	.99770	.99749	.99729
3.8	.99972	.99960	.99949	.99938	.99928	.99918	.99908	.99899	.99890	.99873	.99857	.99841	.99827	.99813
3.9	.99982	.99973	.99966	.99958	.99951	.99944	.99938	.99931	.99925	.99914	.99902	.99892	.99882	.99872
4.0	.99988	.99982	.99977	.99972	.99967	.99963	.99958	.99954	.99950	.99942	.99934	.99927	.99920	.99913
4.1	.99992	.99988	.99985	.99982	.99978	.99975	.99972	.99970	.99967	.99961	.99956	.99951	.99946	.99942
4.2	.99995	.99992	.99990	.99988	.99986	.99984	.99982	.99980	.99978	.99975	.99971	.99968	.99965	.99962
4.3	.99997	.99995	.99994	.99992	.99991	.99990	.99988	.99987	.99986	.99983	.99981	.99979	.99977	.99975
4.4	.99998	.99997	.99996	.99995	.99994	.99993	.99992	.99992	.99991	.99989	.99988	.99986	.99985	.99984
4.5	.99999	.99998	.99997	.99997	.99996	.99996	.99995	.99995	.99994	.99993	.99992	.99991	.99990	.99990
4.6	.99999	.99999	.99998	.99998	.99998	.99997	.99997	.99997	.99996	.99996	.99995	.99994	.99994	.99993
4.7	.99999	.99999	.99999	.99999	.99999	.99998	.99998	.99998	.99998	.99997	.99997	.99997	.99996	.99996
4.8	.99999	.99999	.99999	.99999	.99999	.99999	.99999	.99999	.99999	.99998	.99998	.99998	.99998	.99997
4.9	.99999	.99999	.99999	.99999	.99999	.99999	.99999	.99999	.99999	.99999	.99999	.99999	.99999	.99998
5.0	.99999	.99999	.99999	.99999	.99999	.99999	.99999	.99999	.99999	.99999	.99999	.99999	.99999	.99999

Table D-8. Two-Sided Probability Integral, $\rho = 0.8$

a \ n	2	3	4	5	6	7	8	9	10	12	14	16	18	20
0.1	.01051	.00155	.00024	.00004	.00001	.00000	.00000	.00000	.00000	.00000	.00000	.00000	.00000	.00000
0.2	.04093	.01177	.00356	.00111	.00035	.00011	.00004	.00001	.00000	.00000	.00000	.00000	.00000	.00000
0.3	.08816	.03662	.01596	.00716	.00327	.00151	.00070	.00033	.00016	.00004	.00001	.00000	.00000	.00000
0.4	.14794	.07790	.04299	.02438	.01407	.00823	.00485	.00288	.00172	.00062	.00023	.00008	.00003	.00001
0.5	.21571	.13366	.08662	.05763	.03900	.02673	.01848	.01287	.00901	.00448	.00225	.00114	.00058	.00030
0.6	.28735	.19972	.14477	.10758	.08127	.06212	.04791	.03719	.02904	.01792	.01120	.00707	.00449	.00286
0.7	.35963	.27140	.21289	.17089	.13931	.11483	.09544	.07984	.06714	.04806	.03483	.02547	.01876	.01389
0.8	.43021	.34472	.28601	.24233	.20824	.18078	.15815	.13920	.12311	.09740	.07796	.06294	.05116	.04180
0.9	.49757	.41682	.36008	.31694	.28252	.25416	.23025	.20973	.19190	.16233	.13879	.11962	.10375	.09043
1.0	.56076	.48583	.43233	.39107	.35770	.32984	.30604	.28535	.26712	.23627	.21099	.18979	.17169	.15603
1.1	.61924	.55067	.50107	.46242	.43088	.40433	.38147	.36144	.34365	.31321	.28789	.26631	.24759	.23113
1.2	.67269	.61070	.56534	.52968	.50038	.47556	.45407	.43515	.41826	.38918	.36477	.34379	.32543	.30915
1.3	.72102	.66560	.62460	.59212	.56526	.54240	.52251	.50492	.48917	.46192	.43891	.41903	.40156	.38598
1.4	.76424	.71523	.67860	.64936	.62503	.60422	.58605	.56992	.55543	.53026	.50891	.49038	.47403	.45941
1.5	.80248	.75961	.72724	.70121	.67943	.66071	.64430	.62968	.61652	.59355	.57399	.55695	.54187	.52834
1.6	.83597	.79887	.77058	.74766	.72838	.71173	.69708	.68399	.67216	.65146	.63374	.61826	.60451	.59215
1.7	.86498	.83322	.80876	.78881	.77193	.75729	.74436	.73277	.72227	.70381	.68796	.67405	.66167	.65050
1.8	.88985	.86295	.84204	.82486	.81025	.79752	.78623	.77609	.76687	.75061	.73658	.72424	.71321	.70324
1.9	.91094	.88840	.87072	.85609	.84359	.83265	.82291	.81413	.80612	.79196	.77969	.76886	.75916	.75036
2.0	.92865	.90997	.89517	.88286	.87227	.86297	.85466	.84715	.84028	.82809	.81748	.80808	.79964	.79197
2.1	.94336	.92804	.91579	.90554	.89668	.88886	.88185	.87549	.86967	.85929	.85022	.84217	.83491	.82829
2.2	.95545	.94301	.93300	.92455	.91721	.91072	.90487	.89955	.89467	.88593	.87827	.87144	.86527	.85964
2.3	.96528	.95530	.94719	.94031	.93430	.92896	.92414	.91974	.91569	.90842	.90203	.89630	.89112	.88637
2.4	.97319	.96527	.95877	.95323	.94837	.94403	.94010	.93650	.93318	.92720	.92192	.91718	.91287	.90892
2.5	.97950	.97327	.96812	.96371	.95982	.95633	.95316	.95025	.94755	.94269	.93838	.93450	.93096	.92771
2.6	.98447	.97962	.97559	.97211	.96903	.96626	.96373	.96140	.95925	.95534	.95186	.94871	.94584	.94320
2.7	.98834	.98461	.98149	.97878	.97636	.97419	.97219	.97035	.96864	.96554	.96276	.96024	.95794	.95581
2.8	.99133	.98850	.98610	.98401	.98214	.98045	.97889	.97746	.97612	.97367	.97148	.96949	.96767	.96597
2.9	.99362	.99148	.98966	.98807	.98664	.98534	.98414	.98303	.98199	.98009	.97838	.97683	.97539	.97406
3.0	.99534	.99375	.99239	.99119	.99010	.98911	.98820	.98735	.98655	.98510	.98378	.98258	.98146	.98043
3.1	.99664	.99546	.99445	.99355	.99274	.99200	.99131	.99067	.99006	.98896	.98795	.98703	.98618	.98539
3.2	.99759	.99674	.99599	.99533	.99473	.99418	.99366	.99318	.99273	.99190	.99114	.99045	.98980	.98920
3.3	.99829	.99768	.99714	.99665	.99621	.99581	.99543	.99507	.99474	.99412	.99356	.99304	.99255	.99210
3.4	.99880	.99836	.99797	.99762	.99730	.99701	.99673	.99647	.99623	.99577	.99536	.99497	.99462	.99428
3.5	.99917	.99886	.99858	.99833	.99810	.99789	.99769	.99750	.99732	.99699	.99669	.99641	.99615	.99590
3.6	.99943	.99921	.99902	.99884	.99868	.99852	.99838	.99825	.99812	.99788	.99767	.99746	.99727	.99710
3.7	.99961	.99946	.99932	.99920	.99909	.99898	.99888	.99878	.99869	.99853	.99837	.99823	.99809	.99796
3.8	.99974	.99963	.99954	.99945	.99938	.99930	.99923	.99917	.99910	.99898	.99887	.99877	.99868	.99859
3.9	.99982	.99975	.99969	.99963	.99958	.99953	.99948	.99943	.99939	.99931	.99923	.99916	.99909	.99903
4.0	.99988	.99984	.99979	.99975	.99972	.99968	.99965	.99962	.99959	.99953	.99948	.99943	.99938	.99934
4.1	.99992	.99989	.99986	.99984	.99981	.99979	.99977	.99975	.99973	.99969	.99965	.99962	.99959	.99956
4.2	.99995	.99993	.99991	.99989	.99988	.99986	.99985	.99983	.99982	.99979	.99977	.99975	.99972	.99970
4.3	.99997	.99995	.99994	.99993	.99992	.99991	.99990	.99989	.99988	.99986	.99985	.99983	.99982	.99981
4.4	.99998	.99997	.99996	.99996	.99995	.99994	.99994	.99993	.99992	.99991	.99990	.99989	.99988	.99987
4.5	.99999	.99998	.99998	.99997	.99997	.99996	.99996	.99995	.99995	.99994	.99994	.99993	.99992	.99992
4.6	.99999	.99999	.99999	.99998	.99998	.99998	.99997	.99997	.99997	.99996	.99996	.99996	.99995	.99995
4.7	.99999	.99999	.99999	.99999	.99999	.99999	.99998	.99998	.99998	.99998	.99997	.99997	.99997	.99997
4.8	.99999	.99999	.99999	.99999	.99999	.99999	.99999	.99999	.99999	.99999	.99998	.99998	.99998	.99998
4.9	.99999	.99999	.99999	.99999	.99999	.99999	.99999	.99999	.99999	.99999	.99999	.99999	.99999	.99999
5.0	.99999	.99999	.99999	.99999	.99999	.99999	.99999	.99999	.99999	.99999	.99999	.99999	.99999	.99999

Table D-9. Two-Sided Probability Integral, $\rho = 0.9$

a \ n	2	3	4	5	6	7	8	9	10	12	14	16	18	20
0.1	.01435	.00294	.00063	.00014	.00003	.00001	.00000	.00000	.00000	.00000	.00000	.00000	.00000	.00000
0.2	.05462	.02131	.00877	.00371	.00160	.00070	.00030	.00013	.00006	.00001	.00000	.00000	.00000	.00000
0.3	.11381	.06191	.03548	.02094	.01258	.00764	.00467	.00287	.00177	.00068	.00026	.00010	.00004	.00001
0.4	.18384	.12161	.08454	.06045	.04402	.03245	.02413	.01805	.01356	.00771	.00441	.00253	.00145	.00083
0.5	.25811	.19257	.15037	.12054	.09830	.08114	.06758	.05667	.04777	.03432	.02489	.01815	.01328	.00973
0.6	.33236	.26760	.22439	.19263	.16793	.14801	.13152	.11763	.10576	.08653	.07165	.05981	.05021	.04232
0.7	.40426	.34224	.30013	.26866	.24375	.22328	.20599	.19111	.17809	.15630	.13868	.12408	.11175	.10117
0.8	.47263	.41422	.37414	.34392	.31982	.29986	.28290	.26818	.25522	.23320	.21500	.19955	.18619	.17449
0.9	.53679	.48244	.44484	.41631	.39343	.37439	.35813	.34398	.33148	.31021	.29258	.27755	.26447	.25287
1.0	.59636	.54633	.51145	.48482	.46339	.44550	.43017	.41679	.40492	.38460	.36768	.35323	.34066	.32957
1.1	.65108	.60552	.57349	.54891	.52903	.51239	.49811	.48561	.47452	.45552	.43962	.42594	.41395	.40329
1.2	.70084	.65977	.63067	.60823	.59000	.57468	.56149	.54991	.53961	.52193	.50714	.49446	.48337	.47350
1.3	.74562	.70898	.68282	.66253	.64600	.63207	.62004	.60946	.60003	.58375	.57005	.55823	.54786	.53865
1.4	.78550	.75315	.72989	.71175	.69690	.68434	.67346	.66389	.65534	.64059	.62817	.61743	.60796	.59949
1.5	.82067	.79240	.77192	.75587	.74268	.73149	.72178	.71319	.70550	.69219	.68094	.67122	.66269	.65508
1.6	.85135	.82691	.80907	.79501	.78342	.77355	.76497	.75738	.75057	.73874	.72870	.71996	.71223	.70531
1.7	.87785	.85693	.84155	.82938	.81930	.81068	.80317	.79650	.79051	.78010	.77127	.76360	.75681	.75071
1.8	.90050	.88279	.86967	.85923	.85056	.84313	.83663	.83085	.82564	.81655	.80879	.80203	.79604	.79068
1.9	.91967	.90482	.89375	.88489	.87750	.87115	.86559	.86063	.85616	.84836	.84168	.83583	.83063	.82593
2.0	.93572	.92340	.91415	.90672	.90050	.89513	.89041	.88620	.88239	.87571	.87000	.86501	.86057	.85658
2.1	.94903	.93891	.93127	.92509	.91990	.91542	.91147	.90793	.90473	.89910	.89425	.88999	.88619	.88276
2.2	.95994	.95172	.94547	.94040	.93611	.93240	.92912	.92618	.92351	.91882	.91479	.91124	.90806	.90518
2.3	.96881	.96220	.95713	.95301	.94951	.94648	.94379	.94137	.93917	.93528	.93192	.92897	.92633	.92394
2.4	.97593	.97067	.96661	.96329	.96047	.95801	.95583	.95386	.95207	.94891	.94616	.94373	.94154	.93956
2.5	.98160	.97745	.97424	.97160	.96934	.96737	.96561	.96403	.96258	.96002	.95780	.95583	.95407	.95247
2.6	.98606	.98283	.98031	.97822	.97644	.97488	.97348	.97222	.97107	.96902	.96723	.96564	.96421	.96291
2.7	.98954	.98705	.98509	.98346	.98207	.98084	.97974	.97875	.97784	.97622	.97481	.97355	.97241	.97138
2.8	.99222	.99032	.98882	.98756	.98648	.98553	.98467	.98390	.98319	.98192	.98080	.97982	.97892	.97811
2.9	.99427	.99283	.99169	.99073	.98991	.98917	.98852	.98792	.98737	.98639	.98552	.98475	.98405	.98341
3.0	.99582	.99475	.99389	.99316	.99253	.99198	.99148	.99102	.99060	.98985	.98918	.98859	.98806	.98756
3.1	.99698	.99618	.99554	.99500	.99453	.99411	.99373	.99339	.99307	.99250	.99199	.99154	.99113	.99076
3.2	.99784	.99725	.99678	.99638	.99603	.99572	.99544	.99518	.99494	.99452	.99414	.99380	.99349	.99320
3.3	.99847	.99804	.99770	.99741	.99715	.99692	.99671	.99652	.99635	.99603	.99575	.99549	.99526	.99505
3.4	.99892	.99862	.99837	.99816	.99797	.99781	.99765	.99751	.99738	.99715	.99694	.99676	.99658	.99643
3.5	.99925	.99904	.99886	.99871	.99857	.99845	.99834	.99824	.99815	.99798	.99783	.99769	.99756	.99745
3.6	.99948	.99933	.99921	.99910	.99900	.99892	.99884	.99877	.99870	.99858	.99847	.99837	.99828	.99820
3.7	.99965	.99954	.99945	.99938	.99931	.99925	.99920	.99914	.99910	.99901	.99893	.99886	.99880	.99874
3.8	.99976	.99969	.99963	.99958	.99953	.99949	.99945	.99941	.99938	.99932	.99926	.99921	.99917	.99912
3.9	.99984	.99979	.99975	.99971	.99968	.99965	.99962	.99960	.99958	.99953	.99950	.99946	.99943	.99940
4.0	.99989	.99986	.99983	.99981	.99979	.99977	.99975	.99973	.99971	.99969	.99966	.99963	.99961	.99959
4.1	.99993	.99991	.99989	.99987	.99986	.99984	.99983	.99982	.99981	.99979	.99977	.99975	.99974	.99973
4.2	.99995	.99994	.99993	.99992	.99991	.99990	.99989	.99988	.99987	.99986	.99985	.99984	.99983	.99982
4.3	.99997	.99996	.99995	.99995	.99994	.99993	.99993	.99992	.99992	.99991	.99990	.99989	.99989	.99988
4.4	.99998	.99998	.99997	.99997	.99996	.99996	.99995	.99995	.99995	.99994	.99994	.99993	.99993	.99992
4.5	.99999	.99998	.99998	.99998	.99997	.99997	.99997	.99997	.99997	.99996	.99996	.99996	.99995	.99995
4.6	.99999	.99999	.99999	.99999	.99998	.99998	.99998	.99998	.99998	.99998	.99997	.99997	.99997	.99997
4.7	.99999	.99999	.99999	.99999	.99999	.99999	.99999	.99999	.99999	.99998	.99998	.99998	.99998	.99998
4.8	.99999	.99999	.99999	.99999	.99999	.99999	.99999	.99999	.99999	.99999	.99999	.99999	.99999	.99999
4.9	.99999	.99999	.99999	.99999	.99999	.99999	.99999	.99999	.99999	.99999	.99999	.99999	.99999	.99999
5.0	.99999	.99999	.99999	.99999	.99999	.99999	.99999	.99999	.99999	.99999	.99999	.99999	.99999	.99999

Table D-10. Two-Sided Probability Integral, $\rho = \frac{1}{3}$

a \ n	2	3	4	5	6	7	8	9	10	12	14	16	18	20
0.1	.00673	.00059	.00005	.00000	.00000	.00000	.00000	.00000	.00000	.00000	.00000	.00000	.00000	.00000
0.2	.02661	.00461	.00081	.00015	.00003	.00000	.00000	.00000	.00000	.00000	.00000	.00000	.00000	.00000
0.3	.05877	.01510	.00396	.00105	.00028	.00008	.00002	.00001	.00000	.00000	.00000	.00000	.00000	.00000
0.4	.10184	.03437	.01182	.00412	.00145	.00051	.00018	.00007	.00002	.00000	.00000	.00000	.00000	.00000
0.5	.15404	.06374	.02686	.01147	.00494	.00215	.00094	.00041	.00018	.00004	.00001	.00000	.00000	.00000
0.6	.21335	.10353	.05112	.02556	.01290	.00655	.00335	.00172	.00089	.00024	.00006	.00002	.00000	.00000
0.7	.27761	.15307	.08580	.04866	.02784	.01604	.00929	.00541	.00316	.00109	.00038	.00013	.00005	.00002
0.8	.34470	.21090	.13102	.08230	.05213	.03323	.02130	.01371	.00886	.00373	.00158	.00068	.00029	.00013
0.9	.41261	.27500	.18588	.12693	.08736	.06049	.04210	.02942	.02063	.01023	.00512	.00258	.00131	.00066
1.0	.47957	.34309	.24859	.18182	.13395	.09925	.07388	.05521	.04139	.02345	.01340	.00771	.00446	.00259
1.1	.54411	.41285	.31683	.24521	.19104	.14962	.11770	.09292	.07358	.04649	.02961	.01898	.01223	.00791
1.2	.60503	.48210	.38800	.31464	.25667	.21039	.17314	.14295	.11837	.08173	.05685	.03979	.02798	.01975
1.3	.66148	.54902	.45962	.38734	.32815	.27921	.23841	.20419	.17533	.13011	.09723	.07307	.05516	.04179
1.4	.71292	.61214	.52947	.46059	.40252	.35310	.31073	.27418	.24250	.19081	.15109	.12025	.09611	.07709
1.5	.75906	.67040	.59574	.53197	.47690	.42893	.38685	.34973	.31683	.26137	.21686	.18076	.15125	.12696
1.6	.79983	.72316	.65713	.59955	.54883	.50380	.46356	.42742	.39479	.33837	.29148	.25212	.21883	.19048
1.7	.83537	.77009	.71279	.66194	.61640	.57533	.53806	.50409	.47299	.41806	.37113	.33066	.29549	.26475
1.8	.86594	.81116	.76228	.71825	.67827	.64173	.60817	.57719	.54849	.49696	.45194	.41228	.37709	.34568
1.9	.89191	.84656	.80553	.76808	.73367	.70188	.67236	.64484	.61910	.57223	.53056	.49321	.45951	.42894
2.0	.91369	.87665	.84270	.81138	.78230	.75517	.72975	.70586	.68333	.64182	.60438	.57035	.53924	.51064
2.1	.93176	.90187	.87418	.84838	.82421	.80147	.78000	.75967	.74037	.70447	.67167	.64153	.61366	.58778
2.2	.94656	.92274	.90045	.87951	.85973	.84098	.82317	.80619	.78997	.75954	.73147	.70540	.68109	.65831
2.3	.95856	.93979	.92209	.90531	.88936	.87415	.85961	.84566	.83227	.80698	.78341	.76136	.74062	.72105
2.4	.96817	.95356	.93966	.92641	.91373	.90157	.88987	.87861	.86774	.84706	.82765	.80935	.79202	.77556
2.5	.97579	.96453	.95377	.94343	.93348	.92389	.91463	.90566	.89698	.88036	.86464	.84972	.83551	.82194
2.6	.98176	.97319	.96494	.95698	.94928	.94182	.93459	.92756	.92072	.90756	.89504	.88309	.87164	.86065
2.7	.98639	.97993	.97369	.96763	.96175	.95602	.95045	.94501	.93971	.92945	.91963	.91020	.90113	.89238
2.8	.98994	.98513	.98046	.97590	.97146	.96712	.96289	.95874	.95468	.94680	.93921	.93190	.92482	.91797
2.9	.99263	.98909	.98563	.98225	.97894	.97569	.97251	.96939	.96633	.96035	.95458	.94898	.94355	.93826
3.0	.99466	.99208	.98954	.98706	.98462	.98222	.97986	.97754	.97526	.97080	.96646	.96224	.95813	.95412
3.1	.99617	.99430	.99247	.99066	.98888	.98713	.98541	.98371	.98203	.97874	.97553	.97239	.96933	.96632
3.2	.99727	.99594	.99463	.99333	.99205	.99079	.98954	.98831	.98709	.98469	.98235	.98005	.97779	.97558
3.3	.99808	.99714	.99620	.99528	.99437	.99347	.99258	.99170	.99082	.98910	.98741	.98575	.98411	.98250
3.4	.99866	.99800	.99735	.99670	.99606	.99542	.99479	.99417	.99355	.99233	.99112	.98993	.98876	.98761
3.5	.99907	.99862	.99816	.99771	.99727	.99682	.99638	.99595	.99551	.99465	.99381	.99297	.99214	.99133
3.6	.99937	.99905	.99874	.99843	.99812	.99782	.99751	.99721	.99691	.99632	.99573	.99514	.99457	.99400
3.7	.99957	.99936	.99914	.99893	.99872	.99852	.99831	.99810	.99790	.99749	.99708	.99668	.99629	.99589
3.8	.99971	.99957	.99943	.99928	.99914	.99900	.99886	.99872	.99858	.99831	.99803	.99776	.99749	.99722
3.9	.99981	.99971	.99962	.99952	.99943	.99933	.99924	.99915	.99905	.99887	.99868	.99850	.99832	.99814
4.0	.99987	.99981	.99975	.99969	.99962	.99956	.99950	.99944	.99937	.99925	.99913	.99901	.99889	.99877
4.1	.99992	.99988	.99984	.99979	.99975	.99971	.99967	.99963	.99959	.99951	.99943	.99935	.99927	.99919
4.2	.99995	.99992	.99989	.99987	.99984	.99981	.99979	.99976	.99974	.99968	.99963	.99958	.99953	.99948
4.3	.99997	.99995	.99993	.99991	.99990	.99988	.99986	.99985	.99983	.99980	.99976	.99973	.99970	.99966
4.4	.99998	.99997	.99996	.99995	.99994	.99992	.99991	.99990	.99989	.99987	.99985	.99983	.99981	.99979
4.5	.99999	.99998	.99997	.99997	.99996	.99995	.99995	.99994	.99993	.99992	.99991	.99989	.99988	.99987
4.6	.99999	.99999	.99998	.99998	.99997	.99997	.99997	.99996	.99996	.99995	.99994	.99993	.99992	.99992
4.7	.99999	.99999	.99999	.99999	.99998	.99998	.99998	.99998	.99997	.99997	.99996	.99996	.99995	.99995
4.8	.99999	.99999	.99999	.99999	.99999	.99999	.99999	.99999	.99998	.99998	.99998	.99997	.99997	.99997
4.9	.99999	.99999	.99999	.99999	.99999	.99999	.99999	.99999	.99999	.99999	.99999	.99998	.99998	.99998
5.0	.99999	.99999	.99999	.99999	.99999	.99999	.99999	.99999	.99999	.99999	.99999	.99999	.99999	.99999

Table D-11. Two-Sided Probability Integral, $\rho = \frac{2}{3}$

a \ n	2	3	4	5	6	7	8	9	10	12	14	16	18	20
0.1	.00849	.00099	.00012	.00001	.00000	.00000	.00000	.00000	.00000	.00000	.00000	.00000	.00000	.00000
0.2	.03336	.00765	.00183	.00045	.00011	.00003	.00001	.00000	.00000	.00000	.00000	.00000	.00000	.00000
0.3	.07292	.02451	.00859	.00308	.00113	.00042	.00016	.00006	.00002	.00000	.00000	.00000	.00000	.00000
0.4	.12461	.05416	.02450	.01136	.00535	.00255	.00123	.00059	.00029	.00007	.00002	.00000	.00000	.00000
0.5	.18542	.09697	.05272	.02935	.01660	.00950	.00548	.00318	.00186	.00064	.00022	.00008	.00003	.00001
0.6	.25221	.15145	.09438	.06017	.03895	.02550	.01683	.01118	.00747	.00337	.00154	.00071	.00033	.00015
0.7	.32203	.21484	.14842	.10476	.07505	.05433	.03966	.02913	.02151	.01187	.00663	.00373	.00212	.00121
0.8	.39237	.28388	.21213	.16175	.12506	.09767	.07687	.06087	.04844	.03103	.02012	.01316	.00866	.00574
0.9	.46118	.35539	.28205	.22804	.18677	.15442	.12860	.10772	.09066	.06492	.04701	.03434	.02524	.01866
1.0	.52695	.42668	.35470	.29988	.25653	.22136	.19231	.16797	.14735	.11457	.09004	.07133	.05687	.04557
1.1	.58865	.49566	.42715	.37367	.33036	.29438	.26393	.23779	.21510	.17770	.14826	.12463	.10539	.08954
1.2	.64559	.56088	.49717	.44652	.40479	.36954	.33921	.31275	.28939	.24993	.21781	.19112	.16862	.14943
1.3	.69741	.62138	.56322	.51632	.47717	.44371	.41457	.38886	.36591	.32651	.29370	.26584	.24180	.22082
1.4	.74397	.67664	.62436	.58169	.54571	.51466	.48740	.46315	.44133	.40344	.37142	.34382	.31967	.29828
1.5	.78530	.72641	.68005	.64182	.60929	.58100	.55600	.53360	.51334	.47787	.44758	.42121	.39790	.37707
1.6	.82159	.77068	.73009	.69628	.66729	.64191	.61934	.59902	.58055	.54799	.51997	.49539	.47352	.45385
1.7	.85308	.80957	.77446	.74495	.71945	.69699	.67690	.65874	.64215	.61275	.58727	.56479	.54468	.52650
1.8	.88012	.84336	.81334	.78789	.76574	.74612	.72848	.71245	.69776	.67158	.64876	.62852	.61032	.59380
1.9	.90308	.87236	.84701	.82532	.80632	.78938	.77408	.76013	.74728	.72428	.70412	.68614	.66992	.65513
2.0	.92237	.89699	.87581	.85755	.84144	.82701	.81391	.80190	.79082	.77087	.75329	.73754	.72326	.71020
2.1	.93840	.91766	.90017	.88498	.87149	.85934	.84826	.83806	.82861	.81153	.79639	.78277	.77037	.75899
2.2	.95158	.93482	.92055	.90805	.89689	.88678	.87752	.86897	.86101	.84657	.83370	.82206	.81144	.80165
2.3	.96229	.94890	.93738	.92723	.91810	.90979	.90215	.89506	.88845	.87639	.86558	.85578	.84678	.83847
2.4	.97091	.96033	.95114	.94298	.93561	.92886	.92263	.91683	.91140	.90145	.89250	.88433	.87682	.86985
2.5	.97778	.96950	.96226	.95578	.94989	.94447	.93945	.93477	.93036	.92226	.91493	.90822	.90202	.89625
2.6	.98318	.97678	.97113	.96605	.96140	.95711	.95311	.94937	.94584	.93932	.93340	.92795	.92290	.91819
2.7	.98740	.98250	.97814	.97420	.97057	.96721	.96407	.96111	.95832	.95314	.94841	.94405	.93999	.93618
2.8	.99064	.98694	.98362	.98059	.97780	.97519	.97275	.97045	.96826	.96420	.96047	.95701	.95379	.95076
2.9	.99312	.99035	.98784	.98555	.98342	.98143	.97955	.97778	.97609	.97294	.97004	.96733	.96481	.96242
3.0	.99499	.99294	.99107	.98935	.98775	.98624	.98482	.98347	.98218	.97977	.97753	.97545	.97349	.97164
3.1	.99639	.99488	.99351	.99223	.99104	.98991	.98885	.98783	.98686	.98503	.98333	.98174	.98025	.97883
3.2	.99742	.99633	.99533	.99439	.99351	.99268	.99189	.99114	.99041	.98905	.98777	.98657	.98544	.98437
3.3	.99818	.99739	.99667	.99599	.99535	.99475	.99417	.99361	.99308	.99207	.99113	.99023	.98939	.98859
3.4	.99872	.99817	.99765	.99717	.99671	.99627	.99585	.99545	.99506	.99432	.99363	.99297	.99235	.99176
3.5	.99911	.99872	.99836	.99802	.99769	.99738	.99708	.99679	.99651	.99598	.99548	.99500	.99455	.99411
3.6	.99939	.99912	.99887	.99863	.99840	.99817	.99796	.99776	.99756	.99718	.99682	.99648	.99616	.99584
3.7	.99959	.99940	.99922	.99906	.99890	.99874	.99860	.99845	.99831	.99805	.99779	.99755	.99732	.99710
3.8	.99972	.99959	.99947	.99936	.99925	.99914	.99904	.99894	.99885	.99866	.99848	.99831	.99815	.99799
3.9	.99981	.99973	.99965	.99957	.99950	.99942	.99935	.99928	.99922	.99909	.99897	.99885	.99874	.99863
4.0	.99988	.99982	.99977	.99971	.99966	.99962	.99957	.99952	.99948	.99939	.99931	.99923	.99915	.99907
4.1	.99992	.99988	.99985	.99981	.99978	.99975	.99971	.99968	.99965	.99959	.99954	.99948	.99943	.99938
4.2	.99995	.99992	.99990	.99988	.99986	.99983	.99981	.99979	.99977	.99973	.99970	.99966	.99962	.99959
4.3	.99997	.99995	.99994	.99992	.99991	.99989	.99988	.99987	.99985	.99983	.99980	.99978	.99976	.99973
4.4	.99998	.99997	.99996	.99995	.99994	.99993	.99992	.99991	.99991	.99989	.99987	.99986	.99984	.99983
4.5	.99999	.99998	.99997	.99997	.99996	.99996	.99995	.99995	.99994	.99993	.99992	.99991	.99990	.99989
4.6	.99999	.99999	.99998	.99998	.99998	.99997	.99997	.99997	.99996	.99996	.99995	.99994	.99994	.99993
4.7	.99999	.99999	.99999	.99999	.99999	.99998	.99998	.99998	.99998	.99997	.99997	.99996	.99996	.99996
4.8	.99999	.99999	.99999	.99999	.99999	.99999	.99999	.99999	.99999	.99998	.99998	.99998	.99998	.99997
4.9	.99999	.99999	.99999	.99999	.99999	.99999	.99999	.99999	.99999	.99999	.99999	.99999	.99998	.99998
5.0	.99999	.99999	.99999	.99999	.99999	.99999	.99999	.99999	.99999	.99999	.99999	.99999	.99999	.99999

Table D-12. Two-Sided Probability Integral, $\rho = \frac{1}{4}$

a \ n	2	3	4	5	6	7	8	9	10	12	14	16	18	20
0.1	.00655	.00055	.00005	.00000	.00000	.00000	.00000	.00000	.00000	.00000	.00000	.00000	.00000	.00000
0.2	.02593	.00433	.00073	.00013	.00002	.00000	.00000	.00000	.00000	.00000	.00000	.00000	.00000	.00000
0.3	.05732	.01421	.00357	.00091	.00023	.00006	.00002	.00000	.00000	.00000	.00000	.00000	.00000	.00000
0.4	.09946	.03242	.01071	.00357	.00120	.00041	.00014	.00005	.00002	.00000	.00000	.00000	.00000	.00000
0.5	.15066	.06034	.02447	.01002	.00413	.00171	.00071	.00030	.00013	.00002	.00000	.00000	.00000	.00000
0.6	.20903	.09841	.04688	.02253	.01091	.00531	.00259	.00127	.00063	.00015	.00004	.00001	.00000	.00000
0.7	.27251	.14614	.07925	.04334	.02386	.01320	.00734	.00409	.00229	.00072	.00023	.00007	.00002	.00001
0.8	.33902	.20228	.12195	.07410	.04530	.02784	.01718	.01063	.00660	.00257	.00100	.00040	.00016	.00006
0.9	.40662	.26503	.17438	.11557	.07704	.05159	.03469	.02340	.01583	.00729	.00339	.00158	.00074	.00035
1.0	.47354	.33221	.23505	.16742	.11988	.08621	.06223	.04505	.03271	.01735	.00927	.00498	.00269	.00146
1.1	.53826	.40157	.30187	.22828	.17346	.13233	.10130	.07776	.05984	.03566	.02139	.01290	.00782	.00475
1.2	.59956	.47094	.37237	.29599	.23630	.18932	.15215	.12259	.09900	.06494	.04286	.02844	.01894	.01266
1.3	.65654	.53842	.44407	.36795	.30604	.25536	.21366	.17919	.15059	.10691	.07634	.05477	.03945	.02850
1.4	.70858	.60244	.51467	.44143	.37986	.32779	.28355	.24579	.21345	.16174	.12320	.09425	.07236	.05572
1.5	.75536	.66182	.58220	.51387	.45484	.40356	.35880	.31960	.28514	.22792	.18303	.14756	.11935	.09680
1.6	.79676	.71580	.64519	.58315	.52831	.47961	.43617	.39729	.36238	.30260	.25372	.21346	.18012	.15236
1.7	.83288	.76397	.70260	.64761	.59808	.55327	.51258	.47551	.44164	.38216	.33187	.28906	.25242	.22090
1.8	.86397	.80620	.75385	.70615	.66251	.62241	.58546	.55130	.51965	.46289	.41358	.37047	.33258	.29913
1.9	.89038	.84264	.79874	.75818	.72056	.68555	.65289	.62233	.59369	.54144	.49503	.45356	.41634	.38280
2.0	.91254	.87362	.83738	.80350	.77172	.74182	.71364	.68701	.66179	.61517	.57298	.53463	.49961	.46752
2.1	.93090	.89959	.87011	.84227	.81591	.79088	.76708	.74440	.72275	.68225	.64505	.61074	.57897	.54946
2.2	.94594	.92105	.89741	.87489	.85338	.83281	.81310	.79418	.77600	.74165	.70970	.67988	.65196	.62573
2.3	.95811	.93857	.91986	.90190	.88463	.86800	.85197	.83648	.82152	.79300	.76620	.74093	.71704	.69439
2.4	.96785	.95269	.93807	.92394	.91028	.89705	.88422	.87177	.85967	.83646	.81444	.79350	.77355	.75449
2.5	.97557	.96393	.95265	.94168	.93102	.92065	.91054	.90069	.89107	.87251	.85477	.83778	.82147	.80579
2.6	.98161	.97278	.96417	.95577	.94756	.93954	.93170	.92402	.91650	.90190	.88786	.87432	.86125	.84861
2.7	.98629	.97966	.97317	.96681	.96057	.95445	.94845	.94255	.93675	.92546	.91452	.90392	.89364	.88364
2.8	.98987	.98495	.98011	.97535	.97067	.96606	.96153	.95706	.95266	.94404	.93566	.92750	.91954	.91178
2.9	.99259	.98897	.98540	.98189	.97841	.97499	.97161	.96827	.96497	.95849	.95216	.94597	.93991	.93398
3.0	.99463	.99200	.98940	.98682	.98428	.98176	.97927	.97681	.97437	.96957	.96485	.96023	.95569	.95122
3.1	.99615	.99425	.99237	.99051	.98867	.98684	.98503	.98323	.98145	.97794	.97448	.97107	.96771	.96441
3.2	.99726	.99591	.99457	.99324	.99192	.99060	.98930	.98801	.98672	.98418	.98167	.97920	.97675	.97434
3.3	.99807	.99712	.99617	.99523	.99429	.99336	.99243	.99151	.99060	.98878	.98699	.98521	.98345	.98171
3.4	.99866	.99799	.99733	.99667	.99601	.99535	.99470	.99406	.99341	.99213	.99086	.98960	.98835	.98712
3.5	.99907	.99861	.99815	.99769	.99724	.99678	.99633	.99588	.99543	.99454	.99365	.99277	.99189	.99103
3.6	.99936	.99905	.99873	.99842	.99811	.99779	.99748	.99717	.99686	.99625	.99563	.99503	.99442	.99382
3.7	.99957	.99935	.99914	.99893	.99871	.99850	.99829	.99808	.99787	.99745	.99703	.99661	.99620	.99579
3.8	.99971	.99957	.99942	.99928	.99914	.99899	.99885	.99871	.99857	.99828	.99800	.99772	.99744	.99716
3.9	.99981	.99971	.99962	.99952	.99943	.99933	.99923	.99914	.99904	.99886	.99867	.99848	.99829	.99810
4.0	.99987	.99981	.99975	.99968	.99962	.99956	.99950	.99943	.99937	.99924	.99912	.99900	.99887	.99875
4.1	.99992	.99988	.99983	.99979	.99975	.99971	.99967	.99963	.99959	.99951	.99942	.99934	.99926	.99918
4.2	.99995	.99992	.99989	.99987	.99984	.99981	.99979	.99976	.99973	.99968	.99963	.99958	.99952	.99947
4.3	.99997	.99995	.99993	.99991	.99990	.99988	.99986	.99985	.99983	.99980	.99976	.99973	.99969	.99966
4.4	.99998	.99997	.99996	.99995	.99994	.99992	.99991	.99990	.99989	.99987	.99985	.99983	.99981	.99978
4.5	.99999	.99998	.99997	.99997	.99996	.99995	.99995	.99994	.99993	.99992	.99991	.99989	.99988	.99986
4.6	.99999	.99999	.99998	.99998	.99997	.99997	.99997	.99996	.99996	.99995	.99994	.99993	.99992	.99992
4.7	.99999	.99999	.99999	.99999	.99998	.99998	.99998	.99998	.99997	.99997	.99996	.99996	.99995	.99995
4.8	.99999	.99999	.99999	.99999	.99999	.99999	.99999	.99999	.99998	.99998	.99998	.99997	.99997	.99997
4.9	.99999	.99999	.99999	.99999	.99999	.99999	.99999	.99999	.99999	.99999	.99999	.99998	.99998	.99998
5.0	.99999	.99999	.99999	.99999	.99999	.99999	.99999	.99999	.99999	.99999	.99999	.99999	.99999	.99999

Table D-13. Two-Sided Probability Integral, $\rho = \frac{3}{4}$

a \ n	2	3	4	5	6	7	8	9	10	12	14	16	18	20
0.1	.00955	.00127	.00018	.00003	.00000	.00000	.00000	.00000	.00000	.00000	.00000	.00000	.00000	.00000
0.2	.03736	.00973	.00265	.00074	.00021	.00006	.00002	.00001	.00000	.00000	.00000	.00000	.00000	.00000
0.3	.08106	.03071	.01218	.00496	.00206	.00086	.00037	.00016	.00007	.00001	.00000	.00000	.00000	.00000
0.4	.13724	.06655	.03374	.01756	.00930	.00499	.00270	.00147	.00081	.00024	.00008	.00002	.00001	.00000
0.5	.20207	.11654	.07016	.04333	.02721	.01729	.01109	.00716	.00465	.00199	.00086	.00038	.00017	.00007
0.6	.27183	.17780	.12112	.08453	.05996	.04303	.03115	.02270	.01663	.00904	.00498	.00277	.00155	.00087
0.7	.34334	.24641	.18366	.14006	.10845	.08491	.06704	.05327	.04256	.02749	.01798	.01187	.00789	.00527
0.8	.41409	.31853	.25363	.20626	.17014	.14181	.11913	.10069	.08553	.06244	.04612	.03437	.02579	.01946
0.9	.48228	.39095	.32688	.27858	.24053	.20967	.18409	.16256	.14421	.11474	.09231	.07489	.06115	.05020
1.0	.54671	.46135	.40009	.35291	.31495	.28348	.25685	.23393	.21395	.18078	.15432	.13275	.11490	.09993
1.1	.60660	.52818	.47091	.42613	.38960	.35891	.33256	.30959	.28930	.25489	.22666	.20298	.18279	.16534
1.2	.66153	.59048	.53784	.49621	.46190	.43280	.40761	.38545	.36571	.33183	.30356	.27944	.25851	.24010
1.3	.71130	.64771	.60001	.56191	.53025	.50321	.47965	.45880	.44013	.40781	.38058	.35710	.33653	.31825
1.4	.75588	.69963	.65693	.62252	.59372	.56898	.54731	.52804	.51071	.48054	.45493	.43271	.41312	.39561
1.5	.79538	.74618	.70840	.67769	.65183	.62949	.60982	.59227	.57642	.54870	.52503	.50440	.48611	.46971
1.6	.83000	.78744	.75439	.72731	.70436	.68443	.66681	.65102	.63671	.61158	.59001	.57112	.55432	.53919
1.7	.86003	.82360	.79502	.77142	.75128	.73371	.71811	.70407	.69131	.66881	.64941	.63234	.61710	.60335
1.8	.88578	.85495	.83051	.81017	.79271	.77740	.76375	.75142	.74018	.72027	.70302	.68779	.67415	.66179
1.9	.90764	.88183	.86116	.84383	.82887	.81568	.80387	.79317	.78339	.76599	.75083	.73741	.72534	.71437
2.0	.92600	.90462	.88734	.87274	.86006	.84884	.83874	.82957	.82115	.80611	.79297	.78127	.77072	.76110
2.1	.94125	.92374	.90945	.89729	.88667	.87722	.86870	.86092	.85376	.84092	.82965	.81958	.81047	.80214
2.2	.95380	.93961	.92791	.91790	.90911	.90125	.89413	.88761	.88160	.87077	.86122	.85265	.84488	.83775
2.3	.96400	.95262	.94317	.93501	.92782	.92136	.91548	.91008	.90508	.89606	.88806	.88086	.87431	.86828
2.4	.97221	.96319	.95563	.94906	.94324	.93799	.93319	.92877	.92467	.91723	.91061	.90464	.89918	.89415
2.5	.97875	.97168	.96569	.96047	.95581	.95158	.94772	.94414	.94081	.93476	.92935	.92444	.91995	.91580
2.6	.98391	.97841	.97373	.96962	.96593	.96258	.95950	.95664	.95397	.94909	.94472	.94075	.93709	.93370
2.7	.98793	.98371	.98009	.97688	.97400	.97137	.96894	.96668	.96456	.96069	.95719	.95401	.95107	.94834
2.8	.99103	.98783	.98505	.98259	.98036	.97831	.97642	.97465	.97300	.96995	.96719	.96467	.96234	.96016
2.9	.99340	.99099	.98889	.98701	.98531	.98374	.98228	.98092	.97963	.97727	.97512	.97314	.97131	.96960
3.0	.99519	.99340	.99183	.99041	.98912	.98793	.98682	.98578	.98480	.98298	.98132	.97979	.97837	.97705
3.1	.99652	.99521	.99404	.99299	.99203	.99113	.99030	.98951	.98877	.98739	.98613	.98496	.98387	.98285
3.2	.99751	.99656	.99570	.99493	.99422	.99355	.99293	.99234	.99179	.99075	.98980	.98892	.98810	.98732
3.3	.99824	.99755	.99693	.99637	.99585	.99536	.99490	.99447	.99406	.99329	.99258	.99192	.99131	.99073
3.4	.99877	.99827	.99783	.99743	.99705	.99670	.99636	.99605	.99575	.99518	.99466	.99418	.99372	.99329
3.5	.99914	.99880	.99848	.99819	.99792	.99767	.99743	.99720	.99699	.99658	.99620	.99584	.99551	.99519
3.6	.99941	.99917	.99895	.99874	.99855	.99837	.99820	.99804	.99789	.99759	.99732	.99707	.99682	.99660
3.7	.99960	.99943	.99928	.99914	.99900	.99888	.99876	.99864	.99853	.99833	.99813	.99795	.99778	.99761
3.8	.99973	.99962	.99951	.99941	.99932	.99923	.99915	.99907	.99899	.99885	.99871	.99858	.99846	.99835
3.9	.99982	.99974	.99967	.99960	.99954	.99948	.99942	.99937	.99932	.99922	.99912	.99903	.99895	.99887
4.0	.99988	.99983	.99978	.99974	.99969	.99965	.99961	.99958	.99954	.99947	.99941	.99934	.99929	.99923
4.1	.99992	.99989	.99986	.99983	.99980	.99977	.99974	.99972	.99969	.99965	.99960	.99956	.99952	.99948
4.2	.99995	.99993	.99991	.99989	.99987	.99985	.99983	.99981	.99980	.99977	.99974	.99971	.99968	.99966
4.3	.99997	.99995	.99994	.99993	.99991	.99990	.99989	.99988	.99987	.99985	.99983	.99981	.99979	.99977
4.4	.99998	.99997	.99996	.99995	.99994	.99994	.99993	.99992	.99992	.99990	.99989	.99988	.99986	.99985
4.5	.99999	.99998	.99998	.99997	.99996	.99996	.99996	.99995	.99995	.99994	.99993	.99992	.99991	.99991
4.6	.99999	.99999	.99998	.99998	.99998	.99997	.99997	.99997	.99997	.99996	.99995	.99995	.99994	.99994
4.7	.99999	.99999	.99999	.99999	.99999	.99998	.99998	.99998	.99998	.99998	.99997	.99997	.99997	.99996
4.8	.99999	.99999	.99999	.99999	.99999	.99999	.99999	.99999	.99999	.99998	.99998	.99998	.99998	.99998
4.9	.99999	.99999	.99999	.99999	.99999	.99999	.99999	.99999	.99999	.99999	.99999	.99999	.99999	.99999
5.0	.99999	.99999	.99999	.99999	.99999	.99999	.99999	.99999	.99999	.99999	.99999	.99999	.99999	.99999

Author Index

Page numbers in italic refer to the References section.

Subject Index

Abbreviations

abs. values = absolute values
corr. coef. = correlation coefficient
density = density function
distn. = distribution
d.f. = distribution function
exch. normal r.v.'s
= exchangeable normal variables
multi. normal = multivariate normal
prob. = probability
r.v.'s = random variables
stat. = statistics
symmetric = permutation symmetric